KISS FM: FROM RADICAL RADIO TO BIG BUSINESS

THE INSIDE STORY OF A LONDON PIRATE RADIO STATION'S PATH TO SUCCESS

GRANT GODDARD

Radio Books

KISS FM: From Radical Radio To Big Business
by **Grant Goddard**

Published in 2011 by Radio Books

www.radiobooks.org

Copyright © 2011 by Grant Goddard

www.grantgoddard.co.uk

All Rights Reserved. No part of this publication may be reproduced, stored in a retrieval system or transmitted in any form or by any means, electronic, mechanical, photocopying, recording, scanning or otherwise, except under the terms of the Copyright, Designs and Patents Act 1988 or under the terms of a licence issued by the Copyright Licensing Agency Limited, Saffron House, 6-10 Kirby Street, London EC1N 8TS, United Kingdom, without the permission in writing of the Publisher.

British Library Cataloguing in Publication Data:
A catalogue record for this book is available from the British Library

Library of Congress Cataloging in Publication Data:
A catalog record for this book is available from the Library of Congress

ISBN: 978-0-9564963-1-7 paperback

A friend is an enemy you can't see
'Coz what you've got, they'll make you lose
And then turn around and step in your shoes
I said they'll turn around and step in your shoes
So you'd better keep an eye on your close friend
You'd better watch out for your close friend
Don't trust nobody

'Keep An Eye'
Words and music by Nickolas Ashford and Valerie Simpson
© 1968, Reproduced by permission of Jobete Music Co. Inc/EMI Music, London W8 5SW

Smiling faces sometimes pretend to be your friend
Smiling faces show no traces of the evil that lurks within
Smiling faces sometimes they don't tell the truth
Smiling faces tell lies and I've got proof
Beware of the handshake that hides a snake
Beware of the pat on the back
It just might hold you back
Jealousy, misery, envy
You can't see behind smiling faces sometimes
Your enemy won't do you no harm
'Coz you know where he's coming from
Don't let the handshake and the smile fool you

'Smiling Faces Sometimes'
Words and music by Barrett Strong and Norman Whitfield
© 1971, Reproduced by permission of Jobete Music Co. Inc/EMI Music, London W8 5SW

What're they doin'?
They're smiling in your face
All the time they wanna take your place
The backstabbers
Smiling faces sometimes
Sometimes they tell lies
Idle, mean, low-down, dirty lies

'Back Stabbers'
Words and music by Leon Huff, Gene McFadden and John Whitehead
© 1972 (Renewed) Warner-Tamerland Publishing Corp. (BMI) and MIJAC Music (BMI)
All rights administered by Warner/Chappell North America Ltd

CONTENTS

PROLOGUE 7

PART ONE: Pirate Radio: 1984 to 1988 19

PART TWO: KISS FM: 1988 to 1991 111

PART THREE: Aftershocks: 1991 485

EPILOGUE 499

EPITAPH 519

APPENDICES:

Structure of KISS FM Radio Limited: September 1990 521

KISS FM Radio Limited: Shareholdings 523

Bibliography 525

Acknowledgements 527

PROLOGUE

"Successive Governments have now brought us to a three-tier system in broadcasting. First, there was the BBC, which stood alone for many years and became all the wonderful things we know it to be. Then there were the independent local radio companies, which are private enterprise but are regulated by the state ... Now there is a third class of broadcasting company – the thieves. They are against the law. They are regulated in no way by either Government or Parliament ..."

Lord Kennet
The House of Lords
14 January 1985

"The romance of being a disenfranchised outlaw, battling against an unjust law in the interest of free speech and free music, will probably be the best marketing pitch that many pirates could hope for. The image of the outsider is itself deeply rooted in this history of rock'n'roll and youth culture. It's something record companies and some legal radio stations spend a fortune on trying to achieve."

John Marshall
'Hurd On The Grapevine'
Time Out magazine
13 July 1988

Sunday 25 August 1974.
Camberley, Surrey.

It was a Bank Holiday weekend, thirty miles west of London in suburban Surrey. A clever, but quite shy, lanky sixteen-year old boy was twiddling the dial on the FM radio of his family's hi-fi system, hoping to find a station that was playing the soul music he loved. In recent months, the music of black America had enjoyed a boom in popularity across Britain that was unparalleled since the Motown sound had stormed the country a decade earlier.

Back then, in the early 1960s, this boy's parents had purchased a second-hand Uher reel-to-reel tape recorder which they had used to record their favourite soul and pop songs from offshore pirate radio stations, such as Radio London, and from the few music shows broadcast on television. As a result, this boy had grown up in a home that resonated with music from these homemade compilations, almost as if his parents had created their own little household radio station filled with the upbeat, optimistic songs of the 1960s that they adored.

Now, in 1974, soul music once again dominated the British music singles chart. George McCrae's disco anthem 'Rock Your Baby' was at number one for the third consecutive week. It was about to be deposed by a new entry at number two – girl group The Three Degrees' second UK hit 'When Will I See You Again' was an example of the popular Philadelphia soul sound that combined strong songs with a tight rhythm section and lush orchestral arrangements. Climbing to number four in that week's chart was male vocal group The Stylistics' biggest hit to date 'You Make Me Feel Brand New,' a polished, down tempo example of the Philadelphia sound. Behind them, at number ten, was The Hues Corporation's first hit 'Rock Your Boat,' an infectious song with an irresistibly catchy chorus. In the years ahead, all four of these records were destined to become classic soul songs whose uplifting sounds would be requested in clubs, on dance floors and on radio stations around the world.

Despite the popularity of these million-selling soul records and others like them, British radio stations still betrayed a remarkable reluctance to champion black music. Instead, they preferred to play the kind of puerile pop songs that often seemed like a throwback to the craze for novelty that had dominated the 1960s. Radio One, the country's only national pop music radio station, had been established by the non-commercial British Broadcasting Corporation [BBC] in 1967 to serve young listeners, but it avoided regular airplay of the popular soul songs. Instead, it opted for repeated plays of the largely whimsical pop records near the top of that week's chart – 'Born With A Smile On My Face' by Stephanie de Sykes, 'Summerlove Sensation' by The Bay City Rollers and 'Rocket' by Mud. Would these songs be hailed as timeless examples of classic pop music, even ten years after they had been made? Two decades later, such novelty records would become almost forgotten within the vast history of popular music.

The passage of time would demonstrate that British radio had too often promoted quite trivial and momentary songs at the expense of records whose qualities would be admired for generations. One timeless classic – Roberta Flack's 'Feel Like Making Love' – made a mere one-week impression on the top forty singles chart in September 1974, reaching only number thirty-four. Yet, that same week, the number one and two chart positions were held by The Osmonds' 'Love Me For A Reason' and Donny & Marie Osmond's 'I'm Leaving It All Up To You,' recordings that would quickly become forgotten.

The launch of Britain's first commercial radio stations in October 1973 should have introduced a breath of fresh air into the stale British radio system, providing Radio One with much needed UK-based competition for the first time in its history. However, the first and largest of the new commercial music stations, Capital Radio in London, opened with a playlist of music that was just as conservative as that of the BBC, and only marginally different in character. Capital managed to avoid most of the trivial, humorous pop songs that Radio One seemed to adore, but its playlist instead substituted a stream of lightweight American pop acts and singer/songwriters, mouthing evocative lyrics and worthy causes.

At least Radio One was forced to offer airplay to some soul music, if only because it was so obviously popular with the public who funded the station through payment of their annual Licence Fees. It seemed that, at Capital Radio, most contemporary soul music failed to pass the station's 'quality' threshold and was unceremoniously dismissed. Just before its launch, Capital Radio programme controller Michael Bukht, sounding much older than his thirty-one years, had explained the new station's music policy: "It will be pop music for grown-ups. Nothing to switch your mind off or set your teeth on edge. Music to smile by."[1]

For this teenage soul music fan, living in the outer London suburbs, the advent of Britain's first commercial radio stations had proven a bitter disappointment. Though there was little of interest to be heard during Radio One's daytime shows, at least its commitment to diverse music styles stretched to a solitary Saturday afternoon soul show that lasted an hour and a half and was presented by the knowledgeable David Simmons. Things could have been so different on British radio. One of the weekly music papers of the time commented, under the headline 'If Soul Music Is Your Thing, Then New York Is Your Place':

"Bored, tired and frustrated with [the] lack of Black music on Radio One? You'd go mad in New York. All day you can hear sounds like Sylvia, the Spinners, the Stylistics, War, Ernest Jackson, Willie Hutch, First Choice. WWRL is one of the biggest soul stations in the city. All day they blast out the kind of music that regularly you don't hear outside a good black discotheque. And the great thing is that this kind of music isn't just limited to certain stations; you'll hear it all on nearly every station. There's a game the New Yorkers play: it's called button-pushing. You just sit there at your radio and, whenever a tune comes on that you don't want to hear, you have a choice of seven or eight other stations by just pushing a few buttons. You can always find something you want to hear. Yes, folks, New York is the most exciting city in the world – all you need is a radio."[2]

For a teenage British soul fan, starved of exposure to his favourite music, this New York experience was the kind of exciting radio of which he could only dream. For those living in the boring old UK, the diversity of programmes available on American radio seemed incredible, with dozens of stations in each city serving listeners' every musical taste. Soul, pop, rock, country, jazz, classical – the choice was all there for anyone with a radio receiver, at the merest flick of the dial or press of a button.

The appeal and fascination of American radio was so strong for this suburban soul fan that, whenever he had the chance to travel to central London, he always paid a visit to the newsstand on the corner (literally) of Oxford Street and Tottenham Court Road. This was the only place in London where he knew he could buy 'Billboard,' a weekly American trade magazine for the music and radio industries. It was the thickest and most expensive publication he had ever seen, and he would carry each issue home excitedly to devour every page and every article, trying to understand the complexities of the American radio industry he envied so much. Why, he wondered, was Britain so far behind America in its development of radio? Would he ever see the day when London had its own soul music radio station, a treat that every major city in America already seemed to enjoy? Twiddling the dial of his radio in Britain, would he ever find a soul music station that could satisfy his musical interests?

Recently, this soul fan's fanaticism for American radio had been fuelled even more by the introduction of a new feature on David Simmons' Radio One soul show that he made sure he never missed. Each week, Simmons phoned a DJ on a soul radio station in a different American city to discuss the station's programmes and the best new soul record releases, before playing the station's top singles that particular week. Thirty-year old Simmons had taken over the Radio One show in January 1972 from his predecessor Mike Raven and had gradually moved its musical content away from the more traditional R&B/blues axis he had inherited and more towards contemporary soul music.

Every Saturday, using his family's hi-fi system, this sixteen-year old soul fan would record onto cassette tape the entire American radio segment of Simmons' show, lapping up his chat with DJs such as BB 'Birdbrain' Davies on KOKA Radio in Shreveport, Louisiana; 'Big' Al Jefferson at WWIN in Baltimore, Maryland; and 'Boogaloo' George Fraser at KYOK in Houston, Texas. To this teenager, American black music radio held truly mystical qualities.[3]

At the end of each week's feature, Simmons always read out the address of the American station he had been talking to and encouraged his listeners to write. This particular suburban soul fan needed no encouragement – he wrote enthusiastically to every station that Simmons mentioned. He was rewarded with a steady stream of promotional material mailed from America, including radio stations' printed playlists for that particular week, signed photos of its DJs and car stickers. It was this transatlantic correspondence and the irregular copies of Billboard magazine purchased on trips to London that became the main source of inspiration for a teenager obsessed both with radio and with the soul music that British radio chose not to play. His dream was that, one day, the 'powers' in Britain would awake from their slumber and realise that radio could be made much more exciting and more responsive to their listeners' musical tastes. He dreamt of a time that would see the introduction of many more radio stations in the UK, each of which would specialise in playing a different musical style, just as the Americans were already lucky enough to enjoy.

In the meantime, on that Bank Holiday weekend, he continued to twiddle the dial of his family's radio, searching for anything that might be more entertaining than the wall-to-wall pop music offered by both Radio One and Capital Radio. Suddenly, in the gaps between the BBC's multiplicity of transmitters spread across the FM band, he managed to find a strong signal broadcasting music that did not resemble anything the BBC might play. It was some sort of orchestral music, but the sound had been fed through an electronic gadget to create a 'phasing' effect, which had made it incredibly swirly and psychedelic. A voice, sounding bizarrely like a character from a Monty Python television sketch, intoned over the top of the music:

"Do you remember radio in the old days? Snaps, crackles and pops? Interference? Funny noises? The BBC? Radio Three? Well, that's all changed now …"[4]

There was a short gap in the commentary, as the orchestral music faded out, to be replaced by the opening chords of Junior Walker's version of the Motown hit 'How Sweet It Is.' The voiceover resumed:

"… thanks to Radio Invicta. Radio Invicta guarantees to tickle your trannie."[5]

Our excited suburban soul fan had heard this radio station before, but its transmissions had become more infrequent of late. The DJ on the station told listeners he was called Barry Stone and explained:

"Remember, if you've just tuned in, you're listening to Radio Invicta, the sound of soul, precisely the sound of soul. We play only soul music and we're here just for that music."[6]

Then he played a pre-recorded message for his audience, which announced:

"You're listening to Radio Invicta, bringing soul to London on 92.4 VHF. Now here's a few tips to ensure that you receive our soul sounds all day over this Bank Holiday weekend. Our high quality broadcasts are coming to you through one of several transmitters located in central London. These transmitters are operated at different intervals and this means that, to receive us well, you may have to alter the position of your aerial during our transmissions. So, especially if you have a portable radio, make sure that the telescopic aerial is fully extended and that it is placed horizontally. Also, try rotating the aerial until the strongest signal is received. And remember that Radio Invicta is the sound of soul and worth receiving well. So, for any further engineering information, ring our special numbers that are given out throughout the day."[7]

This was the sound of pirate radio, illegal radio, unlicensed radio. Whatever you wanted to call it, these stations certainly had no right within the law to broadcast, and they were not meant to be filling up the spaces on the FM band. Radio Invicta was London's only soul station and reached its audience through an elaborate network of transmitters installed on the top of very high buildings across London. To try and evade the attention of the authorities, Invicta switched its broadcasts from one transmitter to another every hour, on the hour, requiring it to broadcast these elaborate instructions. Listeners often found that their reception of the station suddenly deteriorated once the hourly switch was made, as the new transmitter site might be far from their immediate neighbourhood. Despite these frustrations, Invicta's audience of soul music fans in and around London was loyal and determined to listen.

Once Barry Stone had finished his show, another DJ, Roger Tate, arrived and explained the station's philosophy to listeners:

"Who are Radio Invicta? You may well be asking. Well, we're an all-soul music radio station. We're more of a campaign than a radio station, I suppose. We believe in featuring more good soul music on the radio."[8]

For this suburban soul fan, Radio Invicta was a lifeline to the soul music he felt was being so unfairly ignored by legal radio stations. Its DJs shared with the station's audience an intense passion and enthusiasm for soul music that neither BBC nor commercial radio DJs managed to convey. Invicta's DJs were primarily fans of the music, a factor that overcame the lack of professionalism they sometimes displayed when presenting their programmes.

Invicta was by no means the only pirate station on London's airwaves, but all the other illegal broadcasters seemed to play varieties of pop and rock music. Invicta was the only station to specialise in soul. Some of the other stations' DJs often sounded as if they were more in love with the idea of illegal broadcasting than with providing a genuine alternative to legal radio. Invicta seemed to command respect within the rest of the pirate radio community because it clung doggedly to its soul music format, and it was so obviously a station run BY soul music fans FOR soul music fans.

Occasionally, other pirate stations helped to publicise Invicta's long running campaign for a soul music radio station to be licensed in London. On one occasion, a DJ on FM pirate station London Stereo was heard to comment on-air to his co-presenter:

"Oh, that's interesting! 'Pirates In Stereo' – this is a newspaper article – 'A pirate radio station will be broadcasting to the Borough on Boxing Day in stereo, and the rest of London will be able to hear Radio Invicta when they defy the Post Office once again and go on the air for eight hours. The small group of do-it-yourself broadcasters…….' Yes, well."[9]

By 1974, Radio Invicta had been operating on and off for four years, but was now limiting its broadcasts to only a few hours each Bank Holiday weekend, which made its handful of broadcasts very special occasions for its audience. Our soul music fan in Camberley would spend all his pocket money on a pile of empty cassette tapes, prior to each Bank Holiday weekend, and would record on them as many of Invicta's broadcasts as he could fit. He treasured those tapes and would play them over and over again until the next Bank Holiday when he could hear the station. Then he would start the process all over again.

Radio Invicta's broadcasts had not always been so sporadic. The station had been launched in December 1970 by soul music enthusiast Tony Johns, initially using a low-power, medium wave, valve transmitter of the 'home brew' type that pirate stations usually built themselves in that era. During its first four years, Invicta had broadcast most weekends for only a few hours, but it had quickly attracted a growing audience. Soon, it became the first pirate station to make the switch to broadcasting on the FM band, pioneering the use of solid state, transistorised transmitters in the pirate radio community. Not only was this modern equipment far more compact and manageable for the station staff than the old, high voltage, valve-based technology, but the listener could enjoy much improved, high fidelity FM reception quality.[10]

Then, during one weekend's transmissions, a Radio Invicta volunteer had been caught by the authorities and fined £100, with £100 costs, for possessing a transmitter and using two public phone boxes for the station's phone-in music requests. As a result, Invicta operated with much greater caution between 1974 and 1977, limiting its broadcasts to Bank Holiday weekends when it would transmit continuously over two days and nights. At first, all its programmes for broadcast were pre-recorded by the presenters on cassette tapes a few days beforehand but, later, the station made the leap to broadcasting live and also converted its FM transmitter from mono to stereo. Unfortunately, in 1976, during Invicta's planned forty-eight hour broadcast between Christmas and the New Year, the authorities tracked down the station studio and several of its staff were subsequently prosecuted and fined by the courts.[11]

Throwing caution to the wind, Invicta returned to a schedule of weekly transmissions between September 1977 and 1981, broadcasting for a few hours every Sunday. By Christmas 1981, Invicta even transmitted live from a record shop in London's Kings Cross area for several days without interruption. The success of this marathon broadcast encouraged the station's staff to try and start continuous broadcasting, twenty-four hours a day. However, as Tony Johns recalled:

"Things started going wrong for us. We were busted three times. After each raid, we didn't play for two weeks – we played every other Sunday. But they got us each time we came back."[12]

Invicta's burgeoning popularity amongst London's soul music fans started to attract coverage in the music press, but the station's higher profile also brought its activities to the attention of the authorities. London listings magazine Time Out hailed Invicta as "probably the most professional sounding pirate in the country." The Evening News reported that reception of Invicta's transmissions was 'excellent' in "all GLC [Greater London Council] areas." However, in January 1982, Invicta was raided three times, which Tony Johns blamed on the recent explosion of other pirate radio stations on the airwaves in London: "Why pick on Invicta when there are a dozen other pirates who are just kids fooling around? We provide a service that London's other stations don't."[13]

Radio Invicta had been voted the third most popular black music radio programme in Britain by readers of the weekly music paper Black Echoes, which had somehow calculated that the station attracted 26,000 listeners each weekend. Invicta had recently started to broadcast advertisements within its programmes, charging £30 per minute of airtime, in order to finance its operations, and it was already broadcasting spots from clothes shops, record shops, clubs and music venues. But the persistent raids by the authorities were beginning to take their toll on the station. At the beginning of 1982, Tony Johns commented:

"In the ten years we've been operating, Invicta has suffered precious few raids. Then, this January, three raids in as many weeks. They let us broadcast for six days right through Christmas then, on the first Sunday of the New Year, they tracked us down and confiscated our transmitter. We half expected the second raid last Sunday week … We've lost about £600 worth of transmitting equipment, including our stereo encoder, but we have enough advertising revenue to go on building transmitters as fast as they capture them."[14]

Despite this bluster, Johns seemed to realise that the raids might well prove terminal for Radio Invicta. He explained openly, for the first time, the routine he had followed each week for the last eleven years in order to put his pirate station on the air:

"We go out for twelve hours on Sundays and there's plenty to organise when I finish work on Fridays. Everyone at Invicta has other jobs. I'm a travel agent … The evening is spent wiring up and, at about midnight, five of us tiptoe to our chosen tower block to erect our thirty-foot telescopic aerial. We use a wall-plug for the power supply and make a point of sending regular cheques to the GLC for the electricity we consume. Wiring up usually takes all night because testing the signal from the studio is pretty tricky. Last week, it took 'til nine in the morning to get it perfect and, as I go on[-air] at ten, I usually go without sleep. Each DJ does a two-hour spot and we get a good idea of our following from the calls our telephone girls take. Our hardcore listeners are aged sixteen to twenty-two, both black and white, but we've plenty of mums and dads."[15]

Sadly, during the remainder of 1982, Invicta managed to make very few appearances on London's airwaves. Instead, Johns devoted his time to organising a demonstration of public support for his station:

"We are asking our listeners to petition to have us accepted by the authorities, but [government minister] Timothy Raison has vowed to wipe the pirates off the airwaves. He obviously isn't aware that we have far more listeners on a Sunday than, for example, a Stockhausen concert on the BBC. Radio Three's audiences are often so small they can't even be measured statistically. But ask any teenager in Oxford Street whether they've heard of Invicta and the answer's usually 'yes.' London needs a soul station and Invicta supplies that service. The official stations make token gestures but, good as they are, three hours of Robbie Vincent on [BBC] Radio London and three of Greg Edwards on Capital [Radio] don't compare well with seven days of rock music."[16]

By the summer of 1983, Radio Invicta had raised a petition of 20,000 signatures in support of its bid for legality, but the station's Mike Strawson commented in frustration: "I have tried to speak to the Home Office about it, but it shuts the door."[17]

Invicta was still trying to come on-air each weekend, but had decided to shift its broadcasts to the early hours of the morning between midnight and six o'clock, when it hoped the authorities were less likely to be monitoring pirate radio transmissions. However, the station attracted the attention of Parliament and, in the House of Commons, Invicta was cited on two occasions as one of the pirate stations of which the government was well aware and which it was attempting to close down.[18]

During 1983 and 1984, Parliament's attention was regularly drawn to the activities of pirate stations by MPs who demanded to know what action the Government was taking to combat their illegal broadcasts. In November 1983, Alexander Fletcher, the Trade & Industry Secretary, noted that he had received representations on the subject of pirate radio from the Independent Broadcasting Authority, Capital Radio and members of the public. He went on to list thirty-one illegal stations that his Department knew had made broadcasts in recent months. In January 1984, Fletcher announced that, during 1983, ninety-seven raids had been carried out on pirate stations, leading to convictions of forty people. The previous year, there had only been sixty raids and ten convictions. However, in February 1984, Fletcher had to admit that there were still thirty pirate stations on-air, although three prosecutions had been made in January and twelve were still pending. He promised that the government would "continue to give a high degree of priority to the tracing and prosecution of pirate radio operators." By March 1984, Fletcher said he had received more than eighty representations on the topic of pirate radio, and it was obvious to him that the government needed to show considerably more active determination to combat the illegal stations.[19]

In May 1984, rumours started to circulate that the government was contemplating the licensing for the first time of a number of local community radio stations that could launch as early as 1986. A meeting was called between the Independent Broadcasting Authority, the Home Office, the Department of Trade & Industry [DTI] and representatives of commercial stations to discuss the idea. The DTI had just completed a two-month study into the phenomenon of pirate radio and had concluded that illegal stations were not as great a problem as was often supposed. Its report found that pirates, in reality, caused little interference to existing licensed stations, and that the commercial radio industry's real fear was the competition for advertising revenues that the pirates created. The DTI had already admitted that pirates were hardly a problem when, in answer to an MP's question in the House of Commons about the interference pirate stations caused to emergency police and ambulance radio communications, the government could only cite one such case as a result of an unlicensed Manchester station.[20]

In June 1984, the chairman of the Independent Broadcasting Authority, Lord Thomson, publicly attacked the government's inaction over the closure of pirate stations, and expressed his concern at "the apparent condoning of theft and other instances of law-breaking, accompanied by a worrying unwillingness to deal with the matter." To date, in 1984, the DTI had forwarded twenty-one cases of unlicensed broadcasting to government solicitors for prosecution, involving forty-nine people in total. Lord Thomson criticised such actions as ineffective and said they only "produced a situation which is demonstrably inequitable in the eyes of the law and of the public, and is increasingly difficult to justify."[21]

Then, on Monday 16 July, the government's Telecommunications Act 1984 was passed into law and irrevocably changed the legal status of pirate radio stations. Officers of the DTI's Radio Interference Service (now renamed the Radio Investigation Service) could, under the new law, seize broadcasting equipment without a warrant, powers they had not previously enjoyed. They could also arrest a suspect involved in pirate radio without a warrant, and the penalties available to the courts were increased to a maximum £2,000 fine and/or a three-month jail sentence. These stiffer deterrents immediately produced the desired effect that several years of raids against pirate stations had failed to yield. Many pirates voluntarily closed down on Sunday 15 July 1984, the eve of the new legislation, suitably frightened by the more severe legal consequences of their hobby. Until now, the authorities had always had to obtain a warrant from a court to enter a building and confiscate a suspected pirate radio transmitter. Now, they could simply walk into a suspected pirate station, wherever and whenever they wished, and walk out with all its equipment. The rules of the game had changed drastically and the law no longer worked so much in the pirate stations' favour. It was almost as if they were now considered to be guilty until proven innocent.[22]

Along with many other pirates, on 15 July 1984, London's first soul music station, Radio Invicta, made its very last transmission and closed down. It had survived thirteen years, during which time pirate radio activity in London had been transformed dramatically from the early days, when a mere handful of teenage radio enthusiasts stood guard over valve-operated transmitters in fields on Sunday mornings. By 1984, it had become an industry filled with dozens of profit-driven young entrepreneurs, each of whom believed they could make a lot of money from owning their own pirate radio station. The enthusiasts were increasingly being driven out by more callous, commercial types. By the time Radio Invicta closed, it was no longer London's only soul station. In recent years, Invicta had spawned several imitators – JFM, Horizon and LWR – each of which seemed to have more resources, more money and more inclination to run their station as a business than Invicta had ever had.

Primarily, Invicta had always been a small bunch of soul music fans playing their favourite music to a larger bunch of like-minded people who were their listeners. Invicta founder Tony Johns summed it up when he recalled: "We at Invicta were never interested in free radio as such. We just loved soul music."[23]

Now, Radio Invicta had gone and, despite an optimistic note in City Limits magazine the following week that the station had "closed with assurances that they'll be back soon somehow," it was not to be.[24]

Radio Invicta was never again heard on the airwaves of London. When that station died, so too did a little piece of hope that one particular suburban soul music fan had nurtured in his heart for the last ten years. Would he ever live to see the day when Londoners were allowed to listen to a licensed soul music radio station? In 1973, Capital Radio had been heralded as London's FIRST commercial music station. Now, in 1984, Capital was still London's ONLY commercial music station. The authorities had shown no inclination to allow more stations to be licensed. The death of Invicta, after thirteen years of actively campaigning for the right to become legal, was a severe blow. If Invicta could not change the obstinate and anachronistic system of British radio broadcasting, what on earth could a (now) twenty-six year old suburban soul music fan do to fulfil the dream he cherished of creating a soul music radio station for London?

---

[1] Tim Devlin, "Capital Music To Smile By", The Times, 13 Oct 1973.
[2] [uncredited], [untitled], possibly Disc or Record Mirror, Apr to Jun 1973.
[3] author's notes, 1972 to 1974.
[4] author's recording, 25 Aug 1974.
[5] ibid.
[6] ibid.
[7] ibid.
[8] author's recording, 28 Mar 1975.
[9] author's recording, 11 Jan 1975.
[10] John Hind & Stephen Mosco, "Rebel Radio", Pluto, London, 1985.
"Radio Invicta", Newswave Magazine no. 1, 1979.
[11] ibid.
[12] ibid.
Kirsty White, "Captured: A Pirate Of The Airwaves", London Evening News, 29 Jul 1980.
[13] ibid.
Lennie Michaels, Carl Gardner & Crispin Aubrey, "Air On A Shoe String", Time Out, 23 Mar 1979.
John Blake, "Hitting The Roof", Evening Standard, 21 Jan 1982.
[14] Chris Salewicz, "Rebel Radios", Time Out, 2 Apr 1982.
David Johnson, "Pirates At 10 O'Clock", Evening Standard, 8 Feb 1982.
[15] ibid.
[16] ibid.
[17] Richard Brooks, "Woodland Pirates Raid The Waves With Rock", Sunday Times, 5 Jun 1983.
"Freetime", Punch, 30 May 1984.
[18] Hansard, House of Commons, 16 Nov 1983, 28 Feb 1984.
[19] Hansard, House of Commons, 16 Nov 1983, 20 Jan 1984, 13 Feb 1984, 15 Feb 1984, 6 Mar 1984.
[20] Richard Brooks, "All-Clear For Radio Pirates", Sunday Times, 20 May 1984.
Hansard, House of Commons, 13 Apr 1984.
[21] "The IBA And Pirate Radio", IBA Press Release, 14 Jun 1984.
Hansard, House of Commons, 10 Jun 1984.
[22] "Pirates Face DTI's New Investigators", Broadcast, 20 Jul 1984.
Eleanor Levy, "Pirate Radio R.I.P.", Record Mirror, 28 Jul 1984.
[23] John Hind & Stephen Mosco, op cit.
[24] [uncredited], [untitled], City Limits, 20 Jul 1984.

PART ONE

Pirate Radio: 1984 to 1988

"I believe it does a great disservice to those who wish to promote community radio to suggest in any way that present unlicensed broadcasters are the pioneers of that form of broadcasting."

Lord Lucas
Parliamentary Under-Secretary of State at the Department of Trade & Industry
The House of Lords
14 January 1985

Mr Pendry MP asked the Secretary of State for Trade & Industry if he will give an estimate of the date by which he expects to have eliminated pirate radio broadcasting within the United Kingdom…

Mr Butcher: *"I cannot estimate when unlicensed broadcasting will be eliminated…"*

Hansard
Written Answers
The House of Commons
23 May 1985

30 November 1984.
The House of Commons, London.

During the previous six months, rumours had circulated that the government was planning to introduce legislation to create a new, third tier of radio broadcasting in Britain. It was thought that new, very localised stations might be licensed, operating much along the same lines as land-based pirate broadcasters, complementing the existing, larger national and regional services operated by the BBC and independent companies. Hopes had been raised amongst staff of former pirate stations such as Radio Invicta that, having already voluntarily closed down under threat of stiffer legal penalties, they might at last be allowed to apply for these completely new radio licences.

In the House of Commons, at 2.30 pm on 30 November 1984, Angela Rumbold, Member of Parliament for the Southwest London constituency of Mitcham & Morden, stood up and asked the government "to look urgently at the present system of regulation and licensing in local, independent radio to see whether it fits the principle of encouraging market forces to determine what can be allowed." She argued that the existence of pirate radio "must surely indicate that there is something wrong with our licensing procedures" and she questioned "why only Capital [Radio] and LBC can operate [as commercial radio stations] in London, with eight million people to serve."[25]

Rumbold advocated that a new system of neighbourhood radio stations should be introduced to serve "local communities within ten to fifteen minutes' drive of each other." She challenged the government to explain why such a substantial proportion of the FM band (88 to 108 MHz) had still not been made available to radio stations, despite international agreement that it must be used expressly for that purpose: "There is no adequate reason why Britain is uniquely unable to join the remainder of the world and use the whole [FM] band."[26]

She proposed a radical change to the infrastructure of radio broadcasting, away from the existing system of a small number of large radio stations and towards a new regime offering a larger number of small stations: "The more stations that come on the air in one locality, the smaller will be the coverage of each service. It is a familiar feature in other kinds of radio communication. The time has now come for it to be accepted in specialist, small business, ethnic and voluntary broadcasting."[27]

Rumbold concluded her speech by comparing the existing British system of radio regulation to the censorship that had once been imposed upon the book publishing industry:

"The notion that the government or their appointed bodies can continue closely to regulate local broadcasting will survive for only as long as the idea that printing presses should be allowed to produce only the Bible and approved texts ... The need now is to devise a licensing procedure to allow orderly progress. I ask the Minister seriously to consider the possibility of making a start by issuing some experimental licenses in the London area as soon as possible on the basis of the suggestions that I have outlined."[28]

David Mellor, the Home Office Under-Secretary, replied to Rumbold's question on behalf of the government. He spent the first half of his sixteen-minute response justifying the existing regulatory system for radio broadcasting and defending the "high standards" maintained by existing radio stations. He argued that "pirate operators observe no common standard, pay no royalties and frequently plagiarise news broadcasts," and he stressed that "those who take the law into their own hands must expect to pay such penalties as are imposed." Mellor stated categorically that "the government do not believe that it would be sensible or fair to issue pirate broadcasters with licences to broadcast. To do so, on the basis suggested by the pirate broadcasters, would be progressively to undermine the broadcasting structure that has evolved over the years."[29]

However, in the second half of his speech, Mellor went on to outline a new government plan for a whole range of community radio stations, though he inserted the caveat that his remarks should not be "interpreted as implying that pirate stations will necessarily be legitimised." He proposed the licensing of two new types of radio station: neighbourhood broadcasters serving local communities with low power transmitters operated by local people; and larger stations serving wider areas, providing programmes in a particular musical style or targeting a particular ethnic group. Mellor made it clear that such proposals were still at a very early stage of discussion and that no details had yet been finalised as to the number of stations or their exact locations. He promised there would be more information "at about the turn of the year."[30]

Mellor concluded by reiterating that "the government cannot license pirate stations as they stand." But he added that the government would "look to those with interest and enterprise to explore the potential for community radio. Provided that the illegal broadcasters meet the criteria for community radio – we shall try to make them as light as possible, consistent with the maintenance of standards – it will be open to them to apply in the same way as any other group. However, I cannot, on behalf of the government, offer them preferential treatment, and I do not think that they could expect it merely because they have pre-empted [unused radio] frequencies."[31]

This was the first occasion on which the government had broached the possibility of licensing any sort of specialist radio station that would serve only one particular segment of the population. Until then, the fifty-one local commercial stations that had been licensed by the Independent Broadcasting Authority since 1973 were each required to broadcast programmes of broad appeal to the entire population within the area they served. The phrase 'all things to all people' had become the ethos of the fledgling commercial radio industry, because regulations required each station not to limit in any way its target audience to either a particular age group or to a segment with a particular musical interest. As a result, the output of all commercial radio stations drove very carefully down the middle of the road, avoiding anything with too narrow an appeal, and often ending up with programmes that appealed to the lowest common denominator of their audiences.

For a former soul music pirate station such as Radio Invicta, there was incredible significance in David Mellor's announcement that the proposed new stations would be aimed at "devotees of a type of music who do not hear enough of what they like on existing, more broadly based stations." It was exactly the argument Invicta had employed in its campaign to be legalised, and it was exactly the view expressed by the 20,000 Invicta listeners who had signed the station's petition the previous year. Very little airplay was given to soul music on existing radio services, which is why London needed a station dedicated wholly to this particular musical style in order to satisfy widespread public demand. For London's soul music fans, Mellor's announcement seemed particularly encouraging.[32]

At the same time that the government's plans for a new tier of local radio suddenly seemed as if they might progress with unprecedented haste, the establishment seemed to be losing its long running legal battle against pirate radio. Initially, the tougher laws introduced four months earlier had frightened the majority of unlicensed radio stations into closing down, but many of them had since drifted back onto the airwaves. When the Telecommunications Act had been passed into law in July 1984, only three London stations had ignored it and continued their transmissions. By October 1984, the DTI had raided four pirate stations in South London and, as permitted by the new law, had confiscated all their studio equipment. One of those pirates was soul station Horizon, where the DTI "confiscated absolutely everything out of the studio, brand new cart machines, Technics decks, the lot, leaving just the clock on the wall and a chair."[33]

Despite the severity of these new-style raids, more pirates continued to return to the airwaves until, by November 1984, the DTI said it was aware of eleven stations in operation. By then, it had conducted one hundred raids and prosecuted thirty-seven people in 1984, of which fifty raids on thirty-five stations had occurred since July, when the new law had come into effect. In the House of Lords, Baroness Stedman asked the government: "How many so-called 'pirate radio stations' have been closed down, how many came back on-air, and after how long?" The DTI replied that nine stations were known to have resumed broadcasts after raids, but that it kept no record of the length of time between a raid on a particular station and any return it might have made to the airwaves.[34]

If this renaissance of land-based pirate stations was already making a mockery of the new law, only months after its introduction, there was a far bigger thorn in the government's side caused by a new source of illegal radio broadcasting. This came not from the British mainland, but from the waters of the North Sea, off the coast of Southeast England. Offshore pirate radio, in the form of stations based on sea-borne ships in international waters, had been a peculiarly European phenomenon that stretched as far back as 1958 although, by the mid-1970s, most such stations had died out. Britain had outlawed offshore pirates in 1967 when it legislated the Marine, etc., Broadcasting (Offences) Act, although one remaining station, Radio Caroline, launched in 1964, had stubbornly continued to broadcast during most of the 1970s and 1980s from the North Sea. Although still on-air in 1984, by then Caroline's audience was tiny due to the poor quality of its broadcast signal and the station's haphazard programming. Radio Caroline no longer posed any real threat to British commercial radio, since most of its revenues derived not from paid spot advertisements, but from selling chunks of airtime to religious broadcasters that were not allowed airtime on licensed stations. Despite its illegality, Radio Caroline was passively tolerated by the authorities as a relic of Britain's broadcasting history, a legacy that refused to lie down and die.[35]

However, in May 1983, a new offshore pirate station called 'Laser 558' had also started transmissions from the North Sea and had given the complacent British commercial radio industry the biggest scare of its short life. Laser transmitted an excellent, strong signal that could be heard clearly throughout most of England and Western Europe. Its pop music programming was innovative and well produced, and its ethos was fresh, at a time when British commercial radio sounded very stale. Without any visible means of organised promotion, word of Laser's arrival on the airwaves spread rapidly amongst British radio listeners, so that people of all ages started to tune their radios away from commercial and BBC stations and towards 558 AM. By 1984, the pirate station's audience was already substantial and it was starting to attract advertising that the British commercial radio industry considered to be rightfully its own.

Pirate radio was now assaulting the British radio establishment in two distinct forms – land-based stations located on inner city tower blocks, and Laser 558 anchored out of Parliament's reach in the North Sea. "The summer of 1984 was the summer of radio piracy," wrote one commentator, "when Dread Broadcasting [Corporation], JFM and Horizon belched reggae, electro and soul all over London, and Laser 558 pumped out non-stop pop from the North Sea."[36]

By the time the British government had legislated the Telecommunications Act in July 1984 to try and combat the problem of land-based pirate radio, the popularity of Laser 558 had emerged as a much more immediate and serious problem to solve. Laser's growing audience was causing a notable fall in listenership to many licensed radio stations in Southeast England, and was therefore posing much more of a direct economic threat to commercial radio than land-based pirate radio had ever done. In Parliament, the government was being asked specifically what it would do to close down Laser 558. In the House of Commons, government spokesman Alexander Fletcher noted "the difficulty of proceeding directly against an illicit broadcaster on the high seas." In the House of Lords, Lord Cockfield replied that "direct action against the offshore pirate stations is more difficult as they are broadcasting from vessels anchored in international waters. As such, the United Kingdom has no jurisdiction which would enable the vessels to be boarded and an end to be put to the broadcasts." The government reluctantly had to admit that it was powerless to act directly against Laser.[37]

The clamour from the broadcasting establishment started to increase dramatically, demanding that Parliament do something about Laser 558. Initially, the government had hoped that Laser might just quietly slip away, switch off or run out of money. After a year, it had become obvious that the American-run station intended to be in Europe for the long run and had spent a small fortune establishing itself. Offshore pirate Laser 558 was proving to be a much more stubborn problem for the government to solve than the proliferation of illegal radio stations in Britain's cities.

Land-based pirates appealed mainly to small and very specific segments of the population – soul music fans listened to the soul pirates, Greek people to the Greek pirates, and so on. Whereas, Laser had managed to attract a mainstream audience that had, until now, been quite happy listening to BBC Radio One or Capital Radio in London. Reception of land-based pirates was often unreliable, since a raid by the authorities could take a station off-air for several days or weeks, whereas Laser was a reliable fixture on everyone's radio, interrupted only by occasional bouts of stormy North Sea weather in winter. Advertising airtime on land-based pirate stations was largely being sold to local shops and small independent record companies, whereas Laser was deliberately seeking out multinational brand names to advertise to its pan-European audience.

Over and above the annoyance caused to the British establishment by Laser's remarkable success in attracting both listeners and advertisers was the unbearable fact that the station was American through-and-through. Laser had American management, American

DJs, American jingles and read out a New York City postal address. Its advertising sales operation was based in America, and its programmes cleverly used all the tricks of the radio trade that Americans had learnt from their sixty-year history of commercial radio. In Britain, commercial radio had started little more than a decade earlier, and the licensing system had mandated that (with the exception of London) there was only one commercial radio station for each area of the country. Although British commercial stations did have to compete with BBC radio stations for listeners, they also enjoyed a monopoly over radio advertising in each of their local markets. The rule of the UK commercial radio industry had been 'one market, one station' until the unwelcome arrival of Laser 558 in the North Sea.

Despite the growing popularity of Laser amongst listeners, the British establishment still considered American-style radio to be the antithesis of what Britain's fledgling commercial radio industry should sound like. When commercial radio had been introduced in 1973, the Independent Broadcasting Authority licence regulations mitigated against any station playing too much music, broadcasting too little speech content or targeting too narrow an audience. British commercial radio had effectively been mandated to sound quite similar to existing BBC stations, but with the addition of advertisements. The regulator had published dozens of guidelines and rules that ensured each commercial station provided precisely the type of programmes it thought would benefit listeners. In this way, UK commercial radio was a remarkably reactionary attempt to duplicate the 'nanny' attitude towards listeners that the BBC had pursued for decades. Radio audiences were never asked what they wanted – they were given what was thought to be good for them.

In the early 1970s, many of the people who campaigned against the introduction of commercial radio in Britain had based their objections solely on their hatred of the American commercial radio system. An editorial in Campaign magazine had articulated these fears in the very week in 1973 that Britain's first commercial music station had launched:

"Commercial radio was equated in many minds with staggeringly inane disc jockies, endless hours of Top Twenty pop music, and a barrage of advertising blending confusingly with the programmes ... Clearly, commercial radio in Britain is not going to be that sort of operation."[38]

A decade later, Laser 558 had arrived out of nowhere, matching exactly that description of American radio, and the establishment was shocked that British listeners seemed to love it much more than the carefully regulated, home-grown variety of commercial radio that they themselves had created. Until then, American-style radio had been completely unheard in Britain, except by holidaymakers visiting the United States and by the few people who tuned in at night to American Forces Network radio broadcasts from U.S. military bases in Germany. Now, suddenly, Laser's format of unadulterated Americana was blaring out of transistor radios across the land and, whenever you visited shops, offices, or people's homes, Laser 558 was more likely to be there on the radio than the local commercial station or the BBC.

The UK commercial radio industry was appalled. For eleven years, it had been giving the public what it believed it knew was best for them, working in the shadow of broadcast legislation that deliberately prevented any one of them becoming the sort of pure pop music radio station that Laser 558 was proud to be. The British commercial radio industry trade organisation, the Association of Independent Radio Contractors [AIRC], had already placed the issue of land-based pirate radio high on its agenda, even before the arrival of Laser 558. In February 1984, the AIRC had said it was "increasingly concerned" at the growth in pirate radio operators and it lamented these stations' ability to operate outside laws that restricted its own members from engaging in fair competition.[39]

In March and May 1984, representatives of the AIRC had held joint meetings with the regulator, the Independent Broadcasting Authority [IBA], and with the Home Office and the Department of Trade & Industry, both of which were responsible for enforcement actions against pirate radio stations. It was reported that "AIRC and IBA representatives were dismayed that so little progress had been made and expressed this disappointment forcibly. DTI revealed that, in the past three months, ten cases had been processed for prosecution, but only two had been brought to court, both with convictions."[40]

The DTI blamed its own lack of resources for the low level of action against pirates, and it promised to send warning letters to advertisers who had illegally bought airtime on pirate stations. But the AIRC wanted more direct action against the operators themselves, and it demanded to know why injunctions could not be sought to stop stations from continuing to broadcast, once they had already been convicted. The DTI, having taken legal advice, admitted there was no obstacle to prevent it seeking injunctions "in appropriate cases," and the AIRC suggested that such action should be taken against several pirates that were persistently on-air.[41]

The AIRC and IBA war against pirate radio was already underway in 1984, and the increasing popularity of Laser 558 that year only served to strengthen their resolve. The IBA chairman Lord Thomson spoke out and condemned the "irresponsible and unfair competition" that pirate stations were mounting against licensed UK commercial radio:

"The radio pirates have been operating on small budgets by flouting copyright laws, stealing IRN [Independent Radio News] news bulletins and employing staff at non-union rates. Strong representations have been made to government to curb these illegal operators. It is essential that Independent Local Radio survives as a healthy and viable public service."[42]

The perceived economic advantages the pirates enjoyed over legal commercial stations became the rallying cry of the anti-pirate lobby. It did not seem to matter to complainants that the British public obviously considered Laser 558's programmes superior to those that the commercial stations were broadcasting. The radio industry chose to ignore these competitive issues and the questions posed by Laser's success as to the suitability of their own programme policies. Instead, it chose to whinge that the pirate stations were not playing the radio game fairly by UK rules. It simply was not cricket. In effect, Lord Thomson was complaining more about the detailed government regulatory system imposed upon the UK commercial radio industry and the economic restraints under which it laboured, rather than about the pirates themselves.

The land-based illegal stations employed largely unpaid volunteer staff, used very cheap home-made transmitters, had no excess funds to fritter away, and were making no attempts to conform to the establishment's prescribed 'public service broadcasting' ethic. Furthermore, they were not contributing financially to the expensive, networked IRN radio news service, as every commercial radio station was required to do. Neither did they have to abide by UK copyright laws which required substantial payments for the broadcast of recorded music. Why should pirates be allowed to enjoy all these freedoms, when commercial radio stations could not?

The AIRC director, Brian West, wrote to The Times:

"Licensed UK broadcasters submit to an extensive and onerous set of rules and costs as a condition of their licences; is it fair that unlicensed competitors should evade all these rules and costs? Thus far, the government has effectively aided and abetted this evasion and unfair competition by failing to enforce the law. Hence our campaign."[43]

Frustrated by the inaction of the Home Office and the DTI against both the land-based pirates and offshore Laser 558, the AIRC proceeded to orchestrate a debate on the subject in the House of Lords. Many local commercial radio stations had Lords amongst the local worthies on their boards of directors, and so each company's managing director or chairman was asked to brief his station's friendly peer on the issues that were to be raised in a Parliamentary debate. The AIRC imagined that this sort of political pressure might force the government to make some kind of statement on pirate radio and it hoped that a debate would push the civil servants to take action.

In the event, the ruse worked brilliantly.

---

[25] Hansard, House of Commons, 30 Nov 1984.
[26] ibid.
[27] ibid.
[28] ibid.
[29] ibid.
[30] ibid.
[31] ibid.
[32] ibid.
[33] Eleanor Levy, "Pirate Radio R.I.P", Record Mirror, 28 Jul 1984.
"Pirate Bust Update", Record Mirror, 20 Oct 1984.
[34] Hansard, House of Commons, 13 Nov 1984, 23 Nov 1983.
Hansard, House of Lords, 27 Nov 1984.
[35] Stuart Henry & Mike von Joel, "Pirate Radio – Then And Now", Blandford, Poole, 1984.
[36] Alice Rawsthorn, "Why Pirate Stations Are Off The Airwaves", Campaign, 15 Nov 1985.
[37] Hansard, House of Commons, 2 Mar 1984.
Hansard, House of Lords, 22 Mar 1984.
[38] Editorial, Campaign, 12 Oct 1973.
[39] "Pirate Radio", Inside Radio no. 7, AIRC, 27 Feb 1984.
[40] "Pirate Moves", Inside Radio no. 8, AIRC, 18 Jun 1984.
[41] ibid.
[42] "Television & Radio 1985", Independent Broadcasting Authority, 1984.
[43] Brian West, "Repelling The Pirates", letter, The Times, 12 Jan 1985.

14 January 1985.
The House of Lords, London.

At quarter past seven on the evening of 14 January 1985, Lord Monson wound up a debate on election procedures in Northern Ireland, after which the House of Lords launched into a bizarre one-hundred-and-two-minute discussion about the evils of pirate radio.[44]

Between 1967 and 1975, Lord Aylestone had been chairman of the Independent Television Association when regulation of Britain's newly created commercial radio sector had been added to its remit. He initiated the debate by asking the government what action it was taking against "so-called radio pirates." He declared: "They are radio thieves. They operate without a Home Office licence. Some of them have applied to the Home Office for a licence and have been refused. They have been refused because they do not conform to the government's view of what is necessary to run independent local radio."

Lord Aylestone reiterated the government's view that commercial radio had to be "a balanced service, a service in which there is some recorded music (records), some talk (documentaries), some feature programmes and so on." Whereas, he said, pirate stations concentrated solely on playing music and "they exercise no control whatever over the amount of recorded music. It can be what is known as 'back to back' – the playing of records the whole time." Lord Aylestone argued that the government seemed to be ignoring the threat to the public posed by this uninterrupted pop music: "It is unfair to say that the Department of Trade & Industry [DTI] are doing nothing [to stop pirates] – but are they really doing enough?"

Lord Aylestone had started his speech by declaring "a small financial interest" in an un-named commercial radio station. His line of argument against the pirates was followed by a succession of similar statements from other peers, many of whom similarly had interests in local commercial radio stations. Speakers in this debate included: Lord Willis, a director of Capital Radio; Lord Craigton, a former radio director and now consultant to a consortium bidding for a proposed radio licence in Aylesbury; Lord Kennet, a director of an un-named station; Lord Mulley, a director of Radio Hallam; and Baroness Stedman, a director of Hereward Radio. The latter also spoke on behalf of the absent Lord Ezra, a director of Radio Mercury.

The remaining speakers were Lord Lucas, Under-Secretary of State at the DTI and the government spokesperson for this debate, and Lord McIntosh, who noted slyly: "It may be that only my noble friend Lord Willis and myself are not actually directors of local radio stations, but I do not suppose …" At this point, he was interrupted by an un-named Lord who pointed out that Lord Willis was, in fact, also a station director. Lord McIntosh resumed by saying obliquely that he "did not think there is a great deal of financial benefit to be gained from being a director of a local radio station."

Baroness Stedman was the only speaker brazen enough to admit the true motive behind the Lords' orchestration of this debate: "The Independent Broadcasting Authority [IBA] have made strong representation to the government and direct approaches to the Home Secretary, as have the Association of Independent Radio Contractors [AIRC], but nothing ever happens. If the offshore pirates increase their reach and listeners, then Independent Local Radio [ILR] is bound to suffer in terms of reach and listeners ... the Independent Local Radio stations will want to know the answers, preferably tonight from the noble Lord."

Most of the Lords' wrath was directed against Laser 558, whose perceived sins were that it played too much pop music, it was American, and it had successfully attracted several big-name advertisers. Lord Willis, a director of Britain's largest commercial station, Capital Radio, whose audience had been impacted substantially by the success of Laser, was particularly damning of the pirate's programmes: "What they give us is audible wallpaper; wall to wall pop music. I have nothing against pop music, but the restrictions and regulations under which the established Independent Local Radio network operates lay down quite clearly that we must provide balanced broadcasting." He told the House that "Laser proudly proclaims 'you're never a second away from music,'" as if this statement must be the ultimate act of heresy [in fact, Laser's slogan was: "you're never more than a MINUTE away from music"].

Lord Willis went on to argue that Laser 558 was backed by Wall Street banks whose aim was to ruin the British system of radio broadcasting: "They see a huge prize here in the United Kingdom if they can only establish this station and take command of a big national network. They are prepared to pour millions into Laser, and they are doing so in order to try to achieve that position. They are not little men. They are big men, and the prize is big. If they are allowed to continue, then the fabric of radio is in danger of being destroyed."

Concluding his speech, Lord Willis said: "We have something unique and splendid in our radio system. We have built it up by a careful system of checks and balances, of licensing, and of making sure that even commercial stations have to broadcast a certain amount of talks and educational programming, and so forth. We have built it into a unique system; yet we now seem to be sitting idly by while these pirates – these thieves – move in and destroy that fabric."

Lord Craig quoted from one of Laser's publicity leaflets which explained that "the station operates on the principle that the airwaves are free and beyond regulation." He described this as a "scandalous statement" and "a situation which we in Europe must do something about." Lord Mulley referred to "the enormous spread of the power of Laser" as if it were an evil source of propaganda, rather than a pop music radio station whose programmes were obviously of immense appeal to the general public.

While the Lords' hatred of Laser 558 bordered on the xenophobic, their attitude towards land-based pirates was comparatively lenient and remarkably tolerant. The land-based stations were viewed largely as the product of eccentric Brits and radio hobbyists whose illegal pursuits on the airwaves did little real harm. Even Lord Aylestone, who had drawn up the regulatory system for the launch of commercial radio in Britain, demonstrated a surprising lack of venom towards the land-based pirates: "Some of them are very small and simply broadcast for a few hours over the weekend – no need at all to worry about them. But there are probably fifty stations which are much larger and which are there as a business to make money by selling advertising on the air."

Lord Mulley made a similar distinction and suggested that the punishments meted out to pirate entrepreneurs should be balanced with tolerance of the hobbyists: "I am told there are up to one hundred and thirty stations, most of them run just on Sunday afternoons by enthusiasts. But the real problems come from people who are making a lot of money by these illegal activities."

Lord McIntosh took up the same issue: "I suspect that the practical complications of legislation to permit political enthusiasts to occupy occasional airwaves on a Sunday afternoon would be too great. Therefore, I am suggesting – and here I think that I am following the noble Lord, Lord Aylestone – that we ought not to be worried too much about that sort of breaking the law."

Estimates of the number of pirate stations in existence, how much it cost to establish a pirate station, and how much profit they could earn from advertising were cited in several speeches. However, the Lords' imaginations vastly over-estimated both the costs and the rewards to be reaped from land-based piracy. Lord Craig explained that he was part of a consortium applying for a commercial radio licence in Aylesbury, and he suggested that an alternative route for his group would be to launch a local pirate station at a cost of £5,000: "In running a pirate station, we could give our audience whatever we liked, when we liked, with programmes and quality determined only by our own interests. Moreover, because we would have a low capital, we could make a profit by cutting our advertising rate below those of the competing licensed radio stations."

Without a hint of irony, Lord Craig had just described succinctly the openly competitive way in which commercial radio was organised in many countries of the world, though not in Britain. Commercial stations elsewhere operated in a free market environment, fighting other stations in their vicinity for listeners and for revenue from advertisers. Only in Britain had commercial radio stations been granted a monopoly over radio advertising in their service area. Like Lord Willis before him, Lord Craig objected that "pirates do not have to provide a costly, balanced public service programme."

Lord Kennet had "obtained the best figures that I could," which led him to believe that a pirate station could break even if it earned £10,000 per week, whereas an independent local station required revenue of £17,000 a week. He regretted that these were "rough figures" [in fact, no land-based pirate station had achieved these levels of income]. Lord Lucas noted that radio transmitters were "fairly cheap items – I understand that a one hundred watt transmitter costs only around £2,000" [in fact, basic pirate radio transmitters had cost less than £100 to make].

If the monetary arguments about illegal radio proved to be ill-informed, then Lord Mulley had the audacity to suggest that the general public disliked pirate stations as much as did he and his fellow commercial radio directors: "There seems to be complete unanimity among the IBA, the AIRC, the individual ILR companies, the BBC and the general public that something ought to be done about this serious and growing problem of pirate or illegal radio stations."

Lord McIntosh, more accurately, placed the blame for the growth of pirate radio at the door of the government itself: "It is important that we should distinguish between the large scale money-makers and the various people on the fringes of local radio who are simply existing in the vacuum which, it must be said, has been created by the bureaucracy, the slowness, of both the Home Office and the IBA in extending radio services to those who might well want them."

The previous speaker, Baroness Stedman, had objected to pirates on the grounds that they "could apply for a franchise but they do not bother." Lord McIntosh quashed this fallacy and proposed a practical solution: "If it is true – and I believe it to be true – that there has been a substantial expansion of illegal pirate radio in the last few years, ought it not to be in the interests of government and of the IBA to see to it that the attraction of pirate radio is less? Ought it not to be, for example, that the IBA and the government should proceed faster in the licensing of new radio stations in the smaller communities? I understand that the IBA has been pressing the government for wider powers in relation to community radio, but we still have a very monolithic radio structure in this country. We do not have ethnic radio stations. We do not really have local radio stations operating, as they should do, on a shoestring …"

Several land-based pirate stations were mentioned by name during the debate. Lord Aylestone was damning of London pirate Radio Jackie which, he said, "issues a brochure in which it boasts of its illegality. It boasts of the fact that it has the support of a large number of Members of Parliament in its own area. I can hardly conceive it to be possible that a Member of Parliament, whatever his or her political shade or colour, would be likely to allow his or her name to be used in this respect."

Lord Mulley was aghast that Radio Jackie "has been allowed to operate for fifteen years and now, for a couple of years, it has been operating for twenty-four hours a day and nothing at all seems to have been done about it by the government."

Baroness Stedman said she had been told that "whereas Capital Radio can offer peak thirty-second [advertisement] spots for something like £490, Jackie can offer the same time for £5." She asked: "Why has the Department of Trade & Industry failed to act against Jackie? Why has it held back its powers?"

Lord Kennet added that Radio Sunshine, "operating near Worcester," used a Post Office box number as its mailing address. He asked: "Would a thief be allowed to do that? Would a brothel keeper be allowed to do that?"

Lord Kennet also cited Radio Scargill which, he said, "puts out pro-strike propaganda to the miners" and was "a criminal enterprise."

After more than an hour of debate, Lord Lucas rose to address the House on behalf of the government, and started by tackling Parliament's track record of action against land-based pirates. He acknowledged that the DTI's Radio Investigation Service was understaffed by eight posts and he pointed out that it was also responsible for investigating other sources of radio interference, in addition to pirates. He said that, in 1982, sixty-two illegal transmitters had been located, of which thirty-nine had been un-manned, resulting in ten prosecutions. In 1984, 119 transmitters had been found, of which fifty were un-manned, and there were forty-three prosecutions. Between July 1984, when tougher laws against pirates had been introduced, and January 1985, he pointed out that there had already been sixty raids on thirty-six pirate stations.

Lord Lucas went on to explain the method by which land-based pirates had reduced their risk of being caught: "The unlicensed broadcasters frequently have their stations at different locations from their transmitters, and the two are generally connected by a radio link. There are technical reasons which make tracing such a link very difficult indeed. It takes a good deal of time and effort. Finding the studio itself may possibly require police assistance …"

He then described the problems involved in tracing land-based pirates: "Most stations are not in fact incorporated institutions, and they frequently change hands ... We find it extremely difficult to catch hold of any one person who will accept responsibility for making the transmission. Therefore, it is difficult and frequently not worthwhile taking people to court, because they can just deny authority for having operated the station. Nevertheless, the task of finding the studios is one which will be pursued – and with increasing vigour."

On the pressing question of offshore pirate station Laser 558, Lord Lucas could offer no solution. He explained that the Marine, etc., Broadcasting (Offences) Act 1967 "gives no powers to anyone to arrest ships on the high seas" and that "there are no pirate radio ships generating [sic] within territorial waters." When pressed for a fuller explanation by Lord Willis, Lord Lucas was forced to admit that "it is an impracticability to take an offshore station outside territorial waters to court."

Acknowledging that the debate had in fact been orchestrated by the commercial radio lobby, Lord Lucas said that "the Association of Independent Radio Contractors, which has been most vociferous in this matter, is due to meet my honourable friend the Minister in a matter of weeks." And he concluded: "I must make it absolutely and abundantly clear that we are not as a government to allow illegal broadcasters to flout the law ... I have also given an assurance that the work of the Radio Investigation Service is to be stepped up, because illegal broadcasting is invariably at the expense of others and that is not fair. If allowed to go unchecked, it would soon result in anarchy on the airwaves and this we cannot allow."

The House adjourned, and the commercial radio Lords probably left with the impression that this final hard-line statement of intent by the government would finally accomplish their aim of destroying Laser 558. What they might not have realised was that the Under-Secretary of State's reference to increased activity against pirates referred not to offshore pirate stations such as Laser, over which the Radio Investigation Service had no jurisdiction, but solely to land-based pirates, despite them being far less of an annoyance to the commercial radio industry. The government knew that it was powerless to act against Laser, despite such action having been the main rallying cry of the radio Lords.

Under pressure, the government had chosen the easy way out – the only way out – and pledged itself to do something about pirate radio. Promising something, anything, was far preferable to admitting that nothing at all could be done about Laser 558. And so it happened that land-based pirate radio was about to be beaten with a very big stick.

---

[44] Hansard, House of Lords, 14 Jan 1985 [all quotes within this chapter].

January & February 1985.

Three land-based pirate radio stations had been mentioned by name during the House of Lords debate in November 1984: Radio Jackie, Sunshine Radio and Radio Scargill.

Radio Jackie was based in Southwest London and had been broadcasting regularly during weekends since 19 March 1969, when it had started life as the hobby of a group of teenage radio enthusiasts. They dreamed of running a local pop music station that would be similar to the offshore pirate broadcasters of the era, Radio London and Radio Caroline, and they had created an organisation called the Sutton Commercial Radio Association to champion their cause. Despite occasional raids by the authorities, by December 1982, Radio Jackie had expanded into a twenty four-hour, seven-day local radio service. From September 1983, the station was earning enough revenue from advertising to employ full-time staff. Radio Jackie opened its own shop in Morden and attracted support from the local Sutton Council in its campaign for a radio licence.[45]

Despite its full-time unlicensed broadcasts in South London, Radio Jackie was paid surprisingly little attention by the authorities until the first legal commercial radio station launched in North Surrey in October 1984. Radio Mercury's large transmission area, centred on its studios in Crawley, extended into the corner of Southwest London that Jackie liked to think of as its own patch. Only weeks after Radio Mercury's arrival, the Attorney General, Sir Michael Havers, acting on the commercial station's behalf, served a writ on Radio Jackie's owner, Tony Collis. The document argued that Jackie was broadcasting within Mercury's legally assigned area with programmes and adverts "of a very low standard in respect of content, quality and presentation." Radio Mercury's managing director, John Aumonier, described Radio Jackie as "the most dangerous example of the current airwave anarchy."[46]

On 11 December 1984, three days before the House of Lords debate on pirate radio, Collis had agreed publicly to halt Radio Jackie's broadcasts. The station remained on the air, however, with Collis claiming that he was no longer involved. Radio Jackie's name was then mentioned several times during the House of Lords debate. By now, the pirate station was earning £1,500 per week from local advertising, according to Collis, and it employed four full-time staff and numerous freelancers. Asked why Radio Jackie had been raided so infrequently, Collis replied confidently:

"We feel the Home Office see us as a sensible and responsible working example of commercial community radio. Perhaps they will tolerate us in order to modify the current state of the broadcasting system."[47]

Any anticipated official tolerance of Radio Jackie was quick to evaporate. Of all the land-based, unlicensed stations, Radio Jackie now held prime position at the top of the Association of Independent Radio Contractors' [AIRC] pirate hit list, as a result of intense lobbying initiated by new AIRC member Radio Mercury. It mattered not that Radio Jackie's shop in Morden was more than 20 miles away by road from Radio Mercury's studios in Crawley. A mere eighteen days after the House of Lords debate, the government took decisive action.

At 11.27 am on the morning of Friday 1 February 1985, in the Radio Jackie studio located above a travel agency in Central Road, Worcester Park, station DJ Ron Brown suddenly told his startled audience: "I think we have visitors" and the station disappeared from the airwaves. A loyal Jackie listener, Ian Courdery, was in the radio studio at the time, taking part in a competition. He recalled: "Suddenly there was a lot of banging, and a secretary rushed into the studio and yelled 'We're being raided.'"[48]

Twenty members of the Department of Trade & Industry's [DTI] Radio Investigation Service, accompanied by police, forcibly entered the premises to seize equipment, tapes, records and documents, and then interviewed nine Radio Jackie staff. It was the first raid Jackie had suffered for more than two years, and station co-ordinator Peter Rivers criticised the ferocity of the DTI's actions: "They kicked doors down without asking us to open them and did not produce a search warrant when we first asked them to show us their authorisation." Rivers vowed to return Radio Jackie to London's airwaves as soon as possible, despite the loss of £10,000 worth of equipment: "We will not be intimidated by bully boy tactics. This raid has made us even more determined to keep going."[49]

Despite this raid on Friday morning, Radio Jackie returned to the airwaves the following afternoon, but was raided once again at two o'clock on Sunday morning, less than forty-eight hours after the DTI's first visit. A further £6,000 of equipment was confiscated, and Peter Rivers commented: "This latest raid has made us even more determined to succeed in getting a legal right to broadcast. We know it will be an expensive business taking a case like this to the European Court, but we intend upholding our right to freedom of speech and that small stations should not be run by the BBC or IBA [Independent Broadcasting Authority]."[50]

During the rest of that Sunday, Radio Jackie's management team consulted their local Members of Parliament, Angela Rumbold and Dick Tracey, both of whom had lent their support to the station's long running campaign for a legal licence. It was now two months since the government had outlined its plan to introduce a new tier of community radio stations in response to Rumbold's parliamentary question. With the possibility of a legal licence on the horizon for the first time, Radio Jackie decided with great reluctance to close its operation for good. During one final Radio Jackie broadcast to bid a fond farewell to its listeners, the station's Tony Collis announced a plan to apply to the Home Office for one of the forthcoming community radio licences. At seven o'clock on the evening of Monday 4 February 1985, Radio Jackie officially closed after fifteen years of illegal broadcasting.[51]

Angela Rumbold convened a meeting at the House of Commons with DTI Minister Geoffrey Pattie to investigate Radio Jackie's allegations that, in the course of the DTI raids, officers had kicked down three doors, used a crowbar to gain entry, and had not followed legal procedures for the execution of search warrants. Rumbold commented that "this was not the way to go about enforcing the law. One reads about this kind of thing happening in Russia. We don't expect it in this country."[52]

The DTI responded that correct procedures had been followed, though it admitted that "sometimes it is regrettably necessary to force doors." With the station now off-air, Rumbold said she "hoped and prayed" that Radio Jackie would soon be granted a licence and she emphasised that "these people are professionals and not just a bunch of kids trying to push out pop music."[53]

The following week, a correspondent to The Guardian newspaper declared that Radio Jackie's decision two years earlier to start seven-day a week broadcasts had been "one of the most momentous in British broadcasting history" and he expressed his fulsome admiration for the station: "To say that Radio Jackie was radio of the people, by the people, for the people is not too grand a claim … Radio Jackie has all the right answers."[54]

With Britain's longest running land-based pirate radio station now silenced, the DTI turned its attention to another of the three illegal stations mentioned by name during the House of Lords debate. Lord Kennet had alleged that Sunshine Radio's unlicensed transmissions were interfering with local ambulance communication channels. The station, based in Ludlow, South Shropshire, had made its first broadcast during a Bank Holiday weekend in August 1981 and had re-appeared each subsequent public holiday. Encouraged by the positive public response, Sunshine Radio went on to broadcast every weekend from February 1983, despite suffering two raids when its equipment was confiscated and fines were imposed upon station staff by the courts.[55]

Then, on 21 February 1985, only days before it was due to celebrate the second anniversary of its regular weekly broadcasts, Sunshine Radio announced that it had decided to close down for good in order to pursue a legitimate community radio licence. Station controller Graham Symonds later explained: "We have gone off the air voluntarily; there is no question of us having been raided. We told the DTI of our plans and have now handed over all the transmitting equipment."[56]

On its last day of broadcasting, Sunshine planned to close down after the breakfast show but, when the station presenter arrived at the studio, he found the transmitter was already off the air. An engineer sent to the transmitter site at Villa Farm in Greete found that an axe or spade had been used to sever the essential cable connection between the transmitter and aerial, causing £4,000 of damage. Despite the public announcement that it intended to close voluntarily, Sunshine Radio had been deliberately prevented from making its farewell broadcast. Symonds voiced his concerns about the incident:

"The transmitter came on, there was no aerial and the thing blew itself to bits, causing a lot of damage. I cannot understand why anyone would want to go out there and do this damage because it was closing down anyway. It is just a nasty situation."[57]

However, Sunshine's premature closure was reported as "welcome news" by the licensed local commercial station for the area, Radio Wyvern in Worcester, which had argued that it had been under threat financially from Sunshine's strong signal and low advertising rates. The pirate had claimed a regular listenership of 30,000 people and had argued that it was much closer to its audience than the local BBC or commercial stations. Two weeks after the station's closure, Sunshine's supporters organised a march through Ludlow and a petition of "thousands of signatures" was presented to the government, demanding the station be granted a licence. But no licence was issued and Sunshine remained off the air.[58]

The third pirate station mentioned in the House of Lords debate was Radio Scargill, which Lord Kennet had accused of operating on a radio frequency that was already being used by local commercial station Radio Trent:

"[It] is being pursued by the government with slightly less faint steps than usual. It has been closed twice; it is now back. It does exactly what one would think it would be doing: it puts out pro-strike propaganda to the miners …"[59]

In fact, Radio Scargill (or Radio Arthur, as it was also dubbed) was only a temporary station that transmitted in the Nottingham area on around a dozen occasions during the protracted coal miners' strike of 1984-85. It was named after the National Union of Mineworkers' leader, Arthur Scargill, whose speeches it had often broadcast. It was the way that the station had supposedly infiltrated the commercial radio transmission system that infuriated Radio Trent's managing director Ron Coles:

"It is a sinister development, because it may mean the pirates have found some way of getting in to the independent local radio system ... But it is difficult to stop because it is difficult to trace the broadcasts because they are so spasmodic and seem to be made from different places."[60]

Whether Radio Arthur/Radio Scargill disappeared due to further raids by the authorities or to the eventual conclusion of the miners' strike is unknown but, along with its demise, faded the perceived threat to the established media order that it had embodied.

These events meant that, within a matter of weeks, the three land-based pirate stations that had been cited during the House of Lords debate had all successfully been extinguished. The type of direct action the DTI had taken against Radio Jackie was merely the most public aspect of the government's increased determination to combat the pirates during 1985. Raids on other unlicensed stations were soon taking place across the country, though they failed to quell the public's enthusiasm for pirate radio or the popularity of the music programmes they alone were broadcasting. A feature in The Times newspaper on the pirate radio phenomenon noted that "the real crime is their popularity. Whatever the hazy moral arguments about the pirates' operations, that is one area in which there is no room for doubt. Pirate radio is popular with the British public, very popular indeed."[61]

Even the government's Home Office Minister David Mellor had been forced to acknowledge the popularity of Radio Jackie in his response to questions in Parliament from Angela Rumbold MP:

"I know that station [Radio Jackie] well because many people in my constituency listen to it and make it clear to me that they enjoy it. It gives me no pleasure to have to be critical of that radio station, but I know that my Honourable Friend understands ... that no government minister can do other than deprecate the position of a service outside the law."[62]

Similarly, during a House of Commons debate on the Finance Bill, Austin Mitchell MP had commented: "I have to confess to an illegality by listening to [pirate] Skyline Radio on the way home at night."[63]

While the raids on pirate stations continued, the government was finalising its plans for a new system of licensed community radio stations. On 23 January 1985, only days before the fatal raids on Radio Jackie, Home Secretary Leon Brittan gave a written reply to a parliamentary question that had requested further information about the new scheme. Brittan said the government wanted community radio to develop as quickly as possible, but he also asserted that there was "absolutely no question of legitimising pirates." He explained:

"It is important to distinguish between community radio and the present pirate stations which cause interference, steal news broadcasts and other copyright material, and operate in flagrant defiance of the law. The government will continue to take action against the pirates, in order to retain control of the spectrum for licensed broadcasters ... But there will not be room for any community radio if the pirates have occupied all the [radio broadcast] spectrum beforehand."[64]

Brittan went on to outline the two distinct types of community station the government planned to license – low power, neighbourhood services and higher power "community of interest" stations aimed at "enthusiasts for a particular kind of music." It was the latter which were of particular interest to those London soul music pirate stations contemplating a licence bid.[65]

Commenting on the Home Secretary's announcement, one newspaper suggested that "it has been partly the popularity of the pirate stations that has persuaded the government of the shortcomings of the present two-tier system." But the paper "felt in some quarters that these pirate stations might increase their chances [of being licensed] were they to go off the air during the next few weeks." A report in Broadcast magazine confirmed earlier speculation that it was only "if [pirates] stop broadcasting and re-apply as legitimate groups [that] they will be treated on all fours with everyone else."[66]

Despite these 'carrots' offered by the government, many pirate stations continued to broadcast, regardless, and they suffered even more zealous raids by the DTI. The Independent Broadcasting Authority deputy director of radio, Peter Baldwin, commented: "We are doing our utmost to make sure the government is doing as much as possible to close the pirates down ... We're pleased there has been a crackdown which has been partially, though not wholly, successful." But Baldwin expressed scepticism at the feasibility of the government's plan for a new tier of community stations: "Whether you could find enough programming, advertising and presenters for twenty-four hour broadcasting, I don't know. I doubt it." He went on to emphasise that the Authority still endorsed its original 'one market, one radio station' policy:

"We wouldn't want to be dealing with two current local stations [in one area]. If it's Radio Yeovil [operating as the only commercial station in Yeovil], well, that's okay ... But we couldn't subscribe to competition [for existing local commercial pop music station Swansea Sound] from Radio Swansea, unless it was in Welsh or concentrated on jazz – and there probably wouldn't be sufficient demand for that kind of service."[67]

To the pirate and ex-pirate stations eager to apply for one of the new community radio licences, it was baffling to hear such contradictory statements from the government and from commercial radio's regulator, the Independent Broadcasting Authority.

In London, would a new licence ever really be granted to a soul music station, since it was inevitable that such a newcomer would take some existing listeners away from the city's only commercial music station, Capital Radio?

How could new stations be licensed only if they posed no challenge to the existing commercial broadcasters?

How could the Independent Broadcasting Authority still be thinking it should uphold 'non-competition' between commercial stations in each local market?

Were the new community radio stations supposed to offer deliberately unpopular programmes to their audiences so as not to become too serious a threat to the established commercial stations?

In July 1984, the IBA director general John Whitney had suggested that, were community radio to be introduced, it should be "in such a manner that it adds to the broadcasting dimension without eroding the strengths of the present system." What exactly did that mean?[68]

Suspicions lingered amongst many pirate stations that they were being simultaneously coaxed and hounded off of Britain's airwaves by a government that seemed to be wielding a carrot, a stick and a vague promise of a legitimate radio licence at some time in the future.

But what if such a licence never materialised?

---

[45] Stuart Henry & Mike von Joel, "Pirate Radio Then And Now", Blandford, 1984.
[46] [uncredited], [untitled], City Limits, 4 Jan 1985.
Nick Robertshaw, "UK Pirate Station Sued", Billboard, 22 Dec 1984.
[47] "Radio", The Observer Magazine, 17 Feb 1985.
[48] Adrian Shaw, "Radio Pirate Sunk After Police Raid", London Evening Standard, 1 Feb 1985.
Alex Hendry, "Pirate Jackie Stormed By Raiders", Daily Express, 2 Feb 1985.
[49] Lyn Champion, "Radio Raids", City Limits, 8 Feb 1985.
Robin Stringer, "Pirate Station Closed In Raid By Ministry", Daily Telegraph, 2 Feb 1985.
"Radio Jackie Back On Air", Sunday Express, 3 Feb 1985.
[50] "Raids Herald Campaign On Pirates", The Times, 4 Feb 1985.
[51] "Radio Jackie Decides To Close", Financial Times, 5 Feb 1985.
[52] "Pirate Protests At DTI Radio Raid", Broadcast, 8 Feb 1985.
[53] Tim Rayment, "US Cash Backs Invasion Of Radio Pirates", Sunday Times, 10 Feb 1985.
[54] Roger Allen, "Switching Off All The Right Radio Answers", letters, The Guardian, 15 Feb 1985.
[55] Hansard, House of Lords, 14 Jan 1985.
"Sunshine Radio Off Air In Bid To Go Legal", Shropshire Advertiser, 28 Feb 1985.
[56] ibid.
[57] "We'll Return Say Pirate Radio Bosses", Shropshire Star, 22 Feb 1985.
[58] "DTI Sunset For Sunshine Radio", Broadcast, 8 Mar 1985.
"Supporters Of Pirate Station On The March", Shropshire Star, 16 March 1985.
[59] Hansard, House of Lords, 14 Jan 1985.
[60] John Hind & Stephen Mosco, "Rebel Radio", Pluto, London, 1985.
"Voice Of Arthur Blights The Air", The Guardian, 22 Aug 1984.
[61] David Hewson, "Cut-Throat World Of Pirate Radio", The Times, 4 Jan 1985.
[62] Hansard, House of Commons, 30 Nov 1984, 7 May 1985.
[63] ibid.
[64] Robin Stringer, "Brittan Is Backing Community Radio", Daily Telegraph, 24 Jan 1985.
Hansard, Written Answers, 23 Jan 1985.
[65] ibid.
[66] Richard Brooks, "Brittan Tunes In", Sunday Times, 27 Jan 1985.
"Sounding Out The Community", Broadcast, 1 Feb 1985.
[67] Alvin Gold, "Rules For Radio", New Hi-Fi Sound, Mar 1985.
[68] "Sounding Out The Community", op cit.

March to October 1985.

Despite the government's determination to stamp out land-based pirate radio, the illegal stations' popularity amongst the public continued to grow, and support for their cause started to arrive from some unexpected quarters. John Thompson, director of radio at the Independent Broadcasting Authority [IBA], wrote an article for The Listener magazine entitled 'The Broadcasting Buccaneers' which argued that the pirates' popularity was such that "legitimate radio may have a thing or two to learn." Despite the IBA's own calls for more determined government action against the illegal stations, Thompson expressed admiration for their tenacity:

"The pressures from both the pirates and the community activists are, in one sense, a tribute to the attraction and power of radio in the mid-1980s. In another sense, the newcomers provide not so much a threat as a warning to the legitimate broadcasters. It is one that must be heeded by the programme makers and treated by legislators and policy makers with a mixture of firmness and flexibility."[69]

This was a remarkable acknowledgement by commercial radio's gatekeeper that pirate stations did indeed have something original and creative to offer, something which might challenge the existing radio system that Thompson was charged with regulating.

A further source of encouragement emerged from newly published BBC audience research that demonstrated the extent of the public's attraction to pirate stations. Under the headline 'Radio Listening Figures: Pirates Dig Deep,' the trade publication Media Week broke the news that pirate stations' collective share of radio listening across the UK had risen to 4.5 per cent by December 1984. Separate research by Capital Radio showed that pirates' share of listening in London alone had increased from four per cent in Spring 1984 to ten per cent by November. The BBC's head of broadcasting research, Peter Menneer, commented that "the pirates are principally digging into Radio One, Radio Two and independent local radio."[70]

A less scientific survey conducted in Sutton High Street in Southwest London by a local councillor revealed "massive support" for the recently closed local pirate station, Radio Jackie. Of 129 people interviewed, eighty-eight per cent had heard of Radio Jackie, eighty-nine per cent said they had listened to the station, eighty-five per cent knew it was unlicensed, and ninety per cent thought it should be legalised. Such acknowledgements of the extent of pirate stations' popularity seemed only to spur the Department of Trade & Industry [DTI] into more concerted action against illegal stations up and down the country. Whilst offshore pirate station Laser 558 continued to prove invincible to the British legal system, the government pursued the land-based pirates in order to be seen to be doing something about illegal radio, whatever that might be.[71]

In January 1985, Suffolk radio enthusiast John Morris was fined £50, with £25 costs, by St Edmunds-Bury Magistrates Court for broadcasting illegally from his home in Bardwell. Morris said: "I think I did it as a form of escapism."[72]

In February 1985, Makerfield magistrates fined a member of Wigan pirate Douglas Valley Community Radio £250, plus £50 costs, for infringing the 1949 Wireless Telegraphy Act with the station's broadcasts.[73]

That same month, a thirty-six year old unemployed Egyptian, Salama Bakshish, was fined £300, with £160 costs, by Marylebone magistrates for running an Arabic pirate radio station from his home in Notting Hill.[74]

Elsewhere in North London, shop assistant Khalid Kashmir was fined £300 with £60 costs by Tottenham Magistrates Court for operating a pirate station named Asian Community Entertainment, and he was ordered to forfeit several thousand pounds worth of radio equipment.[75]

On the first occasion in ten years that a jail sentence was used in a pirate radio prosecution, one-month suspended sentences were imposed by Stockport Magistrates Court on Steve Toon and Charles Turner for their involvement in pirate station KFM. Fines totalling £1,800 were imposed, and £20,000 of equipment was confiscated. The case involved DTI raids that had been made in April and November 1984, though a DTI spokesperson denied that this was a sign of the government stepping up its activities against pirates: "Handing out suspended sentences is unusual, but that's the court's decision and nothing to do with the government." A recording of a Granada TV programme that had been filmed in KFM's studio was used to identify the two DJs. Turner's subsequent appeal against his sentence was rejected by Manchester Crown Court.[76]

Six weeks into 1985, the DTI's Radio Investigation Service was already considering thirty potential prosecutions against pirate operators, compared to a total of forty-six prosecutions during the whole of 1984. Even by 4 February, the DTI had already made twenty-three raids on twenty London pirates (including an unlicensed TV station, Thameside Television) and one raid on a Sussex station. This compared to a total 124 raids during the whole of 1984.[77]

In March 1985, twenty-one year old Mustafa Oncu was fined £80, with £40 costs, by Highgate magistrates on separate charges of transmitting without a licence and being an illegal immigrant. Thousands of pounds' worth of equipment was confiscated from the studio of his Muswell Hill pirate station, London Turkish Radio, where he had been caught sitting at the controls, wearing headphones.[78]

Also in London, Tottenham housewife Aliz Giougas was fined £250, with £5 costs, for operating The Voice of The Greek People. The prosecution told the court that her station had already been raided three times and equipment worth thousands of pounds had been forfeited.[79]

At Maidenhead Magistrates Court, David Wilson was fined £150 for operating "disco channel" Radio Reflex in December 1984 from woods located 300 yards away from his home in Knowl Hill. Wilson told the court he had read an article about Radio Jackie and decided to set up a station himself. £2,000 of equipment was seized, along with 146 singles and eighty-six albums. The court chairman warned Wilson: "The court suggests that you forget all about Radio Reflex and find yourself a job."[80]

Having returned to the airwaves after its court case, Stockport pirate KFM was raided once again in March 1985, more studio and transmission equipment was seized, and DTI staff were alleged to have caused considerable damage to the station's premises. KFM issued a defiant statement: "Prosecution of individuals will not achieve the closure of a radio station which has the full support of local businesses, advertisers and the general public."[81]

Three staff of pirate station Sheffield Peace Radio were fined a total of £470, following complaints lodged by local commercial station Radio Hallam. The pirate had initially been established to provide coverage of the 1983 Campaign for Nuclear Disarmament conference held in the city, but had continued to make regular broadcasts.[82]

By the end of March 1985, the DTI had carried out forty-six raids on pirate stations, forty-two of which were in London.[83]

In April 1985, Chrysostomous Chrysostomous was fined £300 with £150 costs, by Highgate magistrates for operating Greek pirate station Voice of The Immigrants in London the previous October. Its equipment was confiscated and Chrysostomous, who had previous convictions for pirate activity, claimed his station was running at a loss of £10,000. Only weeks earlier, senior police officers from Scotland Yard had turned to the station when they needed assistance in solving the New Year's Day assassination of Greek-Cypriot millionaire Aristos Constantiou in North London. The station had obligingly broadcast regular appeals in Greek for information from the community.[84]

In May 1985, the DTI seized illegal broadcasting equipment from a hut behind a public house in Bury, Lancashire that was used by Radio 108. The station, which had been on the air for two days, was run by Greg Adamson, the twenty-two year old son of actor Peter Adamson, who had a role in the popular TV drama 'Coronation Street.' Three months before the raid, Greg had told The Sun newspaper: "I want to join a major [radio] station."[85]

Despite these occasional raids in the provinces, the majority of DTI activity was still in London, and the main targets were evidently the new wave of soul music pirate stations that had sprung up following the demise of Radio Invicta. By 1985, several new stations were attempting to broadcast twenty-four hours a day, which naturally made them easier targets for the authorities' attentions.

One such station was JFM, initials that were often assumed to stand for the 'Jazz Funk Music' that was a mainstay of the station's music policy. In fact, the pirate's name had originally been an abbreviation of Radio Jackie FM, though JFM no longer had any connection with the Jackie organisation. Radio Jackie had been experimenting with FM transmissions since February 1971, and 'RJ-FM' had started life on a Bank Holiday weekend in 1974 as a fifty-watt FM trial. Until then, London pirates had generally broadcast only on medium wave (also called AM), although Radio Invicta had already started to experiment with the better reception quality offered by FM transmission. In August 1975, Radio Jackie had launched a rock music service on its new FM channel, broadcasting five hours of programmes one weekday evening a week, whilst the station's pop music shows continued to run for six hours each Sunday on AM.[86]

In late 1980, ex-Radio Jackie DJ Brian Anthony had re-launched JFM as a soul station, wholly independent of Radio Jackie, that initially had broadcast only on Sundays and Bank Holidays. Many of the station's DJs worked regularly in London soul clubs, and their high profiles very quickly attracted a substantial audience to the station. In its early days, before JFM generated sufficient revenues from advertising spots, each DJ had paid £10 to broadcast their show, realising that they would benefit immensely from the unlimited opportunities the station offered them to publicise their own nightclub appearances.[87]

JFM continued to build an audience for its regular weekend-only broadcasts until a breakthrough by one of the station's legal team helped change the course of pirate radio history. In December 1983, barrister Peter Corrigan discovered a loophole in the 1949 Wireless Telegraphy Act which implied that radio transmitters manufactured in the UK could not be seized until the case had gone to court, or until a specific order was made for confiscation of the equipment. A test case involving JFM was processed in court and proved successful on this point of law, a result which heralded the beginning of seven-day-a-week transmissions by many London pirate stations from early 1984.[88]

By then, JFM's extended broadcast hours had allowed the station to diversify its operations into off-air promotional activities that included two successful funk cruises from Britain to Holland with guest appearances by soul artists including Haywoode, Loose Ends, Second Image, The Cool Notes and Jimmy Ruffin. JFM's business operation was reportedly costing £200 to £300 per week to run by this time.[89]

However, at the very beginning of 1985, JFM's entire studio installation was confiscated by the DTI in what were described as "sinister circumstances." One report alleged that the former owner of another pirate station was intent on destroying his competitors, as a precursor to staging his own return to the airwaves, and had tipped off the authorities as to the location of the JFM studio. Another report alleged that an ex-employee of competing soul pirate Solar Radio was the informer. In the raid, the DTI, supported by police, worked their way through the building they suspected JFM of occupying, systematically cutting the electricity supply to each floor, until they located the pirate's studio. This offered no time for escape to the DJs who were in the studio at the time, Steve Jackson and Herbie & Dave of the Mastermind Roadshow (the latter had been about to present their first show for the station).[90]

Prior to this raid, the DTI had claimed to have received several complaints from the Gas Board about interference caused by JFM to its emergency communication frequency. As a result, JFM obligingly changed both its FM frequency and its aerial system, but these actions failed to satisfy the Gas Board. In December 1984, the DTI, acting on behalf of the Gas Board, served an injunction on JFM's Brian Anthony to cease broadcasting. However, JFM had continued to transmit throughout the financially lucrative Christmas period, forcing the DTI to take direct action to remove not only JFM's transmitter, but also the considerably more expensive audio equipment installed in its radio studio.[91]

Following this devastating raid, JFM failed to make a return to London's airwaves, while another of London's new soul music pirates, Solar Radio, managed to broadcast only sporadically during January 1985. Its own transmission equipment was said to have been constantly interfered with by a rival station. A further soul pirate, Horizon Radio, re-appeared following a four-month absence caused by a devastating studio raid in late 1984 that was similar in ferocity to the one suffered subsequently by JFM.[92]

Then, at the beginning of February 1985, on the same day as the fatal raid on Radio Jackie, the DTI raided Solar Radio's Crystal Palace transmitter site in South London, along with several other pirates including Asian People's Radio, London Greek Radio (for the thirteenth time), Venus Radio (for the second time) and Ace Radio. In addition to the death blow the authorities dealt to Radio Jackie, the day's work was the most intensive action taken against London pirates for a long time, with the DTI supported by helicopter surveillance and extra staff drafted in from its regional office in Liverpool.[93]

Despite the government clampdown, after a couple of weeks' silence, both Solar Radio and Horizon returned to the airwaves with their normal broadcasts of soul music, and they were soon joined by a number of Greek and Arabic-language pirate stations. Another long running station that played soul and reggae music, LWR, also resumed regular broadcasts after a few test transmissions in January, ending the station's temporary absence from London's airwaves.[94]

Solar Radio held its first 'all-dayer' club event on 3 March 1985 at Kisses club in Peckham, South London with appearances by station DJs CJ Carlos, Gary Kent, Graham Gold, Paul Buick and Dave Collins which attracted a capacity crowd. The resident DJ at this venue was Gordon Mac (real name Gordon McNamee) who had also presented shows on Solar's recently silenced rival, JFM.[95]

With Radio Invicta now closed for good and JFM presently off-air, Solar Radio started to attract considerable press attention as London's leading soul music pirate station. A feature in the weekly music paper NME written by Alocin Strebor [Nicola Roberts spelt backwards!] told how the station had been formed in October 1984 by a group of DJs who had worked on Horizon Radio until that pirate's closure. A postscript at the end of the article casually mentioned the existence of an audience survey conducted by the Independent Broadcasting Authority, a copy of which had been "slipped under the NME office door" and which credited Solar with 1,475,000 listeners during its weekend broadcasts. A fortnight later, Record Mirror magazine reported that "IBA research figures from January suggest that the weekend Solar FM 'is a serious threat' to Capital Radio."[96]

The following week, a further feature about Solar Radio appeared in the national newspaper, The Guardian. Station founder Tony Monson estimated Solar's audience as around 125,000 people, and one of the station's DJs, Sammy J (real name Sammy Jacob), enthused about the pirate's popularity: "You just have to walk down Oxford Street or King's Road and you'll hear eighty per cent of the shops blaring us out."[97]

The article cited the IBA survey previously mentioned in NME and Record Mirror, reiterating the weekend audience of one and a half million it attributed to the pirate: "Solar Radio was found to capture six per cent of listeners during weekends, compared to Capital Radio's three per cent, and over half its audience over a seven-day period."[98]

Monson said that, even if Solar Radio's campaign to create a legal London soul station were to prove successful, and even if the government were persuaded to license such a station, he expected that "the wrong people will get the licence." He predicted that "the people who get it will have money and a lot of flannel. I might be wrong but I think it will be a compromise. It won't have any credibility and we'll go on broadcasting."[99]

The day after The Guardian article was published, another Solar DJ, Paul Buick, was fined £50 with £75 costs at Camberwell Green Magistrates Court for operating a radio station without a licence. The case attracted national press coverage which, once again, repeated the assertion that Solar Radio had an audience of one and a half million. Buick was defiant: "Nothing is going to stop us. They are not going to win. We are London's leading alternative radio station and the listeners love us. It's not fair."[100]

Only days later, the truth about the much quoted IBA survey was revealed by trade magazine Media Week. The seven-page document that had been slipped under the door of the NME had not been written by the IBA at all and was evidently a forgery, bearing only a photocopy of the IBA letterhead at the bottom of its final page. The Guardian's media editor was forced to admit publicly that the article he had published by Vron Ware had not been substantiated: "I'm prepared to accept the IBA's version that there's a phoney document going the rounds."[101]

Media Week also suggested that the widespread publicity Solar had enjoyed from the faked survey might lead to closer scrutiny of its activities by the police and the Home Office. Sure enough, only a week later, the DTI raided Solar, LWR, Horizon and four other pirates' transmitters, though the first two of these stations managed to return to the air within forty-eight hours.[102]

By the end of May 1985, the DTI had made seventy-five raids on forty-one pirate stations and had brought thirty-seven prosecutions. In a written reply to a Parliamentary question from Teddy Taylor MP about its anti-pirate activity, the DTI carefully avoided mentioning the thorny problem of the lack of action against offshore pirate Laser 558, preferring to concentrate on the success achieved in its ongoing war against the land-based stations. The DTI's John Butcher said he was "determined to take effective action to stop the unauthorised use of radio which causes interference, annoyance and sometimes danger to authorised radio users."[103]

Asked by Taylor how many letters the DTI had received from the general public on the subject of pirate radio, Butcher replied that there had been "numerous letters in the past, though the number has greatly diminished recently as the improved enforcement powers, which we took in the Telecommunications Act 1984, have proved themselves." The DTI then published the names of twenty pirate stations which it told Parliament were still on-air, eight of which it believed were attempting to broadcast twenty-four hour services.[104]

The sudden proliferation of raids convinced Solar Radio and Horizon to temporarily come off-air for a while to avoid the DTI's attentions, although LWR continued to broadcast. Solar's Tony Monson announced that he would cease presenting the daily breakfast show on the station, a condition that the licensed commercial station Essex Radio had insisted was a pre-requisite for him to host its new Saturday night soul show.[105]

It was only a short time before Solar Radio and Horizon rejoined LWR, all broadcasting once again on London's airwaves, though their transmitters were raided once again in early June. Solar and LWR managed to resume transmissions very quickly, but both were punished with DTI raids on their entire studio installations the following week. Solar DJ Mark McCarthy almost evaded arrest, but then became stuck at the top of the building's ladder.[106]

Solar Radio announced it was to set up a meeting with Members of Parliament at the House of Commons the following month, and would present its case for a London radio licence to the Home Office, the government department responsible for broadcasting policy. In the meantime, the DTI gloated that in 1985, by mid-June, it had already carried out 109 raids on forty-four pirates and had made fifty prosecutions. Thirty-four of those raids had taken place during the previous three weeks.[107]

The intensity of these DTI raids still failed to deter the pirates. After more than a week of there being no illegal stations on London's airwaves, the longest gap in recent months, Horizon, Solar and LWR all returned, though their broadcasts were initially very tentative. During their absence, sales of soul records in London were reported to have been significantly lower than usual, a phenomenon attributed directly to the airplay of soul music that only the pirate stations offered. It was even suggested that one single, 'London Town 85' by Light Of The World, a song that had become something of an anthem for the London soul pirate community, could have been a chart hit, had airplay not suddenly been curtailed by the temporary absence of illegal stations.[108]

The meeting at the House of Commons took place in July 1985, chaired by Angela Rumbold MP. It announced the launch of the Campaign For Successful Radio In Britain, a lobbying group formed by pirates and community radio organisations that included Solar Radio and Radio Jackie. The campaign's demand for the government to legalise more radio stations was quickly rebuffed by Tim Brinton MP, chairman of the Conservative Party Backbench Media Committee, who argued that deregulation of the airwaves would pose too many problems and that there would be no changes to radio legislation for a long time to come.[109]

Roger Gale MP, who had once worked as a DJ on offshore pirate Radio Caroline, counselled caution: "Don't confuse community radio with specialist interest radio. The government could opt for one or the other first. What will you do if you don't get a licence? If you're not successful, don't then go away and set up another pirate station, as nobody will respect you for it."[110]

The day after the House of Commons meeting, the first annual congress of the Association of Independent Radio Contractors was addressed by the Home Secretary, Leon Brittan. He promised the delegates, all from the commercial radio industry, that tough action would continue to be taken against the pirates because, if unchecked, their activities would lead to "anarchy of the airwaves."[111]

Pirate stations were also criticised by Alex Mackay, chairman of the Greater London Council's Finance & General Purposes Committee, which had recently started to fund several community radio projects in the capital. Hoping that the groups he was supporting would be licensed first, Mackay argued that "pirate stations just don't fill the gap in the radio market that the BBC and ILR have failed to satisfy. Their programming is too similar to Independent Local Radio's and they broadcast over too big an area."[112]

Despite these criticisms, the London soul pirates continued to struggle on against the persistent attentions of the DTI. LWR was raided again at the beginning of July 1985, although it had returned to the air by mid-month, accompanied by Solar Radio and Horizon. However, the emerging aggression between the soul stations themselves was beginning to prove as debilitating as the actions of the DTI.[113]

Solar was suddenly forced off the air after its transmission aerial at Crystal Palace had crashed to the ground. Tony Monson was outraged: "At first, we thought it was an accident. But, on closer inspection, we were horrified to see the aerial had been deliberately hack-sawed. It has to be one of our rivals, as this sort of thing has happened before. On Friday, someone broke into our studio and stole our transmitter, but we've managed to get it back. I won't name names, but I know who the culprits are ... I don't want people to think that pirates spend all their time bickering, but it seems that one station is generally trying to make life miserable for us out of sheer jealousy. Last week, a couple of other stations were raided by the Department of Trade & Industry, and it seems someone is trying to get their own back because we didn't get done. We're trying to apply for legislation and the last thing we need is aggravation from jealous rivals."[114]

At the end of July 1985, the government announced that the DTI's Radio Investigation Service, responsible for enforcement against pirate stations, would be scaled down from 340 to 240 staff. However, in a written Parliamentary answer, Geoffrey Pattie, Minister for Information Technology, guaranteed that more resources would nevertheless be devoted to "dealing with pollution of the radio spectrum by those who operate without licences." The ensuing headline in The Times read: 'War Declared On Radio Pirates.'[115]

As if to compensate for this continuing attrition against the pirates, Home Secretary Leon Brittan chose the same week to announce details of the government's long-awaited community radio scheme. Twenty stations were to be licensed in a two-year experiment that would be monitored and assessed, pending further expansion. London was to have three small neighbourhood stations and two larger 'community of interest' stations, one on FM for South London, the other on AM for North London. The details were much as had been anticipated, but the speed with which the government was moving was wholly unexpected. Applications for these new licences had to be submitted by 30 September 1985, only two months hence, and the successful candidates would be announced in December. After years and years of campaigning for new radio services, the lobbyists were suddenly caught off-guard by the government's haste to implement this radical plan to expand Britain's radio system.[116]

The government's dramatic announcement had little immediate impact on pirate radio activity in London, as the stations were still frantically trying to understand whether they stood any chance of winning the new licences. Solar Radio, Horizon and LWR were all raided one Monday in late July, having only just resumed broadcasting after the last series of raids. LWR had just moved to a new studio location, but it took the DTI only six hours to track it down. The increasing regularity of such raids was seriously disrupting the stations' programme schedules and meant that some pirate DJs had not been able to present their shows for more than two months.[117]

At the beginning of August 1985, Solar Radio announced its intention to apply for the South London community radio licence, and Tony Monson invited other potential soul music applicants to join him in a combined bid. Two weeks later, Horizon announced that it too would close down to pursue a licence. The station's founder Chris Stewart explained: "We've gone as far as we can as a pirate station. It's now time to concentrate on becoming legal. It's a sad day for us. But we will be back in 1986, bigger and better and most importantly, legal."[118]

Horizon closed down permanently at the beginning of September 1985, and Solar followed a couple of weeks later. Horizon's farewell music event attracted 3,000 people and there was widespread shock amongst London's soul music fans that their favourite pirate stations had suddenly disappeared altogether from the airwaves. The London FM radio band was a lot quieter and less exciting than it had been for many years.[119]

LWR was the only soul pirate station to continue broadcasting, stating that it had no plans to apply for a licence, and would instead put its energies into organising a September reggae and soul all-day event at the Upper Cut Stadium in London's Forest Gate. Then, LWR's studio was raided in early October 1985 in what were described as "dodgy circumstances," since the premises had formerly been used by one of the other pirates that had voluntarily closed down.[120]

In addition to Solar and Horizon's publicly declared bids for the new community radio licences, rumours started to circulate that BBC Radio London morning show DJ Tony Blackburn was considering a bid in association with ex-Radio Luxembourg DJ Tony Prince. In his recently published autobiography, modestly entitled 'The Living Legend,' Blackburn had said that "if the [Controller] job at [BBC] Radio One is filled, I would like to open a twenty-four hour a day soul music station in London." To the pirate stations' consternation, neither Blackburn nor Prince had participated in the London soul pirate campaign, whose efforts had been instrumental in forcing the government to introduce community radio.[121]

DTI pressure on the few remaining pirate stations continued when, in early October 1985, LWR DJ John Jenkins was fined £200 with £60 costs by Croydon Magistrates Court for operating a radio station without a licence. The court was told that, following complaints of interference from Capital Radio, an illegal transmitter had been found above a butcher's shop in Westow Hill, West Norwood. Wires were discovered leading from a chimney, over the roofs of neighbouring houses, to a building 300 yards away in Church Road where the studio was found above an engraver's shop. All the studio equipment, as well as Jenkins' records and tapes, were confiscated by the court. This was reported to be the twentieth raid on LWR during the last two years.[122]

At the end of October 1985, the DTI announced that it had made 228 raids on pirate stations and had brought 106 prosecutions during the previous twelve months. It had spent £351,900 on enforcement against unlicensed radio stations and now employed 223 staff. Due to the "vigorous action" it had taken against pirate stations, the DTI noted that "few now transmit regularly or for long periods." If the summer of 1984 had been 'the summer of radio piracy' in London, then 1985 had proven to be the pirates' winter of discontent. Three soul pirate stations – JFM, Solar and Horizon – had closed for good during the year, and the only one remaining – LWR – was suffering badly from raids.[123]

Right now seemed like the most inappropriate moment to try and launch a new soul pirate radio station in London. But this was exactly what was about to happen.

---

[69] John Thompson, "On The Crest Of The Radio Wave", The Listener, 24 Jan 1985.
[70] "Radio Listening Figures: Pirates Dig Deep", Media Week, 15 Feb 1985.
[71] Peter Fiddick, "Media File", The Guardian, 18 Mar 1985.
[72] "Suffolk Pirate Radio Man Wanted 'Escapism'", East Anglian Daily Times, 12 Jan 1985.
[73] "Pirates Up In Court", Broadcast, 15 Feb 1985.
[74] "Egyptian Radio Pirate Fined", Daily Telegraph, 22 Feb 1985.
[75] "Pirates Given Gaol Sentence", Broadcast, 1 Mar 1985.
[76] "Pirates Jail Threat", Media Week, 1 Mar 1985.
"Pirates Up In Court", Broadcast, 15 Feb 1985.
"Pirates Given Gaol Sentence", op cit.
"KFM Lose Appeal", Stockport Messenger, 10 May 1985.
[77] "A Revolution Takes To The Air", The Economist, 16 Feb 1985.
Hansard, Written Answers, 7 Feb 1985.
[78] "Turkish Radio Station Closed", Daily Telegraph, 7 Mar 1985.
"DTI Pirate War Gains Impetus", Broadcast, 22 Mar 1985.
[79] "DTI Pirate War Gains Impetus", op cit.
[80] "Pirate Radio Station Shut", Maidenhead Advertiser, 29 Mar 1985.
[81] "DTI Makes More Pirate Raids", Broadcast, 29 Mar 1985.
[82] [uncredited], [untitled], City Limits, 29 Mar 1985.
[83] "DTI Makes More Pirate Raids", op cit.
[84] "Illegal Radio", The Times, 18 Apr 1985.
"Fines Imposed On No-Licence Stations", Broadcast, 3 Mar 1985.
Chester Stern, "Radio Pirates Help Murder Hunt", Mail On Sunday, 20 Jan 1985.
"Radio Killer Plea", The Times, 21 Jan 1985.

[85]"This Is Radio 105, That Was", Sunday People, 26 May 1985.
"Star's Son Risks Jail As 'Pirate' DJ", The Sun, 26 Feb 1985.
[86]"Radio Jackie 227", Newswave Magazine no. 1, 1979.
Tim Rogers, "Radio Jackie 227", Newswave Magazine no. 2, 1980.
author's notes, 11 Aug 1974 & 3 Aug 1975.
[87]John Hind & Stephen Mosco, "Rebel Radio", Pluto, London, 1985.
[88]Tim Westwood, "Foreword" in John Hind & Stephen Mosco, op cit.
[89]John Hind & Stephen Mosco, op cit.
[90]James Hamilton, "Odds'N'Bods", Record Mirror, 19 & 26 Jan 1985.
The Mouth, "Street Noise", Blues & Soul, 5 Feb 1985 & 4 Mar 1985.
[91]John Hind & Stephen Mosco, op cit.
[uncredited], [untitled], City Limits, 4 Jan 1985.
[92]James Hamilton, "Odds'N'Bods", Record Mirror, 19 & 26 Jan 1985, 2 Feb 1985.
[93]Ian Boyne, "Euro-Plea Planned After Raids Close Six Radio Pirates", Daily Telegraph, 4 Feb 1985.
James Hamilton, "Odds'N'Bods", Record Mirror, 9 Feb 1985.
[94]James Hamilton, "Odds'N'Bods", Record Mirror, 26 Jan 1985, 2 & 23 Feb 1985.
[95]James Hamilton, "Odds'N'Bods", Record Mirror, 2 Mar 1985.
Vron Ware, "The Station That Puts Heart Into Soul", The Guardian, 8 Apr 1985.
[96]Alocin Strebor, "Radio", NME, 23 Mar 1985.
James Hamilton, "Odds'N'Bods", Record Mirror, 6 Apr 1985.
[97]Vron Ware, op cit.
[98]ibid.
[99]ibid.
[100]"Pirate DJ Defiant", Daily Star, 10 Apr 1985.
"Pirate Waives Rules", The Sun, 10 Apr 1985.
[101]"Pirate In IBA Research Fraud", Media Week, 12 Apr 1985.
[102]"Pirate In IBA Research Fraud", Media Week, 12 Apr 1985.
"Radio Pirates Are Forced Off The Air", Daily Express, 20 Apr 1985.
"Pirates Are Back On Air", Daily Express, 22 Apr 1985.
"Pirates Raided!", Streatham Clapham & Dulwich Guardian, 25 Apr 1985.
[103]Hansard, Written Answers, 20 & 24 May 1985.
[104]ibid.
[105]James Hamilton, "Odds'N'Bods", Record Mirror, 1 & 8 Jun 1985.
[106]James Hamilton, "Odds'N'Bods", Record Mirror, 15 & 22 Jun 1985.
[107]James Hamilton, op cit.
"Punishing Pirates", UK Press Gazette, 24 Jun 1985.
"Radio Raids", City Limits, 28 Jun 1985.
[108]James Hamilton, "Odds'N'Bods", Record Mirror, 29 Jun 1985, 6 & 13 Jul 1985.
James Hamilton, Music Week, 13 Jul 1985.
[109]"Brittan To Act Against 'Pirate Radio Anarchy'", Campaign, 5 Jul 1985.
James Hamilton, Music Week, op cit.
James Hamilton, "Odds'N'Bods", Record Mirror, 13 Jul 1985.
[110]"Brittan To Act Against 'Pirate Radio Anarchy'", op cit.
[111]"Brittan To Act Against 'Pirate Radio Anarchy'", op cit.
"GLC Hits At Pirates", Broadcast, 12 Jul 1985.
[112]ibid.
[113]James Hamilton, "Odds'N'Bods", Record Mirror, 13 Jul 1985.
[114]"Dismasted As The Pirates Make War", Evening Standard, 23 Jul 1985.
"Aerial Strike", City Limits, 26 Jul 1985.
[115]War Declared On Radio Pirates", The Times, 27 Jul 1985.
"Pirate Radio Inquiry Staff Target Of Cut", Daily Telegraph, 27 Jul 1985.
James Hamilton, "Odds'N'Bods", Record Mirror, 3 Aug 1985.
Hansard, Written Answers, 25 Jul 1985.
[116]ibid.
[117]Tim Westwood, "Zulu Message", Blues & Soul, 6 Aug 1985.
[118]James Hamilton, "Odds'N'Bods", Record Mirror, 3 Aug 1985.
Simon Goffe & Fiona Thompson, "Is There Soul Beyond The Horizon?", City Limits, 23 Aug 1985.
[119]James Hamilton, "Odds'N'Bods", Record Mirror, 24 Aug 1985, 21 & 28 Sep 1985, 12 Oct 1985.
[120]Simon Goffe & Fiona Thompson, op cit.
James Hamilton, "Odds'N'Bods", Record Mirror, 28 Sep 1985, 12 Oct 1985.
[121]The Mouth, "Street Noise", Blues & Soul, 3 Sep 1985.

Tony Blackburn, "The Living Legend", Comet, London, 1985.
[122]"London Weekend Radio Off Air", Streatham Clapham & Dulwich Guardian, 17 Oct 1985.
John Hind, "Hey DJ!", Record Mirror, 26 Oct 1985.
[123]Hansard, Written Answers, 29 Oct 1985.

October to December 1985.

The devastating studio raid that JFM suffered in early 1985, forcing it from London's airwaves, had come as a great disappointment to the station's many fans, who had followed its changing fortunes during four years of broadcasting. In May 1985, JFM had announced that it would return to the air that autumn, and rumours persisted that it would be re-launched under the name Radio Spectrum or Radio Shadow. Instead, JFM founder Brian Anthony decided to apply for one of the new London community radio licences, in competition with bids from both Solar and Horizon to become the capital's first legal soul radio station.[124]

By August 1985, there were rumours that two former JFM DJs, Cleveland Anderson and Gordon McNamee, frustrated by the station's failure to make its promised return, were each planning to launch new pirate stations of their own. In September, McNamee confirmed that his station was to be called KISS FM and would soon commence broadcasts on 94 FM during weekdays. The gossip column in Blues & Soul magazine commented:

"No sooner we say goodbye to Horizon and Solar etc., than we say hello to KISS FM, a new pirate due on-air around the time you get this journalistic feat. Seemingly, KISS FM is not here simply for the beer and has got some pretty hefty financial clout to take care of all those niggling little hiccups which seem to cast dark clouds over fellow nautical broadcasters. According to my shadow-stepping spies, the station's music policy will be quality music, as opposed to wine bar dross. Still, we've heard all that before, have we not? Only time will tell."[125]

Between 1983 and JFM's closure in 1984, McNamee had presented its drivetime show (using the name Gordon Mac) whilst working as resident DJ at Kisses nightclub in Peckham. His DJ career had started at the age of 13 when he had played records at a church hall event in Camberwell. He had set up a one-night a week soul music pirate station called Sound City in 1983, but admitted that "it was busted so often, it eventually had to be closed." The name of his new pirate station, KISS FM, offered an ideal opportunity for him to promote the events he was organising at Kisses nightclub. These included a Sunday night talent contest when McNamee and his partner, a "black blonde" named Kags, gave cash prizes to the best DJs and dancers drawn from the crowd. The pirate station's name was stolen from one of New York City's most successful black music stations whose owners, RKO Radio, had re-launched the former WRKS as KISS FM in August 1981. The 'KISS FM' identity had subsequently been copied by stations all across America, but no radio owner in Britain had used the name until then.[126]

Pirate KISS FM made its first tentative broadcast from North London at 9.30 am on 7 October 1985, when McNamee presented its very first show. The station immediately attempted to broadcast a twenty-four hour service on 94 FM that would fill the void created by the recent closures of Solar Radio and Horizon. However, after only three days on-air, KISS suffered its first Department of Trade & Industry [DTI] raid, as did the still struggling LWR. Both stations managed a return to the airwaves within a few days and, in November, LWR optimistically organised a Sunday nightclub party to celebrate three weeks of uninterrupted broadcasting. Unfortunately, LWR was already off the air again by the day of the party, the victim of yet another DTI raid.[127]

The closures of Solar, Horizon and JFM had definitely created a vacuum amongst London's soul music fans for news and information about the music and the associated events. Several ex-Solar DJs had seen attendances at their club events suffer now that the station was off the air. Like most pirate DJs, they earned little or nothing directly from their radio shows, but the publicity afforded to their club nights served to boost attendances and enhance their professional reputations.

Having seen KISS FM launched from the ashes of JFM, many of the former Solar DJ team decided to organise their own return using a new station name, TKO. They launched the new pirate in November 1985, using Solar's former channel of 102.4 FM. One of TKO's DJs, Segue Steve Goddard, defended the group's decision to go it alone by pointing out that, even if Solar were to win one of the community radio licences, there would be insufficient airtime available for all the ex-pirate's thirty-seven presenters to each have their own show. Unrepentant, Solar founder Tony Monson said that the breakaway group's involvement in new pirate TKO put them "beyond the pale" and he disassociated those DJs from any further involvement in Solar's bid for a legal licence.[128]

Another new pirate station called K-Jazz emerged in late 1985, the first to broadcast an all-jazz format in London. The station was founded by twenty-year old DJ Gilles Peterson, who had started his radio career on Radio Invicta, before presenting jazz shows on Solar Radio. K-Jazz restricted its broadcasts to Sundays, and Peterson said the favourable public response to the first broadcasts had encouraged him to submit a bid for one of London's new community radio licences. K-Jazz's one-day a week operation did not prevent it from being raided by the DTI.[129]

During November 1985, all three of London's twenty-four hour soul pirate stations – long running LWR plus new entrants KISS FM and TKO – suffered further DTI raids. KISS FM initially tried broadcasting from a single location, but quickly changed tactic to alternate its broadcasts from a number of tower blocks in an attempt to evade the DTI raiding parties. This strategy failed as well, so KISS returned to using a single site, though it admitted to still being "hit fairly heavily by the DTI." LWR was having similar troubles and resorted to broadcasting programmes that had been pre-recorded on cassette tapes in order to minimise the possibility of the DTI locating the station's valuable studio.[130]

KISS FM struggled on with its 24-hour broadcast schedule until 11 December 2005, when a particularly harsh DTI raid lost the station "a very substantial amount of equipment" and knocked it off the airwaves completely. During the weeks that followed, KISS FM was nowhere to be heard on the FM band, and its admittance that the DTI raids "had caused financial problems" suggested that its entire existence might have come to a rather unspectacular end after only two months.[131]

KISS FM had promised Londoners that it would be different from its competitors – LWR and TKO – by including a substantial element of live 'mixes' in its programmes, during which its DJs would seamlessly merge one record into the next without missing a beat. The phenomenon was already popular in nightclubs and had been pioneered on radio by KISS FM's namesake in New York City. However, in its initial two-month existence, the London KISS FM had been pre-occupied with the crippling DTI raids and one press write-up noted critically that "there wasn't very much of the promised live mixing." Gordon McNamee later admitted that "some [pirates] aren't that good" during "that first four to six months when a station develops its character. KISS wasn't that great during that period either."[132]

Despite its absence from the airwaves, KISS FM had already started to garner some attention in the press. Campaign magazine mentioned the station as one of several pirates that (unlike Horizon, JFM and Solar) had stayed on the airwaves "concluding that they have little chance of winning licences." Lyn Champion, radio editor of London listings magazine City Limits, wrote an opinion page on pirate radio for community radio magazine Relay. In it, she cited KISS FM as one of the London soul pirates that played "music ignored by the mainstream stations through a combination of commercial motivations, ignorance and disinterest on the part of radio producers and record companies." In a direct reference to KISS FM's Gordon McNamee, Champion noted that "most [station] DJs work on the suburban soul club circuit in places like Kisses" and "most have no professional radio experience." She also judged that pirates "reflect a predominantly white, male, traditional working class perspective" with "clearly defined hierarchies and small scale entrepreneurs at the top" where "women have little part in the on-air proceedings, but more behind the scenes."[133]

Although KISS FM's future remained in doubt following its raid in December 1985, developments elsewhere suggested there might be the real possibility of a legal soul music station in London. The closing date for applications for the government's new community radio licences had been extended from 30 September to 31 October 1985 to allow potential bidders more time to prepare their submissions. Ex-pirates JFM, Horizon and Solar each submitted separate applications for the FM 'community of interest' licence serving South London, in competition with several other community radio groups. As expected, ex-pirate Radio Jackie applied for a neighbourhood licence for Southwest London.[134]

Eight months after the fatal raid on Radio Jackie, the case against the thirteen people caught broadcasting from the station's studio was only just being heard by Sutton Magistrates Court. One of ten DTI witnesses, Robert Mason, told the court he had clambered over the gate of 87 Abbotts Road in Cheam on 1 February 1985 and had found two aerials, one on the roof of the house and the other which spanned the whole garden. The DTI said they had also found and confiscated £5,000 of equipment from the station's studio at 32 Central Avenue, Worcester Park. The court imposed total fines of more than £5,000 on the accused, plus £100 each in costs. Afterwards, Radio Jackie's Peter Stremes said: "It could have been worse. They could have imposed suspended prison sentences on us. But I have noticed, in previous cases, the fines were about £50 to £100 for each offence. In our case, they ranged from £150 to £250 for each offence."[135]

Radio Jackie programme controller Dave Owen (real name David Wright) said he would appeal against his £850 fine because, he argued, "I am unemployed and the fine is out of all proportion to what I can pay." He was optimistic about the station's chances of winning one of the new community radio licences: "We have a petition supporting us, signed by over 50,000 voters in Southwest London. It would be a great shame if those 50,000 didn't get what they wanted." Whilst awaiting the government's decision on their licence application, the staff compiled a Radio Jackie record album featuring extracts of broadcasts from 1969 until the final raid in February. "It's a collector's item," said Owen, "and an ideal Christmas present." The

Jackie team was now running a taxi business from the station's former studio in Worcester Park.[136]

Another pirate radio prosecution that had only just reached the courts concerned the fatal DTI raid on Horizon Radio in October 1984. The DTI had taken £20,000 of equipment from premises in Bellenden Road, Peckham, but no transmitter was produced in court to demonstrate that illegal broadcasting had taken place. The DTI explained that the transmitter had "got lost" on its way from Horizon's studio to the DTI van waiting outside, an explanation accepted by the court. Horizon owner Chris Stewart was found guilty, with £1,000 costs, and all the station's equipment was confiscated. This was the single largest seizure from a pirate station since the government's powers had been extended by the 1984 Telecommunications Act. Stewart said afterwards that he had not expected such a big stick to be used against him, particularly since he had already closed Horizon to apply for a legal community radio licence. His comments were typically forthright when he told the press that "it's a fucking disgrace."[137]

Elsewhere in London, Camberwell Magistrates Court imposed a £150 fine, and £50 costs, on Michael Grant, a local council play leader, for operating pirate station Fame FM from a house in Streatham. The prosecution alleged that the station, another recent addition to the ranks of the capital's soul pirates, "continuously jammed" the emergency radio system operated by the Gas Board, so the magistrate ordered £1,500 of radio equipment to be confiscated. The same court also prosecuted South London pirate Skyline Radio, which had been broadcasting a community-style format since 1983. Equipment worth £7,500 was confiscated, and afternoon DJ Alan Jones was charged under the 1949 Wireless Telegraphy Act. A second raid on Skyline, 46 hours after the first, netted the DTI a further £13,000 of equipment. Station director Mark Ellis commented: "We have used the last of our funds, but there is no way we will give in."[138]

Outside London, the DTI was just as busy. In Birmingham, it raided an unoccupied council flat in Dorset Tower, Camden Street that had been used by a pirate station called People's Community Radio Line for two months. Equipment worth £2,000 was confiscated, along with a further £10,000 from a second raid four months later. In Stafford, a pirate called WX that had operated unhindered from Paul Reynold's garage for four months was raided. In Stourbridge, an AM station run by a thirty-year old man from wooded land in Foxcote Lane was raided at 9.30 one evening. And, in Harrogate, twenty-four year old television engineer Philip Pearson was fined £75 for broadcasting an illegal FM station called Conference City Sound from his top floor flat. Harrogate Magistrates Court heard that the prosecution was only brought as a result of an article that had appeared in the local press about the station's music policy.[139]

Meanwhile, in the North Sea, offshore pop music pirate Laser 558 continued to annoy Britain's legitimate radio industry with its immense popularity. A survey by the independent Broadcasting Research Unit showed that twelve per cent of Londoners listened regularly to Laser (compared to eleven per cent to BBC Radio London). The DTI insisted that Laser was interfering with navigational frequencies used by helicopters over the North Sea, even though Laser's management said it had received no such complaints. A DTI ship, the Dioptic Surveyor, set sail from Harwich on 8 August 1985 to 'observe' the activities of the Laser ship and any vessels that might be servicing it illegally. The harassment technique cost the British taxpayer £50,000 a month but eventually had the desired effect when, in early November, Laser's ship docked in Harwich for essential repairs and was immediately impounded by the Admiralty Marshal. Four men were subsequently arrested, pending prosecution under the Marine Offences Act, for being members of Laser's crew.[140]

Meanwhile, at the station's New York City office, an answering machine message told callers: "Laser 558 is off air because of a combination of circumstances, bad weather, bad luck and logistical problems, but certainly not because of a lack of listener or advertiser support. Our ship is undergoing repairs and maintenance in Harwich harbour. Our staff, American broadcasters and marine crew are all safe and well. Our future plans are indefinite at this moment, but we appreciate your interest and support."[141]

A group of loyal Laser listeners, who described themselves as "P. Smith and six others" from Birmingham, wrote to the Daily Mirror: "We are very sorry that Laser 558 has been put off the air. No wonder it attracted so many listeners when it offered good pop music instead of the inane jabbering of the DJs on local radio." At the Young Conservatives' Eastern Area conference held in Felixstowe, delegates offered "overwhelming support" for a motion that criticised the DTI's "misguided efforts" to blockade Laser's ship. Edwin Hamilton, chairman of the Norwich Young Conservatives, said: "There is a great demand for the type of service that Laser ... can offer. It is not good public relations for the government to be seen to attack a very popular form of entertainment."[142]

The closure of Laser 558 brought to a conclusion a particularly successful year for the government's pirate-busting activities. Although Laser had been the major gripe of the British commercial radio industry, the DTI had been particularly zealous in its activities against land-based stations, making 231 raids on eighty pirates during 1985, resulting in 130 successful prosecutions. London's airwaves were quieter by year-end than they had been for many years. Ex-pirates JFM, Solar and Horizon were all off the air awaiting the outcome of their licence applications. LWR was still on-air, but struggling. TKO was still operating sporadically. KISS FM had closed after a disastrous two months of attempting to broadcast a twenty-four hour service.[143]

1985 had been the year that pirate radio almost died.

---

[124] James Hamilton, "Odds'N'Bods", Record Mirror, 25 May 1985.
Tim Westwood, "Zulu Message", Blues & Soul, 6 Aug 1985, 29 Oct 1985.
Simon Goffe & Fiona Thompson, "Is There Soul Beyond The Horizon?", City Limits, 23 Aug 1985.
[125] Tim Westwood, "Zulu Message", Blues & Soul, 6 Aug 1985.
James Hamilton, "Odds'N'Bods", Record Mirror, 28 Sep 1985.
The Mouth, "Street Noise", Blues & Soul, 15 Oct 1985.
[126] "IBA Incremental ILR Contract Application Form", KISS FM, Nov 1989.
James Hamilton, "Odds'N'Bods", Record Mirror, 28 Sep 1985.
Nelson George, "The Death Of Rhythm & Blues", Omnibus Press, London, 1988.
Robert Ashton, "Root With A Suit", Music Week, 29 Feb 1992.
[127] Tim Westwood, "Zulu Message", Blues & Soul, 29 Oct 1985.
James Hamilton, "Odds'N'Bods", Record Mirror, 26 Oct & 16 Nov 1985.
Guy Wingate, "Lip Service", MixMag, Oct 1990.
Lindsay Wesker, "History Of KISS", Your Guide To Kissing [supplement to Free! magazine], KISS FM, 1 Sep 1990.
[128] James Hamilton, "Odds'N'Bods", Record Mirror, 16 & 30 Nov, 14 Dec 1985.
[129] James Hamilton, "Odds'N'Bods", Record Mirror, 13 Apr 1985.
"Aerial Strike", City Limits, 26 Jul 1985.
Paul Lashmar, "Jazz After Jazz", The Observer, 25 Aug 1985.
[130] James Hamilton, "Odds'N'Bods", Record Mirror, 7 Dec 1985 & 4 Jan 1986.

"Hold It Now, Hit It", TX no. 6, May 1986.
[131]"Hold It Now Hit It", op cit.
[132]ibid.
Mark Heley, "Pirates: The New Generation", Radio & Music, 16 Aug 1989.
[133]Alice Rawsthorn, "Why Pirate Stations Are Off The Airwaves", Campaign, 15 Nov 1985.
Lyn Champion, "Piracy – More Than Just 'Idiots Making Money'", Relay, Jan 1986.
[134]"CR Applicants Question Choice Of Award Panel", Broadcast, 20 Sep 1985.
Terence Kelly & Nick Higham, "Neighbourhoods Reveal The Good Taste Of Radio", Broadcast, 13 Sep 1985.
[135]"Court Told Of Jackie Raids", The Advertiser, 17 Oct 1985.
"Pirate Crew Face Fines Of £5000", Wimbledon Guardian, 24 Oct 1985.
[136]Mark Watkins, "'Jackie' JPs To Face Court Quiz", Sutton & Banstead News, 5 Dec 1985.
"Jackie Slips Disc", Wimbledon Guardian, 12 Dec 1985.
[137]Lysandros Pitharas, "Pirates Get A Broadside And It's A 'Fucking Disgrace'", City Limits, 17 Jan 1986.
[138]"Pirates Jammed Gas Board Radio", Streatham Guardian, 22 Aug 1985.
"Pirates Rule The Airwaves", Streatham Guardian, 6 Jun 1985.
"Off-Air", Time Out, 6 Jun 1985.
"Radio Raids", City Limits, 7 Jun 1985.
"Minority Radio Pirates Raided", Capital Gay, 14 Jun 1985.
"Skyline Resists Raids", Streatham Guardian, 27 Jun 1985.
[139]"Blacks' Pirate Radio Closed Down", Birmingham Evening Mail, 20 Jul 1985.
"Radio Station Is Raided", Birmingham Evening Mail, 29 Nov 1985.
"Backlash Alert Over Radio Raid", Birmingham Post, 29 Nov 1985.
"Pirate Radio Station Raided", Staffordshire Newsletter, 9 Aug 1985.
"Police Swoop On Radio Hideout", Wolverhampton Express & Star, 2 Sep 1985.
"Radio Show – From A Top Floor Flat", Yorkshire Evening Post, 18 Oct 1985.
[140]"Eye, Eye", The Economist, 21 Sep 1985.
Alice Rawsthorn, op cit.
[141]Alice Rawsthorn, op cit.
[142]Letters, Daily Mirror, 11 Nov 1985.
"Pirate Radio Blockade Attacked", Eastern Daily Press, 22 Oct 1985.
[143]"Pirate Raids By DTI Reach 231", Broadcast, 17 Jan 1988.

January to July 1986.

The government's war against the land-based pirate radio stations continued unabated into the New Year. London's two remaining twenty-four hour soul stations, LWR and TKO, struggled on valiantly against regular raids, but both had to resort to broadcasting tapes of uninterrupted music during most of the time they were on the air. Live programmes with live presenters became something of a rarity on these two stations, and most of London's other smaller pirate stations restricted their broadcasts to weekends – a return to the pattern of illegal broadcasting in the early 1980s. An article in the pirate radio magazine TX summed up the situation:

"It now seems clear that the Department of Trade & Industry [DTI] are making a clear distinction between part-time pirates and those operating seven days a week. They seem to feel that there are always going to be people who'll set up stations to run for a few hours at weekends, and there's not much they can do about it. Those pirates probably don't affect audience ratings on legit[imate] stations too much, so it won't really be worth the DTI spending a lot of time in trying to curb them. The major problem for them now is the seven day a week stations. Quite a few took the 'carrot' of community radio [licences] and decided to close down, which was just what the DTI wanted. With everyone excited about community radio, they can go straight in and proceed to close down all the pirates without too much fuss being made. If anyone does complain, then they can simply point to community radio and say that pirates had a chance to go legit[imate] and obviously didn't want it. Of course, there were bound to be disappointed licence applicants, but they should try again at the end of the experiment and, in the meantime, look forward to what the stations who did get the licences have to offer. Can't you just picture [Home Secretary] Douglas Hurd saying that now?"[144]

The same article went on to comment about the extreme measures the DTI had adopted in recent months when raiding pirate stations: "Up 'til quite recently, the Radio Interference Service doesn't seem to have been too worried about tracing studios in the majority of cases. That has all now changed. They are now spending a lot of resources in trying to track down major stations and actually catch staff operating the equipment. To further put people off illegally broadcasting, the way they carry out raids has become increasingly heavy handed. Once they've broken the door down, they'll proceed to strip the studios and surrounding rooms completely bare. The legislation which allows this is grossly unfair and should at least be made more specific with regard to what exactly the DTI are allowed to take."[145]

The issue of exactly how much equipment the DTI was entitled to remove, and what precisely the courts could confiscate, was subsequently resolved in an extraordinary legal appeal considered by two judges sitting at the Queen's Bench Divisional Court. The case concerned Jeffrey Rudd, who had been charged with operating a pirate radio station in Liverpool during two days in November 1984. Rudd had pleaded guilty to the charges and was fined £100 in February 1985, with £40 costs, a decision upheld by Liverpool Magistrates Court on appeal in April 1985. However, Rudd's legal counsel argued that some of the items confiscated during the DTI raid had not been used in connection with the offences, specifically

300 records, seventy audio cassettes (valued at £1,000) and two Goodmans loudspeakers. After lengthy consideration, the judges of the Divisional Court concluded in early 1986 that the term 'apparatus' referred to in the Wireless Telegraphy Act 1949 did include loudspeakers, but excluded records and cassettes. An order was made to delete records and tapes from the list of forfeited items, and Lord Justice Glidewell concluded that "a question of law of public importance was certified." This ruling was good news for the pirate radio fraternity and offered a glimmer of hope to London's remaining soul pirates that were locked in their continuing struggles against DTI raids.[146]

On 16 February 1986, LWR interrupted its usual taped programmes for a live outside broadcast from Kisses nightclub in Peckham, where Gordon McNamee (of now dormant KISS FM) was resident DJ. Three days later, LWR suffered yet another DTI raid. That same week, McNamee unexpectedly found himself out of a job. Kisses nightclub had changed hands and the new owners had different ideas about what would make the venue successful. The club was to be renamed La Plaza and would now cater for "an older clientele." Blues & Soul magazine lamented that "Kisses, that long time funk oasis in the hinterlands of Peckham, is no more." McNamee consoled himself by quickly arranging a regular Tuesday night DJ spot at the Tropicana Beach club in Luton. The unexpected loss of his job at Kisses also meant he could spend more time trying to return his pirate station KISS FM to London's airwaves, after an absence that had already lasted two months.[147]

On Saturday 22 March 1986, KISS re-appeared on 94 FM for the first time since the previous December, announcing that it had abandoned twenty-four hour broadcasts and would now be transmitting only during weekends. The station was raided by the DTI the very next day. The following weekend's broadcasts were equally unlucky. On Saturday 29 March, KISS signed on, using a new frequency of 95.3 FM, but was raided overnight. This new FM channel improved the reception for listeners living south of the River Thames, but proved worse than 94 FM for those in North London.[148]

KISS FM's return, after an absence of three months, brought the station its first significant press coverage. TX magazine put KISS FM on the cover of its May 1986 issue, with a black and white photo of Gordon McNamee sat at the controls of a very basic pirate radio studio. Under front page headlines that screamed "LONDON GETS A KISS!!" and "SOUL, ELECTRO, BOOGIE AND GO-GO FREELY AVAILABLE ON THE RADIO," TX explained: "London's KISS FM takes its inspiration from New York's WRKS – a top rated station famed around the world for its dance music mega-mixes. 'After Los Angeles, New York and Dublin, we felt London just had to have a KISS', says KISS FM Supremo Mr ****** ****" [TX was careful to make no reference to McNamee by name].[149]

Inside the magazine was a further photo of McNamee, accompanied by an explanation of why KISS FM was now broadcasting only at weekends: "They decided that, as the DTI were hitting twenty-four hour stations so much, they'd be better off reducing their hours, so they'd lose less transmitters and be able to have less breaks in programmes ... Unfortunately, it seems that the DTI have followed the soul stations and are concentrating more on weekend stations than before, making life harder for some of the non-profit making stations. KISS FM has also had to cope with the DTI's surveillance staff who go around following DJs in an attempt to try and find out where stations' secret studios are ... Because of these pressures, KISS's programming has suffered at times – it's not easy to happily present a show if you think the DTI could knock on the door at any minute."[150]

KISS FM continued to broadcast on London's airwaves every weekend during April 1986 on 95.4 FM, suffering only one DTI raid on the 26th, when it lost a transmitter. The station now had a regular mailing address for listeners' correspondence – 29 Dysons Road, London N18 – and was beginning to develop a loyal audience for its programmes. In the face of increased DTI raids, all of London's soul pirates, including LWR and newcomers Fame and Starpoint, had chosen to revert to weekend-only operations. This put KISS FM on a par with its competitors, helping it to quickly secure a significant slice of the London pirate radio audience who were now being offered less programme airtime.

A month after its re-launch, on Sunday 27 April 1986, the first KISS FM all-day music event was staged at London's Town & Country Club, featuring "all the top London jocks you can imagine." The DTI raided the station again on Saturday 3 May, but a contingency plan enabled broadcasts to resume within a few hours. That weekend, the DTI was reported to be "extremely active" and was "following DJs to try and locate studios" of several pirate stations, though KISS FM managed to maintain the secrecy of its location.[151]

KISS FM's programmes began to settle into a regular weekend schedule of shows. Saturdays kicked off at midnight with Max LX playing hip hop, and then Joey Jay playing reggae from 2 am, before the daytime soul shows started with Dean Savonne at 7 am, Dennis O'Brien at 9 am, Paul Oakenfold at 11 am, Norman Jay at 1 pm, Jonathan More at 3 pm, Paul Anderson at 5 pm, Colin Faver at 7 pm, DJ Tee at 9 pm and Desmond D at 11 pm. On Sundays, Greeny took over at 3 am, DJ Selwyn at 9 am, Gordon Mac at 11 am, Richie Rich with hip hop at 1 pm, Derek Boland at 3 pm, Danny Rampling at 5 pm, Tosca at 7 pm, Colin Dale at 9 pm and Dean Savonne at 11 pm.[152]

During May 1986, there was only one interruption to KISS FM's weekend broadcasts, when the DTI raided the station's transmitter at nine o'clock on the evening of Sunday 18th, a few hours before programmes were due to end. Other London soul pirates were less lucky with the DTI. LWR was raided frequently and decided to broadcast pre-recorded shows all the time, with the exception of two live outside broadcasts from Cammies nightclub. When LWR tried to resume seven-day transmissions, the DTI tracked down its studio on 7 May and stripped it bare. The station resumed broadcasts with pre-recorded tapes but, on the 18th, the DTI used a crane to remove LWR's aerial mast from its site in Crystal Palace. The DTI used the same tactic against several pirates the same day, with both Fame FM's and Starpoint Radio's masts being removed by crane. Only TKO managed to escape the DTI's attentions by closing down at lunchtime before its transmitter could be located.[153]

In June 1986, KISS FM was not so fortunate. The station was forced off the air at 7.30 pm on Sunday 2nd, and again at the same time the following Sunday, when the DTI confiscated its transmitter. The next weekend was trouble-free, but the DTI struck again at 11 am on Sunday 23rd. DTI raids on KISS FM often seemed to happen during Gordon McNamee's Sunday morning show, encouraging one magazine to ask rhetorically: "Don't [the DTI] like Gordon Mac's programme?"[154]

KISS FM's luck proved more fortunate than London's other soul pirates. Once again, LWR attempted to resume its seven day schedule during June 1986 but, after two weeks of continuous programmes, the DTI raided the station's studio on the 12th. LWR managed to return on the 17th, but was raided yet again on the 21st, forcing it to broadcast tapes of continuous music most of the time it was on-air. TKO suffered similar problems, with visits from the DTI on the 9th and the 17th, that prevented the station from broadcasting many live programmes. To compete with LWR's attempted return to twenty-four hour broadcasting, both TKO and Starpoint Radio had started to broadcast during weekday evenings as well as weekends, but DTI action dogged their plans too.[155]

Whilst LWR and London's newer pirates – KISS FM, TKO and Starpoint – struggled on, trying to avoid the attentions of the DTI, the old guard of former soul pirates – JFM, Horizon and Solar – were still awaiting the outcome of their applications for Britain's first community radio licences. A total of 180 applications had been submitted in November 1985 for the five London licences. In January 1986, the Home Office Advisory Panel had recommended to the Home Secretary that three additional licences should be allocated to London to help satisfy the overwhelming demand. In March, a Home Office spokesperson said that an announcement would be made "in weeks rather than months." On 26 June, a Cabinet committee met to discuss the community radio experiment. Four days later, Home Secretary Douglas Hurd published a written statement in the House of Commons, announcing that "the Government have … decided to give up the idea of an immediate experiment in community radio."[156]

Hurd went on to cite a number of reasons for the cancellation of the community radio scheme: the lack of a regulatory body to supervise the new stations; the need to impose minimum broadcasting standards; the Independent Broadcasting Authority's wish to develop new national commercial stations; concerns expressed by existing independent local radio stations about the effect of new stations on their profitability; and the forthcoming publication of Professor Peacock's report on the financing of the BBC. Hurd said he was "conscious of the disappointment which this statement will cause to some, and of the effort many people have incurred. I would like to express my regret in particular to all those who made applications, and to the advisory panel which considered them. Their efforts have shown that there is enthusiastic and constructive support for community radio, and I hope that we shall be able to devise suitable arrangements for it to take its part in our radio system."[157]

The 180 applicants for London licences were absolutely astounded by Hurd's unexpected statement, as was the entire community radio lobby. The Campaign for Press and Broadcasting Freedom said the decision confirmed its "worst fears that government plans to deregulate radio are about handing the medium over to commercial operators, rather than encouraging diversity and accountability." New Society magazine suggested that the real reason for the decision was "the desire of [Conservative Party chairman] Norman Tebbit to make his rival for the party leadership look foolish. The ex-Heathite [Douglas] Hurd was in sympathy with the aims of many community radio projects to give ethnic groups a voice; but Tebbit, at the last moment and with [Prime Minister] Mrs Thatcher's backing, persuaded the Cabinet to turn Hurd down." Tebbit himself, speaking on a BBC Radio London phone-in show, said: "Don't blame Douglas [Hurd] on his own. It was a joint decision by all of us." Leon Brittan, the former Home Secretary, who had initiated the community radio experiment the previous year, said its cancellation was "a missed opportunity."[158]

The ex-pirate licence applicants were more forthright in their condemnation of the government announcement, and more determined in their resolve. One un-named bidder said: "Frankly, the gloves are off. We will now use any means at our disposal to get our message across." Another said: "The polite lobbying process has been thrown up in our face, but we'll take Leon Brittan's rhetoric about free speech and act on it." Three days after the shock announcement, representatives of the Community Radio Association met Home Office Minister Giles Shaw and civil servants, who conceded that applicants would be offered financial compensation to cover their expenses incurred in the bids. The government also offered development funds to the Community Radio Association and the prospect of continuing talks with the Home Office, though it was obvious that absolutely nothing of the proposed community radio experiment was about to be salvaged.[159]

TX magazine wrote about "the predicted explosion of pirate radio activity in London" as a result of the cancellation of community radio licences. It commented: "Maybe now, after all this waiting, everyone can get back to the real business of making programmes again. For too long, the creative people in non-mainstream radio have been taking a back seat. Now's the time for the pirates to show everyone just what they're capable of, with a wide range of different stations providing a wide range of different programming ... There's no way now that pirate radio will go away, or even decrease, until the government comes up with an alternative."[160]

In the community radio magazine Relay, Colin Gardiner of licence applicant Hackney Radio articulated the feelings of many disappointed bidders: "People have been coming into our office for weeks now saying 'I've heard the news, when are we going on air?' The news they've heard is the abandonment of the community radio experiment. But what they want to hear is community radio, and they want to hear it NOW."[161]

The gossip column in Blues & Soul magazine summed up the reactions of the London soul pirates: "Maggie [Thatcher]'s minions have decided to put community radio on ice – rather than on the airwaves. In other words, some chinless wonder has done something rather uncomfortable in his trousers and decided on the safest course of action ... to make no decision. A Whitehall farce of the grandest proportions!"[162]

In Parliament, Sir John Biggs-Davison MP asked the Home Office if it had evaluated the effect of its announcement on pirate radio activity. In a written reply, the Home Office's Giles Shaw assured the MP that "there is, at this stage, no evidence that the decision not to proceed with the community radio experiment has led to a significant increase in the incidence of unlicensed broadcasting." Shaw promised that a consultative Green Paper on the future of radio broadcasting would be published that autumn and he expressed "hope that unlicensed broadcasting, which can have serious consequences, will not take place, and that those who want to see changes to the present arrangements for radio will contribute to the discussion which the Green Paper is intended to stimulate."[163]

However, as pirate radio magazine TX pointed out, "many stations are proposing to take to the air as pirates" rather than waste further time in pursuit of legal licences. TX suggested that "if stations plan to go pirate, they'll need to plan their operation carefully if they're to stand any chance of surviving," but it noted that "stations may still stand a reduced chance of being raided if there are more of them." The magazine explained:

"There's a great deal of paperwork that goes with each raid [the DTI] carry out, including testing the equipment and recording details about its operation. Time also has to be spent preparing for court appearances, which are then often slow. When they do go out and raid stations, they are slowed down by the traffic in London, hindering them from getting to where they want to go. Then, once they've traced a station, they have to get into the premises. A warrant will be needed from a local magistrate, and police will then need to accompany the DTI men if they're entering private premises. On a busy night in London, they obviously have much greater priorities than stopping people playing records on the radio."[164]

TX concluded: "There is now the potential for the biggest pirate radio explosion yet, providing the stations are properly planned and organised. London may begin to get a decent choice of radio at last!"[165]

---

[144] "The Eric File - Eric Update", TX no. 5, Mar 1986.
[145] ibid.
[146] "Cassettes And Records Are Not 'Apparatus' In Act Against Pirate Radio", The Times, 16 Apr 1986.
[147] "On-Air Stations: LWR", TX no. 5, Mar 1986.
James Hamilton, "Odds'N'Bods", Record Mirror, 15 Feb 1986.
Bob Killbourn, "Jocks' Rap", Blues & Soul, 25 Feb 1986.
[148] "Hold It Now, Hit It" & "KISS FM", TX no. 6, May 1986.
[149] "London Gets A KISS!!", TX no. 6, May 1986.
[150] "Hold It Now, Hit It", op cit.
[151] James Hamilton, "Odds'N'Bods", Record Mirror, 5 Apr & 19 Apr 1986.
"KISS FM", TX no. 7, July 1986.
[152] "Options", TX no. 7, Jul 1986.
[153] "KISS FM", "LWR", "Fame FM", "Starpoint Radio" "TKO", TX no. 7, Jul 1986.
[154] "KISS FM", TX no. 8, Aug 1986.
[155] "TKO", "LWR", "Starpoint Radio", TX no. 8, Aug 1986.
[156] Tim Richardson, "The Story So Far...", Relay no. 13, Aug 1986.
Hansard, Written Answers, 30 Jun 1986.
[157] Hansard, op cit.
[158] Rebecca Coyle, "What They Said...", Relay no. 13, Aug 1986.
[159] Rebecca Coyle, op cit.
Tim Richardson, op cit.
[160] Steve Hamley, "Editorial", TX no. 8, Aug 1986.
[161] Colin Gardiner, "Community Radio Now", Relay no. 13, Aug 1986.
[162] The Mouth, "Street Noise", Blues & Soul, 15 Jul 1986.
[163] Hansard, Written Answers, 25 Jul 1986.
[164] "Access", TX no. 8, Aug 1986.
[165] ibid.

August to December 1986.

In the wake of the government's U-turn on the community radio experiment, many frustrated licence applicants decided to take the law into their own hands and become pirate broadcasters. A new group, calling itself Action Now For Community Radio [ANCOR], decided "to tell Londoners how they had been cheated of community radio" and interrupted the broadcasts of London's commercial music station, Capital Radio, on four occasions with a pre-recorded thirty-second message. ANCOR said it was planning similar action against commercial stations in the Midlands and the Home Counties. Another group, called Platform 88, started weekly transmissions on an unused FM frequency, broadcasting taped programmes made by disappointed licence bidders "to give community radio applicants what the Home Office denied them – their own voice."[166]

An East London group, calling itself the Hackney Broadcasting Authority, also started weekly broadcasts and distributed an explanatory press statement: "There's no option. It's either sit around for another three years and hope for community radio, or start to do something about it." The Community Radio Association started to co-ordinate these activities into a planned day of direct action in October 1986, but it suddenly abandoned the idea in mid-September after receiving a letter from the Home Secretary, Douglas Hurd, saying he was "concerned that the Association is minded to promote a day of unlawful broadcasting. This will not help the development of radio policy in the direction which you want." Representations were also made to the Association by the Department of Trade & Industry [DTI] which "evidently felt that they had quite enough unlicensed broadcasting to deal with as it was."[167]

In a thinly veiled reference to the Community Radio Association's about-turn over its proposed day of action, Now Radio magazine criticised "major community radio lobby groups" for "stalling until they have read what the Green Paper says about the future." It commented:

"Whilst the wait goes on for some, however, there are many who are not prepared to play that game. They did it between the time the government announced that it was to allow twenty-one experimental community radio stations and the time it said the experiment would not go ahead, for the moment at least. These people include the operators of so-called pirate stations who closed down, made their applications to the Home Office and waited ... and waited ... and waited."[168]

The magazine concluded: "If there are people who think they can run good radio stations ... they should stop sitting around smoky bars and get working to show us what they are on about."[169]

The Community Radio Association's decision to discourage direct action and, instead, to pursue further talks with the government left frustrated licence applicants in disarray. The initiatives to "free the airwaves" by ANCOR and Platform 88 quickly fizzled out and the threatened flood of pirate radio stations failed to materialise. TX magazine attacked the Association's ideology as "impractical, unworkable and totally incompatible with the reality of producing a genuine community radio in Britain." It believed the lack of new pirate activity was because "many potential pirates have been put off by the heavy DTI raids recently." TX said it would still "expect a few stations to tentatively test the water and, once they come to terms with pirate broadcasting in the late 1980s, more will follow and most will stay."[170]

The government increased its activity against pirate stations swiftly and decisively after the Home Secretary's announcement in June 1986 to cancel the community radio experiment. The DTI swung into action, hitting the London soul pirates particularly hard.

During July, Starpoint only managed twenty-five per cent of its scheduled broadcasts, TKO thirty per cent, and LWR sixty per cent, though KISS FM managed ninety per cent. Starpoint started the month broadcasting on weekday evenings and all weekend but, as soon as it switched to twenty-four hour operation in mid-July, it was hammered by the DTI. The station managed a live outside broadcast from the 1-0 Club in Catford on the 3rd, but the DTI then removed Starpoint's mast on the 6th with a crane, removed its transmitter on the 15th, and raided it again on the 28th.[171]

LWR switched from pre-recorded tapes to live shows at the beginning of July 1986, but its aerial mast was removed by a crane on the 6th, again on the 11th, and the DTI raided its studio on the 31st when the DJ on-air at the time, Jasper, managed to comment "see you in court" before the plugs were pulled.[172]

TKO's attempt to fulfil its promised twenty-four hour schedule also proved impossible, after the DTI crane removed the station's aerial mast on the 6th, and again on the 11th, forcing the station off the air for long periods. TX magazine commented: "It makes you wonder if it is really worth it trying to broadcast twenty-four hours a day, if all stations end up with are raids which keep them off the air longer than they're on. It's also much easier to locate twenty-four hour a day stations' studios, so staff keep getting caught and they revert at times to continuous music tapes, which get boring and monotonous."[173]

KISS FM, meanwhile, was having more luck with its weekend-only broadcasting policy, suffering only one raid during July 1986 on Sunday 6th at 1.30 pm. The station's signal was consistently of good quality and its programmes were full of adverts. TX magazine commented that KISS FM "have greatly improved since they limited their hours to weekends only, and miss far less time due to raids. Presentation is much higher when the pressures on the DJs aren't so great."[174]

The DTI continued to prosecute participants in pirate radio. Chris England of Radio Shoestring was fined £666, including costs, though the court returned his record collection. LWR DJ Ron Tom became the first pirate radio DJ to be jailed, receiving a three-month sentence, and two staff from London pirate Three Boroughs' Radio were fined a total of £325.[175]

During August 1986, KISS FM transmitted its first live outside broadcast, from Bentley's nightclub during the Bank Holiday weekend of the Notting Hill Carnival. The station switched its frequency back to 94 FM from 95.3 because a new BBC Essex transmitter had just opened on the latter channel. The DTI continued to show interest in the station, raiding its transmitter on Saturday 8th, but KISS continued to suffer less than its competitors, who were still attempting twenty-four hour services.[176]

LWR lost its transmitter to the DTI on 3 August 1986, its studio installation (resulting in the prosecution of DJ Cliff Ringwood) and another transmitter on the 10th, and a further transmitter on the 29th. Despite these setbacks, LWR managed a live outside broadcast from the Town & Country Club which it billed as the First Summer All-Dayer.[177]

TKO lost its studio to the DTI on 5 August 1986, a transmitter on the 10th, and another on the 29th. Starpoint managed a further outside broadcast from the 1-0 Club in Catford but, after three raids in as many weeks, the station was then off the air for several weeks.[178]

In a related incident, on Friday 29 August, a major police operation swooped on Bentley's nightclub in Canning Town, a venue used by LWR for its Thursday night Reggae Squad, and by TKO for its Friday night Roadshow. Both stations were taken off-air by the DTI shortly before the raid on the club, and it was reported that several of the stations' DJs were present in the club when it was visited by the Drugs Squad.[179]

September 1986 was another relatively raid-free month for KISS FM, while LWR, Starpoint and TKO all succeeded in broadcasting more of their twenty-four hour schedules than they had managed for a long time. So far in 1986, the DTI had made 167 raids on sixty-one stations throughout Britain, and had successfully convicted fifty-seven people, the largest fine being £1,000 with costs. The DTI admitted that LWR was one of the stations it had hit the hardest, but it failed to explain why the intensity of its raids had suddenly slowed down since July. Rumours circulated that it was either because the increase in pirate activity anticipated by the government in the wake of the Home Secretary's announcement had failed to materialise, or because the DTI's Radio Interference Service had overspent its budget during the first half of the year and was now having to cut back.[180]

In October 1986, KISS FM celebrated its first birthday with a party at Lacey's nightclub on the 3rd, and a special Sunday evening radio show on the 5th, during which many of the station's DJs gathered together in the studio. The DTI retaliated later that night by raiding the KISS transmitter at 11 pm. The following Sunday, the DTI took a further transmitter in the afternoon but, during the remainder of the month, KISS FM's broadcasts were uninterrupted. A measure of the station's increasing popularity was the decision by a record company to reissue the 1982 Bunny Wailer song 'Back To School' as a direct result of recent airplay on KISS FM.[181]

LWR had a quiet October 1986 too, with only one transmitter raided on the 12th, enabling it to sustain a twenty-four hour service most of the time. TKO was also raided only once, on the 12th, and then managed a return to live programmes. Even Starpoint returned from the dead on 14 October, broadcasting a twenty-four hour service until someone (other than the DTI) stole the station's transmitter during the night of the 26th.[182]

November 2006 heralded the launch of a new weekend-only soul pirate station in London called WBLS, a name (like KISS FM) stolen from a popular black music station in New York City. Just as KISS FM had done a year earlier, WBLS recruited a strong line-up of London club DJs to present its programmes, even persuading popular hip hop presenter Tim Westwood to leave LWR and join its team. WBLS blitzed the media with information and was rewarded with coverage of its launch in many mainstream magazines. While KISS FM had been quietly building a strong underground following since its re-launch in March, WBLS suddenly achieved more notoriety than KISS had ever managed, even before it made its first transmission. The day before the station's launch, WBLS spokesman DJ Dee commented: "We won't get away with it forever. The DTI will be able to track us but, with perseverance and help from the public, we should be able to continue. The market is out there for this type of radio. It's a pity it has to be a pirate."[183]

The WBLS studio and transmitter had been assembled and tested by the time the station threw its launch party at London's Limelight nightclub on Thursday 6 November. Preparations had been made for a live broadcast from the event, once WBLS had started transmitting in the early hours of Friday morning. However, only hours beforehand, somebody broke into the station's studio and smashed all the equipment. To make matters worse, the transmitter engineers contracted by WBLS suddenly decided to pull out of the deal, under pressure from their other pirate station clients who did not welcome a new competitor. Despite these setbacks, WBLS still managed to debut late on Friday and carried on broadcasting until Sunday morning, when the DTI raided its transmitter. Its presenters during those first broadcasts included Mud Club DJ Jay Strongman, Judge Jules from Family Funktion, Jazzie B from Soul II Soul, Gaz Mayall from Gaz's Rockin' Blues, Derek Boland, Dave Dorell and Barry Sharpe.[184]

After an absence of two weeks, WBLS returned on 21 November with a poorer quality signal, and it managed to sustain weekly programmes until 7 December, when a DTI raid on its transmitter dealt the station a fatal blow. One of the WBLS staff complained: "Some of us had to sell bits and pieces of our lives to get this thing off the ground." Despite WBLS having enjoyed what one magazine described as "probably more pre-launch hype than any pirate station since the return of [offshore] Radio Caroline," the high profile pirate disappeared after that raid, and the threat it embodied to the existing soul pirates vanished almost as quickly as it had appeared.[185]

After the closure of WBLS, KISS FM added Tim Westwood to its team and recruited Steve Jackson from TKO (Jay Strongman, Judge Jules and Jazzie B all joined KISS FM from WBLS at a later date). KISS FM's programmes on Saturday were now: 7 am Dean Savonne, 9 am Dennis O'Brien, 11 am Gordon Mac, 1 pm Norman Jay, 3 pm Jonathan More, 5 pm Paul Anderson, 7 pm Colin Faver, 9 pm DJ Tee, and 11 pm Desmond D. On Sunday: 1 am André, 3 am Trevor James, 5 am Greeny, 7 am Dave VJ, 9 am DJ Selwyn, 11 am Tim Westwood, 1 pm Richie Rich, 3 pm Steve Jackson, 5 pm Danny Rampling, 7 pm Tosca, 9 pm Colin Dale, 11 pm Dean Savonne and 1 am 'Madhatter' Trevor. KISS had also organised a new mailing address: PO Box 704, London N19 4SJ. Apart from one DTI raid on the station's transmitter at 1 pm on the 8th, November was a trouble-free month for KISS. LWR, TKO and Starpoint were also on the air for most of the month with twenty-four hour broadcasts.[186]

December 1986 was notable for the return of soul pirate Solar Radio, absent since September 1985, when it had signed off to pursue a legal licence. The station's Tony Monson commented: "We feel very bitter about the government's refusal to carry on with community radio plans." After two weeks of engineering tests, Solar re-launched a full, twenty-four hour service on 15 December that was similar to its previous incarnation, and so became London's fourth full-time soul pirate.[187]

KISS FM continued to operate only on weekends, except that it celebrated its first Christmas on-air by broadcasting almost continuously from 20 December through to the New Year, despite a DTI transmitter raid on the 20th that prevented DJ Tim Westwood from presenting his first scheduled KISS FM show. A further raid on 29 December took the station off the air temporarily for two days.[188]

LWR, TKO and Starpoint were raided on 7 December, but all managed to broadcast extensively over the Christmas holiday period. Ex-Horizon Radio owner Chris Stewart joined

TKO as a DJ, effectively killing rumours that Horizon would return to piracy (as Solar had just done) now that its community radio licence bid had failed.[189]

Prosecutions against pirate DJs continued apace. Starpoint Radio's Chris Philips was fined £450, with £100 costs, by Camberwell Crown Court, but was allowed to keep the records he had brought to the station's studio. At LWR, Jasper was fined £200 for a raid on the station in July, and Cliff Ringwood and Mike Steele were each fined £600 for a similar raid in August. Beyond the soul pirates, DJ Challenger of Northwest London black community pirate station JBC was fined £185, and Harry Marshall of Twickenham community pirate Border Radio was fined £125.[190]

In November 1986, the DTI said it had made 218 raids on eighty-four stations during the previous twelve months, and it published a list in Parliament of the names of all pirate stations it had acted against. Forty-five of the eighty-four stations were in London, fourteen in Liverpool and the rest in other parts of Britain. In London alone, 182 prosecutions had been brought under the Wireless Telegraphy Act 1949, of which ninety-three related to unlicensed broadcasting, resulting in ninety-two convictions and sixty-one cases where forfeiture of equipment was ordered by the court. The DTI now employed 220 staff in its Radio Investigation Service, of which fifty-five were based in London. DTI Minister John Butcher estimated that thirty-four pirate stations were still broadcasting across Britain, and he promised that "raids will continue in all cases until illegal broadcasting activity stops."[191]

Butcher's statistics were contradicted by a report from the Community Radio Association, which noted 115 pirates on-air during the second half of 1986 alone, of which sixty-five were in London. The Association said that the Government was "clearly losing the war" against unlicensed radio stations, and it reiterated the prediction it had made in June that the Government's decision to abandon the community radio experiment would lead to increased pirate activity.[192]

To highlight the impact the pirates had made on the London radio market, TX magazine organised an end-of-year poll amongst its readers to determine the most popular radio station and DJ in the capital. In the station category, KISS FM came first, LWR third, Starpoint fourth, Solar Radio sixth, WBLS eighth and TKO tenth, with the remaining positions taken by pop and rock pirates. In the DJ category, KISS FM held four positions – Jonathan More second, Norman Jay third, Tim Westwood fifth and Gordon Mac seventh. Although DJs from LWR, Solar, TKO, Starpoint and WBLS were each represented amongst the top twenty DJs, no station managed to score as many places as KISS FM.[193]

KISS FM swept the board so successfully in these polls (the previous year it had only managed ninth place) that it begged the question as to what extent the results had been determined by genuine reader votes or by concerted letter writing campaigns by the station's staff. Whatever the answer, KISS FM had scored its first media victory, albeit in a low circulation magazine read only by pirate radio fanatics.

As TX itself commented: "1986 was certainly the year when soul music radio reigned supreme, for the simple reason of the money involved – quite a few thousand [pounds] a week at the top stations."[194]

The eager newcomer WBLS had attracted more publicity than any other pirate station during the year, but the threat it had posed to the existing soul stations had been successfully seen off. KISS FM's determination to pursue weekend-only broadcasts had paid off, after its re-launch in March. If the closing months of 1985 had been a disaster for KISS, 1986 had proven an unqualified success. The station had firmly established itself now on 94 FM and was already preparing for greater things to come.

---

[166] "Jamming Local Radio", Relay no. 13, Aug 1986.
[167] "Community Pirates Take To The Air", Broadcast, 26 Sep 1986.
John Mulholland, "Pirates Fly The Flag?", The Guardian, 20 Oct 1986.
[168] Gavin Cooper, "Pirates … A Word In Your Ear!", Now Radio, 20 Oct 1986.
[169] ibid.
[170] Chris England, "Rumblings", TX no. 9, Sep 1986.
Steve Hamley, "Editorial", TX no. 9, Sep 1986.
[171] "Round Up", TX no. 9, Sep 1986.
"Starpoint Radio", TX no. 9, Sep 1986.
[172] "LWR", TX no. 9, Sep 1986.
[173] "TKO", TX no. 9, Sep 1986.
[174] "KISS FM", "TKO", TX no. 9, Sep 1986.
[175] Chris England, "The Eric File", TX no. 9, Sep 1986.
The Mouth, "Street Noise", Blues & Soul, 15 Jul 1986.
"Round Up", TX no. 9, Sep 1986.
[176] "KISS FM", TX no. 10, Oct 1986.
[177] "LWR", TX no. 10, Oct 1986.
[178] "TKO", "Starpoint Radio", TX no. 10, Oct 1986.
[179] "Pirates In Drugs Bust", TX no. 10, Oct 1986.
[180] "KISS FM", "LWR", "Starpoint Radio", "TKO", "Raid Count", TX no. 11, Nov 1986.
[181] "KISS FM", TX no. 12, Dec 1986.
[182] "LWR", "TKO", "Starpoint Radio", TX no. 12, Dec 1986.
KISS FM, Greater Licence FM Application Form (Appendix), 1 Jun 1989.
James Hamilton, "Odds'N'Bods", Record Mirror, 4 Oct 1986.
[183] Rosalind Russell, "The Pirates Are Having A Party", Evening Standard, 6 Nov 1986.
"More Rebel Radio", Time Out, 5 Nov 1986.
[184] "WBLS", TX no. 12, Dec 1986.
The Mouth, "Street Noise", Blues & Soul, 18 Nov 1986.
[185] "WBLS", TX/Radio Today no. 13, Feb 1987.
John Mulholland, "Radio News", City Limits, 20 Nov 1986.
"WBLS Launches", TX no. 12, Dec 1986.
[186] "KISS FM", "LWR", Starpoint Radio", "TKO", TX/Radio Today no. 13, Feb 1987.
[187] Peter Holt, "Ad Lib", The Evening Standard, 15 Jan 1987.
"LWR", "Solar Radio", "Starpoint Radio", "TKO", TX/Radio Today no. 13, Feb 1987.
[188] ibid.
[189] ibid.
[190] "Court Report", TX/Radio Today no. 13, Feb 1987.
[191] Hansard, Written Answers, 17 & 21 Nov & 9 Dec 1986.
"RIS Made 218 Raids – Official", TX/Radio Today no. 13, Feb 1987.
[192] Jonathon Miller, "Raids Fail To Stop Pirate Broadcasts", The Times, 31 Dec 1986.
[193] "The Chart", TX/Radio Today no. 13, Feb 1987.
[194] "Rewind", TX no. 12, Dec 1986.

January to July 1987.

Soul music pirate radio had existed in London for sixteen years by now. Although the prospect of a legal soul station still seemed as remote as ever, following the government's cancellation of the community radio experiment, it was becoming evident that the pirates were influencing the legitimate radio industry a great deal. BBC Radio London, the non-commercial, local station for the capital, had adopted an increasingly soul-orientated music policy under the influence of morning show DJ, and long time soul fan, Tony Blackburn. The station had also started to organise weekly 'Soul Nites' in club venues for its listeners, a carbon copy of the lucrative events that pirates had been organising to fund their stations. As one magazine commented, club nights were "where the REAL money is made" in pirate radio, and BBC Radio London was said to have financed a complete new outside broadcast unit from the proceeds of its Thursday Soul Nites.[195]

Many former soul pirate DJs were now gainfully employed by legal radio stations. At BBC Radio London, Steve Walsh (ex-Invicta and JFM) was presenting a Sunday night soul show, Gilles Peterson (ex-Invicta, Horizon, Solar and K-Jazz) presented a Tuesday night jazz show, Jeff Young (ex-LWR) had a Saturday lunchtime soul show, and even the station's phone-in host, Robbie Vincent, had worked on Invicta in its early days. At Essex Radio, Tony Monson (ex-Solar) had a Saturday night soul show. At County Sound in Guildford, Lynn Parsons (ex-JFM) had a Saturday night pop music programme. At Invicta Radio in Kent [unrelated to London pirate Radio Invicta], Pete Tong (ex-LWR) was presenting soul shows. KISS FM DJ Tim Westwood had recently contributed to the 'Saturday Live' show on the BBC's national pop music network, Radio One, and Chris Forbes (ex-Solar) now presented an overnight show on London commercial station, Capital Radio.[196]

On 1 January 1987, LWR celebrated its fourth birthday, making it the oldest of London's soul music pirates still on-air. The capital's four full-time soul stations – LWR, Solar, Starpoint and TKO – had been joined recently on the airwaves by a steadily increasing number of part-time stations, most broadcasting only during evenings or weekends with low power transmitters. Making a casual scan across the FM dial in London, a listener would have found stations such as Radio Activity, Flashback Radio, Joy Radio, People's Choice, Quest FM, RJR, Rock II Rock, Studio One, Time Radio, Trax FM, Twilight Radio and WKLR, all broadcasting various forms of black music.[197]

In addition to these music stations, black community pirate stations, such as JBC in Harlesden and Community Development Radio in Southwest London, were broadcasting a mix of black music and community-orientated, speech programmes. TX magazine's prediction the previous year had been correct – London's airwaves were slowly filling up with more and more illegal stations, even though the capital had not experienced the immediate surge in pirate activity anticipated by the government after its cancellation of the community radio experiment in June 1986.[198]

In January 1987, the Department of Trade & Industry's [DTI] Radio Regulatory Division published its first annual report, for 1985/6, which noted that, "in line with the shift towards a greater enforcement role, the Radio Investigation Service has been given a new mandate by

Ministers." The report said the DTI "has carried out a sustained and concentrated campaign against land-based, unlicensed broadcasters" and it reproduced a colour photo of a large pirate radio aerial being removed from the top of a building by a DTI crane. Although the publication of this report was recounted by trade magazine Broadcast under the headline 'Radio Pirates Sunk By DTI's Campaign,' nothing could have been further from the truth.[199]

The DTI had been busy recruiting additional staff to join the London branch of its Radio Investigation Service, whose budget had been substantially increased to improve the effectiveness of its work. On Sunday 25 January, the DTI's increased determination to combat the pirates was evident when London experienced the most concerted campaign of raids yet. On that one day, equipment was taken from KISS FM, LWR, TKO, Direct Line Radio, Studio One, London Greek Radio, Twilight Radio, RFM, Community Development Radio, Quest FM, RJR and a new Greek station. By the end of the day, only a handful of smaller pirate stations remained on the air in London.[200]

LWR and Starpoint returned to the airwaves the following day, believing that the DTI activity had ended for now, but further raids that evening took LWR off the air again and lost Starpoint its transmitter, a mere fifty-five minutes after signing back on. The DTI also raided Time Radio on Monday, Radio Duck on Wednesday, and JBC and Time Radio again on Thursday. The raid on the JBC studio coincided with the presence of a film crew from Channel Four television, who were making a programme about the pirate radio phenomenon. As a result, the entire twenty-minute DTI raid was subsequently broadcast on the 7 February edition of The Bandung File to a nationwide TV audience. By the end of that single week in January 1987, the DTI had made more than eighteen raids in London.[201]

Steve Hebditch, editor of Radio Today magazine (formerly 'TX'), commented: "All the indications are that things are going to get a lot tougher. The DTI's Radio Investigation Service has been recruiting a lot more people and they obviously feel the pirates are getting out of hand. The number of stations is increasing all the time. There are forty or so in London and a lot more around the country. People who closed down to try to get community radio licences are now coming back on the air." A DTI spokesman responded: "There is always an offensive going on. If people are in the business of broadcasting without a licence, we are in the business of stopping them doing it ... If somebody starts broadcasting, it is an occupational hazard that they will be busted."[202]

The treasurer of the Community Radio Association, Richard Hilton, said: "The Home Office's indecision [over community radio] has only succeeded in creating more pirates ... The Home Office led us all up the garden path." The Telegraph newspaper's radio critic, Gillian Reynolds, complained that, trying to locate London commercial station Capital Radio on her receiver, "the route was blocked by half a dozen pirate stations. Did you think that these had all been chased off, closed down, brought to court? Not in London, where they all broadcast telephone numbers, addresses and forthcoming nights out at dance halls." The Evening Standard even reported that ex-pirate Radio Jackie was planning to make a return to broadcasting at the end of March.[203]

During the first three months of 1987, the DTI carried out 119 raids, compared to a total of 209 during the whole of the previous year. Despite this increased level of harassment, KISS FM managed to broadcast successfully every weekend during January and the first half of February. Then, the station's transmitter engineer suddenly quit, and an attempt by a new engineer to put the station back on-air failed. DJs were asked to pay the station for presenting their shows, so as to raise money to employ further engineers, but some objected to such a system and left the station. Rumours circulated for a while that the remaining presenters were planning to leave en masse and join another pirate station, but KISS FM eventually organised a return to the airwaves during March after a five-week break. It had a new programme schedule and a new mailing address – 37 Grand Parade, Green Lanes, Haringey, London N4 – the location of a soul music record shop called Music Power.[204]

In February 1987, the government published its much delayed consultative Green Paper on the future of radio, entitled 'Radio – Choices And Opportunities.' The document proposed "several hundred" new local radio stations, but failed to make a distinction between mainstream pop music stations that already existed in Britain, and new types of service that could play a single genre of music or serve a particular community of interest. The community radio magazine Relay commented: "The Green Paper is no more than what can be expected of this government. In the light of recent challenges to programme content and attempts to muzzle the media, plus the cancellation of the community radio experiment, it's hardly surprising that the Green Paper doesn't REALLY encourage the voice of local communities on radio." Steven Gray of the Campaign for Press & Broadcasting Freedom said: "More does not mean different or better. In the Green Paper, it means more pop and prattle, less diversity and less accountability."[205]

Broadcast magazine asserted that "the Green Paper is expected, if anything, to give the pirates a boost." It asked: "Why pack up now when the government is proposing to license a sector of deregulated, low cost radio in future anyway? Especially when the Home Office made it clear, during the aborted community radio experiment of 1985/86, that a previous history of illegal broadcasting would not automatically disqualify applicants for a licence ... It is hard not to conclude that, whichever authority finally gets the job of licensing community radio, it will be deluged by requests to operate soul music stations ... Pirate radio is not going to disappear."[206]

The most immediate impact of the Green Paper was the reaction of the media, who had suddenly been made aware that pirate radio was not only on the increase again, but could become the blueprint for the type of new stations the government proposed to introduce. As a result, the activities and workings of pirate stations came under much closer public scrutiny than they had ever done before.

Newspapers reported that "pirate radio transmissions have been seriously interfering with a vital landing system at Heathrow Airport over several months." One paper warned that "the situation is serious" and reported that DTI staff had located and closed down the pirate station in Brixton, South London which had been causing the interference. However, in another newspaper report, a spokesman for the Civil Aviation Authority denied that the interference was a danger to aircraft: "It was just annoying and it should not have been there. But it has been stopped."[207]

DTI action against the pirates continued during May 1987. In the courts, DJC from Starpoint was fined £850 for illegal broadcasting and remanded in custody for "assaulting a DTI member." Barry James, also from Starpoint, was fined £50, plus £250 costs, after being caught changing the station's pre-recorded tapes for transmission. On the airwaves, heavy raids took place on Sunday 3 May against KISS FM, Greek Radio For London, British Greek

Community Radio, London Greek Radio, Flashback Radio, Rock II Rock, TKO, RFM, Radio Shoestring, Studio One, RJR, Quest FM and several smaller stations. TKO returned on the 6th, along with LWR, which had been off the air since April due to internal problems, but the DTI moved in again on the 11th. TKO managed to remove its transmitter without being caught, but the DTI staff returned to their car to find that its tyres had been slashed.[208]

At the beginning of June 1987, five Law Lords unanimously upheld the Court of Appeal ruling made the previous April that the courts had no powers to seize pirate stations' records and tapes, because they were not "broadcasting apparatus." Jeffrey Rudd of Liverpool, whose original conviction for illegal broadcasting dated back two years, could at last have his records returned to him. Dismissing the DTI's appeal, Lord Goff said: "I recognise this conclusion may create problems for the enforcing authorities." A DTI spokeswoman admitted that the ruling was a significant boost for pirate stations: "Records and tapes are often the most expensive part of their equipment, transmitters being worth only pennies in comparison …This ruling removes an important economic weapon from the enforcement authorities." She added that the confiscation of pirate stations' record and tape collections had, until now, been one of the DTI's most important sanctions.[209]

Pirate radio also made the headlines when The Evening Standard investigated the 'powerplay' system, whereby record companies paid pirate stations to play their records. A reporter from the newspaper, posing as an independent record company, rang three London pirates and discovered that "if you've got the cash, the stations have the time to play your single." He found that LWR charged £500 a week for fifty-six plays, one at the end of each of its eight daily shows. An LWR spokeswoman told him: "The only way to guarantee play on the station is to pay for it. Everyone knows pirate stations charge for playing some records. We think we're providing a service for new talent." TKO charged £300 a week and guaranteed twelve plays per day. A TKO spokesman said: "The major record labels certainly use our service and it's often the only way new records receive any play." KISS FM said it charged £100 for a single to be played every two hours during its weekend transmissions, which it claimed attracted 200,000 listeners. A KISS spokesperson said: "The major record companies prefer this method rather than straight advertisements." The British Phonographic Industry, representing the record companies, denied all knowledge of such business deals. Its spokesman countered: "It's a new one on us and sounds highly unlikely. It would be illegal anyway, and I don't think our members would get involved in anything like that."[210]

In July 1987, Channel Four television screened an hour-long documentary made by the Birmingham Film & Video Workshop called 'The Black And White Pirate Show' which examined the history of illegal radio and the role of black pirate stations in the 1980s. Media critic Nick Higham noted that "the real question posed by the programme is whether the clubs and pirates together have the potential to provide more than an escapist focus for disenchanted black youth. Might they develop into a political focus as well? Or is the pirates' aim no more than that of their predecessors back in the 1960s – to get established stations to play more of the kind of music their listeners like or, failing that, to have fun broadcasting and then go legit[imate] themselves?"[211]

The Evening Standard published a follow-up article to the programme, claiming that London pirates believed the BBC national pop music station Radio One to be "prejudiced against black dance music." LWR owner Zak told the newspaper: "All the London clubs are swinging towards soul, house and rap music because that's what people like now. Yet Radio One have this continual favouritism for bland, monotonous pop like [the group] Curiosity Killed The Cat to the exclusion of good soul ... Pirates have influenced musical trends so much that, now, more than half the chart is dance music. Due to this, I've heard the BBC are trying not to promote too many black records at the moment." KISS FM DJ 'Madhatter' Trevor commented: "Radio One seldom encourage young DJs. Admittedly, they've got [ex-pirate reggae DJ] Ranking Miss P, but she's just a token pirate who's made it." Radio One chief assistant Dave Price responded: "The pirates tend to have a very narrow definition of soul, and a lot of dance tunes are too long and repetitive for radio. I'd say we've done more for soul in the country to the casual listener, if not the specialist."[212]

Out of the blue, at the end of July 1987, came the government's most remarkable and most vitriolic attack on pirate radio to date. This was conducted not on the tower block roofs of London, nor in the country's courts, but in a press briefing called by DTI Junior Minister John Butcher. He told journalists that DTI staff who raided pirate stations were being subjected to a "reign of terror" and said that "some of the things seem to have more in common with Chicago in the 1920s or 1930s than with the streets of London or Birmingham."[213]

Unidentified "government sources" subsequently gave journalists details of several incidents which Butcher claimed were causing DTI staff to live in fear of intimidation for themselves and their families. The incidents allegedly occurred when:

- Four DTI staff had been ambushed by gangs in two cars off the Edgware Road in London. One car had stopped in front of the DTI, the other behind, and two officers were then dragged from their car and beaten with baseball bats. One suffered a permanently crushed elbow.
- One DTI officer, working alone in Birmingham, had been dragged from his car by a gang who smashed his false teeth and stole his vehicle. He later died from a heart attack. "He never got over it," commented one DTI source.
- One DTI officer had been climbing a ladder at a South London tower block when he had it pulled from under him.
- DTI vehicles were being chased by gangs, after being spotted carrying out routine work. Terrified officers had to drive through red traffic lights to evade their pursuers.
- DTI staff were receiving threatening phone calls from pirate radio operators.
- A British Gas engineer was told he would be "done over outside" after an argument on the phone with a pirate operator about radio frequencies.
- DTI officers, pursued by a gang, took refuge in a police station, but the gang followed them in and started a row. When the police intervened, the gang alleged that the DTI staff had harassed one of their number.[214]

Butcher told the press: "It's now happening more and more, and things are getting more and more violent. We are concerned that some of these people should be prosecuted ... I want the public to understand that the work of this department is to protect the public at large. They have an extraordinarily difficult job, but it is applied with common sense and realism. This recent phenomenon is very disturbing, and we need the help of the public at large to support the Radio Investigation Service. What they are doing is in the interests of the public."[215]

Butcher also alerted the media to the existence of a book entitled 'Radio Is My Bomb,' published by Hooligan Press several months earlier, which described itself as a 'Do It Yourself Manual For Pirates.' This seventy-two page publication was a hotchpotch of articles about pirate radio, many of which had appeared previously in pamphlet form. From it, Butcher quoted to the press one paragraph, under the heading 'Confrontation,' that said:

"A good trick if you can get away with it. The DTI and police (they normally only bring a few) are wide open to attack (the mouse becomes the cat!) when coming to get you ... The good thing is that, if pirates start attacking them, they have to bring many more police with them and can only do it when spare police are available ... If you're going to attack them directly, make sure you're well masked and tooled up, and have enough skill and numbers to get past them. Go straight for the police officers and disable them, before they can make their 'officer in distress' call (take or smash their radios, or have someone jamming their frequencies). Other direct ways of hitting back are: attacking the DTI at their bases, attacking their vehicles at their depot, obtaining home addresses/phone numbers of chief officers and harassing them, etc. etc. Remember, they have the entire state apparatus backing them up, any form of direct attack should therefore be anonymous and never spoken of or boasted about later. Or before hahahahahahaha."[216]

The press lapped up the DTI stories and ran extensive details of the alleged violence under exactly the sort of headlines the DTI had probably wanted: 'Chicago-Style Terror Of Radio Pirates' said The London Evening Standard; 'Pirates Scourge Of The Radio Waves' said The Scotsman; 'Pirate Radio Investigators Terrorized' said The Times; 'Pirate Radio Investigators Ambushed' said The Daily Telegraph; 'Thugs On Rampage In Pirate Radio War' said The Sun; 'Radio Pirates In Terror War' said The Daily Express; 'Terror Of The Radio Pirates' said Today; and 'Radio Pirates Go To War!' said The Daily Mirror. Even the American trade publication Variety chipped in with 'Brit Radio Pirates Threaten, Attack Govt. Inspectors,' and a staid magazine such as Electronics & Wireless World joined the melee with a story headlined 'Spectrum And Physical Abuse Increases.'[217]

Despite such horror stories, not all the media swallowed the DTI line without comment. An editorial in The Daily Telegraph suggested: "There is something not quite right about sudden revelations from the DTI that their radio engineers are being terrorised by certain pirates, aided and abetted by anarchist groups ... Were there to be a licensing system, even a strictly limited one, action against those outside it might command more of the public support which is now being sought against the thugs." An editorial in Broadcast magazine admitted: "The pirates we have come across are remarkably like Joe Public and a long way from the type of people who would want to bash a DTI engineer with the nearest piece of transmitter." Steve Hamley (alias 'Steve Hebditch'), editor of Radio Today, commented: "It's not in the interests of most pirates to carry on like that. There is a growing frustration among pirates about whether they're going to be given a licence or not. But they realise that violence isn't going to help their case."[218]

The pirate stations themselves tried to dismiss the DTI allegations. Gordon McNamee of KISS FM said: "We know we are doing something illegal. If we are taken off the air, we accept it. They have their job to do. I have heard stories of violence, but never thought it was true. It does not seem violent from where I am sitting. We are a very easy going station." Tony Monson of Solar Radio commented: "Longer running stations like ourselves, KISS FM, TKO and

LWR are run by responsible people with one eye firmly fixed on future community radio licences. We certainly wouldn't jeopardise our potential in this way." A spokesman for LWR said: "The accusations are absolutely ridiculous. We have never used violence, and have no intention of using violence, against any government official. To claim that pirate radio stations are doing this is just an excuse to attack us." Solar Radio DJ Clive Richardson added: "We would never advocate trying to stop government agents physically from performing what is only their duties." Fresh FM DJ Lyndon T suggested that the DTI "could be doing it in retaliation against recent TV coverage of the case for pirate radio."[219]

The trade union representing DTI staff, the Institution of Professional Civil Servants, said it was concerned about the existence of the 'anarchist' pamphlet and demanded "adequate protection" for its members if they faced danger. However, a union spokesman accused John Butcher of attempting to make "political propaganda" out of the issue, and he insisted that there were presently only 160 Radio Investigation Service inspectors, not 200 as Butcher had said, and that the government had plans to reduce that number to 132. The union's assistant secretary, Peter Downton, said he was very suspicious about the timing of Butcher's comments: "We want to know why he is raising these old-hat cases at this particular juncture. What we are concerned about is not just attacks, but the gradual rundown of the service. The government has told us it wants staff cuts of between thirty and fifty in the next two or three years." The union's assistant general secretary, Tony Cooper, added that the Radio Investigation Service's workload required 300 engineers and noted that 280 staff had previously been employed, before the department had been transferred to the DTI from British Telecom in 1984.[220]

The day after his initial outburst, John Butcher revealed part of the real motive behind his accusations. During a radio interview, he hinted that continued pirate radio violence might delay the government's introduction of community radio, as envisaged in its Green Paper. He said: "The irony is, it is this government which is most minded further to liberalise the airwaves and consider the options for community radio." The veracity of Butcher's tales of violence was seriously impacted when the police subsequently asserted they had not linked the case of the DTI officer's death from a heart attack with the man's work investigating pirate radio. Also, DTI data revealed that, in 1984, there had been only one violent incident against DTI staff, in 1985 there were two, in 1986 three and, in the first three months of 1987, there were seven.[221]

Radio Today magazine pointed out that, in the one case where a DTI official's car had been followed, there was no intention of violence. In another case of a DTI officer having been assaulted, the person concerned had already been charged. It noted that pirate stations themselves were becoming increasingly concerned about the heavy-handed way the DTI carried out recent raids. The chief Radio Investigation Service officer in London had recently been convicted of assault on one pirate station operator. During the DTI raid on Border Radio in Twickenham in September 1986, serious damage had been caused to the station owner's home. He was later admitted to hospital with a complaint thought to have been brought on by the ferocity of the raid. Radio Today reported that the DTI admitted they could not cope with the large number of pirates on the air, and a DTI officer had urged the Community Radio Association not to condone unlicensed broadcasting because the government agency would not be able to cope with the consequences. The police also admitted that they were unhappy having to devote manpower to assisting the DTI in closing down stations, particularly since several pirates had helped police officers solve crimes by broadcasting public appeals for information in their programmes.[222]

Predictably, the British commercial radio industry was eager to support the DTI stories. Ian Rufus, managing director of Birmingham commercial station BRMB, wrote in The Independent newspaper: "It was only a matter of time before the activities of the illegal broadcasters resulted in violence and tragedy. Despite their (groundless) claims that they serve the community with a variety of entertainment and good works, the truth is that the 'pirates' operate outside the law to make a fast, and often crooked, buck. They inhabit a shady world of dubious business practices which will inevitably attract those who will not stop short of violence to protect their activities … The sad thing is, though, that as long as the 'pirates' persist with their irresponsible and illegal operations, the chance of the wishes of the new [community] broadcasters ever being realised is remote." When it came to arguing the case for retaining the status quo of 'one market, one commercial station,' existing licensees such as Rufus were never slow to trash any potential competitors.[223]

As Radio Today magazine commented: "These allegations could mark the start of a major campaign, with the [DTI] channelling their efforts into a huge round-up with the aim of silencing [the pirates] for good … The [DTI] could not embark on such a campaign without greater support from the public … Turning the public against the pirates does look like the main reason behind the allegations … This is where the [DTI] has probably failed. There is still massive support for the pirates. From the young kids today who've grown up listening to the stations, to people who remember how the pirates were treated in the 1960s when they were young. The pirates will never go away until listeners have a legal alternative."[224]

---

[195] Clive Glover, "Selections", TX no. 12, Dec 1986.
[196] ibid.
[197] "Cuts", "RX", TX/Radio Today no. 13, Feb 1987.
[NB: LWR had existed in a previous incarnation as London Weekend Radio, under different ownership during the early 1970s, when it was a Sunday-only pop music pirate in West London, broadcasting on AM.]
[198] ibid.
[199] "Radio Investigation Service", Radio Regulatory Division Annual Report 1985/86, Department of Trade & Industry, 1986.
Nick Higham, "Radio Pirates Sunk By DTI's Campaign", Broadcast, 4 Jan 1987.
[200] Steve Hamley, "Aerial Warfare", TX/Radio Today no. 13, Feb 1987.
[201] ibid.
"Looks Unreel [sic]", City Limits, 5 Feb 1987.
[202] "Pirates Ride Out Storm On Airwaves", Music Week, 28 Jan 1987.
[203] "Broadside For Pirates On The Air", Evening Standard, 6 Feb 1987.
Gillian Reynolds, [untitled], Daily Telegraph, 20 Jan 1987.
Peter Holt, "On The Air", Evening Standard, 25 Feb 1987.
[204] "Radio Off", City Limits, 14 May 1987.
"KISS FM", TX/Radio Today no. 13, Feb 1987.
"KISS FM", "Farewell KISS?", Radio Today no. 14, Aug 1987.
[205] Rebecca Coyle, "What Shade of Green For Community Radio", Relay no. 16 (Insert), Feb 1987.
Rebecca Coyle, "Bricks & Bouquets", Relay no. 17, Apr 1987.
[206] Nick Higham, "Why The Pirates Will Stay With Us", Broadcast, 20 Mar 1987.
[207] Mark Rosselli, "Heathrow Alert Over Pirate Radio Waves", The Independent, 17 Apr 1987.
David Wallen, "Pop Pirates On The Air Land Planes In A Jam", London Daily News, 18 Apr 1987.
[208] "Newsdesk", "London Diary", Radio Today Update no. 14½, Jun 1987.
[209] "Pirate Radio Stations Win Lords Ruling", Liverpool Express & Star, 4 Jun 1987.
"Confiscation Ruling Is Boost For Radio Pirates", The Independent, 5 Jun 1987.
"Power To Curb Radio Pirates Slashed", The Guardian, 5 Jun 1987.

"Broadcasting", The Independent, 8 Jun 1987.
[210]"Power Of The Pirates", Evening Standard, 10 Jun 1987.
"Row Over Pirate Payola", New Musical Express, 20 Jun 1987.
[211]Nick Higham, "Jolly Roger Radio", The Listener, 9 Jul 1987.
Ken Johnson, "The Day Pirates Captured The Capital", London Evening News, 13 Jul 1987.
[212]"Radio One Rapped By The Pirates", Evening Standard, 23 Jul 1987.
[213]"Pirates Scourge Of The Radio Waves", The Scotsman, 28 Jul 1987.
John Williams, "Chicago-Style Terror Of Radio Pirates", Evening Standard, 28 Jul 1987.
[214]Philip Webster, "Pirate Radio Investigators Terrorized", The Times, 28 Jul 1987.
Karl Waldron, "Radio Nasties", Time Out, 5 Aug 1987.
[215]Ben Preston, "Radio Anarchy", Bristol Evening Post, 28 Jul 1987.
Philip Webster, op cit.
[216]"Radio Is My Bomb", Hooligan Press, Apr 1987, p.31.
[217]Nicholas Comfort, "Pirate Radio Investigators Ambushed", The Daily Telegraph, 28 Jul 1987.
Trevor Kavanagh, "Thugs On Rampage In Pirate Radio War", The Sun, 28 Jul 1987.
Ted Daly, "Radio Pirates In Terror War", The Daily Express, 28 Jul 1987.
Lynne Carlisle, "Terror Of The Radio Pirates", Today, 28 Jul 1987.
"Radio Pirates Go To War!", The Daily Mirror, 29 Jul 1987.
Elizabeth Guider, "Brit Radio Pirates Threaten, Attack Govt. Inspectors", Variety, 5 Aug 1987.
Pat Hawker, "Spectrum And Physical Abuse Increases", Electronics & Wireless World, Sep 1987.
[218]"Policy On Pirates", The Daily Telegraph, 29 Jul 1987.
"Violent Piracy", Broadcast, 31 Jul 1987.
Steve Clarke, "Kept Afloat By Adverts, Gifts", Evening Standard, 29 Jul 1987.
[219]John Williams, op cit.
Ronnie Smith, "Radio 'Thugs' Claim Denied", The Morning Star, 29 Jul 1987.
"'Propaganda Stunt' Claim Pirates", New Musical Express, 8 Aug 1987.
Martin Wainwright, "Radio Pirates Surprised At Highlighting Of Attacks", The Guardian, 29 Jul 1987.
[220]David Graves, "Protection Call For Radio Men", The Daily Telegraph, 29 Jul 1987.
"Pirates Scourge Of The Radio Waves", op cit.
Martin Wainwright, op cit.
Mark Rosselli, "Pirate Radio Checks Hit By Reduction In Staffing", The Independent, 29 Jul 1987.
[221]Howard Foster, "Attacks 'Are Like Chicago'", The Times, 29 Jul 1987.
[222]"Pirate Radio Violence", Radio Today no. 15, Aug 1987.
[223]Ian Rufus, "Shady Radio World", letters, The Independent, 31 Jul 1987.
[224]"Pirate Radio Violence", op cit.

August to December 1987.

The government's sordid attempt to turn the public against pirate radio by making exaggerated claims of violence against the stations' staff had completely backfired. John Butcher's pronouncements only served to fuel the media's interest in the pirate radio phenomenon, and it only helped to further romanticise the swashbuckling image the stations themselves liked to project.

The News On Sunday paper reported: "What was once a wacky hobby for music loving youngsters has become a big money-spinner, with some stations claiming profits of more than £3,000 a week. And the scent of shady money has drawn in the gangsters. Popular pirate stations like Solar, LWR and KISS FM reach hundreds of thousands of record-buying young Londoners. Disc jockeys, who are also big names on the club scene, pay to present shows on the big stations. Record shops are keen to advertise and record companies treat them like legal stations – offering free records (and the occasional bribe). One example of the power of the pirates is Steve Silk Hurley's 'Jack Your Body,' which was not played on BBC Radio One until after it had made the top of the charts. And one of London's legal stations, Capital Radio, even turned to the pirates to advertise a Latin music show that it was sponsoring, after tickets failed to sell."[225]

This newspaper story carried the subheading 'Government forces are planning to launch a crackdown on illegal disc-jockeys like these, who bring a sense of real fun to broadcasting.' It concluded: "Mr Butcher is probably backing a loser. Pirates are still supplying listeners with what they want. Turning this huge audience against the illegal broadcasters will be harder than Ministers think."[226]

It was KISS FM and Solar Radio that benefited financially from carrying advertisements for the Capital Radio salsa concert. The commercials were booked by concert promoter Brian Theobald, who reportedly paid each station £50 a day. KISS FM's Gordon McNamee commented: "I couldn't believe it. It's crazy that Capital can't advertise their own things." Solar's Tony Monson added: "We were aware that we were advertising a Capital Radio event, but the people who gave us the advertisement said the response [to Capital's own adverts] had not been very good." Capital Radio spokesman Mike Whitehead would only say: "The suggestion that Brian Theobald has been advertising on pirate radio comes as a complete surprise to us."[227]

Throughout the 'pirate violence' debacle, the DTI continued its more conventional actions against the illegal stations, making a total of 197 raids (154 in London) during the first half of 1987, compared to 209 during the whole of the previous year. Despite such harassment, KISS FM appeared to be sufficiently organised to appear on the airwaves every weekend, and this regularity increased the station's popularity, despite it only broadcasting two days per week.[228]

The FM band in London was brimming over with dozens of new pirate stations, most of which were playing soul or reggae music, but many of which seemed to be overstretching their capabilities by trying to provide twenty-four hour services. The quality of some stations' output was very poor, their transmissions caused dreadful interference, and their music and

DJs were unprofessional. Radio Today magazine listed fifty-eight pirates as active in London during late 1987, thirty-one of which were playing soul, reggae or some form of black music. Nineteen stations were trying to run daily services: established names such as LWR, Starpoint, TKO, plus a host of newcomers such as Chicago '87, City Radio, Faze One, Fresh FM, Girls FM, Quest FM, RJR, Rock II Rock, Sky FM, Soul FM, Time Radio, Traffic Jam, Trax FM and WNK.[229]

The influence of London's soul pirate stations on the legitimate radio industry continued to grow. In September 1987, BBC Radio One recruited ex-pirate DJ Jeff Young from BBC Radio London to present its new Friday night soul show, and it added a new 'real soul' show on Sunday presented by Andy Peebles. London pop music station Capital Radio recruited ex-pirate DJ Pete Tong from BBC Radio London to present its Saturday night soul/dance music show. Capital also poached Tim Westwood from KISS FM to present a new weekend show to be broadcast live from a London club each week, an innovation that pirate stations had been doing for many years. Capital re-introduced a soul oldies show called 'Soul Circle' on Friday evening, presented by Peter Young, and it launched a new Sunday morning jazz show presented by Alex George. Suddenly, legal radio stations were offering more airtime to the soul and black music they had previously ignored.[230]

A correspondent to Radio Today magazine commented: "I saw in the last issue that you were saying that Capital [Radio] never has any new ideas. I now hear that they're going for a dance music format on a Saturday night with DJs like Tim Westwood and Chris Forbes, and a live link-up with a London nightclub from 1 am. Am I totally stupid, or wasn't this done by the pirates first, and didn't these DJs start out on the pirates? Another first for Capital. Nice one, guys."[231]

KISS FM responded to the loss of Tim Westwood, and Capital Radio's increasingly dance music-orientated output, by recruiting seven new DJs. The pirate's weekend broadcasts now started earlier, at midnight on Friday night. The new schedule was: Saturday midnight Nick Power, 2 am Dean Savonne, 4 am Lindsay Wesker, 7 am Dean Savonne, 9 am Dennis O'Brien, 11 am Gordon Mac, 1 pm Norman Jay, 3 pm Jonathan More, 5 pm Dave VJ, 7 pm Colin Faver, 9 pm Richie Rich and 11 pm Sammy LR; and on Sunday, 1 am Colonel Crashbeat [an alias for cassettes of back-to-back music], 7 am Lindsay Wesker, 9 am DJ André, 11 am Jay Strongman, 1 pm 'Madhatter' Trevor, 3 pm DJ Tee, 5 pm Steve Jackson, 7 pm Tosca, 9 pm Joey Jay and 11 pm Dean Savonne. One of these new recruits, Lindsay Wesker, was a former deputy editor of Black Echoes magazine, who had just lost his job that July from the promotions department of A&M Records.[232]

KISS FM began to attract considerably more interest from the mainstream press. The London Daily News ran a feature on DJ Norman Jay and his Saturday afternoon programme 'The Original Rare Groove Show.' Regular airplay on Jay's show of obscure soul oldies such as Maceo & The Macks' 'Cross The Tracks' and The Jackson Sisters' 'I Believe In Miracles' had encouraged Polydor Records to re-issue these songs as singles and within a compilation album. KISS FM's Gordon McNamee explained: "'Rare groove' is that track that nobody picked up on when it was released, then you hear it played and you know you should have bought the album." Jay said: "'Rare groove' has taken its natural course, everyone wants it, everyone is talking about it, but no one can understand where it is coming from. The answer is that it's coming from the street, and it's very easy for people like me to see what is happening on the street."[233]

78

The Sun newspaper printed a full-page story headlined 'Why Radio One Is On Its Death Bed' in which it noted that "pirate stations like KISS FM, Solar, LWR, Starpoint, JBC, Caroline and Laser are on the air almost twenty-four hours a day. Millions of kids tune into them." The author, ex-pop music star Jonathan King, complained: "Why won't the government license dozens of small VHF stations in every city, each one a low-range, low-powered FM unit?"[234]

London listings magazine City Limits ran a double-page spread on pirate radio, including a large photo of KISS FM DJ Jonathan More sat in the station's studio. Clearly visible on the studio wall behind him was a large notice, handwritten in thick felt pen: "<u>DON'T</u> TALK ANY SHIT. NO DRUG STORY'S [sic]. NO SEX OR SEXIST COMMENT. NO DRINK STORY'S [sic]. <u>MUSIC</u>." Commenting on the flood of pirate radio stations on the capital's airwaves, LWR's Zak said: "TKO are just a carbon copy of LWR. And when stations like Fresh FM just go on the air with the same old approach, that's bad. Everyone should have a different approach. We respect KISS FM because they do their own thing, and Solar because they're so professional. But things have got really staid."[235]

The success of KISS FM's occasional club nights, and increasing public awareness of the station, encouraged Gordon McNamee to develop further his business activities. He rented a small office unit at 12 Greenland Street, in the trendy Camden Town area of North London, to use as the administrative base for both KISS FM and a new company he had registered called 'Goodfoot Promotions.' Formation of the new company was arranged by two off-the-shelf incorporation specialists who changed its name formally from Cityoffer Limited to Goodfoot Promotions Limited. On 28 September 1987, McNamee appointed himself as Goodfoot's sole director, and his wife Kim as company secretary. Fifty-three of the company's ninety-eight shares of £1 were held by McNamee, with the remaining forty-five distributed equally amongst several of the KISS FM DJs. Trevor 'Madhatter' Nelson, Dean Savonne, Tony Harrison (alias DJ Tee), Norman Joseph (Norman Jay), Joel Joseph (Joey Jay), Jonathan More, Colin Faver, Selwyn Samuels (DJ Selwyn), and Paul Walton held five shares each.[236]

Goodfoot was a useful, legitimate 'front' for KISS FM activities, and a means of diverting legitimate earnings from lucrative club events into meeting the overheads of the pirate radio operation. The first regular club event McNamee organised under this new arrangement was a Saturday night residency called 'The Base' at the HQ winebar, only a few hundred yards up the road from Goodfoot's office in Camden. From its debut on 26 September 1987, the club night ran successfully every week for ten months. The Independent newspaper reviewed The Base as "the best of Camden's plethora of night-spots" and "cheaper and less pretentious than the West End," whilst noting that "pirate radio people KISS FM claim they play 'hard noise on big plastic.'"[237]

Despite McNamee having appointed himself Goodfoot's sole director, and having taken the majority of the company's shares, he liked outsiders to believe that KISS FM was organised as a sort of co-operative. McNamee told City Limits magazine: "It all functions democratically. The shareholders vote, even on new DJs." The magazine dutifully explained: "A number of KISS FM DJs also own shares in the pirate. And, while five shareholders are white, an equal number are black." KISS FM was described as "the station which carries the swing for many soul fans today ... The illegal weekender can boast healthy ad sales (from clubs, record shops, promoters and mainstream films) and a roster of thirty 'name' DJs."[238]

One of the DJs recently recruited to KISS FM was Jazzie B, founder of the sixteen-person 'Soul II Soul' crew that had been organising club nights in London for the last five years. Its regular Sunday event, held at The Africa Centre in Covent Garden and described by City Limits as "this year's upfront club," had built upon a reputation, earned the previous year, organising warehouse parties with Norman Jay and Family Funktion. Jazzie B explained that "classes, as well as races, started to mix. And I believe we were the instigators: a black street crew and a white, middle class bunch. People checked us as a form of rebellin'... What we say is, look, we are ALL somebody. Tune in and let this music tell you THAT."[239]

While KISS FM seemed to be enjoying an uninterrupted run of success on the airwaves, some of London's other illegal stations were not faring so well. The Times reported that someone had started "stealing unattended transmitters and selling them back to the pirates at up to £600 a time." Jazz station K-Jazz, re-launched recently on 94.3 FM after a two-year absence, complained that its transmitter and aerial had been stolen by a rival station. K-Jazz's Stuart Lyon explained: "We'd only played two tunes before our transmission site in Crystal Palace was invaded. I'm not going to say who did it, except that it was a well known soul station. After we went off the air, one of our engineers rushed round to the site and found a guy shinning down the roof. When approached, he seriously threatened our engineer's health. It's appalling that another pirate station can behave like this ... This kind of Mafiosa activity is disappointing, negative and gives credence to the authorities' view that pirate stations are run by irresponsible hooligans." Blues & Soul magazine's gossip column hinted at the possible involvement of KISS FM by commenting: "Why stations have to stick around the 94 FM frequency is beyond me."[240]

In a two-page article in the trade magazine Campaign, pirate station LWR claimed it had one and a half million listeners in London, but only earned £700 "in its best weeks," despite owner Zak driving a Porsche with a car phone. LWR was reported to have lost 173 transmitters and nine studio installations to the DTI. Zak explained why he persistently broke the law: "It's the satisfaction of knowing you're number one, of eroding the established stations, of being able to hear LWR everywhere in London and knowing it's something you've engineered." Another profile of Zak in The Observer newspaper described the former accountant as an "ultra elegant Motown mogul look-alike in sharp suit, candy striped tie, huge padded shoulder top coat" with "a pocket bleeper that bleeped every five minutes."[241]

Meanwhile, KISS FM was diversifying its activities by organising a Black Music Record Fair on 29 November at a venue two doors away from its office in Camden. The station celebrated its second birthday with two separate events in November – a club night at The Wag open to the public, and a private party at Lacey's for the station's DJs and friends. One newspaper described the public event as "the first opportunity for many to see the normally faceless DJs who play on the station" and mentioned the "long queues outside the nightclub." At the private event, Gordon McNamee instituted a light-hearted prize-giving ceremony to recognise individual KISS FM DJs' achievements during the year. There were awards to Steve Jackson for 'Giving Gordon Mac The Most Grief,' to Trevor Nelson for 'Most Disorganised DJ,' to Norman Jay for 'Best Radio Interview,' to Joey Jay for 'Best Reggae Show,' to Matt Black for 'Best Mixer,' and to Manasseh a special 'Endurance' prize.[242]

Over the Christmas period, when radio advertising was at its most lucrative, KISS FM abandoned its weekend-only policy and broadcast programmes continuously from 18

December to 3 January. The station organised two special club events during the festive period – one before Christmas called 'Plan Nine From Outer Space' at the club Paramount City (described by City Limits as "a wild night of live radical KISS-style groove"), the other before the New Year at The Wag (described as "probably one of the best parties to be going down over the Christmas period"). Additionally, KISS held special festive versions of its residency night at the HQ winebar, where Christmas Eve night included a "special female Santa Clause giving away presents" and, on Boxing Day, the admission price was lowered from £6 to £2 "for anyone wearing fancy dress." All these KISS FM events were heavily promoted on-air in the station's shows, as well as in a full-page advertisement on the back of the December 1987 issue of Soul Underground magazine, the second edition of this new London-based monthly.[243]

The first professional publicity material for KISS FM was organised by Sandra Charlemagne, who helped McNamee in the Greenland Street office and who arranged for photographer Rory Moles to take a group shot of the station's DJs. The resulting black and white photo, featuring twenty-six of the KISS FM crew standing in front of the huge KISS FM banner, proved very productive when it was printed in many publications during the following year.[244]

KISS FM's biggest publicity coup occurred at the very end of 1987, when London's Evening Standard newspaper held its annual readers' poll. The results, published in the paper's last issue of the year, included a 'best radio station' category. Capital Radio won this section, with KISS FM second, BBC Radio One third, Radio Caroline fourth, LBC fifth, BBC Radio London sixth, BBC Radio Three seventh, pirate LWR eighth, BBC Radio Two ninth and pirate Time FM tenth. The paper commented: "The amazing success of KISS FM proves that the pirates are not just a passing phase and that Radio One should wake up."[245]

KISS FM's achievement, taking second place in a poll organised by London's only evening newspaper, was a watershed in the pirate's history, eclipsing the surprise first place it had enjoyed in the (much lower circulation) TX magazine poll one year earlier.

By the end of 1987, Gordon McNamee had ensured that his station's prospects looked very healthy, even in the increasingly crowded London pirate radio marketplace. Just how successful could an illegal radio station such as KISS FM become?

---

[225] Mike Taylor, "Into Battle, Pirates Of The Airwaves", The News On Sunday, 2 Aug 1987.
[226] ibid.
[227] "Capital Clanger", Evening Standard, 8 Jul 1987.
[228] Jane Lyons, "Pirates Of London", City Limits, 30 Jul 1987.
[229] Jane Lyons, op cit.
"AM/FM", Radio Today no. 16, Nov 1987.
[230] James Hamilton, "BPM", Record Mirror, 5 Sep 1987 & 3 Oct 1987.
[231] Mike Hardy, "The Song Remains The Same", letters, Radio Today no. 16, Nov 1987.
[232] "KISS FM", Radio Today no. 16, Nov 1987.
The Mouth, "Street Noise!", Blues & Soul, 4 Aug 1989
[233] Jessica Berens, "Grooves From The Underground", London Daily News, 19 May 1987.
[234] Jonathan King, "Why Radio One Is On Its Death Bed", The Sun, 8 Jun 1987.
[235] Jane Lyons, op cit.
[236] Goodfoot Promotions Limited, Company no. 02162147, Companies House records, London.
[237] Jonathan Taylor, "7-Day Saturday Night Fever", The Independent, Apr 1988 [exact date unknown].
Bob Killbourn, "Jocks Rap", Blues & Soul, 27 Oct 1987.
[238] Cynthia Rose, "Dancefloor Justice!", City Limits, 5 Dec 1987.
[239] ibid.

[240] "Bylines", The Times, 14 Oct 1987.
"Scuppered By The Soul Mates", Evening Standard, 29 Oct 1987.
"Pirates Switched Off", Melody Maker, 7 Nov 1987.
The Mouth, "Street Noise!", Blues & Soul, 10 Nov 1987.
[241] Nick Higham, "Twilight Zone Of Pirate Stations", Campaign, 6 Nov 1987.
Sue Arnold, "Shattered Images", The Observer, 29 Nov 1987.
[242] "Faceless Wonders", South London Press, Nov 1987 [exact date unknown].
Rose F Christie, "Jive Talk", City Limits, Nov 1987 [exact date unknown].
[243] "Plan Nine From Outer Space", "KISS FM Party", City Limits, Dec 1987 [exact dates unknown].
KISS FM advertisement, Soul Underground no. 2, Dec 1987.
[244] Rory Moles, "The KISS DJ Line-Up", 1987 [exact date unknown].
[245] "The 1987 Readers' Poll", Evening Standard, 30 Dec 1987.

January to March 1988.

Following its success in The Evening Standard readers' poll, KISS FM pursued potential advertisers much more aggressively. Helen Needham, who helped handle the station's advertisement sales, prepared the first KISS FM 'media pack,' a handful of photocopied sheets that extolled the virtues of advertising on the station. In her covering letter, addressed to potential new advertisers, Needham described KISS FM as "the capital's definitive dance music station" and explained: "KISS FM is the foremost Specialist Music station in London, attracting an audience with an overiding [sic] interest in the arts, clubs, music, fashion, magazines and sport."[246]

The media pack included a sheet headed 'WHO WE ARE' which described KISS FM as "the leading alternative dance music station" and continued:

"KISS FM was launched in October 1985 in the belief that Londoners' demand for Dance Music should be better served. KISS FM has succeded [sic] in both reflecting and stimulating the diversity of the Dance Music scene. Our huge success has resulted in:

- The Evening Standard annual readers poll 1987 voting KISS FM the Most Popular Music Station second only to Capital Radio.
- An unmatched reputation for authoritative Dance Music programming.
- Bringing a specialist music form to the attention and the delight of our increasing audience.
- Increasing popularity in Dance Music which has boosted the sales of both mainstream and specialist record importers, distributors and retail outlets.
- Exerting considerable influence on the programming policies of established mainstream radio stations.

With a rosta [sic] of no less than thirty-two of the capital's top DJs and presenters from the club and music world, KISS FM has huge cult status and a devoted audience with an avid interest in Dance Music, and a serious commitment to the lifestyle."[247]

A further sheet, headed 'KISS FM Advertising Rates,' explained that seventeen plays of a thirty-second advert over one weekend's broadcasts would cost £150, or eleven plays for £100, or eight plays for £80. KISS FM charged an advertiser £25 to produce the audio for one thirty-second advert, and the media pack advised: "If you are about to take airtime on KISS FM for the first time, it pays to ensure that your adverisment [sic] does you justice. Make sure that it is distinctive and that it clearly projects your image and product or service."[248]

Responding to its higher public profile, KISS FM extended its hours once more, now broadcasting each weekend from 7 am on Friday to 1 am on Monday morning. The new programme schedule was: Friday 7 am Lindsay Wesker, 9.30 am Gordon Mac, 12 noon Matt Black, 2 pm Danny Rampling, 4 pm Jonathan More, 6 pm Judge Jules, 8 pm Bobbi & Steve, 10 pm Jazzie B; then Saturday 12 midnight Nick Power, 2 am Patrick Forge, 4 am [guest DJ], 7 am Eli Hord, 9 am Sammy Lyle, 11 am Gordon Mac, 1 pm Norman Jay, 3 pm Paul Anderson, 5 pm Max LX & Dave VJ, 7 pm Colin Faver, 9 pm Richie Rich, 11 pm Steve Jervier; and Sunday 1 am Daddy Bug, 3 am Manasseh, 5 am [guest DJ], 7 am Lindsay Wesker, 9 am DJ André, 11 am Jay

Strongman, 1 pm 'Madhatter' Trevor, 3 pm DJ Tee, 5 pm Colin Dale, 7 pm Steve Jackson, 9 pm Joey Jay, 11 pm Dean Savonne.[249]

The station produced a range of KISS FM merchandise, featuring the KISS FM station logo and the slogan 'RADICAL RADIO,' which it sold by mail order. A full-page press advertisement for the products – black T-shirts, black sweatshirts, key rings, car stickers and badges – was published on the back cover of the January 1988 issue of Soul Underground.[250]

Gordon McNamee formed a second company called KISS Records Limited in partnership with Heddi Greenwood, who had previous experience in the record industry. Their idea was that the new record label could capitalise on the growth of the 'rare groove' phenomenon in London by re-issuing hard-to-find soul songs from the 1970s and 1980s. KISS FM was an ideal medium to promote such records, and the station's endorsement of the products would signify a guarantee of quality to soul music fans. McNamee and Greenwood appointed themselves as directors of the company, each holding £1 in shares, with Greenwood acting as company secretary, working from the Greenland Street office.[251]

Media interest in all aspects of pirate radio continued to grow. Black magazine Scope ran a five-page feature that profiled several London stations and concluded: "Pirate radio is an ever growing phenomenon and, whether you love them or hate them, the fact that they have such a massive impact on listeners cannot be denied and is testimony to their escalating popularity ... There are so many illegal broadcasting stations, playing more or less the same kind of music; perhaps they could merge and set up fewer, more effective stations?"[252]

The newsletter of broadcasting pressure group Voice of the Listener commented: "Some listeners to VHF Radio in Britain have had exceptional interference from 'pirate' broadcasters over the past eighteen months. This phenomenon has increased, as equipment has grown in sophistication, and the commercial rewards increased, but the means to tackle it through the courts have until recently remained the same ... Radio Three from [the FM transmitter at] Wrotham suffers particularly badly. It is quite inaudible at times, in parts of South London, because the high ground of the Crystal Palace area is a favourite site for illegal transmitters. Indeed, last year's Proms [classical music concerts] were spoilt for many."[253]

Adding to the feeling that there was an excess of pirate radio activity in the capital, The Evening Standard reported that soul station Horizon Radio was about to be re-launched: "The station, originally closed down two years ago following government pressure, has substantial financial backing and is set to poach some of the best DJs from pirate rivals, including KISS FM, Solar and LWR." However, two days later, the paper reported that Horizon owner Chris Stewart was in fact in Spain, opening a new English-language station called the Horizon Broadcasting Corporation in Marbella. Stewart commented: "London pirate radio has gone to the gutter ... There used to be healthy competition between the pirates, now there's just aggravation. And take that so-called 'rare groove' they play. The pirates were describing a 1980 record called 'Give Me Your Love' by Sylvia Striplin as 'rare groove.' It was selling at £75 a time, yet I had three copies on my bottom shelf. That was when I thought something was wrong." Stewart was scathing of KISS FM owner Gordon McNamee who, he said, used to work for him as a warm-up DJ: "Gordon learned everything he knows from me. He got the whole idea of KISS FM from me."[254]

Pirate radio also figured in the recent success story of twenty-two year old Derek B [alias Derek Boland], who had worked as a London club DJ since the age of fifteen, had presented shows on KISS FM and had been the driving force behind the previous year's ill-fated pirate station WBLS, before starting to make his own hip hop records. His song 'Goodgroove' reached number sixteen in the UK singles chart in early 1988, and the follow-up, 'Bad Young Brother,' sold just as well. Commenting on his experience with WBLS, Derek B said: "My radio station failed and that really pissed me off because I lost a lot of money. I began to lose confidence in myself because I thought 'Nah, this ain't for me.'"[255]

Britain's legitimate radio industry continued to be critical of pirate radio. Mike Owen, programme controller of Birmingham commercial pop music station BRMB, said he was looking forward to the introduction of the new radio stations the government had promised in its Green Paper the previous year: "This is an exciting development which should be good for us, and we will be pleased to see the death of the pirates once and for all. I think the new legislation will lead to pretty severe penalties which don't exist at the moment ... There are either rules, or there are not rules. We have to pay £300,000 a year to broadcast, and it also costs us £1,000 per day in performing rights, and yet we have got people operating with impunity. It is getting increasingly irritating. In London, there are more than fifteen pirate stations – in effect, they are crooks."[256]

London commercial station Capital Radio asked its staff and listeners to record as much information as they could about pirate stations they heard operating in their area. Capital said it would compile regular reports and forward them to the Department of Trade & Industry [DTI], demanding it act to close down these stations. A Capital Radio spokeswoman commented: "We have had several complaints about these foreign radio stations causing interference to our signal on 95.8 FM." The 'foreign' stations were thought to be Greek-language pirates operating from North London.[257]

BBC Radio London DJ Tony Blackburn became embroiled in a scrap with the pirate stations when LWR DJ Ron Tom said of him: "He's a smutty fool, a fossil who's not changed his presentation in fifteen years. Soul's about unity, not inane, rude chatter. Blackburn puts himself on a pedestal first and the music last. He doesn't talk the language of soul kids on the street. All of us pirates think Blackburn should be taken down a peg. He's no soul man, just a show man." To which, Blackburn replied: "I am an established soul DJ, a national figure, and I don't have to justify myself to these gentlemen."[258]

The 'powerplay' aspect of the pirates, whereby record companies paid stations for playing their records, suddenly re-surfaced, seven months after the phenomenon was first exposed by The Evening Standard. A regional current affairs show on commercial TV, 'The London Programme,' investigated the 'powerplay' system that the larger pirates had operated for several years. Amrik Rai, manager of new black music group Krush, admitted he had paid LWR to play the act's record 'House Arrest,' which had subsequently reached number three in the singles chart. Rai said: "For six weeks, the pirates played 'House Arrest' every day. It was a blanket play. It cost £400 – worth every penny." LWR, which had just celebrated its fifth birthday, willingly claimed that its 'powerplay' of the Krush record was the only reason the song had become a hit.[259]

The reporter on the TV show was offered airplay for a record every two hours for a week on a South London pirate for a three-figure sum, while a rival station in Northwest London offered five plays a day for £150 a week. The documentary also reported on the increasingly common phenomenon of pirate station owners attacking their rivals' facilities.

One DJ recalled how he had exited his station's studio to inspect the transmitter equipment, after the signal had unexpectedly gone off the air, when he was confronted by a man carrying a knife, who said: "I'm from another station, mate. Don't mess with me or I'll stab you."[260]

Pirate stations were dismayed at the TV programme's obsession with the 'powerplay' system and its exaggeration of a few violent incidents. LWR's Zak commented: "We DO take money for playing records, but listeners know that, because we play it as a 'Powerplay' record. We have a long waiting list of people trying to get their records on because we only have two 'Powerplays' per week. We'd lose all credibility if we played more." Eddie of LWR added: "To me, they're making something out of nothing. When folding money goes into the pockets of mainstream DJs, that's 'payola.' When it's paid into the station, according to an advertising rate card, and played on our 'Powerplay' slots in between other ads, then clearly it's an ad."[261]

On 19 January 1988, Home Secretary Douglas Hurd made his long-awaited announcement in Parliament about the government's plans for the future of radio. Hurd said that 500 responses had been received, following the publication of the Green Paper eleven months earlier, and he agreed that "there are many tastes and interests which existing services can at best satisfy only to a limited extent." He promised that "in due course, several hundred new stations are in prospect" and said that new legislation would be introduced by the summer of 1989, based on the proposals in the Green Paper: "We aim to provide, alongside the existing BBC services, opportunities for national commercial radio and for the expansion and deregulation of local radio. All these services will be free of the existing constricting statutory requirements which have been applied to independent local radio. They will instead be subject to light regulation designed to protect the consumer rather than direct the broadcaster ... The key test which stations will have to pass to obtain a licence to broadcast is that of widening the range of consumer choice. They will have to live up to their promises to their audiences if they want to keep those licences."[262]

Hurd went on to say: "New local and community services will be given the opportunity to start broadcasting to enhance the range of programming and the diversity of consumer choice. The number of services, and their scale, will depend on local demand and wishes." He also announced the establishment of a new regulator, to be named 'The Radio Authority,' which would oversee the expansion of commercial radio, replacing the current activities of the radio division of the Independent Broadcasting Authority. He concluded: "Our proposals are, above all, intended to benefit the listener. It may take a little time for the public to become accustomed to new kinds of service ... but we believe that the expansion of radio which I have outlined can only be to the good of broadcasters and listeners alike."[263]

The media quickly seized upon Hurd's announcement as an open invitation to pirate radio stations to become legitimate. The Evening Standard noted that the pirates' significance was increasing because ten per cent of Londoners now listened to such stations. It commented: "De facto, the pirates are the base from which any future authority that grants new London radio licences will draw. However, buccaneering entrepreneurs of the airwaves are already fiercely jockeying for position inside an illicit, and therefore totally unregulated, market. So fiercely that competitive operations, it's alleged, routinely use gangster-rock style tactics to keep the opposition off the air. Stations have been shut down; people are being threatened. This is the ruthless competition of the free market taken to its logical conclusion

... At stake are not only the huge revenues anticipated in the deregulated radio ad revenue market of London in the 1990s, but ready cash from record companies."[264]

In The Independent newspaper, journalist Martin Wroe reported the Home Secretary's statement that "pirates are welcome to apply" and profiled KISS FM as a potential candidate. Alongside a photo of KISS FM's Gordon McNamee and Norman Jay in a makeshift radio studio, Wroe noted that the DTI had confiscated the station's equipment on one hundred occasions during its two-year history, but that KISS FM had recently been voted second best radio station by readers of The Evening Standard. According to Wroe, "advertising may bring in £1,000 a weekend" and "KISS FM is banking its profits to prepare for an application."[265]

The Economist magazine also reported KISS FM's success in The Evening Standard poll and suggested that "disc jockeys on Radio One, the BBC's most popular radio station, were mortified to learn that many people preferred programmes such as KISS FM's cult 'rare groove show' to their own fare of synthetic pop music." The article continued: "The share of London's audience listening to Capital Radio, its biggest independent station, has dropped from twenty-five per cent to fourteen per cent in the past two years. Listeners have defected in droves to pirate music stations such as Fresh FM, Passion, Solar, Time and LWR ... A main reason for the popularity of the pirate stations is that their disc jockeys talk less (as Radio One's DJs have just been told to do) and play newer, more exciting music than those on the official stations."[266]

The Observer newspaper reported that "a new function of pirates is making hit records. Maceo & The Macks' 'Across The Tracks' is just one of the 1987 hits created by pirates; and the 'rare groove' boom of summer 1987 is a whole trend created by one pirate: KISS FM." A photo of KISS FM DJ Norman Jay in the station studio was captioned with a comment that "the major pirates, KISS and LWR especially, are London-wide and powerful."[267]

In the magazine What's On In London, KISS FM's Gordon McNamee commented on his station's high placing in the recent Evening Standard poll: "The response we get sometimes is amazing. When we came second in the Standard poll, we were shocked. We'd expected to be top of the pirates, but not beat a major station like Radio One. As for exact listening figures, we can't be sure but, using the same equation as the BBC, that one letter equals 1,000 listeners, then we must be approaching the half a million mark. Some weekends, we've had over 500 letters." Commenting on Douglas Hurd's announcement of new radio licences, McNamee said: "I think we'll be putting in an application for a licence because we DO serve the community, we might not be a 'community station' as such, but we do play a type of music that a particular community is into."[268]

The Sunday Telegraph suggested that "under the new legislation proposed for radio broadcasting, the cloak and dagger stuff of pirates could be re-robed as legitimate broadcasting within two years. But TKO DJ Rick Robinson was worried that a legal licence would restrict a station's transmission to no more than a few miles in radius: "A range of three or four miles would render the advertising side useless. And, if we don't have advertisers, we wouldn't be able to pay performing rights fees. I think we'd be restricted to such an extent that we would have to continue as a pirate."[269]

The established commercial radio industry was determined that pirates should not be allowed to apply for the new licences. Ron Coles, chairman of the Association of Independent Radio Contractors [AIRC], mentioned previous occasions when pirate operators had allegedly beaten up DTI officers and thrown transmitters from the roofs of buildings without regard for passers-by. Brian West, director of the AIRC, added: "The pirates are illegal, a nuisance, and a menace to the broadcaster. They engender sympathy from the listener because they are tilting at authority, but the public doesn't realise the danger ... It is completely unfair and they deserve no sympathy."[270]

The widespread media coverage afforded to the pirate radio phenomenon was not the kind of publicity the government had expected to follow its announcement of new community radio licences. Since its success in the Evening Standard poll, KISS FM had attracted the most media coverage of all the pirates. One magazine suggested that "KISS FM jock Gordon Mac is fast becoming a TV celebrity, what with all his appearances as a representative of pirate radio." Another publication commented: "At one point, it seemed impossible to switch on the TV or open a magazine without seeing the face of KISS FM's Gordon Mac."[271]

The government was not at all pleased. Thirteen days after the Home Secretary's announcement of new radio licences, the war of attrition against pirates was stepped up by DTI Junior Minister John Butcher, who announced: "The Radio Investigation Service will act vigorously to clear the frequencies of unlicensed users. Particularly in view of the Home Secretary's announcement of 20th January on broadcast radio policy, I very much hope that unlicensed broadcasters will voluntarily stop broadcasting since they, with other interested parties, may soon have an opportunity to make applications to establish legal stations. At present, they are squatting on frequencies assigned for legal stations ..."[272]

Butcher told Parliament that the DTI had "reviewed the resource need of the Radio Investigation Service," it was "strengthening manning levels in the London area" and was "investing some £400,000 in new equipment which should assist in the tracing of unlicensed radio operators." Another Junior DTI Minister, Francis Maude, revealed that seventy-seven prosecutions had been brought against pirate operators during 1987, resulting in seventy-five convictions. These announcements produced the desired headlines in the press – 'DTI Hots Up Pirate Hunt', 'Curb On Pirates' and 'Butcher Promises Tougher Measures On Pirate Radio' – but they failed to persuade the pirates to voluntarily quit the airwaves. The broken promises made by the government only two years earlier, when it had cancelled the community radio experiment, were still fresh in many stations' minds, and so there was no way they would countenance being duped once again.[273]

The DTI responded by strengthening its resolve to stamp out the pirates. It appointed a former Metropolitan Police officer to work full-time to examine the business aspects of pirate stations. DJs caught during raids were now being fined an average of £234 by the courts, though the DTI really wanted to trap the businessmen behind the stations, who were thought to be earning thousands of pounds per week. An un-named senior DTI official said: "From now on, we shall not just be going after the transmitters. We are making determined efforts to catch the people who control the stations, and those who fund them. We suspect that some of the big record companies may be involved because it is well known that you can pay to have records promoted on the illegal stations."[274]

As if to emphasise its renewed hard-line approach, the DTI announced that it wanted to hear from anyone with information on the whereabouts of Chris Stewart, the man behind former London soul pirate Horizon Radio. A warrant was issued for Stewart's arrest, relating to unpaid court fines and costs in a successful prosecution against him in 1985 for pirate radio activity. The DTI also won a test case against pirate London Greek Radio, when a magistrate agreed that an illegal station's offices could be raided as part of a DTI investigation. Soon afterwards, Southeast London pirate station Faze One was raided and, along with studio and transmitter equipment, the DTI seized a large amount of paperwork and arrested two people. The DTI's tactics proved less successful in a prosecution against London listings magazine Time Out for having published the radio frequencies of offshore stations Laser 558 and Radio Caroline two and a half years earlier. This case, reported to have cost £1m, was thrown out by Sittingbourne Magistrates Court as a result of a legal technicality.[275]

The pirates remained on-air in London and they continued to be sceptical about the government's plans to offer them legal licences. The Parliamentary timetable anticipated that a White Paper would be published by Easter 1988, presented to Parliament as a Bill in the autumn, become law by September 1989, and the first new stations could be on-air by the end of the year. However, as one un-named pirate station manager commented, when asked about the Government's plea for pirates to quit the airwaves:

"That's what we did last time, and look what happened – they cancelled the community radio experiment. If they think we'll fall for that one again, they've got another thought coming. There's no way we're leaving the air until they come up with an alternative."[276]

---

[246] Helen Needham, standard letter to potential advertisers, KISS FM, [undated].
[247] Helen Needham, "KISS FM - WHO WE ARE", Media Pack, KISS FM, [undated].
[248] Helen Needham, "KISS FM Advertising Rates", Media Pack, KISS FM, [undated].
[249] "KISS FM", Radio Today no. 17, Apr 1988.
[250] KISS FM advert, Soul Underground, Jan 1988.
[251] Kiss Records Limited, Company no. 02213441, Companies House records, London.
[252] Seltzer Cole, "Pirates Of The Airwaves: A Look At London's Pirate Radio Stations", Scope, Jan 1988.
[253] "The Pirates, Or Unlicensed VHF/FM Broadcasters", Newsletter, The Voice of the Listener, Spring 1988.
[254] Peter Holt, "New Sound On The Horizon", Evening Standard, 5 Jan 1988.
"New Horizons", Evening Standard, 7 Jan 1988.
Paul Trynka & David Bowker, "All Jazzed Up And Ready To Go", Radio & Music, 19 Jul 1989.
[255] Jane Wilkes, "Derek B: Licensed To Ill", Record Mirror, 9 Jan 1988.
[256] Graham Young, "Keelhaul The Radio Pirates!", Birmingham Evening Mail, 11 Jan 1988.
[257] "Capital Radio In Pirate Witch Hunt", Now Radio, 24 Nov 1987.
[258] "Pirate War On DJ Tony", Evening Standard, 26 Nov 1987.
[259] James Dalrymple, "Arresting Way To Plug A Hit Single", The Independent, 15 Jan 1988.
Steve Clarke, "It's A Hit – Thanks To Payola", Evening Standard, 14 Jan 1988.
"Rainbow Madness", Evening Standard, 7 Jan 1988.
[260] James Dalrymple, op cit.
Caris Davis, "Pirate Power", Evening Standard, 21 Jan 1988.
[261] Rebecca Coyle, "Radio News", City Limits, 21 Jan 1988.
[262] Written Questions, Hansard, 19 Jan 1988.
House of Commons, Hansard, 21 Jan 1988.
[263] ibid.
[264] Caris Davis, op cit.
[265] Martin Wroe, "Pirates Who Storm The Open Airwaves", The Independent, 13 Jan 1988.
[266] "Grooving Down The Gangplank", The Economist, 23 Jan 1988.
[267] Sue Steward, "Music", The Observer, 24 Jan 1988.
[268] Jon Homer, "Pirates On Parade", What's On In London, Feb 1988.
[269] Megan Tresidder, "Pirates Set To Sail Into Legal Wavebands", Sunday Telegraph, 24 Jan 1988.
[270] Martin Wroe, op cit.
[271] James Hamilton, "Odds'N'Bods", Record Mirror, 30 Jan 1988.
Steve Hamley, "Radio On TV", Radio Today no. 17, Apr 1988.
[272] Written Answers, Hansard, 1 Feb 1988.

[273] Written Answers, op cit.
"DTI Hots Up Pirate Hunt", Broadcast, 5 Feb 1988.
Nigel Nelson, "Curb On Pirates", Sunday People, 7 Feb 1988.
"Butcher Promises Tougher Measures On Pirate Radio", Music Week, 20 Feb 1988.
[274] "DTI Receive Massive Cash Injection In Battle Against Pirates In London", Now Radio, 16 Feb 1988.
[275] "Arrest Warrant For Former London Pirate", Now Radio, 16 Feb 1988.
"Arrest Warrant Over Horizon", Radio Today no. 17, Apr 1988.
"DTI Given OK To Raid Stations' Offices", Radio Today no. 18, Sep 1988.
Katie Price, "Radio Reforms?", City Limits, 7 Mar 1988.
Andy Gliniecki, "Court Takes Time Out", Time Out, 16 Mar 1988 ? [date uncertain].
[276] "Government Announces Radio Explosion", "Pirates Face £400,000 Crackdown", Radio Today no. 17, Apr 1988.

March to July 1988.

KISS FM had succeeded in significantly raising its public profile during recent months, through a spate of media interviews by Gordon McNamee, and by organising more club nights. After the Department of Trade & Industry [DTI] had declared its determination in February 1988 to track down the profits being made from pirate radio, stations realised the importance of being able to demonstrate publicly that they were not profiting from their illegal activities. The government was emphasising the 'community' aspect of the new radio licences on offer, which suddenly encouraged pirate stations to add hitherto unnecessary community activities to their operations.

KISS FM responded by organising a one-off club event called Rhythm Rage at Busby's club in Charing Cross Road, from which funds were donated to the Joint Stock Theatre Company. Similarly, profits from the KISS FM Easter Hop at The Wag club in Wardour Street were donated to The Soho Project in a cheque presentation ceremony organised to achieve maximum press coverage. Less philanthropically, KISS FM organised two nights called The Renegades Jam at The Africa Centre in February and April 1988 in conjunction with the Viva Express organisation.[277]

Individual KISS FM DJs were also starting to enjoy critical and commercial successes on their own account. Coldcut (the alias of DJs Jonathan More and Matt Black) produced a single entitled 'Doctorin' The House,' featuring singer Yazz, that reached number six in the singles chart during March 1988. Two months later, a Coldcut remix of several old James Brown hits, entitled 'The Payback Mix,' reached number twelve. Coldcut had established their reputation during 1987 with a series of innovative underground dance twelve-inch singles – 'Say Kids, What Time Is It?' 'Beats And Pieces' and 'That Greedy Beat' – released on their own Ahead Of Our Time label. At every opportunity, Coldcut publicised KISS FM by talking about the radio station in press interviews, and by wearing sweatshirts emblazoned with the station logo in photo sessions.[278]

Two other KISS FM DJs, Daddy Bug and 'Madhatter' Trevor, were now working for Red Records and featured heavily in a blaze of publicity that accompanied the record shop's grand opening at 47 Beak Street in Soho during April 1988. Another KISS FM DJ, Jazzie B, released his first record, 'Fairplay,' in May under the name of his sound system, Soul II Soul. In one of his first press interviews, Jazzie B told Record Mirror: "We've been running nightclubs for years, even before all the warehouse parties started out. Making a record is just a natural progression. Soul II Soul is geared towards the aim of creating our own record company, with its own shop, distribution and so on. Some people think we're just a bunch of black geezers who've made a few quid and have jumped in the deep end making a record, but we all take this seriously."[279]

The legal radio stations responded to the upsurge of public interest in pirate radio by increasing the amount of programming they allocated to soul and dance music. In January 1988, Capital Radio added a new Friday night hip hop show to ex-KISS FM DJ Tim Westwood's existing Saturday night slot. In February, Radio Luxembourg introduced a new Saturday night soul show presented by Mike Hollis.[280]

Realising that its plea to pirates to quit the airwaves voluntarily had been altogether ignored, the government decided to adopt a more threatening tone. Home Office Minister Timothy Renton, speaking at a conference organised by pressure group The Voice of the Listener, made an announcement aimed at illegal stations: "We are considering that any pirate, broadcasting after a certain date, would be automatically exempted from applying for a licence." Renton called the pirates a "nuisance and a menace," though the stations themselves remained unrepentant. Zak of LWR commented: "The government is simply dangling a carrot in front of us. We have to be very wary of such statements and get the government to clarify their plans and timescale for community radio." Zak said that LWR had been raided 187 times since 1983, and had to finance itself by charging £8 for each play of a thirty-second advertisement.[281]

Scare stories about pirate radio started to re-appear in the national press. The most incendiary was a news report in The Daily Telegraph which stated: "Criminal gangs are trying to seize control of more than twenty pirate radio stations operating in London to skim off the thousands of pounds being paid to plug reggae and soul records and money from lucrative advertising contracts, the police said yesterday." The report was confused about the pirates' 'powerplay' system, which it described as a 'racket,' and it alleged: "Gangs first moved into five pirate stations operating in West London, where complaints of intimidation and assaults were made to police ... Pirate radio stations in other areas of London, such as Tottenham and Wood Green, are now also under threat from gangs." An unnamed senior police officer commented: "The pay-off for constantly playing a record, sometimes five times in the course of an evening, is very substantial and an easy target for black criminal groups. The whole thing is a recipe for violence and we are attempting to put a stop to it before it gets out of hand."[282]

Another organisation that suddenly appeared anxious to stamp out the pirates' 'powerplay' system was the record companies' royalty collection agency, Phonographic Performance Limited. Its managing director circulated a letter to all its record company members, attaching a list of eighty-six known pirate stations, pointing out that "any assistance given (e.g. supply of records) to any of these stations may result in prosecution under the Wireless Telegraphy Act 1949." Regardless, many record companies continued to service the pirates with records, knowing full well that these stations offered airplay, particularly for black music, that was unattainable on legal stations.[283]

Independent record company Music of Life Records openly admitted that its Derek B single 'Get Down' had succeeded because of exposure it received on pirate radio. Chris France of the company explained: "The pirates have been a tremendous benefit to us ... We get very strong pirate support because we do each other a favour. They play the kind of music we produce and they give us our most important promotional outlet ... We don't advertise much, except with KISS FM. We don't actually spend much money, but we send the pirates a lot of records."[284]

KISS FM's Gordon McNamee conveniently sidestepped the whole 'powerplay' issue by claiming in an interview that his station was not involved in the activity. This assertion seemed to contradict an Evening Standard article, published a year earlier, which had reported that KISS charged £100 for a record to be played every two hours. Now, McNamee told the press: "We don't do payola ... Sure, if our DJs happen to like a record they get sent, they'll play it, and I'm not saying some DJs don't overplay some stuff, but it's not common ... It takes away their identities to play new releases against their will."[285]

The resolve of the pirate stations to continue broadcasting, and to ignore government promises of licences and increased harassment by the DTI, was revealed to be entirely justified. On 21 May 1988, The Times newspaper disclosed that the Home Secretary, Douglas Hurd, was about to abandon his previously announced plan to introduce legislation later in the year to license 'hundreds' of new radio stations. Stuart Woodin of the Community Radio Association commented: "We are quite devastated. It is yet another broken government promise. There will be great pressure on people within our movement who have been waiting patiently to unashamedly go pirate." Woodin predicted that at least fifty new pirate stations would start broadcasting within the next twelve months. The Association's chairman, Bevan Jones, said its official policy was still anti-pirate, but that it had decided to turn a blind eye to any members who went on the air illegally: "If individuals or communities feel it is the only way, we understand their motives."[286]

However, the anticipated rush of new pirate radio activity failed to materialise for the simple reason that most potential licence applicants were already on the air illegally, none having responded to the government's earlier request to stop broadcasting. In London, around thirty pirates could be heard most weekends, two thirds of which were broadcasting soul or reggae music. Admittedly, the quality of most stations' broadcasts was significantly lower than a few years earlier, when there had been only a few stations in operation. One unnamed record company executive commented: "In the days of Solar, JFM and Horizon, the stations were always on, you knew who would be on at a certain time and they wanted to play new music. With the current 'rare groove' situation, all that many of the DJs want to do is to play the most obscure oldie they can find."[287]

DTI activity against pirate stations continued unabated. During the first five months of 1988, 137 raids were mounted against thirty-nine stations in London, in addition to thirty-three raids on twenty-four stations in the rest of the country. In Parliament, the DTI was asked what action it was taking against pirate Radio Britannia in South London and against "the increase of pirate radio broadcasting in Birmingham." Despite the postponement of the promised new radio legislation, Dame Jill Knight still asked the Home Office if it would "introduce regulations to remove from community radio stations the right to apply for licences if they continue to broadcast unlicensed after a specified date." For the government, Timothy Renton replied that proposed future legislation would include a provision "disqualifying persons convicted of offences of unlawful broadcasting from obtaining licences from the Radio Authority."[288]

The cost to the government of the DTI's Radio Investigation Service was escalating, though the huge growth in pirate radio activity had not been accompanied by a similar increase in the number of successful prosecutions. Figures released to Parliament showed that the DTI's costs of "enforcement activity against unlicensed broadcasters" were:

1985/86	£600,000
1986/87	£600,000
1987/88	£800,000

whereas the numbers of legal proceedings were:

    1983   40 prosecutions, 40 convictions
    1984   48 prosecutions, 47 convictions
    1985   136 prosecutions, 135 convictions
    1986   79 prosecutions, 74 convictions
    1987   77 prosecutions, 75 convictions.[289]

Parliament was also presented with a table showing how often thirty-three London pirate stations, that were still active, had been raided by the DTI in successive years. The figures differed significantly from the numbers of raids that stations themselves claimed to have suffered, and included:[290]

	1988 [first half]	1987	1986	1985
KISS FM	3	18	11	11
LWR	15	15	14	14
Solar	3	13	2	12
Starpoint	3	5	10	-
TKO	8	8	11	1

The glut of pirate stations in London, and particularly the growth in poor quality pirate stations, was causing problems not only for the DTI, but also for the long established soul pirates and for radio listeners. Zak of LWR complained: "There used to be friendly competition. We'd warn other stations about any bust. Now these smaller stations, who've no intention of getting a legal licence, are sabotaging and shopping others. The sooner these gangster stations go, the better, to let the genuine community free radio stations pursue their goal of going legal."[291]

Even the normally pro-pirate magazine Radio Today complained: "Listening to Radio One FM round at my gaff means constantly having to fight with my telescopic aerial to get rid of the Greek thing next to them! ... It is getting harder to find empty frequencies upon which to squat nowadays – too many pirates on them already!! Since the majority of them all sound the same, and are highly financed by sponsored plays and club contra deals, it means the new and innovative up-and-coming stations can't find anywhere to broadcast at all. Sad really how the big bullies spoil it for everyone, isn't it?"[292]

Pirate radio was enjoying an unprecedented boom and it looked as if the introduction of new, legal stations was still many years away. However, in June 1988, a brief reply in Parliament offered an unexpected glimmer of hope. Replying to a question from Mark Fisher MP about possible pilot schemes for community radio, the Home Office Minister Timothy Renton said: "It did not prove possible to proceed in 1986 with the proposed community radio experiment, and we have no plans to revive it, but we have indicated to the Independent Broadcasting Authority and other interested organisations that we will look, without commitment, at any proposals in advance of the proposed broadcasting legislation for further developing the independent radio broadcasting sector within the current framework of the

Broadcasting Act 1981." Nothing further was elaborated on the topic, which made it look suspiciously like another government ruse to induce pirate stations into believing legalisation was still an imminent possibility.[293]

This notion was fuelled further by Home Secretary Douglas Hurd's address to the Radio Festival in July 1988. Hurd said that the Home Office and DTI were considering new measures to strengthen existing legislation against pirate broadcasters, and he promised the DTI's Radio Investigation Service an additional £400,000 and an increase in staff numbers. He said: "I am considering seriously the suggestion that anyone convicted after a certain date of an offence of unauthorised broadcasting should automatically be disqualified from a Radio Authority licence for a period. I do not want those who break the law to be able to profit from their activities. Some of these pirate radio stations may think they will benefit by building up an audience which will stand them in good stead when the Radio Authority starts to issue licences. Although the desire to jump the gun may be understandable in some cases, it really cannot be excused ... But I must make it clear that we are determined to combat unauthorised broadcasting." Hurd said that new legislation to expand the number of licensed radio stations would not be introduced before 1990.[294]

John Gorst MP, chairman of the House of Commons Media Committee, explained: "It's a question of priorities. Douglas Hurd obviously couldn't persuade the Cabinet to move the [Radio] Bill further up the Parliamentary timetable. Everybody feels that their case should be treated as a priority, but this issue has clearly lost out to other, more important legislation." Hurd's announcement was greeted with anger by the Community Radio Association, which reiterated its belief that community broadcasters were likely to resort to piracy, faced with a further two-year delay in legislation.[295]

Time Out magazine pointed out that the extra £400,000 budget for the DTI Radio Investigation Service would cost the government more than the establishment of a new Radio Authority that could start issuing legal licences to the pirates right away. The magazine's radio columnist John Marshall wrote: "London's booming pirate radio sector is in for a stormy patch. Or it will be, if the Home Secretary gets his way. But Douglas Hurd's announcement last week of a new hard line on illegal broadcasting misses the point more than somewhat and shows that, in their confusion about what to do with radio, the government is falling back on the old myth that it still has the option of using the law effectively."[296]

Marshall concluded: "As long as the government clings to old myths about being able to control radio, and tries to wield the big stick, it will get itself into more and more of a mess. Rather, it should remember some techniques of social control from British history. Enfranchise the outsiders and discover, perhaps, that you've been fighting shadows, not dragons."[297]

---

[277] KISS FM, "Greater London FM Application Form", Appendix, 1 Jun 1989.
[278] Tim Jeffrey, "The First Cut Is The Deepest", Record Mirror, 27 Feb 1988.
[279] Red Records, advertisement, Blues & Soul, 16 Apr 1988.
Tim Jeffrey, "Soul II Soul", Record Mirror, 4 Jun 1988.
[280] James Hamilton, "Odds'N'Bods", Record Mirror, 23 & 30 Jan 1988.
[281] "Turn Off", Sunday Times, 27 Mar 1988.
Michael Leapman, "New Threat To Pirate Pop Stations", The Independent, 26 Mar 1988.
Richard Brooks, "Air Raid Warning", The Observer, 3 Apr 1988.
[282] John Weeks, "'Payola' Of Pirate Radio Lures Gangs", Daily Telegraph, 18 Apr 1988.

[283] letter from JB Love, Managing Director, PPL to members, 15 Apr 1988.
[284] "Music Of Life? Label Mates And Pirate Pals", London Student, 5 May 1988.
[285] Marek Weitler, "KISS - Mouthing Off", London Student, 5 May 1988.
[286] "'Pirates' Threat To Air Waves", The Times, 21 May 1988.
Nick Higham, "London Pirates 'Rush' Is A Flop", Broadcast, 10 Jun 1988.
[287] Nick Higham, op cit.
author's notes, May & Jun 1988.
Graham Gold, "Legal Pirate Waves?", Root Magazine, Apr 1988.
[288] Nick Higham, op cit.
Written Questions, Hansard, 24 May & 21 Jun 1988.
[289] Written Questions, Hansard, 27 Jun 1988.
[290] Written Questions, Hansard, 4 Jul 1988.
[291] Jolly Dodgers", Evening Standard, 22 Jun 1988.
Chris England, "Talk Back", Radio Today no. 18, Sep 1988.
[292] ibid.
[293] Written Questions, Hansard, 27 Jun 1988.
[294] Steve Clarke, "Broadside For Radio Pirates", Evening Standard, 6 Jul 1988.
Maggie Brown, "Hurd Warns Pirate Radio Operators", The Independent, 7 Jul 1988.
Martyn Palmer, "War On Radio's Pirate Cheats", Today, 7 Jul 1988.
Jane Thynne, "Hurd 'Determined To Combat' Pirate Radio Broadcasters", Daily Telegraph, 7 Jul 1988.
Peter Fiddick, "Pirate Stations Face Crackdown", The Guardian, 7 Jul 1988.
[295] Brian B, "News", Soul Underground, Aug 1988.
Jane Thynne, op cit.
[296] John Marshall, "Hurd On The Grapevine", Time Out, 13 Jul 1988.
[297] ibid.

July to November 1988.

Media interest in KISS FM continued to grow apace. A full-page feature on the station in MixMag, the monthly magazine of the Disco Mix Club, explained that the record 'Bass (How Low Can You Go)' by club DJ Simon Harris, which had reached number twelve in the singles chart during April 1988, had originated from an advertisement broadcast on KISS FM. Harris had produced a thirty-second promotion for KISS FM's weekly club night The Base which included his voice announcing: "The Base has arrived." This catchphrase caught on amongst London's club-goers and so Harris decided to make an entire record to capitalise on its popularity.[298]

In a half-page feature on KISS FM in i-D magazine, Gordon McNamee explained the reasons behind the station's existence: "Nobody else was mixing on the radio at the time, so our music policy was lots of mixing and no 'envelope music' – none of the shitty records that got sent through the post by record companies ... Originally, we wanted to play old LP tracks that nobody else was playing, but now Norman Jay's 'rare groove' has become like a monster – we can't kill the fucker off and we're sick to death of it!" Asked about KISS FM's audience, McNamee said: "We haven't pitched ourselves at any particular crowd. We just went for the best DJs who happened to be in or around a particular scene. For want of a better word, we're now getting the 'trendies.'"[299]

Listening to KISS FM (or, more accurately, CLAIMING to listen to KISS FM) had undoubtedly become a trendy pastime that Londoners liked to raise in casual conversation. The station's logo was increasingly visible around the capital on T-shirts, sweatshirts and caps that the station was selling in their hundreds, and in press advertising for its events. The station struck a deal with the weekly London listings magazine City Limits, whereby KISS FM broadcast regular adverts for the publication, in return for City Limits printing a quarter-page advert for the station in each issue. The text of the KISS FM press advert heralded the pirate as "the happening of the '80s, forging ahead to the '90s" and solicited listeners' names and addresses to add to the 'KISS FM Mailing List.' Correspondents were promised regular newsletters about the station and a 'Legalise KISS' badge.[300]

Radio Today magazine organised its second readers' poll, and KISS FM was once again voted the most popular radio station, followed by LWR, Time Radio, Starpoint and Solar. In the DJ category, KISS FM's Matt Black came second, Jonathan More fourth, Norman Jay seventh, and Gordon McNamee tenth. McNamee commented on the results: "We're really pleased about it. It's good to know radio connoisseurs still appreciate our kind of radio."[301]

KISS FM's off-air activities continued to expand with a special May Day club night held at Munkberry's in London's West End, a second record fair at The Cut in Greenland Street in June, and a competition for listeners to design a new logo for the station. The resulting entries were displayed at the HQ wine bar in Camden during a Bank Holiday Monday afternoon, accompanied by KISS FM DJs playing jazz music.[302]

The tiny office in Greenland Street shared by KISS FM, Goodfoot Promotions and KISS Records was becoming increasingly crowded. KISS FM DJ Lindsay Wesker was spending an increasing amount of time there, following his aborted attempt in February 1988 to launch a record promotion company called Plateau Promotions in conjunction with club promoter Bryan O'Conner. Gordon McNamee had also persuaded a new recruit, twenty-three year old Rosee Laurence, to join his growing business. The two had met when Laurence was working in the South London office of GM Records, one of the city's main wholesale suppliers of imported soul records bought by club DJs like McNamee. Laurence took on the vague, but demanding, role of McNamee's secretary, personal assistant and press officer, providing him with the experience in office organisation that he lacked himself.[303]

In June 1988, KISS FM attracted media attention that was not so welcome, when The Daily Mail newspaper discovered that well known TV comedian Lenny Henry was nominally the 'chairman' of the pirate station. It reported that Henry "could face heavy fines in a Department of Trade investigation after admitting last night that he is the boss of a pirate radio station." Henry said he had been approached by KISS FM merely to lend his support: "But I only agreed to be chairman if it was as a figurehead. I wanted to support them in the quest to become a legal station. There is no question of me earning any money from it or supporting the station financially." KISS FM DJ 'Madhatter' Trevor claimed that Henry regularly visited the station to meet its DJs and to "discuss music." A spokeswoman for the Department of Trade & Industry [DTI] insisted: "He could still be prosecuted, even if he is just the figurehead chairman. We will treat him the same as any other offender."[304]

The Daily Mail claimed that KISS FM had a "regular audience of 200,000," whilst another publication said that "conservative estimates put their audience at around the 500,000 mark." Although KISS FM had certainly built a large audience, and an even larger reputation, since its re-launch in 1986, such figures remained pure speculation. McNamee was not averse to such exaggerations of his station's audience, since the hyperbole only helped him sell advertising airtime at higher prices.[305]

On air, KISS FM perpetuated the myth that it had thousands of listeners writing in constantly to its programmes, though this was not always the truth. For example, an on-air competition was organised at the end of June 1988 to coincide with the London launch of a new Prince film 'The Sign O' The Times.' Listeners were asked to write in, naming two artists signed to Prince's Paisley Park record label, to win a special Prince T-shirt. During the next weekend's broadcasts, the ten winners were announced, but the names included 'Heather Forestwood' and 'Jackie Greenwood' – two variations on Heddi (Heather) Greenwood, McNamee's partner in KISS Records – and 'Nick Crossland,' the graphic artist who designed KISS FM's publicity material. By then, Rosee Laurence had already written to the film's publicity company, PSA, thanking it for the T-shirts "permitting us to hold a very successful competition on the radio."[306]

KISS FM started to develop close links with the monthly London magazine Soul Underground that had launched at the end of the previous year. The station had already advertised in the publication and, from April 1988, a business arrangement was agreed with its publisher, whereby Heddi Greenwood sold advertising in the magazine using a second telephone line installed in the Greenland Street office. To compound the relationship, KISS FM DJ Lindsay Wesker was appointed assistant editor of Soul Underground in May, having previous experience as a journalist on the weekly black music paper Echoes. For its part, KISS FM promoted the magazine heavily on-air and sent out subscription forms to listeners on the station's mailing list. However, by June, the relationship had already soured and KISS FM quickly severed all links with Soul Underground. Greenwood and Wesker both lost their responsibilities for the magazine, which continued to publish independently.[307]

Instead, Greenwood and Wesker devoted more time to the KISS Records record label, which issued its first album release in July 1988 entitled 'Salsoul 1,' a compilation of eight 1970s and 1980s singles from the New York label Salsoul. The record included a sleeve note by KISS FM DJ Norman Jay and it credited Lindsay Wesker with 'A&R Co-ordination.' Although Gordon McNamee and Heddi Greenwood were the only partners in the record company, Record Mirror magazine nevertheless reported that "Lindsay Wesker (playwright Arnold's little boy) has co-founded the new KISS Records label, debuting with – it has to be said – a very intelligent compilation LP of Salsoul oldies." The undue prominence afforded to Wesker within KISS Records was compounded when, two weeks later, Record Mirror reported that "Lindsay Wesker has moved with KISS Records and Goodfoot Promotions to Unit 14, Blackstock Mews, Blackstock Road, London N4."[308]

The move from Greenland Street to the new office three miles away across North London in Finsbury Park was necessitated by a pressing need for more space, and was enabled by the larger sums of money that KISS FM was now earning from its radio and off-air activities. Officially, only Goodfoot Promotions and KISS Records operated from the Blackstock Mews address. Pirate station KISS FM retained the mailing address of Music Power Records and continued to use Gordon McNamee's home telephone number on-air to solicit advertising. However, in practice, all three businesses were now operated from Blackstock Mews and were run by the same team – Gordon McNamee, Heddi Greenwood, Lindsay Wesker and Rosee Laurence.

The idea of naming the record label 'KISS Records' soon turned out not to be such a good move. Because the KISS FM radio station was illegal, assumptions were made in some quarters that the KISS record label was also some kind of illegal activity. Legal radio stations, in particular, were reluctant to play a record that might promote an illegal competitor, and so the promotional potential of the first album release was not fulfilled. The decision had to be made to change the company's trading name to Graphic Records, although the company itself remained registered as KISS Records Limited. Two further compilation albums of old soul tracks were released during the next few months, entitled 'Boogie Tunes' Volumes One and Two, this time on the new Graphic Records label. Nevertheless, Record Mirror magazine referred to "Gordon Mac's newly renamed Graphic Records label" and the cover of the first release included a prominent photo of KISS FM DJ Paul Anderson, which only accentuated the KISS FM connection.[309]

KISS FM published its first newsletter in July 1988, named '94' after the station's FM frequency, which was sent free to everyone on its mailing list. The four-page folded A3 sheet was edited by Lindsay Wesker and Guy Wingate, who had been assisting in the administration of KISS FM and whose company, Ellerdale Productions, co-promoted many of the station's club events. The front-page editorial, credited to Gordon McNamee (but most likely ghosted by Wesker), declared:

"Over the past two years, it has been a constant struggle. You are one of a mailing list of 3,500 and there are many, many more KISS FM listeners. The fight to provide a specialist music station to the capital has been very frustrating. We made the decision to be three days a week twelve months ago and have only run for sixty-six hours – uninterrupted – as often as possible. The reason for the breaks in transmission are many. It's hard to pinpoint precisely who is breaking the transmission, we know the DTI are responsible for most of the busts, but we have reason to believe that 'outside forces' are also at work. Obviously, nothing hurts us more than losing communication with our listeners and, for all the time we've been off-air, we apologise sincerely. Life without KISS FM is as empty for us as it is for you but, as long as there is a need for a specialist music station in London, we will try to provide the service we know you require."[310]

On its inside pages, the newsletter included the latest KISS FM programme schedule, with the recent additions of a show by Heddi Greenwood on Sunday morning and a bhangra music show by Ashok Kumar early on Saturday morning. Also mentioned were news of the latest music recording activities of KISS FM DJs and instructions on how to order KISS FM merchandise (though the price of sweatshirts had risen from £9.50 to £12 in a matter of months). Commenting on the recent competition to design a new KISS FM logo, and the exhibition of entries at the wine bar, the newsletter noted: "On that day, we displayed the winning logo. Since then, we have changed our minds and, for that, we must apologise. We are still deciding and the final decision has had to be delayed until we have finished moving offices." In fact, KISS FM retained its original logo, adapted from the New York station of the same name, and the 'winning logo' was quietly forgotten.[311]

While KISS FM became more organised, extending its business activities into new areas, the government remained just as determined to stamp out illegal radio because, as The Sunday Times reported, "pirate stations are sprouting as never before." In August 1988, the DTI requested to the government that the forthcoming Broadcasting Bill should include several new legal provisions. It wanted to make advertising on pirate stations a specific offence, it wanted to be able to confiscate pirate stations' record collections, and it wanted to abolish the rule restricting prosecutions to the period six months after a raid. As if to emphasise the greater risks piracy now commanded, Wood Green Crown Court turned down an appeal by pirate London Greek Radio against a fine of £25,000 imposed after a raid on the station's offices in July.[312]

Whilst the illegal radio business faced tougher times and heavier fines, the legal stations increased even further their commitment to the soul music that the pirates had been pioneering for years. At Capital Radio, Chris Forbes was given a new Friday night house music show, and Alex George was given the whole of Saturday night to play black music while, on Saturday night, Tim Westwood's hip hop show and Pete Tong's soul show were both extended. On Radio Luxembourg, the recently introduced weekly soul show was expanded to Friday, Saturday and Sunday nights.[313]

Legalisation of the pirates still seemed an increasingly remote possibility until, in September 1988, the Independent Broadcasting Authority [IBA] unexpectedly revealed that it had pursued an earlier invitation by the Home Secretary to find ways of licensing more radio stations in advance of new legislation. The IBA had submitted to the Home Office a proposal to license twenty new 'incremental' stations to broadcast within geographical areas already served by existing commercial stations (an apparent pre-requisite of existing legislation). A number of these new services would be earmarked for 'community of interest' stations serving both ethnic and non-ethnic audiences. A press statement declared:

"The IBA looks forward to a swift and positive response from the Home Office and would like to press ahead quickly, advertising a number of 'incremental' contracts regularly each month throughout the coming winter and spring. The IBA believes its proposals are in the interests of both listeners and potential radio broadcasters, during what could otherwise be a fairly stagnant period in commercially funded radio development."[314]

Some pirate stations were understandably sceptical about the proposed scheme. Zak of LWR commented: "We will continue and won't believe what the government says. We know about its promises – they have been full of hot air." KISS FM DJ 'Madhatter' Trevor concurred: "They kicked us in the teeth once before." And Stuart Woodin of the Community Radio Association added: "Quite frankly, we have been down this path before and we are not getting overly excited." However, KISS FM's Gordon McNamee suggested: "If the Home Office agrees to the licences, we will definitely apply and, if coming off the air is going to help, then we will do that. It's not like we are drug pushers and don't want to become legal – we do want to be legal." A spokesman for the IBA explained: "As it stands at the moment, we have no intention of preventing pirates from applying. But, when considering their applications, we would have to take into account that they were broadcasting outside the law. It's a fact that the law is the law."[315]

In the meantime, KISS FM was busy expanding its lucrative off-air activities. The station organised an out-of-town event in Basildon, Essex that cheekily included former KISS FM DJ Tim Westwood (now working for legal Capital Radio) at the top of the bill. Then, ending one year's residency of The Base club at the HQ wine bar, KISS FM switched venues in Camden to launch Second Base at the larger Dingwalls nightclub on Saturday nights. The media were glowing in their reviews of the new club night. Time Out magazine said it was "recommended," City Limits promised "bigger, brighter, bolder and better boogie music," i-D said it was "continuing the radical radio musical manifesto," Record Mirror called it "solidly funky" and Blues & Soul called the night "SERIOUS boogie," printing a photo of KISS FM's Gordon McNamee, Rosee Laurence, Lindsay Wesker and Paul Anderson, posing with a new station banner specially made for the event.[316]

In the second edition of its newsletter '94,' KISS celebrated its third birthday with an editorial entitled 'Another Year Older, Another Year Wiser' which proclaimed:

"We learnt long ago not to get too enthusiastic about press reports concerning the dishing out of new licences. We learnt long ago that radio is the bottom of the government's priority list. We don't knock politicians for that ... The powers-that-be would find KISS FM a very well run operation with delicious coffee, good phone manners, very reasonable advertising rates and a very long guest list. Now that we're another year older, we know a few more things. We know: a) who we can rely on to turn up on time; b) who works best at certain times of the day; c) who we can rely on to keep a dancefloor full and who is best qualified to completely clear it; d) who we can rely on for good ideas and physical help; e) where best to promote gigs; f) who best to take advertising from; and g) who our friends are."[317]

KISS FM organised three separate events to celebrate its third birthday – a warehouse-size Friday club night at The Arch venue in South London; a special edition of its regular Saturday night Second Base at Dingwalls which was attended by six hundred people; and a Sunday event at Hammersmith Palais featuring three live bands – Push, The Brand New Heavies and The James Taylor Quartet – that drew a crowd of a thousand. Additionally, there was another in-house KISS FM Annual Awards ceremony, once again held at Lacey's club. 'Madhatter' Trevor won the Best Show Award, Paul Anderson won Best Mixer, Tony Farsides won Worst Mixer, Jazzie B won an award for wearing the biggest trainers, DJ Tee won the 'Endurance Award' for broadcasting non-stop for six and a half hours, Jay Strongman won the 'Spreading The Word Award,' Heddi won the award for 'Best Newcomer,' Coldcut won the 'Rise To Fame Award,' and DJ André won the 'Most Disorganised DJ Award.' The winner who drew the most applause was Rosee Laurence for a special 'Behind The Scenes Award.' At the end of the night, Gordon McNamee was presented with an engraved silver disc by the station staff for "being the best station controller and looking after us all over the past three years."[318]

The gossip column in Blues & Soul magazine described the event as "thirty rather embarrassing minutes of awards" and added: "The award for the most rapid departure from the lig went to Gordon Mac himself, who legged it as soon as the official business was over in order to stand outside Spectrum [club] selling copies of 'Boogie Tunes 2,' the new KISS-sponsored compilation [album]." These comments produced an indignant response from McNamee which the magazine printed in its next issue: "Graphic Records is a record company; Gordon Mac and Heddi Greenwood are DJs who jock on KISS FM; Graphic Records is owned by Gordon and Heddi and was founded with their own personal savings. Graphic Records is NOT KISS FM's record company. KISS FM is owned by eight DJs on the station, of which Gordon Mac is but one. It's very simple. In fact, the other shareholders of KISS FM are a little fed up at being connected with Graphic Records."[319]

McNamee's response was over-the-top, considering how recently he and Greenwood had changed the name of their record company from 'KISS' to 'Graphic,' and considering that it continued to operate out of the same office as KISS FM. KISS FM continued to promote the Graphic releases heavily on-air and in its publicity material, so there was bound to be confusion over the relationship between the station and the record label. Despite what McNamee had told Blues & Soul, there were now nine shareholders in Goodfoot Promotions, the 'front' company for KISS FM. Seven DJs (Joey Jay, 'Madhatter' Trevor, Dean Savonne, DJ Tee, Norman Jay, Jonathan More and Colin Faver) still held five shares each, but McNamee had increased his shareholding from fifty-three to sixty-four shares, and his wife Kim now held one share. For McNamee to state that he was "but one" shareholder in KISS FM was misleading, since he still held the overwhelming majority of shares and remained the company's only director. Goodfoot Promotions Limited, more than ever, was McNamee's company.[320]

Pirate radio activity continued much as usual in London until, on 2 November 1988, the Home Secretary, Douglas Hurd, issued a written statement in Parliament, approving the IBA's proposal to establish twenty new community radio stations. Hurd agreed that "they provide a way, in advance of new legislation, of broadening the choice available to radio listeners." He believed the new services would "benefit the radio industry as a whole, provide valuable new broadcasting opportunities for minority communities and enhance listener choice, as far as practicable, in advance of the major changes needing legislation." Hurd said the licences would be "open to anyone previously, but no longer, involved in unlawful broadcasting," but that he wished to prohibit "those continuing to act outside the law." He proposed that anyone convicted of a pirate radio offence after 1 January 1989 could not hold a radio licence for the following five years, nor could they be employed by a licensed station for the same period.[321]

The Home Office confirmed that "the new stations should come on-air next year." Only a week after the Home Secretary's announcement, the IBA invited potential licence applicants to write to it with basic details of the area they wished to serve and the type of programming they would like to broadcast. The twenty new stations would fall into two categories: 'community of interest' stations covering an area of twelve kilometres radius, and 'small geographical/community' stations covering a six kilometre radius. The IBA placed large advertisements in The Sunday Telegraph and The Guardian newspapers, outlining the new 'incremental' radio scheme and inviting "letters of intent."[322]

After so many false starts and dashed hopes in recent years, could it really be true that this latest plan to introduce specialised radio stations might come to fruition, when all such proposals to date had failed? Could London really be witnessing the possibility of a legal soul music station for the first time in British radio history? Or would those hopes be dashed unexpectedly at the last minute, as had happened so many times before?

---

[298]Dave Seaman, "KISS FM: The Story So Far", MixMag, March 1988.
[299]John Godfrey, "The Crucial KISS", i-D, Mar 1988 ?? [exact date unknown].
[300]KISS FM advert, City Limits, 12 May 1988.
[301]Steve Hamley, "Life At The Top" "The Chart", Radio Today no.18, Sep 1988.
[302]Bob Killbourn, "Jocks Rap", Blues & Soul, 21 Jun 1988.
"Greater London FM Application Form", Appendix, KISS FM, 1 Jun 1989.
[303]James Hamilton, "Odds'N'Bods", Record Mirror, 13 Feb 1988.
[304]Steve Absalom, "Lenny Copies TV Role With The Radio Pirates", Daily Mail, 17 Jun 1988.
Terry Tyldesley, "Jail Threat Over TV Star's KISS FM Link", South London Press, 1 Jul 1988.
[305]Steve Absalom, op cit.
[306]Steve Absalom, op cit.
Jon Homer, "Pirates On Parade", What's On In London, Feb 1988.
"To All DJ's - Please Read", competition script, KISS FM, 30 Jun 1988.
"KISS FM Competition", competition results script, KISS FM, 7 Jul 1988.
letter from Rosee Laurence, Goodfoot Promotions to Ros, PSA, 4 Jul 1988.
[307]Soul Underground, Apr, May, Jun & Jul 1988.
"Soul Underground: Subscribe!", leaflet, KISS FM, [undated].
[308]"Salsoul 1", LP, KISS Records no. LIPS1, May 1988.
James Hamilton, "Beats & Pieces", Record Mirror, 16 30 Jul 1988.
[309]"Boogie Tunes 1", LP, Graphic Records no. LIPS 2, Sep 1988.
"Boogie Tunes 2", LP, Graphic Records no. LIPS 3, Nov 1988.
Graphic Records advert, Blues & Soul, 22 Nov 1988.
James Hamilton, "Beats & Pieces", Record Mirror, 3 Sep 1988.
[310]Gordon Mac, "The Fight To Stay On Air", 94 no. 1, Jul 1988.
[311]"Programmes On KISS 94 FM", "Recording Activities", "KISS FM Merchandising", "No-Go Logo", 94 no. 1, Jul 1988.
[312]Paul Donovan, "Pirates Try To Repel The DTI Boarders", Sunday Times, 24 Jul 1988.
"Pirate Radio Faces New Clampdown On Ads", Campaign, 5 Aug 1988.
"DTI Steps Up Pirate Fight", Broadcast, 12 Aug 1988.
Andy Gliniecki, "Battle Stations", Time Out, 17 Aug 1988.
[313]The Mouth, "Street Noise!", Blues & Soul, 11 Oct 1988.
James Hamilton, "Beats & Pieces", Record Mirror, 8 15 Oct 1988.
[314]"IBA Unveils Plan For New Radio Stations", Press Release no. 59/88, IBA, 13 Sep 1988.
[315]Vivek Chaudhary, "Popular Radio Stations Fear Being Passed Over In Licence Handout", The Voice, 20 Sep 1988.
Jonathan Hunt, "Every Day Is A Risk For The Radio Pirates", Haringey Post, 22 Sep 1988.
Shyama Perera, "Radio Pirates Vie For Licence To Speak", Guardian, 28 Sep 1988.
[316]"KISS", Time Out, Aug 1988 [exact date unknown].
"Second Base", City Limits, Aug 1988 [exact date unknown].
"Second Base", i-D, Dec 1988.

James Hamilton, "Beats & Pieces", Record Mirror, 3 Sep 1988.
Bob Killbourn, "Jocks Rap", Blues & Soul, 13 Sep 1988.
[317] "Another Year Older, Another Year Wiser", 94 no. 2, October 1988.
[318] Cynthia Rose, "Radio On", City Limits, 17 Nov 1988.
"Reviews" & "The KISS FM Awards 1988", 94 no. 3, Dec 1988.
[319] The Mouth, "Street Noise!", Blues & Soul, 22 Nov & 6 Dec 1988.
[320] Goodfoot Promotions Limited, Company no. 02162147, Companies House Records, London.
[321] Written Questions, Hansard, 2 Nov 1988.
[322] "Home Secretary Approves Community Radio Schemes And Issues Warning To Pirate Broadcasters", Press Release, Home Office, 2 Nov 1988.
"IBA Invites Expressions Of Interest From Potential New Radio Operators", Press Release no. 75/88, IBA, 9 Nov 1988.

November & December 1988.

The Home Secretary's announcement of new 'incremental' radio licences created shock waves within pirate and community radio groups on two accounts. Firstly, the immense speed with which the government had suddenly agreed to introduce new stations, after years of prevarication; and, secondly, the requirement that pirate stations wishing to apply for the licences would have to quit the airwaves within only a few weeks. The mood of the radio groups lobbying for licences was one of cautious optimism because, although they had no wish to be made fools of once again, they nevertheless hoped that there existed a real possibility on this occasion of becoming legitimate broadcasters.

The Community Radio Association welcomed the government's announcement, and its chairman Steve Byrom commented: "It has been a long wait for such an obvious stop-gap measure. Now, for the first time in the history of British broadcasting, there is a limited opportunity for groups of ordinary people to own, manage and run a radio station which genuinely reflects their lives and community." The Association regretted that "only a limited number of licences will be available" because it believed this would "provide little incentive for many unlicensed operators to come off the air." It described the five-year ban on pirates convicted after 1 January 1989 as "draconian."[323]

Unsurprisingly, the five-year ban was "unreservedly welcomed" by the commercial radio trade body, the Association of Independent Radio Contractors [AIRC], whose director Brian West said: "This has to be right, and we're only surprised it has taken so long since the Home Office first mooted the idea at the beginning of the year. Of course, as we have said many times, under a deregulated system, enforcement will have to be stepped up, otherwise some pirates won't lose any sleep over the ban, but will simply continue to broadcast illegally as they do at present."[324]

The AIRC gave only a "guarded welcome" to the government's proposal for twenty new stations. One member, Colin Walters (managing director of Manchester commercial station Piccadilly Radio) went so far as to allege that the Independent Broadcasting Authority's [IBA] proposals were "illegal under the Broadcasting Act" and said he would urge the AIRC to challenge the proposals in the courts.[325]

Potential pirate radio applicants for the new licences held mixed opinions. KISS FM's Gordon McNamee was delighted: "It's wonderful news. It's going to be a wonderful Christmas this year. I shall be meeting with our shareholders to plan our application. I only hope the licences will be going to the small outfits and not the Capital Radio's of the world ... We just hope it isn't a re-run of 1985, when pirates went off the air and licences were never granted." Zak of LWR was more sceptical and worried that large companies might win the new licences: "People like us have soldiered on for years and we have been picked on more than other stations. If the government won't plug the hole in the market we have found, we will continue." Lee of South London black music pirate Rock II Rock complained: "The government will only allow you to broadcast to a small area. You just couldn't stay in business. It's not worth coming off the air in January to then find they don't give out the licences until the January after."[326]

Media interest in pirate radio continued to focus on alleged acts of violence. The Star newspaper reported that "pirate broadcasters have turned highbrow [BBC] Radio Four into a round-the-clock reggae station" because "prattling dreadlocked DJs are using the same frequency as the Beeb's flagship." It said the DTI was ordering an investigation after receiving "a flood of complaints" from listeners in Hackney, East London. The Sun reported that "a government inspector dropped dead as he raided a pirate radio station." Thirty-seven year old Roy Threlfall apparently collapsed as he and other DTI colleagues climbed fourteen flights of stairs to storm a pirate station based in a Manchester tower block. The station's DJ John Paul commented: "I'm sorry about the man dying, but I'm sick of being hassled." A new London pirate, Red Hot FM, complained that its competitors were stealing its equipment. Station manager Eugene Rodgers said he had encountered two men, armed with crowbars, who had run off with the transmitter and equipment worth £1,500.[327]

KISS FM had encountered similar problems in recent times from inter-pirate warfare. Gordon McNamee explained: "Over the past six months, KISS FM has had equipment disappear that we don't believe was taken by the [DTI's] Radio Investigation Service. I think mainly it gets ripped off and resold for a quick profit. We have also heard stories of pirates attacking each other." McNamee was certain that the pressure on pirates from the government would increase after the 1 January 1989 deadline: "When they busted London Greek Radio, they took every filing cabinet out of the actual studio. And, when they took it to court, the station got a £14,000 fine, plus £10,000 costs. It's on appeal, but that's your pointer for 1989."[328]

One press article about the competitors for new radio licences revealed that, "since pirates may apply only if they are not broadcasting, KISS FM have taken a vow of silence effective from New Year's Day. But the choice to gamble on legalisation was not made by [Gordon] Mac alone. Eight others co-own the station, five of them black Londoners. And their recommendations were 'ratified' by thirty DJs." McNamee commented: "When we started KISS, we didn't set out with the intention of breaking the law. We just saw that there was a need for a specialist black music station and went about trying to fill the gap. I think the fact that we've beat all the legal stations in readers' polls in many major magazines intimates that we're on the right track. It was a relief when [Home Secretary] Douglas Hurd made his statement. It means that we have a chance at least to go for some form of legalisation … We felt now is our last chance of going legal, which is what we always wanted. As a station, we've never been stronger. We've got a great team of DJs and enormous support from listeners, the media and even the record companies … If we do get a licence, the service can only improve. But pirate radio is bound to lose some of that romance."[329]

The third edition of the KISS FM newsletter '94' explained, in a front-page editorial, the full reasons behind the station's decision to quit London's airwaves at the end of the year, and the station's hopes for the future:

"For the last three years, KISS FM has been broadcasting on the frequency of 94 on the FM waveband, providing a service to those that like listening to dance and black music all day long, and look for more in a radio presenter than the ability to sound professional. For the last three years, KISS has provided a much appreciated public service. The achievements of KISS and its DJs are well documented. We shock legal stations in readers' polls, our functions fill massive venues, our DJs write and/or produce Top 75 hits, our DJs write themes for television programmes, our DJs create musical trends, we merchandise the cleverest T-shirts, we run the most successful club residencies and many of our DJs run or are employees of successful specialist record shops. No other station – legal or illegal – can boast such a talented, knowledgeable, industrious and charismatic DJ roster."

"Radio One, Capital Radio and [BBC] GLR still fail to cater for many Londoners. There is a substantial audience – tens of thousands – that does not want to listen to commercial rock and pop at any time of the day, and is not satisfied with being spoon fed the occasional dose of black music artists that have 'crossed over.' Where else can you hear hard-to-find, mid-1970s singles by the JB's? Where else can you hear unreleased album tracks produced by Leroy Burgess? Where else can you hear highly skilled, twenty-minute uninterrupted mixes on a regular basis? For the last three years, being as adventurous and creative as possible, KISS has gone on despite the disapproval of the DTI and other illegal broadcasters."

"On Sunday November 13th – in The Sunday Telegraph – and on Monday November 14th – in The Guardian – the IBA ran an advertisement stating that they would be establishing around twenty new stations. The ad invited potential applicants to notify the IBA of their interest. KISS FM have notified the IBA of their interest. The next step is for the IBA to send us an application form. The IBA have told applicants that they cannot be illegally broadcasting on the day they send in their application form so, on Sunday January 1st [1989], KISS FM will cease being an illegal radio station. We will shut down and stay shut down until the twenty licences are issued. We have been told that successful applicants will be notified within two months so, during that period, we will attempt to further our cause without the aid of the airwaves. We will stage functions, collect letters and signatures of support, and hope to release a record encompassing the talents of the recording artists that DJ on KISS FM."

"For any of you that have relatives or friends in positions of influence – particularly if they work in arts-related organisations or government bodies – please get in contact with us on 01-431-4441. We are trying to collect letters of support from people in positions of power. Naturally, your letters of support are of equal importance. Please type/print your letters and make them as business-like as possible."

"Hopefully, in a few months time, KISS FM will be granted the licence it so richly deserves and, with the aid of proper studios and proper transmitting equipment, we'll be able to provide our service to the whole of London clearly, and in stereo – and without any disruption."

"Fear not! Very little will change if KISS FM becomes legal. In fact, the weekends will be practically the same. The most significant change will be the introduction of regular weekday shows between 7 am and 7 pm. These shows will run from 7-10 am, 10-1 pm, 1-4 pm, 4-7 pm. During these shows, fifty per cent of the tracks will come from a KISS FM playlist. This playlist will be constructed weekly by a committee of DJs. This playlist will contain dance and black music records that are on the ascendancy. Either new records that have been well received or hit records that are going UP in the charts. This playlist will also include the hottest imports. Only the DJs playing Monday-Friday 7 am to 7 pm will be obliged to feature fifty per cent playlist music."

"Once the licences have been issued, and doubtless there will be one granted to a dance music station, the DTI will make every effort to put the pirates out of business. We have no intention of broadcasting in the face of such pressure. Thus, the countdown to January 1st will be KISS FM's last broadcasts as an illegal radio station. Even if we don't get a licence, we will not be coming back on. For those last remaining days, to the best of our abilities, we will attempt to become a twenty-four hour station".

"The time following January 1st, though, will be far more important than the countdown to it. After January 1st, we will be attempting to maintain our relationship with our listeners, even though we'll have no way of actually speaking directly to them! During that period, your support will be crucial. We hope you'll come to all the KISS FM functions. These functions will be the only way London can hear KISS FM. We have little doubt these nights will be as intense and passionate as those functions in the days when black music used to be underground!"

"We hope you'll listen to these last broadcasts and we hope we can count on your support once we have come off air!" [330]

The KISS FM newsletter explained that the station's move to quit the airwaves was a "radical decision" and it elaborated: "It was not a decision made in haste. After a month of long meetings, discussions and arguments, we're a bit tired, but full of enthusiasm and confidence that we have made the right decision." Ensuring that it went out in a blaze of promotion, KISS FM organised three events to celebrate its departure from London's airwaves – the 'Au Revoir KISS FM' night at The Wag club on 28 December, and two special nights of the station's Dingwalls Saturday residency on Christmas Eve and New Year's Eve, all of which were well attended.[331]

The last few days of KISS FM's broadcasts between Christmas and the New Year were very emotionally charged, with all the station's DJs playing their favourite records and reminiscing about their most memorable moments from the station's three-year history. When the time came to turn off the station's transmitter for the very last time, the whole crew of KISS FM DJs and helpers assembled together in its makeshift radio studio. 'Madhatter' Trevor broadcast the last few words, when he announced: "And finally, from everyone in the studio, after three. One ... two ... three". There was a huge chorus of "bye" from everyone present. Trevor then said: "From your 'Radical Radio'... Bye from me, 'Madhatter' Trevor. You've been wicked, and you've been wonderful. Okay, bye from me. Keep the faith ... in KISS." Then there was a countdown from everyone in the studio: "Six ... five ... four ... three ... two ... one" and the KISS FM station jingle produced by Coldcut was played for the very last time. An eerie silence descended upon the 94 FM channel as the transmitter was turned off. KISS FM was suddenly gone. It was the end of an era for the radio station.[332]

The dilemma that had faced soul pirate broadcasters such as KISS FM was articulated by Soul Underground magazine: "Pirates all over the country face a difficult decision. If they stop broadcasting from January 1st, there will be at least a six-month delay until they can resume, and no one can guarantee that they will receive a licence. If they continue to broadcast and are caught, they will miss out on the Government's 1990 bonanza ... Six months of radio silence seems a daunting prospect, not least for the DJs. A bemused [KISS FM DJ] Norman Jay didn't know what he was going to do with his Saturday afternoons. He speaks for many who, over the years, have manned the decks at all times of the day and night to bring us outstanding music. In many ways, 1988 will signal the end of an era for the pirate scene ... We can only hope that the next six months pass quickly and someone in the IBA has both the knowledge and the wisdom to put the right stations back on air."[333]

It was true. 1988 was the end of an era for pirate radio in London. Exactly what the future held in store for KISS FM nobody knew. There was sadness after the station's closure, but there was also hope that the event would soon herald a re-birth, and an even brighter future, for KISS FM in London. Fingers were crossed and the faithful wore their little pink and green 'Legalize KISS FM' lapel badges with pride. KISS FM had undeniably become one cause that was worth fighting for.

---

[323] "Incremental Contracts - A Step In The Right Direction", press release, Community Radio Association, 2 Nov 1988.
[324] "AIRC Gives Guarded Welcome To Home Office Community Radio Proposals", press release, AIRC, 3 Nov 1988.
[325] "AIRC Gives Guarded Welcome …", op cit.
Angella Johnson, "IBA Plans 20 New Community Radio Franchises", The Guardian, Nov 1988 ?? [exact date unknown].
[326] Shyama Perera, "Radio Promise Silences Pirates", The Guardian, 3 Nov 1988.
Terry Tyldesley, "Pirates To Snub Licence Scheme", South London Press, 8 Nov 1988.
[327] "Reggae Four!", The Star, 14 Nov 1988.
"Pirate Tragedy", The Sun, 17 Nov 1988.
Deanna Fishel, "Pirates At Civil War", Sounds, 19 Nov 1988.
[328] Alex Bastedo, "Radio Gaga", Offbeat, January 1989 ?? [exact date unknown].
Cynthia Rose, "A Legal KISS", New Statesman & Society, 23 Dec 1988.
[329] Cynthia Rose, op cit.
Vie Marshall, "Pirate Radio - Who Will Rule The Waves?", The Voice, 10 Jan 1989.
Sheryl Garratt, [untitled], The Face, Jan 1989.
James Delingpole, "Signing Off With A KISS", Daily Telegraph, 31 Dec 1988.
[330] "KISS FM Closes Down", 94 no. 3, Dec 1988.
[331] "Editorial" "Previews", 94 no. 3, Dec 1988.
[332] author's recording, Dec 1988.
[333] Brian B, "Radio Fun", Soul Underground, Dec 1988.

PART TWO

KISS FM: 1988 to 1991

Tony Monson of London soul pirate station Solar Radio:

"The wrong people will get the licence. The people who get it will have money and a lot of flannel. I might be wrong but I think it will be a compromise, it won't have any credibility ..."

Vron Ware
'The Station That Puts Heart Into Soul'
The Guardian
8 April 1985

Journalist: *"Would LWR be satisfied if a London-wide black music station was licensed?"*

Zak of London soul pirate radio station LWR: *"Run by who?"*

Jane Lyons
'Pirates Of London'
City Limits
30 July 1987

"IBA; please, please have the guts [to award KISS FM a licence]. You won't be disappointed. We won't have a financial crisis after six months, we won't alter our proposed music format, we won't preach, we won't abuse our position and we won't accept payola. In short, we won't resemble some of the stations that have already been given a licence".

Lindsay Wesker, KISS FM
'The Campaign So Far'
The Written Word no. 5
May/June 1989

5 December 1988.
Brixton, London.

It was a cold, dark winter evening when I made my way on the London Underground to Brixton, south of the River Thames, for a public meeting about the new 'incremental' radio licences. Ostensibly, I was attending because of my job as radio editor of City Limits magazine. Each week, I wrote half a page of news about the London radio scene and previewed some of the forthcoming week's radio programmes that I thought might be of interest to readers. I had only just taken on this job, following the decision of my predecessor, Rebecca Coyle, to marry and return to her native Australia. City Limits paid £48.41 per week for my labours, with no expense allowance. I soon found that I was spending around a quarter of my earnings travelling to work in London, buying magazines and newspapers to keep up with radio industry developments, and going to meetings such as this one.

To supplement this meagre wage, I also worked three days a week for a record company, organising its press and promotion campaigns, and I regularly wrote articles about radio for magazines such as For The Record (a monthly for music retailers), Jocks (a monthly for DJs) and NME (a weekly music paper). Writing about the radio industry enabled me to unearth a lot of detail about the events going on behind the scenes, and I hoped that this wealth of information would eventually lead me to what I really wanted – a full-time job in radio production. The imminent licensing of several new London stations, if it ever happened, seemed the ideal opportunity to break back into the radio industry. That evening's meeting about the incremental radio scheme seemed as if it might be a good starting point to try and further my career aspirations.

More than a hundred people crowded into one room of the Bon Marché building in Brixton for what the event organiser, the Community Radio Association [CRA], had unimaginatively entitled 'The Third London Community Radio Forum.' There was already a great deal of expectation amongst the radio community in London that, after their many years of campaigning, new opportunities might at last be about to present themselves for the licensing of more stations. The meeting attracted representatives from several London pirate stations, including WNK, Red Hot FM and KISS FM, as well as some commercially minded licence applicants and many community radio groups.

Publicity material for the event had captured the evident mood of anticipation: "Now that the government has given the go ahead for the Independent Broadcasting Authority [IBA] to award twenty or more 'incremental contracts' to community stations, five to six of which will be in London, the time is ripe for potential bidders to get together to find out more about the implications of a trebling of the number of stations in London."[334]

The CRA predicted that there would be 150 "serious applicants" for the five or six London licences, and it was keen to capitalise on potential bidders' thirst for hard information to entice them along to this meeting. Its publicity asked: "Will it be a free for all, even a shambles, in London, or will, as both the CRA and IBA hope, different groups and interests co-operate and work together?"[335]

The whole room was hushed as Paul Brown, the IBA head of radio programming and the evening's main guest speaker, gave an explanation of the system for radio groups to apply for the new licences. Brown explained that there would be five new incremental stations licensed in London over the next twelve months. Two of these would have London-wide coverage, one on AM, the other on FM. One was likely to be a service shared between London's many ethnic communities, while the other could potentially be a specialist music station. Additionally, there would be three very localised services on FM, two of which were likely to be advertised specifically for ethnic programming. Brown said that discussions were due to take place over the next three days between the IBA and the industry's three main lobby groups: the CRA, the Association for Broadcasting Development and the Association of Independent Radio Contractors [AIRC]. Following these talks, the specific geographical locations of the new stations would be announced.

Brown pointed out that the shortage of available radio frequencies would limit the extent of the new scheme, and that the Department of Trade & Industry [DTI] still had to agree to the use of empty FM and AM channels for use by these new stations. He warned that, particularly in London, this hurdle could slow down the rate of expansion of further new radio services, and he admitted that the IBA was as frustrated by this bottleneck as were the potential applicants. "Don't hold it against me," he said. "You want both of [the London-wide services] to be FM, but we are being told we can't have two FMs ... Whatever we want, if there aren't the frequencies to service it, we won't get it."[336]

At the end of his speech, Brown was bombarded with very specific questions from the audience about the exact structure of the IBA incremental radio scheme. He gave frank answers, offering generous amounts of information about those aspects that the IBA had finalised so far. He also voiced an opinion regarding what he considered to be the poor timing of the government move to introduce new radio stations, just when the state of the economy was far from at its best: "How is the new radio, community or otherwise, going to pay for itself? I'm not entirely sure that non-BBC radio output is financially all that rosy at the moment."[337]

Brown reminded the audience that commercial radio had experienced a rocky start when it had first launched in the UK in 1973, just prior to the 'Three-Day Week' when most of the country's workforce was forcibly put on part-time hours. He recalled how the next expansionary phase of radio had occurred in 1981/82, which had similarly coincided with a recession. Brown drew attention to the fact that the interest rate was presently very high and was expected to rise even further, making the financial outlook for a commercial radio station to launch during the next year not particularly good.

The majority of those present at the event were excited more by the thought of the new radio stations they wanted to run, than by the economic hazards their business plans might encounter. Brown's words of warning were largely dismissed as the sort of caveat any good public servant would offer when introducing new government policies that entailed entrepreneurial risk. His explanation of the structure of the incremental scheme was far more warmly received and, although the details were still sketchy, there was sufficient new information to make most participants think that it had been worthwhile travelling to Brixton that winter evening.

The question of what sort of groups the IBA would declare eligible to apply for the new incremental licences was a particularly contentious issue amongst both the pirate and community broadcasters at the conference. They feared the IBA might open bids to the existing commercial stations, which would enable them to use this new scheme to strengthen their existing monopolies and keep out potential competitors. Such suspicions were fuelled by comments from another member of the conference panel, Philip Bacon, who was present in two capacities – as chairman of the radio industry's professional body, The Radio Academy, and as assistant editor of London commercial talk radio station LBC. He said: "You must expect existing contractors to take an interest in [the incremental scheme]. Why shouldn't they, unless the government bars them from doing so? LBC is as interested as Capital Radio or anybody else."[338]

The licensed commercial stations had already made it perfectly clear through their trade association, the AIRC, that they intended to grab as large a slice of the new incremental scheme for themselves as the IBA would allow them. In a press statement, AIRC director Brian West had commented: "Our members have a wealth of experience and resources, and a number of them have already established fruitful dialogues with intended community franchise applicants."[339]

West had already stated that, if existing commercial stations within the AIRC failed in their attempts to maintain their monopoly over the commercial radio industry, then they would view the newcomers with outright hostility. He declared: "If they think they're coming in to attack the soft underbelly of independent radio on the cheap, they're mistaken."[340]

At the Brixton event, the IBA's Paul Brown sought to calm fears that the commercial radio industry would be allowed to hijack the whole incremental scheme: "The AIRC write extremely good press releases but, basically, we made it quite clear at the outset, in advance of the whole scheme going forward, that we saw no value and no way in which we could prevent anybody from applying for an incremental contract, independent local radio as much as anybody else. They will apply."[341]

Brown said he had received 520 letters of intent from potential licence applicants in the three weeks since the IBA had placed its newspaper advertisements. He expressed surprise that only about 125 of these were interested in opening stations in London. He also made it clear that the IBA intended the incremental scheme not to merely provide more of the same sort of radio stations that already existed: "We need new people doing new things on the radio, as many of them as possible, and as many new sounds as possible." Brown went on to offer hope to the many applicants who were bound to be unsuccessful in their bids for the mere handful of new licences on offer. He said there was still a possibility of between five and ten further stations being licensed in the capital by December 1991, some of which could be London-wide.[342]

In his introduction to the event, the Community Radio Association's Stuart Woodin similarly outlined the potential that existed for the incremental scheme to herald a new type of radio station that involved the community and listeners in its operation: "This is already happening on some of the unlicensed stations, where listeners regularly bump into each other, perhaps at a club gig, in a record shop, or at the station itself."[343]

Pirate radio stations' interest in bidding for the new licences was much in evidence at the meeting. Jo Douglas of North London reggae pirate WNK asked if there would be 'no-go' areas of the capital where the IBA considered it too politically sensitive to offer new radio licences. Pat Chapelle of pirate Red Hot FM commented that one London-wide FM licence was insufficient to satisfy the unfulfilled demand for many different specialist music stations in the capital. Delroy Alexander of the Deptford Community Radio project asked the question that was uppermost in most pirate operators' minds – what would happen to the majority of pirates who were unlikely to win a licence?: "At the moment, there seem to be a hell of a lot of pirate radio stations on the airwaves. How are you going to guarantee that pirates are going to shut down? Or how is there going to be peaceful co-existence?"[344]

Paul Brown replied, rather evasively, that it remained the DTI's responsibility to take action against pirate broadcasters. He added that the IBA was not responsible for the relationship between any future licensed ex-pirate broadcaster and those pirates that decided to continue transmitting illegally.

After the main panel discussion, the audience broke into eight discussion workshops, covering a range of issues relevant to the incremental radio scheme. I chose to attend one entitled 'Why Music Is Important To Community Radio,' chaired by KISS FM's Gordon McNamee and Format Radio's Lawrence Hallett (it was only later I learnt that Hallett was one of KISS FM's resident pirate radio engineers). About a dozen people gathered their chairs into a circle in the main hall to discuss a longstanding issue: the community radio movement, as typified by the Community Radio Association, seemed obsessed with promoting talk-based radio, to the neglect of music-orientated stations. The fear was expressed that the IBA might award the incremental licences to talk-based community radio applicant groups associated with the CRA, rather than to any of the much larger number of music-orientated applicants, most of whom were pirates.

KISS FM was cited as an example of a licence applicant where the music content of its programmes was far more valuable to the station's audience than any speech content it might broadcast. Did that make KISS FM's licence bid any less valid? At the end of our discussion, all the different groups re-convened together, and a summary of our topic was presented to the other delegates: "Clarity of programming was felt to be important, particularly in terms of creating new, and not necessarily commercial, stations which would have an identity of their own and not end up as a glorified Capital Radio."[345]

Following the report from each discussion group, the conclusion to the evening's meeting was presented by Nick Higham, media correspondent for BBC TV. His closing words articulated the still unanswered question of how furtively the incremental scheme was linked to the government's determination to stamp out pirate radio: "What happens to the pirates? With four or five licences on offer in London, and thirty or forty pirate stations, I cannot see that this or, indeed, any future scheme is the automatic answer to the problem of illegal broadcasting."[346]

The meeting broke up, with many participants saying how pleased they were with the high turnout, how useful was the new information gleaned from Paul Brown's responses, and how lively was the debate. I had noticed that KISS FM's Gordon McNamee was sat directly behind me during the closing session. We knew each other by name now since, at the workshop group, each person had identified themselves before the discussion had started. So, before leaving, I said goodbye to him and his companion, Rosee Laurence.

"You should come up to the office some time," McNamee said to me, "so we can have a proper chat."

I said I would be pleased to accept his invitation and I promised to phone him to arrange a convenient date and time.

"That would be great," said McNamee affably. "Come and see us, and you can have some tea and toast."

I replied that I would enjoy that very much. We parted and, as I stepped back into the cold night air and made my way home across London, I could not help thinking what a nice, ordinary guy McNamee seemed to be, and how much I was looking forward to finding out exactly what kind of business operation he was running at KISS FM.

---

[334] letter from Stuart Woodin, Community Radio Association to Matt Preston, City Limits, 3 Nov 1988.
[335] ibid.
[336] author's recording, 5 Dec 1988.
[337] ibid.
[338] ibid.
[339] "AIRC Gives Guarded Welcome To Home Office Community Radio Proposals", AIRC press release, 3 Nov 1988.
[340] "CRA Fury With IR Over Community Stations", Broadcast, 11 Nov 1988.
[341] author's recording, 5 Dec 1988.
[342] ibid.
[343] ibid.
[344] ibid.
[345] "Report Back: 3rd London Community Radio Forum", Community Radio Association, London, Apr 1989.
[346] author's recording, 5 Dec 1988.

1 January 1989.

If the government was to be believed, 1 January 1989 should have seen the radio broadcast bands completely clear of pirate stations. The reality proved to be somewhat different. Some illegal London stations, following KISS FM's lead, did shut down with a certain amount of ceremony during the closing hours of 1988, and the FM radio band did become remarkably quiet for most of New Year's Day. A DJ on black music pirate Big Apple FM, which decided to continue broadcasting beyond the deadline, commented on-air about those stations that had closed down: "We wish Time Radio a lot of luck for the future in 1989, and also Fresh FM. I understand JBC went off last night as well, and Traffic Jam also went off last night. So we wish them all a lot of luck. They're all fighting for that key – a licence – and, you never know, 1989 could be that year when Brent, in particular, could be the first area to have their own legal twenty-four hour station."[347]

However, contrary to the DJ's expectations, the Northwest London Borough of Brent was definitely not one of the twenty-six areas earmarked by the Independent Broadcasting Authority [IBA] for a new radio licence, rendering completely pointless all these pirate stations' decisions to leave the airwaves before the New Year deadline. This DJ's comments were typical of the disinformation that was circulating amongst most of the London pirate stations about the proposed new licences. The same DJ continued his on-air conjectures: "If all the stations get licences, then I suppose the need for pirate radio will cease. But then again, I ask you one question: will this happen?"[348]

The death of pirate radio certainly did not happen in January 1989, however much the government had wanted it to. Illegal radio activity in London continued pretty much as it always had done. The closure of some of the bigger stations – including KISS FM, London Greek Radio, LWR, Solar, JBC, South London Radio and WNK – in order to prepare their licence bids attracted considerable media attention, but many of the smaller pirates carried on broadcasting just as before. The Department of Trade & Industry [DTI] continued to raid stations, just as they had always done, persecuting London Greek Radio to the bitter end of its pirate existence by raiding the station three and a half hours before it was scheduled to voluntarily close down for good to make its licence bid.[349]

During the first three days of 1989, twenty-four pirates were heard in London, only marginally fewer than the thirty that had been on-air in December 1988. In the first nineteen days of the New Year, the DTI made seventeen raids on eleven London pirate stations. Media coverage was no help in sorting fact from fiction. A New Year's Day story in The Mail On Sunday newspaper, entitled 'Radios Silent As Pirates Call Truce,' documented the voluntary closedown of LWR, which was described as "the largest land-based [pirate] station in the UK." The article claimed that LWR had been raided 457 times in its six-year history, and asserted that "the fines for illicit transmission for DJs after today include a five-year ban on working for any legal station and the confiscation of records."[350]

Contrary to these scare stories appearing in the media, neither the fines nor the authorities' ability to seize the radio pirates' possessions had changed at all on 1 January 1989. The only difference was that a pirate operator successfully prosecuted after that date could not be involved in any of the new licensed stations for a period of five years from the date of the offence. It was only in the Republic of Ireland that the law had been changed in 1989 to increase the maximum penalty that Irish courts could levy on pirates to a £15,000 fine and a two-year jail sentence. This had a dramatic impact on pirate activity in Ireland after the New Year, forcing the closure of one hundred illegal stations, twenty-five of which were in Dublin. The British government had been planning to introduce similarly harsh penalties in a new Radio Bill, but legislation had been delayed by Parliament's decision to subsume new radio laws into a much broader Broadcasting Act that it would debate soon.[351]

Nevertheless, the DTI was in a heartily self-congratulatory mood about the supposed demise of the pirates, despite overwhelming evidence to the contrary. The New Year edition of the DTI internal staff newspaper included a photograph of Under Secretary of State for Industry, Robert Atkins, visiting the store room of the Radio Investigation Service [RIS] Warrington branch, where he was examining a seized pirate radio transmitter. Barry Maxwell, head of the RIS, commented: "Serious radio interference to authorised radio services (including emergency services) by pirate broadcasters will shortly form part of a publicity campaign, spearheaded by Mr Atkins, to make the public more aware of the harmful effects of pirate radio." Bizarrely, the photo showed Atkins standing next to a life-size cardboard cut-out of a uniformed policeman writing in his notebook. The caption explained that this figure was used only when the RIS was particularly short-staffed.[352]

Some of the London pirate stations that had closed down at the end of December 1988 soon started to make cautious returns to the airwaves under different names, and many of their DJs adopted new aliases, though their voices were easily recognisable to their fans. A spokesperson for the DTI said: "They aren't fooling us! We know who they are, and it's only a matter of time ..."[353]

On 12 January 1989, Robert Atkins announced that the government intended to seek additional legal powers that would enable the courts to prosecute the supporters and advertisers involved in pirate radio. He reiterated that the existing penalties were a maximum £2,000 fine and up to three months in jail, and trumpeted "a record year of raids against illegal broadcasters." Atkins said that raids had increased from 391 in 1987 (of which 332 were in London) to 444 in 1988 (355 in London). Altogether, 117 people had been prosecuted in 1988, with the resultant costs and fines totalling £79,500. He gloated that, during the summer, Highgate Magistrates Court had ordered £25,000 in fines against a single station, London Greek Radio, following an "in-depth investigation."[354]

At the DTI press conference announcing these successes, Atkins sternly criticised comedian Lenny Henry for glamorising pirate radio in his BBC TV comedy series 'The Lenny Henry Show.' Henry's character Delbert Wilkins was a DJ on the fictional pirate station, Brixton Broadcasting Corporation, also known as Crucial FM, about which Atkins complained: "It has been suggested to the BBC that they should consider their position. Lenny Henry is a very funny man, but he is glamorising a problem."[355]

Atkins said it was "ironic" that the BBC had been a regular complainant to the DTI about interference to its broadcast transmissions from pirate radio activity whilst, at the same time, it was portraying a pirate station in one of its own programmes. He hinted ominously that, if the Corporation did not kill off Henry's pirate radio sketches, the matter "would have to be elevated to a higher profile." Atkins similarly attacked the ITV drama series 'Emmerdale

Farm' which, he said, had included a pirate radio station in one of its storylines and had portrayed a fictionalised raid by the DTI. He complained that "it suggested some of my officials were breaking up and damaging [pirate radio] equipment."[356]

The press was also told by Barry Maxwell of the RIS that, although pirate stations were still operating in Leeds, Manchester, Liverpool and Birmingham, the number on-air in London had successfully been reduced from more than thirty to between eighteen and twenty. The DTI once again raised the spectre of pirate radio involvement with organised crime, claiming that London police were in fear of "a wave of violence caused by racketeers trying to cash in on pirate station profits in return for protection."[357]

The BBC responded to DTI criticism of Lenny Henry's television show by pointing out that, at the end of the comedian's last series, Henry's character Delbert Wilkins had turned his back on pirate radio and had joined BBC World Service radio. Atkins, who had obviously not been following the series very closely, responded meekly that he was "delighted" by the news.[358]

Despite the continuing DTI campaign against pirate radio, support continued to come from unlikely sources, such as former pop star Jonathan King in his Sun newspaper column: "I'm furious! How dare puffed-up, stuffy windbag Minister Robert Atkins slam our pirate radio operators? Politicians know nothing and care nothing about radio." Unfortunately, King's enthusiasm for anti-establishment broadcasters seemed partially attributable to his revelation that the BBC's newly re-launched local station for London, GLR, had turned down his offer to present its breakfast show. King also displayed an alarming intolerance of the IBA's plan to license new stations specifically for Britain's ethnic minorities: "They will license community radio which encourages foreigners not to learn or speak English, not to adapt to their new country, but to continue as if they had never left their old one and merely use our facilities and money."[359]

King asked his readers to send him the names and frequencies of their local pirate stations, so that he could print them in his column, but his campaign quickly fizzled out and failed to deter the government's continuing war against illegal radio. The Minister for Broadcasting, Timothy Renton, was invited by The Radio Academy to be its guest speaker during a luncheon held at London's Savoy Hotel on 9 February 1989. Renton took the opportunity, whilst addressing an audience made up entirely of BBC and commercial radio executives, to attack "the mischief of the pirates" which, he said, not only affected legitimate broadcasters, but also interfered with emergency services and aircraft communications.[360]

By then, forty-five pirate stations were active in the London area, making the government's resolve to destroy unlicensed radio once and for all begin to look particularly hollow. Many of the pirates who had quit the airwaves before the New Year deadline were beginning to realise that obtaining a legal radio licence was not the routine administrative matter they had expected. As a result, they returned to illegality and, once again, the airwaves began to be filled with pirate radio activity.[361]

Besides, predictions started to be made that the IBA would award the new London licences to some kind of 'old boy network' and that the winners had already been decided, despite the fact that the IBA had not yet advertised any of the licences. Black community pirate station JBC, based in Harlesden, had come off-air in December along with many others, but one staff member, O'Brian, commented: "Everybody knows who will get the licences, and they'll get them without having to apply and prove themselves like the rest of us. The government aren't interested in giving franchises to stations that'll play soul and reggae."[362]

Concerns were being voiced that applications from the pirates might lose out to establishment names such as Virgin's Richard Branson, composer Andrew Lloyd Webber and millionaire businessman Lord Hanson, all of whom were known to be making bids for London licences. A proposal was made publicly by LBC presenter Syd Burke that pirate stations should join together to make a single, more effective bid against well-financed business interests: "There are a lot of people who stand to get licences who've never been heard of before, just because they have money and expertise … The objective in the short-term should be to ensure that as many licences as possible go to the black community."[363]

One example of just such co-operation was the merger of Brixton ex-pirate Passion Radio with the Afro-Caribbean Community Association Radio Project in a joint bid for the South London ethnic radio licence. Passion DJ Pete argued: "It's better for the community to join together, rather than being divided. That way, someone from outside the area could come in and get the licence."[364]

In a similar development, a meeting was held at London's Diorama Arts Centre on 15 February 1989 to discuss the idea of a 'Channel Four for pirates' licence bid, whereby airtime on a new legal station would be shared equally between participating groups. Representatives from pirate stations Red Hot FM, Swinging Radio England and the Dread Broadcasting Corporation attended. One participant, Andy Howard of SBS, commented: "In the long term, it would be best for pirates to pull together on a scheme like this, as they would get more credibility for the next lot of licences."[365]

The group believed that it was only the outcome of "pressure from the pirates and the community radio movement" that had precipitated the incremental radio scheme, and that the London-wide FM licence "should be awarded to a station which represents these people, rather than the 'Bransons' or 'Hansons.'" But, defeating its own argument somewhat, the group said that "the IBA and the Home Office see the pirates as divided, amateur, criminal and deviant." Seven reasons were offered as to why a combined pirate application would offer the best chance of success:

- "it is difficult to fill a seven-day/twenty-four hour schedule with good programmes;
- mixed format specialist music stations are successful overseas;
- many existing pirates already have mixed formats;
- contemporary audiences have eclectic tastes in music;
- stations only need successful shows in peak hours to attract advertisers;
- a joint application will give everyone something now. It will be a good starting point for applications for further licences in the future;
- do we want to go back to being pirates?"[366]

These reasons were fairly dubious, even to the most ardent pirate radio enthusiast, and the group managed to totally demolish its own flimsy arguments for a Channel Four-type operation by admitting that "the aim of the station will be to provide as much paid employment to as many people as possible."[367]

Although invited to participate in this scheme, KISS FM made the decision to go it alone with its own application. After the station's brief and abortive liaison with Soul

Underground magazine the previous year, Gordon McNamee did not feel at all inclined towards co-operative working. KISS FM had achieved a higher public profile in recent months than any other pirate station, and McNamee felt he had more reason to be optimistic about winning a licence on his own account than did any of the other ex-pirates involved in this group.

Accusations of a licence carve-up continued to fly, with the publication in the trade magazine Broadcast of a letter from Graham Gold, who was in competition with KISS FM to apply for a soul music station in London under the name "S.O.U.L." Gold wrote: "It has been thought for some time that it was a pre-judged affair and that the contract would go to Andrew Lloyd Webber's Classic FM … though a pre-judged issue has been denied by the IBA …"[368]

The other worry expressed by many in the pirate community was that the whole incremental radio licence scheme was merely a ruse to encourage illegal stations to leave the airwaves. They questioned whether anyone really believed the government was about to grant licences to stations that, only a matter of months earlier, had been flaunting their illegality.

But there were, nevertheless, a few ex-pirates who were becoming increasingly optimistic about their chances of becoming legal. JBC's entirely misplaced expectation that it would win a licence as a community radio station serving the London Borough of Brent meant it had gone as far as advertising in the press for station staff. Although it was already publicly known that Northwest London had not been earmarked by the IBA for any of the new licences, JBC's self-styled 'media consultant' Paul Broome advertised several staff posts in the press, including station manager, program [sic] director, producer for an eight-track production studio, technicians and announcers.[369]

Asked what JBC would do if the IBA turned down its application for a licence, station co-ordinator Challenger said: "We'll cross that bridge when we come to it."[370]

---

[347] Grant Goddard, "Pirate Radio Update", Jocks, Jun 1989.
[348] ibid.
[349] "London Pirates Close Down", Radio Today Newsletter no. 1, 4 Jan 1989.
"Pirates Return To The Airwaves, Despite Government Warnings", Now Radio, 25 Jan 1989.
[350] Grant Goddard, "Pirate Update", City Limits, 12 Jan 1989.
"Pirates Return To The Airwaves …", op cit.
Sasha Nott, "Radios Silent As Pirates Call Truce", Mail On Sunday, 1 Jan 1989.
[351] Joe Joyce, "Irish Pirates Fade Out For The Sake Of Auld Lang Syne", The Guardian, 2 Jan 1989.
[352] Barry Maxwell, "Radio Investigations", DTI News, Jan 1989.
[353] "Pirate Count Still High", Now Radio, 11 Jan 1989.
[354] "No Let-Up In Fight Against Radio Pirates", DTI Press Notice, 12 Jan 1989.
[355] Maggie Brown, "Minister Unveils Pirate Radio Advertising Ban", The Independent, 13 Jan 1989.
[356] Gary Jenkins, "A Crucial Mistake", Daily Mail, 13 Jan 1989.
[357] Richard Evans, "Delbert Wilkins Under Fire", The Times, 13 Jan 1989.
Maggie Brown, op cit.
"Radio Will Be Licensed For A Clean Record", Television Today, 19 Jan 1989.
[358] Richard Evans, op cit.
Gary Jenkins, op cit.
[359] Jonathan King, "I Back Radio Pirates", The Sun, 19 Jan 1989.
[360] Edwin Riddell, "Pirates Ignore DTI Threats", Broadcast, 17 Feb 1989.
[361] Grant Goddard, "Tune In", City Limits, 9 Feb 1989.
[362] Vie Marshall & Dotun Adebayo, "Old Boy Network Rattles The Pirates", The Voice, 17 Jan 1989.

[363] ibid.
David Upshal, "Pirates – Unite Instead Of Fight", The Voice, 21 Feb 1989.
[364] ibid.
[365] "Greater London FM Incremental Licence", C4FM press release, [undated].
"Pirates Pull Together For Channel Four Radio Plan", Now Radio, 15 Feb 1989.
[366] "IBA Incremental FM Licence For Greater London", C4FM Press Release, [undated].
[367] ibid.
[368] Graham Gold, "Black Music Station Plea", letter, Broadcast, 10 Mar 1989.
[369] Display Advertisement, JBC, Now Radio, 22 Feb 1989.
[370] Vie Marshall & Dotun Adebayo, op. cit.

January 1989.

It was January before I found time to take up Gordon McNamee's invitation to visit him at the KISS FM office. Although the radio station had been off the air since the New Year, it continued to use the address of Music Power Records in Haringey for correspondence, despite the bid for a licence being co-ordinated from the office at 14 Blackstock Mews. Most of the streets around the Finsbury Park area of North London looked remarkably filthy and run-down and always seemed to be strewn with litter and peopled by drunks and oddballs. But Blackstock Mews was an oasis of calm, occupying a quiet, secluded cul-de-sac alongside 100 Blackstock Road that had recently been renovated into two terraces of small business units.

KISS FM's premises at number fourteen were remarkably spacious, occupying two floors linked by an old, wooden staircase. Downstairs was dominated by a large, dark, rectangular breezeblock-built room that fronted onto the Mews and seemed to be used by the station merely as a storage space, filled with all sorts of junk. Behind it was a much smaller room without windows, used as a basic radio studio and as a secure space for storing vinyl records. Its walls were covered with soundproofing material to help deaden the room's acoustics, and there were pieces of KISS FM's now disused pirate radio equipment everywhere – disco mixers, battered cassette desks, turntables – that all looked the worse for wear from several years' heavy usage by dozens of different DJs.

The top of the staircase led straight into one huge room, with a very high pitched roof, a skylight, and two massive wooden doors at one end that opened out onto the space above the narrow Mews. This floor must once have been the mezzanine of a warehouse, where goods were loaded from street level, using a rope and pulley system, to swing them from the Mews up through the double doors. Windows on three sides of the room provided the open-plan office with a huge amount of natural light, and its height made the available workspace appear much larger than it actually was.

A large black, skull and crossbones flag was hung above the top of the staircase as a reminder of KISS FM's pirate ethic, and the logo of Goodfoot Promotions had been painted to a height of several feet on one of the whitewashed walls. A handful of battered office desks were scattered around the centre of the room, all facing inwards towards a large empty space in the middle. Littered around the edges of the room were a photocopier, a fax machine, an old sofa in one corner, and a stereo system with huge loudspeakers perched high up against one wall. A kitchenette unit and tiny bathroom had been partitioned off at one end of the room, but the overall feeling was of a huge surplus of space, filled mainly by those few office desks randomly arranged in the middle.

Gordon McNamee greeted me fulsomely and set about organising the tea and toast he had promised when we had first met in Brixton. His desk was noticeably bigger than the others in the room, and he sat behind it in an old-fashioned armchair, rather than the plastic office chairs that the others used. He thanked me for the positive articles I had written about KISS FM for various magazines in recent months, and we chatted for a while about the prospects of the station winning one of the new licences.

I had seen a couple of McNamee's television appearances a few months earlier when the media had blitzed the issue of radio piracy, and I had coincidentally stood next to him in one of the bars of the Royal Albert Hall during the previous year's Disco Mix Club Awards. But this was the first time I had a chance to study him up close and personal. McNamee seemed to dress rather shabbily in voluminous, garishly patterned, knitted sweaters, combined with nondescript trousers and shiny shoes. Where his thick hair had once been an unreformed uncut shag, he had more recently let it grow very long and woven it into dreadlocks which he tied back into a ponytail, a style more commonly associated with black Rastafarians than with white, working class London lads. His facial features were rather rodent-like, with beady eyes and a prominent nose, while several days growth of beard hid an emerging double-chin that testified to the overweight body he was struggling to hide under his loose-fitting clothes.

McNamee may not have been particularly good-looking, but his effusive charm overcame these deficiencies. His manner was to encourage and cajole you in a broad London accent, with all the artfulness of an East End market stall trader trying to sell you imported fake watches, whilst describing them as bargain priced, once-in-a-lifetime, genuine Rolexes. McNamee was obviously a born salesman, inveigling information out of people, convincing them he could do something for them, whilst coolly calculating exactly how much profit he could pocket for himself from the deal. He often described his business methods as 'ducking and diving' or 'wheeling and dealing,' and he conveyed an aura that, despite having little formal education, the university of life had certainly taught him to spot every opportunity to turn a quick profit, make a quick buck, or earn a few grand. McNamee told me he had started his career as a salesman in a shoe shop and it seemed as if, ever since, he must have been refining those same persuasive skills and applying them to his other business activities. He was now a savvy, streetwise hustler – not a businessman in the traditional sense, but an opportunist who would never let pass an easy chance to profit, even if his gain was to be made at someone else's expense.

Drawn in by his charm, I shared with McNamee my considered opinions about the ways I anticipated the new London licences would be awarded. Despite his success developing KISS FM's public profile, McNamee appeared to have little contact with the established radio industry, and his positive reputation seemed mostly limited to the music industry and the alternative/underground media in London. It must have become obvious to McNamee, during the course of our conversation, that I had a good working knowledge of the radio industry and that I had some good contacts in the legitimate radio business that he was eager to break into, now that KISS FM was poised to evolve from its pirate past. McNamee had never worked in the established radio business, so he asked me what experience I had in broadcasting, and I gave him a brief summary of my career to date.

Ever since I was very young, I had been an avid radio listener and music fan. I could remember my parents listening enthusiastically to the pop songs played by the 1960s offshore pirate stations, Radio London and Radio Caroline, and I recalled the excitement in our household that accompanied the opening of Britain's first legal pop music station, BBC Radio One, in 1967. Like many children growing up in the 1960s, I became a fanatical listener to the evening English language service of Radio Luxembourg, often falling asleep at night with the radio still playing on my pillow. In my teens, I loved the excitement created by the second wave of offshore pirates – Radio Northsea International, Radio Atlanta and Radio Mi Amigo.

My first break into radio came in 1972 when, still at school, I started presenting radio programmes for London pirate stations including Radio Concord, Swinging Radio England, and the first incarnation of London Weekend Radio. These early land-based pirates were Sunday-only pop music stations broadcasting on medium wave, and probably had few listeners outside of other pirate radio fanatics.

Together with a school friend, Jeremy Mitchell, who was skilled in electronics, we assembled a basic radio studio, using Garrard SP25 Mark IV turntables, Sony microphones, cassette decks, Akai 4000DS reel-to-reel tape recorders, and a home-built mixing desk. Jeremy and I made lots of our own radio jingles and experimented for hours with multi-tracked voices and echo effects. Though neither of us were particularly proficient DJs, we produced rather esoteric radio programmes that included lots of the soul, reggae and African music that I loved. Before long, we were being asked by several London pirate stations to supply our pre-recorded programmes on cassette for broadcast, and our makeshift studio facility was in demand from aspiring pirate DJs who did not have their own equipment. We excelled at making music-focused programmes and, during the summer, we had set up our studio equipment on the roof of my family's bungalow in Surrey, where we recorded ambient shows for pirate stations that included the noises of birds and planes passing overhead. My home had been used, from time to time, as a broadcast site for some of the pirate stations in which we were involved, after Jeremy had helped me suspend a 100-foot 'longwire' aerial between two tall pine trees in the garden.

Several years later, on completion of my studies, my first full-time job was with local commercial station Metro Radio in Newcastle as deputy head of music. I was asked to present a weekly rock programme for the station and, wanting to be innovative, I launched the first show on British radio dedicated to the independent music charts, at a time when 'new wave' artists were mostly ignored by mainstream radio. My show offered public exposure to a wide range of talented local musicians in Northeast England, and I regularly included interviews and demo tapes produced by promising local acts, including Prefab Sprout and Pauline Murray.

Two aspects of Metro Radio's operation had shocked me, in comparison with my earlier experiences with London pirate radio. One was the station's ignorance of what was happening locally, exacerbated by the lack of direct contact it had with its audience. Metro's studios had been built in the former offices of a scrap metal business on an outlying industrial estate several miles from Newcastle city centre, a location which completely discouraged listeners from dropping by to say 'hello.' To try and counter this lack of local awareness, I started to compile a weekly local concert guide which I read out during my show, mailed to listeners, and pinned to notice boards in local record shops. Although I encouraged other presenters on the station to mention local concerts on-air, I never heard any daytime DJ use my guide.

The other aspect that I had not expected was that the majority of the staff at Metro Radio demonstrated very little interest in music, and surprisingly little enthusiasm for the medium of radio. Most of the presenters seemed to care little for the records they were playing, and I never witnessed any discussion within the station about the techniques of radio production, or how Metro could better target its audience. One daytime presenter seemed more interested in acquiring as many records as possible, including large parts of the station's music library, allegedly to trade for cattle feed that he could use on his Northumberland farm.

My first professional radio experience at Metro Radio had been a grave disappointment. I wanted to work in a radio station that, like the London pirates I had encountered, was brimming with enthusiasm for radio and music, full of creativity, and staffed by a team of people who had determination to succeed. Metro Radio was a sluggish monopoly, the only commercial station in the area, with a music format that was so old fashioned that it bordered on the eccentric. Not long after I joined Metro, the company became embroiled in an industrial dispute with its staff over pay increases, which quickly escalated into a strike. Once resolved, the owners swiftly implemented retributions, dismissals and the enforced redundancies of many staff, which led to an appalling workplace atmosphere. One record company representative commented to me that Metro was the only radio station he had ever visited where he could walk the length of the building and not hear any of the staff listening to their own station's output. There was even one occasion when the station's transmitter went off-air and none of the staff realised until a listener phoned in and asked me why they had been hearing 'dead air' for the last quarter-hour.

When I joined Metro Radio in 1980, its music playlist system was archaic, with slots allocated each hour to 'instrumental' and 'vocal standards' records. The station's long playlist of current hit records ran to several pages. As a result, its output paled in comparison with the more contemporary and hit-orientated format of national BBC Radio One, which is why Metro Radio's audience had been in decline. One of my first tasks was to implement a more streamlined playlist system to strengthen the station's sound, throwing out the idiosyncratic aspects of its music scheduling. Metro's new, slimline playlist of only thirty current hit records drew strong criticism from the music trade press and, as a result, some record companies (including EMI) boycotted the station because they felt there were too few opportunities for their new records to be played. However, the streamlined playlist worked well with listeners, Metro's audience started to grow again, and my pioneering system of a thirty-song playlist of current hits was soon adopted by most other commercial stations.

The other revision to the playlist system that I introduced was the creation of a database of old hit records, along with a scheduling system to ensure that each 'oldie' was played regularly. Until then, each presenter had had the freedom to choose their own oldies for their shows, which resulted in many of them favouring a narrow selection of songs from the significant periods in their own lives. As a result, many familiar records that listeners might have liked to hear had gone unplayed. I spent several weeks selecting hundreds of titles worthy of being called 'oldies' and organised a complex system to rotate these songs evenly across the station's output. Much of what I implemented at Metro Radio had been learnt from detailed accounts I had read of music selection systems used in commercial radio in the United States.

These changes had an immediate, positive impact on Metro Radio's audience, which started listening in greater numbers and for longer periods of time, according to industry research. A paper written in June 1981 by the Independent Broadcasting Authority about the audience for Metro Radio commented:

"The past year has represented something of a breakthrough for Metro Radio, as regards the size of audience attracted. Since 1978, its previously most successful year, the station had been achieving unspectacular audience figures. However, a fairly dramatic increase in listenership was recorded in the Autumn 1980 JICRAR survey, with Metro's 'weekly reach' rising sharply, from 44% to 52% ... The hours of listening for which the average Metro listener tuned in also rose in 1980-81, to 11.4 hours per week. With both the size and the loyalty of its audience increasing, Metro was able to claim a 28% share of all radio listening within its survey area, the highest since the station's establishment."[371]

A further report written by the Independent Broadcasting Authority for its Local Radio Advisory Committee in the Metro Radio service area noted:

"Of all the nineteen Independent Local Radio stations that took part in both the Spring and Autumn [1980] JICRAR surveys, Metro Radio's audience figures show the greatest improvement ... Not only did Metro's audience size increase considerably during 1980, so also did the length of time for which its listeners chose to tune in ... In general, these audience figures must be regarded as highly encouraging. Metro may feel very satisfied with the significant increases in the number of adult listeners, and in the amount of time they spend listening to the station ..."[372]

If Metro Radio felt 'very satisfied' about these improvements to its audience ratings, it was certainly not communicated to me. At the end of 1980, I was called into the office of the station's managing director, Neil Robinson, for the first time. Metro Radio's senior managers ate their lunches in a separate dining room from the rest of us, and Robinson worked on a different floor from the programming staff, so we had never had an opportunity for conversation. At this meeting, Robinson expressed his anger about an article concerning Metro Radio that had been published in a music industry trade magazine that week. It was headlined 'Metro Sticks By Smaller Playlist' and said:

"One week, about six months ago, Metro Radio's playlist suddenly dropped from fifty-two singles and six station hits to a very stringent and selective list of forty [sic] titles. However, in spite of the expected industry grumbling, music organiser Malcolm Herdman feels that the move has helped strengthen the overall sound of the station and therefore broadened its appeal ... While the audience response has been reportedly good – results of the next JICRAR survey are confidently awaited, there are certainly some [record company] pluggers who felt cheated by the cutback."[373]

I thought Robinson would have been pleased to see Metro Radio's success reported in the press, but his anger was the result of the article's penultimate paragraph, which said:

"The playlist is compiled each Thursday morning by Malcolm Herdman, managing director Grant Goddard and programme controller Mic Johnson. The gang of three listen to a stack of new releases, some which have come recommended by the record companies, some by the presenters at the station."[374]

Robinson asked me why I had told the magazine that I was Metro Radio's managing director. I explained that I had not even spoken to the reporter. It was my boss, Malcolm Herdman, who had been interviewed by the magazine, which is why he had been quoted in the article. I had no idea why the magazine mistakenly believed I was the station's managing director, but it was certainly not an error of my making. Robinson told me that I was to be made redundant at the end of the month. He did not thank me for my work turning around the station's audience figures. I was out.

Metro Radio had employed more than seventy staff when I had joined in 1980, but the management wanted to reduce that number to forty-seven by 1982. Neil Robinson attributed these reductions to "natural wastage," though many staff saw them as retribution for their involvement in the successful strike action at the station.[375]

At Metro Radio, I had witnessed, at first hand, the sluggishness of the British commercial radio industry and how uncreative it was without any direct competitors in each local market. It was a world away from the competitive American radio business that I had read about avidly in Billboard magazine since I was a teenager. I was very disillusioned by the callous way the station's management treated its employees, and by the lack of passion that most of the station's staff displayed for the medium of radio.

One notable exception at Metro Radio was the station's senior producer, John Coulson, who also presented a weekend rock music show that combined an extremely eclectic mix of music and talk. Coulson often interspersed his highly personal selection of rock music records with long extracts read from books such as Hunter S Thompson's classic story of gonzo journalism, 'Fear And Loathing In Las Vegas.' It was the first time I had heard anything so inspired and creative attempted on British commercial radio, and it gave me hope that there must be other passionate people, like Coulson, who realised that running a successful radio station was a very different business from manufacturing meat pies or selling shoes.

Coulson seemed to be regarded as a 'weirdo' by many of the staff he worked with at Metro Radio and he was shunned by most of them, often eating his lunch alone at a table in the staff canteen. He had joined Metro at its launch in 1974 and had won awards for his radio work but, having become increasingly isolated in a hostile and remarkably unsympathetic working environment, he died tragically of an accidental heroin overdose in 1984. Coulson had been forced to resign from Metro Radio in 1981, following a court appearance for heroin possession and, despite his immense talent, he had been unemployed for the three years preceding his death. Coulson's work at Metro Radio, and his belief in the potential creativity of radio, inspired me immensely during my short time at the station. His tragic death and forced exile from an industry to which he had contributed so much talent made me more determined than ever that radio was exactly where I should direct my skills.[376]

Two other incidents at Metro Radio had brought home to me the darker side of the radio industry and the power that some record companies believed was wielded by local commercial radio stations. On one occasion, a newly appointed local promotion representative of CBS Records assured me that he could organise the dispatch to my home address of his company's entire back catalogue of albums, worth many thousands of pounds, if I would add certain new CBS single releases to the station's playlist. I was shocked at the audacity of this bribe and informed my boss, Malcolm Herdman, who ensured that the rep was banned from visiting Metro Radio ever again.

In a separate incident, just as I was leaving the station to go home one Friday afternoon, the receptionist asked if I would see two visitors waiting for me in the foyer. There, I found two young women with plunging necklines and very short skirts, who said they had been sent from London by a small record company to help promote one of its new single releases. They pouted, flirted, and asked me if I knew any "hot places" to go in Newcastle where they could show me "a good time." I was so shocked by this blatant offer of sex that I hurriedly declined the invitation, rushed out of the building, and left them to prey on any passing DJ who might be less reticent to indulge them.

Now, sitting in the KISS FM office eight years later, I explained to Gordon McNamee that Metro Radio had been my baptism of fire into the world of commercial radio, and I had swiftly learnt how things were, how things were not, and what I could contribute to make them how I thought they could and should be. Since then, I had worked for the Voice of Peace radio station in Israel, I had been employed on a one-year contract as programme manager at London cable community station Radio Thamesmead, I had worked short-term contracts at Capital Radio for the last two years, and I had produced music programmes with Rough Trade Records for broadcast on an FM station in Japan.

During my years working in radio, I had presented and produced programmes; recruited, trained and managed staff; drawn up and overseen budgets; written, produced and voiced adverts; and co-ordinated special projects and funding applications. McNamee seemed interested in my skills, offered me another cup of tea and asked me what I was doing right now. I explained that I was currently working for a record company, was on the staff of City Limits magazine, and was also writing radio stories for several magazines. I explained that I was really seeking a job working full-time in radio, rather than writing about it, but that there had been no suitable vacancies of late. Without any prompting on my part, McNamee asked if I was interested in becoming involved in KISS FM.

I told McNamee that I had always believed London deserved a dedicated black music station, ever since my own initial involvement in pirate radio, making my own programmes and listening enthusiastically to London's first soul station, Radio Invicta, all those years ago. I had voraciously bought soul records ever since the late 1960s, when I had first discovered the delights of the Stax and Motown record labels. The second music concert I had attended was James Brown's stunning appearance at London's Royal Albert Hall in 1971 and, since then, the type of music KISS FM played had continued to be a very important part of my life. Right now, I believed that there was a real chance that one of the new licences would be awarded to some sort of soul or reggae radio station, and so I offered to assist McNamee in any way that I could in order to help KISS FM win a licence.

McNamee promised he would get back in touch with me about my involvement in KISS FM, and we left the arrangement as vague as that. He knew where I could be reached, and I was not anticipating a job offer from the station at this early stage. Primarily, I was a soul music fan and I was a pirate radio fan who would have loved to witness KISS FM become London and Britain's first legal soul music radio station. It was as simple as that. Anyway, despite its spacious office in Finsbury Park, it was common knowledge that KISS FM was being run on a shoestring budget, particularly since quitting the airwaves a few weeks earlier. I was not even considering the possibility of earning a living from any involvement in KISS. McNamee seemed like a nice guy, and I just wanted to help him out with his plans for a legal radio station.

Before I left the office and headed back to City Limits magazine, McNamee introduced me to the other staff working for KISS FM, Goodfoot Promotions and Graphic Records. I had already met his personal assistant, Rosee Laurence, at the Brixton conference the previous month and had spoken to her several times since then on the phone. McNamee introduced me to Heddi Greenwood and Lindsay Wesker, and we exchanged polite greetings. I had absolutely no idea how closely the five of us would become entangled in our respective destinies at KISS FM. On that day, it was just a casual visit to another radio licence applicant that I had wanted to check out for myself. The tea and toast had been great. As I left the office, McNamee said I was always welcome to pop in again for more. I walked away, wondering to myself if KISS FM really could win a licence, and wondering exactly how McNamee wanted to involve me in the station. What part would I play in the radio station's future?

---

[371] David Vick, "Metro Radio: Audience Research", Independent Broadcasting Authority, Draft Paper (81), 22 Jun 1981.
[372] David Vick, "Metro Radio: Audience Figures – Note By The IBA Staff", Independent Broadcasting Authority, Tyne/Wear Local Radio Advisory Committee Paper 1(81), 13 Jan 1981.
[373] Patricia Thomas, "Metro Sticks By Smaller Playlist", Record Business, 15 Dec 1980.
[374] ibid.
[375] "Radio Cutbacks – No News Is Good News??", Durham Street Press no. 31, Sep/Oct 1980.
[376] Steve Forshaw, "Drug Overdose Killed DJ", The Journal, Newcastle, 25 May 1984.
"DJ Lost His Fight To Beat Drug", Northern Echo, Newcastle, 25 May 1984.

January 1989.

Now that KISS FM was no longer on-air, the station having put behind it three years of pirate radio activity, Gordon McNamee switched his priority to pulling together a radio licence application. He knew that the document would have to prove sufficiently impressive to compete against an anticipated deluge of bidders, many of whom would have considerable public reputations and heavyweight financial backing.

On 10 January 1989, McNamee met David Evans, a family friend who was chairman and managing director of Centurion Press, a successful contract print and publishing company based in London's West End, with an annual turnover of £20m and a payroll of more than a hundred staff. Evans had left school at the age of fifteen to become an apprentice printer, before founding Centurion Press in 1971. McNamee took to the meeting a draft copy of the cost and revenue budgets he had calculated would be appropriate for a full-time legalised version of KISS FM. He desperately needed a financial backer who would be willing to invest their money in the station, and Evans was a natural first port of call, given his involvement and successful track record in legitimate business. Evans would be able to offer an indication to McNamee of how appropriate the budgets were that he had drafted.

The meeting with Evans proved to be very productive and became the catalyst for a change in McNamee's vision of exactly what sort of business KISS FM was destined to become, should it win a licence. Until then, McNamee had been planning to run the legalised KISS FM along the lines of a pirate station that just happened to have a radio licence. He had anticipated that the station would continue to function on the kind of shoestring budgets with which he had been accustomed to working in the pirate radio business. McNamee had thought that a legalised KISS FM should broadcast only to the most central area of London, just as it had done as a pirate, and that it would need office space only slightly larger than its existing home in Blackstock Mews.

Evans became the first of several people from the world of business who, consulted by McNamee, would tell him that they visualised the legalised KISS FM as an operation that would bear more similarities to the kind of commercial companies of which they themselves had direct experience. Evans had no knowledge of the radio industry and was probably imagining that KISS FM would need to be a station organised along similar lines to Capital Radio, with plush offices in the centre of London and a team of highly paid executives. It did not occur to him that Capital only enjoyed these privileges because it was the largest commercial radio station in Britain, it was the only commercial music radio station in London, and it had been enjoying the fruits of its monopoly position for the last fifteen years. Evans knew only that Centurion's offices were modern, well equipped and filled with well paid staff, and he saw no reason why KISS FM should not be organised the same way.

The proposals and assumptions contained in McNamee's initial budgets, which he shared with Evans, may have been remarkably naive, but they directly reflected his own experience of having run KISS FM as a weekend-only pirate radio station in London. KISS FM had always financed itself from its own means, so McNamee had made an assumption that "no bank loans or overdraft facilities will be necessary in the first year," and that income from sponsorship deals and sales of KISS FM merchandise (T-shirts, hats, etc.) would be negligible for the legalised station. Evans proceeded to increase all of McNamee's budgeted costs to amounts he considered to be far more realistic. McNamee's proposed share capital of £10,000 was upped to £25,000; rent of premises was doubled to £40,000; gas and electricity budgets were doubled; marketing costs of £6,000 were upped to £16,000; and legal costs were increased from £2,550 to £4,000.[377]

It was the cost of staffing the legalised KISS FM that proved to have been underestimated most significantly. McNamee had anticipated that the station would employ four production assistants, one secretary, one receptionist, one sales person, a part-time cleaner, a part-time bookkeeper, plus McNamee and his personal assistant. The KISS FM DJs would be paid £20 per hour on a freelance basis, the bookkeeper would receive £9.20 per hour for twelve hours per month of work, the cleaner £4.10 per hour for three mornings a week, and the whole business was to occupy a 2,000 square foot building. The one remaining cost was the only one that Evans thought was over-budgeted. McNamee had insisted that the station would need three security guards to protect its premises twenty-four hours a day on a rota basis. Evans queried the £54,600 annual cost of providing such extravagant security, but McNamee was adamant about the importance of keeping out his enemies and rivals, the most important lesson he had learnt from his pirate radio days.[378]

Evans increased several of McNamee's staff costs by a factor of ten. He insisted that a proper accountant was vital to run the business properly, and so the cost of a bookkeeper was upped from £2,880 to £30,000. The single salesperson's basic salary was upped from £3,272 to £30,000 (McNamee scribbled "Super Sales" against this new amount in his notes). McNamee's own remuneration of £18,000 as managing director of KISS FM was improved by the addition of a company car worth £12,000, a change that signalled the earliest hint of a metamorphosis from pirate radio enthusiast to company man. However, at that stage, neither McNamee nor Evans seemed to realise that a radio station serving London would find it difficult to operate effectively with so few staff.[379]

Three separate cashflow forecasts had been prepared by McNamee to accompany the budgets, demonstrating the outcomes of differing levels of success in selling advertising airtime on the station. At the bottom end, if only two minutes per hour of adverts were sold, the station would earn £48,591 in its first year, to be set against costs of £93,896. In the best case scenario of six minutes advertising per hour, revenue would be £145,773, against costs of £111,035, generating an operating profit for the station in its first year. Evans felt that, because the station's running costs had had to be increased so substantially, McNamee's proposed advertising rates were likewise too low. The cost of a thirty-second advert in the breakfast show was increased from £25 to £150, daytime adverts from £15 to £50, and overnight spots from £10 to £20. This earliest draft of the station's budget assumed that only £100,000 of start-up capital would be required and, even in the worst of the three scenarios, this investment would be recouped after only eight months on-air.

Despite the evident shortcomings of McNamee's budget, Evans said he was keen to participate in KISS FM's bid for a radio licence. He committed his company Centurion's support as a shareholder and said he would consider taking a personal stake in the company as well. He suggested that it would be appropriate to arrange for Centurion's financial director, Martin Strivens, to look at the financial aspects of the licence application in far more detail. With

Evans and Strivens assisting him, McNamee now had the nucleus of a team with business experience who could start to plan the station's future. As a long time family friend, McNamee trusted Evans' intentions and judgement far more than any other potential investor who might be interested in a legalised KISS FM. Because Strivens was in Centurion's employ, McNamee was willing to accept Evans' word that the accountant was trustworthy and could make a valuable contribution to the work at hand.

The day after the meeting between McNamee and Evans, a letter arrived at KISS FM's Blackstock Mews office from the Independent Broadcasting Authority [IBA], announcing its advertisement of the first five incremental radio licences for Manchester, Hounslow, Bristol, Rutland and Stirling. In the letter, Peter Baldwin, the IBA's director of radio, outlined the timescale of the scheme, whereby applicants were to be given two months to apply, once a licence had been advertised, with the winner announced by the IBA one month later. There was no cost to submit an application for a licence, but the winner would have to make a one-off payment to the IBA of £4,000, and then pay an annual sum of £23 per 1,000 adults living within the area to which the station planned to broadcast. A detailed specification document and blank application form was available on request from the IBA. Baldwin warned that many of the hopeful licence applicants were bound to be unsuccessful: "Please remember that this is only an interim development. The government intends to appoint a new Radio Authority, which should be in business by January 1991, able to operate under less demanding regulation with a growing number of frequencies at its disposal. If you are unlucky at this stage, many more radio opportunities should develop in two years' time."[380]

McNamee's next task was to request the full application form and accompanying details from the IBA, in order to determine exactly what information was required from applicants. That same day, McNamee asked his personal assistant, Rosee Laurence, to write and distribute a letter to everybody on the KISS FM mailing list, requesting that they pledge their support in writing for the station's licence bid, and informing them of the productive meeting he had had the previous day with David Evans. McNamee believed that Centurion's backing was all the station needed to win the licence, and he was keen to demonstrate his absolute trust in Evans. The letter told the station's fans: "KISS FM have complete financial backing to set-up [sic] from David Evans, chairman and managing director of Centurion Press ... David Evans' company has no connection whatsoever with the record or radio industry. He is a family friend of station manager Gordon McNamee and will become a shareholder, should KISS FM gain a licence. David Evans' investment is not being borrowed, thus there will not be substantial amounts to repay following KISS FM's legislation [sic]."[381]

Within the letter, this information was typed entirely in capital letters to emphasise its importance, and it went on to list thirty-nine noteworthy people from whom letters of support for KISS FM's licence bid had already been received. Most of those named worked in the record industry or were journalists writing for music or style magazines, though the list also included Sir Roy Shaw, former secretary general of the Arts Council, and film director Lindsay Anderson.[382]

Two weeks later, Rosee Laurence produced a revised version of the letter that included additional names, bringing the total number of supporters to sixty-four. Attached was another circular, addressed to "whom it may concern" from "the shareholders of KISS FM," expressing the station's confidence in the funding of its licence bid: "We have financial backing for a legal version of KISS FM. As our cash flow projection shows, we know how much money is required and we are assured of the necessary finances from David Evans, owner of Centurion Press."[383]

Evans and McNamee discussed the funding of the licence bid in more detail with Centurion's financial director, Martin Strivens, who made further upward revisions to the budgets. Strivens, like the other two, had no experience in the commercial radio industry, but could see that some of the estimates needed more attention. Although of British nationality, Strivens had studied for his Bachelor of Commerce degree at The University of Witwatersrand in Johannesburg. He had qualified as a chartered accountant in 1976 after four years' articles with a large firm of accountants in Johannesburg, before moving to London to work for Ernst & Whinney. Now, aged thirty-seven, he was a director of all the companies within the Centurion Group, and his benefits included a Porsche company car.

KISS FM had implemented very few corporate policies for its business dealings during its pirate radio days, but one which it had always subscribed to was firm opposition to the racist political regime in South Africa. KISS FM had refused to accept advertising from South African companies and would have nothing to do with persons or organisations connected with the country. Because of this, Strivens' past connections with South Africa would have to be played down within the radio station, and McNamee felt that it was fortunate that Strivens displayed very little trace of a South African accent in his speech.

The management nucleus of McNamee, Evans and Strivens was soon supplemented by the appointment of Keith McDowall CBE as chairman designate of the legalised KISS FM. The argument was voiced by Evans and Strivens that, despite the ex-pirate station's adopted slogan of 'radical radio,' it was more important now to impress upon the IBA that the new company was endorsed by the establishment. After all, Capital Radio's chairman was Sir Richard Attenborough, LBC's Chairman was the Right Honourable Christopher Chataway, and they thought that KISS FM needed someone of similar standing to take on the role of an establishment figurehead.

McDowall had run his own public relations consultancy since 1988 and claimed to have useful contacts at the IBA that would help KISS FM with its licence application. He had worked as a journalist for twenty years, before entering the Civil Service to work in a succession of government information departments. Before taking early retirement, he had spent seven years with the Confederation of British Industry, where he was deputy director general, before leaving in 1988. The Queen had awarded him the CBE the same year and now, at the age of fifty-nine, he was looking for a new business venture in which to become involved.

Despite the fact that, like Evans and Strivens, McDowall had no radio industry experience and no knowledge of the black music industry, Evans felt that McDowall would be a very useful person to assist with the KISS FM licence bid, using his contacts in public life and the world of public relations to lend legitimacy to its publicity campaign. The fact that McDowall wanted to be a shareholder in the station was an additional benefit.

The nascent KISS FM management team now needed to recruit someone with a solid reputation in the commercial radio industry, so as to demonstrate to the IBA that there was sufficient sector experience within its board to enable the ex-pirate's paper application to be turned into reality. Coincidentally, Capital Radio DJ Dave Cash approached KISS FM at the same time to offer his assistance with its licence application. For a consultancy fee of £5,000, a seat on the company board and a guaranteed contract of employment if KISS FM should win the licence, Cash promised he would lend his name and his experience to the bid, as well as the informal assistance of his contacts in the IBA's radio division.

Though he spoke with a North American accent, Cash was London born, but had moved to Canada at the age of sixteen and had entered the radio industry after quitting the University of Columbia. He returned to Britain in the mid-1960s to work on the offshore pirate Radio London, and was voted fifth most popular DJ at the time by the music paper NME. Stints on Radio Luxembourg and the newly launched BBC Radio One followed. When Capital Radio opened as Britain's first commercial pop music station in 1973, Cash's defection from the BBC to take up the post of production manager at the new station attracted much publicity, and his weekday show drew a substantial audience. However, by 1989, Capital was employing a much younger type of DJ for its daytime shows and Cash, now aged forty-four, had been relegated to a night time slot on the company's AM oldies service, Capital Gold.[384]

The four-man steering group at KISS had little knowledge of Cash's achievements or his reputation within the radio industry. To them, he was someone whose CV offered many years' radio experience and who was presently employed by Britain's largest commercial station, Capital Radio. Cash's promise to utilise his contacts at the IBA was thought to be particularly useful for KISS FM, as would be his assistance in drawing up the licence application form. It was agreed that Cash would be paid the requested fee for his work and would take up the post of programme director on the company board, if KISS FM's application were to prove successful. In order not to jeopardise Cash's current employment with Capital Radio, the management team agreed to keep his involvement in KISS FM strictly confidential, and his name would be excluded from all publicity surrounding the station's licence bid.

At this stage in the licence application process, my own role within KISS FM was one of unpaid adviser to Gordon McNamee. Through my work writing about the radio industry, I was regularly coming across news and information about various groups' intentions and plans to bid for the London licences, which I then passed on to McNamee (except in cases where applicants had insisted I maintain confidentiality). I was also buying all the weekly media trade magazines that covered the radio industry, which not only provided me with leads for radio stories, but also provided me with insights about media industry developments that I could pass on to McNamee. Although the Blackstock Mews office seemed to be awash with magazines covering music and lifestyle topics, the broadcasting trade press went unseen, which probably explained why KISS FM had so far earned little coverage in periodicals such as Broadcast, Media Week and Campaign.

On a practical level, I had obtained my own copy of the full licence application form and explanatory notes from the IBA, and had started to consider how best KISS FM should present its bid. The application form comprised twenty-five pages, divided into fourteen sections, with spaces allotted for answers to a series of very specific questions. Within these spaces, KISS would have to prove to the IBA the worthiness and integrity of its bid, as well as the relevance of its proposed music format to radio listeners in London. The bidding process was going to be a highly competitive exercise with, perhaps, up to a hundred different groups applying for a single licence. I asked myself: what would make KISS FM's application stand out from the rest in such a crowded contest?

I considered that, in the likely scenario of intense competition for the London licence, KISS FM had two distinct advantages over other applicants, both of which would need to be emphasised within the available space on the application form. Firstly, KISS FM had already accumulated a substantial history in broadcasting since 1985, and had proven that it could organise itself as a radio station. It should matter little that the station had been illegal and had only operated at weekends. The vast majority of competing applicants would be submitting hypothetical paper proposals for stations they had never tried out on the airwaves in any shape or form. KISS FM had already been broadcasting its intended music format for several years in the real world and, therefore, it was proposing a proven and successful formula.

The second factor was KISS FM's intimate knowledge of the radio audience to which its programmes were intended to appeal. All of the people involved in the pirate incarnation of KISS FM were dance music fans, and many of them also worked within the dance music industry as artists, writers, producers, record shop staff and club DJs. It was essential to demonstrate to the IBA that a high level of compatibility already existed between the station and its audience, which would undoubtedly pave the way for KISS FM's success. The station's personnel were not mere observers of the music they played on the radio, but active participants who were themselves shaping the contemporary soul music scene in London.

I was certain that many of the other licence applicants would be proposing music formats of which they themselves had little intimate knowledge. Many bids would be the result of market research that purported to identify a specific gap in the London market for a radio station playing a particular style of music. The applicant group would then be happy to adopt this format, as readily as it would any other, if the evidence showed there to be an audience of sufficient scale to make the station commercially viable. Such applicants would probably argue that one did not have to be a country & western fan to make a successful licence bid for a radio station playing that type of music.

But KISS FM wanted ONLY to run a soul and dance music radio station. It was not interested in any other music format, no matter how financially viable another musical style might appear to be. The task, therefore, was for the KISS FM application to demonstrate convincingly that the station's staff knew more about its particular musical niche than other competing bidders knew about their own chosen music formats.

The IBA application form was rigidly designed and there was little space allotted to demonstrate, in answer to the questions, these two qualities that I felt could win KISS FM the licence. So, I concluded that the KISS FM bid should, instead, consist of two separate documents: the standard IBA application form answering the assigned questions, plus a completely distinct 'appendix' that would allow KISS FM to state its case in its own way. The form itself was restricted to twenty-five pages length, but an appendix could be made as thick as a telephone directory in order to demonstrate the weight (literally) of KISS FM's case for a London radio licence.

In my spare moments at work, I made full-size mock-ups of the two application documents that I had imagined. I gave them to McNamee as my suggestion for the KISS FM licence bid. Both were enclosed in stiff covers with a huge KISS FM logo on the front, the thinner document with 'APPLICATION FORM' written on it, the much larger one inscribed

'APPENDIX.' Within the application form, I had drafted answers to several of the IBA's questions. Within the appendix, I had drawn up a suggested list of contents for seven sections:

- A   KISS FM Personnel & Their Achievements
- B   KISS FM Press Releases
- C   KISS FM Newsletters & Magazines
- D   KISS FM Press Coverage
- E   KISS FM Selection Of Letters Of Support
- F   The British Dance Music Industry:
  - 1   Record Companies
  - 2   Promotion Companies
  - 3   Periodicals
  - 4   Existing Radio Coverage
  - 5   London Record Shops
  - 6   London Clubs
- G   KISS FM Sponsored Or Promoted Events.[385]

McNamee liked my ideas and quickly adopted my two documents as the template for KISS FM's licence bid. Work in the KISS FM office started on gathering all the information that would be needed to fill the telephone directory-size appendix. If nothing else, the two-part application should certainly impress the IBA by its sheer size. KISS FM had to be able to demonstrate that it was completely au fait with all aspects of Britain's dance music industry. The appendix to the application would be like a 'Yellow Pages' of the dance music scene, demonstrating KISS FM's intimate knowledge and that the station, through its pirate broadcasts, had already become a focal point for the whole movement.

At last, KISS FM's application for the London radio licence was underway.

---

[377] Gordon McNamee, [untitled], KISS FM, Jan 1989.
[378] ibid.
[379] ibid.
[380] Letter from Peter Baldwin, IBA to KISS FM, 10 Jan 1989.
[381] Letter from KISS FM to mailing list, 11 Jan 1989.
[382] ibid.
[383] Letter from KISS FM to mailing list, 26 Jan 1989.
[384] Keith Skues, "Radio Onederland", Landmark, 1968.
"DJ Dave Moves On", Daily Mirror, 28 Jul 1973.
[untitled], Record Mirror, 28 Jul 1973.
[untitled], Daily Express, 30 Jul 1973.
[385] Grant Goddard, mock-up of KISS FM licence application, [undated]

February 1989.

Several of the London pirate radio stations that had closed down by the 1 January 1989 deadline had already declared their intention to bid, like KISS FM, for the one London-wide FM licence soon to be advertised by the Independent Broadcasting Authority [IBA]. It was difficult to estimate exactly how many of them would be able to raise the finance necessary to turn their plans into viable proposals. Would several applicants proposing the same soul/dance music format make it more likely that the IBA might grant the licence to one of them? Or, would several small-scale soul music applicants, competing against each other and all of them up against better financed bids from major companies, only diminish the chance of any one of them winning?

One certain bidder against KISS FM for a soul radio licence in London was going to be ex-pirate station Solar Radio, headed by forty-five year old DJ Tony Monson. Solar had made an earlier bid for a licence in 1985, under the aborted Home Office community radio experiment, and had subsequently returned to a pirate existence, broadcasting a seven-day soul music service for most of its life. Solar played softer and more jazz-influenced black music than KISS FM, which had tended to include harder underground sounds, pushing the barriers of soul music towards their limits. Tony Monson was the younger brother of Lord Monson, and had started his radio career in 1963 working for ZBM Radio in Bermuda. After a brief spell on British offshore pirate station Radio 355, Monson went on to present programmes for BBC Radio Medway, Radio Orwell, Essex Radio and Capital Radio in the 1970s and 1980s. He was recognised as an authority on soul and jazz music and had compiled the weekly 'Street Sales' dance chart for Echoes music paper for many years.

Monson had launched Solar Radio in 1984, and the station's community radio application in 1985 had involved other soul and jazz DJs including Jude James, Mark McCarthy, Helen Mayhew, Clive Richardson, Dave Collins, Marc Damon, Paul Buick, CJ Carlos, Bob Jones and Tomek. The station had resumed illegal broadcasts from November 1986 but, by October 1988, had been plagued by raids, some of which Monson believed to have been executed by rival pirate stations, rather than by the Department of Trade & Industry [DTI]. Solar's morale was left badly shaken, as Monson recalled: "By February [1988], the station was all but in ruins. In March, we got a studio raid, after only a few hours of being on the air. Bit by bit, a number of the more 'materialistic' DJs had disappeared from the station ... In October 1988, Solar got its final bust. When, literally days later, the new community [incremental radio licence] project was announced, it seemed the right time to call things to a halt."[386]

By December 1988, Monson had secretly decided to join the KISS FM application rather than mount a separate Solar Radio bid. Several of Solar's DJs, including Gilles Peterson and Bob Jones, had already joined KISS FM, which seemed to Monson to be more effectively organised to mount a licence bid than his own group. Differences remained between the favoured music policies of the two stations, as Monson noted: "If KISS could best be described as the 'radical alternative,' Solar tried to set itself up as being the 'quality soul alternative' ... If KISS had the majority of the trendy club-goers at any one time, Solar was trying to cater for the soul fans who couldn't handle the intensity of the club scene."[387]

As part of the secret deal struck by KISS FM's Gordon McNamee to fold Solar Radio into his own licence bid, it was agreed that Monson would be named as one of the key personnel on the KISS FM application form, and that he would be offered a daytime show on the station. Monson's interest in the more melodic aspects of soul music would be reflected in the weekday programmes he would present on KISS FM, were it to win the licence, as he explained: "You will hear, effectively, the best that KISS FM offered in its unlicensed days, only this time as an all-embracing legal outfit – with the more 'radical' approach being confined to evenings and weekends."[388]

Having subsumed Solar Radio's aspiration for a London licence into his KISS FM bid, McNamee was keen to disarm other potential competitors who wanted to operate a dance music format similar to his own. Another aspiring applicant was thirty-four year old DJ Graham Gold, who had already declared his intention to apply under the station name 'S.O.U.L. – The Sound Of Urban London.' Gold had worked as a DJ for Solar, written for Blues & Soul magazine, and had stood in for Capital Radio's soul presenter on a couple of occasions. He lived in Rickmansworth and worked full-time for a London music video jukebox company called Diamond Time. According to his own notes: "Gold began putting together an application under the acronym S.O.U.L. in case their [sic] was prejudice against the KISS FM appliation [sic] as it had been an unlicenced [sic] broadcaster. After it became clear that his worries were unfounded, he took his work to Gordon Mac at KISS."[389]

Gold offered the preparatory documents he had written for his S.O.U.L. licence application to McNamee as his part of the deal to combine forces. His contributions included a four-page commentary on the popularity of dance music, entitled 'Our Industry,' and some correspondence with parties who had demonstrated an interest in establishing a dance music station. Gold was incensed by the thought that composer Andrew Lloyd Webber's planned classical music station might win the London licence over a soul music applicant. As well as having written to Broadcast magazine expressing these fears, Gold also wrote directly to the IBA accusing it of a "pre-judged decision." His letter sought to draw to the IBA's attention the fact that he was no longer acting as a representative of Time Radio, a pirate station based in Harlesden that had continued broadcasting after the 1 January deadline: "Stupidly, they have decided to continue broadcsting [sic] so I have dissassociated [sic] myself with this group and have subsequently approached three companies with my ideas ... The investors I have approached are all, for the record, white-owned companies with proven track records, one of whom's [sic] turnover last year exceeded two million pounds."[390]

Gold had been driving a hard bargain with KISS FM's McNamee over his proposal to combine forces and, afterwards, most of what Gold had promised to McNamee turned out to hold little substance. Gold had made the research he had completed sound far more substantial than was warranted, and the great weight he placed on his experience working in commercial radio and his contacts in the radio industry proved to be largely inconsequential. He had presented only a handful of shows on legal radio and, as Record Mirror had commented: "Graham Gold ... had half a second of fame as DJ of the week on [the TV show] 6.20 Soul Train."[391]

McNamee knew that he needed more radio professionals involved in the KISS FM bid who could contribute notable industry experience outside of the pirate radio scene, and Gold had made it sound as if he provided just such expertise. A deal was eventually agreed between the two, and KISS FM issued a press statement announcing the news: "Now KISS FM is very happy to bring aboard another veteran. Graham Gold has been a professional DJ for seventeen years ... Bringing with him technical expertise, broadcasting skills and extensive musical knowledge, Gold will be a valuable addition to the already impressive roster of DJs." The press release also announced the merger with Tony Monson's Solar Radio and concluded: "The KISS FM application is three applications in one, uniting three audiences and countless years of experience."[392]

One important aspect of the deal that was not announced publicly was McNamee's private agreement that Gold would present the KISS FM weekday breakfast show, should it win the licence. This programme is traditionally the flagship of a radio station's output, since more people listen to radio during those hours than at any other time of the day. The agreement potentially represented a considerable career boost for Gold. Both he and Monson had secretly been offered two of the station's prestigious daytime shows, in preference to KISS FM's existing team of presenters who had worked for the station since its pirate days. To those loyal DJs, it would have seemed unthinkable if they found out that McNamee had suddenly 'given away' the task of presenting some of the station's most high-profile shows to 'outsiders.'

Gold himself found it very difficult to keep the news about the terms of the deal to himself and, writing an internal briefing document for KISS FM, he hinted at his own delight in securing such a major responsibility: "Our broadcasters for the main twelve hours 7 am to 7 pm will all be professionals who's [sic] obvious love of the music has become apparent over the years."[393]

At the same time, the controversy around comedian Lenny Henry's role as honorary president of KISS FM resurfaced. His portrayal of a pirate radio DJ in his television show still seemed to pose a serious question mark over his future involvement in the station. Although KISS FM was no longer broadcasting illegally, it was reported in one publication that: "[The DTI] are also understood to be unhappy at Lenny Henry's links with former unlicensed station KISS FM, where he is president."[394]

More worrying for KISS FM were the continuing rumours that a large existing business was pre-destined to win the London-wide FM licence over a new entrant to the radio industry such as KISS FM. In the first newsletter to be mailed to KISS FM listeners after the station had voluntarily closed down at the end of 1988, an editorial posed the question: "Do KISS really stand a hope against Andrew Lloyd Webber's Really Useful Company, or Capital Radio's application for another station?"[395]

With this new issue, the newsletter changed its name from '94' to 'KISS FM's Written Word' and transformed itself from a basic two-sheet newsletter into a proper twenty-four page magazine. The idea was to turn the venture into a desirable, soul music-orientated magazine that could generate paid-for advertising, rather than for it to remain merely a free publicity sheet for KISS FM activities. Now that the radio station was off the air and no longer generating income from the advertising spots it had broadcast, McNamee needed new financial ventures to cover the costs of running the station's office. The magazine's editorial explained that "the name '94' is obviously no longer suitable, especially since that frequency, which we vacated in December, has now been taken up by an outfit who have chosen to defy the tough, new government laws."[396]

DJ Judge Jules enlarged upon the personal impact of KISS FM's departure from London's airwaves in an account of his typical day: "I rub the sleep from my eyes, trying to replace drama with reality. It's Friday morning and, for a semi-conscious moment, I contemplate my show that evening on the Radical Radio. I roll out of bed and turn on the radio to ensure that the authorities haven't taken us off-air. To my horror, I hear a voice welcoming the listener to Lazer 94 FM. This brings me back to Earth with a crash landing. Of course, we're off the air applying for a licence."[397]

Lazer, a twenty-four hour black music pirate station, had been broadcasting to London on 95.4 FM during December 1988, but KISS FM's decision to quit the airwaves had enabled it to move its transmissions to the clearer channel of 94.0 FM. Although no KISS FM DJs were involved in Lazer, it was considered important for the station's licence campaign that no one suspected KISS FM of continuing to broadcast illegally under a different name, as other pirate stations were doing.[398]

The first issue of 'KISS FM's Written Word' also updated its former listeners about the progress being made with the licence application: "In the past two months, the KISS staff have found ALL the necessary finances to start-up a radio station. We have researched radio in Britain thoroughly and we now know precisely how much it costs to run a station the size of, say, Capital Radio."[399]

The information on radio station costs came directly from Capital Radio DJ Dave Cash's involvement in the KISS FM bid, but the tone of the statement was indicative of a gradual change in McNamee's vision for KISS FM. Increasingly, his earlier notion of a licensed KISS FM as a legalised version of the former pirate operation was being replaced by a new concept that considered the re-launched KISS FM to be a serious competitor against London's only commercial pop music station, Capital Radio. Suddenly, it was no longer enough purely to legitimise KISS FM's former pirate status. Now the station was supposed to be taking on the world, as the newsletter explained: "The technical side – the money, the equipment, the people – is all taken care of. We could start transmitting tomorrow! We could start competing straight away! (And certain parties would feel the pinch immediately!)"[400]

Behind these words of confidence and bluster, the reality was still rather different. Gordon McNamee was grappling with the budgets and the proposed staffing of the station, both of which were consistently being increased. Week by week, KISS FM was becoming a much bigger business proposition on paper, and a much more costly venture. McNamee's initial business plan in January had comprised twelve full-time staff, two part-timers, plus the thirty-five ex-pirate DJs. Following further consultations with David Evans and Martin Strivens of Centurion Press, the station's major shareholder, the business plan had been expanded over the last two months to now support twenty-eight full-time employees and thirty-five freelancers.

McNamee himself still planned to take a salary of £18,000 as managing director, and to pay his personal assistant Rosee Laurence £10,000 (though this was upped to £13,000 in a later revision). The rest of the station was now divided into four departments: music programmes, spoken word programmes, finance and sales. A new job as head of music programming was pencilled in at £12,000 (later upped to £15,000), a post to be offered to either Lindsay Wesker or Tony Monson. Reporting to this person were five daytime DJs paid

£13,000 each, thirty freelance DJs paid £100 per week each, one record librarian paid £10,000 and four programme assistants paid £10,000 each.

The post of "head of news & spoken programmes [sic]" was to be paid £12,000 (later amended to £15,000) and had been pencilled in to be offered to me, although McNamee had not informed me. Beneath me, there were planned to be two producer/presenters (paid £10,000 each), jobs to be offered to Lyn Champion and Tony Farsides. There were three additional journalists/presenters paid £6,000 each (later upped to £8,000), posts to be offered to Sivan Lewis, Lisa I'Anson and Eko Eshun, plus five freelance journalists.

On the advice of Centurion's financial director, Martin Strivens, the finance department was beefed up considerably from McNamee's original plan to employ one part-time bookkeeper working six hours a week at a salary of £2,880. There was now a head of finance paid £30,000, a full-time bookkeeper paid £10,000 (later upped substantially to £15,000), two filing/typing assistants paid £6,000 each (upped to £8,000), and a typist paid £8,000 (upped to £10,000). Touchingly, McNamee pencilled in his mother to take the bookkeeper post, offering her the third highest paid post in the company. With these changes, Strivens had created a finance department of comparable size to that which he was used to running at Centurion, seemingly with little regard for a radio station's needs.

The sales department now consisted of a sales manager paid £30,000 (dropped to £20,000 and then again to "maybe £15,000 plus commission"); two sales persons paid £12,000 each, and a further two sales persons paid £10,000. The station's engineering requirements were to be sub-contracted to an outside company at a proposed cost of £5,000 per annum, bringing the total annual staffing costs alone to nearly half a million pounds.

The radio company's board of directors, to whom McNamee would be accountable as managing director, was now planned to include the shareholders and a few 'worthy' names that it was considered might help KISS FM win its licence bid. The shareholders were McNamee, David Evans, Martin Strivens and Keith McDowall, while question marks were placed against other possible names – Lenny Henry and Tony Prince.

These revised budgets more realistically reflected how expensive it would be to establish a new radio station in London. However, if KISS FM were to successfully cover such large overheads, it would now be necessary to sell its advertising space at a much higher return than had originally been anticipated. The station would definitely have to sell more airtime than the two minutes per hour anticipated in one of the earliest cashflow forecasts, if it were to become a profitable business. For KISS FM to sell a high volume of radio advertising in the London market, in competition against two other commercial stations (Capital Radio and LBC) that had had the market to themselves since 1973, the station would have to be very aggressively marketed to potential clients and advertising agencies. More and more, it was starting to look as if KISS FM would be forced to compete with Capital Radio, particularly for advertising revenue, and this necessitated an organisational structure that would be comparable to that of Capital itself.

Centurion Press alone was unable to commit the necessary sums of capital required to establish KISS FM at this much elevated level of commercial operation. It was imperative now to involve an additional established media business that could offer substantial capital investment in KISS FM, but that would not take control of the company. The burden of KISS

FM's start-up costs needed to be spread much more widely than Centurion Press and the personal stakes of the station's directors.

The task now facing McNamee, Evans, Strivens and McDowall was to sell the idea of investment in KISS FM to others, and to make the case forcefully that, although such investment required large sums of money, the financial rewards could be even greater if the station competed successfully with Capital Radio. The selling of KISS FM as a potentially highly profitable business venture was about to begin. The idea of running KISS as a pirate station with a licence was being discarded very quickly. Gordon McNamee was witnessing the transformation of his weekend London pirate station into a potential media empire, and he was seeing his potential salary as managing director increase as the scale of the proposed enterprise grew.

KISS FM – welcome to the world of business.

---

[386] "Solar: Soul, Jazz & Rhythm And Blues Music For London", Licence Application, Jun 1985.
Tony Monson, "No Compromise", KISS FM's Written Word no. 4, Feb 1989.
[387] ibid.
[388] ibid.
[389] Graham Gold, "Application Notes", briefing document, [undated].
[390] Graham Gold, "Black Music Station Plea", letters, Broadcast, 10 Mar 1989.
letter from Graham Gold to David Vick, IBA, 10 Jan 1989.
[391] James Hamilton, "Odds'N'Bods", Record Mirror, 4 May 1985.
[392] "Sound Of Urban London (S.O.U.L.) Pacts With KISS FM", KISS FM Press Release, 7 & 11 Apr 1989 [two versions].
[393] Graham Gold, "Application Notes", op cit.
[394] "New Plans To Kill Pirate Stations", Radio Today no. 1, 4 Jan 1989.
[395] "One Licence Under A Groove", KISS FM's Written Word no. 4, Feb 1989.
[396] The Editors, "Editorial", KISS FM's Written Word no. 4, Feb 1989.
[397] Judge Jules, "Where Has All The Music Gone?", KISS FM's Written Word no. 4, Feb 1989.
[398] "Airwaves", Radio Today no. 1, 4 Jan 1989.
[399] "One Licence Under A Groove", op cit.
[400] ibid.

March 1989.

Until then, Britain's radio industry had developed incredibly slowly, compared with the experiences of other nations. The country's first popular music channel, BBC Radio One, had not launched until 1967 and, in contrast to North America, the introduction of commercial radio to Britain had followed the introduction of commercial television by some twenty years. Radio broadcasting in the United Kingdom had not yet been allowed to develop into a particularly challenging or innovative medium. This had made it all the more surprising to witness the breathless speed with which the Independent Broadcasting Authority [IBA] was suddenly pressing ahead with its advertisement of the new incremental radio licences. An initial announcement of the scheme in September 1988 was followed, the next month, by an invitation for interested parties to contact the Authority. Then, just before Christmas 1988, the IBA had published details of the geographical location of the licences.

On 10 January 1989, the IBA had advertised the first five of the twenty licences it planned to offer. Applications were invited from bidders in Manchester and Hounslow (in West London) who wanted to serve local ethnic groups, and from bidders in Bristol, Rutland and Stirling who could propose any format. The closing date for applications for this first batch was 13 March 1989, the winners to be announced in April. The IBA had advertised a second batch of five licences on 6 February 1989, consisting of ethnic services in Coventry and Haringey (North London), and any format for the Isle of Wight, Sunderland and Tendring (in Essex). Applications for these had to be submitted by 10 April 1989, with the winners announced in May.[401]

Never before had the broadcast regulator offered so many new commercial radio licences within such a short space of time. It was a remarkable change from the usual, stifling slowness with which new broadcasting innovations had, until then, been developed in Britain. However, it was also becoming obvious that this new 'incremental radio' scheme would produce only a short-term, one-off expansion of radio services, rather than herald the beginning of a determined push to enlarge, almost infinitely, the commercial radio industry. A Home Office spokesperson explained that the twenty incremental licences were "a limited response" and blamed it on the scarcity of available radio frequencies: "It is unlikely that the IBA would be given the go-ahead to issue further licences."[402]

On 6 March 1989, the IBA held a press conference at its Knightsbridge office to announce the third batch of licences it was advertising – an ethnic service for the whole of London, an ethnic station for Bradford, and services of any format in Belfast, Kettering and Stockport. The closing date for these was 8 May 1989 (except for London, which was 5 June), with the winners to be announced one month later. The London licence, for the AM medium wave band, was specifically designated for use by a number of different ethnic minority broadcasters who would share a single channel. The IBA would act as broker for these groups, bringing them together to form a management team that would run the station co-operatively. This particular licence was of no interest to those applicants in London, such as KISS FM, who wanted to operate music services that required the higher quality FM band.[403]

The handful of journalists who attended the IBA press conference were offered cups of tea and were invited to ask questions of the three IBA executives who were present. Most of the discussion centred on the difficulty the IBA faced in its role as matchmaker for the ethnic groups interested in the London-wide AM licence. But there was also a query about the cost involved in establishing a new radio station in the capital, to which the IBA's director of radio, Peter Baldwin, answered: "I would imagine, speaking off the top of my head, it would be prudent for £100,000 to be available for a pan-London station, if you are thinking of a transmitter, a site, an aerial, premises and studios."[404]

One of the journalists present, Bob Tyler from the trade magazine Music Week, suggested that an applicant was likely to require capital of at least £1,500,000 to establish the London-wide FM station whose licence the IBA was to advertise the following month. But the IBA's head of programming, Paul Brown, replied: "I dispute your capital costs. I think that's a gross over-exaggeration of what it will actually cost." However, as KISS FM's Gordon McNamee was quickly discovering, if the staff costs alone for a new station's first year of operation amounted to around £500,000, the figure Tyler had cited for a station's launch capital was not so fanciful. Tyler went on to express his fear to the IBA officers that such large sums of money were completely out of the reach of most former pirate stations, who had duly come off the air by the 1 January 1989 deadline in the hope of winning a licence. He argued: "We're not actually talking about community radio in London. We're talking about big business radio ... If they [the pirates] are unsuccessful, they are all going to be back on the air again in autumn."[405]

The IBA's Paul Brown replied that, although the current incremental radio experiment was limited strictly to twenty or twenty-one licences, unsuccessful applicants could still apply for further licences that would be advertised at some point in the future. But Tyler persisted with his point, suggesting again that the London-wide FM licence was actually out of the reach of most potential ex-pirate applicants. Brown said he disagreed with this hypothesis, and the IBA's principal radio development officer, David Vick, added: "We've just received a copy of KISS FM's 'Written Word' magazine. They clearly don't feel that it is out of their reach. They clearly believe they can get the money to run the operation profitably. They clearly believe they can put in a credible application. So I think the pirates aren't claiming that they're being priced out of it. They feel they can compete fairly for it."[406]

Vick had been referring to the latest issue of the KISS FM magazine which had proclaimed proudly that "all the necessary finances to start up a radio station" had already been secured. Despite this public statement, behind the scenes at KISS FM, the search was continuing for at least one further major investor to provide capital for the bid. Bob Tyler's estimate of the finances necessary to mount a licence bid in London were proving to be much more realistic than the IBA's own figures.[407]

That week's issue of the trade magazine Broadcast included a four-page pull-out supplement about the incremental radio scheme, entitled 'The Great Air Race.' It predicted pessimistically: "A licence to lose money is how community radio has been described. Cynics predict that, when the cash runs out, the big boys will move in for the pickings. The pitfalls are enormous ..."[408]

Broadcast had assessed the potential applicants for each of the IBA's incremental licences and had predicted the possible winners. For the London-wide FM licence, Andrew

Lloyd Webber's Classic FM was considered "front runner." Other bidders were said to include: the Channel Four-type grouping of former pirates, another classical music bid, an easy listening service owned by Lord Hanson, rock music station London Rock Radio, an arts station run by the Institute for Contemporary Arts, and Capital Radio in pursuit of another London licence. KISS FM was referred to inaccurately as one of the "out-and-out pop and rock applicants." Amongst the advice the article offered to applicant groups was a suggestion to "make sure your team includes at least one first class journalist, capable of capturing your aspirations with the clarity they deserve."[409]

A subsequent editorial in Broadcast magazine, under the headline 'The Big Sell-Out,' took up the argument articulated by Bob Tyler at the IBA press conference: "Community radio is being sold out to businessmen and consortia with stakes in independent radio stations. Many of the proposals for the first incremental contracts are as close to the community and ethnic groups they purport to serve as Chris Tarrant [breakfast DJ on London station Capital FM] is funny." The article cited examples of bids anticipated for the Bristol licence from existing West Country commercial stations Severn Sound and GWR; an application for Hounslow that involved the Daily Telegraph newspaper and Wembley Stadium; and a bid for Manchester that included Red Rose Radio, Mersey TV, and a radio advertising saleshouse.[410]

The Broadcast editorial complained that too many licence applicants seemed to be proposing black music formats, and it referred to the letter from Graham Gold that it had published earlier in the month: "A correspondent wrote to Broadcast several weeks ago, pointing out that black music accounts for thirty-eight per cent of music sales, yet gets hardly any airtime on BBC radio. If this is true, then the community stations will offer a real alternative to the national stations." It concluded, confusingly: "It is crucial that the IBA recognises that a black music station and a black community station are two very different things, and the former is a cop-out."[411]

KISS FM had always identified itself as a specialist music station that played black music. It had never sought to call itself a community radio station and it certainly had no aspirations to act as a medium for London's black community. The only community KISS FM served was the capital's large number of black music lovers. Confused commentators, such as this one writing in Broadcast, were quite typical of the media establishment's inability to understand that fans of black music were not confined to Britain's black community. They failed to recognise that black music was liked and enjoyed by many sorts of people, all of whom were neglected because of existing radio stations' reluctance to play their favoured genre.

The confused and contradictory attitude of the press towards ex-pirate station bidders for the incremental radio licences was an issue that desperately needed to be tackled by launching a publicity campaign which conveyed accurate and informed facts. In order to correct these misconceptions, much of the work undertaken in the KISS FM office during this period was devoted to raising the station's profile, particularly in the quality periodicals and the media trade press. It was essential to overcome the common prejudice of media professionals that pirate radio stations were run by people who were little better than common criminals. Now that KISS FM was no longer on the air, it was important to maintain its public profile by contacting as many journalists and acquaintances in the media as possible.

The trade magazine Media Week responded by including KISS FM in its round-up of applicants for the London licence, but it suggested that the station's expertise in dance music was a negative, rather than a positive, factor: "Gordon Mac, who was station manager when KISS was broadcasting, and who would be managing director of a new, licensed station, is first and foremost an enthusiast for the music KISS would provide; the audience it would produce seems an afterthought."[412]

The European trade journal Music & Media reported that KISS FM was assembling "a team of DJs and producers from former pirate and independent stations" to provide a "balanced dance and soul music sound." Another industry magazine noted that KISS had raised £450,000 of funds from Centurion Press, but still rated its chances of winning as no more than fifty-to-one: "A sprightly outsider. KISS FM is the people's choice, but that won't count for much when money matters most ... The group lacks the funds and establishment clout to impress the IBA. Big money competitors, and what he perceives as back door lobbying, has left KISS' Gordon Mac feeling 'despondent,' but he insists on going it alone."[413]

London listings magazine Time Out reported that KISS FM was "chasing £2 million in backing" and that, having signed up Centurion Press, it was still in need of another major shareholder. Gordon McNamee was said to hope his backers ended up with less than fifty per cent of the company's shares: "We're all music people, so we want to make sure we're not run over by a group that says: 'We're backing this and we want it to be all this way.' There's the threat that big business could come into it and say 'Let's change our format, let's change our style, and we'll make more money.'"[414]

Even the music and style press, which had always been supportive of KISS FM in its pirate days, were now more sceptical of its chances in the race for the London-wide FM licence. The Face magazine suggested: "Whether KISS – or any soul station – will be successful in their application is more doubtful ... Even if a pirate does succeed, it will have to broadcast within the limits of 'needletime' and IBA rules."[415]

Blitz magazine noted that KISS FM was "up against some really big, powerful businessmen," but that McNamee was "not planning to screw up his life's dream." It reported: "If KISS is not selected, the station will not return to the airwaves ... Mac is confident that, if Lady Luck doesn't deliver just yet, KISS will have its licence within five years under the government's further deregulation of radio."[416]

In addition to this publicity drive, KISS FM's other activity was the continuing and expanding promotion of club nights that featured the station's DJs at several central London venues. These events served two purposes, now that the station was off the air. They kept the KISS FM name alive in the public eye, and they generated substantial sums of cash that were needed to pay for the office overheads. In January 1989, a regular Saturday club night called Garage Grooves had started at The Borderline, a bar beneath the Break For The Border restaurant on Charing Cross Road. KISS DJs Colin Faver, Judge Jules and Mixmaster Tee were booked to perform on a rota basis, and public interest was stimulated by a live appearance of the American soul group Blaze.

By February 1989, a second residency had been organised at The Borderline on Thursday nights, called Low Rider, with KISS FM DJ Jay Strongman. The music played was a mix of traditional soul, funk and R&B, with guest DJs added to the bill each week. Soon, a third Borderline night was added on Fridays, called Upfront, that played late 1970s disco tunes now being revived under the name 'boogie.' Regular DJs for that were KISS FM's 'Madhatter' Trevor and Stafford from OBJ, plus occasional guests. Additionally, the KISS FM Saturday night club Second Base was still running at the Dingwalls venue in Camden, having built up a huge following since its launch the previous August. Several one-off KISS FM events were also organised, including a Valentine's Day party and two record fairs at Jacksons Lane Community Centre in North London, two World Beat nights at The Borderline, a mid-week Rap Review at Dingwalls, and two Bank Holiday parties at the Fridge in Brixton.

Each Monday morning, the KISS FM office would be overflowing with cash generated from these weekend activities, and the money would be carefully counted by McNamee's personal assistant, Rosee Laurence, before being paid into the bank. As its imminent licence application noted, KISS FM financed much of its operation through running these very lucrative club nights. The example quoted in the bid document illustrated the potential for profit: "At a 1,000 capacity venue – with admission £6 – a function can expect door revenue of £6,000. After costs, this can leave a club-runner with – at the very least – a net profit of £2,500. Club-running had become an occupation [for KISS FM]." Much of the publicity campaign surrounding KISS FM's licence bid was financed from these successful club nights, but the station still needed a significant new shareholder who was prepared to commit much larger sums of start-up capital. The search continued for a further investor to add to Centurion Press.[417]

At this stage, my involvement with the KISS FM licence bid was still as a casual, unpaid adviser to Gordon McNamee. I was following closely all the developments in the race for new licences to write my weekly column in City Limits magazine, my monthly half-page in For The Record, and any occasional space I could secure in Jocks magazine. Since our initial meeting in January, McNamee and I had spoken regularly on the phone, and I had provided information and advice where I felt it would be of use.

In March 1989, an advertisement appeared in the press, seeking staff to work for a new radio industry magazine. There had been several attempts to publish a radio-only trade publication since the launch of commercial radio in 1973, all of which had ended in failure. The industry had still not become large enough to sustain substantial amounts of paid-for advertising, or to build a large enough circulation to make such a publication financially viable. Then, EMAP plc, a major publisher of consumer magazines and regional newspapers, announced plans to launch Radio & Music, a fortnightly, glossy magazine aimed at the music radio sector. EMAP had established its reputation as one of the twenty fastest growing companies in the UK, with an annual turnover of £189m. It believed the time was right for a radio publication: "The radio industry is undergoing a radical change and deserves a radical voice to reflect the new environment ... We will be the sole magazine devoted to the radio industry in all its guises ..."[418]

I was eager to secure further outlets for my writings about the radio industry, so I rang the phone number in the recruitment advert. I spoke to Brian Davis, the magazine's managing editor, and arranged to meet him at EMAP's John Street office at 6 pm on 22 March. There, on the top floor of MEED House, I found a group of advertising executives selling space in EMAP magazines by phone with a ferocity and aggressiveness I had never before witnessed. Davis greeted me warmly and the two of us moved into the penthouse meeting room, where he expanded upon the philosophy behind the magazine's launch. I ran through my experience in radio and my writings about the radio industry, and I expressed interest in writing for the magazine in either a full-time or freelance capacity. Davis showed me the draft layout of a pilot issue scheduled for April publication, and he asked my opinion of some of the planned content.

He expressed interest in employing me in some capacity on the magazine, and asked me to submit two examples of my work: an opinion piece on one aspect of the radio industry that I felt was pertinent to the magazine's readership; and a list of twenty editorial items I felt should be included regularly in the new publication. I obliged by writing an editorial on the conservatism of commercial radio playlists, and I drafted a list of twenty suggested features that included:

- "sit in on a particular show & examine success/failure
- pick a city/area & examine the radio market
- details of artists' radio promotion tours
- who's pushing what – record companies/pluggers' hitlists
- giveaway sampler CDs."[419]

I sent my suggestions to Brian Davis and awaited his response. I was still keen to be more involved in KISS FM, but it was not earning me any money. Right now, some additional income from writing about radio would be particularly useful for me. I was hoping that Davis might offer me a post or, at the very least, some freelance work.

While I awaited a response to the ideas I had sent to Davis, the competition for the London-wide FM radio licence was intensifying.

---

[401] "IBA Advertises First Five Incremental ILR Contracts", IBA press release no. 02/89, 10 Jan 1989.
"IBA Advertises Second Batch Of Five Incremental ILR Contracts", IBA press release no. 15/89, 6 Feb 1989.
[402] "IBA Faces Block Over Franchises", Broadcast, 24 Feb 1989.
[403] "IBA Advertises Third Batch Of Five Incremental ILR Contracts", IBA press release no. 22/89, 6 Mar 1989.
[404] author's recording, 6 Mar 1989.
[405] ibid.
[406] ibid.
[407] "One Licence Under A Groove", KISS FM's Written Word no. 4, Feb 1989.
[408] "The Great Air Race", Broadcast, 3 Mar 1989.
[409] ibid.
[410] "The Big Sell-Out", Broadcast, 31 Mar 1989.
[411] ibid.
[412] Robin Hunt, "Model Beginnings", Media Week, 10 Mar 1989.
[413] Jon Henley, "KISS Wants To Set Up Dance Radio", Music & Media, 4 Mar 1989.
William Owen, "Punters Guide To The Great Race For London FM", Radio & Music, 13 Apr 1989.
[414] Sid Smith, "Kiss And Tell", Time Out, 26 Apr 1989.
[415] Sheryl Garratt, [untitled], The Face, Jan 1989.
[416] David Davies, "KISS", Blitz, Mar 1989.
[417] "KISS FM Greater London FM Application Form: Appendix", KISS FM, 1 Jun 1989.
[418] Brian Davis, "A Radical Voice For Radical Times", Radio & Music, 13 Apr 1989.
[419] Grant Goddard, "20 Things I'd Like To Read About", 28 Mar 1989.

March & April 1989.

At the KISS FM office in Blackstock Mews, work continued on various aspects of the licence application. One important task that needed to be tackled was an assessment of precisely how much advertising revenue a legal incarnation of KISS FM could expect to attract. Budgets had been prepared for the costs of setting up the radio station, but would KISS FM be able to earn enough money from selling advertising spots to cover its overheads? The practice in the British commercial radio industry was for each local station to employ its own team of salespersons to sell airtime to local advertisers (shops, offices and businesses in its own vicinity), whilst national advertisers (such as Coke, Ford, The Sunday Times and Esso) booked their airtime through a radio saleshouse contracted to the station. There were a handful of such saleshouses, mostly based in London, each of which handled contracts for a subset of local commercial stations, dealing directly with large companies and their advertising agencies.

Independent Radio Sales [IRS] was one of the largest radio sales houses which, in London, sold advertisements for the talk station LBC, one of the city's two commercial stations. Both IRS and LBC were owned by Crown Communications plc, a media group that also held minority shareholdings in several other local commercial broadcasters. On 1 March 1989, a lunch was organised between a member of the IRS sales team, John Quinn, and a representative of KISS FM, Guy Wingate, to discuss how much advertising the ex-pirate might be able to attract. Wingate had been heavily involved in KISS FM during its pirate existence and had co-edited the station's '94' newsletter, though he was now working as a journalist for MixMag magazine.

Quinn estimated that IRS could sell £5m worth of 'blue chip' national advertising on KISS FM in its first year, with the saleshouse taking between ten and fifteen per cent of that amount as commission. He suggested that IRS could employ a separate sales force dedicated solely to selling airtime on KISS FM. Quinn proposed that, if KISS FM were to contract IRS as its exclusive sales house, he would enrol the parent company, Crown Communications, into providing assistance with the station's licence bid. Wingate noted this offer in his minutes of the meeting: "If a 'provisional' deal can be struck with IRS for the handling of blue chip accounts, they have signalled a willing commitment to use all their available (and considerable) fire-power in helping to secure a licence for KISS FM. They also have suggestions about who we use for writing the proposal [the licence application]."[420]

Quinn also offered his company's assistance in the possible future syndication of KISS FM programmes to overseas radio stations, and he suggested that Crown Communications might be interested in taking a shareholding in the station's licence bid. Wingate's notes showed him to be justifiably cautious about this particular offer: "I subsequently suggested that, in the unlikely event of this offer being accepted, Crown Communications plc would have to sign a contract restricting them from ever mounting any form or manner of takeover operation, so as to protect the interests of the other [KISS FM] shareholders."[421]

Of more interest to Wingate was Quinn's revelation that Crown Communications was currently seeking approval from the Independent Broadcasting Authority [IBA] to change the format of its LBC FM channel to a specialist music station, whilst maintaining its established talk and news format on its AM frequency. Quinn suggested that KISS FM might want to participate in the new music station, though Wingate noted Crown's doubts about the ex-pirate's standards of professionalism: "They seem to be uncertain as to whether the KISS FM DJs are polished enough to present the Monday through Friday 10 am to 5 pm shows. This is, therefore, something they would have to be VERY STRONGLY convinced of by listening to tapes, auditions etc. I did mention the fact that Dave Pearce and Chris Forbes, amongst others, had expressed an interest in joining a legal KISS FM and would, hence, be obvious material for the Monday to Friday daytime slots."[422]

These proposals from IRS were one of several topics discussed at a meeting of the KISS FM steering group on 15 March 1989, attended by David Evans and Martin Strivens of Centurion Press, Gordon McNamee of KISS FM and chairman designate Keith McDowall. It was quickly agreed that a national sales house, such as IRS, was required for the station, and Strivens and McDowall were delegated to negotiate an appropriate deal. As for the licence application itself, McNamee agreed to prepare a draft version of the form which McDowall would then discuss with his "IBA contacts to establish whether the language and content are broadly acceptable to the IBA." McNamee also told the meeting that 3,000 square feet of office space would be required for the station's premises, and it was agreed to contact estate agent Gross Fine to establish the cost.[423]

Some time was spent discussing the composition of the radio station's board of directors. It was eventually agreed that there should be "fair representation of an ethnic minority, a woman, a known radio broadcasting expert and possibly a representative from education and sport." It was noted that these "board members must be seen to be responsible etc." McNamee's proposal to re-appoint KISS FM's honorary president, comedian Lenny Henry, was accepted, as was the proposal that Tony Prince be appointed as the board member with radio expertise. Forty-five year old Prince had spent two years working as a presenter on offshore pirate Radio Caroline in the 1960s, before moving to Radio Luxembourg in 1968, where he stayed for sixteen years, latterly as programme director. Subsequently, he had launched the Disco Mix Club [DMC], a DJ subscription service, and its associated magazine, MixMag.[424]

A more contentious issue for discussion was the shareholding structure of the company. McNamee was insistent that seven KISS FM DJs should be allotted shares in the new legalised station, since they were existing shareholders in Goodfoot Promotions Limited, McNamee's 'front' company for KISS FM. Besides, he argued, 'Madhatter' Trevor Nelson, Jonathan More, Colin Faver, 'DJ' Tee Harris, brothers Joey and Norman Jay, and Dean Savonne had all been an integral part of KISS FM since its pirate beginnings three and a half years earlier. McNamee had already approached these DJs with an earlier recommendation from the steering group that they each be given a one per cent stake in the new company, but he now reported back that "his DJs were less than happy" with this arrangement. So, it was agreed that their stakes should be increased to two per cent each, plus a one per cent share of the company's profits. The revised shareholding structure was now: McNamee – forty-eight per cent; Centurion Press – thirty-three per cent; the seven DJs to share fourteen per cent; and McDowall – five per cent.[425]

The station's budget was also discussed at the meeting and lengthy explanations were necessary as to why KISS FM required new "uplifted turnover/profit figures." It was thought that the company's likely funding requirement would now be £350,000, and Strivens agreed to go away and calculate a new set of figures.[426]

The next day, Strivens asked Centurion's group accountant, Jeff Rajpoot, to set up a new company named 'KISS FM Limited,' while he worked on revising the shareholder structure of the station, in accordance with the percentages that had been agreed at the meeting. The total share capital necessary would now be £50,000, supplemented by £150,000 of secured convertible loan stock (£130,000 from Centurion and the rest from McDowall). The remaining £150,000 was to be arranged through a lease fund and a bank overdraft.[427]

The following week, Keith McDowall reported to the other steering group members some new information that he had gleaned from his contacts at the IBA. He had been told that an advertisement for the London-wide FM radio licence would be published in the 3 April edition of The Evening Standard newspaper. It was anticipated that eighty groups would apply. McDowall noted: "The depth of the [winner's] financial resources will be important. The IBA does not want an embarrassing TV-AM flop on its hands. It will therefore want to see demonstrated that the applicant not only has start-up cash, but major financial resources for the longer term." McDowall also suggested that KISS FM should create an advisory committee, with members "covering diverse fields like the ethnic aspect, unions and other groupings." At Centurion, David Evans scribbled "very interesting" on his copy of McDowall's memo.[428]

On 31 March 1989, Gordon McNamee contacted the other steering group members by fax, updating them as to what he had achieved since their last meeting. He noted that Ralph Simon of the music publishing company Zomba Music had been in touch with him, "trying to talk his way into the organisation." However, the IBA had informed McNamee that record and music publishing companies were not allowed to be shareholders in radio licences. Simon "was very insistent, claiming that he was sure he could get involved in some way" and had asked McNamee to arrange a meeting for him with David Evans. On other matters, McNamee reported that contact had been established with several journalists working for broadsheet newspapers, many of whom seemed interested in running stories about KISS FM's licence bid. McNamee also noted that KISS FM would be featured in the next edition of Channel Four Television's 'The Media Show,' which was to address the topic of the new London radio licences.[429]

The following day, a letter arrived at the KISS FM office from David Vick, the IBA's principal radio development officer. It said: "You have previously contacted us to indicate your interest in applying for an incremental independent local radio contract covering the Greater London (VHF/FM) area. I am pleased to tell you that this is among the contracts which we are advertising next week." The IBA press release enclosed with the letter explained that the new station would broadcast to a potential audience of 6,450,000 adults. An accompanying map showed the station's service area as stretching from Hoddesdon in the north to Caterham in the south, and from Slough in the west to Basildon in the east. Although this area was smaller than the one that the IBA had granted in 1973 to the London pop music station Capital Radio, it was significantly larger than KISS FM's proposal to serve only the Central London area. The press release noted that each applicant's proposed station "should increase the diversity of radio choice available to listeners in the Greater London area." The closing date was 5 June 1989, and the winner would be announced in July. That left KISS FM only two months to finalise the details of its application.[430]

The TV programme 'The Media Show' that McNamee had mentioned in his memo proved to be good publicity for KISS FM. The programme was introduced by presenter Muriel Gray in her typically upbeat style: "Part of the reason that pirate radio, often run from the luxury of a bedroom or a garage, has flourished in Britain is that official radio doesn't exactly offer a huge choice to the listener. Babbling fools playing bland music on one hand, and upper class English voices discussing P.G. Wodehouse on the other, doesn't quite echo the diversity of tastes in a modern multi-racial country."[431]

Although McNamee and DJ Norman Jay were interviewed about KISS FM, most of the programme focused on the heavyweight competition it faced from Andrew Lloyd Webber's classical music bid, Richard Branson's Virgin group, and a rock music bid funded by a TV facilities company. The show alleged that there existed "a built-in bias towards those who already have the necessary financial backing," and it cited a comment made by the IBA director of radio Peter Baldwin: "If there is big money in whichever group you care to choose, then that will achieve what our chairman George Russell has said recently – that the quality of money is there to sustain a good service – and so it doesn't worry us at all that some big names have entered the field."[432]

The need to expand KISS FM's capital base was beginning to look more and more essential in order for the station to win a licence, and the race was on to find another major investor who would prove compatible with McNamee and Centurion Press.

In a seemingly unrelated occurrence, I attended the opening ceremony of the fifth UK Music Radio Conference on the evening of 4 April 1989, organised by the Radio Academy at the HMV Megastore record shop in London's Oxford Street. The event itself was largely an opportunity for the radio industry to indulge in mutual back-slapping, but I was there in the hope that it might provide some source material for a radio article. I bumped into Brian Davis, managing editor of publisher EMAP's new magazine Radio & Music, to whom I had not spoken since our initial meeting the previous month. I had yet to receive a response from him to the ideas I had submitted. Davis introduced me to his associate publisher, Peter Gould, and we exchanged small talk about the magazine's impending launch. Recognising me across the crowded room, KISS FM's Lindsay Wesker came to join our conversation and, once I had introduced him to the others, the topic switched to the ex-pirate station's prospect of winning a London FM licence. Gould was very enthusiastic about KISS FM's chances and showed particular interest in learning that the station was seeking a further investor. He suggested that a meeting with his superiors at EMAP could prove productive.

After that initial chance contact, EMAP was very quickly drawn into discussions about involvement in the KISS FM licence bid. On 12 April, Gordon McNamee met Keith McDowall once more to discuss progress made with the licence application, and McDowall agreed to arrange a meeting with EMAP chairman Sir Frank Rogers. McNamee and McDowall also talked about potential new board members in more detail, while McNamee promised to chase up a reply from Lenny Henry about his position as honorary president. McDowall's suggestions for new board members included: Walter Hayes, former vice president of public affairs at the Ford Motor Company; Dennis Trevelyan, the former First Civil Service commissioner; Sir Barney Hayhoe, Conservative MP; Lord Pitt, whom McDowall described as the "first coloured peer in Lords"; musicians Johnny Dankworth and Cleo Laine; Lord Mellish, former MP for Bermondsey; Brenda Dean, SOGAT union general secretary (and McDowall's wife); Harry

Morton, retiring general secretary of the Musicians' Union; and jazz musicians Humphrey Lyttleton and Dave Shepherd. Like McDowall, none of these suggested directors for KISS FM had previous experience in the radio industry.[433]

McDowall arranged the appointment with EMAP chairman Sir Frank Rogers a few days later, but informed McNamee that his presence was not required, since Martin Strivens would accompany him to the meeting. Despite McDowall's and Strivens' lack of detailed knowledge about KISS FM and the radio industry, Rogers quickly agreed to be a director, if EMAP could take a shareholding in the radio station equal to the amount already held by Centurion Press.[434]

A couple of days later, John Quinn of radio saleshouse IRS followed up his earlier meeting with KISS FM's Guy Wingate by creating a draft ratecard that showed the revenues he anticipated the station could earn during its first year of operation. Quinn still estimated the total to be between £3m and £8m, dependent upon how selective the discounts offered to advertisers might be. He calculated that KISS FM should charge an advertiser £250 for a single thirty-second advertisement broadcast in the station's weekday breakfast show. Only three months earlier, McNamee had calculated the station's first budget on the assumption that such an advert would cost £25. The difference showed how quickly KISS FM was growing, in terms of the commercial dividends its stakeholders were expecting to reap from the station.[435]

The search continued for appropriate board members to add to the station's management team. McNamee knew that the one person who could simultaneously lend the station authority with the establishment, whilst reinforcing the ex-pirate's street credibility, was comedian Lenny Henry. Therefore, it came as quite a blow when Henry's agent, Robert Luff, turned down McNamee's invitation for his client to join the KISS FM board. Luff's letter said: "My client Lenny Henry, who is very committed to professional engagements at the moment, has asked me to write on his behalf … He appreciates your invitation to join your board, but quite frankly his present commitments are such that he could not possibly consider taking on any further responsibilities. However, he sends his best wishes and sincerely hope [sic] that you will succeed in establishing your black music station."[436]

It was unclear whether Henry's decision was, to any extent, influenced by the public rumpus a few months earlier over his television portrayal of a pirate radio DJ, or by earlier revelations of his figurehead role in the pirate incarnation of KISS FM. The rejection letter disappointed McNamee bitterly, since Henry's name had already been publicly associated with the station as its honorary president, and it might seem as if the comedian had purposefully withdrawn his support from the station's bid to become legitimate.

Two days prior to Henry's agent writing the letter, the government had launched another attack on pirate radio. In a written Parliamentary Answer, the Secretary of State for Trade & Industry, Lord Young, said that he had received a number of presentations about the increasing number of unlicensed stations. He pointed out that the 444 raids made during the previous year represented an all-time record for the DTI, and he promised new, tougher legislation: "In the forthcoming Broadcasting Bill, the government will be seeking additional powers to make it an offence to supply goods and services for the operation of an unlicensed station, to advertise on an unlicensed station, or to solicit others to do so and to be engaged in the operation of an unlicensed station."[437]

That week, twenty-seven pirate stations were reported to be operating in London and, although the 'old guard' of soul pirates – KISS FM, Solar, LWR and TKO – were no longer active, there were plenty of newcomers who had arrived to take their places. Stations such as WLR, Peoples FM, Star, Crystal, Medina, Big Apple, and Supreme all operated black music formats in North London; while Lightning, Rock II Rock, Sky and Tropical served the South. The weekend-only station, Starpoint FM, was one of the few long running stations to have continued broadcasting beyond the 1 January 1989 deadline. Strong rumours persisted that LWR was currently preparing a licence application in competition with KISS FM, though no one seemed to be aware of the details.[438]

At KISS FM, now that a second major investor had been recruited in the form of EMAP, work could concentrate on finalising the licence application form. In early April 1989, EMAP launched the pilot issue of Radio & Music magazine although, strangely, its editorial was not particularly positive about KISS FM's chances of winning the London FM licence. From a personal perspective, I was frustrated to find that, during this and the magazine's following issues, several feature ideas which I had proposed had been used. The magazine's managing editor, Brian Davis, had never contacted me again.[439]

Although the prospect of paid work for Radio & Music had failed to materialise, I was being kept increasingly busy working on KISS FM's licence application (though unpaid).

---

[420] Guy Wingate, "Summary Of Ideas Proposed By Crown Communications plc", 1 Mar 1989.
[421] ibid.
[422] ibid.
[423] "Minutes Of A Meeting Held On 15th March 1989", KISS FM, 15 Mar 1989.
[424] ibid.
Rodney Collins, "Radio Luxembourg 1979", Radio Luxembourg, London, 1978.
"KISS FM Greater London Licence Application", KISS FM, Jun 1989.
[425] "Minutes Of A Meeting Held On 15th March 1989", op cit.
[426] ibid.
[427] "Suggested Share Holders Equity Structure For KISS FM", 16 Mar 1989.
[428] "KISS FM" memo, 23 Mar 1989.
[429] letter from Gordon McNamee, 31 Mar 1989.
[430] letter from David Vick, IBA to KISS FM, 31 Mar 1989.
"IBA Completes Advertisements Of Incremental ILR Contracts ...", IBA press release no. 34/89, 3 Apr 1989.
[431] "The Media Show", Channel Four TV, 9 Apr 1989.
[432] ibid.
[433] Keith McDowall, "Note of mtg with Gordon McNamee 12.4.89", 12 Apr 1989.
[434] fax from Keith McDowall to KISS FM, 14 Apr 1989.
[435] fax from John Quinn, IRS to KISS FM, 14 Apr 1989.
[436] letter from Robert Luff to KISS FM, 20 Apr 1989.
[437] Hansard, Written Answers, 18 Apr 1989.
[438] Grant Goddard, "Radio", City Limits, 6 & 20 Apr 1989.
[439] William Owen, "Punters Guide To The Great Race For London FM", Radio & Music, 13 Apr 1989.

April & May 1989.

KISS FM had been off the air for several months by now, but the station's growing number of club nights continued to prove phenomenally successful. In addition to club events organised under the station's own name, many of its DJs were busy organising their own clubs and music recording activities.

Jazzie B's group, Soul II Soul, had scraped into the bottom of the British top seventy-five singles chart during 1988 with its first two single releases, 'Fairplay' and 'Feel Free,' and these songs had already become club anthems in London. It was the group's next single release, in March 1989, entitled 'Keep On Moving,' featuring vocals by lovers rock singer Caron Wheeler, that turned Soul II Soul into international pop stars. Spending three months on the chart, the record peaked at number five, and its ground-breaking style influenced the tempo and sound of a lot of soul and dance music over the next few years.

Two other KISS FM DJs, Jonathan More and Matt Black, who produced records under the name Coldcut, had already achieved a number six chart placing the previous year with 'Doctorin' The House' featuring singer Yazz. Their follow-up single, 'Stop This Crazy Thing,' with vocals by Junior Reid, had reached number twenty-one. Coldcut's next single, 'People Hold On,' released in March 1989, reached number eleven and brought to the world's attention its featured singer, Lisa Stansfield.

Another KISS FM DJ, Richie Rich, had dented the chart in 1988 with his rap single 'Turn It Up,' and had reached number twenty-two with his re-mix of The Jungle Brothers' song 'I'll House You.' Now, Rich was busy promoting a new solo track, 'Salsa House', which reached the top fifty later in 1989.

KISS FM's roots reggae crew Manasseh had mixed a version of Yazz's single, 'Fine Time,' which was included on the twelve-inch pressing and had reached number nine in the singles chart during February 1989.

Another KISS DJ, Bob Jones, had been responsible for finding the old American soul song, 'The Only Way Is Up,' which Yazz had covered and had made a number one single in 1988.

All these artists' records had been played extensively on KISS FM in its pirate days, which had helped them build their followings amongst London club-goers. It seemed rather unfair that many of these artists were now experiencing significant success in the pop music charts, just when KISS FM was off the air and could no longer directly promote their records. Everyone was pleased to witness these friends' mainstream successes but, at the same time, there was disappointment that KISS FM could not somehow share in it. More than that, McNamee seemed somewhat jealous that many of his DJs had created successful businesses out of their work for KISS FM, whilst he himself could only cling to the hope of winning a radio licence. All around him, his DJs were experiencing creative success. Steve Jackson was recording under the name The Garden Of Eden; Norman Jay was remixing MFSB's 'Love Is The Message,' overlaid with a Martin Luther King speech; Manasseh had released a reggae LP 'Sound Iration In Dub'; Jay Strongman had released a single 'East West'; and Coldcut were working with Neneh Cherry. McNamee must have felt desperate for a taste of this kind of success.

With KISS FM off the airwaves, it was becoming more problematic for the office staff at Blackstock Mews to maintain regular contact with the station's large team of DJs. In April 1989, McNamee sent a note to them all, requesting their attendance at a KISS FM general meeting to be held one Monday evening in the office. The letter admitted that "we haven't been together in the same room for quite a while" and noted: "All people who have anything to do with KISS FM are invited, which includes DJs, Word team and new members."[440]

On the morning of 24 April 1989, the Independent Broadcasting Authority [IBA] announced the winners of the first four incremental licences it had advertised in January. The Bristol licence was awarded to ex-reggae pirate station For The People whose bid had been up against five other competitors. The ethnic licence for Hounslow in West London was won by Asian ex-pirate Sina Radio over eleven other bidders. In Manchester, soul station Sunset Radio beat nine other applicants in a successful outcome to its many years of campaigning for a licence. The other winner, in Stirling, was a community radio group. These results were very encouraging for KISS FM's campaign, as they demonstrated that the IBA was prepared to legalise both ex-pirate stations and black music applicants. These licence successes, albeit outside of London, were one of several positive pieces of news that Gordon McNamee could impart to the general meeting held that evening, and would help offset the disappointment that Lenny Henry was no longer involved in KISS FM.[441]

The meeting was held in the downstairs room of the Blackstock Mews office, which was cleared of all its accumulated junk and rubbish for the occasion. Office chairs, used by staff in the upstairs office, were brought down for people to sit on, supplemented by a collection of some twenty orange vinyl stacking chairs that KISS FM had inherited. The only drawback was that these chairs were designed for use by young children, so that their miniature seats were barely a foot about ground level, making them very uncomfortable to sit upon for any length of time. More than thirty people drifted into the meeting during the course of the evening, and had to sit in the cramped and sweaty atmosphere of this unventilated room. Several DJs brought their mobile telephones and pagers with them, which would periodically ring and interrupt the flow of the discussion. McNamee had bought a substantial supply of canned beer and orange juice for those present, which naturally made the whole affair increasingly boisterous as the evening progressed.

The meeting started much later than advertised and resembled more of a chaotic stage show than an organised committee. McNamee stood at the front, facing everyone, and spent the evening rambling through a list of topics scribbled on the piece of paper held in his hand – the closest the meeting had to an agenda. This shambolic get-together was held together by McNamee's ability to skilfully manipulate the crowd he faced. He projected a stage persona that was a cross between a streetwise sixth form teacher and a football club manager addressing his team. Hecklers were dealt with by sharp one-liners; voices of dissent were listened to, but their arguments were countered not by reasoned argument, but with amiable jokes; private conversations that broke out in corners of the room were stamped upon by a quick witty rebuke.

McNamee was incredibly adept at handling this sort of event – he was an entertainer, a showman and a clever raconteur. He could work this crowd of his associates very easily, appealing to their vision of him as a like-minded comrade and an amiable friend whilst, at the same time, earning for him their respect as their leader and boss. McNamee's confidence in his own act increased visibly as the evening went on and greater quantities of alcohol were consumed. By the end of the meeting, he had the audience eating out of his hand.

The bulk of that meeting was spent running through the progress that had made been with KISS FM's licence application since the station had voluntarily left the airwaves almost four months earlier. McNamee explained that KISS had acquired two new shareholders, Centurion Press and EMAP, and he introduced several of the new people (including me) who had become involved in the station during recent months. The mood of the meeting was generally optimistic, though worries were expressed that the London FM licence would inevitably be awarded to an establishment figure such as Andrew Lloyd Webber. Copies were distributed to everyone present of the latest issue of KISS FM's Written Word magazine. The get-together also gave many DJs a chance to catch up on each other's club and recording activities, now that they no longer had the forum of the station's weekly broadcasts.

Later that week, Zomba Music renewed its interest in securing a stake in KISS FM. The company's executive director Ralph Simon spoke to Martin Strivens at Centurion Press about his desire to join the station's licence bid, and followed this up the next day with a three-page memo that detailed the Zomba Group's businesses. Simon's keenness to strike a deal was evident in the sign-off to his letter: "We believe that our broad range of professional services will not in any way produce conflict within the framework of your application to the IBA. I would appreciate if you would revert to me after your meeting, to advise if we can progress our hoped-for involvement in the consortium applying for the required operating licence/franchise."[442]

Strivens could only reiterate to Simon the information that McNamee had already given him following his initial enquiry. The IBA was quite specific in barring companies directly involved in music publishing or record production from holding any substantial shareholding in commercial radio companies. Their reasoning was that such companies could abuse their position by exerting influence over their radio station's programming and playlists, to their own commercial advantage.

In early May, a further meeting was held in the downstairs room of KISS FM's Blackstock Mews office. This time, the desks from the upstairs room were carried downstairs and pushed together in the shape of a rectangle, with a large space in the middle. McNamee sent out a note to a select few, asking them to attend a "commitee [sic] meeting" to discuss the progress that was being made with the licence application. This was to be a very different meeting from the informal one held a couple of weeks earlier in the same room, since only around a dozen of the people most intimately involved with the application were invited. In addition to the KISS FM office staff and the steering committee, Dave Cash was there as programme director designate, Tony Monson represented the Solar Radio element of the bid, and Graham Gold, accompanied by DJ Dave Gregory, similarly represented the S.O.U.L. licence bid.[443]

The meeting discussed several areas of the application process, but steered clear of any detail about the bid's financial arrangements or the company's shareholders. It was agreed that the KISS FM bid needed to be accompanied by an intensive publicity campaign to raise the station's profile, particularly in the establishment press, to the level that was currently being achieved by Andrew Lloyd Webber's competing bid. It was also agreed that a 'corporate brochure' should be produced to convey the spirit of the ex-pirate station, but which should also communicate the most important pieces of information about the structure and purpose of the KISS FM bid. This would be accompanied by a cassette audiotape that would give people an idea of how KISS FM would sound, were it to win the London FM licence.

One of the problems KISS FM had regularly encountered was journalists' misunderstanding that the ex-pirate was some sort of ethnic radio group, rather than a music station that had more in common with Capital Radio or BBC Radio One. A similar problem arose from the inability of many in the media to understand that the term 'black music' did not refer to music that was only listened to by London's black population. An exasperated McNamee had told 'The Media Show' a few weeks earlier: "It's difficult to explain to people that there's such a big culture of people that love music. It's a way of life for them ... this isn't just black people or white people. It's a whole cosmopolitan culture that love music."[444]

McNamee also wrote a letter to the trade magazine Broadcast, which it published as a follow-up to its March editorial on community radio: "KISS FM evolved from London's black music community and, undoubtedly, much of our massive audience comes from the black music community, but we are not an ethnic station and we do not plan to programme for racial communities ... We are proud to be called a 'community' station, but we are emphatically a 'specialist music' station."[445]

It was important that the proposed KISS FM brochure should prove as impressive as anything produced by its competitors for the London licence. At the same time, the brochure needed to explain very precisely why London needed a dance music station, rather than a classical music or rock music station. With less than a month to go before the closing date for licence applications, there was a tremendous amount of work that still needed to be done. At the end of the meeting, Dave Cash handed out a photocopied note to those present that listed the phone numbers at which he could be contacted. Alongside Capital Radio's switchboard number, he had written: "careful – cool message only." During the meeting, McNamee had explained why Cash's involvement in the KISS FM bid must remain a secret. If his current employer, Capital Radio, ever knew that he was involved in a potential competitor on London's airwaves, he was likely to lose his job.

The budget set aside for KISS FM's licence application was £11,954, of which £5,000 was accounted for by Dave Cash's fee. £2,025 was allocated to the corporate brochure, £1,154 to the accompanying cassette tapes, and £2,075 for the design and printing of the application itself, including the planned appendix of telephone directory proportions. EMAP had agreed to contribute £3,490 towards these costs, but the remainder were to be met by Centurion Press, who would absorb the application's typesetting and printing costs by handling the work within their own company.[446]

The most pressing need was to have some good quality colour photos of the personnel involved in the KISS FM licence bid. Up until then, the station had still been using two black and white group photos of the DJ team that had been shot a couple of years earlier. By now, these photos had appeared in the press many times and it was time to organise some new ones. The Sunday after the committee meeting, everyone involved in KISS FM was asked to assemble at the Blackstock Mews office at 1 pm for a new group photograph.

Sunday 7 May 1989 turned out to be one of the hottest days of the summer. I arrived at the KISS FM office in the morning to help with preparations for the photo session. Blackstock Mews was only a short cul-de-sac, all of whose properties had been converted into small business units and workshops. At the far end of the street was an L-shaped turning area for cars, and a whitewashed wall that would serve as an ideal backdrop for a group photograph. All the office chairs were carried outside to the end of the Mews, along with three large KISS FM banners that were usually hung inside venues on KISS FM club nights. Balanced on a ladder, I hammered the banners into the whitewashed wall and arranged the chairs in front of them, in preparation for the photo session.

Many station DJs were unable to attend because of other commitments or because of the short notice they had been given. By early afternoon, we had gathered together twenty-nine people, all of whom were asked to don either a T-shirt or a cap emblazoned with the KISS FM logo. The patient photographer took three different shots of the KISS FM staff – one of the whole team, one of just the DJs, and one of the talks team. Everyone was sweltering in the intense heat, which was made worse by the whitewashed wall and the lack of a breeze at the end of the Mews. McNamee positioned himself in the middle of the front row for the group shots and, while the rest of us wore T-shirts and jeans, he played the part of the station's managing director by dressing in a suit and tie. The photos turned out very well, except that you could see the sun reflected in the pool of sweat on McNamee's forehead.

Once the outdoor group photographs had been completed, a second photographer worked inside the Blackstock Mews office, taking individual head-and-shoulder portraits of the KISS FM DJs and the station's office staff. Those DJs who had been unable to attend that Sunday were photographed separately at the beginning of the following week in North London's Livingston Studios. Both sets of photographs were quickly developed and printed, ready to be incorporated into the design of the KISS FM brochure.

The booking of the photographers and design of the brochure was co-ordinated by Lyn Champion (née Armstrong), who had known McNamee for several years, although she had not been part of the pirate KISS FM team. Champion had worked as radio editor of City Limits magazine in the mid-1980s and had written extensively about unlicensed radio, before joining BBC Radio Four in 1987 to produce a new youth programme, 'WPFM,' that sounded quite similar to the output of London's soul music pirate stations. In 1988, she had left the BBC to become a partner in a music video production company called Pressure, and she was now assisting KISS FM's licence campaign in her spare time.

Champion knew a design company in Manchester that was prepared to work on KISS FM's brochure for no payment, but in anticipation of the good publicity it could earn from the project. She provided the designers with a written brief:

"This brochure is to be sent out (with a seven-minute sound cassette summarizing the sound of KISS) to advertiser/radio industry people/press/business people and record companies as well as the public ... KISS has three weeks to apply for this licence – it's in the middle of a very competitive campaign, against Andrew Lloyd Webber's opera station and a rock AOR station (yawn zzz). The brochure needs to be forceful, authoritative and businesslike, whilst conveying the fresh, new radical, stylish and happening feel of the station! EASY!"[447]

Champion used her substantial powers of persuasion to convince the design company that this was a project worthwhile it taking on, and she dangled the prospect of KISS FM's radio licence which, "if it happens, we're talking mega-bucks and mega karma." In addition to the colour photos of the KISS FM team that the brochure would include, it was planned to incorporate a montage of colour images that were pertinent to the station's image. For a couple of days, everyone in the KISS FM office searched through their photo collections and hundreds of back issues of old music magazines, tearing out anything that they felt communicated the spirit of the radio station.[448]

On the other side of the brochure were to be printed a number of short paragraphs that explained the station's history, its successes and its plans for the future. I set to work writing what would quickly become thirteen mission statements that summarised the positive aspects of KISS FM's licence bid. Within only a few days of the photo session, all of the brochure's elements were packaged together and sent to Manchester – photos, text, the station logo and dozens of photographic images.[449]

While the KISS FM office staff were being kept busy organising the station's publicity campaign, Gordon McNamee was still pre-occupied with finalising the management structure of his dream radio station.

---

[440] letter from Gordon McNamee to "Dear All", 17 Apr 1989.
[441] "IBA Awards First Batch Of Incremental ILR Contracts", IBA Press Release no. 41/89, 24 Apr 1989.
[442] fax from Ralph Simon, Zomba Group to Martin Strivens, Centurion Press, 27 Apr 1989.
[443] letter to Grant Goddard from Gordon Mac, KISS FM, 20 Apr 1989.
[444] "The Media Show", Channel Four TV, 9 Apr 1989.
[445] Gordon McNamee, "KISS Was Created For The Community", Broadcast, 14 Apr 1989.
[446] "Pre Launch Expenditure", KISS FM, [undated].
[447] memo from Lyn Champion to Roy Patterson & Associates, [undated].
[448] ibid.
[449] Grant Goddard, "Blurb For Corporate Brochure", 9 May 1989.

May 1989.

To complete KISS FM's licence application, there were two outstanding matters that Gordon McNamee still had to resolve: the company's board of directors; and the management structure the station would operate if the bid were successful. The composition of the board involved several difficult considerations, all of which had to be satisfied simultaneously. McNamee did not want to lose control of the company, making it important that he include, amongst the directors, as many trusted associates as possible. At the same time, each major shareholder required a seat on the board as a pre-requisite for their investment in KISS FM. Additionally, it had been agreed that the board should appear representative of the different interests in the station and must include at least one prominent person from London's black community.

During the course of the application process, the list of proposed board members was amended regularly, reflecting the influence exerted at any one moment by those interests representing money and power. An early version had proposed ten board members: McNamee himself, two representatives of shareholder Centurion Press, two representatives of shareholder EMAP, individual shareholder Keith McDowall, KISS FM DJ Trevor Nelson, sportsman Garth Crooks, an "IBA man" and a separate chairman. Later, this was amended to nine board members: McNamee, McDowall as a shareholder and chairman, Martin Strivens representing Centurion Press, Sir Frank Rogers representing EMAP, Dave Cash as programme director, Trevor Nelson, the station's (yet to be appointed) sales & marketing director, plus two independent directors selected from three names – footballer John Fashanu, ex-Radio Luxembourg man Tony Prince, and McDowall's friend Dennis Trevelyan.

McNamee had argued that Trevor Nelson should be a full board member, acting as the representative of the seven KISS FM DJs who were to take shareholdings in the company. This arrangement also helped McNamee feel more secure about his power over the board, since he knew he could count on Nelson as a loyal friend, in addition to Martin Strivens, as an employee of family friend David Evans, and on Evans himself. Of the suggested board names, John Fashanu accepted the invitation and agreed to attend the company's planned six board meetings per year for an annual payment of £6,000. Tony Prince also took up the offer and agreed to campaign for KISS FM's licence bid in the pages of his magazine, MixMag.[450]

By the time the KISS FM licence application was completed, the idea of including the company's sales & marketing director on the board had been dropped, leaving eight named board members. The inclusion of such mature directors as Sir Frank Rogers (aged sixty-nine) and Keith McDowall (aged fifty-nine) pushed up the board's average age to forty-two, which hardly appeared to reflect KISS FM's slogan 'The Sound Of Young London.' For McNamee, this was the price that had to be paid for mounting a heavyweight bid that would stand a chance of winning. Only two directors, Cash and Prince, had previous experience in the commercial radio industry, and neither was to be a shareholder in the company. Cash was on the board as a pre-condition of his one-year employment contract with KISS FM, while Prince was a non-executive director who was extremely busy expanding his Disco Mix Club company through the acquisition of a chain of record shops. There was no guarantee that either of them would be contributing their radio industry expertise to the day-to-day development of KISS FM in the long run.

Nevertheless, with the board composition finalised, McNamee turned his attention to the station's management structure. In the early days of the application process, this had proven a relatively simple task. McNamee's initial plan to run the new KISS FM along the lines of a pirate station with a licence had meant he could promise almost everyone working in the KISS FM office a relatively senior position within the operation. Since then, a number of 'outsiders' had provided assistance to McNamee with various aspects of the licence bid, a development that had forced him to promise positions within the company to a wider circle of people. Tony Monson had been offered a full-time post as a daytime DJ in return for folding his Solar Radio bid into KISS FM's. Graham Gold had been promised the job of breakfast DJ for having similarly merged his S.O.U.L. licence bid with KISS FM's.

Additionally, McNamee knew that Lyn Champion's track record in BBC Radio would lend authority to the KISS FM application. He had not paid Champion for her assistance with the brochure, so he felt he had to promise her a senior position producing KISS FM's speech output. Similarly, McNamee knew that my experience in commercial radio would lend additional weight to KISS FM's application, and so he had to find a carrot to tempt me to continue assisting him without pay. McNamee also realised that this influx of newcomers, in addition to the new shareholders, was bound to create tensions amongst the existing KISS FM staff. They justifiably felt that they had played a large part in making the pirate station such a success story, and they would not take kindly to McNamee offering highly paid jobs to 'outsiders.' However, McNamee understood that his ex-pirate radio staff alone could not win KISS FM the licence. Of necessity, he was being forced to make accommodations and compromises here and now in order to win the station a licence in the future. His loyal staff would have to be appeased at a later date.

Of the three full-time KISS FM staff working in the Blackstock Mews office that were impacted by these changes, it was Lindsay Wesker who could have felt the most aggrieved. He had joined KISS FM as a DJ in 1987, having previously presented programmes for Radio Invicta, LWR and JFM since 1983. Between 1982 and 1984, Wesker had worked as deputy editor of the weekly music newspaper Black Echoes, but had quit to work in the artist & repertoire divisions of two major record companies, WEA and A&M. However, he had exited both companies and was subsequently offered a full-time job by McNamee, working in the KISS FM office. For the last two years, he had acted as label manager for KISS FM's fledgling record company, Graphic Records, and he had co-edited KISS FM's newsletter, The Written Word.

In one of McNamee's earliest plans for the legalised station's management structure, drafted soon after pirate transmissions had ended, Wesker had been provisionally named as KISS FM's head of programming, responsible for the huge team of DJs and all the programmes they presented. Wesker probably thought that such a post within the station was entirely appropriate for him, since he may have felt he knew as much about dance music as many of the station's DJs, and he certainly held firm beliefs as to how the station should sound. He had already communicated many of his ideas about the future shape of a legalised KISS FM in the columns of the station's newsletters. Wesker saw his own lack of experience in the established radio industry as a positive asset, since he was determined not to allow KISS FM to sound anything like the existing stations in London.

More recently, faced with an influx of new people to accommodate, McNamee had had to create new positions, whilst moving around Wesker and other existing post-holders within his staffing plan. While the budgets, salaries and overall size of the planned new KISS FM continued to grow (along with shareholder expectations), McNamee could accommodate some extra jobs, but it necessitated changes. In addition to Graham Gold's secretly agreed role as breakfast show presenter, he had been offered the title of senior producer. Gold's partner in the now defunct S.O.U.L. licence bid, DJ Dave Gregory, was offered the job of senior presenter. Tony Monson was similarly offered a role as senior producer, in addition to his guaranteed daytime show.

Initially, Lyn Champion had been pencilled in by McNamee as yet another station producer, but her experience in producing talk programmes quickly elevated her position to head of news & spoken word. Champion also persuaded McNamee to name her acquaintance, Christine Boar, as assistant to the head of news. Boar had previously worked at BBC Radio One, but had left to join the ill-fated Radio Radio satellite station, and so she was now seeking a new job. McNamee had initially pencilled me into the KISS FM team as head of news & spoken programmes, until he realised that Champion's experience was more suited to that role. Once McNamee understood that I knew how the various component parts of a commercial radio station worked, he gave me the catch-all title of general manager. The idea was that McNamee would be in overall charge of the company, but that I had the necessary industry experience to run the day-to-day radio operations.

However, Dave Cash's new role in the licence bid and his insistence upon a one-year contract as the station's programme director had forced McNamee to make further amendments to the staff plan. My post could no longer be titled general manager, since Cash's position was to be superior to mine and I was to be made accountable to him. McNamee decided that, if Cash were to be programme director, then I would be programme controller beneath him. The logic was that Cash might know a lot about commercial radio, but he knew little about dance music and, at the age of forty-four, was not particularly in touch with 'The Sound Of Young London,' which was KISS FM's rallying cry. At the age of thirty-one, I was younger than Cash, plus I had a very good knowledge of the soul and dance music the station played.

The one person whose role in KISS FM was diminished by these changes was Lindsay Wesker. Before the arrival of Dave Cash and me, Wesker had been promised the post of head of programming (or head of music & programming, as it had been described in some instances). This would have made him directly accountable to McNamee, with responsibility for the station's entire output. The revised plan positioned two new managers between Wesker and McNamee – Dave Cash and me. As a result, Wesker's new title was head of music, a position within the company that was now on a par with Lyn Champion, who also reported to me. I was accountable to Dave Cash who, in turn, was accountable to McNamee. Wesker had suffered not only a diminution of responsibility, but his proposed salary of £15,000 had remained static, whilst it seemed that everyone else's had risen as a result of the whole business plan having been enlarged.

Although no animosity broke out openly, I could feel that Wesker had not taken his effective demotion particularly kindly. The appendix to the licence application, which Wesker had helped to collate, included a section entitled 'The Team Behind KISS FM' which offered biographies of the key personnel within the station. I was conspicuously absent from the list (as was Dave Cash in order to retain his confidential involvement), despite the inclusion of other new recruits such as Lyn Champion, Tony Monson and Graham Gold. Tellingly, Lindsay Wesker's job title was still listed as head of programming. These omissions seemed too pertinent to be coincidental.[451]

The issue of salaries was less contentious amongst most staff, because the amounts promised had continuously increased over recent months, as the licence bid itself had grown in size and expectations. By the time the completed application form was submitted to the Independent Broadcasting Authority [IBA], Gordon McNamee's planned salary as managing director had risen to £40,000, from its initial figure of £18,000 only five months earlier. Dave Cash was to earn £27,500 as programme director, Martin Strivens was to receive £35,000 as financial director (upped from an earlier draft of £30,000), and the unnamed sales & marketing director was to receive £30,000. Lindsay Wesker, Lyn Champion and I were each to earn £15,000, whilst McNamee's personal assistant, Rosee Laurence, was to be paid £13,000. The company's worst paid staff worked in the programming department, where researchers were budgeted at £8,000 each, and a full-time record librarian was to be paid only £6,000. There were glaring inconsistencies within the salary scheme; for example, the station's two typists were to be paid £10,000 each, although the breakfast show DJ would earn only £17,000.

The final business plan now comprised thirty-seven full-time staff and forty part-time staff which, if it had been realised, would have made KISS FM the local commercial station in Britain with the largest staff complement. Over its first full year of operation, the wages and salaries bill alone was now estimated to be around £1m. In the plan, these high costs were to be covered by similarly high revenues that it was expected would be earned from the sale of advertising spots on the station. Despite the optimistic forecasts that radio sales house IRS had provided, which anticipated KISS FM's first year revenues to be between £3m and £8m, the application included a more conservative estimate of £2.5m. This income would be supplemented by £403,000 from KISS FM club nights and the sale of station merchandise, bringing the first year's total revenues to nearly £3m. On this basis, KISS FM was expected to show a profit by its eighth month on-air, and it would be able to repay its investors after only two years in business. The £1.4m of finance necessary to launch the venture would be provided by £412,500 in share capital, £377,500 in loan stock, £350,000 in leasing agreements, and a National Westminster Bank overdraft facility of £250,000.

Just as these details of the KISS FM application were being finalised, two further potential investors suddenly appeared on the horizon. One was the radio advertising saleshouse BMS, the industry's main competitor to IRS. Following its consultation with IRS in March, KISS FM had similarly asked BMS to provide its own estimate of KISS FM's potential revenue and proposed advertising rates. In recent press reports, it had appeared that BMS and its Canadian-born chief executive Terry Bate were seeking shareholdings (both corporately and personally) in many of the incremental radio applicant groups across the country. Scepticism was rife within the radio industry about Bate's motive for such a move. It had been suggested that the existing commercial stations that formed BMS's client base had the most to gain from the failure of the new radio stations with which they would have to compete. BMS had already announced that it held a ten per cent stake in Sunset Radio, the soul station that had just won the new Manchester licence. Either Bate or BMS chairman Terry Smith was to take a seat on Sunset's board, and the trade paper Broadcast went as far as printing Smith's photo above a caption that said: "Smith: to head Sunset Radio?"[452]

Bate approached Gordon McNamee and suggested that BMS could take a stake in KISS FM's application. Initially, his offer was accepted and the station's proposed funding was amended to allow BMS a £90,000 shareholding and £125,000 of loan stock, entitling it to fifteen per cent of voting rights. But then, at a very late stage, Bate insisted that BMS had to be offered a larger stake in the company. This threat was rebuffed, negotiations broke down entirely and Bate withdrew his offer of investment. Whatever Bate's intentions, he effectively messed up the final stages of the budget to be included in KISS FM's licence application. By now, it was too late to revise all the financial figures, so that the planned BMS shareholding had to be relabelled "unallocated." It had to be explained privately to the IBA why such a substantial element of the station's shareholding still appeared to be undetermined.[453]

The second new investor was incorporated into the bid more productively. Cradley Print plc, a Birmingham magazine printing company associated with Centurion Press, took up £30,000 in shares and £40,000 in loan stock, giving it five per cent of voting rights. This commitment did not entitle the company to nominate a director to the KISS FM board, and so offered useful additional capital whilst not diluting the existing board members' control.[454]

Cradley was the company that Centurion Press had sub-contracted to print KISS FM's corporate brochure, and there was tremendous excitement in the Blackstock Mews offices when the finished product was delivered later in May. It was easily the glossiest publicity that KISS FM had produced to date. The finished brochure was more of a full-colour, double-sided poster, approximately A3 in size, that folded like a concertina down to a convenient size to mail out in a long envelope. The printing paper was of high quality and the colour reproduction was excellent. Everyone at KISS FM agreed that it looked far more impressive than any publicity that had so far been produced by competing applicants for the licence.

The other aspect of the station's publicity campaign that still had to be produced was the cassette audiotape intended to give journalists an idea as to how KISS FM would sound on-air if it won the licence. An appropriate space had been left at the bottom of the colour brochure design, specifically so that a cassette could be attached before the package was mailed out. The tape was to comprise two parts: a montage of announcements by KISS FM DJs that would demonstrate the diversity of the music that they played; preceded by a spoken introduction that would state the case for KISS FM to be awarded the London licence. In one draw of his office desk, Gordon McNamee had kept dozens of cassette tapes of KISS FM programmes recorded when the station had been a pirate. However, a quick listen to these cassettes convinced me that the recording quality was not good enough to re-use them.

This meant that a new set of recordings had to be made from scratch, requiring all the KISS FM DJs to arrange individual times to come to the tiny back room studio on the ground floor of the Blackstock Mews office in order to record a typical example of their radio programme. The resulting tapes were then passed to Graham Gold, who agreed to edit them in his home studio. Gold's first attempt at this production work proved unusable because the samples taken from each DJ's programme were far too long, making the tape run substantially beyond the seven minutes' duration that was required. Gold's second attempt proved more satisfactory, so that the work now focused upon the spoken introduction to be placed at the beginning of the tape.

Lindsay Wesker drafted a script for the introduction that filled three typed pages, which he passed to McNamee for approval. Asked my opinion, I told McNamee that I felt it was far too long and far too defensive, displaying a tendency to affect an air of moral superiority and make cheap jibes against KISS FM's competitors for the London licence. Rather than having made a hard-hitting positive case for KISS FM to win, the script criticised other applicants for employing "dubious statistical information" and accused them of seeking the licence "because it's a neat addition to their business portfolio." I also felt that the script dwelled too much on competitors' suggestions that "KISS FM will not have the experience and know-how to run such a station" and that it should not criticise commentators who "foolishly suggested that KISS FM play a narrow spectrum of musics."[455]

I turned Wesker's efforts into something that I felt was a more positive affirmation of KISS FM's achievements, shortening it to two pages of double-spaced script, and submitted this new version to McNamee. I had calculated that this script ran to around three minutes, which was still probably too long. McNamee felt that my abbreviated script needed more detail in several places, and so he re-introduced some of Wesker's original paragraphs that I had removed. The end result was a compromise that proved to be an unsatisfactory hybrid of two very different approaches. Rather than make a pro-active decision one way or the other, McNamee seemed to have drifted into a solution that partially pleased both me and Wesker, but that did KISS FM little justice.[456]

The cobbled together script was sent to Tony Prince to voice. McNamee felt that Prince was the appropriate person to use because he was an established DJ, a respected member of the music industry and a KISS FM board member. Since time was running short, Prince's recorded introduction was sent straight for duplication alongside the completed music section that Gold had prepared earlier. It was only once hundreds of copies of the finished cassettes arrived back at the KISS FM offices that it was realised how dreadful the finished tape sounded. Prince had injected no natural warmth into the script when he had read it, and his voice sounded thin and unconvincing. The introduction now ran for more than five minutes, which was far too long for something so dreadful.

The other aspect of the tape that sounded strange was McNamee's insistence that a snatch of his favourite record be used at its very beginning. This would have been fine, had the track been an example of a hot new dance music track that KISS FM alone had championed. But the KISS FM 'theme tune' that McNamee chose was Fontella Bass' jazzy 1965 recording of the ballad 'Our Day Will Come,' originally an American number one pop hit for Ruby & The Romantics two years earlier. The combination of this laughably middle-of-the-road song, Tony Prince's uninspired introduction, and a succession of KISS FM DJs sounding particularly stilted as they presented obviously faked programmes was a recipe for disaster. The whole tape now lasted almost twenty minutes and proved to be one of the station's rare public relations disasters. Because the cassette duplication had already been completed, and because special inlay cards had already been printed for each tape box, the project had to be seen through to its bitter conclusion.

For several days, everyone in the KISS FM office devoted their entire working time to the packaging and mail out of almost a thousand press packs. I even took a day off work from my part-time job at the record company to assist in the huge operation, which was still not completed by the closing date for licence applications. Within each pack, a printed sticker with the KISS FM logo and the legend 'The Sound Of KISS FM' had to be stuck onto the correct side of the cassette. Then, an eight-panel inlay card with photos of the KISS FM team had to be folded carefully into the cassette box with the tape. This was then attached to the folded colour brochure using a couple of adhesive pads. Each package was slipped into a long envelope, sealed with a tiny thumb-sized sticker printed with the station's logo, and then finished off with an address label and a twenty-eight pence stamp. At the end, all one thousand packages had to be carried by hand to the nearest Post Office, one hundred yards along Blackstock Road from the office, for mailing.

The brochure had turned out brilliantly, even though the cassette tape was somewhat embarrassing. At least the overall package succeeded in elevating KISS FM's image in the media. It easily outshone all the competitors' publicity campaigns. But would all this hard work prove sufficient to win KISS FM the licence, when it was up against so many formidably financed, extremely commercial applicants?

---

[450] letter to John Fashanu from Martin Strivens, Centurion Press, 30 May 1989.
[451] Appendix no. 6, "Appendix: Greater London FM Application Form", op cit.
[452] fax from Terry Bate, BMS to KISS FM, 12 Apr 1989.
"Community Winners Get IR Help", Broadcast, 26 May 1989.
[453] "KISS FM: Summary Of Initial Funding", KISS FM, [undated].
[454] ibid.
[455] untitled draft, 31 May 1989.
[456] "Tony Prince's Introduction For KISS FM Tape", 31 May 1989.

May & June 1989.

After the meeting in March 1989 between John Quinn of IRS and Guy Wingate of KISS FM, Crown Communications had asked commercial radio's regulator, the Independent Broadcasting Authority [IBA], for permission to launch a youth-orientated music-based service on the FM transmitter of its London talk station LBC. Such a proposal might have enabled KISS FM to secure some airtime in London if it lost its own bid for an FM licence. The IBA turned down the proposal, insisting that LBC continue to carry its news and information service on FM, though it did grant permission for the station's AM transmitter to broadcast music for up to forty-nine per cent of each day. In practice, this concession proved impractical to implement, since music radio required the higher quality signal afforded by FM transmissions. The IBA response effectively killed off any potential deal whereby KISS FM could have provided programming to LBC under contract, should it not win the London-wide licence.[457]

Better news arrived from the IBA in May 1989, when the four winners of its second batch of incremental licences were announced. In London, the ethnic licence for Haringey was awarded jointly to London Greek Radio and WNK, both of which were former pirate stations. This decision, along with the London licence awarded the previous month in Hounslow to another ex-pirate station, proved very encouraging for KISS FM.[458]

During the final few weeks before the licence application deadline, the KISS FM staff spent much of their time completing detailed answers to the questions posed in the IBA's twenty-five page form. Several evening meetings were held, attended by the station's key personnel, to thrash out sentences and paragraphs that were felt to be representative of KISS FM's philosophy. These decisions were inevitably preceded by much discussion.

McNamee was becoming increasingly concerned that another bidder, London Jazz Radio, would win the licence. This competing group had secured considerable press coverage in recent weeks, and former KISS FM DJ Gilles Peterson had joined their bid as a company director and presenter of the station's youth-orientated jazz programmes. To counter these developments, McNamee decided to place considerably more emphasis on jazz music in the KISS FM application, in order to demonstrate to the IBA that the station could adequately cover this style of music alongside the others in its programme plans.

One of the evening meetings at Blackstock Mews eventually agreed upon a definitive description of KISS FM that the IBA required to be answered in no more than forty words and which became the 'Promise of Performance' of each applicant. It was decided that: "KISS FM is a music-based, urban contemporary station covering the whole spectrum of dance/black music from jazz through reggae to soul, reflecting the style and fashion of cosmopolitan London."[459]

The final part of this description had initially been drafted as "young London" by McNamee, but others in the group felt this phrase to be ageist, so a Thesaurus was brought to the meeting to identify a more suitable word. Until then, KISS FM's slogan had always been 'Radical Radio' which, as a pirate station, it had emblazoned across its T-shirts, car stickers and publicity. However, concern had been expressed within the steering group that this slogan might appear to the IBA to be too uncompromising to win KISS FM the licence, so it was reluctantly agreed not to mention 'Radical Radio' anywhere in the application.[460]

The other part of the application form that still needed attention were two pages that required a description of the applicant's programme plans. One of these pages was wasted by KISS FM listing thirteen musical styles (house, hip hop, jazz, soca, etc.) and laboriously noting which of the station's "principal DJs" presented a programme playing each music genre. Proposals for four "theme shows" were added underneath, seemingly to fill the allotted space. The second page provided a chronological narrative of a typical day's broadcasting on KISS FM, but which failed to offer a guiding philosophy or detail about the station's programming policy. At McNamee's behest, jazz music was mentioned surprisingly often in this section, which now promised a Monday evening jazz chart, a Sunday lunchtime jazz special, and a jazz show each weekday evening.[461]

The last minute rush to complete the application form had taken its toll, and the overall impression of the KISS FM submission was a lack of attention to detail in answering the IBA's very specific questions. For example, a whole page which the IBA had allotted for each applicant to explain their station's intended audience was barely half-filled by KISS FM's miserly three paragraphs. A half-page space in which applicants were asked to explain how their station's projected revenues were calculated had been answered tersely by KISS FM in two sentences. Although the completed application form rather understated KISS FM's case for a London licence, the attached appendix made up for this deficiency by its sheer weight and detail. In several hundred pages that, together, were one-inch thick, it managed to relate detailed information about KISS FM's most significant history. The appendix ended up weighing 1.3 kg, some way towards the telephone directory-like dimensions I had envisioned, and copies were delivered to the IBA in their own custom-made briefcases.[462]

Unfortunately, there were a few glaring inconsistencies between the application form and the appendix, a product of the split that had already developed within the station's organisation. Apart from the programming areas already mentioned, the application form had been drafted by the steering group – McNamee, Strivens, Evans and McDowall – in conjunction with Dave Cash. Whereas, the appendix had been collated by the KISS FM office staff, with most of the written work prepared by Lindsay Wesker. A lack of communication between the two parties was evident. The four-page 'Brief History Of KISS FM' in the appendix had forecast that the station's audience, by the end of Year One, would be 671,500 adults (or 8.5% of London's population). However, the application form had based its calculations on an audience of one million listeners (fifteen per cent of the population). There were also discrepancies in the station's senior staff and their job titles, which differed between the two documents. In the history of the station in the appendix, neither Lyn Champion nor I were mentioned and, as noted, the biographical section failed to include me either.[463]

Aside from these errors, the appendix did offer a remarkably comprehensive account of KISS FM's history. it included twenty-three pages of press cuttings, a complete set of all KISS FM's magazines from '94' to 'The Written Word,' thirty-five pages of flyers (some reproduced in colour) produced by KISS FM to publicise its club events, and twenty-three pages of technical specifications for the station's proposed studios. Additionally, the full results were included of an audience research survey that KISS FM had commissioned from Market and Opinion Research International shortly before the application deadline, at a cost of £2,875. In it, 296 Londoners aged between fifteen and twenty-four years had been asked eight questions about their radio and music preferences. Thirty-four per cent had said they listened to KISS FM when it was a pirate station, forty-nine per cent preferred the soul, funk and rare groove music that KISS FM played, and seventy-one per cent said they supported KISS FM's bid for a licence.[464]

The appendix should have included copies of the eighty-five letters of support for KISS FM's application from notable persons that had been received. The originals had been stacked in a cardboard box and taken to Centurion Press' premises in the West End, from where the production of the application had been organised. However, the box had been accidentally left on the floor one night, and the company's cleaners had mistakenly assumed it was rubbish and had thrown it out. Unfortunately, no photocopies of these letters had been made, so a list of the correspondents' names was all that could be included in the appendix.[465]

The application form and the appendix were each held together with black spiral bindings. On the covers of both, the red and blue KISS FM logo was superimposed over the sheet music of McNamee's theme song for the station, 'Our Day Will Come.' Accompanying these two documents was a sheet of stiff board emblazoned with the words 'The Sound Of KISS FM' in red, to which was affixed a copy of the cassette audiotape that started with that same song. On the morning of Monday 5 June 1989, McNamee delivered eight copies of the application documents to the IBA office in London's Brompton Road, directly opposite Harrods department store. David Vick, the IBA's principal radio development officer, wrote a receipt to "Mr G. McNanee [sic], KISS FM."[466]

It was only five months since KISS FM had closed down as a pirate station, but there already seemed to be a world of difference between the weekend-only radio station it had been then and the business organisation that it had already become. After submitting the documents to the IBA, McNamee returned briefly to the KISS FM office before heading home to pack his suitcases. The next day, accompanied by his wife, he flew off for a two-week holiday at his parent's villa in Spain.

I had agreed to take a week's holiday from my part-time job at the record company to help run (unpaid) the KISS FM office during the first week of McNamee's absence. Much of my time was spent completing the huge mail-out of publicity brochures and accompanying cassettes that had taken far longer to organise than we had anticipated. To help deal with the steady stream of phone enquiries that the KISS FM office was receiving from journalists, I wrote and produced a set of briefing documents about the station's licence bid. Four double-sided sheets tackled, in turn, 'The Case For KISS FM,' its proposed programmes, its intended audience, and its financing. Each one was photocopied onto pink paper using black and red ink, and I included an optimistic quote that I created and attributed to McNamee: "We already have four years' solid experience of broadcasting as an unlicensed station. Our reputation is well established as a popular radio service that plays many types of music largely ignored by existing stations. We are literally ready and waiting to go – all we need now is the IBA licence."[467]

That week, there was also a new thirty-two page issue of KISS FM's magazine 'The Written Word' to mail out to the thousands of people on the station's mailing list. In an editorial column, the publication's editor, Lindsay Wesker, argued KISS FM's case for a licence: "KISS FM is not just a group of one-track minded business people solely making a bid for profit.

Not that we don't have the business acumen and the experienced personnel required to run a radio station, but our main aim has always been to provide the music that London wants, and that is what we shall do."[468]

In a separate two-page article that explained the details of KISS FM's campaign for a licence, Wesker (anonymously) lambasted three magazines – Broadcast, Cut and Media Week – for their predictions that KISS FM's bid would not succeed. Wesker's writing traits, recently demonstrated in his introductory script for the audiocassette, were in evidence once again: "What makes people feel that we're not qualified to do the job? Do they think we're incapable of employing people with independent local radio and BBC radio experience? Logging-in records, putting cartridges in cartridge machines and extracting stories out of the daily newspapers. Gosh, it all sounds like very hard work. Those buttons on the cartridge machine: one is green, one is red, which one should I press? Which is the right way to put the cartridge in? Gosh, it all sounds so daunting."[469]

In fact, despite this bluster, both the logging of records and the use of cartridge machines that play advertisements and jingles in a radio studio were activities that KISS FM DJs had never experienced. As a pirate station, KISS FM had used ordinary domestic cassette players for playing adverts, and it had never had to note down the records it played, which legal stations were obliged to do for their music royalty payments. Wesker and the other KISS FM staff had learnt about these responsibilities of legal radio stations from me during recent months, in preparation for the licence application. The article ended with a naive appeal to the IBA to award the London licence to the supposedly perfect KISS FM: "IBA, please, please have the guts. You won't be disappointed. We won't have a financial crisis after six months, we won't alter our proposed music format, we won't preach, we won't abuse our position and we won't accept payola. In short, we won't resemble some of the stations that have already been given a licence."[470]

It quickly transpired that the contest for the London FM licence was the most intense of all the IBA's twenty-one incremental radio contracts. Thirty-two applications had been submitted on 5 June 1989, including many that involved well known music, business and broadcasting personalities. Their presence attracted substantial media coverage to the licence competition, much to the detriment of KISS FM's less star-studded bid.

The Sunday Times printed photographs of six such personalities and outlined the respectability of many of the applicants: "But just look at whose money is up there waving in the breeze: Rothschilds, Pearson, the Really Useful Group, Virgin, the Evening Standard, WH Smith, Hanson, Capital Radio, Time Out magazine, Radio City from Liverpool, Yorkshire TV. And look at the names. David Maker's Golden Rose (classical music) has Dame Kiri Te Kanawa, André Previn, the Christies of Glyndebourne and Henry Wrong of the Barbican on the board. Their closest rival, the Radio City Consortium, has Joan Bakewell as chairman, David Aukin of the National Theatre, Jane Glover, Carl Davis, Simon Jenkins and Jocelyn Stevens."[471]

This article, written by respected radio critic Gillian Reynolds, went on to dismiss the applications by former pirate stations that were said to be "jumping up and down and yelling about squatters' rights." Reynolds wrote that "KISS FM (soul music) is claiming an IBA carve-up," perhaps a conclusion drawn from reading Lindsay Wesker's prose in 'The Written Word' magazine, a copy of which she had been sent. More damagingly, Reynolds expressed concern about the "quality of money" offered by some applicants: "In the old 1960s pirate days, the fear that money from organised crime was being laundered through some radio stations did as much to bring about their closure as arguments about invasion of the airwaves and non-payment of copyright on records. These days there is the additional fear of money from Libya, Syria and Iran finding its way too." Although Reynolds did not express this concern about any specific applicant, there was understandable anger amongst the KISS FM team that such scaremongering should be used to tar all the applications from ex-pirate stations. On the phone from Spain, McNamee asked Lindsay Wesker to contact Reynolds and clarify KISS FM's entirely legitimate sources of funding.[472]

Coverage elsewhere of the licence race proved to be far less hysterical. The Observer newspaper felt that "the odds would favour a classical or jazz station rather than one offering rock or hip hop" and documented the success of jazz radio formats in America.[473]

Broadcast magazine printed the colour photo of the KISS FM team that had been taken on that swelteringly hot day in Blackstock Mews, and it described the station's bid as "strongly fancied." However, it commented: "With disco singles flooding the charts and playlists, the appeal of KISS may now be too narrow. The fact that a rival, Rhythm Radio, has publicly said so will not help its chances." A subsequent article in Broadcast dismissed the bids by KISS FM and rock applicant Q102 because they were said to "propose channels which are variations on a theme of rock and pop." Ten other applicants, mainly offering classical and easy listening formats, were listed as potential licence winners.[474]

In a full-page analysis of the London licence applicants, Media Week magazine said that "the most obvious posturing is that of KISS FM." Lindsay Wesker was quoted saying "there will be anarchy if KISS does not get a licence" and predicting that "there will be a huge surge of pirate activity." The article did not predict a winner.[475]

Martin Wroe, the journalist who had given KISS FM its first national newspaper coverage eighteen months earlier, wrote an article in The Independent that outlined the merits of several applicants, including KISS FM, and asked: "But will the men in suits at the IBA dare plump for hip hop and salsa over, for example, the host of classical music applications to choose from?" To which the IBA's head of radio, Peter Baldwin, responded: "My principal radio development officer is a fan of reggae and black soul music. There's no possibility of my being immune to that interest. KISS FM stands as good a chance as anyone."[476]

The most positive support for KISS FM's application came unexpectedly from BBC TV's media correspondent, Nick Higham, who, in an article for The Guardian newspaper, named KISS FM as "the runner which any tipster might do well to nap." He argued that the existence of thirty pirate stations in London provided evidence of the demand for "leading edge" music such as reggae, soul, house, hip hop and rare groove. His article concluded: "They [KISS FM] have acquired the backing of a substantial publishing company, EMAP, and of EMAP's chairman Sir Frank Rogers – as well as footballer John Fashanu, former Capital presenter Dave Cash as programme director and Tony Monson, the man behind the rival pirate Solar Radio, as 'senior presenter.' It's a combination of programme format, names and big money the IBA may find hard to resist."[477]

Higham was an acknowledged radio industry expert, having previously worked as radio editor of Broadcast magazine. His positive comments provided exactly the sort of encouragement the KISS FM team needed to counter other commentators' obsessions with the high quality of the classical and rock music bids. However, Higham's article raised immediate problems within KISS FM because it named Dave Cash as a "former" Capital Radio presenter. Cash's involvement in the KISS FM bid was still meant to be confidential, as he continued to present an overnight show on Capital Radio's AM oldies station. An internal memorandum had already been circulated within KISS FM that explained the basis of the station's press campaign. Its first item had noted: "Do not use Dave Cash and Dave Pearce" (Dave Pearce was a presenter on the BBC London station GLR who also intended to join KISS FM if it won a licence).[478]

KISS FM had planned to inform the IBA of these two presenters' involvement in its bid through a confidential letter, so that their names could be omitted completely from the application form. However, at some point during the preparation and printing of the document at the office of Centurion Press, this arrangement must have been forgotten, so that both names had been listed in the application with biographies and job titles (Pearce was described as the station's senior presenter). Copies of applicants' documents were freely available for inspection by the public in the IBA library, which must have been how Higham had gleaned the information about Dave Cash's involvement in KISS FM. Higham probably assumed that Cash was no longer working for Capital Radio, since his current DJ work for the station had been strangely omitted from his biographical details.

Cash was understandably furious about this complete breach of confidentiality, which he had consistently emphasised to the KISS FM steering group was essential if he were to keep his job at Capital Radio. The following week, the crisis deepened further when Broadcast magazine ran a story on page two headlined 'KISS In Clash With Capital Over Cash.' To date, Edwin Riddell, the publication's radio editor, had failed to write anything positive about KISS FM's licence bid. Higham's revelation about Dave Cash's involvement had given him a further opportunity to write something negative: "KISS FM is locked in a tug-of-war battle with Capital Radio over its programme director, only days before the IBA decides the winner of the London FM franchise. In its application to the IBA, KISS said its programme director would be Dave Cash … It is believed that Cash withdrew after Capital threatened to dismiss him if he remained with the consortium."[479]

Unbeknown to anyone else in the KISS FM office, Lindsay Wesker had taken a phone call from Riddell earlier that week, and had spoken to him in the absence of McNamee, who was still on holiday in Spain. Wesker's comments were quoted substantially in the article, contradicting Riddell's own information. Said Wesker: "All I can say is that there's no way Dave [Cash] would commit himself to us and then withdraw. He is categorically going to be programme director if we get the licence." Wesker also claimed that KISS FM had been in contact with other staff at Capital Radio, whom he said "are obviously unhappy with the station, despite its success." He denied that KISS was planning to directly target Capital Radio's audience, and he claimed that Cash had informed Capital of his involvement with KISS FM before the latter's licence application had been submitted.[480]

After the article's publication, the phone lines between Spain and Blackstock Mews were red hot for several days as McNamee discussed the situation with Wesker and me. I was furious that Wesker could have jeopardised KISS FM's bid by talking so freely to a journalist who was known not to be particularly sympathetic towards the station. Furthermore, Wesker had consulted neither McNamee nor me (in McNamee's absence) before talking to Riddell on the record. Wesker claimed not to have realised that Riddell was fishing for quotes to substantiate a scoop that had ended up trailed on Broadcast's front cover as 'KISS In Cash Row.' For me, this defence seemed particularly weak, given Wesker's journalistic experience on a weekly music paper.

Whatever the real reasons behind the faux pas, the waves it created were substantial. Dave Cash needed to maintain his well-paid DJ job at Capital Radio and so he had to formally renounce any involvement in the KISS FM bid to his employers and to the press. KISS FM chairman Keith McDowall had to write to the IBA to clarify the presenter's on/off involvement in the station's licence application. The IBA's head of radio programming, Paul Brown, replied to McDowall, acknowledging that the change in Cash's status had been noted.[481]

The actions of Centurion Press and Wesker had caused the sudden removal of KISS FM's programme director, one of the station's key staff positions, from its licence bid. The change undoubtedly weakened the application and must have reduced KISS FM's chance of winning the licence. At the same time, Cash's sudden withdrawal also meant that there was now one less person in the company's management structure positioned between Wesker and McNamee. The week's events had effectively removed one of the two newcomers who had deprived Wesker of the position for which he had originally been destined, in charge of the station's programming. There was now only one person left between Wesker and McNamee who was still denying him this job – and that person was me.

---

[457] "LBC Rebuffed", Broadcast, 14 Apr 1989.
[458] "IBA Awards Another Four Incremental ILR Contracts", IBA press release no. 47/89, 15 May 1989.
[459] "Greater London FM Application Form", KISS FM, 1 Jun 1989.
[460] ibid.
[461] ibid.
[462] ibid.
[463] ibid.
[464] ibid.
[465] ibid.
[466] Receipt, David Vick, IBA, 5 Jun 1989.
[467] "The Case For KISS FM", KISS FM press release, [undated].
[468] "Editorial", The Written Word no. 5, May/Jun 1989.
[469] "The Campaign So Far", The Written Word no. 5, May/Jun 1989.
[470] ibid.
[471] Gillian Reynolds, "Singing All The Way To The Bank", Sunday Telegraph, 21 May 1989.
[472] ibid.
[473] Richard Brooks, "Interesting Station, Good Prospects", The Observer, 14 May 1989.
[474] "London FM Bids Pile Up In Search Of Magic Formula", Broadcast, 26 May 1989.
"IBA Faces FM Juggling Act", Broadcast, 16 Jun 1989.
[475] Richard Gold, "On The Station Sidings", Media Week, 23 Jun 1989.
[476] Martin Wroe, "Making Radio Contact With 5m Listeners", The Independent, 12 Jul 1989.
[477] Nick Higham, "Radio Daze", The Guardian, 12 Jun 1989.
[478] "Press Release Info Package", KISS FM memorandum, [undated].
[479] Edwin Riddell, "KISS In Clash With Capital Over Cash", Broadcast, 23 Jun 1989.
[480] ibid.
[481] letter from Paul Brown, IBA to Keith McDowall, KISS FM, 16 Jun 1989.

June & July 1989.

Gordon McNamee returned from his vacation in Spain, looking very suntanned but seeming little rested. He said he had spent a lot of time pacing the rooms of his parent's villa, worrying about the KISS FM licence application. There were several weeks to go before the Independent Broadcasting Authority [IBA] was expected to announce its award of the London FM licence, and the tension brought on by the waiting was becoming unbearable. One of the biggest problems facing McNamee was what he should do if KISS FM failed to win the licence. He had already stated publicly that he would not return the station to its former pirate existence, but what other option was there for a radio station without a licence to broadcast? The possibility of KISS FM leasing airtime from London commercial radio station LBC had been scotched by the IBA, which had also made it quite clear that further London radio licences were unlikely to be advertised for several years.

McNamee talked vaguely about moving to Spain if KISS FM's licence bid failed, where he could live in his parents' villa and set up a radio station or a club. After another London soul pirate station, Horizon Radio, had closed down a few years earlier, its founder Chris Stewart had moved to Marbella and had set up a Spanish version of the station. McNamee wondered if he could do something similar. Once this current burst of new, incremental radio licences was over, it looked as if the British radio industry would return to developing very slowly, so that McNamee would have little reason to stay in London awaiting a further opportunity to legalise his station.

In recent months, there had been a noticeable increase in pirate radio activity in London. After several months' absence, four black music stations – Fresh FM, Classic FM, RJR and Twilight – had all returned to the airwaves in April 1989, having realised that there was little or no chance of them winning a legal licence. By June, twenty-two pirates were audible on London's airwaves during a typical weekend.[482]

In a written Parliamentary Answer, Lord Young, the Trade & Industry Secretary, said he had received "a number of representations" from licensed broadcasters about this recent increase in pirate activity. He stated that the Department of Trade & Industry [DTI] had carried out a record 444 raids the previous year, and he outlined further legislation to combat their activities: "In the forthcoming Broadcasting Bill, the government will be seeking additional powers to make it an offence to supply goods and services for the operation of an unlicensed station, to advertise on an unlicensed station or to solicit others to do so and to be engaged in the operation of the unlicensed station."[483]

In May, only days before the IBA had announced the winning applicant for the Bradford incremental licence, seven DTI officials and eight police officers had raided Bradford pirate station Eastern Community Radio and had confiscated £2,000 worth of equipment. Nottingham pirate Heatwave Radio was raided the same day, for the fifteenth time. By June, the DTI had carried out 274 raids on 102 pirate stations, of which 204 raids were on sixty-three London stations. The Voice of The Listener pressure group was moved to comment: "Despite claims to the contrary, the government is not winning the war against the pirates."[484]

On 4 July 1989, the Home Secretary, Douglas Hurd, addressed an audience of commercial radio industry delegates at the London Congress meeting of the Association of Independent Radio Contractors [AIRC]. He admitted that, despite the five-year licence ban that had been imposed from 1 January 1989, pirates "continued to cause concern" and he noted: "During the first five months of this year, raids by the Radio Investigation Service [RIS] were up fifty per cent compared with the same period last year. We intend to use the Broadcasting Bill to strengthen the hand of the RIS and the police in getting pirates off the air."[485]

Hurd confirmed that new legislation would make it an offence: for an owner or manager of premises to knowingly allow it to be used by a pirate station; to advertise on a pirate or supply it with goods and services; and to have pirate radio equipment available for use. Search and seizure powers would be strengthened; records, tapes and equipment would be liable to forfeiture; and the maximum penalty would be increased to two years' imprisonment and/or an unlimited fine. Hurd told his audience of commercial radio managers: "As respectable folk running legal radio stations, you have never had much sympathy with pirates. But, of course, the public has had a sneaking admiration for them which you and I have not been able wholly to extinguish. That should change now."[486]

This was the closest a Home Secretary had ever come to admitting that the government could not stop its citizens liking pirate radio, and that commercial radio had not lived up to the challenge that the pirates had posed. Commenting on the proposed new laws, "former pirate radio DJ" Jazzy M said: "This is taking things to the extreme. If we were pushing drugs over the air or something, I could maybe understand it, but some pirates do a good service ..." David Lubich, editor of Soul Underground magazine, said he believed that pirates had been tempted off the airwaves by the promise of legal licences, only to see heavier laws prevent them from returning to illegal broadcasting: "I think the pirates have been very naive, as everyone knew that the government wasn't going to hand out much in the way of FM contracts. The better stations have been forced to stay off the air with the promise of contracts that might never materialise. The DTI will be given more powers to do even more raids."[487]

The evening after Douglas Hurd's speech, I took the train to Cardiff to attend the Radio Festival, an annual conference for the British radio industry's programme makers. In my suitcase were bundles of KISS FM leaflets I planned to distribute to journalists and radio people during the three-day event. One of the conference's opening speakers was James Gordon, managing director of Radio Clyde, who was a vociferous spokesman for the established commercial radio industry. He spoke of the problems he expected former pirate radio stations to face if they won incremental licences: "Former pirate operators will find that living within the law ironically carries a cost penalty. They'll have to pay copyright fees for the first time, perhaps charges for a news service. I think it's a pity that the penalties fall on those who observe the law, rather than on those who break it. And I'm sure we all welcome Douglas Hurd's announcement at the AIRC Congress yesterday of a range of measures to curb the growth of pirate radio. Already, I'm afraid, there is evidence that there is an element of gang warfare creeping into the pirate radio scene. And the longer the government delays in [taking] really forceful action to rid our airwaves of pirate radio, the more difficult it is going to be."[488]

Gordon believed that the commercial radio sector was being expanded too rapidly by the IBA, and that the incremental stations would face severe problems as a result: "The economic facts of life will mean that quite a lot of stations are going to lose substantial amounts of money ... I genuinely regret to forecast that, of the twenty-one incremental licences, I foresee that a quarter of them, on their present funding, will be out of business within two years. And I say that with no pleasure. In many cases, it will be perfectly decent people who will be losing their money."[489]

In the audience, listening to Gordon, were representatives of several of the newly licensed incremental radio stations: Lindsay Reid and John Henry of Birmingham's Buzz FM, Mike Shaft of Manchester's Sunset Radio, and several staff from Bristol's For The People. There were also delegates in attendance from many of the London licence applicants, all of whom were awaiting the outcome of the bids with as much trepidation as was KISS FM: Stephen Games of London Classical Radio, Keith Harris and Richard Barbrook of Rhythm Radio, and Alex Pascall of Academy Broadcasting.

Mike Shaft was the only person from a new incremental station to have been invited to speak from the platform during the Radio Festival. The following day, he seized the opportunity to rebuff Gordon's pessimism about the incremental radio scheme: "I believe it still hasn't sunk in to a lot of people that these incrementals are going to happen. Whether you like us or not, we're going to be on your dial real soon. So please don't ignore us because we're not going to go away. The next couple of years, the incrementals will be making their statement. We'll be the first new development in radio for about twenty years. I think it's long overdue and I'm delighted to be here."[490]

Several speakers at the Festival had already voiced their opinions, both from the stage and from the floor, that a classical music format was the preferred choice for the London FM licence. Some of these proponents declared their own personal interests in pending licence bids, whilst other supporters from the existing commercial radio industry understood that classical music posed the least threat to their own businesses. Mike Shaft explained that the format of his own station Sunset Radio, due on air within a couple of months, mixed black music with speech programmes for the ethnic communities of Manchester. Then he offered his own opinion about the London incremental FM licence: "These incrementals were meant to add to what was already there. I don't see another specialist classical station coming on-air as adding to what's already there. We have [BBC] Radio Three ... I don't think we need another classical radio station."[491]

Much of the informal discussion that took place outside of the seminars, in the conference hall bar, over lunch and during tea breaks, centred on speculation about the impending winner of the London FM licence. There was also discussion about what would happen to the dozens of unsuccessful applicants, particularly those, like KISS FM, that had already renounced a return to piracy. A couple of weeks earlier, a lone press article in Broadcast magazine had speculated that "there is now a strong possibility that further FM frequencies for London and elsewhere will be allocated in the next two or three years."[492]

Then, on the second day of the Festival, copies of that week's edition of Broadcast arrived in Cardiff. Everyone was shocked by its front-page headline: "DTI OFFERS FIVE MORE RADIO FREQUENCIES FOR LONDON." The sub-heading illuminated the story: "DISAPPOINTED BIDDERS FOR FM AND AM FRANCHISES COULD BE GIVEN SECOND CHANCE." The article explained: "If a dramatic offer by the DTI is accepted, the capital could get more than the two new stations due to be announced by the IBA next week ... It is thought that the Government would like to offer at least one more London franchise quickly in order to sugar the pill of its new crackdown measures against pirate radio announced this week."[493]

No more light was thrown on these claims until the Festival's final day, when Gillian Reynolds prefaced her conference summary with some additional information: "The front page of Broadcast certainly set everyone thinking. Were there going to be five additional frequencies allocated from the DTI for the London incremental applicants? Well, as the afternoon wore on and as the sources opened up, it seemed to have become apparent that we may hear an announcement next week that there will be additional frequencies. Maybe not five, but watch this space and remember where you heard it first."[494]

A further story inside the new issue of Broadcast speculated that the IBA's short-list for the London FM licence comprised Rhythm Radio, Melody Radio, KISS FM, London Jazz Radio and an unspecified classical music applicant. Once more, Broadcast dismissed KISS FM's chance of being the outright winner: "The choice of Rhythm would be less controversial than that of KISS FM. The IBA could feel that KISS would be tempted to go head on for Capital's audience."[495]

Before leaving Cardiff, I called the KISS FM office from a public phone in the entrance lobby of the conference hall to tell McNamee the latest news that Reynolds had just announced about additional London licences. Standing within earshot of me was a journalist, dictating an article by phone to the news desk of his paper, predicting that London Jazz Radio would be the winner of the London licence. His sources sounded very authoritative, so I warned McNamee of the unwelcome news. During the next few days, I scanned all the daily newspapers, searching for the journalist's story, but without success.

I returned to London and caught up with the latest developments at the KISS FM office. The station's new non-executive director, Tony Prince, had at last published the article he had promised in his newsletter, MixMag Update, supporting KISS FM's licence bid. It took the form of a one-page open letter to the IBA, setting out the case for a dance music station in London, and ended with the plea: "So here we are, hoping that DANCE music will win your votes and, in particular, that the group behind KISS FM become entrusted with that new and exciting FM frequency. Thank you."[496]

The IBA had forewarned licence applicants that its decision would be announced the following Wednesday. I arranged to join Gordon McNamee for an evening meal on the eve of the announcement. After finishing work at the record company, I met him at the KISS FM office and we walked around the corner to a tiny Italian restaurant just off Blackstock Road. After six months' involvement in the KISS FM bid, this was the first social occasion I had shared with McNamee. It was also the first time I had received any kind of compensation for my work on the licence application, as McNamee paid the restaurant bill.

McNamee seemed very pessimistic about KISS FM's chance of winning the licence against all the other bidders, and he had the air of someone who had already resigned himself to the idea of losing. Almost all of the media coverage had favoured applicants other than KISS FM, and there was an underlying feeling that the establishment had failed to grasp the magnitude of young Londoners' passion for the black music we wanted to broadcast. Paradoxically, KISS FM's genre of music had never been more popular in London. Having reached number five in the singles chart with 'Keep On Moving,' KISS FM DJ Jazzie B's group Soul II Soul was now in its fourth week at number one with the follow up, 'Back To Life.' The highest climbing singles in that week's top thirty chart included songs by Chaka Khan, Bobby Brown, Karyn White, A Guy Called Gerald, Michael Jackson, Monie Love, De La Soul and LA Mix.

Trade magazine Music Week had just published a twelve-page dance music supplement that had recognised the growth of the genre's popularity and the role that pirate radio had played in its success. Mark Moore of the group S'Express felt that national BBC radio was "hopeless" when it came to dance music and commented: "We have to go Top Twenty before we even get B-listed ... Not even a great plugger can fight radio's attitude to dance." Johnny Walker, head of A&R at Polydor Records, believed there was now less radio exposure for new acts since KISS FM had gone off-air. Tim Simenon of the group Bomb The Bass said: "The big stations have always tried to ignore dancefloor records, though now they've got no option but to play them. But the pirate stations were there first for us. It's the clubs and the pirates that matter, as far as I'm concerned."[497]

McNamee and I sat in the Italian restaurant, chewing over the unfairness of the British radio system and the way in which public demand for new stations was continually being suppressed by the government's incredibly slow expansion of the commercial radio system. We also touched upon personal matters for the first time and exchanged experiences of our relationships with women. I had just broken up with my girlfriend of three years, after a particularly bitter confrontation that had shocked me profoundly. Since Easter, London's rail and underground system had suffered a series of one-day strikes that had brought the city to a complete standstill once a week. On returning home one evening to the flat I shared with my girlfriend, I had found a note informing me that me she was staying overnight with a friend, because she was working the late shift in her job and thought the following day's strike would prevent her from getting home.

However, that evening, I happened to notice that the packet of condoms stored in the bathroom cabinet had been disturbed and, on inspection, I found that several of them were missing. When she returned the next day, I confronted my girlfriend with this evidence and she admitted she had spent the night with a work colleague who was still in his teens, and with whom she had planned to have sex using my condoms. Later, I discovered that my girlfriend had been harbouring sexual desires towards this work colleague for at least the previous year of our relationship, and that she had specifically asked her employer to change her shift pattern so that the two of them could spend the night together.

I was outraged that she had deceived and cheated me so blatantly. I had told her that our relationship ended there and then. However, she refused to move out of the flat that we shared as joint tenants, so the two of us were now living together in a horrible atmosphere. I no longer wanted anything to do with her, but she refused to get out and go her separate way. It felt as if a complete stranger had suddenly invaded my living space, so I tried to stay out of the flat as much as possible, since I could no longer trust her to tell me the truth about anything.

McNamee told me that he had suffered similar experiences at the hands of former girlfriends who he felt had treated him badly. Then, he regaled me with a story of how he had once thrown an ex-partner's possessions out onto the pavement outside their shared house after he felt that their relationship had ended. In unfolding the events to me, I became aware that McNamee seemed to relish the power that he felt he could wield over women, and the revenge he knew he could wreak, in retribution for things that had happened to him in the past. I was startled to see a vicious side to McNamee that I had never before glimpsed, where he seemed almost to revel in hurting people for wrongdoings that others had inflicted upon him many moons ago. For the first time, I realised that McNamee might actually enjoy hurting people for no good reasons. This revelation came as quite a shock.

After our evening of chat, McNamee and I parted and made our separate ways home, knowing that the next time we spoke to each other, things could never be quite the same. Either KISS FM would have won the licence and our lives would be changed forever. Or we would face failure and have to turn our individual attentions to other tasks and new projects. Tomorrow was the big day that the IBA would announce the winner of the London FM licence.

---

[482] Grant Goddard, "Notes", City Limits, 4 May 1989, 22 Jun 1989.
[483] Hansard, Written Answers, 18 Apr 1989.
[484] "Raids On Pirates Rise", Broadcast, 12 May 1989.
"Raids Silence London Pirates", UK Press Gazette, 12 Jun 1989.
[485] "Home Secretary Proposes Crackdown On Pirate Radio In Broadcasting Bill", Home Office press release, 4 Jul 1989.
[486] ibid.
[487] "Government Gets Tough With Pirates", Television Today, 17 Aug 1989.
[488] author's recording, 5 Jul 1989.
[489] ibid.
[490] author's recording, 6 Jul 1989.
[491] ibid.
[492] "IBA Faces FM Juggling Act", Broadcast, 16 Jun 1989.
[493] Edwin Riddell & Sean King, "DTI Offers Five More Radio Frequencies For London", Broadcast, 7 Jul 1989.
[494] author's recording, 7 Jul 1989.
[495] "Rhythm Radio Claims Place On IBA's London FM Shortlist", Broadcast, 7 Jul 1989.
[496] "An Open Hearted Letter To The IBA", MixMag Update no. 94, 4 Jul 1989.
[497] Stuart Lambert, "Keep In Touch!", Dance Supplement, Music Week, 15 Jul 1989.

12 July 1989.

A little after 6 am on Wednesday 12 July 1989, Gordon McNamee phoned the office of the Independent Broadcasting Authority [IBA] from his home. He had been assured that someone would be at work in its radio division by this hour in order to answer enquiries about the licence decision. However, an answering machine message told him to call back during office hours. That day, London's train and underground systems were paralysed by another one-day strike. McNamee's personal assistant, Rosee Laurence, had managed to catch an early bus to the KISS FM office, where she found that an envelope embossed with the IBA logo had already been delivered by the postman, though she left the letter unopened until her boss arrived.[498]

McNamee got out of bed and drove across London to the KISS FM office, but the roads were already snarled up with traffic because of the strike, so he did not reach Blackstock Mews until nearly eight o'clock. Opening the IBA envelope, he only had to reach the second sentence of the two-page letter from its director of radio, Peter Baldwin, to understand its message: "I am afraid the decision is, for you and your colleagues, a disappointing one."[499]

The IBA had decided to award the London-wide FM licence to London Jazz Radio whose application, Baldwin wrote, "offered the prospect of the best radio service to increase the choice available to listeners in London." However, on the second page of the letter, there was an interesting piece of information: "It seems probable that additional frequencies for London-wide services could be released for early allocation by the Radio Authority [the IBA's successor]. You may have read the recent trade press speculation concerning the availability of further frequencies for independent radio use."[500]

That morning's IBA press release enlarged upon the same point: "Recognising the range of audience tastes in Greater London that will still remain largely unserved following this contract award, members of the Authority placed on record that, had more than one frequency been available, they could have selected further successful groups from those they considered. Members made a strong recommendation that, if more channels were available, consideration should be given to their release."[501]

McNamee phoned me straight away at home with the bad news and sounded incredibly dispirited that London Jazz Radio had won the licence, particularly since former KISS FM DJ Gilles Peterson was involved in the bid as a shareholder and company director. The IBA had announced a press conference to explain their decision, to be held at 2.30 that afternoon in their Knightsbridge office. Despite London's strike-bound roads, I embarked upon a succession of bus journeys that lasted several hours, but managed to arrive at Brompton Road just in time for the start of the meeting. The difficult travel conditions meant that very few journalists attended, though the IBA staff kindly offered us tea and biscuits, and the ensuing informal discussion in room number 736 lasted around fifty minutes.

The IBA director of radio, Peter Baldwin, pre-empted any questions that journalists might have wanted to ask about the award of the licence to London Jazz Radio by announcing, at the outset of the press conference, without a hint of irony: "We never disclose the internal machinations of the Authority's decision making process. Neither do we issue a batting order of who came second or third." Nevertheless, Baldwin's assertion did not prohibit questions along similar lines. The IBA press release had referred to London Jazz Radio's "good range of music styles derived from and related to jazz." Asked to explain this statement in more detail, the IBA head of radio programming, Paul Brown, responded: "In assembling their application, they did a lot of research which told them that an audience would prefer to have a jazz radio station that provided a wide spectrum of jazz including, for example, Afro-Caribbean rhythms, salsa and also some of the big band favourites and standards. That seemed to us to be a useful alternative to what already existed, as far as London listeners were concerned."[502]

The phrase "Afro-Caribbean rhythms" sounded suspiciously like a musicologist's term for dance, soul and reggae music – exactly the styles that KISS FM had proposed in its own bid. It seemed as if part of the appeal of London Jazz Radio's application to the IBA was the way it had proposed to amalgamate a huge variety of black music styles within a single radio station. Another factor that distinguished its application from most of its competitors was the large number of establishment figures involved in its management structure. London Jazz Radio's board of directors included a Lord, an MP, two CBE's and an MBE. The station's advisory panel included three Sirs, two Lords, one Viscount, one CBE, one MBE, a bishop, five MPs and actor Michael Caine. Many of these names were also shareholders in the company.[503]

At the press conference, journalist Bob Tyler asked pointedly: "Is this the way for the next ten years that radio is going to develop? Has everybody got to have a Lord or an MP on its application to get a licence?" The IBA's Paul Brown replied flatly: "London Jazz Radio did not receive the contract because it has got Lords and MPs on its board. There are other Lords and MPs involved in other applications."[504]

Time Out magazine's radio editor, Sid Smith, suggested that the substantial audience for London's black music pirate stations would be aggrieved by the IBA decision to license London Jazz Radio, rather than one of the former pirate stations that had been attempting to become legitimate. He pondered whether there might be a further upsurge in illegal radio activity on London's airwaves. Peter Baldwin replied:

"It was a factor that was considered in great detail. KISS FM put in a very strong application and we have made representations to the Home Office. [IBA] Members felt very strongly that there were a number of applicant groups who could have been offered a contract, and we are seeking government's agreement to the release of additional frequencies so that we can broaden the offers that we can give to these applicant groups. That is widening the choice generally. One has no idea where KISS FM will come in that. But I'm bound to say that, given the government's attitude towards pirate broadcasting, and the five-year ban for anyone who does broadcast after the 1st January, I think it would be imprudent for anyone [ex-pirate] to go back on the air [illegally] if they have an aspiration towards [legal] broadcasting."[505]

The way in which Baldwin had singled out KISS FM was startling, since there had been several other ex-pirate broadcasters amongst the thirty-two applicants for the London-wide FM licence. It almost seemed as if the IBA was apologising for not having awarded the licence to KISS FM, and was telling the station quite directly not to contemplate a return to piracy. Baldwin went on to explain in more detail what he had been hinting at:

"Our professional knowledge tells us that two more FM frequencies could be available in a short space of time. It would be a matter for government to decide, but the frequencies could be made available within six to nine months. There are people on them who are proposing to move off. It's a complicated subject because there are other people going to temporary [frequency] positions whilst they get ready to go to somewhere else in the long term. It is a jigsaw, but life is never easy. The first hurdle is government policy, as to whether they wish to usurp the role of the Radio Authority by offering frequencies they had intended to hold back for issue when the Radio Authority comes into being. The IBA's view is: should the listeners of London, who haven't got certain genres of broadcasting, have to wait eighteen months for that moment to arrive? And that's a matter on which there will have to be a judgement made."[506]

The Radio Authority was the new public body planned by the government to replace the existing IBA Radio Division from 1 January 1991. Baldwin's message was becoming a lot clearer. The government must be planning to let the newly formed Authority allocate further London licences in 1991, but there was now a possibility that their award could be brought forward. The decision seemed to rest upon whether the IBA's lobbying of the Home Office would prove successful.

In answer to a question from Brian Belle-Fortune of Soul Underground magazine about the IBA's rejection of KISS FM's bid, its principal radio development officer, David Vick, replied: "Our own research confirms the potential popularity and viability of a black/dance music station, and that's one of the reasons why we are anxious to make more contracts available if the frequencies can be found."[507]

Belle-Fortune persisted in arguing that the IBA must have been insufficiently briefed about the extent and popularity of the dance music scene in London because of its underground nature. Vick replied with another message of encouragement: "There's clearly a very intense following for black/dance music and KISS FM ... Our research fully confirms the potential audience for a black/dance music station in terms of sufficient numbers to sustain that station. There is no doubt at all that London can support a legitimate black/dance station."[508]

A further issue was raised by freelance journalist Daniel Nathan about a black music applicant's chance of winning any future licence. Because the North London licence had already been awarded to black applicant WNK, and the South London licence to another black consortium, Nathan asked whether the IBA might consider that these licensees would already cater sufficiently for black music radio programming. Paul Brown replied succinctly: "We perceive the difference."[509]

The press conference ended and the small number of assembled journalists chatted together and compared notes, before re-entering the overcast, strike-bound city outside. From Knightsbridge, I caught another series of buses that eventually delivered me to the KISS FM office in Finsbury Park. The long journey gave me plenty of time to contemplate the IBA officers' words. I had started the day with a large dose of pessimism, following McNamee's phone call conveying the bad news about KISS FM's application. However, now I was beginning to feel surprisingly optimistic about KISS FM's chances of winning a second bite at the licence cherry. It was difficult to ascertain exactly how confident the IBA really was of gaining government approval to advertise those extra London licences now, rather than later. There had already been so many delays and U-turns in the government's radio broadcasting policy during recent years that nothing seemed at all certain any more. However, the press conference had spent more of its time discussing KISS FM's losing bid and the situation of black music ex-pirate stations than it had discussing the winning jazz applicant. Although the immediate situation offered KISS FM no opportunity to return to the airwaves as a legal station, the IBA seemed to be nurturing an obvious desire to see the ex-pirate succeed (eventually). It was too good an opportunity to ignore.

The atmosphere in the KISS FM office seemed particularly gloomy when I arrived there at the end of the afternoon. I explained to Gordon McNamee exactly what had been said at the press conference and the hope that the IBA seemed to hold for offering us another chance to win a licence in the future. However, McNamee remained immersed in the gloom of his own failure and could not see any potential positivity in the situation. The office received a constant stream of phone calls, faxes and visits from people expressing their commiserations. Many of the KISS FM DJs phoned in to find out exactly why the station had failed in its bid and why London Jazz Radio had won. Journalists were calling up for quotable comments from a losing applicant such as KISS FM, and McNamee obliged with a few barbed epithets.

Dave Pearce, the DJ presently working for BBC London station GLR who had been included in KISS FM's application as a future member of staff, phoned to ask McNamee if he wanted to talk on-air about the IBA decision during his show that evening. I felt that it was essential for KISS FM not to be seen to attack London Jazz Radio for having won the licence, or to attack the IBA for its decision. So I wrote a few quotes for McNamee to say during Pearce's programme that I felt were conciliatory in tone, but which expressed the opinion that Londoners should be allowed to have more radio services from which to choose. The rest of us sat listening to the radio show in the office, while McNamee talked live on GLR and I scribbled little notes for him to use in his discussion while the arguments progressed on-air.

Three bottles of champagne sat unopened, perched on the corner of McNamee's desk, where they remained unnoticed for the rest of the week. The office staff spent the rest of that evening consoling each other and answering dozens of phone calls from well-wishers and disappointed listeners, before we had to battle our separate ways home using the paralysed London transport system. It had been a dismal day. Everyone was overwhelmed with disappointment and wonderment that the goals for which the KISS FM team had worked so hard could have been so easily dismissed by those in authority.

The press reaction to London Jazz Radio's win over KISS FM was mixed. The dance music magazines and style press that had always supported KISS FM expressed their disappointment. The quality newspapers generally welcomed the decision to license a station for jazz, which their journalists probably understood and appreciated far more than dance music.

The first report, published in that day's Evening Standard, described the IBA decision as "a surprise" since the newspaper had anticipated that the licence would be won by KISS FM or Classic FM.[510]

Media Week magazine similarly thought that London Jazz Radio's win "came as something of a surprise," as it had previously selected an adult-orientated rock music service or a former black music pirate station as its favourite bets.[511]

In The Guardian newspaper, KISS FM's Gordon McNamee was quoted saying: "London's airwaves need something young and lively, and there are a lot of people out there who want dance music. But we'll come back next time there's an opportunity. One day, I want there to be a station for jazz, for house, for rap, for reggae."[512]

Soul Underground magazine said that the IBA decision had caused "shock and disappointment mingled with amazement," but added that an IBA spokesman had said it would be "a shame if KISS FM were to wind down its most impressive effort." London Jazz Radio's founder Dave Lee said, somewhat cryptically, of KISS FM: "I'm sure that they've lost out only for a short period of time."[513]

Jocks magazine said that the dance music industry had "reacted with dismay" to the IBA decision and it quoted record producer/artist Simon Harris: "Today is a day of mourning for black music. The IBA have got so wrapped up in their rules and regulations that they've completely missed the point." Gordon McNamee told the publication that he was very disappointed not to have won the licence, but that there would no question of KISS FM returning to the air as a pirate: "We're very deflated at the moment because we really believed we had an excellent chance, especially since [black music] stations like ours had won franchises in Manchester and Bristol, but we will be applying again as soon as possible."[514]

Even veteran DJ Tony Blackburn, then presenting shows for London's Capital Radio, was moved to comment: "I was amazed that the new London FM was a jazz station. I think KISS FM should have got the licence. I would have thought it would have been a soul station. If I'd been the IBA, that's the one I would have given. The problem is, if they don't give a proper legalised soul station soon, there's going to be more and more pirate radio stations."[515]

Keith Harris, who had led another of the unsuccessful applicant groups, Rhythm Radio, suggested to Time Out magazine how black music fans might react to the licence award: "A lot of people are going to be very angry. This is an area of music which is disenfranchised. That's why the pirates set up in the first place. And this IBA decision hasn't addressed that situation in the slightest. An unnecessarily volatile climate has been created between the pirates and the DTI."[516]

McNamee predicted that London would experience an upsurge in pirate radio activity, but denied that KISS FM would return to illegal broadcasting: "We'll apply for the next frequency, whether it's in three months, six or eighteen. If he had twelve Lords a-leaping, we might have got the licence this time. We'll play the game, the game of England. And we'll hope."[517]

The involvement of peers, MPs and wealthy businessmen in London Jazz Radio's application was a source of immense irritation to McNamee, as he told Radio & Music magazine: "You just have to look at the people behind the station to see how different they are from us. I think there's a real need for a jazz station and I don't think the award is unfair, but it's MPs and Lords whose names seem to count."[518]

Rhythm Radio's Keith Harris thought that London Jazz Radio's immense financial backing had guaranteed their success: "The feeling we have is that we were competing for a completely different station. It doesn't seem to be a coincidence that the station which spent most on its campaign, reputedly £50,000, won the contract."[519]

Much of the finance for London Jazz Radio's bid was provided by wealthy financier David Heimann, in whose plush Mayfair office I had met the station's founder, Dave Lee, several months earlier to discuss its bid. Lee told me then that Heimann could finance London Jazz Radio for several years without the station needing to earn a penny in advertising revenue: "David Heimann is a very important businessman who is underwriting the costs of our radio station because he loves jazz. He thinks that it's a civic duty, apart from a personal joy, that London should have such a station."[520]

Lee had also told me how important the role in his group's campaign for a jazz licence had been of a fourteen-person, all-party parliamentary group that he had established. I subsequently wrote an article for City Limits magazine that questioned the extent of this parliamentary lobby group's influence on the licence decision, which resulted in a letter of complaint from the IBA to the magazine's editor.[521]

Easily the most undignified response to KISS FM's failure to win the London licence came from the chairman of one of the other unsuccessful bidders. David Astor of Classic FM commented: "I've nothing against these KISS people. I don't even know who they are, to be honest. I just think there's too much pop music about – white or black – it all sounds the same to me. You can't walk into a shoe shop without being subjected to blaring pop music – it's such a dreadful imposition."[522]

When a respected establishment figure such as Astor felt he could publicly demonstrate such total contempt for contemporary popular music, was it really any surprise that the powers that be had denied former 'Radical Radio' pirate station KISS FM the chance of a licence?

---

[498] author's recording, 12 Jul 1989.
Grant Goddard, "Kissed Off", NME, 26 Aug 1989.
Grant Goddard, "Airwaves", Jocks, Sep 1989.
Grant Goddard, "Radio On?", City Limits, 3 Aug 1989.
[499] letter from Peter Baldwin, IBA to KISS FM, 11 Jul 1989.
[500] ibid.
[501] "IBA Announces Decisions On Incremental ILR Contracts In Greater London And Scotland", IBA press release no. 63/89, 12 Jul 1989.
[502] author's recording, 12 Jul 1989.
"IBA Announces Decisions On Incremental ILR Contracts In Greater London And Scotland", op cit.
[503] "Press Release", London Jazz Radio, [undated].
[504] author's recording, 12 Jul 1989.
[505] ibid.
[506] ibid.
[507] ibid.
[508] ibid.
[509] ibid.
[510] Steve Clarke, "All That Jazz For New London Radio", Evening Standard, 12 Jul 1989.
[511] Richard Gold, "A New Boy In The Band", Media Week, 21 Jul 1989.
[512] John Fordham, "More Of All That Jazz", The Guardian, 17 Jul 1989.
[513] Brian Belle-Fortune, "Kiss Of Death", Soul Underground no. 23, Aug 1989.
[514] "KISS FM Fails To Win A Licence", Jocks, Aug 1989.
[515] Sarah Davis, "Rebel With A Cause", Music Week, 19 Aug 1989.
[516] Sid Smith, "London Jazz Radio", Time Out, 19 Jul 1989.
[517] ibid.
[518] "Did Money Do The Talking For London Jazz?", Radio & Music, 19 Jul 1989.
[519] ibid.
[520] author's interview with David Lee, 6 Apr 1989.
[521] Grant Goddard, "How The Parliamentary Jazz Band Swung It", City Limits, 20 Jul 1989.
[522] Paul Trynka & David Bowker, "All Jazzed Up And Ready To Go", Radio & Music, 19 Jul 1989.

July 1989.

The day after the Independent Broadcasting Authority [IBA] press conference, I spent the morning at home considering precisely what the regulatory officers might have meant when they had referred to the possible availability of further London FM frequencies. Where exactly were these frequencies, and would their usage mean that some existing stations might have to change channels to make way for new broadcasters? I phoned the engineering information departments of the IBA and the BBC, both of whose staff were very forthcoming in helping me piece together the various components of the FM waveband jigsaw in London. The previous day, the IBA officers had mentioned two further FM channels, one of which I thought I had just identified.

BBC Radio One had recently started broadcasting on FM for the first time, until then having used only the AM medium waveband since its launch in 1967. In London, the station was temporarily using the 104.8 FM channel with a relatively low power transmitter of 2,000 watts from the BBC's South London aerial mast at Crystal Palace. This channel was only an interim arrangement until a permanent, much higher power transmitter of 120,000 watts was installed at Wrotham in Kent that would cover the whole of Southeast England. Once that change was implemented in November 1989, Radio One's permanent frequency would switch to 98.8 FM, leaving its former channel of 104.8 free for another station in London.

What would this 104.8 FM channel be used for once BBC Radio One had moved to its new, permanent home? The BBC engineering department's plans showed that nothing had been planned for that frequency, other than a very low power, fifty watt transmitter at High Wycombe in Buckinghamshire. This was intended to relay the future broadcasts of BBC Radio Surrey & Berkshire, a new station that had been planned for many years, but which I considered was likely to fall victim to local radio budget cutbacks within the BBC. Surely, this 104.8 FM channel could instead be used for a new London station, broadcasting from the same Crystal Palace transmitter site that the BBC had already successfully used for its temporary broadcasts of Radio One. Now that I knew one of the two frequencies to which the IBA had alluded the previous day, I believed that KISS FM should start campaigning for the channel to be allocated to a new London station, rather than just left empty.

That afternoon, I went to the KISS FM office to explain my research to Gordon McNamee and to suggest that the 104.8 FM channel offered the station a specific objective around which to mount a further public campaign. McNamee listened and seemed to agree with me, but he showed little enthusiasm for the idea. He already appeared to have resigned himself to the notion that no amount of campaigning would repair KISS FM's failure to win the licence.

Fortunately, the other staff in the Blackstock Mews office were more enthusiastic about my idea, so I set to work and prepared a two-page press release to launch this new campaign. It expressed KISS FM's sadness at losing the London-wide licence, whilst simultaneously stating the argument for the government to award more FM radio frequencies in London. It read, in part:

"KISS FM and its listeners are extremely disappointed that the IBA decided NOT to award it the Greater London FM radio contract ... The IBA maintain they cannot grant more licences until they are allocated more frequencies by the Home Office. Radio One's 104.8 FM was allocated to them as a temporary frequency. Radio One will be relinquishing this London frequency in November and there are no plans for its alternative use ... KISS FM INSISTS that the Home Office allocate 104.8 FM to a deserving cause."[523]

Also included in the press release was a positive quote about KISS FM's future that I attributed to McNamee: "Whether it takes three months or three years, we will carry on campaigning until we are given the chance to be a legal radio station in London."[524]

While I organised this new press campaign for the 104.8 FM frequency at one desk in the KISS FM office, Heddi Greenwood decided to formulate a complementary strategy that would respond to the dozens of listeners who had contacted the office, asking how they could help. She drafted a one-page letter addressed to Douglas Hurd, the government's Home Secretary, who was responsible for broadcasting policy. It read:

"Dear Mr Hurd. In view of the IBA's decision NOT to grant the Greater London FM licence to KISS FM, I believe they have made the wrong decision. The IBA may feel they have catered for me by granting London Jazz Radio a licence, but there is a big difference between their style of broadcasting and 'dance music radio.' The IBA have publicly stated that they have identified two FM frequencies that could be allocated to new stations. As it is within your power to allocate these frequencies to the IBA, I hope you will attend to this urgent matter. Please help me – and many others – by co-operating with the IBA. Please speed up your plans regarding London's airwaves. Yours sincerely, ..."[525]

Greenwood wrote this letter as a template, with blank spaces left for each individual to write their signature, name, address and the date. Then she duplicated thousands of copies of the letter and organised a volunteer task force drawn from KISS FM staff and fans to take batches of letters to all of London's dance music record shops and clubs over the coming weekend, asking members of the public to pledge their allegiance to the campaign.

By the following Wednesday, Greenwood's dedication and hard work resulted in more than three thousand individually signed letters addressed to the Home Secretary. Exactly one week after the IBA announcement of the London licence award, Greenwood persuaded McNamee to visit the Home Office headquarters at Queen Anne's Gate to deliver all these letters, bundled into a cardboard box that had formerly held photocopying paper. Greenwood arranged for a photographer to capture the event and, although McNamee did not get to see Hurd himself, he did speak to Hurd's private secretary, who took receipt of the box and promised to pass its contents on to the Home Secretary. KISS FM was the only one of the losing licence applicants to have mounted such a high profile campaign, and it felt really good to be doing something positive, rather than wallowing in defeat.[526]

That evening, McNamee had convened a meeting of all the DJs and staff at the KISS FM office. The New Music Seminar was taking place in New York the same week, resulting in the absence of several members of the team – Jonathan More, Matt Black, Jazzie B, Dave VJ and Richie Rich – who had been enjoying recent successes in the music charts. Unsurprisingly, the meeting was comparatively short and low-key, consisting largely of McNamee's blow-by-blow account of the IBA's London licence announcement and KISS FM's subsequent campaign for further licences to be offered. There was much indignation amongst those present that the government had deceived the pirate radio community into thinking that a legal black music station was a distinct possibility in London. Several DJs said they thought that it was foolish of KISS FM to consider waiting for a further opportunity to apply for a licence, given how many promises the government had broken in the past.[527]

McNamee repeated his assertion that he had no intention of returning KISS FM to pirate broadcasting, and he also told the DJs that they were now free to pursue work with other legal radio stations, if they so wished. If KISS FM were to reform at some point in the future, McNamee promised that they would all be invited back to become involved in the station, so long as they had not contravened the government's ban on pirate broadcasting in the meantime. The meeting dissolved in an unusual mood of gloom and disappointment. McNamee had told everyone that there would be no further DJ meetings until or unless new developments happened that required the team to reform. It was an emotional evening, and there was a horrible air of finality about the proceedings that left McNamee looking extremely despondent by the end of the evening. His words sounded like a final goodbye to all the KISS FM staff, after having worked together as a team for more than three years.

McNamee also decided to close down the Written Word magazine that had, until then, acted as a promotional vehicle for KISS FM's activities, its clubs and its campaign for a licence. One final issue was printed to inform the station's fans of the full facts surrounding the failed licence bid. For this swansong, Lindsay Wesker wrote a two-page article entitled 'The Conclusion Of The Campaign' that summarised KISS FM's history and the licence application process that had ended in failure. He ended the piece plaintively:

"Nobody will be able to say that KISS FM didn't do their homework. No one will be able to say that KISS FM didn't try their hardest. No dance/black music organisation has come so close to being legal. For the last three-and-a-half years, whether on-air or not, we have served the interests of our public. Seven days a week, twenty-four hours a day, whether grooving in a club or under a pile of 6,000 envelopes, we really have tried our hardest."[528]

The front cover of this final, thirty-two page issue of the newsletter was inscribed in three-and-a-half inch high letters "NO LICENCE FOR KISS FM." Inside, photos were reproduced of the KISS FM team that had been taken for the publicity brochure. There was also an editorial:

"For as long as KISS FM is without a licence, we know there will still be hundreds of thousands of Londoners that do not have a radio station they can relate to … Even if you hear KISS FM DJs on other legal radio stations, do not despair, this does not signal the dissolution of KISS FM. If KISS FM gain a licence, all of these presenters will be invited to rejoin the team. There will be no more Written Word until further notice, we will just sit and watch and wait. OUR DAY WILL COME."[529]

Although The Written Word newsletter was closed down, the KISS FM campaign I had launched for additional London radio licences continued to run and I was pleased that it had started to attract considerable attention in the media. I was particularly encouraged to hear Dave Lee of London Jazz Radio reiterate his opinion that there would be a further London station licensed within six months, and that it would be awarded to KISS FM.[530]

The IBA had been told by the Department of Trade & Industry [DTI] not to discuss publicly the availability of individual FM frequencies, but the DTI's own spokesman, David Thompson, commented: "The 104.8 channel has not been re-allocated, but it is very close to frequencies held aside for community radio. We have to take into account future users." Home Office spokesperson Rosemary Waugh was far less forthcoming about the possibility of further London stations: "Even if everything were to go smoothly, it seems highly unlikely that any more stations could go on-air before the Broadcasting Bill has gone through Parliament and a new Radio Authority has been established. That means next spring at the very earliest, and probably not until the autumn of 1990."[531]

The following week's edition of Broadcast magazine proclaimed on its front cover: "GOVERNMENT TURNS DOWN IBA'S EXTRA FRANCHISE OFFER." The article reported that, at its meeting with the IBA, the Home Office had raised an objection that the introduction of additional London commercial stations would take away advertising revenue from the three, new national commercial radio channels that were going to be proposed in the Broadcasting Bill. My subsequent enquiries to both the IBA and the Home Office brought fierce denials from both parties that there was any truth in this report. IBA spokesperson Stuart Paterson said: "No decision has yet been made. We're still in discussion with the Home Office to see whether further FM frequencies for Greater London could be made available." The IBA's principal development officer David Vick added: "We are very keen for the process to be concluded as quickly as possible, as it seems likely that we will be legally required to re-advertise [any new licences]. It is categorically not the case that there are London FM 'runners-up' who will be automatically awarded any licence. All thirty-one of the other applicants for the first frequency will be in with a chance."[532]

Until then, the one disappointing outcome of the KISS FM campaign for further London FM licences had been the lack of a formal reply from the Home Secretary's office to the thousands of letters of support that McNamee had delivered. Out of the blue, two weeks later, a letter arrived from Douglas Hurd's private secretary which stated: "We are, of course, aware of the keen interest in this matter, but frequencies for this type of service are at a premium. The Home Office, in close liaison with colleagues at the DTI, is urgently considering whether there is a way additional contracts can be issued at this time, and we hope to be able to reach a decision as soon as possible."[533]

Four days later, much to the surprise of the entire radio industry, the Home Secretary approved the notion of two additional London-wide FM stations, to be awarded by the IBA in the near future. Douglas Hurd said that the huge number of applications for London Jazz Radio's licence had illustrated the existence of a "strong and high quality demand" for more radio in the capital. He continued: "More stations mean not more of the same but wider real choice. The new stations will take us two steps closer to the new regime for radio which will follow new legislation. That will offer more opportunities for several hundred radio stations to be established across the country."[534]

The IBA said that it "warmly welcomed" the Home Secretary's decision and was pleased to have been given an opportunity to continue the task of expanding listener choice. It noted: "The quality and variety of the thirty-two applications received for the one 'community of interest' incremental independent local radio contract for Greater London advertised in April ... demonstrated that considerable scope exists for serving a broader range of audience tastes in the capital."[535]

The speed with which these two new FM frequencies had been approved by the government seemed incredible. The news was greeted with jubilation by everyone involved in

KISS FM. It was impossible to know how great a part the station's publicity campaign had played in changing the Home Office's mind although, for Heddi Greenwood and me, it felt as if our dogged determination to respond positively to the original licence disappointment had been completely vindicated. A Home Office spokesperson would only say: "There was no way of knowing before that there were so many attractive and high quality proposals. It was subsequently clear that there was a demand for frequencies and the IBA put up a good case."[536]

The IBA's principal development officer, David Vick, admitted that its argument to the government for additional licences had been "an outside shot" but he added: "We will be much harsher this time on the actual substance of the application. On the previous round of licences, some applicants took the opportunity to try and influence the Authority by including all sorts of extras." This was probably a reference to both the audiocassette and the huge appendix that KISS FM had included in its submission alongside the basic application form.[537]

Gordon McNamee commented on the decision: "We'd virtually given up. Obviously I'm very pleased. Congratulations to the IBA for doing it." Within days, the IBA wrote to KISS FM, along with all the other unsuccessful applicants, promising to supply further information during the next couple of weeks about the application procedure it would adopt for these two new London licences.[538]

Once again, speculation started to spread in the media as to the potential winners from this next round of radio licences. Broadcast magazine predicted it would be a classical music service and a "music station such as KISS FM." Media Week magazine suggested a short-list that included classical, easy listening and dance music formats. The Financial Times mentioned KISS FM and easy listening Melody Radio. The Evening Standard specifically cited KISS FM.[539]

A leader column in Broadcast magazine welcomed the Home Office decision to offer more London FM licences and it demanded that Douglas Hurd continue to offer even more new radio services at a similar pace of development. A contrary viewpoint was expressed the following week in The Independent newspaper by Radio Clyde managing director James Gordon, who reiterated the gloomy speech he had made at the Radio Festival: "It has to be asked whether there is really evidence of pent-up demand from listeners for more localised neighbourhood stations ... I suspect that listeners will quickly become bored with radio if it is too introverted ... Eight to ten London-wide stations would be enough to cater for most tastes."[540]

Gordon should have read the final issue of The Written Word that had included two pages of letters from KISS FM supporters, bemoaning the fact that their favourite radio station had not been awarded the first London-wide FM licence. One fan, Julian Harcourt of Hitchin, wrote: "I have just heard that the FM licence has gone to London Jazz Radio and not KISS and, aside from feeling entirely gutted, cannot believe that a minority music like jazz has got the licence ... All I can say is: keep up the campaign and justice will be done one day."[541]

Whatever James Gordon might have thought, the two new licences that the Home Office had just unveiled suddenly gave KISS FM the second chance it needed to try and ensure that justice might possibly be done. Second time around, surely KISS FM must win!

[523] "KISS FM To Lobby For 104.8 FM", KISS FM press release, 13 Jul 1989.
[524] ibid.
[525] "A Letter To The Home Secretary, Douglas Hurd", KISS FM, [undated].
[526] Grant Goddard, "Radio On?", City Limits, 3 Aug 1989 [photo caption].
[527] Grant Goddard, "Kissed Off", NME, 26 Aug 1989.
[528] "The Conclusion Of Our Campaign", Written Word no. 6, Aug 1989.
[529] "Foreword", Written Word no. 6, Aug 1989.
[530] Paul Trynka, "What Next For The Losers", Radio & Music, 19 Jul 1989.
[531] Mark Heley, "IBA Faces Race For Two More Frequencies", Radio & Music, 19 Jul 1989.
[532] Edwin Riddell, "Government Turns Down IBA's Extra Franchise Offer", Broadcast, 28 Jul 1989.
Grant Goddard, "Radio On?", City Limits, 3 Aug 1989.
Mark Heley, "More London Frequencies: Home Office Decision This Week", Radio & Music, 2 Aug 1989.
[533] letter from Catherine Bannister, Home Office to KISS FM, 3 Aug 1989.
[534] "More Radio For London Says Home Secretary", Home Office press release, 7 Aug 1989.
[535] "IBA To Advertise Two More Incremental Radio Contracts For Greater London", IBA press release no. 70/89, 8 Aug 1989.
[536] Edwin Riddell, "Hurd Gives Go Ahead For More Franchises", Broadcast, 11 Aug 1989.
[537] Mark Heley, "Two More London FM Licences By Christmas", Radio & Music, 16 Aug 1989.
[538] ibid.
Liz Roberts, "FM Hopefuls Cheer Promise Of More London Contracts", Media Week, 11 Aug 1989.
letter from David Vick, IBA to KISS FM, 8 Aug 1989.
[539] Edwin Riddell, op cit.
Liz Roberts, op cit.
Raymond Snoddy, "IBA To Offer Two More London FM Contracts", Financial Times, 8 Aug 1989.
Steve Clarke, "Music In The Air For London", Evening Standard, 21 Aug 1989.
[540] "Radio Freedom", Broadcast, 11 Aug 1989.
James Gordon, "Planners On The Wrong Wavelength", The Independent, 18 Aug 1989.
[541] "X Talk", Written Word no. 6, Aug 1989.

August 1989.

There was a momentary lull in the usually frenetic activity at the KISS FM office, whilst we awaited the next Independent Broadcasting Authority [IBA] announcement that would give specific details of the application procedure for the two new London FM licences on offer. Gordon McNamee turned his attention to other matters, since he understood that there was still no guarantee of KISS FM winning the licence, even on its second attempt.

On several occasions, I had mentioned to McNamee my belief that there existed significant untapped commercial potential in KISS FM's magazine, 'The Written Word.' A year earlier, the publication had started life as a single A3 sheet newsletter, entitled '94,' that had been produced on a word processor and had been printed without photographs. At that time, it had been intended solely as an update for the station's fans and its main feature had been the KISS FM programme schedule. As the station's mailing list increased in size, so too had the content of the magazine. By the final issue of The Written Word, the thirty-two pages had included lots of photos, record reviews, interviews and information about the London dance music scene. There were also several pages of paid-for advertisements which had helped to defray the increasing costs of printing and postage.

For several years, I had been fascinated by the proliferation of free magazines in London, with weekly titles such as 'Ms London,' 'Girl About Town' and 'Midweek' handed out during the morning rush hour to thousands of commuters at London's railway and underground stations. For revenue, these magazines depended entirely upon the advertising space they sold, but their distribution costs were low and their print runs were huge. An increasing number of more specialist magazines were being produced and financed in this way. Travelling through Waterloo railway station one day, I had been handed a free entertainment and what's on magazine that was aimed specifically at high earning commuters living in the suburbs. In my area of Northwest London, I regularly received a free copy of a general interest, colour magazine aimed at homeowners in the locality.

One of the problems KISS FM had encountered with The Written Word was the huge cost of sending out thousands of copies of each issue individually to every person on the station's growing mailing list. I believed that these expenses could be reduced dramatically by distributing the magazine as a free giveaway to a wider readership that would pick it up from dance music record shops, music venues and clubs in London. Many more copies would have to be printed to circulate the magazine in this way, but the advertising space within it could be sold at a much higher price, since it would be reaching many more readers. Instead of being solely a KISS FM publicity vehicle, the enlarged publication could be London's first giveaway magazine to be aimed specifically at the city's dance music community.

McNamee liked my idea and could see the potential it offered him to earn much needed revenue to cover the overheads of running the KISS FM office. After several weeks discussing with him my proposal for the magazine, McNamee asked if I would like to launch the project and be its editor. I had experience in this field, having been editor of the student newspaper and student handbook whilst at university, and having launched an independent music magazine in Northeast England. I accepted McNamee's job offer and handed in my notice to the record company where I had worked during the last two years. McNamee said he would pay me £100 for three days' work each week, plus eight per cent of the net profits generated by the magazine. Although this worked out to be less money than I had earned from the record company, I believed that the new job would improve my career prospects and provide an opportunity to be more closely involved with KISS FM.

Besides, my recent experiences with the record company had left me frustrated and eager to explore a new work opportunity. Back in 1985, whilst working in Israel, I had discovered a female singer named Ofra Haza whose music, a kind of 'Middle East meets West' sound, I believed would be marketable in Europe. Since then, I had worked hard promoting her music and had succeeded in achieving airplay on national radio in the UK and positive press coverage. By 1989, one of the Ofra Haza songs I had found in Israel four years earlier had reached number fifteen in the UK singles chart. It was released by the independent record company for which I had been working. I asked the company for some compensation towards all the work I had done to make this artist a success, including a UK artist interview tour I had arranged in early 1989. The directors had met and decided to offer me a cheque for £200. I felt insulted by this amount, particularly as my years of work had given the company its biggest chart hit in a long time. Worse, the credit for Ofra Haza's chart success was being taken in press interviews by someone else working at the record label. Now, all I wanted to do was quit the company, having earned almost nothing from four years of work having created Israel's biggest international pop music star, and yet not having even gained any recognition.[542]

I started work at the Blackstock Mews office on 22 August 1989, the first occasion I had earned money from KISS FM, despite having been involved in the business since the beginning of the year. I had been spending more and more time in the office, working with the other staff, but had never been offered remuneration. I looked forward to becoming a proper employee, although the one person in the organisation who did not seem to welcome my appointment as editor of the new publication was Lindsay Wesker. He had been editor of The Written Word, until its recent closure, and he probably felt that this experience, combined with his previous work for the Black Echoes music paper, should have made him the ideal candidate for this new post. McNamee told me privately that he was well aware of Wesker's antipathy towards my appointment, but assured me that he wanted fresh blood to be in charge of the project.

The day after I handed in my notice to the record company, I convened an evening meeting at the KISS FM office to discuss the new magazine. After a considerable amount of brain-storming, Heddi Greenwood suggested it could be titled 'Free!' reflecting not only the fact that it was to be a giveaway magazine, but also the notion of personal freedom to which dance music fans would be able to relate. Her suggestion was accepted unanimously. It was agreed that the first monthly issue would be published at the beginning of October 1989, that the print run would be around 30,000, and that the magazine should divorce itself entirely from the KISS FM campaign for a radio licence that had dominated The Written Word. Everyone felt that it was most important for the magazine to be viewed as an authoritative, independent guide to the London dance music scene. Heddi Greenwood would handle the advertising sales for the magazine, and McNamee had appointed Lindsay Wesker its deputy editor in a gesture of reconciliation. I set to work writing a substantial business plan that outlined the magazine's purpose and ethos, which would also be used in presentations to potential advertisers. Over several pages, I defined the editorial content of Free!, its intended readership and the reasons I believed it would prove so successful.

Now that I had become the fifth paid worker in the KISS FM office, McNamee arranged a second-hand desk and phone extension for my arrival. I was now working at Blackstock Mews on a regular basis, from which I gained a greater insight into the way in which the members of the KISS FM team worked and their respective roles within the organisation. The biggest shock was discovering the limitations of Gordon McNamee's literacy. He admitted to having "bummed out of school most of the time," but claimed to have left Walworth Comprehensive School in South London with Certificates of School Education in physics, mathematics, woodwork, technical drawing and English.[543]

However, in the KISS FM office, when McNamee read aloud from letters he had received, or when he read out parts of magazine articles he wanted to draw to others' attention, he frequently stumbled over long sentences and he mispronounced uncommon words. Additionally, his writing, always in capital letters and always scribbled in brown ink from a Pentel pen, was almost indecipherable. For example, McNamee's handwritten notes about KISS FM's shareholders had read: "EMAP – A MAGER COMSUMER MAGGAZINE PUBLISHER ... CRADLEY PRINT PLC – ONE OF THE BIGGEST MAGGAZINE PRONTERS BASED IN BRIMINGHAM ... EMAP IS AGRUBLY THE MOST SOCSESSFULL EXERBITION CO. 45 COUNCURMER MAGS, 45 BESENESS MAGS." Even dealing with music industry terminology, McNamee seemed to have problems. Reggae became "REGGIA," African became "AFFRICAN," and garage was "GARGE." His difficulty with spellings prevented him from writing his own correspondence, and he could use neither a typewriter nor word processing software.[544]

McNamee's lack of skills in written English was compensated by another factor that came into play within the KISS FM office – the closeness of his relationship with his personal assistant, Rosee Laurence. I soon learnt that, in 1987, there had been considerable resentment from those involved in running KISS FM at the time when McNamee had unexpectedly offered Laurence a full-time job within the small organisation. Questions were asked as to why he wanted to employ a twenty-two year old who had no previous work experience as a DJ or in pirate radio. There were plenty of more skilled and experienced people who could have been recruited. This initial antipathy had eventually blown over. McNamee regularly turned up for work each morning accompanied by Laurence, usually left in the evening with her, and would often disappear at lunchtime with her. McNamee regularly brought his dog, Aster, to the office with him, and it was always Laurence who had to take the pet for a walk, had to take it outside when it wanted to go to toilet, and had to clean up the mess when it frequently fouled the office floor.

McNamee sat serenely behind his large desk in the open plan office at Blackstock Mews and, whenever he had an idea or some task that needed doing, he would bark across the room to Laurence, demanding she carry it out. His frequent orders included anything and everything, from making endless cups of tea for him, going out to buy his lunch or putting his favourite record on the office hi-fi system, to typing out letters, making endless phone calls and organising his diary for him. One of McNamee's favourite expressions was 'hands-on work,' which he told everyone was the successful way in which he organised KISS FM. He regularly told outsiders that anyone who became involved in the radio station would have to do all the hard graft themselves, and not expect to be able to order around others to carry out deeds for them. However, McNamee himself singularly failed to work in this way. He might have had some good ideas and devised some grand schemes, but it was inevitably Rosee Laurence who was burdened with the task of executing them. She was the only person he entrusted to count and bank the thousands of pounds earned each weekend from KISS FM club nights; she had to draft and type all the station's correspondence; and she had to organise all the station's publicity and office systems. Evenings and weekends, she also had to be the door-person at KISS FM events, since McNamee entrusted no-one else to take customers' money.

On the frequent occasions when the relationship between McNamee and Laurence was not running particularly smoothly, a frosty atmosphere would envelop the entire office. McNamee would shout even more loudly at her across the room, and would tell her how inadequate she was, chastising her in front of everyone else for not carrying out the most minor of tasks to his complete satisfaction. During these periods, Laurence would become noticeably red-eyed, and would often sob quietly whilst sitting at her desk, then rush into the toilet or disappear completely from the office for hours at a time. One lunchtime, I visited my bank branch in Finsbury Park and found Laurence standing on the pavement outside, completely motionless at a junction busy with lorries, buses and cars, leaning over the protective railings, and staring blankly at the congested traffic. She was lost in her own thoughts and looked as if she had been in that same position for several hours.

Laurence accompanied McNamee to all the meetings he attended, because he needed her to make literate notes of what he had said and the actions he had committed himself to doing. Besides, it usually ended up being Laurence herself who would carry out the plan of action on his behalf. Even when KISS FM organised evening or weekend events, Laurence would inevitably be present alongside McNamee. In the office, although McNamee could often be overheard talking to his wife on the phone, there was only one occasion I can recall her ever visiting, very briefly, Blackstock Mews.

If Laurence seemed to live an almost slavish existence responding to McNamee's every command, then Lindsay Wesker's role was much more one of the faithful lieutenant to his boss. McNamee seemed to believe that, by employing Wesker, he had rescued him from the disillusionment suffered when his 'dream job' working in the music industry had failed to work out. Like Laurence, Wesker worked extremely long hours in the office for what he viewed as the noble cause of KISS FM. Wesker seemed not that interested in the profit he could derive from working, so McNamee exploited mercilessly his goodwill and dedication to black music. Wesker was clever and often came up with good ideas, which McNamee had a tendency to acquire and peddle as his own schemes, without any explicit objections from Wesker. Despite them being the same age, Wesker seemed to play the role of pupil to McNamee's teacher and, at the slightest beckoning, Wesker would scamper over to his boss's desk and eagerly promise to do whatever was asked of him.

To Wesker, his work for KISS FM appeared to be a calling rather than a job, and McNamee was his mentor rather than his employer. I developed a nagging feeling that, even if McNamee were to ask him to do something really dreadful, Wesker would go right ahead and do it, as long as he could be convinced that it would help 'the cause,' which Wesker viewed purely as creating a soul and dance music radio station for London. KISS FM seemed not to be a commercial business in Wesker's eyes, and it often appeared that he felt his authority over others within the station should derive from his impeccable knowledge of black music. Radio industry experience or business skills seemed unnecessary to him – he was in this purely for the love of the music. This appeared to render Wesker both very useful and entirely unthreatening to McNamee's status within KISS FM, for Wesker would willingly do all the work without wishing to usurp McNamee's own desire for power, money and glory.

Then there was Heddi Greenwood who, at thirty-two, was the oldest person in the office and had the most experience in business. Despite Greenwood having joined the organisation as McNamee's partner in KISS/Graphic Records, he seemed perpetually suspicious of her and tried his utmost not to involve her in any task that might usefully employ her business and organisational skills. Maybe McNamee viewed her experience and expertise as a threat to himself, since she obviously knew so much more about running a company than he did, which might be why he continually belittled and frustrated her. Despite having worked as a DJ on the pirate KISS FM, Greenwood's name had been left out of the station's licence application. In the office, she shared the workload equally with everyone else and had as much involvement in the running of the station as did the others. Because she was nominally his business partner, McNamee seemed to like annoying and infuriating her by denying her any additional status. For her part, Greenwood was sympathetic to Rosee Laurence who, ten years younger than her, seemed to be embroiled in a tortured relationship with McNamee through sheer naivety. However, Greenwood distrusted Wesker immensely and had first-hand experience of the ways McNamee would use him as a weapon to carry out his own dirty deeds.

The other person often to be seen in the Blackstock Mews office was KISS FM DJ Paul Anderson, who used the two-story building as his home. Commonly known by the nickname 'Trouble,' an epithet he sometimes lived up to, Anderson was much in demand as a club DJ and record remixer. Though not around the office much during the day, he and his friends tended to arrive there during early evening and used the open-plan space as their living room and recreation area. Soon after starting work at KISS FM, I would arrive first thing in the morning and find that papers and notes I had left on my desk the previous night had disappeared, been torn up, or had phone numbers and messages scribbled on them that were unconnected to me. The others in the office explained that they too suffered this problem as a result of Anderson's nocturnal activities. To avoid these irritations, each night before I left work, I cleared all the papers off the top of my desk and into its drawers. I soon learnt that, by solving one problem, I had simply created a different one. Mine was the only clear desk in the office that had a usefully clean, flat surface. Now, when I arrived each morning, sat down, and rested my arms on the empty desk top, my shirt sleeves would become coated with tiny particles of white powder, mixed with something that looked like cigarette ash. So, in addition to clearing my desk every night, I now had to introduce a ritual of wiping the desk surface clean with a damp cloth every morning, after I arrived. The others in the office must have thought I was being incredibly tidy but, in reality, I wanted neither to lose my working papers, nor have suspicious substances smeared on my shirtsleeves for the rest of the day.

Apart from these minor inconveniences and the sporadic bad feeling that permeated the office when McNamee and Laurence periodically fell out, KISS FM provided a very enjoyable work environment. The phones were ringing continually, the photocopier was always busy, and the stereo system was usually blasting out some newly acquired dance record or one of the remaining pirate stations. For these reasons, it was thoroughly pleasant working there most of the time.

I was busy putting together the blueprint for the new Free! magazine. I visited a cheap photo-typesetting company in Brighton, commissioned quotes from printing companies, called meetings in the office of potential contributors, and commissioned a logo design. McNamee was becoming increasingly enthused about the potential profit offered by the new magazine, and so he quickly became more involved in its day-to-day running. He had almost stopped talking about KISS FM altogether and, despite our awareness that the new London FM licences were in the pipeline, McNamee directed the whole office's efforts into this new publishing venture.

One extremely hot and sunny weekend in late August, the KISS FM staff spent the whole of Saturday and Sunday transforming the hitherto unused downstairs room at Blackstock Mews into an office for Free! All the accumulated rubbish was completely cleared out and the dark, dreary room was repainted – ceiling, walls, floor, everything. McNamee bought a job lot of small second-hand desks, which were moved outside to the Mews for us to paint in gloss black. The office stereo system was rigged up outdoors to provide us with musical entertainment, and McNamee dug out some old cassette recordings of programmes from KISS FM's pirate days, which he had kept in his desk drawers, to entertain everyone.

Some brand new shelves and storage units were purchased from the IKEA furniture store, which McNamee and I assembled in the new downstairs office. There was one piece of furniture with which McNamee became obsessed: the construction of a huge, rectangular glass-topped table, more than six feet in length. It was the closest he could achieve, for now, to the impressive pieces of furniture he had admired in the opulent boardrooms of KISS FM's new, corporate shareholders. Between the clear glass table top and its felt underlay, McNamee spent hours carefully positioning press articles about KISS FM and pages from The Written Word magazine, along with some of the station's publicity materials. Once the glass top had been screwed down to the base, the whole thing looked remarkably like a personal shrine to the KISS FM pirate radio station that McNamee used to run and to the commercial radio business to which he aspired.

One chapter in his business career now having ended, McNamee seemed determined to bury the deep disappointment of the failed KISS FM licence bid and, instead, to put all his energies into turning my idea for Free! magazine into the money-spinner he longed for. The dream of KISS FM radio was very quickly being forgotten.

---

[542] Grant Goddard, "Ofra Haza: The Making Of World Music's First International Star", Grant Goddard: Radio Blog, 27 Dec 2010.
[543] Robert Ashton, "Root With A Suit", Music Week, 29 Feb 1992.
[544] Gordon McNamee, handwritten notes, [undated].

August & September 1989.

On 21 August 1989, the Independent Broadcasting Authority [IBA] made its long awaited announcement about the details of the two new London-wide FM licences it was advertising. The IBA director of radio, Peter Baldwin, wrote to KISS FM, outlining the revised application procedure and informing potential bidders that the closing date was 13 November. The IBA had increased the number of copies it required of the completed application form from eight to twelve, and Baldwin's letter warned: "Applicants should not submit any extra pages, prefaces or appendices giving information additional to that requested in the application form, or enclose any other material such as full research reports, cassettes or publicity documents with their applications ... The inclusion of supplementary material at the outset may render the application liable to disqualification." It was a clear warning to KISS FM not to submit the huge appendix or audiocassette tape it had included on the last occasion. As a result, the answers each applicant provided within the standard application form would prove even more critical than before.[545]

Straight away, Gordon McNamee wrote to all the KISS FM DJs, asking them to attend a meeting on 5 September to discuss the new licence application and "other projects in hand." By this, he meant the impending launch of Free! magazine, which still needed more contributors and help with its organisation and distribution.[546]

For his part, Keith McDowall, KISS FM chairman, had been busy since the announcement of London Jazz Radio's licence win, with an examination of that group's application form and its proposed structure. He became convinced that the company's forty-two person advisory panel, which The Guardian newspaper had described as "prestigious," had been an important factor in the success of its application. London Jazz Radio had declared that the composition of this advisory panel showed "that jazz knows no bounds. It is the music of the people, ageless and classless; it can be happy or sad, joyful or thoughtful." In reality, the panel was heavily skewed towards MPs, Lords, and the cultured jazz elite. McDowall believed that a similarly constructed advisory group could help KISS FM immeasurably to win its second bid for a licence, and so he set about recruiting suitable members.[547]

Comedian Lenny Henry was the first person McDowall approached, despite his agent's negative response to the earlier invitation for Henry to serve as a KISS FM company director. This time, McDowall's letter was sent directly to Henry and read, in part: "You probably saw that KISS FM did not get the new London FM station – it went to London Jazz – but we only just missed it ... What we lack perhaps is 'street credibility.' London Jazz scored because it was able to use names like that of actor Michael Caine and several Members of Parliament. We have since learned that they are supporters rather like the fan club of a football team. We have decided that KISS FM needs an advisory committee broadly representative of London folk – residents who can put a view from every angle – ethnic, age, sex and interests of every kind."[548]

Aside from the rather condescending tone of this letter to one of the UK's top comedians, McDowall failed to grasp the fact that "street credibility" was the one characteristic that KISS FM already had in abundance, much more so than other competing licence applicants. Unless, perhaps, he was referring to the kind of streets lived in by Lords, MPs, OBEs or CBEs, like himself. McDowall went on to persuade Gordon McNamee to support this plan, asking him to suggest more 'names' who could be approached to join the committee. In turn, McNamee listed the advisory committee as one of the topics on the agenda of the DJ meeting he had called, where suggestions from those present included Island Records founder Chris Blackwell, pop musician Paul Weller, actress Patsy Kensit, Dianne Abbott MP, newsreader Trevor McDonald and boxer Frank Bruno.[549]

However, the majority of the meeting was spent discussing the prospect of KISS FM winning a licence on its second attempt. McNamee explained to his audience the pros and cons of the situation, but seemed to lean much more on the side of potential failure than success. The positive points were: KISS FM was said to have been amongst the top five applicants on the first occasion (though this had not been confirmed by the IBA); the IBA's own research had confirmed the feasibility of a dance music station; and the award of a licence to KISS FM could be used as a scapegoat for further government clampdowns on pirate radio activity in London. McNamee indicated that the negatives were: established stations such as Capital Radio were suddenly including more dance music in their output, which might be thought to alleviate the need for a station like KISS FM; and the fact that three new London stations (London Jazz Radio, WNK in Haringey, and South London Radio in Brixton) already planned to include substantial amounts of black music within their output.[550]

According to McNamee, WNK and South London Radio had already written jointly to the IBA, demanding that the two, newly advertised London-wide FM licences should not be awarded to any kind of black music applicant, since a newcomer such as KISS FM would damage these stations' audience figures and their potential to generate advertising revenues. Apparently, the IBA had refused to make any such promise. McNamee went on to assure the DJs again that they were welcome to take up jobs on newly licensed stations, but that those companies' contracts might forbid them from moving back to KISS FM, should it win a licence. He suggested that the DJs wait until Christmas before taking up other offers of radio work, since the outcome of KISS FM's second bid would be known by then.[551]

McNamee also announced that there would be no party to celebrate KISS FM's fourth birthday that year, and that the station would maintain a deliberately low public profile in the run-up to the submission of its application. This was in marked contrast to the station's previous licence bid, and reflected both the station's shortage of funds and the feeling that KISS FM had already won the publicity war. This time around, the effort would be concentrated more carefully on putting together a winning application. Finally, McNamee explained the rebirth of The Written Word magazine as Free!, the venture that was now occupying my entire time working at the KISS FM office. When I had accepted the job of editor, McNamee had promised that I would also be spending some of my time working on the second licence application, but the launch of Free! was proving to be very demanding and there was still little sign of action within the organisation about the radio licence.[552]

McNamee hardly ever mentioned KISS FM any more, and the only aspect of the second licence application that seemed to occupy him was satisfying the chairman's desire to assemble an advisory committee. Since the failure of the first bid, there had not been a single office meeting to discuss what had gone well or badly in the previous campaign, or to analyse what had been the good and bad points of the application. Whenever I broached the subject of the second licence bid with McNamee, he would shrug it off and change the subject to the potential success of Free! magazine, which had overtaken KISS FM as his pet project. This state of affairs frustrated me immensely, because it seemed as if McNamee had lost interest in making a second licence bid at all. He had already discarded KISS FM's past and the possibility of winning second time around. In fact, McNamee had confided in a close friend, Joe Strong, manager of Dingwalls venue in Camden, that losing the licence had left him "absolutely devastated" and "absolutely inconsolable."[553]

I was perplexed. I arranged to meet a fellow journalist and radio worker, Daniel Nathan, whom I had known since moving to London in 1986, and with whom I felt I could discuss this problem. As the two of us walked across Blackheath one weekend, I ranted to Nathan about how incredibly close I thought KISS FM was to winning a licence on this second occasion, and how frustrating it was that McNamee seemed intent on wasting the opportunity. I had been the only member of the KISS FM team to attend the IBA press conference announcing London Jazz Radio's win (Nathan had been there too) and it was obvious to me how much enthusiasm some of the IBA staff had shown towards KISS FM's bid. This time, there was likely to be a similar number of applicants for the two new licences and, unless KISS FM could submit an almost perfect application, the IBA would feel duty bound to award licences to other groups who proved that they were better organised.

Talking to Nathan clarified, in my own mind, the gravity of the situation. These two new London licences were likely to be the last on offer until some time in the mid-1990s. To throw away the chance of winning a black music station for radio listeners in London at this stage would be utterly crazy, particularly after so many people had campaigned for so many years in the hope of just such an eventuality. I decided that, even if McNamee was prepared to remain slumped despondently in his office chair, consigning KISS FM to a space in his glorious past, I certainly was not. If he wanted to wallow in his own despair, that was fine with me. He could carry on playing nostalgic tapes of his old KISS FM shows to everyone in the office, as he had been during recent weeks, but I was determined to do something more positive about winning the station a licence.

On returning to work the following week, at the first opportune moment, I confronted McNamee across his desk in the open plan KISS FM office. Why was he not doing anything about the second licence bid? Did he not believe KISS FM could win? If everyone else still had faith in KISS FM, was he not letting them all down? Was any work being done on a revised application? Was not Free! magazine merely a short-term distraction? Almost anyone could start a new magazine, but how many people could win a radio licence? Why had he slumped into total inaction? As I questioned McNamee, I could sense the other staff at their desks in the office trying to bury their heads in work and look as if they were not listening to our conversation. I explained to McNamee that I thought he was throwing away the biggest business opportunity he was ever likely to encounter in his life. I told him that, of the people within the KISS FM office, I seemed to be the best qualified person to organise and co-ordinate the second licence application. For the moment, that work seemed to me to be a far more appropriate use of my skills than editing Free!, particularly as nobody else seemed to be doing anything about the KISS FM bid.

I suggested to McNamee that someone else should be brought in to edit Free! magazine while I devoted my full attention to re-working the KISS FM licence application. I had already prepared the groundwork for the new magazine during the last month, and the project could easily be handed over to another editor at this stage. On the other hand, if we did not act on the KISS FM bid now, we would never be offered another chance.

During this monologue, McNamee listened to me, smiled a lot, but said virtually nothing in reply. I could sense that, deep inside, he was incredibly angry that anyone should even dare to challenge his authority in this way. I had seen him act this way before, but only when directing his anger towards others who had displeased him. Instead of showing any response of anger or emotion, McNamee just glowered at you and clammed up. It was his usual cold shoulder treatment – ex-communication rather than confrontation – and you had to wonder whether he was already plotting some ghastly revenge to extract upon you in the future for your supposed crime. McNamee continued to be wholly unresponsive to my questions, so I told him that I planned to start work immediately on KISS FM's application and that, initially, I planned to do some research in the comparative peace of my home. I promised I would willingly explain and hand over all the tasks I had completed on Free! magazine to whomsoever he wished. After all my suggestions, McNamee still offered me no response, so I gathered together my work and left the office.

After that 'meeting,' it was almost a week before I heard anything at all from McNamee. I had been busy working at home, as I had planned, and although I had regular telephone conversations with the other staff in the KISS FM office, McNamee had carefully avoided any contact with me. To me, this sort of behaviour appeared incredibly childish – McNamee seemed to be putting the vanity of his own ego above the need for his radio station to win a licence. Then, late one evening, he phoned me from home. He offered no explanation or apology for his attitude towards me that day in the office, and he gave no reason as to why he had failed to contact me at all during the intervening week. Our conversation was unemotional and businesslike. He told me that, from now on, he would pay me £100 for spending three days each week working on the KISS FM licence application. He said he wanted more of my time, but I explained that I had other work commitments during the week on which I could not renege. He made it sound as if this arrangement had just come to him in a flash of inspiration, and that his offer was obviously too good for anyone to turn down.

He also told me that I would no longer be involved in Free! magazine in any capacity. He wanted me to visit the office and hand over all my paperwork to the newly appointed editor, who would be Lindsay Wesker. Finally, he disclosed the caveat that must have taken him almost a week to concoct. When my work on the licence application ended in November, I would no longer be paid by KISS FM, and neither could I resume the editorship of Free! magazine. In essence, I was being allowed to have my own way in the short term but, in the end, I had been made to sacrifice a permanent job at KISS FM. I would be forced to look elsewhere for work once the licence application process was over. This did not worry me excessively because I sincerely believed that KISS FM could win the licence this time around, whereas McNamee seemed already to have resigned himself to failing on the second occasion. This new arrangement cut my pay to a basic £100 per week, because I would no longer draw the percentage of profit that McNamee had previously agreed I would derive from Free! magazine. I was not told the details of the deal that McNamee had struck with Wesker to take over editorship of Free!, but Wesker could not hide his delight at assuming the position he must have felt he had always deserved.

However, when the much delayed first issue of Free! was eventually published at the beginning of November, Wesker's tendency to indulge himself shone from the inside of the magazine. He contributed one page of his own photos and three and a half pages of his record reviews to the beginning of that first edition. These reviews included glowing critiques of a single released by KISS FM's own label, Graphic Records, and of a track recorded by Wesker's partner, Claudette Patterson. I was no longer allowed any involvement in Free! and my name was deleted from the magazine's masthead, in disregard of my work developing the original idea and setting the project in motion. Free! had been my 'baby' and I had had to sacrifice it for KISS FM. From then on, Wesker spent most of his time in the downstairs Free! office at Blackstock Mews, while the rest of us continued to work upstairs on the business of KISS FM and Goodfoot Promotions.

During the week that McNamee had been incommunicado, I had visited the IBA Library and had read through all thirty-one of the other applications for the first London-wide FM licence. Most of them had commissioned market research to support their argument for a particular format, and many of them had attached the full analysis tables as an appendix to their bids. Several of these reports demonstrated the popularity of dance music in London, particularly amongst those aged between fifteen and thirty-four years. These were the first useful sources of information I researched for the second KISS FM application. Although these data were taken from competitors' work, I credited the research of London Jazz Radio, Stream FM, Crystal FM and London Rock Radio in KISS FM's finished application document. The statistics showed that the public support for a dance music radio station in London was undeniable, regardless of who had been commissioned to carry out the research.

After my rapprochement with Gordon McNamee, I returned to working in the KISS FM office to collate as much information as I could about the station's first unsuccessful licence bid. Although I had been involved in drafting answers to many of the questions posed in the application form, I had never seen all the paperwork for the bid. I asked McNamee if I could look through the filing system that I assumed had been organised in the office for the first KISS FM application. He laughed loudly and told me that no filing cabinet existed full of neatly labelled suspension files, as I had imagined. Instead, he pointed to a pile of loose, unordered documents stacked on the floor of the office, behind his desk, climbing about a foot up the wall. This was the paperwork for the first application, and my first task was to organise it into some sort of order.

The other information I needed was a copy of the finished KISS FM application form from the last bid, and a copy of the huge appendix that had accompanied it. McNamee pulled out his own private copies from a shelf unit alongside his desk, and told me that my need for these last remaining copies of the documents was greater than his at that moment in time. I took both documents and started flicking through them on the train journey home, hoping they might offer me some inspiration.

The application looked pristine, as if it had been completely untouched. Then I came across the page that outlined KISS FM's intended staff structure, showing each job in the company and how much it would be paid. In pencil, McNamee had scribbled out two of the station's seventy-seven staff positions. One was the programme director, a position created specifically for Dave Cash, but which was no longer required since he had dropped out of the bid. That change was understandable. However, the other post McNamee had crossed out was the station's programme controller, the job for which I had been earmarked. No new posts had been added to the diagram, no jobs had been re-titled and no other amendments had been made. It was clear that, in the new scheme, Dave Cash and I no longer held positions within the company. These changes left KISS FM's head of music, Lindsay Wesker, reporting directly to McNamee, who now acted as both the company's managing director and programme director.

I was shocked to have found out accidentally that I seemed already to have been ousted from the KISS FM master plan. What should I do? During the weeks and months that followed, McNamee made no mention of this revised staffing structure, so I started to forget about its implications. Maybe these had been mere doodlings that McNamee had made immediately after the failure of the first licence application. I had no idea.

It was only much, much later I would learn that these scribbles held far more significance for my future than ever I could have imagined at the time.

---

[545] letter from Peter Baldwin, IBA to KISS FM, 21 Aug 1989.
[546] letter from Gordon McNamee to 'Dear All', 24 Aug 1989.
[547] John Fordham, "More Of All That Jazz", The Guardian, 17 Jul 1989.
"News From London Jazz Radio", London Jazz Radio press release no. 2, [undated].
[548] draft letter from Keith McDowall, KISS FM to Lenny Henry, 1 Sep 1989.
[549] minutes of KISS FM DJ Meeting, 5 Sep 1989.
[550] ibid.
[551] ibid.
[552] ibid.
[553] Robert Ashton, "Root With A Suit", Music Week, 29 Feb 1992.

September 1989.

One Monday morning in September 1989, one of the KISS FM DJs arrived at the Blackstock Mews office with news of something that had happened to him during the weekend. Bill Tuckey (alias 'Billy T') was one of the three reggae fanatics who owned the Manasseh sound system and had presented a very popular Saturday night roots reggae show on KISS FM in its pirate days. Tuckey had recently enrolled himself into the editorial team of Free! magazine and could be found working in the magazine's downstairs office most days. That Monday, Tuckey came upstairs to share with us some news.

He had attended a private party at the weekend in Hampstead and had wandered onto the balcony of the house to get some fresh air. Looking across to the neighbouring house, Tuckey could make out a figure stood on the adjacent balcony that looked remarkably like Richard Branson, the entrepreneur behind the Virgin Group of companies. Tuckey called across to him and cordially invited him to come next door and join the party, an offer which, much to Tuckey's surprise, Branson accepted immediately. Some time later that evening, the two had talked about radio and Tuckey had explained his involvement in the KISS FM licence application, a subject that had seemed to fascinate Branson.

Virgin had been one of the thirty-one applicants competing against KISS FM for the first London-wide licence, having proposed a rock music station called Crystal FM. Although Branson's involvement had brought the bid a certain amount of publicity, Virgin had never been considered one of the frontrunners because there were several other applicants proposing a rock format whose applications looked more impressive. Branson told Tuckey that he would be very interested in becoming a partner in the second KISS FM bid, and he suggested that someone from the radio station should call his private office to arrange a formal meeting to discuss the matter. When Tuckey recounted this chance meeting to everyone in the KISS FM office, we were amazed and a little sceptical that Richard Branson would want to become involved in our licence application, rather than continue to bid for his own radio station.

As Tuckey had suggested, McNamee contacted the personal office of Branson, who followed through the invitation, as he had promised, and instructed his staff to set negotiations in motion to formalise Virgin's stake in KISS FM. This process echoed EMAP's involvement in the first licence application, in that it had introduced the station to a significant investor through a chance meeting, rather than a systematic plan. On 25 September, Gordon McNamee and Martin Strivens of KISS FM met Charles Levison, managing director of Virgin Broadcasting Limited, the company within Branson's group that focused on radio and television. The details of Virgin's involvement in the KISS FM bid were finalised there and then to both parties' satisfaction.

Forty-eight year old Levison desperately desired a high-profile media project to be involved in that would bring his division a much needed success story. The previous year, Virgin Broadcasting had launched Radio Radio, with Levison as its chairman, which was an ill-fated, satellite-delivered radio service designed for local commercial stations to re-broadcast overnight instead of their own locally produced programmes. The station failed to attract advertisers and was sold shortly before its closure. Virgin Broadcasting had also been involved in Music Box, an early attempt to provide a satellite-delivered music video station along the lines of MTV. Levison was a director of the company, which failed commercially and was downgraded to the role of an independent television production house. Then there was Super Channel, another satellite-delivered TV entertainment channel, of which Levison was joint managing director. It too failed and ownership was eventually transferred to an Italian media conglomerate.

The Crystal FM bid having failed earlier in the year to win the London-wide FM licence, Levison must have realised that KISS FM's chance of winning second time around would be greater than a re-submission of the Virgin bid. To him, it probably seemed a safer bet to be involved as a partner in KISS FM, rather than to risk being a total loser in the highly competitive London FM licence bidding war. Aside from Virgin's own ill-starred ventures, Levison's only other radio industry experience was an earlier role as director of the local commercial station, Radio Mercury, whose complaints had forced London pirate Radio Jackie off the airwaves. Levison was a lawyer, but had moved into the entertainment industry, most notably as chief executive of WEA Records, where he had overseen the successful launch of American soul singer Randy Crawford's career in the UK.

Levison agreed terms with McNamee and Strivens, under which Virgin would subscribe to ten per cent of KISS FM's share capital in return for a directorship on the station's board. Levison indicated that he would be willing to take a larger holding, up to twenty per cent, if it were offered him, but agreed that Virgin had no desire to be the company's majority shareholder. He also promised that Virgin would neither re-submit its Crystal FM application, nor be involved in any other competing bid for the two new London licences. It was agreed that Virgin's involvement in KISS FM would not be made public until a joint press statement was published at a future date. Levison came away from the meeting with the distinct impression that KISS FM would be capitalised at £2.5m, although the station's first licence application showed total funding of only £1.4m, of which £790,000 was to be raised from share capital and loan stock. Levison followed up the meeting with a letter of confirmation to Martin Strivens, in which he promised KISS FM "£250,000 for the 10% share."[554]

Virgin's new shareholding meant considerably more to McNamee and Strivens than the ten per cent of KISS FM it meant to Levison. They saw it as a green light to make their planned radio station bigger and better resourced, enabling many of its senior staff to be more highly paid. Strivens revised the budgets upwards and produced a new cashflow forecast that made Virgin's £250,000 stake look much more like a ten per cent share than would have been the case if it had simply been grafted onto the financial plan from KISS FM's first application. All the budget estimates were increased, some by spectacular amounts, so that the station's level of funding now more closely resembled the millionaire-financed proportions of London Jazz Radio. McDowall, particularly, still considered the jazz station to be the role model for a successful bid for a radio licence.

KISS FM's total financing was upped by more than a half from £1.39m to £2.17m. Its share capital was nearly tripled from £412,500 to £1,117,500, and the bank overdraft facility was increased by £100,000 to £350,000. The company was once again being made bigger, as well as becoming a business that encompassed much greater financial risks, but which also offered bigger potential rewards to its investors. Most of the increased costs of the company were accounted for by inflated salaries of a handful of executives.[555]

Gordon McNamee's salary as managing director increased from £40,000 to £55,000, while the sales & marketing director's earnings were raised from £30,000 to £40,000. Financial director Martin Strivens' salary rose from £35,000 to £40,000. Lindsay Wesker's head of music post and Lyn Champion's head of features job now both paid £22,500, instead of £15,000 in the previous application. Dave Cash's defunct £27,500 programme director position, which I inherited, was renamed 'programme controller' and its salary increased to £30,000. It remained the lowest paid of the three departmental heads – finance, sales & marketing and programming – despite the incumbent's responsibility for the largest number of staff. Even Rosee Laurence's salary as personal assistant to McNamee rose from £13,000 to £16,000, while two typists' pay was raised from £10,000 to £12,000.[556]

Some additional personnel were added. The sales department was increased from one person paid £12,000 to a team of five, each paid £20,000. The finance department added an additional accounts assistant and a secretary. A receptionist suddenly appeared in the scheme. Programming was the only department to have its personnel reduced, from twenty-three full-time and forty part-time staff in the first application to twenty-one full-time and twenty-seven part-time now.[557]

The company's projected costs for its first full year of operation were increased from £2.7m to £3.5m though, at the same time, it was not anticipated that KISS FM could earn more money from selling advertising airtime than it would have in its first application. Projected Year One revenues were maintained at £3m, and Year Two revenues were cut from £3.7m to £3.4m. These new figures characterised a large-scale radio station that still believed it could make a trading profit by the end of its first year on-air, and could eliminate its accumulated losses by the end of its second year. This was all very different from McNamee's initial plan for KISS FM nine months earlier, whose overheads had been estimated to be less than £1m a year, and whose managing director was to be paid £18,000.[558]

The stakes were substantially higher now, the risk of failure would be greater, and even a relatively minor error in calculating the station's costs or revenues could turn the business from its projected path of profitability into a serious loss-making venture. However, the individual rewards for KISS FM's senior staff were substantial enough to make the business an enticing proposition, since they would be able to earn considerable sums from it in a short space of time, even if the station itself failed in the long run.

While Martin Strivens grappled with the financial aspects of the second licence bid, I proceeded to revise the other parts of the application form that dealt with the station's programming plans. I suggested to McNamee that a group meeting should be convened one evening to 'post mortem' the first application form and to critically note the areas where there was obvious room for improvement. I felt that KISS FM needed a clear plan of action if it was going to submit the finished document by the 13 November deadline.

The post mortem meeting was held on 6 September in the downstairs office at Blackstock Mews used by Free! magazine. A group of key KISS FM staff assembled that evening around McNamee's beloved glass-top table. They were destined to meet together in exactly the same spot many more times during the next few months. Those people were: Gordon McNamee, his personal assistant Rosee Laurence, Lindsay Wesker as head of music, Lyn

Champion as head of talks, and myself as head of programming. The remaining person who worked in the KISS FM office, Heddi Greenwood, was reduced to only occasional involvement in these meetings. McNamee had still not offered Greenwood a role in the running of the legalised radio operation, despite her having devoted as much time as anyone else around the table to the organisation of KISS FM's licence campaign.

McNamee still seemed remarkably unenthused about the prospect of KISS FM winning a licence, so I chaired the post mortem meeting and ran a critical eye over the previous application. I felt that not enough hard research had been included which could have been used to argue why London should have a black music station, rather than any other music format. Several of the questions had been answered far too bluntly, and there were evident inconsistencies within KISS FM's arguments that had not been addressed. The meeting also looked through the blank application form that the Independent Broadcasting Authority [IBA] had revised slightly since the station's first bid. There was now additional space available to answer some of the financial and programming questions, and more detailed responses were required in several places. The IBA had recognised some inadequacies in its original form and had corrected these for the last two licences it was offering in the incremental radio scheme.

That first meeting agreed that the best way to move the KISS FM bid forward was to work our way methodically through the application form, examining each question in turn. We decided to meet as a group once a week to discuss a draft answer that I would have already prepared to a specific question. The meetings would also offer me the chance to present to the others the research I was collating that would support KISS FM's case. McNamee agreed to go along with this plan of action, and seemed happy enough to let me do all the work that it involved. These weekly meetings would restrict themselves to the programming aspects of the bid, whilst McNamee would liaise with Martin Strivens over the revision of the application's financial section. It was agreed that a further meeting would be held in one week's time to tackle the answer to the first of the IBA's questions.

The seriousness of this post mortem meeting set the tone for the hard work that was about to be put into KISS FM's second licence application over the next three months. During the first licence bid, the KISS FM office had been totally absorbed with the publicity and public relations aspects of the station's campaign. The application form itself had been completed at the last minute as a mish-mash of half-formulated ideas provided by different people within the group. This time around, there was no publicity campaign to accompany the bid, so work could be concentrated on making the application form as impressive as possible. There was no doubt that KISS FM had already succeeded in substantially raising its profile within the media since renouncing pirate broadcasting at the end of 1988. The task ahead for the station's staff was to live up to the expectations so many people harboured that KISS FM would definitely win a London radio licence second time around.

Personally, I was very disappointed to no longer be involved in the launch and organisation of Free! magazine. However, I firmly believed that KISS FM would win the London licence if I could come up with the necessary facts and figures in this second version of the application form. There would always be another opportunity in the future for me to launch a new publishing project. Right now, this might be the last opportunity I would have to win

London a black music radio station. The hard work had only just begun, and a lot of responsibility was suddenly resting upon my shoulders.

---

[554] letter from Charles Levison, Virgin Broadcasting to Martin Strivens, Centurion Press, 29 Sep 1989.
[555] "IBA Incremental ILR Contract Application Form", KISS FM, Nov 1989.
[556] ibid.
[557] ibid.
[558] ibid.

September & October 1989.

KISS FM chairman Keith McDowall remained pre-occupied with adding worthy people to the advisory committee he had created. He wrote a letter to several of the suggested names, similar in content to his earlier note to Lenny Henry, promising that "this committee would gather no more than twice a year, for which, of course, we would pay an honorarium fee ..." The most recent suggestions for potential recruits included Olympic gold medallist Tessa Sanderson, TV personality Jonathan Ross, and comedians Adrian Edmondson and Harry Enfield, all of whom were added to McDowall's mailing list. One person who had already replied positively was Sammy Harari, managing director of the advertising agency TBWA, who agreed to take up the job "for less than £2,500 [per annum]."[559]

McDowall received many rejection letters in response to his requests. Bob Hoskins' management said that the actor spent too limited an amount of time in the UK to be involved. Harry Enfield's office mistook McDowall's letter as an invitation to join London Jazz Radio and replied that "jazz is not particularly high on his list of interests." The biggest disappointment arrived in the form of a two-sentence letter from the Lynne Franks PR Company: "Many thanks for writing to Lenny Henry and asking him to support KISS FM on an advisory committee. Unfortunately, Lenny is unable to commit himself to this, due to numerous other previously arranged commitments."[560]

It had been understandable, from the earlier approach, that Lenny Henry might not have sufficient time to devote to being a non-executive director of KISS FM. Surely he could attend two meetings a year of its advisory committee. The letter was less of a blow to McDowall than to McNamee, who had always been proud to have Henry's name associated with the station since its pirate days. Now that KISS FM might be on the verge of becoming legitimate, it would have been fantastic to involve Henry in some way. Much to McNamee's immense disappointment, it was not to be.

Despite McDowall's enthusiasm for imitating what he considered was London Jazz Radio's winning strategy of creating an advisory committee for its station, he found that very few of the people he approached would accept his offer to be involved in KISS FM, even in return for payment. Since it was now only weeks until the application deadline, the whole notion of an advisory panel had to be quietly shelved.

However, one person who was becoming increasingly involved in KISS FM's licence application was a young American, Tim Schoonmaker, who EMAP had appointed to manage its stake in the company. Having moved to London to study a degree in business, Schoonmaker had stayed in the country after his studies, married and joined EMAP, where he had risen to the post of development director and worked from the office of the EMAP chairman, Sir Frank Rogers, who was on the KISS FM Board. Though his experience was in publishing rather than radio, Schoonmaker was enthusiastic about the concept of KISS FM and contributed extensively to the station's marketing and sales strategy, which was explained in much more detail in the second licence application. He started to visit the KISS FM office frequently and showed himself to be a shrewd, sharp, methodical analyst who saw straight through any bullshit explanations that were presented to him as fact.

As a peripheral activity to its extensive local newspaper holdings in the Midlands and East Anglia, EMAP already held stakes in several commercial radio companies. These had been minor investments within the public company's overall portfolio – twelve per cent of Mid Anglia Radio, ten per cent of Suffolk Radio, three per cent of Midlands Radio, and two per cent of Radio Broadland. In August 1989, Schoonmaker had started to look more closely at the UK commercial radio market and had found that, although the industry had only broken even in 1985, it had made a profit of £40m by 1989. Those radio stations in which EMAP had stakes had generated a profit of £2m the previous year, and Schoonmaker said he was keen for the publishing group to launch new radio stations in the future: "You can imagine us being amongst the best in radio. We haven't got all the skills in-house at present but, hopefully, we'll learn quickly through these stakes we've acquired [in radio stations]."[561]

EMAP's proposed investment in KISS FM eclipsed all of its existing radio holdings by value, by percentage control, and in terms of the high public profile that a new London radio station would attract. EMAP had been particularly successful in launching a series of youth-orientated magazines in the 1980s – Smash Hits, Just Seventeen and Looks – all of which appealed to teenagers by offering bright, no-nonsense editorial accompanied by lots of colour photography. EMAP's move into youth-targeted radio seemed a natural progression. Tim Schoonmaker's involvement in KISS FM presented an ideal opportunity for him to learn, from the inside, how the British radio industry worked. If KISS FM were to win the licence, EMAP would set up a new radio division within the company to consolidate and expand its radio holdings, and Schoonmaker wanted to steer this subsidiary towards further investments in the growing commercial radio industry.

During his visits to the KISS FM office, Schoonmaker would usually be seeking to elicit information about what the station's intended strategies were on a series of issues. The first challenge he set for me was to explain precisely from where the audience for KISS FM was going to come. He wanted to know which existing radio stations KISS FM's potential audience was listening to at present, and how many of them would make the switch to KISS FM. The week after the post mortem meeting, I prepared a three-page document for Schoonmaker entitled 'Where Does KISS FM's Audience Come From?' Using some of the research submitted by competing applicants in the first round of licence applications, mixed with analysis of official audience research about Londoners' radio listening habits, I suggested that KISS FM would attract listeners from five distinct sources, as follows.[562]

Capital FM, London's only commercial pop music radio station, had a substantial young listenership, with fifty-five per cent of fifteen to twenty-four year olds tuning in each week. The station played a lot of dance music hits, and there were undoubtedly many dance music fans who listened to the station because it was the nearest they could find to a legal, dance music radio format. The advent of KISS FM would mean they no longer had to tolerate the pop records on Capital FM that they had had to put up with until now, but which they did not really like.[563]

Secondly, Radio One, the BBC's national non-commercial pop music channel, played less dance music than Capital FM, but it too attracted a relatively young audience. KISS FM would probably draw fewer listeners from Radio One than it would from Capital FM, though there would certainly be a proportion of the audience that would defect.[564]

Thirdly, the BBC's local station for London, Greater London Radio [GLR], had been completely revamped a year earlier. In its previous incarnation as BBC Radio London, the station had included a substantial element of dance and reggae music in its programming. This had been abandoned in favour of a combined rock music and talk format. There was a considerable audience that was disenfranchised by the new-style GLR, but which had probably found no other station that effectively fulfilled its craving for dance music. Although GLR's audience had always been small, some of it was certainly going to turn to KISS FM.[565]

Fourthly, despite the government's threat of increased penalties, London still had many black music pirate stations, though it had always been difficult to establish the size of their audiences because they were not recorded in official listening surveys conducted by the legitimate radio industry. In recent months, the pirates' broadcasts had become increasingly sporadic in London, and there were no stations that could sustain twenty-four hour broadcasting to the extent that Horizon, Solar and JFM had in the mid-1980s. Many pirate radio fans would turn to KISS FM, not only because of the station's own pirate history, but also because its signal would prove more reliable than illegal alternatives.[566]

Finally, there were a substantial number of dance music fans who had probably given up listening to music radio completely, and had turned to their own records and cassette tapes for entertainment. They lacked a single radio station that satisfied their interests. This group would also turn to KISS FM, though only if a high-impact marketing campaign could be implemented that made them aware of the station's existence.[567]

I estimated that the combination of all these sources of listeners would provide KISS FM with an audience of one million Londoners who would tune to the station every week by the end of its first year of operation. This 'one million by the end of year one' figure was subsequently adopted as the goal that KISS FM pledged publicly it would achieve. The station would be broadcast to approximately 5.9 million people in the London area, so it needed around seventeen per cent of them to find something on KISS FM to which they liked to listen, if my plan was to work. Although one million listeners sounded like a huge audience for KISS FM to achieve, it was considerably less than the audience each week in London for Capital Radio (2.9 million), BBC Radio One (3.1 million), or middle-of-the-road music station BBC Radio Two (2.9 million). Even the former BBC Radio London had attracted 1.2 million listeners before it had been re-launched as GLR. By comparison with these figures, KISS FM's target of one million listeners seemed achievable, particularly given twelve months to attain it.[568]

The most difficult aspect to assess was exactly how much Londoners' radio listening habits would be impacted by the sudden influx of new 'incremental' radio services licensed by the Independent Broadcasting Authority [IBA]. The choice of legal radio stations in London had remained virtually the same since 1973, when commercial radio had first been introduced. Suddenly, the number of stations available on the radio in London was to be doubled within the space of a year. Who knew exactly how listeners would react to that? I had few answers yet in that respect. Tim Schoonmaker accepted the arguments I had made in my document about KISS FM's audience, and my key points were written almost word for word into the application form.

I continued to collate further research to argue KISS FM's case for a London black music radio station. At the IBA press conference called to announce the winner of the first London-wide FM licence, its principal radio development officer, David Vick, had said that the lack of jazz programmes on existing stations had been one of the deciding factors in the award to London Jazz Radio. Vick had said: "We also looked at the statistics on what is available at the moment. In terms of jazz, somebody who wants to listen to jazz can, at the moment, hear four and a half hours of it a week on established stations. The extent of deprivation in terms of access to the music was another factor. The same argument can clearly be made about black/dance music on legal stations. I wouldn't deny that for a moment."[569]

KISS FM's first licence application had not quantified how little black music was being broadcast on London's radio stations. Because so many dance music records were crossing over to the pop charts, it would prove impossible to measure how much of each station's entire output was devoted to black music. That would have required monitoring all stations' broadcasts for a day, or even a week, and the proportion would vary according to how many dance music records filled the singles pop chart in any one week. Instead, I decided to examine how many hours of each London radio station's output were occupied by programmes exclusively devoted to black music. This was of more relevance to radio listeners who were interested in black music, because they would want entire programmes, rather than the odd song or two on Capital FM or BBC Radio One that would inevitably be followed by three pop or rock music records.

For this research, I consulted old radio programme schedules published by the stations themselves, I looked at back issues of The Radio Times archived in the IBA library, and at radio programme guides printed in the media sections of old newspapers that were catalogued at the British Library. Using these sources, I built up a picture of exactly how many black music programmes a radio listener could have listened to on all available radio stations in London during the previous ten years.

BBC Radio One, Capital Radio and GLR all had a decreasing proportion of their output devoted to black music programmes. At the present time, BBC Radio One had three soul shows (presented by Robbie Vincent, Andy Peebles and Jeff Young); GLR had two dance shows (Dave Pearce), one reggae (Ranking Miss P) and one world music programme (Jo Shinner); and Capital Radio had two hip hop shows (Tim Westwood), two soul (Peter Young and Alex George), one dance (Pete Tong), one reggae (David Rodigan), and one Motown oldies show. These few programmes represented the diminishing proportion of specialist black music programming on each London station: BBC Radio One had suffered a fall from seven per cent in 1988 to only four per cent now, Capital Radio had dropped from six per cent in 1985 to five per cent, and GLR was currently six per cent compared to an incredible thirty-two per cent in 1986 when, as BBC Radio London, it had programmed daily black music shows.

In total, you could now hear thirty and a half hours of dedicated black music programmes a week on London's music stations, representing just under five per cent of their total broadcasting hours. More importantly, all these programmes were scheduled on Friday, Saturday and Sunday, leaving black music fans with no relevant radio programmes to listen to on weekdays. Furthermore, eight of the total thirty and a half hours were scheduled during unsociable hours, between midnight and six o'clock in the morning. The research showed demonstrably what I already knew from my own experience as a black music fan and an avid radio listener. The opportunities to hear black music on the radio had diminished substantially, particularly since the re-launch of BBC Radio London with a new name and new format. Although the total for black music, of thirty and a half hours' radio output, was not as low as the four and a half hours a week of jazz music cited by the IBA, it demonstrated the lack of coverage for a genre that enjoyed considerably more widespread popularity in London than jazz.

These figures successfully proved that dance music was being increasingly marginalised by the established radio industry. It was equally important to demonstrate the opposite end of the equation – at the same time, dance music's popularity in London was increasing dramatically. Anyone who was interested and involved in the dance music scene knew this to be true from their own direct experience – there were now more records being released, more nightclubs opening, and more dance music record shops opening in the West End of London. However, anecdotal evidence alone would not be sufficient to convince the IBA.

The definition of any particular genre of music is always open to fierce debate, which is why I needed to adopt an industry standard for 'black music,' rather than try and invent one myself. I examined back issues of the weekly music industry trade magazine Music Week to see if there was a noticeable upward trend in black music's general popularity. I had kept my own copies for the previous two years and, for the period before that, I consulted copies archived in the National Sound Archive of the British Library. Music Week had launched its 'Disco & Dance' chart in February 1983, and had published a weekly singles and albums listing ever since. When the disco craze finally subsided in mid-1986, the name of these two charts had been abbreviated to 'Dance.' Despite such occasional name changes, there had always been records in the British pop charts that were regarded as soul, rhythm & blues, dance or black music. At the time when Music Week's dance charts were launched in 1983, black music records constituted around eighteen per cent of its Top Forty pop singles chart. Although there had been subsequent fluctuations in this proportion, the overall trend had been noticeably upward since then. By September 1989, sixty per cent of the Top Forty chart was made up of dance music singles, the highest proportion ever.

I believed that it was important to demonstrate to the IBA that the huge popularity of dance music was no flash-in-the-pan phenomenon, and that the widespread interest in dance music stretched as far back as the early 1960s, when R&B first took hold within the British club scene. The IBA would not award a licence to a radio station they might feel was only riding on the popularity of a transitory trend in contemporary music. Music Week magazine had published regular supplements that examined the consumer market for particular musical genres. In September 1989, it had noted: "Not since the 1970s disco boom and the success of artists such as The Bee Gees have the charts been so full of dance product ... Over the coming year, all the signs are that dance music's impact on the charts ... will be even greater."[570]

I presented the results of all this research systematically to meetings of the KISS FM application team, crowded around the glass-top table in the Free! office. I would type up all the details on my battered manual typewriter at home, photocopy them at the office, and then distribute them to the others, ready for discussion. The meetings would last for many hours and often became bogged down in discussion of very minor points, sometimes about the meaning of a particular word. Everyone around the table was passionate about black music and had their own idea of what KISS FM meant to them. That made it particularly easy for discussion of a particular topic to become sidetracked by issues that might be relevant to the dance music culture, but had little direct bearing on the KISS FM application to the IBA for a radio licence. The most important thing that I needed to accomplish was to come out of each meeting, however long it might take, with an answer, or part of an answer, to one of the IBA's specific questions.

Following the post mortem that had set the ball rolling, the weekly meetings took place as planned for the first two weeks. However, it quickly became obvious that there would be insufficient time to debate all the necessary points. By the third week, we convened meetings on two evenings. By the fourth week, we were meeting three times. Thereafter, we seemed to be gathered around that glass table almost every night of the week. The process of planning KISS FM's policies was proving to be incredibly productive, but was also very exhausting. I spent the days researching facts and figures to use in the application, drafting answers to each question, and making sure that everyone was aware of the topic to be discussed. Then, in the evenings, I would chair the meetings, many of which started at half past six and finished well past midnight. The outcome of these discussions would then have to be typed up the next day and circulated to everyone in the group, to ensure that it was an accurate record of what had been agreed.

As more and more of these meetings took place, Gordon McNamee's interest in the licence application seemed to be rekindled. The intensity of the discussions was infectious. Everyone around the table eventually became convinced that KISS FM would definitely be the licence winner this time around, if only we could hammer out the main points of our case and distil them into the spaces provided on the application form. There had always been a lot of talk in KISS FM's press statements about the way the radio station worked as a close-knit team. This series of intense evening meetings demonstrated that there was substance behind those clichés. There were also a lot of laughs to be enjoyed, alongside the serious work at hand, with the making of endless cups of tea and coffee to keep us awake, and a steady stream of take-away meals brought in from the many restaurants along nearby Blackstock Road.

Right there in that little office, we felt that we were deciding exactly how the legalised KISS FM would take London by storm. Any worries we might harbour about the involvement of big businesses – EMAP and Virgin – in the company completely evaporated from our minds at that time. KISS FM was all about black music, and it was all about radical radio. These two elements were what we lived and breathed, and also what we knew would make the station a huge success. Huddled around that glass-top table, we really believed then that no one, no one at all, could take those things away from us. We were totally obsessed and absorbed in KISS FM's future success. It was a success that all of us were longing to share.

---

[559] standard letter from Keith McDowall, KISS FM to potential advisory committee members, Sep 1989.
letter from Tim Schoonmaker, EMAP to Keith McDowall, 19 Sep 1989.
[560] letter from Hutton Management to Keith McDowall, 9 Oct 1989.
letter from PJB Management to Keith McDowall, 17 Oct 1989.
letter from Lynne Franks PR to Keith McDowall, 19 Sep 1989.
[561] "EMAP Antenna Homes On Radio", Splash: News For EMAP People, Feb 1990.
[562] Grant Goddard, "Where Does KISS FM's Audience Come From?", 13 Sep 1989.
[563] ibid.
[564] ibid.
[565] ibid.
[566] ibid.

[567] ibid.
[568] ibid.
[569] author's recording, 12 Jul 1989.
[570] "Dancers Take A Spin In The Albums Market", Music Week, 30 Sep 1989.

October 1989.

Although Virgin Broadcasting had agreed in September 1989 to take a ten per cent stake in KISS FM, throughout October the company persisted in trying to increase its shareholding to twenty per cent. KISS FM could certainly have welcomed the extra cash Virgin wanted to inject, but Gordon McNamee resisted the idea, determined not to increase further the voting rights in the company held by 'outsiders.'

While these negotiations with Virgin rumbled on, McNamee and KISS FM financial director Martin Strivens arranged a meeting with another potential shareholder, Group W. It was a division of Westinghouse Electric, the corporation that had launched America's very first commercial radio station in 1920. Group W already owned fourteen stations in major US cities and was looking to expand its radio business into Europe. Broadcasting legislation restricted shareholdings in British commercial licensees by non-EEC [European Economic Community] companies, such as Group W, to small minority stakes, a factor that McNamee found more to his liking than Virgin's possible intention to eventually control the whole company. The meeting with Group W vice president of planning, Dave Graves, proved interesting, although the company eventually decided to invest In London Jazz Radio, which had already won its licence, rather than KISS FM, which was still only one of many hopefuls.

With the deadline for the KISS FM licence application approaching rapidly, it was important to finalise the deal with Virgin. Its stake hovered precariously between ten and twenty percent for a while, until a compromise of fifteen percent was finally agreed. There was a sting in the tail for Virgin, because it was now to be charged an additional 'premium' for its shareholding, justified by the fact that it was a latecomer to join one of the licence bids that had already been hotly tipped to win. This successfully produced more capital for KISS FM from Virgin, without McNamee having to relinquish power in the company's boardroom.

McNamee's desire to retain control over the radio station, despite his dependence upon other people's investment to launch the company, was cleverly incorporated into KISS FM's two-tier shareholder structure. There were to be 'A' shares, each of which cost £1.50 and entitled the holder to six votes; and 'B' shares which also cost £1.50 each, but which only entitled the holder to one vote. In the boardroom, the holder of an 'A' share would have six times as much clout as the holder of a 'B' share. McNamee ensured that he was the company's biggest holder of 'A' shares. Although he invested only £30,000 in KISS FM, a mere four per cent of the company's capital, he was entitled to twenty per cent of the votes. On the other hand, Centurion Press and EMAP, who were both investing £180,000 in KISS FM, held only 'B' shares, entitling each of them to only twenty per cent of the votes, the same proportion as McNamee.[571]

The remainder of the shares were allocated just as carefully in order to support McNamee's plan to retain control of the company. The other holders of the privileged 'A' shares were: McNamee's family friend David Evans, whose £2,250 investment gave him one and a half per cent of votes; Evans' employee at Centurion Press, Martin Strivens, whose £1,500 equalled one per cent; and the seven KISS FM DJs, each of whom invested £1,000 for one per cent. All of these 'A' shareholders were parties that McNamee believed he could trust to support him in the boardroom. The remainder of the 'B' shares were taken by: Cradley Group Holding plc, an associate company of Centurion, providing £45,000 for five per cent; KISS FM chairman Keith McDowall, whose £22,500 equalled two and a half per cent; and Virgin Broadcasting, whose £135,000 (exclusive of the premium) equalled fifteen per cent. There was a final tranche of £72,000 of 'B' shares which was described on the application form as "unallocated."[572]

The shareholders that McNamee felt he could depend upon to support him were: his family friend David Evans; Evans' company, Centurion Press; Centurion's associated company, Cradley Group; Evans' employee Martin Strivens; and the seven KISS FM DJs. Between them, they held 54.5 per cent of the votes, despite contributing only a little over a third of the company's share capital. However, if ever the other corporate shareholders – Virgin and EMAP – together with KISS FM's chairman were to gang up against McNamee, they would not win a vote in the boardroom. The shareholding structure seemed ideal in giving McNamee power over the company, without him taking responsibility for the substantial financial risk that the venture involved.

In the application form's financial section, written by Martin Strivens with McNamee's input, the IBA was told that the unallocated £72,000 of shares "will be placed privately after the licence has been granted." In answer to a question on the form about KISS FM's ownership, it was stated that one of the key factors in the shareholding structure was "making a significant proportion of ownership available to key personnel who will be responsible for ensuring the success of the station." In reality, it was unclear whether this £72,000 had been a spare amount inserted purely to make the figures add up neatly, or whether there was a genuine intention to offer these shares to some of the staff within the company. Apart from the minuscule holdings being offered to some of the station's DJs, McNamee had never mentioned to anyone in the KISS FM office the possibility of buying a substantial stake in his company.[573]

At the time, there was far too much urgent work to complete the application form for the office staff to pay close attention to these financial arrangements. One of the most important tasks was to describe accurately the programme format that KISS FM would adopt, were it to win the licence. In the first application, the station's output had been variously described as "black/dance music" and an "urban contemporary station." Confusion persisted in some sections of the media as to whether KISS FM was some kind of black or ethnic radio, rather than a specialist music station. Hence, it was decided to use a unique term for the station's format in the second licence application that would prove less open to misinterpretation. From now on, KISS FM would proclaim itself a 'dance music station.'

The station's detailed programme plans also needed to be sharpened considerably. In its first application, KISS FM should have had the edge over other applicants in this area, since it had already been putting its programming ideas into practice as a pirate station since 1985. However, its set of answers to the IBA questions had been very disappointing. This time around, it was vitally important to define much more precisely the station's programming philosophy. Preparing an answer to this one question required several evening meetings at Blackstock Mews, and it involved more passionate debate than any other response on the application form. The IBA had increased the space allocated for this answer to three pages, two of which McNamee decided should be devoted to a double-page, fold-out programme schedule printed in colour, with the one remaining page providing a written explanation.

After much discussion, and an incredible amount of haggling over the meaning of individual words, it was agreed that the answer to the programming question would start: "The most important element of KISS FM's programmes is the many and varied styles of music embraced by the term 'dance,' e.g. soul, R&B, funk, reggae, ska, world music, hip-hop, house, gospel, soca, blues and salsa. Within each week's output, there is a range of programmes that appeal to both the general listener and to those who have more specific musical tastes. This is achieved by a mix of playlist-based and specialist interest shows that complement each other and satisfy quite specific communities of interest ..."[574]

A further eight paragraphs explained, in more detail, that the KISS FM programmes broadcast on weekdays between 5 am and 7 pm would be heavily reliant on a playlist, whilst shows during weekday evenings and weekends would be devoted to different specialist music styles. Much of the language used in this explanation, such as the phrase 'communities of interest,' was deliberately inserted as terminology that the IBA had previously used to describe radio programming styles.[575]

The explanation of the KISS FM music playlist was reworked to combat a commonly voiced argument that the station's output would merely duplicate the dance music records already being played by other radio stations. The application form now noted: "The content of the playlist differs significantly from those of existing stations by concentrating on brand new dance records not receiving airplay elsewhere, new artists and emerging styles ... offering a content significantly different from existing radio services."[576]

Altogether, there was now considerably more detail about KISS FM's programming plans, compared to the first application. A lot of the answers encompassed sensible proposals that I felt served two purposes – they would make the station successful and, simultaneously, they would appeal to the IBA. While I wrestled with the language used to answer these important questions, McNamee became absorbed in the fold-out programme schedule he had promised to design. After several days spent messing around with rulers, coloured pens and a roll of tracing paper, he proudly presented me with his finished work. Unfortunately, the large grid he had drawn had its axes round the wrong way. I had to tell him that the days of the week normally run down the side of the page, and the hours of each day along the top, rather than the other way around. McNamee's second attempt proved more successful, and he then spent several days filling in each square with different coloured pencils, according to the genre of music to be played. The finished chart looked like some kind of psychedelic chess board but, for now, I was happy to let McNamee carry on with his unscientific method of determining the station's programme schedule. I knew that, if KISS FM were to win the licence, much more attention would have to be paid to these details. Until then, I was happy that McNamee was obviously enjoying himself.

Once the answers to all the questions had been finalised, a meeting was arranged on 16 October at the Blackstock Mews office with KISS FM chairman Keith McDowall for him to read over our work. Although he was happy with most of the document, sixty-year old McDowall did insist that all references to 'streetwise' and 'acid house' were removed. To us, it was obvious that the word 'streetwise' summed up KISS FM's attitude very precisely, but McDowall insisted that it was too anti-establishment. I hastily made the necessary revisions and prepared new copies of the application form. McNamee presented these to a meeting of the station's investors the following afternoon. The finished document was given final approval and everything seemed to be on schedule to submit the application to the IBA the following month.

Apart from EMAP's Tim Schoonmaker, who visited the KISS FM office quite often, it was rare for any of the other investors or board members to be seen at Blackstock Mews. McNamee was the only person in the office who met them regularly, and he would arrange meetings at their offices rather than at our own. The outcome of all these meetings, such as the one that considered the final draft of the application form, was relayed to the rest of us in the office with a bare minimum of detail from McNamee. We usually gleaned more detailed information by overhearing McNamee's phone conversations in the open-plan office, or by asking his personal assistant, Rosee Laurence, in whom he seemed to confide everything.

There was one unusual occasion, on 3 November, when the office staff was allowed to meet some of 'the backers' at a radio industry lunch organised by The Radio Academy at the Savoy Hotel in the Strand. A table was booked for KISS FM and McNamee was accompanied by Rosee Laurence, Lindsay Wesker, Lyn Champion and me. Also present were EMAP's Tim Schoonmaker, Centurion's Martin Strivens, non-executive director Tony Prince, chairman Keith McDowall and Virgin's Charles Levison, whom I sat next to. The dinner passed uneventfully and everyone seemed to get on well together, talking about their involvement in KISS FM and their hopes for a successful licence application this time around. Then, at the end of the lunch, just as we left our seats, a tall, suited, lanky young man with an Irish-American accent approached our table and asked if he could have a few words with me. I obliged and he introduced himself as Garret O'Leary, who worked alongside Charles Levison at Virgin, although I did not catch his exact job title.

O'Leary said he was aware that I had completed a lot of original research for the KISS FM application, including an analysis of the presence of dance music on existing radio stations in London. I assumed that Levison must have told him of the summarised results of this research that he had approved within the draft application form. O'Leary said he wanted to have copies of all my research documents and, without explaining why he might need them, he demanded they be sent over to his office later that afternoon. I told him that, unfortunately, I could not comply with his demands. Firstly, the research was confidential to KISS FM's licence application and was not intended for public consumption. My research could prove particularly useful to any other bidder planning to compete against KISS FM's application. Secondly, I told him that the decision on what information KISS FM released was McNamee's, and not mine. O'Leary did not appreciate my response and pressed upon me further his need to have the information as quickly as possible. I shrugged off his demands, but it was obvious that O'Leary must have been used to telling people what they should do for him, rather than asking them politely and explaining why he might need such confidential information.

By the time I had returned to the KISS FM office later that afternoon, there was already a phone message from O'Leary and a follow-up fax demanding copies of all my research. I told McNamee what had passed between the two of us at The Savoy and explained my reasons for not wanting to grant O'Leary access to my work. It was hard to understand why O'Leary's boss at Virgin, Charles Levison, who was a perfect gentleman, would employ such a 'difficult' assistant. I hoped that McNamee would deal firmly with the situation by telling O'Leary to back off. However, the following week, I continued to receive further phone calls at the office from O'Leary, which I eventually had to refuse to take, and further faxes demanding copies of my work, which I ignored. It was a minor irritation, but totally unnecessary, particularly given the stress we were all under to complete the licence application on time.

My next task was to co-ordinate the typesetting of the application form. Centurion Press had a subsidiary company, Senator Graphics, that used computer typesetting equipment to reproduce graphs, charts and diagrams. On Monday 6 November, I left home very early in the morning to travel by train and Underground across London from one end to the other, in order to reach Senator's offices by half past eight. In the middle of a horribly rundown area of South London, full of boarded up offices and tiny workshops around Waterloo station, I found the company's hi-tech facilities based in the top floor of an otherwise disused office block. I was introduced to two young Essex lads who were both soul music fans and who seemed thrilled to be asked to work on KISS FM's licence application. They were completely at home with all the technical gadgets that surrounded them and they started to type the document into their computers straight away. I selected the typefaces, the layout and the style, and we set to work on the project as a team of three. While the other two inputted data, I proof checked what they had just done. When it came to the diagrams, we experimented with different ways to lay out the pages until the results looked impressive.

For the last two months, I had been carrying around the constantly updated master version of the licence application form in a cheap, battered yellow and black A4 ring-binder purchased from a stationery shop near the KISS FM office in Finsbury Park. Now, it felt particularly satisfying to see all the dog-eared sheets of paper I had revised so many times in the binder suddenly being transformed into beautifully printed pages of type. I set up shop on one of the spare desks in the two boys' office. There were still several points in the financial section of the application form that either did not make obvious sense, or which contradicted other statements within the document. For the rest of the day, there was a constant stream of faxes and phone calls between Martin Strivens, Tim Schoonmaker and me in order to iron out these details. Apart from a short break at lunchtime to buy sandwiches from the café next door, we worked right through the day and late into the evening. Although their shifts officially finished in the afternoon, the two young typesetters were happy to stay at work to try and get the job finished. By very late that evening, it was obvious that more time would be necessary. We packed up work for the day and I struggled back across London, fighting the tiredness that threatened to overwhelm me, until I finally reached home.

The next morning, I got up early again and crossed London to reach Senator Graphics by half past eight. The completion of the job seemed in sight now and, with a fresh start that day, the work seemed to fly by much more quickly. There were endless bottles of Lucozade brought in to keep the three of us going, and Luther Vandross' 'Greatest Hits' album blasted across the office the whole day from a CD player the company had thoughtfully installed for its hard working staff. With the two soul boys singing along to the Vandross songs they knew and loved, and me scribbling away in red ink on the proofs they were producing, we completed the work by the end of that second afternoon. Printing plates were made for each of the application form's forty-eight pages, which I took by taxi to Centurion Press's office in the

West End. I also made several photocopies of the finished pages to take back to the KISS FM office for everyone to see.

By the end of that week, the completed application form arrived at the Blackstock Mews office from the printers. This time around, there was no huge appendix, just the relatively slim application form upon which all our futures depended. The sheet music from the song 'Our Day Will Come,' which McNamee had insisted be printed across the cover of the first application, had been replaced by a simple red and blue KISS FM logo printed on a plain white background. Inside, the document followed a straightforward question and answer format, broken only by McNamee's fold-out programme schedule printed in garish blocks of yellow, blue, pink and purple. Everything on the form looked great, and the small typeface I had selected helped to impress that each of the IBA's questions had been answered fully and at length.

The next Monday morning, 13 November, McNamee and I travelled in his car from Blackstock Mews to the IBA office in Brompton Road to deliver twelve copies of the finished application form. The building's entrance lobby was crowded with other applicants handing over their own documents, along with a few journalists who were talking to each group of bidders as they arrived. The IBA's David Vick once again signed a receipt for our application forms and we soon returned to the KISS FM office, having discovered that there were around thirty-five other competitors for the two FM licences.

I felt a huge sense of relief now that the application process had been completed. It had been less than two months since I had quit the job of launch editor of Free! magazine in order to devote all my time and energy to KISS FM's second licence bid. So much work had been accomplished during that short period of time. The team had sat around the table in the Free! office during so many evenings for so many hours, thrashing out a clear idea of what sort of radio station KISS FM would be if it won. We had all grown much closer during those last few weeks of heated discussions, considered debate and bitter argument. We had become a genuinely tight-knit team. It seemed that all we needed now was the green light of an FM radio licence to be able to turn our detailed plans into reality. The hard work was all over for now. The waiting had only just begun.

---

[571] "IBA Incremental ILR Contract Application Form", KISS FM, Nov 1989.
[572] ibid.
[573] ibid.
[574] ibid.
[575] ibid.
[576] ibid.

November & December 1989.

The day after the licence application had been submitted, a letter arrived at the KISS FM office from the Independent Broadcasting Authority's [IBA] principal radio development officer, David Vick: "I am writing formally to acknowledge receipt of your application for one of the two incremental independent local radio contracts for Greater London, advertised in August ... A committee of Members of the Authority will make their decisions about the contract awards, following a detailed staff appraisal of the applications, probably in mid-December. We shall then write to let you know the outcome as soon as we can."[577]

The IBA had received forty applications, many from groups that had also bid earlier in the year for the first London-wide FM licence. Of particular interest to KISS FM were those bidders who proposed dance music formats. One applicant, 'LFM – The Soul of London,' included a fifteen per cent stake from Zomba Music, the record company whose persistent interest in KISS FM had been rejected by Gordon McNamee. One of that applicant's key personnel was Greg Edwards, who had worked as a soul DJ on London's Capital Radio for many years. Another dance music bidder, Music Broadcasting, planned to use the on-air name 'Solar FM.' Its co-ordinator, ex-Solar Radio DJ Clive Richardson, had written to McNamee in September 1989, offering to combine its bid with that of KISS FM if McNamee would offer him a ten per cent shareholding. McNamee had rejected that offer, but it was interesting to see that former KISS FM consultant Dave Cash's wife Monica was involved in Solar FM's bid as a minor shareholder.[578]

Equally intriguing was a black music bid by Sunset Radio, which had recently won the incremental licence in Manchester, following a long campaign by local DJ Mike Shaft. Sixteen per cent of the group's capital was subscribed by radio saleshouse BMS, which had nominated Terry Bate as its board member. Bate and BMS had almost invested in KISS FM's first application, but Bate had dropped out after being refused a substantial shareholding in the company. Subsequently, Bate had invested in the newly licensed North London incremental, WNK, where he also had a seat on the board. He said he expected to spend time helping other incremental stations on the air, with the aim of "seeing them all succeed in spades." The London application for Sunset Radio said the station planned "to open a shop front in Finsbury Park" which, rather coincidentally, was the location of the KISS FM office.[579]

Most of the other bids were not direct competitors to KISS FM as they were offering rock, classical or easy listening music formats. To me, it seemed likely that the IBA would decide, firstly, which formats they believed the two new London stations should broadcast, before determining which particular company should be awarded each licence. The important thing was for KISS FM to be the clear winner amongst the dance music applicants, if this was one of the two formats chosen by the IBA. Looking at the competing applications, it seemed to me that KISS FM had made a much better case for the licence than had either Sunset Radio or Music Broadcasting.

My work at KISS FM was now at an end. Under the informal arrangement I had made with McNamee in September to co-ordinate the second licence bid, my employment with KISS FM effectively finished on the day the application form was submitted. I had earned £900 in total for my work over the last nine weeks. Now I was no longer on the KISS FM payroll. My remaining sources of income were from articles I was still writing for magazines such as City Limits, NME, Jocks and For The Record. If the KISS FM application proved successful, I believed that there would be plenty of future work for me to do to help launch the radio station.

Just before I had finished my work for KISS FM, McNamee promised me that I would be given a shareholding in the company in gratitude for my extensive work on the second bid, if it proved successful. I was thrilled to hear McNamee's offer, because I felt that I had produced a licence application that was much improved over Dave Cash's attempt the first time around, and at a considerably lower cost to the KISS FM shareholders. I believed that the future looked good for me personally if KISS FM won this licence.

Nevertheless, there was still a possibility that the second application would fail, forcing me to quickly find another job. My writing work alone would not be able to provide enough income on which to live. However, in the meantime, there existed a period of uncertainty until the IBA announced the winning applicants for these final two new licences. My future hung in the balance until then. The previous year, I had accumulated several weeks of holiday entitlement from my staff position at City Limits magazine, which now made it an ideal time to take a vacation. It had been two years since I had last travelled abroad and, as it was now November in London, I ideally wanted to go somewhere the climate was hot and the cost of living was cheap.

Just after KISS FM's first licence application had failed, a man from The Gambia had rung the Blackstock Mews office to ask if he could meet and talk to someone about a radio project he was planning. McNamee and I had spent a morning in July 1989 talking with George Cristiansen about his idea to open West Africa's first commercial FM radio station. He was visiting Britain to find business partners and possible investors for the project. At the time, KISS FM itself was still looking for investors, so there was little we could offer him. Since then, I had kept in touch with Cristiansen because I had an interest in the pop music of The Gambia and Senegal. I was also intrigued by his plan to name his station 'Radio One.' Cristiansen had cleverly obtained a copy of the on-air jingle package used by Britain's BBC Radio One. He had also acquired a large quantity of Radio One car stickers which he could use for publicity in The Gambia, once he had guillotined the FM frequency printed along one edge.

I bought a last-minute return air ticket to The Gambia for £199 and spent three weeks there, enjoying a fascinating and restful time, lazing in the sun on a beautiful sandy beach. I stayed in a local (non-tourist) hotel and enjoyed Cristiansen's hospitality at his compound. My holiday was marred only by one incident. One evening, I was walking with another British guest who was staying at the same hotel to a local restaurant that had been recommended. The streets were shrouded in complete darkness because not only were there no streetlights, but the country endured daily electricity supply cuts of several hours' duration. A thief must have heard our English voices and seized the opportunity to rob us as we walked along the road. My companion's purse was ripped from around her neck with a knife, while I was stabbed in the hand. We had no idea how badly injured we were because of the complete darkness. However, we soon found a policeman not far along the road, to whom we explained what had happened, but he swore at us and told us that tourists were not welcome in his country and that we had got what we deserved. Returning to our hotel, I found that my injuries were not serious, but they prevented me from bathing in the sea during my final week there.

There were a few days in The Gambia when I wondered whether I would be able to return home as scheduled. The government abruptly decided to close its border with neighbouring Senegal, and the country's armed forces were placed on alert, resulting in squads of armed soldiers marching around the streets at all hours. As quickly as it had escalated, the threat subsided and life returned to relative normality. The holiday proved to be the ideal antidote to both the pressures of the KISS FM licence application and the continuing antagonism I was suffering from my former girlfriend, who was still refusing to move out of our flat.

While I was several thousand miles away in West Africa, the press in Britain were speculating wildly about the winners of this second round of licence applications. The Evening Standard had already predicted wrongly that "competition ... is likely to be less intense than it was for the first round." It argued: "Many would-be broadcasters have apparently considered that it is not worth applying, because they believe that one licence is almost certain to go to former pirate station KISS FM, a runner-up last time, while the other contract will be awarded to one of the groups offering to run a classical music service." In the event, there had been even more applicants this second time around.[580]

Media Week magazine described KISS FM as "the ex-pirate hotly tipped to win a franchise"; Music Week called it "the widely tipped dance music station"; and Now Radio said it was "hotly tipped as one of the successful bidders." However, Broadcast magazine decided that classical bidder Classic FM had "emerged as a likely favourite to win," in a reversal of its earlier assertion that "KISS FM is favourite." Gordon McNamee commented about KISS FM: "We will definitely not be going back as a pirate. For one, it's no fun, and secondly, I want to get on with other projects."[581]

Radio & Music magazine, owned by KISS FM shareholder EMAP, had to declare its financial interest, though it described the station as "a front-runner, although many existing services have a similar music policy." It also reported that the IBA considered that "the existence of 'localised' ethnic stations like Choice FM and WNK will not affect black music applications."[582]

North London black community station WNK had launched on 6 November 1989 with seemingly little publicity other than a back page advertisement in Echoes music newspaper. It shared an FM frequency with a Greek station, so its programmes could only be heard in four-hour blocks, between four and eight o'clock in the morning, midday and four in the afternoon, and from eight until midnight. Its format consisted entirely of soul and reggae music, with negligible community information, making it sound similar to any one of London's many black music pirate stations.

The winner of the Brixton licence, South London Radio, was planning to open its black community station under the name 'Choice FM' in March 1990 with a music format similar to that of WNK. Neither Choice FM nor WNK relished the thought of KISS FM winning a London-wide licence, fearing that its dance music format might eclipse their own commercial potential. Patrick Berry, managing director of Choice FM, was still trying to persuade the IBA that it should not award either of the two new FM licences to a black music station. Asking the IBA to "seriously consider" the consequences of their decision on other London stations, Berry said: "I believe it would have a serious impact on us, and a worse one on WNK, who are only on-air twelve hours a day … We will not be able to compete sufficiently for a peak time audience. We would have no alternative other than to go for a wider format such as pop."[583]

More significantly, a wider economic problem was looming large for the new incremental radio stations. It was the threat posed by a recent downturn in advertising revenues, which the existing commercial radio industry was already beginning to suffer. Radio advertising revenues in the UK had grown by nineteen per cent to £134.2m between 1987/88 and 1988/89, following a twenty-nine per cent increase the previous year. However, Britain's largest commercial station, London's Capital Radio, had announced in November that such growth within the sector was unlikely to continue "in view of the slowdown in advertising generally and the uncertain economic climate." Broadcast magazine commented: "If a shakedown does occur, the hardest hit stations could be the new incrementals, many of which are now preparing to go on-air after making business plans at a time of unprecedented growth in the radio industry." Mike Powell, managing director of Guildford commercial station County Sound, said that only those incremental radio stations "projecting sensible costs and prudent revenues" would survive. He predicted that the radio industry was in for a "sticky eight to nine months."[584]

None of these voices of doom and gloom about the future of the radio industry reached me while I was enjoying my holiday in The Gambia. After three sun-soaked weeks, I caught my return flight home on Friday 15 December. There were unexplained delays at Banjul airport and, for several hours, passengers had to sit on the tarmac runway in the baking sun, there being no departure lounge. It was not until the early hours of Saturday morning that I arrived in London, pleased to be back after the much delayed flight.

Blearily reaching home, I noticed that the flat's front door no longer seemed to have a curtain across the inside of its window. I turned the key, went inside, and realised that many other things were missing as well. In the kitchen, the wooden dining table had vanished, the saucepan stand and vegetable rack had gone, and there was very little cutlery to be found. There was a note in my former girlfriend's handwriting that I did not need to read to understand what had happened. She had finally left the flat during the three weeks I had been away, but she had taken much of the contents of our home with her.

I cautiously opened the door to the spare room, to find that shelf units, a filing cabinet and a writing desk had gone. In the bedroom, the double bed was still there, probably because it was too large to remove easily as I had assembled it within the room. More shelving had gone and two bedside tables were no longer there. I was mightily relieved to find that my stereo system and record collection looked untouched. Then, opening the door to the living room, I was amazed to find that the entire room had been totally stripped bare. There was no longer a carpet, curtains or furniture – not even a lampshade. The room was completely empty, the only remaining fittings being the curtain track and a bare light bulb swinging from the ceiling in the centre of the room.

I was far too tired after the long journey, and too pleased with my restful holiday, to immediately become angry about the situation. This flat had been the first unfurnished, rented accommodation I had taken in London, and I had invested all my savings in redecorating the place and purchasing all its contents. For the first few months living there, my lack of funds had left the place almost bare and I had slept on a mattress on uncarpeted floorboards. Now, most of the household items I had built up over the last few years had gone. I returned to the kitchen and decided to read the note from my former girlfriend. It started: "I have moved out. Things that were jointly purchased, divided as follows …" Then it listed several household items. However, the list bore little relation to the items that had disappeared from the flat, and the note quickly became irrational and bitter: "I have taken the kitchen table since you always wanted to chuck it out." Predictably, she had not left me either a forwarding address or phone number.[585]

There was no fresh milk in the flat which might have enabled me to find solace in a much needed cup of tea, so I crawled into bed, tried to forget about the loss of so many of the flat's contents, and fell asleep. It was late at night, already early Saturday morning, and I realised that I would have to spend the next day sorting out exactly what I had lost and what I was going to do about the situation.

It was only just daylight when I suddenly realised that the phone was ringing. It seemed to take me ages to drag my weary body out of bed, as the phone continued to ring long and hard. Who on earth would want to phone me at this early hour on a Saturday morning? I toyed with the notion that it might be my former girlfriend, who seemed determined to inflict as much hurt on me as possible, despite our relationship having ended abruptly through her own infidelity and lies.

But it was not her. It was Gordon McNamee, calling me from his mobile phone. He said he was standing in the middle of his local park, walking his dog, accompanied by his mother. I could hear in the background that it was pouring with rain. McNamee asked if I had the home phone number of any of the IBA staff so that he could find out whether KISS FM had won the licence. I asked him why he was so anxious to find out at such an early hour in the morning. McNamee told me that Music Week magazine's radio correspondent, Bob Tyler, had rung him at home at around eight o'clock that morning to find out if he knew who had won the licences. McNamee admitted that he had heard nothing, despite knowing that the decisions had been made by the IBA at its Thursday meeting and should be announced imminently. McNamee told me that he had stayed at the KISS FM office all day Friday, but there had still been no phone call from the IBA, so he assumed that KISS FM had lost the licence for the second time, and had returned home.[586]

Bob Tyler had phoned McNamee a second time at around nine o'clock that morning to say that he had just heard a rumour that KISS FM had won a licence, though there was still no means of official confirmation. McNamee, feeling agitated and frustrated, had decided to get out of bed and take his dog for a walk in the local park. Halfway across the park, it had started to pour with rain. Then, just as he, his mother and his dog had run for shelter, McNamee's mobile phone had rung again. This time it was Richard Brooks, media editor of The Observer newspaper, offering his congratulations to McNamee on KISS FM's win of one of the two licences, and asking for a comment to include in the next day's issue. McNamee thanked Brooks for his call, but emphasised that he himself had not been told the news and so would have to obtain official confirmation from the IBA before he could say anything publicly. Brooks assured him that he had seen a letter sent to one of the losing applicants which definitely stated that KISS FM and easy listening applicant Melody Radio were the two winners. McNamee promised to ring him back as soon as possible.[587]

There was jubilation in the park, despite the torrential rain. McNamee and his mother leapt up and down with excitement, watched by an astonished old man who was also sheltering from the storm. The old man asked them what all the fuss was about and, when McNamee told him he had just won a hotly contested radio licence, the old man offered him a celebration roll-your-own cigarette and apologised for not having a cigar. Now, McNamee needed to find out from the IBA if the news was true, and why it had been broken to him by a journalist, rather than in an official IBA communication. That was when he had rung me. I told McNamee that I probably had the home phone number of one of the IBA officers, if the paperwork had not disappeared from my flat, so I would find it and try to obtain official confirmation. I quickly found the home phone number of the IBA press officer, Stuart Patterson, on the top of an old press release he had sent me. I called him and, although he himself refused to confirm or deny whether KISS FM had won, he promised to arrange for someone from the IBA radio division to call me as soon as possible.[588]

It was only a few minutes later that David Vick, the IBA's principal radio development officer, called me. At first, he was pre-occupied with explaining to me the protocol of the IBA announcement, and did not tell me outright that KISS FM had won:

"Hi, it's David Vick from the IBA. I gather you're the only people who haven't got the news officially yet ... I've just had a quick word with Stuart, obviously ... We've told the winners that they might expect calls from journalists. What we're anxious not to happen, and maybe it's a false hope now, is for journalists to ring losers before they've got their letters. But clearly, the Christmas post is so unpredictable that our best laid plans have fallen apart this morning."[589]

"I didn't ring Stuart as a journalist," I interrupted. "It was the KISS FM side ... Did we get it or didn't we?"

"Yes, of course you did," answered Vick.

"Oh, brilliant," I screamed. I was elated. Until now, I and the rest of the KISS FM team could only have dreamed of this moment when the IBA would ring us to say that we had won a radio licence. Now, it had really happened. I was very tired. I was still shattered from the long journey home. I had only just woken up, but I was also incredibly happy that my hard work on the licence application had won out in the end.

"Congratulations," said Vick, while I gasped with joy at the other end of the call. He remained far more composed than I was right now, and he continued to explain the detail of the announcement: "I don't know how The Observer got hold of it. Clearly, one of the losers has talked to The Observer fairly early on this morning, because they've been hot on the trail from quite early on. So congratulations on that."

I was still laughing and whooping at my end of the conversation, as Vick continued: "We normally do ring winners on Saturday morning but, this time, we've been playing it so laid back and ultra cool that I hadn't actually planned to do that. All the letters seem to have got through, but clearly some of the most serious applicants have given business addresses, and they're the ones who haven't actually got the letters. You're not unique. We've had a vexed Lord Hanson [of Melody Radio, the other winner] ring us this morning, asking what's going on and why is he being rung by journalists."

Vick continued: "You and Lord Hanson have been in the identical situation this morning of being rung by The Observer and others at the crack of dawn, and not known what was going on … What we didn't want was for losers who haven't got their letters this morning to find out from the newspapers either on Sunday or ideally on Monday … We had a terrible botch-up with the Post Office on one of the previous months. And, this time, I rang the district postmaster yesterday afternoon and said 'look, we've got another run of letters going through.' And he said he'd do his best to catch them the moment they arrived at the sorting office and hustle them straight through for us. And he's clearly done the job with unfailing skill and everything's arrived this morning. But the ones going to business addresses, yours and Hanson's and some of the other quite serious applicants, have ended up hearing about it through the grapevine as a result."

"Oh, this is brilliant," I gasped. I was still far from composed and I was barely taking in Vick's pre-occupation with the minor points of the procedure. We had won! That was all that was important to me right there and then. We had won! Vick continued regardless: "We told everybody our press release would be [published] Tuesday morning. But I've spoken to Peter Baldwin [IBA director of radio] and Stuart [Patterson], and that's clearly crazy now, so we're going to issue the press release early Monday morning. So, if you could bear to at least smile inwardly and say as little as you can to the press until then …"

I was muttering words of agreement without really taking in all the detail that Vick was relating. He could tell my excitement was getting the better of me, so he suddenly changed gear: "Well done. We'll obviously have a lot to do with each other in the months ahead. One of the things we've said in the letter is that, if you could come in [to the IBA office] and meet us all in the next couple of weeks, that would be super."

"We would love to," I replied, still giggling uncontrollably. Once more, Vick was keen to discuss the nitty gritty, right here and now on a Saturday morning: "Very well done. It was an excellent application. The trouble is that you're going to get a lot of griping comment now from people saying that they [the IBA] only did it to keep the pirate lobby happy. The fact was that it was a bloody good application that got it on merit, because we certainly wouldn't have given it to you if the application hadn't been deserving of it."

It was incredibly pleasing to hear Vick credit the KISS FM application after all the hard work I had put into it. I felt that, finally, I had been vindicated for my insistence to McNamee that the whole licence application had to be as perfectly presented as possible on this occasion. I thanked Vick for his kind comments, and he continued: "I think, to be honest, that the extra six months actually did you a lot of good. Not that the first application was bad or anything but, in this one, you had clearly learnt so much over the last six months, and you had strengthened it in so many ways. And, fortunately, by majoring on the new release aspect of the daytime [music] playlist, you've given us a very solid peg to hang the 'diversity' point on. Because, when Capital [Radio] and others predictably start complaining, we can actually point to the fact that you are going to be playing the music before it gets in the charts, and they will play it after it gets in the charts, which gives greater diversity."

Since its launch in 1973, Capital Radio had been London's one and only commercial pop music station, and it was still eager to defend what it considered to be its own rightful territory – a monopoly over playing pop music in the capital. The IBA was charged with widening the choice of radio stations available to listeners, whilst not duplicating the existing output of Capital Radio. The emphasis I had placed in the KISS FM application on the station's championing of new music had proven to be precisely the argument the IBA could use to defend a decision to award KISS FM the licence. Admittedly, Capital Radio did play dance music within its programmes, but it only played songs that were already in the Top Forty singles chart. KISS FM would be playing mostly new releases, before they gained widespread popularity. My strategy for the KISS FM application had worked exactly as I had intended, which Vick confirmed as he continued to relate the detail: "The press release actually says that KISS FM has been chosen as a station that will be in the forefront of music tastes and that's your market position, as we define it."

McNamee must have returned home by now, so I gave his home telephone number to Vick and thanked him for calling me so promptly. It was absolutely brilliant news and I was still utterly ecstatic. I tried to phone McNamee straight away, but Vick must have managed to get through to him first. I continued re-dialling for several minutes, until the phone eventually rang. McNamee was shouting down the phone to me over the top of a loud conversation I could hear in the background:

"Grant, you cunt," he greeted me, in his typically perverse way. "We've got it! I can't believe it! David Vick just phoned me and we went through the whole lot. I can't fucking believe it."[590]

There was loud laughter in the background and McNamee already sounded drunk on the news, in spirit, if not in reality: "You've got a job! Your gamble worked out. We've all got a job. Fucking wonderful! It's wonderful! It's just unbelievable. I'm going to be down at Dingwalls [nightclub] tonight and the whole world will be, I should think. I'm going to phone everyone today. I'll talk to you later on. I've got to phone all the bosses, and I'll talk to you later."

McNamee was right. My gamble had paid off. I had believed that KISS FM could win the licence, if only someone was prepared to work hard on the application this time around. Then, when McNamee had failed to take up the challenge, I had decided to take on the task myself. While McNamee had been pre-occupied with his initial failure, I had been determined to turn KISS FM's second application into a winner. Asked subsequently what had persuaded the IBA to award KISS FM a radio licence, David Vick answered: "A well researched application and musical knowledge."[591]

It was pleasing to know that my strategies had been proven correct. It was my detailed research and my belief in KISS FM's musical expertise that had swung the licence bid. Now, here I was, having learnt the good news only hours after arriving back in the country. If KISS FM had lost its licence bid this second time around, I would have had no job to return to. Plus, my flat had been deliberately and spitefully emptied. But these things did not matter to me any more. The dream I had cherished for so many years of a legal black music radio station in London was about to become a reality at last. I had played my part in turning that dream into reality. I was absolutely thrilled. For me, it was literally a dream come true.

---

[577] letter from David Vick, IBA to KISS FM, 14 Nov 1989.
[578] two letters from Clive Richardson, Music Broadcasting Ltd. to KISS FM, 3 Sep 1989.
[579] "Bates Sits Back", Radio & Music, 11 Oct 1989.
[580] Steve Clarke, "Tuning Up For Radio Battle", Evening Standard, 6 Nov 1989.
[581] Liz Roberts, "Media Owners Vie For London Radio Franchises", Media Week, 17 Nov 1989.
Bob Tyler, "London FM: All Things To All People?", Music Week, 25 Nov 1989.
"Interest In London FM Bid Wanes", Broadcast, 27 Oct 1989.

"Loose Ends", Now Radio, 11 Oct 1989
"Classic FM Favourite To Win New London Licence", Broadcast, 15 Dec 1989.
[582]Julian Clover, "Seconds Out For London FM", Radio & Music, 8 Nov 1989.
Julian Clover, "Money Counts For London FM", Radio & Music, 22 Nov 1989.
[583]"Choice In London FM Threat", Radio & Music, 6 Dec 1989.
Bob Tyler, "Concern Grows As New Stations Go 'Out-Cremental'", Music Week, 16 Dec 1989.
[584]Sean King, "IR Faces Slowdown In Advertising Growth", Broadcast, 8 Dec 1989.
[585]letter from XXXXX XXXXXX to Grant Goddard, 6 Dec 1989.
[586]Grant Goddard, "Legal, Decent, Honest & Funky", Free!, Feb 1990.
[587]ibid.
[588]ibid.
[589]author's recording, 16 Dec 1989.
[590]ibid.
[591]Lisa Brinkworth, "Sealed With A KISS", Soul Underground, Sep 1990.

December 1989.

The news about KISS FM's win of the London FM licence spread like wildfire through London's dance music community. The phone lines between everybody involved in KISS FM were red hot during the rest of that Saturday, as word quickly circulated that the station had succeeded on its second attempt. Once I had phoned my family and friends to tell them the exciting news, I turned my attention to the much more mundane task of sorting out my rather bare flat. I also started to unpack the suitcases which had been standing in the hallway since my arrival the previous night.

The first thing I needed to do was to secure the flat properly, since my former girlfriend still had two sets of keys for the front door. The last thing I wanted her to do was to return while I was out and remove anything further that might take her fancy. Unfortunately, opening the door to the hallway cupboard, I found that all the useful household tools had already gone with her. There was no ladder, no iron, no ironing board, no painting implements and, most importantly, no screwdrivers, chisels, hacksaws or drill.

That day, and during the months that followed, I experienced the same disappointment on many occasions when I looked around the flat for things I used to own. Just when I needed a particular implement for some household maintenance or repair job, I would find it missing and have to buy a replacement at the local hardware shop. To add insult to injury, my former girlfriend had even taken the £24 do-it-yourself manual we had purchased to help us maintain the flat.

That Saturday, once I had purchased a new set of screwdrivers, I set about removing and replacing the front door locks to the flat. My next door neighbour emerged to find out what was necessitating all the hammering and chiselling on a Saturday morning. I explained that my former girlfriend had removed much of the flat's contents while I had been away. He told me he had seen her and some helpers spend the better part of a day shifting everything down four flights of stairs and into a large van parked outside. To him, it had simply looked as if she was moving out. Of course, he had no idea who owned most of the goods that were being carried away.

In the evening, I was keen to forget about the losses I had suffered in the flat, so I was eager to attend KISS FM's club night at Dingwalls in Camden. It proved to be a particularly boisterous affair. All the KISS FM staff and DJs were there. Gordon McNamee ordered crate after crate of champagne to share with those around him. I had not seen the rest of the team for the last three weeks, so it was wonderful to be there and join with everybody congratulating each other on the success of the licence application. The celebrations went on very late into the night. I eventually caught a taxi home, arriving just before the sun rose the next day. I was still thrilled that KISS FM had won the day.

The Sunday newspapers devoted more coverage to the winner of the other London FM licence, Melody Radio, than to KISS FM's achievement. Melody had proposed an easy listening music format and was owned by Lord Hanson, a high profile businessman. The group's public relations had been handled by Michael Shea, former press secretary to The Queen. Only Richard Brooks in The Observer found room to comment on KISS FM's win: "Its critics say that it replicates the type of music played by Brixton-based community station Choice FM which was awarded a licence by the Independent Broadcasting Authority [IBA] five months ago. Another new London station, Jazz FM, also has a remit to play a proportion of black and soul music."[592]

Choice FM's managing director Patrick Berry predictably declared himself "totally flabbergasted at the decision and appalled at the weak rationale" of the licence award to KISS FM. Referring to London's other commercial music radio stations – WNK, Capital Radio – and his own Choice FM, he said angrily: "With KISS FM, there's four of us. Everyone's playing the same records. The IBA seem to be strangling us at birth ... It's not really KISS FM we're facing – it's Virgin, EMAP and Centurion Press. They can outwage [sic] us in terms of presenters and can offer bigger promotional incentives ... This is a most unbelievable situation. We are not even on-air yet and the IBA have done this. What chance will we have of competing for an audience or advertising against a London-wide black dance station?"[593]

The IBA director of radio, Peter Baldwin, responded that both Choice FM and WNK had been awarded licences quite specifically as community radio stations to serve the black populations of South and North London respectively. He argued: "Any intention by these two stations that they would simply be black dance stations is misguided. They must appeal to all age groups in their local ethnic community." David Vick, the IBA principal radio development officer, added: "WNK and Choice cover a million people each and are specifically for ethnic groups. KISS FM is a music station and not ethnic."[594]

London Jazz Radio, which was planning to launch its new station under the name 'Jazz FM' the following year, seemed far less concerned that KISS FM might encroach upon its audience. The station's head of music, David Lee, commented: "We are not going to change our music policy. In fact, KISS FM listeners might be encouraged to explore a few jazz idioms and tune to us."[595]

Attempting to strike a conciliatory note with Choice FM's enraged managing director, KISS FM's Gordon McNamee responded: "I think there is enough room for us all together. I was pleased for the other music stations when they won. I think our second application was much better than the first one – perhaps our increased backing may have helped."[596]

The weekend's excitement at winning the licence naturally spilled over to Monday, as the KISS FM staff started to arrive at the Blackstock Mews office. That morning, the postman belatedly delivered the formal, four-page letter from the IBA deputy chairman, Lord Chalfont, which explained the decision to award KISS FM the licence:

"It gives me great pleasure to send this letter to you ... You and your group have clearly put much thought and preparation into your proposals. After taking account of a very full appraisal of all the applications by the IBA's radio staff, assisted by our financial and engineering specialists, my colleagues and I concluded that the proposals submitted by your group, KISS FM, and the other successful applicant, Melody Radio, together offered the prospect of the best radio services to increase the choice available to listeners within the Greater London area, on a self-financing and technically sound basis. I congratulate you and your team upon a deserved success."[597]

However, Lord Chalfont went on to point out that KISS FM's ownership structure, as proposed in its application form, might fall foul of restrictions imposed upon the IBA by the Broadcasting Act 1981. He requested a written assurance from KISS FM that EMAP's substantial stake in the station would preclude it from taking any similar substantial stake in other commercial radio companies, because limitations existed on the cross-media holdings of publishers such as EMAP. Secondly, he wanted further clarification of the relationship between KISS FM shareholder Virgin Broadcasting, the latter's parent company, the Virgin Group, and Virgin's music and record activities. Music and music publishing companies were forbidden by law from making investments in commercial radio, as Lord Chalfont explained: "The activities of the Virgin Group could make it a disqualified body within the terms of Section 20 of the Broadcasting Act 1981. For Charles Levison to take up his proposed directorship in KISS FM, he should play no part as a director of the Virgin Group, and should be, and remain, wholly unconnected with any disqualifying activities undertaken by the Virgin Group."[598]

KISS FM's second licence application had been accompanied by a three-page letter to the IBA that had set out in detail the complex relationship between the various companies within the Virgin Group as of November 1989. The IBA obviously felt that further explanations were necessary. Many of these cumbersome ownership restrictions on commercial radio were soon to be lifted anyway, once the government executed its plan to replace the IBA Radio Division at the end of 1990 with a new Radio Authority, whose remit was to regulate the industry with a 'lighter touch.'[599]

Lord Chalfont's letter went on to explain that KISS FM would shortly be sent a £5,000 invoice "to cover the IBA's costs of advertising and awarding the contract" which required payment within twenty-eight days. It seemed slightly bizarre that the winners alone should be burdened directly with the cost of the IBA's long-winded licence application process, but this was typical of the agency's quasi-governmental status. Lord Chalfont's letter also reiterated a point that David Vick had raised during his telephone conversation with me on Saturday, that a meeting between the IBA Radio Division staff and KISS FM would be useful. He signed off with his best wishes for the station's success: "You and your colleagues will be pioneering a new form of radio and a new way of getting a station under way. You, like the IBA, will be learning as you go along. For our part, we shall aim to offer you all the assistance and encouragement we can, as you prepare for the launch of your new station. May I wish you every success in this venture and, once again, offer my warmest congratulations on your successful application."[600]

The IBA press release, publication of which had been brought forward one day, as David Vick had intimated in his phone call with me, also arrived by fax in the KISS FM office on Monday. After stressing the high quality of all forty applicants, it explained: "The Authority's eventual decision was in favour of Melody Radio ... and KISS FM, which has offered to provide a service of dance music directed mainly at a young audience, and including a high proportion of newly-released records designed to place the station at the forefront of trends in that area of music." The press release emphasised that these two licences were the very last to be awarded as part of the IBA's incremental contract scheme. This emphasised that KISS FM had only just achieved legality by the skin of its teeth. There would be no more London radio licences advertised for at least the next several years, and KISS FM would become the very last of the new stations to take to the airwaves.[601]

Once all the staff had arrived at the KISS FM office, we convened a meeting in the Free! office, sat around the same glass-topped table at which the details of the winning licence application had been hammered out night after night during the preceding months. It seemed an appropriate place to start a new topic for discussion: what should we do now that the licence had been won? It was agreed that we needed a well defined strategy for dealing with enquiries from the press in the wake of the IBA announcement. Already, that morning, the office answering machine cassette tape had been filled with requests from journalists for comments and interviews about the licence win. I felt that it was important for all comments about KISS FM to come from one spokesperson, who should be Gordon McNamee. Other winning applicant groups had made themselves look foolish in recent months by providing the press with quotes from different members of their team that had contradicted each other concerning their station's policies. I was also mindful of the unwanted press coverage KISS FM had attracted over Dave Cash's involvement in the first licence application, following Lindsay Wesker's unguarded words with a trade journalist.

The meeting agreed that McNamee should be the only spokesperson for KISS FM and that all press enquiries would be referred to him alone. It was also agreed that a press statement would be issued as quickly as possible, which I was delegated to write and which Rosee Laurence would type and distribute. It was only one week away from Christmas Day, so there was little that could practically be achieved in forging the station's future before the New Year, other than to deal with the immediate avalanche of enquiries the office was receiving. I set to work writing a press release, headed "KISS FM WINS THE FRANCHISE AT LAST!", that outlined the station's history and its successful campaign for legality. The only new information I included was the station's commitment "to commence its broadcasts in the second half of 1990." I included a quotation that many press reports subsequently used, and which I attributed to McNamee: "It's the best Christmas present London's dance music fans could have been given. The IBA's decision vindicates the huge public support that KISS FM has attracted over the last four years. Our listeners and supporters have played an essential part in our success and we owe them immense gratitude."[602]

Once the press release had been written and was being faxed to the press, McNamee took me to one side in the office and said he wanted me to start working full-time for KISS FM straight away. He explained that he needed me to work very closely with him to turn the promises contained in the station's licence application into reality. He realised that the scale of the work that lay ahead for the station was very daunting, and he recognised that this work needed someone with experience in commercial radio, rather than the pirate radio background to which he had been confined. I explained that there were still outstanding journalistic commitments I had to fulfil which prevented me from starting full-time work for KISS FM immediately. I was required contractually to give one month's notice to City Limits magazine to resign my post of radio editor. The other magazines I was still writing for regularly would also need time to find replacement journalists for my radio columns.

McNamee remained insistent that he needed me to commit myself full-time to KISS FM as soon as possible, and he promised I would be paid a proper wage from 1 January 1989 onwards. He explained that, although I would not yet receive the £30,000 salary for the programme controller post that had been designated for me in the business plan, I would probably be paid around half that amount while I worked as an assistant to him. I checked my diary and explained to McNamee that, if I were to resign my job with City Limits straight away, I could start working full-time for KISS FM from the third week in January. Until then, I could commit four days a week. McNamee agreed to this arrangement, so I phoned my section editor at City Limits to explain what I planned to do and confirmed it in a handwritten fax sent that morning. I suggested to my editor that he replace me with Daniel Nathan, who had written the radio pages during my holiday in The Gambia and who already knew the magazine's systems.

During the remainder of the day, I phoned the other publications to which I contributed, and promised to fulfil my outstanding commitments, recommending they use either Nathan or Music Week's radio correspondent, Bob Tyler, for future radio articles. When it came to writing my final column for City Limits, I explained to readers: "I'm off to join KISS FM, the station that will kick ass in the 1990s. Keep listening!" I was pleased to be returning to a full-time job working within the radio industry, something I had desired for a long time, rather than writing about radio from the sidelines.[603]

The celebration of KISS FM's licence victory continued to occupy the station staff the rest of that week. Letters, cards and congratulatory phone calls flooded the office, and a steady flow of champagne bottles arrived from record companies involved in dance music. It became a full-time occupation for us just to deal with the huge volume of correspondence, enquiries and requests from journalists for comments.

The music and style press was considerably more enthusiastic about KISS FM's win than the quality newspapers had been. In its round-up of "the happenin' occurrences that made '89 fine," the Metropolis column of the Evening Standard included "KISS FM finally getting their licence." Time Out magazine offered the KISS FM team its congratulations and a round of applause, but noted cautiously: "It's a decision well worth celebrating for it will have delighted a large section of the community and should do a whole lot for (dance) music in London at a time when British dance music is making real strides. Of course, there will be fairly radical changes to the KISS FM format but, for now, let's just celebrate the future …"[604]

Record Mirror was pleased that "KISS FM's ceaseless campaigning has finally paid off" and Music Week reported that "at last, sense has prevailed." Blues & Soul magazine called it "a momentous moment, a piece of history in the making, that marks the coming of age of dance music, the acceptance by wider society that the music is here to stay." Then it reminded its readers: "Let's not forget all the people who have worked so hard throughout the 1980s to bring about this situation, from the early pirates like Invicta, JFM (where Gordon Mac first started in the Kisses days), Horizon (where Chris Stewart demanded high standards for pirate broadcasters) and Solar (and a special mention must go to Tony Monson for working so long and hard for this result)." Echoes newspaper offered its congratulations to KISS FM but noted that "it'll certainly be interesting to hear how an ex-pirate station fits into the commercial world of the capital's radio scene."[605]

One of the few voices of dissent was that of Tony Blackburn, a successful soul music DJ on BBC Radio London in the mid-1980s, who was now working for London oldies station Capital Gold, one of KISS FM's future competitors. He wrote in Jocks magazine: "Now that KISS FM are legal, it will be interesting to see how they face up to the challenge of broadcasting for the first time on a truly competitive basis. Gone are the days when they paid nothing for playing records. Gone are the days when a truly amateur DJ, sitting in a makeshift studio in someone's bedroom, was tolerated because he was a 'pirate.' And gone are the days when DJs on the station was [sic] paid little or nothing for their services. Now that KISS FM is legit, it will have to put out a truly professional sound to attract audience and advertisers alike."[606]

It was difficult to accept Blackburn's comments as anything other than sour grapes that he had played no direct role in winning London its first soul and dance music radio station. In his autobiography, published four years earlier, Blackburn had written that he ideally wanted a job running the BBC's national pop music station, Radio One, or a soul music station in London.[607]

However, as Blues & Soul magazine had correctly pointed out, it was the pioneering work of the London soul pirate stations, from Radio Invicta onwards, which had spearheaded the long running campaign for a legal black music station in London. Despite Blackburn's evident affinity for soul music, there was nothing he had done personally to further that particular cause. Now, he seemed somewhat jealous that KISS FM had won the licence, and maybe he wanted a slice of the action he felt he deserved. Unfortunately for Blackburn, there was no space for him in KISS FM's plans. KISS FM had developed its own way of doing things, and Blackburn's negative comments only made us want to succeed even more on our own account.

---

[592] Jane Thynne, "Big Band Radio Drowns Classics", Sunday Telegraph, 17 Dec 1989.
Geordie Grieg, "Classics Draw Short FM Straw", Sunday Times, 17 Dec 1989.
Richard Brooks, "Soul And Muzak Win Radio Bids", The Observer, 17 Dec 1989.
[593] Richard Gold, "SIRS Lands Sales For Disputed FM Station", Media Week, 5 Jan 1990.
Susannah Richmond, "Why New Stations Must Find A Niche Or Tread The Road To Self-Destruction", Campaign, 6 Jan 1990.
Bob Tyler, "Feathers Fly As KISS And Melody Take To The Air", Music Week, 6 Jan 1990.
[594] Richard Gold, op cit.
Sean King, "Franchise Award Dismay", Broadcast, 22 Dec 1989.
[595] Bob Tyler, op cit.
[596] "Media Forum On The New London Radio Market", Campaign, 6 Jan 1990.
[597] letter from Lord Chalfont, IBA to KISS FM, 15 Dec 1989.
[598] ibid.
[599] letter from Gordon McNamee, KISS FM to IBA, 8 Nov 1989.
[600] letter from Lord Chalfont, op cit.
[601] "IBA Announces Decision On Incremental ILR Contracts For Greater London", IBA press release no. 103/89, 18 Dec 1989.
[602] "KISS FM Wins Franchise At Last!", KISS FM press release, 18 Dec 1989.
[603] Grant Goddard, "Notes", City Limits, 18 Jan 1990.
[604] "Metropolis", Evening Standard, 29 Dec 1989.
David Swindells, "Happy Kissmass!", Time Out, 3 Jan 1990.
[605] James Hamilton, "Beats & Pieces", Record Mirror, 6 Jan 1990.
James Hamilton, "James Hamilton Column", Music Week, 6 Jan 1990.
The Mouth, "Street Noise!", Blues & Soul, 16 Jan 1990.
"Vinyl Meltdown", Echoes, 20 Jan 1990.
[606] Tony Blackburn, "Blackburn", Jocks, Feb 1990.
[607] Tony Blackburn, "The Living Legend", Comet, London, 1985.

December 1989 & January 1990.

On the evening of the Tuesday before Christmas, everyone who had been involved in KISS FM's winning licence application was invited to a celebration drink at the Blackstock Mews office. The ground floor Free! office was cleared of all its furniture and stocked with a huge volume of alcoholic drink purchased by Gordon McNamee. This was supplemented by several crates of Rolling Rock lager that its distributor had agreed to supply without charge, in return for inclusion of the brand's logo in publicity for future KISS FM club nights.

That evening at the office was the first occasion that people involved in all the different aspects of KISS FM had met together in one room. The DJs, the office staff, the investors and the company directors all mingled together, attempting to hold polite conversations that crossed their different worlds. The joy of finally winning a London radio licence on the second attempt overcame any immediate fears harboured by the original KISS FM team that the new investors might pose some sort of threat to the station's 'pirate' ethos. Nevertheless, it still felt rather like an intrusion to see several suited and grey-haired men at a party in the downbeat and funky Blackstock Mews office.

The next day, a letter arrived from David Vick, the principal radio development officer of the Independent Broadcasting Authority [IBA], containing some technical information about the licence. He explained that London Jazz Radio, due on-air in 1990, had just agreed the size of its Total Survey Area [TSA] with the IBA. The TSA represented the geographical boundary around London in which the station would define the extent of its listenership for the purpose of selling advertising airtime and conducting audience research. Each new commercial radio station was required to agree the limits of its TSA with the IBA, before being allowed to refer to it in its publicity and sales materials.

London Jazz Radio had just agreed a large area, illustrated in an accompanying map, which stretched far beyond the limits of Greater London, eastward into Essex as far as Southend, southward into Surrey as far as Guildford, westward into Berkshire almost reaching Reading, and northward as far as Luton in Bedfordshire. The total population within this area was 9.72 million people, including 7.97 million adults over the age of fifteen. Vick explained in his letter: "As your station's coverage will be very similar to London Jazz Radio's, it would seem to make sense for you to share the same TSA. It will clearly make marketing more comprehensible to advertisers if the three new Greater London FM stations can use a uniform TSA."[608]

This proposal offered KISS FM a substantial increase to its potential audience from the 7.5 million people, including 6.0 million adults, that had been offered in the IBA's original licence advertisement. An invitation to adopt a larger TSA was very enticing, because any radio station would welcome an opportunity to broadcast to a greater potential audience. However, there were two impacts of the proposal, one of which might not seem so important right now, but which might be once KISS FM had been on the air several months.

The radio industry's agreed methodology for audience research was to count a station's listeners who were aged fifteen and over. The standard metric of a station's listenership was called 'weekly reach,' the number of people within the TSA who listened to that station during the course of a single week. It did not matter whether a listener tuned in to the station for only half an hour during a week, or listened every day for the entire week. Both listeners had been 'reached' by the station during the course of a week, and both were added to the station's 'weekly reach' figure.

This weekly reach statistic could be expressed in two different ways – as an absolute number (such as one million) or as a percentage of all the potential listeners within the station's TSA. In its business plan, KISS FM had forecast that it would achieve a weekly reach of one million people by the end of its first year of operation. I had estimated this number using the IBA's original (smaller) TSA, which required the station to attract one million listeners out of a total possible six million adults, equivalent to a weekly reach of seventeen per cent.

If KISS FM's TSA were to be increased to nearly eight million adults, the target of one million listeners per week would prove slightly easier to achieve because now there were more potential listeners within the station's broadcast area. One million listeners would now be equivalent to a lower weekly reach of twelve and a half per cent. On the other hand, if KISS FM still wanted to maintain its target in percentage terms, as a seventeen per cent weekly reach, it would be necessary to increase the absolute weekly reach to 1.35 million adults per week.

One way or another, KISS FM had to restate its target audience if it wanted to accept the IBA proposal of an enlarged TSA. After some discussion, the station's management decided to focus, from now on, exclusively on the one million target audience and to forget about the promised weekly reach in percentage terms. As a result, the magic number to be used in all KISS FM publicity was 'one million' by the end of the first year on-air, which would make my task of attracting listeners slightly easier.

The argument in David Vick's letter for a common TSA to be adopted by all three, new London-wide FM stations – London Jazz Radio, KISS FM and Melody Radio – was compelling. If a potential advertiser wanted to compare the cost effectiveness of booking a campaign on each station, it would be far easier to make an evaluation if the TSA was identical for all three. In this way, the compatibility of their TSAs should offer benefits to all three stations. By the following month, all the new London-wide stations had accepted the IBA proposal so that, henceforth, KISS FM's potential audience was eight million adults, making it the UK's (joint) third largest commercial radio service behind Capital Radio and LBC, both of which operated more powerful transmitters that could be heard by 9.58 million adults in and around London.

Important as was the impact on the business plan of this enlarged KISS FM transmission area, the psychological effect it had on the station's staff and on the rest of the radio industry was much more profound. One year earlier, KISS FM's stated aim had been to win a licence to broadcast only to the central London area, which would have been roughly comparable to the range of its pirate transmissions. Since then, through a succession of amendments to its incremental radio scheme, the IBA had defined larger and larger coverage areas for the new London stations. Now, KISS FM's new licence made it more of a station for southeast England, rather than London alone, and it would be heard by around a fifth of the population of the whole of the UK.

Within the company, the danger was that the enlarged TSA might convince some that they were now working for one of the largest, most popular radio stations in the country, rather than for a specialist music station that was aiming to attract a quite narrowly defined audience interested in dance music. Simultaneously, the larger TSA helped to convince some observers in the radio industry that KISS FM was undoubtedly planning to be a direct competitor to London's Top 40 chart music station Capital Radio, rather than remain a new, small-time player in the London radio market.

Campaign magazine noted that "many are worried that KISS FM will damage local stations, and some predict it could have a devastating effect on Capital Radio." Radio & Music magazine felt that KISS FM "obviously poses the most serious threat to Capital FM."[609]

Within KISS FM, the station's budgets and the salaries of senior managers had already seen substantial increases since the earliest plans had been laid barely a year earlier. The new, enlarged transmission area merely seemed to confirm the proposition that the station had acquired major league status. Media Week magazine confirmed this elevation of KISS FM, but noted the potential pitfalls: "There are, of course, dangers in moving from what was an underground movement, for which illicitness was certainly a factor in its popularity, to becoming part of the radio establishment, with powerful financial backers holding a majority of shares in the company. One danger is that the shareholders will exert too much influence over the station's output to maximise revenues, driving it to become more commercial at a time when listeners who liked the pirate image might look towards other pirates."[610]

Media Week also hinted at McNamee's own potential vulnerability within the company, the bigger an operation KISS FM was destined to become: "For the first time, McNamee will be reporting to a board of directors and, while nobody is under the illusion that the new contract will be a licence to print money, targets will have to be achieved and some, particularly ex-pirates, are sceptical about the influence McNamee will have if things do not go according to plan. McNamee does not appear too worried about his prospects. He believes that the target of one million listeners by the end of the first year of legal broadcasting is realistic ..."[611]

However, it was the gossip columnist of black music magazine Blues & Soul who expressed the same thoughts much more bluntly: "Now the responsibility rests with the KISS FM board of directors to ensure that the station truly represents an alternative to Capital and GLR. I must admit that I find it very hard to take Gordon McNamee seriously as the managing director of a legal radio station, even though every photograph shows him wearing a Coles suit. Still, at least it proves that I can really become prime minister!"[612]

The same columnist went on to note that "there are a lot of people on the fringes of the station who will be clamouring for their opportunity" to be a DJ on KISS FM. It was true that the Blackstock Mews office had already been inundated with phone calls and letters from aspiring programme presenters, only a few days after the licence award had been announced. The standard answer given to each enquirer was to ask them to send a cassette tape and CV, which would be dealt with in due course, once KISS FM was closer to going back on the air.[613]

Having dealt with personnel work before, the most useful thing I achieved before the Christmas break was to write standard letters to all those people who had enquired about job opportunities. I also set up a basic filing system so that, when the time came to deal with these enquiries, I could find the details of those people skilled in particular areas of radio work that the station required.

Time Out magazine reported the situation: "'We've never been so popular,' says KISS FM's wonder-woman Rosee Laurence. 'I do find it funny. It's so different to the time before we got the licence.' The KISS FM crew ... are now coping with ansaphone tapes full of DJs' demos and requests – and they're pleading for a cease-fire while they search for a new building and get the nitty-gritty business sorted out."[614]

Gordon McNamee told Record Mirror magazine: "All of a sudden I've got a million DJs who want to know me!"[615]

In addition to enquiries from hopeful DJs, the office was flooded with phone calls and letters from all sorts of companies wanting to sell the newly legalised station anything and everything from office premises to stationery. Hustling salespeople (usually men) would do their utmost to make an appointment with anyone in the office who happened to answer their phone call. As a result, I was forced to waste an entire morning with a computer equipment salesman who was keen to demonstrate his goods in the office. He had arranged an appointment with me through whomever in the office had answered his phone call and who had then left a note in my diary. Eventually, I had to tell him that his product was completely irrelevant to KISS FM's future needs and that I was sorry he had wasted both his and my time.

Very quickly, the celebrations in the Blackstock Mews office for KISS FM winning the licence turned into celebrations for Christmas. Our serious work was curtailed by the early closure of many of the businesses that we needed to deal with in order to get the station launched. McNamee sent me a Christmas card with an inscription in his favoured brown ink Pentel pen: "Grant, Happy Xmas and let's kick ass in the 90s. Love, Gordon."[616]

The KISS FM office was closed between Christmas Eve and the New Year, while McNamee concentrated on running a series of special KISS FM Christmas club nights during clubland's most lucrative period of the year. The largest of these events was KISS FM's Win Or Lose Party held at the Wag Club with a £10 entrance fee. It had been planned long ago, prior to the IBA licence announcement, to be either a celebration or a drowning of sorrows, depending upon the result.

When the Blackstock Mews office reopened in the New Year, McNamee's first action was to write to all the KISS FM DJs and staff, asking them to attend a full meeting of the station on the evening of 15 January. The mood in the office remained jubilant, and this feeling was conveyed in McNamee's letter: "Happy new year to one and all. What a great start to the year!"[617]

During the Christmas office closure, McNamee had decided that he wanted to poach two DJs currently working for London's Capital Radio to present KISS FM's weekday daytime programmes. He asked me to get in touch with one of them, Peter Young, who was hosting the Friday night soul show on Capital FM, and a weekend show on its AM counterpart, Capital Gold. I tried phoning Young at Capital on several occasions after the end of his show, but the station's ruthlessly efficient night security man refused to put me through to the DJ.

I did not want to put an approach in writing to Young, for fear of jeopardising his position at Capital. Having seen how unhappy the station had been about Dave Cash's involvement in KISS FM, at a time when it had been only one of many licence applicants, I had no wish to create a worse problem now that KISS FM had won a London licence. I tried to contact Young through another DJ at Capital, David Rodigan, whose home phone number I still had from having written an article about him for City Limits magazine the previous year. Rodigan was Capital's expert presenter of reggae music and, coincidentally, was the other DJ that McNamee wanted to poach from the station.

McNamee had quickly become insistent that the legalised KISS FM would need the services of 'name DJs' to present its daytime programmes, in order to tempt listeners away from Capital Radio and BBC Radio One. However, these plans had to be conducted in strict secrecy, not only to avoid the two DJs' current employer, but also to avoid the wrath of the existing KISS FM DJs, who McNamee knew would not take at all kindly to 'outsiders' being offered the highest profile programmes when the station reopened.

The press was already speculating as to which DJs KISS FM would draft into its re-launch plans. Blues & Soul magazine guessed wildly that KISS FM would recruit Capital Radio's Pete Tong, Peter Young, Martin Collins, Mick Brown and David Rodigan, ex-Radio One DJ Robbie Vincent, ex-Capital Radio DJ Chris Forbes, and ex-Radio Essex DJ Dave Gregory. City Limits, more accurately, suggested David Rodigan alone.[618]

To avoid the possibility of my phone conversations being overheard in the open plan KISS FM office, I made arrangements from home for me and McNamee to meet Peter Young at a bar near the Capital Radio office on Tuesday 9 January. McNamee parked outside the Grafton Hotel in Tottenham Court Road at one o'clock, while I wandered around the lobby bar looking for Young, whose face I knew only from publicity photos. He arrived a few minutes late and then the three of us convened to a nearby Italian restaurant for lunch.

The meeting was very friendly as we discussed the sorry state of the UK radio industry, what a dreadful place Capital Radio was to work, soul music and KISS FM's plans for the future. McNamee explained why he felt Young would be the right DJ to present KISS FM's daily afternoon show and pointed out that, although the initial salary on offer would not be huge, the station was expected to be very profitable by its second year. Young was enthusiastic, but made no immediate commitment to join McNamee's newly legalised venture. The three of us parted amicably after lunch and Young promised to be in touch, though McNamee and I already had an inkling that he was also being courted by London Jazz Radio.

Just before our meeting with Young, McNamee and I had paid a visit to a potential office for KISS FM, our first such sojourn. The music publishing company Chappell was soon to move out of offices at 14 New Burlington Street, just off Regent Street, in the heart of the city's West End. The large, old rambling building we inspected would make a perfect home for the radio station, we agreed, and its lobby would be an excellent shop front for the sale of KISS FM merchandise. An offer was made to the owners.

KISS FM appointed the estate agent Gross Fine, on the recommendation of shareholder Centurion Press, to handle the search for a suitable property. Half-page advertisements were placed in several trade magazines, specifying that premises of between six and ten thousand square feet were required, located close to London's West End, with twenty-four hour access, a long lease, and car parking space for at least six vehicles.[619]

London had a huge surplus of office space, though most of it was inappropriate to KISS FM's needs, in one way or another. Every day, details of dozens of premises arrived by post and fax at Blackstock Mews, but most were ruled out because they included no on-site car parking spaces. McNamee was insistent that KISS FM's new office had to have its own parking area, where he and other senior managers could park their company cars in absolute security. This restriction alone ruled out almost all the properties of which details were being received, regardless of their location or price.

Three days after our viewing of the New Burlington Street office, an initial KISS FM meeting with the IBA radio division staff was organised, as suggested by David Vick in his pre-Christmas phone call to me and in his subsequent letter. At quarter past ten on Friday morning, I met McNamee, financial director Martin Strivens and chairman Keith McDowall in the lobby of the Hyde Park Hotel in Knightsbridge, where we ordered a round of tea and discussed what we would say to the IBA. I was wearing a new suit that I had purchased over Christmas, specifically with this occasion in mind.

Just before eleven o'clock, we marched nervously down the street to the IBA office in Brompton Road, where three of the radio staff showed us to the same desk in the same room at which, six months earlier to the day, they had announced London Jazz Radio's win of the first London-wide FM licence, rather than KISS FM. Tea was served once again, and the meeting assumed a cordiality that overcame any fears we might have harboured beforehand.

Apart from the search for suitable premises and potential new presenters, the Christmas holiday had stymied any major progress in turning KISS FM's plans into reality. Therefore, much of our conversation focused on fuller explanations of some of the answers we had written in the KISS FM application form. The only substantial comment made by the IBA was a query about the size of the station's proposed staff complement. Did we not consider forty-two full-time and twenty-seven part-time staff rather a lot of employees for a specialist music station? It was agreed that the KISS FM board would reconsider the matter. The meeting ended with words of encouragement and optimism from the IBA staff about our plans and business projections.

Once McNamee and I were alone, returning to the Blackstock Mews office in his car, we both commented on how strange it suddenly felt to be dealing with the IBA staff on such an informal level. Although they had always been helpful to us during the application process, the IBA staff had always made it perfectly clear that KISS FM was only one of many hopeful bidders that were coveting a radio licence. Last year, KISS FM, like all the other applicants, was an outsider that wanted to break into the radio business. Now, having won a licence, we were suddenly inside the radio industry and we were already being treated as 'one of them.' Within the space of the last few weeks, we had switched sides and had joined the same radio industry which we had always criticised so harshly until now.

That IBA meeting, more than all the celebrations that had preceded it, finally brought home to us the realisation that the war for a legal black music radio station in London had been won. We were now inside the treasured citadel and it felt as if we almost had our hands on the Holy Grail. It was a very new experience for both McNamee and me. And, for both of us, it already felt absolutely fantastic.

---

[608] letter from David Vick, IBA to KISS FM, 20 Dec 1989.
[609] Susannah Richmond, "Radio Industry Raps IBA Over Hanson's FM Franchise Victory", Campaign, 22 Dec 1989. Mark Heley & Julian Clover, "Stirring Up The Capital", Radio & Music, 5 Jan 1990.
[610] Richard Gold, "Pirate KISS Goes Legit", Media Week, 12 Jan 1990.
[611] ibid.
[612] The Mouth, "Street Noise!", Blues & Soul, 16 Jan 1990.
[613] ibid.
[614] Dave Swindells, "Nightlife", Time Out, 10 Jan 1990.
[615] Richie Blackmore, "Sealed With A KISS FM", Record Mirror, 6 Jan 1990.

[616] Christmas card from Gordon McNamee to Grant Goddard, Dec 1989.
[617] memo from Gordon McNamee to KISS FM Team, 4 Jan 1990.
[618] The Mouth, op cit.
Rose Christie, City Limits, 4 Jan 1990.
[619] advertisement, Estates Gazette, 27 Jan 1990.
advertisement, Radio & Music, 31 Jan 1990.
advertisement, Music Week, 3 Feb 1990.

January 1990.

The following Monday evening, Gordon McNamee chaired a meeting of KISS FM DJs that was convened, as usual, in the ground floor office at Blackstock Mews used by Free! magazine. It had been a month since the announcement of KISS FM's licence win, but the mood was still celebratory and, to help lubricate the euphoria, there was a plentiful supply of Rolling Rock lager from the station's first sponsorship deal.

A few days earlier, McNamee had ordered fifty sweatshirts, each emblazoned with the KISS FM logo and the inscription 'LEGAL AT LAST!,' and made of the cheapest, thinnest grey cotton material he could source. McNamee's personal assistant, Rosee Laurence, was given the task of carefully distributing one of these items of clothing to each DJ and member of staff at the meeting, and she painstakingly made sure that no one tricked her into giving them two.

The meeting consisted mostly of McNamee offering a progress report on the continuing search for suitable office premises, and the announcement that the station planned to re-launch on-air in August or September 1990. The KISS FM team was reminded that all enquiries they might receive from journalists for quotes or interviews were not to be answered individually, but should be referred to McNamee or Rosee Laurence. It was stressed that all KISS FM public announcements would be issued from the Blackstock Mews office, and it was emphasised how important it was that no one must reveal any of the radio station's plans to either the press or competing broadcasters.

At the end of the meeting, everyone moved out of the stuffy, sweaty downstairs office into the cold night air of Blackstock Mews, crowding around the arched entrance that led into the quiet Mews from busy Blackstock Road. With plastic cups and bottles of lager still in their hands, the happy and jubilant KISS FM team were captured on camera by photographer Dave Swindells. The resulting colour pictures eventually appeared in the Sunday Correspondent and in i-D magazine, accompanying features on the station's re-launch.[620]

During the weeks that followed, the main priority was the continuing search for suitable premises. The KISS FM board had decreed that a lease would have to be signed by Easter if the station was to be ready to re-launch in September.

In the office, heaps of unsolicited letters and tapes continued to flood in, not only from potential DJs, but also from secretaries, engineers, research companies and office furniture suppliers, all of whom wanted to profit from KISS FM's licence win. Inevitably, it was the DJs who pestered the office the most. However famous or obscure might be the DJ who phoned me or wrote to me, my response was always the same – send me a cassette of your work and a CV, and your letter will be answered in due course. Many of the dozens of hopeful DJs who rang me were eventually forced to admit, after questioning, that they had no knowledge of dance music. Some of them found it impossible to comprehend that KISS FM was licensed to be a specialist music station and would not be playing pop music. I had no interest in employing a DJ who had no knowledge, of or love for, the station's music.

One such DJ who phoned me was Nick Abbot, having just been fired from GLR's breakfast show. He was insistent that he was the right person for KISS FM to employ. I asked him what relevance his previous work for a news/rock music station such as GLR had for a job with KISS FM, and he responded that he had played dance music in his former show. I explained that I needed more from a DJ than having played a few dance music records. He became quite stroppy and continued to insist that he deserved a job with KISS FM!

Another DJ, Mike Raven, phoned me and offered his services as a presenter. Raven had been part of BBC Radio One's original presentation team when the station had launched in 1967. I vividly remembered listening to his smooth voice presenting excellent, weekend rhythm & blues shows that exposed black American music not played anywhere else on the radio at the time. When I suggested he send me a tape and a letter, outlining what sort of music he might want to play in one of KISS FM's weekend specialist music shows, for which the station would pay £50 per programme, he complained bitterly and said that no real radio station would survive paying its staff such pitiful amounts. I explained to him the economic realities of KISS FM, as a specialist music station, but he became agitated and the conversation ended sourly. He never did send me a tape or letter. I was saddened that a radio legend, for whom I had always had such a high regard, could prove so unreasonable in person.

A couple of days after the DJ meeting, McNamee and I visited another potential home for KISS FM at the former Gilbey's Gin factory in Camden. The huge building had been converted into several floors of offices, none of which were yet occupied. The opulent entrance lobby now incorporated a glass-panelled section of floor, underneath which could be seen the water of the Grand Union Canal that was Camden's trademark feature. The view of London from the building's top floor was magnificent, but McNamee was reluctant to take a single floor within premises that would have to be shared with other businesses. He was still searching for his ideal vision of a new home for KISS FM and he was not willing to compromise.

I spent the rest of that week preparing to attend the MIDEM music industry trade fair held annually in the town of Cannes on the south coast of France. Even before KISS FM's licence win, I had planned to attend the event for the first time as a press delegate to write about a three-day radio conference that was part of the proceedings. I knew that it was worth taking with me some publicity material about KISS FM, since there would be personnel from many European radio stations in attendance who might prove useful industry contacts in the future. I assembled a large bundle of the KISS FM publicity brochures that had been left over from the first, unsuccessful licence bid, and packed them in my bags to go to France.

The radio conference was organised by Unique Broadcasting, the British independent radio production company, in conjunction with Broadcast magazine, which was why many of the speakers were drawn from the UK radio and music industries. I had attended music conferences before, but the sheer size of MIDEM was spectacular, attracting delegates not only from all parts of Europe, but from places as far away as Australia and Africa. The venue, right on the French Riviera, was beautiful and the whole event was a wonderful experience.

On the second day of the radio conference, a panel convened to address the issue of 'Targeting The Listener' that included Richard Park, programme director of London's Capital Radio. It was little more than a month since KISS FM had won its licence, but Park could not resist making a barbed comment about his future competitor: "KISS FM's Promise of Performance says they won't play any records in the top fifty so, boy, are they going to be different from KIIS FM in Los Angeles who won't play any records that are out of the top fifty."[621]

The 'Promise of Performance' that Park was referring to was the definition required by the Independent Broadcasting Authority [IBA] of each new radio station's format. It was the definition that had been inserted into the first page of the licence application form and which had to use no more than sixty words. Despite Park's assertion on the conference panel, KISS FM's Promise of Performance had stated: "KISS FM is a dance music station – an exciting new style of radio for the nineties. Its dance music of varying tempos spans the last four decades, whilst always being on the cutting edge of tomorrow's trends. KISS FM's innovative mix of dance music and talk reflects the style and fashion of cosmopolitan London."[622]

Park's comment stemmed from his desire that KISS FM should avoid playing the best selling hit singles that his own station, Capital Radio, depended upon for its huge popularity. However, there had been no mention in KISS FM's Promise of Performance, or anywhere else in its application form, of implementing a music policy that would not play hit records.

It was true that, in the aftermath of the IBA award of the licence to KISS FM, Gordon McNamee had intimated in press interviews that the station would stop playing dance records once they became national pop hits. In making these statements, McNamee had followed the IBA's advice that KISS FM should deliberately distance itself from Capital Radio's policy of playing chart music. The IBA had wanted KISS FM to stress its commitment to new music, which is why McNamee had told The Evening Standard: "The difference between Capital Radio and us is that they play music that's in the top fifty. We'll play it before it gets there. Once it's in the charts, we'll stop playing it."[623]

Similarly, McNamee had told Radio & Music magazine: "Once a record gets into the top fifty, it'll be dropped from our playlists. It'll then move into Capital's territory." He had said to Music Week: "If a record enters the top fifty, we'll drop it from our playlist. We'll be playing records before they enter the chart." And to Media Week: "Once it gets into the top forty, we'll drop it, because then it becomes Capital's territory."[624]

I knew that, in making these assertions, McNamee had overstated his case somewhat, since no radio station in its right mind would deliberately avoid playing songs that were obviously popular with the public. Additionally, there would regularly be dance music records that leapt straight into the singles chart during their first week of release, and there was no way that KISS FM could afford not to play these 'hot' songs. I knew that McNamee's quotes came from his lack of experience in legitimate music radio and that, when KISS returned to the airwaves, it would have to play all the dance music hits, much as Capital Radio was already doing.

For now, Richard Park had cleverly picked up on McNamee's quotes in the press and was peddling the story that KISS FM was destined to be an unsuccessful radio station because it was planning to deliberately avoid playing popular hit records. Nothing could have been further from the truth, particularly at a time when dance music records made up the majority of the pop charts. Park's comments were mildly annoying although, ultimately, they demonstrated that he must consider KISS FM a serious future competitor to Capital FM.

On the last day of the radio conference, the morning presentation was delivered by Alec Kenny, media director of advertising agency Saatchi & Saatchi. He tackled the thorny issue of why commercial radio had consistently failed to attract advertisers' attentions as much as had commercial television. Using slides and videos, his message was informative and stark – the UK radio industry was not working hard enough to attract customers to buy its airtime. His presentation was quite critical, but he showed an evident passion for the radio medium.

At the end of his talk, I approached Kenny at the front of the conference theatre and asked him if he was aware of KISS FM's recent licence win and its plan to launch in September. In order to make an impact on its potential audience in London, KISS FM would require the services of an advertising agency such as Saatchi & Saatchi. Since he demonstrated an evident interest in the radio market, I asked him whether his agency would be interested in pitching for the contract for KISS FM's launch marketing campaign. We exchanged phone numbers and Kenny promised to get in touch once we were both back in London.

I had been suffering from an increasingly bad cold during the MIDEM conference, so the morning coffee break thankfully gave me a chance to escape from the confines of the dark, stuffy theatre and let me take in some fresh air on the mezzanine floor outside. Although the weather was mild, I was wearing an old KISS FM sweatshirt from the station's pirate era, emblazoned with the 94 FM logo, to try and keep my cold at bay. A young man approached me whilst I was standing on the mezzanine and, seeing my sweatshirt, asked if I was Grant Goddard from KISS FM. I said I was, and he introduced himself as Mark Heley, a journalist with Radio & Music magazine. I had read many of his articles and knew that he had interviewed Gordon McNamee about KISS FM on several occasions. His employer, EMAP, was now a shareholder in the radio station.

After the merest of pleasantries had passed between us, Heley suddenly said to me: "You've got to be careful!" I looked at him with puzzlement. He emphasised: "You've got to be really, really careful!" I was none the wiser and must have appeared quite dumbfounded. "Your involvement in KISS FM," he continued. "You've got to be very careful about what happens to you."

I was rather embarrassed by this sudden outburst from someone I had only met for the first time a few minutes earlier. All around the two of us, radio industry people were spilling out from the conference theatre and onto the mezzanine. Heley had not been talking to me in a whisper. Everybody milling around us could easily hear what he had been saying to me. Heley himself was too pre-occupied with delivering his message to me to be, in any way, subtle or discreet. He continued: "You've got no idea what's really going on behind the scenes at KISS. And you've got to realise what a precarious position you're in there."

I tried to contemplate exactly what Heley was hinting at. It was the forcefulness of what he was saying that struck me the most. This was certainly not a quiet word whispered from a colleague within the industry. Although I had never met him before, Heley obviously had definite information that he wanted to impart to me. It felt dramatically as if a prophet of doom was suddenly rising up in front of me – someone who had seen into the future and knew of some unspoken atrocity that was yet to happen.

I tried to manoeuvre Heley along the mezzanine and towards the stairway, away from the crowd of radio industry people sipping their coffees whilst awaiting the start of the next conference session. Heley and I were now in a slightly less central spot for our conversation.

"But isn't it Gordon [McNamee] whose head will be on the block if KISS FM fails?" I asked Heley. "Isn't it Gordon who is caught between the need for outside shareholders to invest their money, and the fear that they will eventually take over the whole business if he shows the slightest sign of failing to make KISS FM a dazzling success?"

"No, it's nothing like as simple as that," expanded Heley, still seeming exasperated by the hopelessness of my involvement in KISS FM's fortunes. "You wouldn't believe how much more complicated it is than that. I can't tell you how I know, or even what I know. But, believe me, you're being used and, unless you are really, really careful, you'll be the one who comes out the worst from the whole business."

I put on a brave face against Heley's words of doom and gloom. I explained that I had already been named in the KISS FM application form as the station's programme controller. I told him that, although I did not yet have an employment contract, McNamee had already asked me to work full-time, assisting him in putting the station's plans into action. However, beneath this veneer of confidence, I was badly shaken by Heley's passion to pass on his warning to me. Here I was, in the South of France, as far away from the day-to-day work of KISS FM as I could get, and yet Heley had obviously sought me out especially to deliver this message.

Heley said he could not elaborate further than what he had already said, but again he implored me to act with caution during my involvement with KISS FM. We went on to exchange small talk about the conference, the radio industry, the magazine for which he wrote, and the beauty of being in Cannes at that time of the year. The half-hour coffee break ended, and we both returned to the conference theatre for more panel discussions about radio.

My head was clouded by the cold I had contracted and my sore throat. The previous day, my health had been sufficiently poor that I had spent the whole afternoon snuggled up in my hotel bed, sucking Strepsils, drinking Lemsips and watching the French music video channel MCM on the room's multi-channel colour TV (I had only a tiny, black and white portable television at home). What Heley had just told me did not really sink in immediately. I was still buoyed by the euphoria surrounding KISS FM's licence win. It still seemed that KISS FM's success was one of the most important things that had happened in my life. I still felt that anything was possible now, and that the radio industry was there for KISS FM to grasp with all its might.

It was only during the next few days, once I had got over the thrill of attending MIDEM for the first time, and once my cold had started to subside, that Heley's message began to take on a darker meaning. I realised that Heley obviously knew something quite specific about KISS FM, its 'big business' plans, the board's possible ulterior corporate motive, and my future within it. Heley knew McNamee well and he also worked for EMAP, one of KISS FM's major shareholders. I could not dismiss what Heley had said, but the nature of his warning was nevertheless very vague. All I knew now was that I would have to be careful.

Heley's words had been much more specific than another warning I had received previously from an unconnected source. The previous summer, just when I had started to become heavily involved in KISS FM's licence campaign, a colleague in the radio industry had warned me, over a drink in a local Harrow pub, to be wary of the people I was associating with at KISS FM. Paul Leaper, who worked at BBC GLR, advised me that KISS FM was obviously not a 'kosher' radio company and he suggested that I could not expect it to work along the same kind of gentlemanly lines that he or I might take for granted in the mainstream radio industry.

Both warnings heightened a nagging doubt in the back of my mind about the fate of other people I knew had previously been involved in KISS FM, but who now seemed to be entirely persona non grata to Gordon McNamee. I had learnt that someone called Tosca had been a partner in the original pirate version of KISS FM, but Tosca was now only mentioned by McNamee in moments of disgust or anger. None of KISS FM's current publicity ever mentioned Tosca, not even as a former partner.

There were others who had seemingly fallen from McNamee's favour and had been wiped from the KISS FM history book. During recent months, while re-organising into an ordered filing system the massive mess of papers that had been stashed behind McNamee's desk, I had seen Guy Wingate's name at the bottom of many old KISS FM documents. Wingate was no longer involved in KISS FM on a day-to-day basis and he now worked for MixMag magazine. At some point in KISS FM's past, Wingate seemed to have been the most literate and media-aware person within the station. I found papers demonstrating that he had written KISS FM's 'manifesto' to become a legal station, and that he had created the station's newsletter which had become such an important part of the campaign for a licence.

Now, when Wingate's name came up occasionally in the KISS FM office, McNamee was dismissive of his abilities and accused Wingate of having unspecified ulterior motives when he had worked for the station. Despite having obviously been such a key team member of the pirate era KISS FM, McNamee had refused point blank to involve Wingate at all in the licence application process. McNamee had also refused Wingate's offer to be a shareholder in the new company. McNamee had then refused to let Wingate be involved in the launch of Free! magazine, despite it being the direct successor to Wingate's pioneering work creating the KISS FM '94' newsletter.

Similarly, I was concerned about McNamee's continuing negative attitude towards Heddi Greenwood, who still worked in the Blackstock Mews office, but whom McNamee wanted to deny any involvement in the legalised KISS FM. It sometimes seemed as if McNamee had already written off Greenwood, even though she continued to work for him, for no reason whatsoever.

Ghosts past and ghosts present – such as Tosca, Wingate and Greenwood – seemed to inhabit McNamee's world. He seemed to rewrite the history of KISS FM continually as time marched on, carefully discarding all trace of former colleagues who had fallen from grace.

In France, had I been warned that I too would suddenly be transformed from being an important part of the KISS FM team to becoming another of McNamee's ghosts? I reasoned that McNamee himself knew nothing about the workings of commercial radio. He needed me to get KISS FM on the air. That much I knew for sure and, however minimal that morsel of reassurance might have been, I realised that I would simply have to get on with the work at hand, in spite of Heley's warning. As for the future after that – I would try to heed the advice I had been given and be very, very careful.

---

[620] Dave Swindells, "Newsflash", iD, Mar 1990.
Cynthia Rose, "Pirate Enterprise", The Sunday Correspondent, 29 Apr 1990.
[621] author's recording, 23 Jan 1990.
[622] "IBA Incremental ILR Contract Application Form", KISS FM, Nov 1989.
[623] Steve Clarke, "The Kiss Of Life As Radio Station Reopens", Evening Standard, 27 Dec 1989.
[624] Mark Heley & Julian Clover, "Stirring Up The Capital", Radio & Music, 5 Jan 1990.
Bob Tyler, "Feathers Fly As KISS And Melody Take To The Air", Music Week, 6 Jan 1990.
Richard Gold, "Pirate KISS Goes Legit", Media Week, 12 Jan 1990.

January & February 1990.

I returned from France on Saturday 27 January 1990, energised by the MIDEM radio conference and pleased that KISS FM's licence win had brought the London ex-pirate station to the attention of the European commercial radio industry. I realised that there was an awful lot of work to accomplish now in order to re-launch KISS FM by September or October, and I knew that my time would increasingly be absorbed turning the dream of KISS FM into a reality.

Early on Monday morning, I met my bank manager for the first time. The previous week, just before having left for France, McNamee had asked me how much money I would be able to invest in shares of the new KISS FM company. I told him that I would have to find out how much money my bank would loan me, since I had no significant savings of my own. McNamee implored me to determine as quickly as possible how many shares I could buy. He said he was anxious to ensure that the shareholdings in the new company were finalised as soon as possible, so I had made the appointment to meet my bank manager just before leaving for MIDEM.

McNamee had not made it clear whether the shares he was suddenly offering me were to be in addition to the shares he had already promised me in return for my work co-ordinating the successful licence application. Or, were the shares being offered me now intended to be a chance to buy my reward at a discounted price? Whichever was the case, I knew it was an opportunity too good to miss. KISS FM, I believed, was destined to become a very successful radio station, and I wanted to share in the financial rewards that my work would bring.

I showed my bank manager the KISS FM business plan, the cashflow forecasts and the detail of the licence application form. I explained to him my position in the company, my significant role in winning the company's radio licence, and my responsibility for ensuring that the station would be launched on-air and attract a substantial audience. The bank manager did not seem particularly impressed by the KISS FM venture, but he asked me how much money I wanted to borrow. I plucked a figure out of the air and told him I wanted £10,000. McNamee had not suggested a value for my shareholding but had only asked me how much I could invest.

The bank manager pointed out to me that I had no security to offer against such a loan. He noted that I owned no property or valuable possessions. In the end, with some reluctance, he said I could borrow £5,000 from the bank in the form of a personal loan, which he would expect to be matched by £5,000 of my own money to purchase £10,000 of shares. He suggested that I repay the loan over five years, at a total cost to me of £9,692 and at an interest rate of 23.8% per annum. He insisted that my expected monthly salary cheque must be paid directly into my bank account, and that repayment of the loan would have to be made at £161.54 per month.

The loan offer did not sound like a particularly good deal to me, but I had no other means to raise the necessary funds. I anticipated that, if KISS FM were to prove a successful business, the shares in the company would eventually be worth far more than I would pay for them. From the meeting at the bank, I travelled to the KISS FM office where, that afternoon, I told McNamee that I could raise £10,000 to buy KISS FM shares. I did not tell him that I had no idea where I was going to find the £5,000 matching amount that the bank expected me to contribute, but I would just have to deal with that problem when the occasion arose.

McNamee spent the rest of the afternoon attending a board meeting of the newly formed company at the office of shareholder Centurion Press in George Street. Since the New Year, McNamee had become less and less talkative about exactly what happened at these meetings. Everyone in the office had noticed that he would become very edgy on the day of the meeting and, afterwards, he would seem very sullen and uncommunicative. We were never allowed to see the agenda for these meetings, never allowed to see the minutes that were written up afterwards, and there were never any debriefing sessions for us to be told what was going on.

The next day, I met McNamee at the office in Farringdon of another KISS FM shareholder, EMAP, which was the first occasion I had visited Tim Schoonmaker in his workplace. We were there to meet an American radio syndication company, Westwood One, which viewed the current expansion of commercial radio in Europe as an ideal opportunity to sell its products into a new market. Schoonmaker had arranged for McNamee and me to meet Richard Rene, whom Westwood One had dispatched to London to set up a new European office. From the other side of the huge, wooden boardroom table adjacent to Schoonmaker's office, Rene made his sales pitch to us, explaining how Westwood One was already the market leader in radio programming in America and could help KISS FM achieve the same success in London. He shunted cassette copies of his company's syndicated shows across the shiny surface of the table to me and McNamee, and he suggested we sign a contract to broadcast them.

I listened politely to Rene's sales talk and then explained that KISS FM was in no way attempting to be a clone of an American 'urban' radio station. It was important to recognise that the two radio marketplaces – America and London – were completely different and that an American chart show such as the one his company produced would prove largely irrelevant to Londoners. I explained that Britain had its own home-grown dance music scene that bore little resemblance to the music which was presently popular in America. Whereas 'urban radio' in America was a euphemism for black radio, in London we knew that stations like KISS FM attracted a multi-ethnic audience. Rene should realise that we were creating a specialist music station for London, rather than a copy of American black radio, despite our KISS FM brand having been stolen from the New York City station of the same name.

McNamee offered a more conciliatory reply and promised to listen to the tapes himself to see what Rene's company had to offer. However, I was shocked that Westwood One did not seem to consider the subtleties of selling its products in overseas markets. It seemed to believe that its staff could steam in to any European country and sell radio shows in exactly the same way as it did at home. Westwood One had ensured that it maintained a high profile at the previous week's MIDEM conference, and its products were also the topic of a three-page feature in the current issue of Radio & Music magazine, where the company's Norman Pattiz had launched his opening gambit for selling product to us: "I think giving KISS a licence was a great move and I think that format will become a major player in the London market."[625]

In the same issue of Radio & Music was a two-page sales pitch by Colin Walters, the former managing director of Manchester commercial station Piccadilly Radio, who had just launched a radio consultancy service to advise new stations. Walters also seized the opportunity to praise potential customers for his services, when he said: "The Independent Broadcasting Authority has allocated new franchises to Melody and KISS, promising respectively easy listening and black dance ... This is a tremendous broadening of choice in a London which less than two years ago offered nothing more than unsplit [simulcast on AM and FM] Capital and LBC."[626]

It appeared that Walters desperately wanted to become involved in EMAP's plans to invest in commercial radio, so it came as no surprise when EMAP's Tim Schoonmaker introduced him to McNamee and me at another meeting in his office. Walters based his sales pitch upon his ability to employ American systems of music research, whereby snippets of records were played down the phone to a station's potential listeners, who were then asked to say how much each record appealed to them. The station then played only those tracks that achieved the highest scores in this research.

I told Walters that I was already aware of this method of 'call-out' research, but that I felt that it was largely irrelevant to KISS FM. I could see that it might be of use to stations that wanted to 'play safe' and not broadcast any record considered to be too unfamiliar or out of the ordinary, much like the programming policies of Britain's existing local commercial stations. However, KISS FM's licence remit was specifically to play new music, new styles, and to take risks with music that existing radio stations ignored. It was KISS FM's role to lead musical tastes, rather than to reflect the existing likes and dislikes of the general audience for radio. Only a tiny proportion of KISS FM's daytime output was going to consist of old records, whilst the vast majority of the station's output would be devoted to recordings only released during the previous few weeks. Market research such as that offered by Walters was irrelevant to a new type of specialist radio station such as KISS FM.

After our meetings in the EMAP office, McNamee, Schoonmaker and I moved to the traditional London pub next door in Farringdon Road for a late lunch. There was virtually nothing left on offer from the pub's menu at that late hour, and there were no vegetarian dishes, so I made do with a soft drink while the other two tucked into some hot food that looked and smelled remarkably gruesome. The meetings with Rene and Walters had identified quite clearly two phenomena that KISS FM would experience over and over again during the coming months. Firstly, many radio industry people considered that, although KISS FM had won the licence on its own merit against stiff competition, nevertheless it must desperately need the assistance that experienced professionals such as Walters could provide. Because KISS FM had been a pirate radio station, the industry was assuming that the station's management must be stupid, ignorant and gullible.

Secondly, there was an assumption that KISS FM was really going to sound just like every other local commercial station in Britain, despite the fact that it had been licensed to play dance music. Walters knew not the slightest thing about the London dance music scene, but he still believed that KISS FM should rely on him to research the music policy the station would adopt. He was ignoring the fact that KISS FM had grown out of London's dance music culture. At KISS FM, if you did not know your hip hop from your house music, you certainly had no place within the station's programming team. KISS FM was definitely not destined to be just another radio station that played pop music, like its competitors. Dance music, not pop music, was the central plank of the station's whole philosophy.

This lack of understanding about KISS FM was evident in the continuing flood of demonstration tapes I was receiving from hopeful DJs wanting to join the station. The vast majority of applicants still failed to demonstrate any knowledge of dance music or any appreciation of KISS FM's specialist music policy. Most surprising to me were the number of applications I was receiving from American candidates who seemed to think that, because the station's name derived from New York City, KISS FM must want to employ an all-American team of DJs. It was quickly becoming clear that the concept of a specialist music station such as KISS FM, playing dance music, was not at all an easy notion for the radio industry to comprehend.

On our way back from EMAP to the KISS FM office in McNamee's car, I asked him when I was going to be paid for my work in January. It was now the thirtieth of the month and the next rent payment was due to my landlord in a couple of days' time. McNamee responded by telling me, in a remarkably roundabout way, that I was not going to be paid at all that month. He explained away this revelation, quite casually, as the fault of the company's board of directors who, he said, had not yet raised all the capital necessary to finance the new company. McNamee told me that there was presently no money in the kitty, so no one could yet be paid.

I asked him when the money would come through, and he replied that he hoped to have everything in place to pay wages to the staff for February. So, I asked, would I be paid retrospectively for my work for the station during January? No, McNamee said bluntly, since there was nothing in the budget to pay wages in retrospect. He explained that the decision had not been up to him alone and that it was now a matter for the whole board of directors. Progress with the financing of the new company had simply not moved as swiftly as had been anticipated.

McNamee's words sounded liked mere excuses to me. I was angry and I suddenly felt completely betrayed by him and his earlier promises to me. It was McNamee who, in December, had begged me to devote all my attentions to KISS FM as soon as possible. It was McNamee who had promised me that I would be paid for the whole of January. I had voluntarily given up other work I would have been paid for, writing for several magazines, in order to devote my time fully to KISS FM. These were things that McNamee had demanded of me. I had put myself out to comply with his demands. Now, suddenly, I was learning, after the end of the month, that I was to be paid nothing at all?

I was furious with McNamee. My financial situation was already dire. I had just paid £129 for my return flight to the MIDEM conference, though now I could no longer recoup this expense by writing articles for magazines, as I had originally planned. After my former girlfriend had moved out of the flat we had shared, I now had to meet the monthly rent payment of £280 by myself. She had also left me several bills to settle – the quarterly telephone bill now due was £138, the highest amount I had ever had to pay, and the quarterly electric bill of £66 was also due. I owed £572 Income Tax to Inland Revenue for the 1987/88 tax year, and my season ticket for daily train travel to the KISS FM office was costing me £68 a month.

During the previous month, I had been forced to spend considerable sums replacing necessary household items that had disappeared along with my former girlfriend. A kitchen table, crockery, cutlery, an iron, an ironing board, lampshades and curtains were amongst the items I had already bought. The living room was still completely bare, exactly as my ex-partner had left it. Until now, I had had neither the time nor the money to even start replacing its former contents. If I was not going to be paid at all for my work in January, I would certainly not have the means to buy the remaining household essentials.

I felt that McNamee had ripped me off and, to make matters worse, he did not seem particularly concerned about it either. He made no offer to me to somehow claw back the earnings I had lost from my work in January. Neither did he offer to loan me money whilst the board was still raising the capital to finance KISS FM. According to McNamee, the first money I would receive from the new company was still a month away at the end of February and yet, in the meantime, he expected me to continue working for KISS FM as if nothing untoward had happened. McNamee had robbed me blind.

We were still sat in McNamee's car on the journey back to the KISS FM office from EMAP. I was tempted to tell him to stop the car so that I could get out. I was tempted to walk away, not only from McNamee, not only from his car, but from the whole of KISS FM. Forever. Then, remembering Mark Heley's words to me in France, I realised I should act carefully. Maybe McNamee wanted me to walk away now that his former pirate radio station had successfully won the London radio licence. And what would I have achieved then?

Over the following days and weeks, many more promises that had been made to me were broken. Despite the urgency with which McNamee had asked me to raise funds to buy shares in the new company, he no longer mentioned the matter and, when I asked, he shrugged off his promise with more excuses. During the visit to my bank manager, I had stressed the urgency of the situation and my need to arrange a loan quickly, but McNamee now showed no interest whatsoever in my money. My bank eventually wrote me a follow-up letter, asking whether the loan I had requested was still required.[627]

It had suddenly become impossible to ascertain the truth from McNamee about exactly what was going on at the regular meetings he was having with the other directors of the new company. While the rest of us at Blackstock Mews continued working on the day-to-day running of the KISS FM office, McNamee increasingly inhabited a world totally apart from us. He had become incredibly secretive, he was evasive when we asked him questions, and he was wholly uninformative about the detail of the radio station's plans.

The offer McNamee had made to me to buy shares in KISS FM never materialised, and the bank loan I had negotiated remained unused. The promise McNamee had made to me that I would receive a shareholding in the company in return for my success co-ordinating the winning licence application was similarly broken without explanation – I was never offered shares in the station. The promise from McNamee to pay me a full-time wage from 1 January 1990 had completely vanished.

For the first time since I had become involved in KISS FM, McNamee was reneging on his word to me, and in several quite spectacular ways. Mark Heley's words of warning to me at MIDEM were already being substantiated by McNamee's latest actions, a matter of only a few weeks later. McNamee had needed me last year to win him the radio licence, and I now began to feel that he had tricked me into working for him for a paltry sum of money, with only a promise that I would be properly rewarded at a later date. However, now there were no signs of those promises being fulfilled. I realised that I had obviously become not so vital to McNamee's current pre-occupations, whatever they might be.

Within a matter of weeks, the KISS FM I had known and loved – the struggling underdog, the popular pirate station, the friendly crowd of music-lovers – was already showing signs of turning into a very different kind of workplace and a very different kind of business. The only person in the KISS FM office who knew what was really going on was McNamee. And he was resolutely saying nothing.

---

[625] Mark Heley, "Go West", Radio & Music, 17 Jan 1990.
[626] Colin Walters, "The Style Council", Radio & Music, 17 Jan 1990.
[627] letter from Lloyds Bank, Harrow to Grant Goddard, 30 Apr 1990.

February 1990.

Despite the concerns expressed by the Independent Broadcasting Authority [IBA] at our first joint meeting that KISS FM might be planning to employ too many staff, the station's board of directors subsequently decided to increase the number of employees in certain areas of the company. The licence application had proposed that a single director would be responsible for both the advertising and marketing functions of the station, but the board later decided to split this into two separate jobs. Advertisements were placed in the media trade press to recruit for the newly created posts of 'head of advertising sales' and 'head of marketing,' and applicants were told that they must "fit in well with the KISS FM team." The contact person for enquiries was Tim Schoonmaker at EMAP, who had more experience in advertising sales and marketing than anyone in the KISS FM team.[628]

Gordon McNamee's issues with literacy and his lack of management experience, combined with the fact that he had not previously worked in licensed radio, understandably gave him a sense of insecurity about his newly elevated position as managing director of what would soon be one of the largest commercial radio stations in the country. McNamee was careful to express such doubts only to the other KISS FM office staff, and not to his board members. He started to talk a lot about sending everybody in the office, including himself, on management courses to prepare us all properly for the station's launch, but nothing ever came of the idea.

Amongst the KISS FM staff, Heddi Greenwood was particularly keen to attend a marketing course of some kind, but McNamee refused to approve her request for the station to fund the cost. In fact, McNamee had still not appointed Greenwood to a post in the new KISS FM structure. At the same time, McNamee's personal assistant, Rosee Laurence, said she was keen to learn some radio skills. She had no previous experience of radio presentation or production, and her on-air work during the pirate days of KISS FM had been limited to a few voice-overs for station jingles. For Laurence, McNamee readily agreed to sanction some evening and weekend courses in basic radio production.

The positions of Greenwood and Laurence in McNamee's favours could not have been more different. His snub of Greenwood's aspiration to be more involved in KISS FM's launch marketing campaign was typical of McNamee's attitude to his erstwhile business partner. Meanwhile, Laurence was being regularly encouraged by McNamee to expand her horizons. The previous year, when Jocks magazine had approached KISS FM for inclusion in a feature about female DJs, it was Laurence whom McNamee selected for interview, despite her not being a DJ. A photo of Laurence ended up appearing on the magazine's full-colour cover, whilst KISS FM's only genuine female DJ, Greenwood, had been completely omitted from the article.[629]

During recent months, the remaining worker in the Blackstock Mews office, Lindsay Wesker, had become totally absorbed in his role as editor of the monthly magazine Free! and he was now spending little time on KISS FM matters. The February 1990 edition of the magazine presented the first opportunity for KISS FM to explain, in its own words, exactly how it had won its radio licence. Wesker wanted to write the article, but McNamee intervened and insisted that I should pen the two-page feature. Despite the magazine having been my original idea, this was the only occasion I was asked to contribute to Free!, and then only because McNamee had insisted. Wesker seemed incredibly territorial about the project he now viewed as 'his baby,' and he appeared to like to do as much of the work on the magazine himself as was possible.[630]

The only time that the rest of the office staff became involved in Free! magazine was at the very end of each month, when a huge lorry would arrive and reverse into the narrow Blackstock Mews. Then, everyone would have to share the task of unloading 30,000 finished copies of the new issue into the office, ready for distribution. The magazines were bound into bundles of several hundred, but the printer's bindings were razor-sharp and the whole exercise would leave everyone exhausted and sweating profusely, inevitably with several cut and bleeding fingers. From my perspective, it was pleasing to observe that my notion of a free dance music magazine had proved a success. Although advertising revenue was still proving difficult, the venture was particularly popular with the public while KISS FM remained off the air. There was even a competing magazine in London, called Rave! (also with an exclamation mark), that had launched in the wake of Free!'s groundbreaking success.

Although KISS FM was still pre-occupied with finding premises for its enlarged operation, the station's future competitors on London's airwaves had already started to amend their programming in anticipation of the former pirate's imminent re-launch. At the beginning of February 1990, the IBA's David Vick sent McNamee a press cutting from The Daily Mirror newspaper, accompanied by a handwritten note that simply said: "Interesting.....!!" The article, headlined 'Dancing To A New Tune,' explained that BBC Radio One was increasing its commitment to dance music, in a sudden reversal of its former music policy: "Much criticised for being out of tune with the current craze for dance music – which makes up sixty per cent of the charts – Radio One is catching up at last, re-jigging its schedules and producing a new playlist dominated by dance singles."[631]

Despite Radio One having reduced its commitment to dance music at the end of the previous year by axing Robbie Vincent's long running soul show, the article announced that Jeff Young's Friday night dance music programme was about to be extended. Also, Gary Davies' weekday lunchtime show was to devote its 'Non-Stop Half Hour' almost entirely to dance music. A BBC spokesperson explained: "Radio One realises dance music is the big thing and we're reflecting that. We've been slagged off for ignoring it, but I'm glad to say that's all changing."[632]

Commenting on these sudden moves to include more dance music in Radio One's output, Norman Cook of the British dance act Beats International told NME: "It's no surprise to me. It's a sign of the times ... And with dance stations like KISS FM getting official licences, maybe Radio One are feeling the threat." A letter to the same publication from a reader named 'Matt' argued: "Radio One (and Capital, come to that) are going to have their butts kicked right out of the London ratings war when KISS FM comes on-air, and serves them right too. Cynical last ditch attempts to retain their (up to now) captive audience are going to impress no one, except possibly the out-of-touch lame brains who run 'Britain's Favourite Station.'"[633]

For the KISS FM team, the competition to attract listeners was anticipated to come less from Radio One than it would be from London's commercial station, Capital Radio.

Whereas the BBC national station was very sluggish and out of touch with new musical trends, Capital was far more aware of the music market and could react very quickly to changes in public tastes. Already, dance music fans in London were commenting that Capital now seemed to be playing far more dance music in its daytime programmes than it did before KISS FM had won the licence. To investigate whether or not this was true, I started to collect the weekly playlists from the reception areas of Capital Radio and Radio One on my way into work. I would then compare these playlists with that same week's singles chart to determine whether either station was becoming significantly more dance-orientated than was the pop music market as a whole.

For KISS FM to compete effectively with Capital Radio's sixteen-year monopoly as London's only commercial music station, it would be necessary to organise an extensive advertising campaign to coincide with the station's launch. KISS FM's licence application had budgeted £450,000 for this purpose, and a paragraph written by EMAP's Tim Schoonmaker had explained that the station's image would be projected to the public by employing such key words as "alive, outgoing, vibrant London, style-leading, fashion-creating, knowledgeable, street-credible and alternative."[634]

Schoonmaker had already started to co-ordinate the selection of an advertising agency to plan and execute KISS FM's launch campaign. By the beginning of February 1990, he had interviewed six possible contenders and was preparing to draw up a short-list. Following my chance meeting with Alec Kenny at the MIDEM conference, I contacted Saatchi & Saatchi in London, which also became involved in making a pitch for the new radio station's business.[635]

Within a fortnight, Schoonmaker's short-list comprised two agencies – Simons Palmer Denton Clemmow & Johnson and Saatchi & Saatchi. An opportunity for each company to present its work in person to KISS FM was arranged for Monday 19 February. Then, at the last minute, Simons Palmer Denton Clemmow & Johnson unexpectedly withdrew from the race, allegedly because the agency already managed the account of London news/talk radio station LBC, which must have decided that KISS FM was a future competitor. With only one contender remaining, the date of the final interviews had to be postponed. It was imperative that there be a competitive pitch for an agency to win KISS FM's business, so the search had to be resumed for further agencies to add to the current short-list of one.[636]

The remarkably low-key launch of North London black community station WNK the previous November had demonstrated how essential it was for a new radio station to organise a coherent publicity campaign it if wanted to be successful. WNK's negligence meant that few people in London were even aware of the station's existence, let alone listened to it. Another of the new stations, Choice FM in South London, had just started test transmissions and it too seemed to be planning a very low budget launch. WNK and Choice FM were only of passing interest to KISS FM because each was only broadcasting to a small part of London. However, another new station, Jazz FM, was more pertinent because, like KISS FM, it was going to broadcast London-wide. Jazz FM's promise to play a wide spectrum of 'jazz-derived' music, rather than only pure jazz, meant that it could choose to schedule a substantial proportion of dance music within its output. There was a real danger that Jazz FM might try and grab KISS FM's potential audience even before the latter station had the chance to re-launch.

A news report in Broadcast magazine, headlined 'More Soul For Jazz FM,' confirmed the KISS FM team's worst fears. Citing Jazz FM's own audience research, which had shown that soul and blues music appealed to many potential listeners aged between twenty and sixty years, the article noted: "Jazz FM is to play a high percentage of soul and blues music to broaden the station's appeal to non-jazz fans. The London incremental will launch on March 4th with a weekday daytime output heavily biased towards soul and blues …"[637]

That same week, we learned that Capital Radio soul DJ Peter Young, whom McNamee had wanted to recruit to KISS FM, had agreed to join the daytime presentation team of Jazz FM. Young had not been back in touch with either McNamee or me since our lunch together, so the news came as no surprise. The radio industry was already aghast at the high salaries and generous benefits that Jazz FM was offering its newly recruited personnel, and we realised that there was no way that KISS FM could compete on that score for Young's services.

Having lost Peter Young to Jazz FM, McNamee was particularly keen for me to arrange a meeting with the other Capital Radio DJ, David Rodigan, whom he wanted to present a daytime show on KISS FM. It was Rodigan who had kindly put me in touch with Young after Christmas, whilst explaining that he himself was too pre-occupied with the birth of a new baby to discuss the possibility of working for KISS FM. The news about Jazz FM's recruitment of Young hastened the need to talk to Rodigan, whom McNamee was convinced would prove an invaluable addition to the KISS FM team.

Coincidentally, details were sent to Blackstock Mews of another potential KISS FM office building that was located right behind Capital Radio's studios on Euston Road. The empty premises in Drummond Street had even been used in the past by Capital Radio for its Christmas Helpline operation, though the offices were presently leased to Thames Television, which no longer needed them. The location was very central, very accessible and met McNamee's awkward requirement to have its own private car park. The only issue was that to work in the shadow of the very radio station that was being viewed as KISS FM's main competitor might prove rather daunting, particularly as Capital Radio was housed in the base of Euston Tower, a huge skyscraper that dwarfed the surrounding area.

The day that McNamee visited Drummond Street for the first time, 1 February 1990, was also the day he instructed staff in the Blackstock Mews office to answer the phone with the words 'KISS FM' for the first time. Until then, we had continued to answer as 'Goodfoot Promotions,' even after the licence win. It appeared that the station's board of directors had finally agreed to start funding KISS FM as a separate entity. The board had also agreed to absorb all of Goodfoot's assets into the new company, and McNamee told me afterwards that he had driven a particularly hard bargain by valuing all of Goodfoot's fixtures and fittings, mainly re-painted second-hand office furniture, at a very high price.

I was still being kept very busy at the Blackstock Mews office, processing the flood of job applications that were by now arriving at a rate of thirty or more a day. Because the company still employed no secretaries or administrative assistants, it was time consuming for each member of staff to type, photocopy and mail all the correspondence themselves, whilst having to deal with the torrent of phone enquiries the station was receiving. Having myself been a regular recipient of job rejection letters, or received no response at all from potential employers, I was determined to make KISS FM's 'personnel department' more friendly. In reply to each person who showed an interest in working for the station, I sent a letter and a photocopied list of magazines and newspapers in which radio jobs were advertised, which I hoped would assist them in the gruesome task of job hunting, even if KISS FM could not make direct use of their skills.

McNamee became interested in the idea of a television documentary that would relate 'The KISS FM Story' and he started making appointments with potential production companies. KISS FM's head of talks designate, Lyn Champion, was still working full-time for her video production company, Pressure, and had discussed with McNamee the idea of making such a programme herself. He rejected her involvement in favour of a larger company that he felt could ensure the programme was shown on television to coincide with the station's launch. McNamee also met the journalist Cynthia Rose, who had written several sympathetic articles about KISS FM and who now worked for The Face magazine, to discuss a film collaboration, but nothing more came of it. Instead, Rose suggested that The Face could run a large feature, to coincide with KISS FM's launch, in the form of a diary that noted all McNamee's preparations and work leading up to the big event. McNamee agreed, but then delegated the task to me to keep notes of the day-to-day developments within the station. Tasks such as this, which involved writing, organisation and planning, were usually passed to me to do. My workload was increasing substantially. The challenge for me now was to keep making progress simultaneously with the dozens of tasks I needed to co-ordinate to launch the station.[638]

McNamee's documentary project was eventually assigned to Mentorn Films, a London television production company that produced a weekly regional what's on show entitled '01 For London' that was presented by Mark Webster. McNamee knew Webster from the days when the latter had reviewed records for Blues & Soul magazine, and McNamee believed him to be the ideal front man for a documentary about the radio station. At the same time, McNamee told me that he wanted Webster to co-present KISS FM's weekday breakfast show with Graham Gold when the station was launched. This was not a recommendation, but an instruction from McNamee. There was no discussion. It might appear that McNamee had already offered Webster the job, in return for him endorsing KISS FM on television, in exactly the same way as he had already rewarded Gold for not bidding against KISS FM's licence application. I realised that I was to have no say as to which DJs should present the station's most high-profile programme, the weekday breakfast show. I also realised that it was I who would be held responsible if the programme failed to attract an audience. I just had to bury my head in other important work.[639]

Finding suitable premises was still the number one priority, because the details of the studio installation and office arrangements could not be planned until we knew exactly what sort of size and shape building we were going to occupy. An offer was still pending for the first premises McNamee and I had viewed, presently occupied by Chappell Music, and the owners had told us that another potential tenant who had viewed the building before us had pulled out of the race. As a precautionary measure, KISS FM also made a formal offer for the Drummond Street office, despite it being so close to Capital Radio. It was already early February and we were rapidly nearing the Easter deadline the board had set for signing an office lease.

The music and style magazines were already starting to speculate as to how the newly legalised KISS FM would sound and whether it would differ substantially from its pirate days. Blitz magazine asked: "The question remains as to how the station will identify itself going into the Nineties, as previously the favourite line on the station has been 'the radical response to the Eighties.'" Echoes newspaper, in a review of two new dance music singles by Innocence and Rosalind Joyce, asked rhetorically: "Are these the grooves that will drive KISS FM?" It ended another record review with the statement: "KISS FM would have put this in the charts." In Radio & Music magazine, a feature on music station formats asked: "KISS FM. How tightly formatted are they going to be? Are you talking about aggressive rap? They can play mainstream bands like Soul II Soul?" i-D magazine reported: "Some have suggested that the legal station will be more commercial than the pirate's 'radical radio' broadcast policy of across-the-board dance music from house to rap to soul." The Face magazine reasoned, more knowledgeably than other commentators, that "the new, legal KISS FM cannot of course keep up the same shambolic mix of chaos and club sounds seven days a week."[640]

These issues, and others facing the station, were the topics being discussed in increasingly long and regular meetings between various combinations of KISS FM staff in the Blackstock Mews office. On Monday 5 February, McNamee and I had a very long meeting with KISS FM's head of talks designate, Lyn Champion. This was our first opportunity, since winning the licence, to discuss in detail the planned speech programming of the station. The licence application had proposed that, on weekdays, there would be a fifteen-minute speech programme every lunchtime and a thirty-minute speech programme each evening. At weekends, there would be a lunchtime show with speech, supplemented by a one-hour round-up of the week's events on Sunday. In our discussions of these plans, it quickly became apparent that McNamee had no idea how much more time consuming and expensive it was for a radio station to produce speech programmes than music shows. With music programmes, you could simply put on a record that lasted four minutes, after which you might talk for thirty seconds before starting yet another record. With speech programming, there is no music upon which to fall back. Every single second has to be filled with some kind of talk, discussion or narrative. This is why speech programmes require a huge amount of planning and production.[641]

During the meeting, Champion was very anxious that she should be given the necessary resources to produce successful speech programming, but McNamee was keen to cut corners at every opportunity. Although the budgets had been enlarged in KISS FM's business plan for some areas of activity such as marketing and sales, the board were demanding cutbacks in other (to them) seemingly less important areas. McNamee felt that the talks department was ripe for pruning. He quickly became exasperated with Champion's insistence that every little detail should be thrashed out and agreed beforehand, and that every need within her department must be taken account of now. Not knowing anything about the intricacies of speech production, McNamee accused Champion of merely wanting to follow "the BBC way of doing things" which, to him, seemed to involve needless expenditure on unnecessary resources and not enough sheer hard work by the managers themselves. McNamee invoked his 'hands on' theory to Champion, whereby he expected all the executives working for KISS FM to get stuck in and do the work themselves, rather than them merely sitting back and ordering their staff to get their hands dirty.

I had some sympathy with both sides of the argument. On the one hand, McNamee was completely out of his depth arguing that KISS FM's speech output only needed a particular number of staff and a particular amount of equipment. McNamee had never made a speech radio programme in his life. However, he persisted in arguing that Champion was only trying to build up her own little empire within the station, rather than her simply requesting the resources necessary to get the job done. On the other hand, I could see that Champion was prone to making excessive demands and she seemed to want the maximum amount of resources to complete a task, rather than compromise with a lesser amount. It was true that Champion had only worked in radio for the BBC, where resources were routinely offered to producers seemingly with little thought as to the cost of individual items. She had not worked in commercial radio, where staff had to struggle and 'get by' with the limited resources that were available. McNamee and Champion had first met before I had become involved in KISS FM, and I had assumed that the pair must already have established a good, working relationship. However, it seemed impossible for the two to agree upon anything, and McNamee seemed ridiculously suspicious of Champion's expertise in an area that he knew nothing about.

I was already becoming caught in the middle of their crossfire. In the company's management structure, Champion was accountable to me and, in turn, I was accountable to McNamee. I could sense that there were definitely going to be problems in this area and that they might take a lot of hard work to resolve. McNamee wanted an element of speech programming on the station – about that there was no doubt. The licence application had made a firm commitment to broadcasting speech programmes within the station's dance music format. Organising such programmes, when neither McNamee nor anyone else on the board of directors was experienced in speech radio, was going to prove a real headache. How could the board expect such programmes to be made, and made successfully, if they could not understand that a certain level of resources would be necessary to do such work? And why was McNamee being so unreasonable with Champion, when it was he who had decided to hire her in the first place, specifically because of her expertise and experience in producing speech programming for young people? I sensed that there were going to be difficult days ahead.

---

[628]KISS FM advertisement, Campaign, 26 Jan 1990.
KISS FM advertisement, Marketing Week, 26 Jan 1990.
KISS FM advertisement, Radio & Music, 31 Jan 1990.
[629]Vie Marshall, "Female DJs", Jocks, Aug 1989.
[630]Grant Goddard, "Legal, Decent, Honest & Funky", Freel, Feb 1990.
[631]David Vick, IBA compliments slip, 8 Feb 1990.
"Dancing To A New Tune", Daily Mirror, 7 Feb 1990.
[632]ibid.
[633]"Broadcasting House", NME, 17 Feb 1990.
Matt, "Talk Radio", letters, NME, 3 Mar 1990.
[634]"IBA Incremental ILR Contract Application Form", KISS FM, Nov 1989.
[635]"KISS FM Goes In Search Of Shop For Launch", Campaign, 2 Feb 1990.
[636]"KISS FM", Marketing Week, 16 Feb 1990.
"Simons Palmer Denton Clemmow", Campaign, 9 Mar 1990.
[637]"More Soul For Jazz FM", Broadcast, 16 Feb 1990.
[638]"KISS FM Diary", The Face, September 1990 [my diary notes had been attributed to "Gordon McNamee, Grant Goddard, Lindsay Wesker, Rosee Laurence and Heddi Greenwood"].
[639]"Radical Radio: The Story Of KISS FM", television programme, Mentorn Films, 1990.
[640]"KISS FM", Bylines, Blitz, Feb 1990.
Chris Wells, "Singles", Echoes, 10 Feb 1990.
Paul Trynka, "Top Of The Formatters", Radio & Music, 14 Feb 1990.

Dave Swindells, "Newsflash", i-D, Mar 1990.
Sheryl Garratt, "Radio", The Face, Mar 1990.
[641]"IBA Incremental ILR Contract Application Form", KISS FM, Nov 1989.

February 1990.

Having concluded the rather fraught meeting with Lyn Champion, Gordon McNamee headed straight to EMAP's office in Farringdon, where interviews were about to take place to appoint KISS FM's head of advertising sales. EMAP's Tim Schoonmaker had handled the application and short-listing process until now, and McNamee was the only person from the KISS FM office invited to participate in the final interviews. He returned to Blackstock Mews at the end of the day, revealing little about the selection process, except that he needed to find out more about the background of some of the applicants. He asked me what I knew about Radio City, the commercial station in Liverpool, so I told him what little I had gleaned from press reports and from the one occasion I had listened to the station.

I had been busy scheduling appointments with each of the former pirate KISS FM DJs to discuss what sort of programme they were interested in presenting when the station returned to the airwaves. Trends in dance music were prone to very rapid change, so I could not assume that a DJ who had presented a show of, say, house music in KISS FM's pirate days would still be interested in the same style of music more than a year later. It was necessary to make individual appointments with each of the station's thirty-odd DJs to meet me at Blackstock Mews to discuss exactly what they would like to do on the new KISS FM. I made notes about each person in the back pages of my diary because I knew that, eventually, I would have to fit all their different interests into a single coherent programme schedule for the station.

At the most recent DJ meeting, McNamee had repeated the promise he had originally made before the licence win, that every DJ who had worked for the pirate KISS FM when it closed would automatically be offered one weekly show on the newly legalised station. Additionally, he had explained that there would be vacancies for several full-time presenters to host the station's high profile weekday daytime shows. McNamee had suggested that those DJs interested in applying for these vacancies should let me know. This was why, in the back of my diary, I was also drawing up a short-list of possible candidates for the handful of on-air jobs which would be more prestigious and better paid. The licence application had promised that the new KISS FM would comprise five daily shows on weekdays, each presented by the same person on all five days, in a style known in the radio industry as 'strip programming.'[642]

However, McNamee's desire to appoint 'outsiders' to some of these plum positions automatically precluded many of the vacancies being filled by loyal KISS FM loyal DJs. Although Peter Young had recently signed to Jazz FM rather than KISS FM, McNamee was still keen to tempt David Rodigan away from Capital Radio. Additionally, unknown to the KISS FM DJs, Graham Gold and Mark Webster had already been promised the breakfast show; Tony Monson had been promised a daytime show; and McNamee was also keen to offer Dave Pearce, presently working for London radio station GLR, another of the daytime positions. These clandestine appointments did not leave many opportunities for internal candidates, a fact that McNamee realised would cause much resentment amongst his loyal team when they discovered that newcomers were destined to take the most highly paid DJ jobs on the station.

Nevertheless, Dave Pearce's credentials as a future KISS FM DJ were impeccable. He had started his radio career with London pirate station Radio Jackie in the early 1980s, before moving to BBC Radio London at the time the station was playing more soul music than any other legal station in London. In 1988, after the BBC had appointed a new management team, the station was renamed Greater London Radio [GLR] and a very different, rock-orientated music policy was introduced. Pearce's shows were marginalised until, in September 1989, his daily evening slot was axed, leaving him with only one weekend programme. At the time, GLR's new programme organiser, Trevor Dann, had commented: "If KISS FM had got the franchise and we were about to have a twenty-four hour dance station, I would still want a Dave Pearce dance programme and a rap show."[643]

However, once KISS FM had won a licence on its second attempt, Dann's comments were quickly shown to be empty promises. Despite Pearce's seven years with the station, it had become obvious that the BBC wanted him out of GLR before KISS FM re-launched in the autumn. To fill his time, Pearce had started a dance record company called Reachin' Records from a tiny basement office in West London's Nottingham Place. I arranged to meet him there on Wednesday 7 February and we adjourned to a nearby Italian restaurant to discuss his future with KISS FM.

Pearce was very keen to present the station's afternoon drivetime show, since he felt particularly experienced in producing a daily programme that would appeal to teenagers listening to radio on their return from school. This was precisely the audience he had attracted to his shows on BBC Radio London and GLR. Knowing that McNamee had very definite ideas of his own as to which DJ would be placed where in KISS FM's daytime schedule, I could only listen to Pearce's arguments and stress that no DJ could yet be promised a specific time slot. Having suffered a setback to his career from the re-organisation of BBC Radio London into GLR, Pearce was incredibly keen to make the move to KISS FM, where he felt he would be allowed to play the dance music that he knew and loved. Over lunch, he suggested many ways to promote the station and its dance music programmes to potential listeners. It was a real joy to talk to someone who understood how radio worked, and I knew there and then that Pearce would be a definite asset to the re-launched KISS FM.

On my return to the Blackstock Mews offices, I noticed that builders were working on the construction of a brick partition across the back wall of the ground floor office used by Free! magazine. The partition created a long, though very narrow, space that McNamee told me would be used to hold private meetings, when it was deemed inappropriate for a confidential conversation to take place in the open-plan first floor office. This seemed to be a symptom of the subtle changes that were evolving within the radio station. Until the licence win, McNamee had never been happier than when he was the centre of attention in the upstairs office, barking orders to the rest of us and listening in on everyone else's conversation around him. He had always made sure that he was the focus of activity in the room and he had always made sure that he knew about everything that was going on. Now, increasingly, McNamee was out of the office during most of the day, usually in meetings elsewhere, and he was sharing less and less information about KISS FM's development with the rest of us in the office.

That evening, I convened the first KISS FM 'programming meeting,' intended to discuss some of the decisions that needed to be made before the new programme schedule could be decided. The meeting was supposed to start at half past five, but the office was still frenetically busy by then and Lyn Champion had not yet arrived. In the end, it was nearly seven o'clock before the office cleared and the answering machine could be switched on. A small group consisting of McNamee, Champion, Lindsay Wesker, Rosee Laurence and me drew some chairs together at one end of the huge upstairs office. I set up a makeshift easel to hold a large A2-size writing pad, on which I was going to scribble some of my ideas in felt pen.

None of the other participants had worked in the commercial radio industry so that, even before we could tackle the precise detail of the KISS FM programme schedule, it was important for me to ensure that we all understood exactly how a commercial radio station worked. Only once all of us had grasped the essential principles of commercial radio could we then start to construct the kind of radio station we needed. I apologised in advance if the evening meeting seemed to be a lecture, but I felt that this was a necessary pre-requisite to the detail that would need to be decided during future meetings.

I started by showing the others how basic economic theory could be applied to every good or service bought or sold in a marketplace. Every good sold across the counter of a local shop has three characteristics: a buyer, a seller and a price. The same characteristics apply equally to services, such as dry cleaning or plumbing – a deal is made to exchange money for a service once a particular buyer and a particular seller have agreed upon a mutually acceptable price. This is the law of economics.

Then, I asked Lindsay Wesker how he would apply this theory to the business of a commercial radio station. What, I asked him, was being sold, and who were the buyer and the seller? He replied that the seller was the radio station, that the buyer was the station's audience, and that the good being exchanged was the radio programme to which the buyer listened. He added that the price of the exchange was the degree to which the station's programme was attractive and enjoyed by the listener. If the station's programme proved to have insufficient appeal to a listener, they would no longer listen to that station and would retune their radio to another station, where they might find something more suited to their tastes.

I had asked Wesker the question because I had anticipated that he would respond in this way. He was someone who seemed to place artistic merit above commercial worth. He appeared to listen to music with an ear for its intrinsic pleasure, rather than its ability to reap financial rewards. As a result, perhaps the records that had been released on KISS FM's label Graphic Records were artistically very good, but their sales had proven to be disappointing, despite the acclaim they had received within the narrow world of dance music industry peers.

Using liberal quantities of paper covered with boxes and arrows drawn in colour felt pens, I explained that the relationships between the different component parts of commercial radio were, in reality, very different from the way they appeared to outsiders. A commercial radio station made its money from selling advertising space on its airwaves, and its income derived from making deals with advertisers. If a station carried no advertisements, it would quickly go out of business. So it was this aspect of the station's operations that was fundamental to its very survival, not its programmes.

The seller was definitely the radio station, but the buyer was not the listener. It was the advertiser that booked a campaign of commercials on the station. Money was only passed from the advertiser to the radio station once a deal had been struck at a competitive price for a certain number of advertisements. But what was the good that passed in the opposite direction? In simple terms, the station gave up thirty seconds of its airtime to the advertiser in exchange for the money it paid, but the deal was more intricate than that. An advertiser would never waste money booking an advertising campaign on a radio station that had no listeners. However cheap a thirty-second advert might be offered by a station that had been proven to have no listeners, an advertiser would not be interested. What the advertiser was interested in were the listeners that the station attracted. Listeners who, by default, would be listening to the advertisement sandwiched in between their favourite songs. What the advertiser was actually buying was the station's audience, not just a thirty-second piece of airtime.

So, returning to the economic theory, the seller is the radio station, the buyer is the advertiser, and the exchange involves money passing in one direction and the station's audience passing in the other. Put simply, a commercial radio station sells its audience to its advertisers. The second question an advertiser asks a radio station, after wanting to know the price of an advertisement, is: how many people are going to hear my advert? Of the four people watching my little lecture, three looked somewhat stunned by my revelation. The fourth, Gordon McNamee, retained an air of detached disinterest, as if he was not learning anything from what had been said.

It was Lindsay Wesker who asked: "Where does the station's programming fit into all this, then?" I told him that the programming did not really enter into the station's basic economic function. He protested that a radio station was nothing without its programmes and that, surely, it was the programmes and the DJs that were absolutely essential to a station's success. I told him that although, as head of programming designate for KISS FM, I would love to be able to agree with him, the notion that programming was a commercial radio station's most important asset was simply not true. The most important part of a commercial radio station's operation was always its sales department. Without its sales force and its sales director, a commercial radio station had no ability to earn revenues. It could have the best programmes of any radio station in the world, but it would not stay in business a single day without a sales department to earn it money.

Wesker asked me how programming fitted into the theory that I had explained, and which he seemed to have difficulty believing was the way that commercial radio operated. I told him that, above all else, a radio station's sales department needed the largest possible audience to sell to potential advertisers, and the sales staff did not care how that audience was achieved. The station's programmes were merely the bait required to attract listeners. Think of a radio station's programming as the colourful wrapper on a chocolate bar that might persuade a hungry person to buy one brand rather than another in a sweet shop. That was all that radio programming meant to a commercial radio station. It was the 'front' for the station's real raison d'être – making money. In order to attract listeners, programming was an expensive but necessary evil to most stations' management. If you are a fisherman, you try and get away with using the cheapest bait to catch a fish. In the same way, if you are a commercial radio station, you try and attract the biggest audience by using the cheapest possible programming.

There were blank stares and a certain amount of disbelief amongst my audience, so I tried to illustrate how a station's programming department is always bottom of the pile in its list of priorities. Take, as an example, London's commercial music station, Capital Radio. When it launched in 1973, it had a lot of specialist music shows and speech-based programmes in its schedule, which it was forced to broadcast by the regulatory body, the Independent Broadcasting Authority. Over the years, Capital had saved itself money by dropping almost all of these shows and replacing them with cheaper, chart-based music programmes. It was far easier and cheaper to extend an existing pop music show by a couple of hours, using the same DJ and the same format, than to schedule a jazz show that needed a specialist presenter. Capital Radio was much more profitable now, and its costs were lower.

Take the example of a commercial radio station that was facing financial difficulties. It might not be earning as much revenues as it had anticipated and it was destined to lose more and more money, week on week. It would be forced to make cutbacks of some sort or it would go out of business, so what would it do? It would cut back on the aspects of its operation that did not directly earn the company its revenue, of which the most obvious was the programming department. At the same time, it wanted to earn more revenue than it had done to date, in order to be able to pay its bills. So, not only would it cut back on its programming, but it would put additional resources into its sales department to try and earn more money. As a result, at the same time as making several staff redundant in its programming department, it might hire more staff in its sales department. Overall, this would not only save the station money, but it would also shift the emphasis of the station's activities further away from the programme content and more towards those activities that directly generated money.

Someone in my audience suggested that such a shift of resources must surely damage the station's audience, particularly if the resources of the programming department were cut back too much or for too long a period. I replied that this was certainly true, but that a station's immediate need for revenues usually took precedence over its long-term plans. Put simply, if you thought you were soon to go out of business, you took steps to cut your costs and increase your revenues as quickly as possible, without really giving a second thought as to how your station's audience might react in the long term.

Worse than that, a station that had already succeeded in attracting a substantial audience might feel that it no longer needed to spend as much money on its programming. Such a station might feel that the bait of 'good programming' had already worked, that the audience had already been won over, and that the bait was no longer needed. In this case, even if the station was doing well, both financially and in terms of audience numbers, it might still decide to cut back its programming department and channel more resources into its sales operation, believing it could make even more profit on the back of the success it had already achieved. Only when its audience figures started to decline might the station consider it was worth diverting a little more money back into programming.

So, I concluded, a commercial radio station's sales department was usually the engine of the whole business operation and it had the most weight to throw around. The programming department, whilst it might seem important to the listener, was nowhere near as important to the station itself. As a result, whenever a station faced problems of one sort or another, it tended to be the programming department that suffered, and never the sales department.

"So it's always programming that gets the chop," interrupted Wesker, suddenly realising the essence of what I had been saying, and grinning madly now that he had understood my message.

"Yes, it's always the programming department that gets hit in the end," I agreed. "Whether it performs well or badly, programming is too often seen as being the radio station activity that is most dispensable and, too often, it suffers the axe. If you read stories in the newspapers about staff cutbacks at radio stations, nine out of ten times it is the programming people who are being sacked or laid off, almost regardless of what may be the station's real problems."

This brought to a conclusion the first KISS FM programming meeting. We had started late, and we were now finishing even later. During the whole evening, McNamee had contributed virtually nothing to the discussion. Now he asked me if, the next time we met, we could move on to the subject of KISS FM's programming and what we were going to do about it. I said we could, but I reiterated that it was important for the whole group to grasp some basic facts about the commercial radio industry that we were about to join. McNamee did not appear to be particularly enthused by that evening's lecture.

Lyn Champion asked me if I wanted a lift to Finsbury Park tube station in her car, an offer I gratefully accepted. As we were about to leave the KISS FM office, Lindsay Wesker said 'good night' to us, and I noticed that he was still smiling to himself, seemingly pleased with some of the things I had explained during the meeting.

"So it's always programming that gets the chop," he mused out loud. I told him that this had certainly been my experience of the commercial radio industry to date. "But that's not what will happen at KISS FM, is it?" Wesker asked me. "KISS FM is different, isn't it?"

I shrugged and walked out of the building, into the cold February night air of Finsbury Park. It was late, I was tired and it was going to be a long journey home to Harrow.

---

[642]"IBA Incremental ILR Contract Application Form", KISS FM, Nov 1989.
[643]Grant Goddard, "Dirty Dancing", City Limits, 14 Sep 1989.

February 1990.

KISS FM's technical requirements – the building of radio studios, equipping them and linking them to a transmitter – were another area of work that still needed attention. The task fell to me, not because I knew much about electronics, but because (once again) I was the only person within the start-up team who had worked in a commercial radio station. The initial KISS FM business plan had provided for the employment of a chief engineer and two assistants. However, in an attempt to save money, McNamee had decided not to fulfil the station's technical needs in-house, as was normal practice, but rather to contract out the work to an external company. To this end, McNamee had appointed Phoenix Communications, a small business run by Lawrence Hallett and Martin Spence, the two engineers who had masterminded KISS FM's transmitters during its pirate days. This arrangement was an example of McNamee's keenness to 'payback' some of the people who had supported his pirate radio operation.

Until recently, Phoenix Communications had been based in a workshop in East London, where Hallett and Spence had manufactured dozens of radio transmitters for KISS FM and many other London pirate stations. The duo had decided to transform their secret operation into a legitimate business from 1 January 1989, the cut-off date imposed by the government for pirates to voluntarily cease broadcasting. Phoenix was now hoping to win contracts from many of the newly licensed incremental radio stations to design, install and maintain their studios and transmitter equipment. McNamee's decision to contract out the KISS FM work gave Phoenix its biggest contract to date. Hallett and Spence must have hoped that the size and prestige of working for London-based KISS FM would help win them further business from other clients across the country.

I held an initial meeting with Hallett and Spence at the KISS FM office to discuss the contracting-out arrangement, a conversation which lasted five hours. No previous example existed of a legal radio station that had sub-contracted all of its technical work, so the idea seemed fraught with danger for a new station as inexperienced as KISS FM. However, McNamee had insisted that this was the only way that the new company could afford to satisfy its engineering needs. He had expressed total faith in Hallett and Spence's ability to deliver the necessary services, despite them not having undertaken a project of this magnitude. McNamee knew very little about the technical aspects of radio, and so my initial meeting made me realise that it would be me who ended up being the station's management person for engineering matters.

My main concern was Hallett and Spence's unexpected announcement that they were about to move their company from East London to Worcestershire, more than a hundred miles away. They assured me that this re-location would not cause them problems fulfilling their contract with KISS FM (unknown to me, they had already agreed with McNamee that one room in KISS FM's new premises would be designated as Phoenix Communication's London office, staffed by one of their future employees). They explained that the move to Worcestershire was necessary because it was more central to the whole country than London, making it easier for them to service the other contracts they expected to win elsewhere.

However, I was not so sure that a company based so far away was going to be that meticulous in responding to the specific needs of a station in far away London.

During the meeting, the three of us looked through the engineering specifications that Phoenix had prepared for inclusion in the KISS FM licence application, and we discussed the sort of equipment that would be needed in the station's broadcast studios. It was still difficult to be specific about the exact requirements until the new premises had been finalised. The question of which equipment KISS FM installed, and what size to build the studios, would be determined very much by the sort of building within which they were to be housed. The issue of suitable premises still seemed a long way from being settled, despite the insistence of the station's board that a decision must be made by Easter at the latest.

McNamee and I had just visited another potential premises in Camden High Street, only a short walk from KISS FM's former office in Greenland Street. Next door to a public library, the building's upstairs floors were available to rent, each divided in half by a staircase that ran up the middle of the building. The only tenant was Autocar magazine, though we were told that it would move out shortly. The advantage of the building was that it fronted a very busy High Street near the centre of London, and that there was retail space on the ground floor that could be used to display and sell KISS FM merchandise. There were also car parking spaces to the rear of the building, an attribute that McNamee felt was essential, though these spaces would have to be shared with the eventual occupants of the building's other floors.

McNamee liked the idea of the radio station being based in Camden once again, as it was a particularly trendy part of London where KISS FM still held its weekly Second Base club night at the Dingwalls venue further up the High Street. However, McNamee felt that one whole floor of the building would prove too large for KISS FM's requirements, while half a floor would not be large enough. I thought the office space was almost perfect for KISS FM, but it seemed as if McNamee was becoming increasingly fussy about the specifications he was looking for in a building, so we left Camden High Street unsatisfied.

I caught the Underground back to the Blackstock Mews office, while McNamee went to be photographed for a personal profile in GQ, the monthly magazine devoted to men's fashion. When the issue was published, the photo portrayed McNamee dressed as a suave businessman, while the accompanying article pointed out that "independent radio is a potential licence to print money." It explained: "Capital Radio, which KISS FM will be challenging head-on come August, made fifteen million pounds in profits before tax last year, sixty-two per cent higher than the previous year's figure. If it works, and the economy stays above water, KISS FM should be a gold mine."[644]

After the photo session, McNamee went to a meeting with the creative team of Saatchi & Saatchi, the advertising agency that was keen to win the KISS FM launch account. He returned to the office later in the day, bubbling with enthusiasm for some of the agency's ideas. He regaled us with examples, such as its plan to wheel-clamp cars all over London with a special fake KISS FM clamp on the day the station re-launched, and to paint the station's logo right across the Cromwell Road, one of the busiest commuter routes into the capital. McNamee told us that the Saatchi & Saatchi team would visit Blackstock Mews over the coming weeks to talk to us about our own ideas for the launch of the station and to find out for themselves exactly what made KISS FM such an exciting venture.

At the end of the day, the office was visited by Nick Ware, producer of a weekly BBC Radio Four youth programme called 'WPFM.' He interviewed McNamee for an item about pirate radio that was to be included in the next edition of the show. McNamee told him: "By the end of this year, there will be ten commercial radio stations [in London]. We wonder whether the public are ready for this all, and we just hope that we're not one of the casualties. We feel very, very positive, purely because we are a tried formula, to a point, and we've got a listenership there ready to go for it." Radio critic Ken Garner was more sceptical in his contribution to the programme, describing KISS FM as "a very successful right-on pirate station for a good two or three or four years. It didn't get [a licence] at the first go, [but] got lucky the second time around. There's going to be a lot of pressure on them to be absolutely terrific from the first second [on-air]."[645]

One of the key decisions for KISS FM's financial success would be the appointment of a radio saleshouse for the station, contracted to book advertising campaigns from big national companies and earning a commission for their work. There were several saleshouses serving the UK commercial radio industry and, in order to decide which was most appropriate for KISS FM, Tim Schoonmaker organised two days during which each company made a lengthy presentation to the KISS FM team. These pitches were held in a windowless conference room in London's Royal Horseguards Thistle Hotel and were attended by McNamee, Martin Strivens, Keith McDowall and me from KISS FM, along with Schoonmaker from EMAP. A radio industry veteran, David Maker, was also invited to attend in order to share with us his opinions, even though he was not involved in KISS FM.

For two days, a succession of smiling, suited salesman regaled us with stories of how wonderful KISS FM was going to be, how much money they could make for us from selling our advertising airtime, and how perfectly they understood what KISS FM was all about. Unfortunately, most of their knowledge of the station proved to be wide of the mark. One saleshouse, The Radio Sales Company, predicted that KISS FM's audience in its first year would be 670,000 adults, despite the station having already publicly declared its target figure as one million listeners. It also envisaged KISS FM as a down-market station, despite our publicity having already stated that we expected to attract upper and lower class listeners in roughly equal proportions. Its forecast was that the station's advertising revenue in the first year would be £1.9m, despite the station's business plan requiring more. The Radio Sales Company had recently won the contract to represent another new London station, Jazz FM, which was designed to appeal to up-market, middle-aged listeners. It must have judged KISS FM as an opportunity to complement Jazz FM's older, affluent listenership with our station's supposedly down-market, youthful audience. The evident danger was that, for The Radio Sales Company, KISS FM would be a lower priority than Jazz FM, since the saleshouse had already guaranteed the latter £1m of advertising revenue in its first year.[646]

Another saleshouse, New Media Sales, made a more optimistic forecast that KISS FM would sell £3.3m of advertising in its first year, growing to between £4m and £6m by the second year. The challenge was that the company presently had no other radio sales contracts because it had concentrated primarily on the television sector. The KISS FM team considered this to be a distinct disadvantage, since television advertising could earn a saleshouse much more revenue than the launch of a new radio station ever could. Similar reservations were expressed about the credentials or intentions of several of the other saleshouses that made presentations to the group.[647]

After much discussion, and with some reluctance, the decision was made to award the national advertising contract to Independent Radio Sales [IRS], a saleshouse owned by Crown Communications, the parent company of London's commercial talk station LBC. IRS had offered KISS FM several incentives over its competitors. It had a track record as it already sold advertising for LBC and roughly half the local commercial stations across the country. IRS also promised to sell KISS FM's advertising using a dedicated sales team that would devote all its attentions to the one new station and no other.

Additionally, IRS promised to supply KISS FM with a 'customised' service of news bulletin through its sister company, Independent Radio News [IRN]. Until recently, IRN had enjoyed a monopoly in producing hourly, three-minute news bulletins broadcast by all local commercial stations. In the last few weeks, a competitor called Independent Television News had entered the market and had already successfully signed up seven new incremental stations to broadcast a radio version of its long established TV news bulletins. As a result, IRN had suddenly become keen to offer incentives to new stations that would subscribe to its service. The deal on offer meant not only that KISS FM would be offered the existing IRN news service completely free of charge, but that IRN would arrange for a special, customised version of news bulletins to be supplied to the station, designed to appeal to a younger audience than its standard, networked reports.

The other offer that IRS threw into the deal was the supply of a satellite receiving station that KISS FM could use to receive audio recordings of new national commercials that were beamed simultaneously to stations across the county. The system, operated by a separate company called Satellite Media Services, was intended to replace the former, labour intensive practice of a saleshouse sending out individual tapes of new commercials to every station on which they were to be broadcast. The satellite receiving station would normally cost around £20,000, but IRS promised that it would be supplied free of charge to KISS FM as part of the overall deal.

McNamee was particularly impressed by the IRS promise that its salesman John Quinn would be promoted to head the proposed KISS FM sales team. McNamee knew Quinn from the latter's freelance work as a club promoter in London. Ten months earlier, it was Quinn who had met KISS FM's Guy Wingate to discuss the possible involvement of IRS in the station's first licence application. McNamee was in no doubt that Quinn understood the potential of KISS FM and the audience it planned to attract much more so than the other salespeople who had been seen during two days of presentations. As a closing touch, at the end of its pitch, the IRS team presented everyone in the room with a special blue sweatshirt, printed with the logos of both IRS and KISS FM above the words "the winning combination." Once a decision was made to do business with IRS, it was up to McNamee and Schoonmaker to sort out the details of the contract.

The next morning, I arrived for work at the KISS FM office to find that I was the first one there. Despite working full-time for the station, I had still not been entrusted with a set of keys to the office, so I routinely had to wait for McNamee, Wesker or Greenwood to arrive. That morning, on walking into Blackstock Mews, I had found that the security grilles padlocked across the KISS FM office entrance had been entirely covered with dozens of plastic, inflatable, red pairs of lips, ranging in size from a few inches to more than a foot across. A cryptic note had been left stuffed into one of the grilles that read: "Your account is worth more than a million smackers to us."

I knew then that this was an example of the bizarre work of the Saatchi & Saatchi creative team. After all, it was 14 February, St Valentine's Day, and the advertising agency must have considered that the occasion presented a unique opportunity to demonstrate the 'kissing' theme that it wanted to employ in the station's advertising campaign. Once McNamee had arrived in his new company car, accompanied by his personal assistant Rosee Laurence, he found a camera upstairs and took photos of the artwork gracing the front of our office, while the occupiers of adjacent business units, arriving for work, stared at us as if we were all completely mad.[648]

By comparison to that morning's Saatchi & Saatchi stunt, the rest of the day in the office was very routine. Rosee Laurence spent most of it talking to representatives of franking machine companies. The volume of outgoing mail from the KISS FM office was growing daily, and it was becoming too cumbersome to stick stamps on all the letters for posting in the nearest post box. Gordon McNamee suddenly realised that he was overweight and launched a short-lived fitness campaign to play a game of squash each afternoon. There was the usual, constant stream of people visiting the office, including a student from the media course at Goldsmiths College and a member of the parliamentary Bow Group, wanting to know more about the station's plans. In the evening, I was invited by Daniel Nathan, who had recently succeeded me as radio editor of City Limits magazine, to visit Goldsmiths and talk to students on his radio course about KISS FM. I found that many of them had been fans of the station in its pirate days, and they were particularly keen to know whether KISS FM would be 'selling out' by playing more commercially orientated music and by employing mainstream DJs from other radio stations.

The same fears were being expressed in recent magazine articles about the station. MixMag noted that "KISS have stated publicly that it is not their policy to 'buy in' DJs from other stations (a fact that will preclude such luminaries as Jeff Young, Pete Tong and Tim Westwood from transferring in)." The article predicted (wrongly) that the station was making sufficiently fast progress to launch in late summer and noted that "the other strong hint was that a DJ who is currently on-air with one of the main competitors was amongst the front-runners to hold down daily strip shows." It added: "All that remains to be seen now is whither Robbie Vincent?"[649]

i-D magazine reported that "some have suggested that the legal station will be more commercial than the pirate's 'radical radio' broadcast policy," a suggestion rebuffed by a quote from KISS FM's Lindsay Wesker: "There's no need to water down the music. We won't be going mainstream and there's no way we'll be playing pop music." However, in The Face magazine, Gordon McNamee admitted: "We've got a difficult task ahead, treading a line between commercial demands and the clubs we all came from."[650]

Blues & Soul magazine expressed an even more forthright opinion in its gossip column: "Listening to [new North London incremental] WNK, test transmissions for [South London incremental] Choice, and the promises coming from KISS HQ, one thing in particular strikes me … Londoners are about to drown in a sea of bland, middle of the road pop/soul and pop/house. The problem stems from the very way that radio stations are set up in this country, with the profit-making ideal as the prime motivator. The end result is a board of directors, desperate to attract good advertisers, ensuring that daytime programming conforms to the lowest common denominator theory – that you play music that as many people as possible are prepared to listen to, or that as few people as possible find offensive ... If there is one thing we should have learnt from the Eighties pirate radio explosion, it is that there is a large minority of listeners in London who do not want to listen to lowest common denominator radio stations. There is a danger of getting so carried away in the euphoria of legal dance music stations, at last, that we turn a blind eye to the problems."[651]

When Gordon McNamee saw this opinion piece in Blues & Soul, he picked up an orange marker pen and drew a thick line around these very words. The question was: did McNamee view this as a scenario that, following KISS FM's legalisation, he wanted to avoid at all costs? Or, did he know that, despite his bold statements about maintaining the station's integrity, KISS FM was about to be transformed into a very different station from the 'Radical Radio' of its pirate heyday?

---

[644]Matthew Gwyther, "Dance Music Master", GQ, May 1990.
[645]WPFM, BBC Radio Four, 14 Feb 1990.
[646]"A Radio Sales Company Presentation To KISS FM", The Radio Sales Company, 13 Feb 1990.
[647]"A Proposal For KISS FM from New Media Sales & Hallett Arendt", New Media Sales, 13 Feb 1990.
[648]Cynthia Rose, "Pirate Enterprise", Sunday Correspondent, 29 April 1990.
[649]"KISS Line Up", MixMag Update, 22 Feb 1990.
[650]Dave Swindells, "Newsflash", i-D, Mar 1990.
Sheryl Garratt, "Radio", The Face, Mar 1990.
[651]The Mouth, "Streetnoise!", Blues & Soul, 13 Mar 1990.

February 1990.

On the morning of Monday 19 February 1990, KISS FM gained a new employee, Fran Andrews, whom McNamee had recruited to be the receptionist, telephone answerer and general helper in the office. Andrews was a bubbly, outgoing sixteen-year-old who had only recently left school and had no previous experience of working in an office. What she did possess was an obsessive enthusiasm for anything to do with KISS FM, having attended almost all of the station's club events, and she was already on first name terms with several of its DJs. McNamee had recruited Andrews because she was happy to work full-time in the KISS FM office for a wage of around £20 per week. He mercilessly exploited her enthusiasm for the station, with little regard for whether she was the most appropriate person to be on the 'frontline' of KISS FM, answering the business' telephone and personal enquiries.

McNamee needed Andrews to relieve the pressure of work from his personal assistant, Rosee Laurence, who had become over-burdened. Not only was Laurence still dealing with most of the general enquiries about KISS FM that flooded into the office each day, but she was kept even busier organising McNamee's increasingly hectic diary, as well as writing all his correspondence. On top of this, McNamee was now playing a far less central role in organising KISS FM's continuing weekly club nights at the Borderline and Dingwalls venues. Someone still had to book the appropriate DJs for these clubs each week, inform the press of the details and then, on the night, take the money on the door and pay the DJs. With McNamee doing less of this work, it fell to Laurence to execute these tasks. Then, the morning after each club night, Laurence had to count and bank the cash takings. Despite KISS FM being off the air, the station's club nights were still immensely popular with the public, and thousands of pounds in cash was passing through the KISS FM office each week.

I had still received no wage from KISS FM since the station had won its licence more than two months ago. The new company's finance director, Martin Strivens, phoned me from his office at Centurion Press to say that I would only be paid for my work in February once I had written him a letter confirming that I was self-employed. I explained to Strivens that I had been allocated a 'Schedule D' code number by Inland Revenue since 1980, proving that I had been granted self-employed status. I explained that, during recent years, I had worked as a freelance journalist for several magazines owned by some of the largest publishing companies, including IPC and United Newspapers, all of whom had accepted the 'Schedule D' code as sufficient proof of my self-employed status. Strivens was having none of it. He insisted that I write him a letter declaring my personal liability for taxation. In order to be paid for my work for KISS FM in February, I wrote the exact words that Strivens had requested: "I agree to undertake consultancy work for KISS FM for the period to 31st March 1990. During this period, I will receive payment on a Schedule D basis, under which I take responsibility for relevant Income Tax and National Insurance contributions. The arrangement to be reviewed at the end of the period."[652]

I felt that Strivens' attitude to this financial matter was particularly petty and demeaning, given that I was supposed to be a member of the station's senior management team. Strivens was treating me as if I were merely a temporary, casual worker and his proposed 'review' of my employment status seemed bizarre, given that I had already been named as KISS FM's head of programming in the winning licence application. Something did not feel at all right.

That morning, Gordon McNamee had attended a meeting of the company's shareholders, about which he made no comment on his return to the office in the afternoon. Instead, he distributed a set of documents to Laurence, Wesker and me, telling us that they were our employment contracts, and asked us to sign and return them to him as soon as possible. The only person in the office not to be given a contract was Heddi Greenwood, whom McNamee still planned to exclude from any involvement in the new KISS FM.

My copy of the contract was attached to a covering letter on KISS FM notepaper that had been signed by McNamee and read: "Your employment with the company will commence on 1st April 1990. Initially, you will be assisting me on programming matters. From 1st June 1990, you will be appointed head of programming. Initially, your wages will be £300 per week, paid monthly in arrears. From 1st June 1990 you will be paid a salary of £30,000 per annum, monthly in arrears, subject to review in October each year, commencing October 1991. In addition to this, you will receive a company car to the value of £10,000 as part of your remuneration."[653]

The £30,000 figure was the salary that had been stated in the licence application for my post, though it seemed unfair to pay me only half that amount until June 1990. I had still received no pay for my work in January, I had received none of the bonus promised to me for winning the licence, and McNamee had reneged on his promise to let me buy shares in the company. The only fillip of encouragement was the addition of a company car to the package, an extra that had not previously been mentioned in the station's budgets. I could only guess that this was intended as some kind of compensation for all the broken promises made by McNamee.

If the covering letter held mild surprise for me, then the attached contract of employment came as a complete shock. It consisted of twelve weighty paragraphs, each divided into several sub-sections, all crammed onto six pages using a word processor. The document mainly referred to my employment by "the company," rather than KISS FM, though there were occasional references to "Centurion," indicating that the contract must have been rather hastily adapted from a standard form used by Centurion Press. Many of the clauses seemed draconian and were rooted in a kind of old-fashioned worker/slave mentality, rather than the modern media company that KISS FM was supposed to be.[654]

Whilst my normal working day was stated to be 9.30 am to 6 pm Monday to Friday, with an hour for lunch "at a time convenient to the company," I was also required to work "for additional periods of time as are reasonable should the necessity arise," without any mention of additional pay or time off in lieu. I was also told that "incoming personal telephone calls are only allowed under exceptional circumstances" and that my four weeks holiday per year included "one week compulsory holiday over the Christmas period." If I were sick, "the company reserves the right to make 'check-up' visits to your home." If I left KISS FM's employment, I was prevented for the whole of the next year from being able to "deal or contract with any person" who still supplied their services to the station, prevented from employing anyone who had worked for KISS FM, and prevented from enticing customers away from the station.[655]

The most distressing paragraph in the contract was entitled "grievance procedure" and appeared to me to be completely unworkable. It stated that, if I had any grievance, I should "discuss this with the managing director" who was Gordon McNamee. Then, "if the grievance has not been settled within five working days, then it may be referred in writing to Gordon McNamee for settlement by him and his decision shall be final and binding." Furthermore, if I received a written warning of dismissal, I could "appeal in writing to the managing director," Gordon McNamee, who would arrange for the case to be investigated and notify me of his decision.[656]

The contract enforced a workplace situation within which I was to be totally beholden to McNamee. Not only was he my immediate boss, but it was to him I had to address any grievance, and also to him I had to address any subsequent appeal about his own decision about such a grievance. Similarly, if I were dismissed, it would be by McNamee since he was my boss, but the contract stated that it was he to whom I must address an appeal about his decision to dismiss me. This situation was plainly ridiculous since the contract appointed McNamee as judge, jury and ombudsman of my employment with KISS FM. I suggested to McNamee that perhaps there had been a drafting error in the contract and that the typist at Centurion might not have realised that he, McNamee, was my line manager as well as the managing director of KISS FM. I suggested that my ability to make an appeal should be addressed instead to either the company chairman or the board of directors. I also pointed out to McNamee the many occasions in the contract where the word "Centurion" had not been replaced by the typist.[657]

Later that week, McNamee gave me a revised version of the same contract. All references to "Centurion" had been purged, but the paragraph referring to the grievance procedure remained unchanged. I asked McNamee why the mistakes in this section had not been corrected as well, but he told me that there had been no errors. I repeated to him my worries about the practicality of such an arrangement. I suggested that someone else within the company should be included in the grievance procedure, so that it was not he alone involved at all stages of a dispute. He seemed hesitant, but promised he would take up the matter with the company's board at its next meeting and would let me know the outcome.

The terms of the contract worried me, particularly the grievance procedure, so I discussed my concerns with other staff in the office. Lindsay Wesker said that he too was concerned about the rather strident wording of the document and, like me, he felt that it did not sound like the sort of contract KISS FM should be issuing to its most loyal staff. However, he and Rosee Laurence signed their contracts anyway, just as McNamee had requested, and returned them. I was still apprehensive about the relationship implied in the contract between myself and McNamee, particularly when I turned back to the covering letter which stated that I would be "assisting" McNamee "on programming matters." Surely, as KISS FM's head of programming, I should be given more direct responsibilities of my own, rather than merely acting as McNamee's adviser? Why was my job title 'HEAD OF programming' if I was only meant to assist McNamee in this area of activity? The whole status of my employment with KISS FM was beginning to look decidedly dodgy.[658]

The following evening, McNamee, Laurence, Wesker, Champion and I assembled in the upstairs office after work for our second programming meeting. Once again, I had prepared a series of graphs and charts, this time to explain to the others the general patterns of listening to radio stations. I had drawn several graphs of Capital Radio's listenership, as a typical example of a pop music station in London. They showed that, on weekdays, Capital's largest audience was at breakfast time, after which the volume of listening declined steadily throughout the day, though there was a slight upturn during the evening rush hour, before the audience continued its decline into the night.

I explained that I was anticipating KISS FM's listening pattern to be somewhat different from that of Capital Radio. The evidence I had examined, particularly from radio stations in America that had youth-orientated, black music formats, showed a different pattern, with audiences increasing, rather than decreasing, as the day progressed. A dance music radio station would attract a younger audience than that for a top forty radio station, and young people tended to listen to music during the evenings, rather than watch television. At the other end of the day, dance music fans seemed not as bothered about listening to the radio first thing in the morning, as were listeners to top forty stations. As a result, KISS FM should expect that, unlike pop music stations, its breakfast show might not capture the biggest audience of the day, since this listening peak might well occur during evening hours.

Additionally, KISS FM needed to think carefully about the way that one programme would follow another in the schedule. In its pirate days, KISS FM had broadcast very dissimilar programmes, playing completely different styles of music, side by side within its weekend-only schedule. Now that the station was to be on the air twenty-four hours a day and seven days a week, it was important to try and keep the audience listening for as long a time as possible. A reggae music fan would obviously enjoy a reggae show on the radio, but might turn off if it were followed immediately by a jazz programme. In building its new programme schedule, KISS FM needed to consider exactly what sort of listeners tuned in to hear particular shows. Then, the schedule had to be arranged in such an order that each programme would 'inherit' the greater part of the previous show's audience. Admittedly, this was a difficult task to do, but it would prove essential if the newly legalised station were to successfully attain its target of one million listeners per week.

That evening's meeting started to draw up the basic building blocks of the new KISS FM programme schedule. McNamee was keen simply to replicate the draft programme schedule he had created for inclusion in the licence application. Whereas, I expressed the view that it was vital to determine what goals the station sought to achieve, and then to place the programmes accordingly. After much discussion, we agreed that the nightly magazine programme, 'The Word,' should be scheduled at 7 pm, since this was the hour by which the majority of the London workforce had returned home and would be considering what to do with the rest of their evening. The show would provide information about concerts, clubs, films and other events going on in the city, and it would act as an essential source of knowledge for listeners deciding how to spend their leisure time.

We also discussed the issue of how many different shows the weekday daytime broadcasting schedule should comprise. I was keen to have only four programmes between 6 am and 7 pm, but McNamee insisted that we stick to the plan that had been included in the licence application and broke the day into five shows. No decision was reached on this matter during the meeting so, afterwards, I asked McNamee why he was insisting on five shows rather than four. He told me that he had already promised the breakfast show to Graham Gold and Mark Webster, that he had already promised Tony Monson a daytime show, and that he still wanted to recruit David Rodigan from Capital Radio and Dave Pearce from GLR. These DJs would fill four daytime programmes, but McNamee recognised that he dare not offer all the peak slots to 'outsiders' without creating a huge rumpus amongst the loyal team of DJs from KISS FM's pirate days. So, McNamee explained, there would have to be an additional fifth daily show to accommodate at least one DJ from the existing team, and to demonstrate that he had not neglected them totally.

It was very late when the meeting finished and I felt exhausted. These sessions made me feel like a lecturer in media studies, teaching the other staff the basic facts about commercial radio, how it was organised and why certain things were done in a particular way. Having laid before them the various courses of action and the reasons for considering each option, I then had to cajole the group into making a positive decision that would further KISS FM's objective to attract one million listeners. These meetings were hard work for me because I knew more about commercial radio than the other participants. Yet, here we were together, planning one of the biggest radio station launches that London had ever seen. However, to cap that evening's meeting, McNamee had indicated firmly to me that he had already made up his mind about many important programming issues. Despite any reservations I might express, he had insisted that it was going to be done his way and no other. The whole process was exhausting.

The next day, McNamee spent the whole afternoon meeting KISS FM's shareholders and, once again, returned to the office saying very little about what had happened. I phoned Capital Radio DJ David Rodigan at home and arranged for McNamee and me to meet him for lunch the next day, to discuss the possibility of him joining KISS FM. The three of us met in the Camden Brasserie on Camden High Street, just a few blocks away from KISS FM's first office in Greenland Street. Although neither McNamee nor I had met Rodigan before, the meeting quickly became very relaxed once the DJ discovered that both of us were big fans of reggae music. Rodigan expressed a fear that his long running reggae show was becoming increasingly marginalised within Capital Radio's programme schedule by the station's latest management team. On the other hand, he was very enthusiastic about KISS FM having won the London FM radio licence.

McNamee explained that, although KISS FM was not offering its DJs salaries anywhere near as large as those that Capital Radio could afford, the station would have a much greater commitment to reggae music than Capital and it could guarantee Rodigan's reggae show a priority time slot within its schedule. Additionally, we were keen for Rodigan to present a daily programme on the station that would mix all styles of black music, rather than reggae alone. Although Capital had asked Rodigan to present occasional daytime shows of pop music, there were few opportunities at the station for Rodigan to break out of the specialist reggae genre which the management viewed as the appropriate use of his talents. Instead, Rodigan was now presenting more mainstream music shows for the British Forces radio station, BFBS, and he gave me two cassette tapes to listen to of recent programmes he had recorded at their London studios.

After we had bade farewell to Rodigan, McNamee and I walked along Camden High Street, both feeling somewhat elated. We had just met one of our long-time radio heroes and, more importantly, he had seemed very keen to work with us to ensure KISS FM's success. McNamee and I chatted about how we had both been addicted to Rodigan's reggae shows and we realised that we both still possessed cassette recordings of some of his shows that dated back to his earliest days as a DJ on BBC Radio London.

Back at the office that afternoon, the creative team from Saatchi & Saatchi paid a visit to find out more about KISS FM's plans. There was also a visit from another advertising agency called BBDO which had expressed their interest, somewhat grandly, in making a pitch for our account. A few days earlier, a motor cycle courier clad in leather and a crash helmet had rung the door bell at Blackstock Mews, and had strode into the office to deliver a large flat, but very thin, package to McNamee. The courier had then left the building without saying a word, much to the surprise of everyone there. McNamee ripped off the wrapping and, inside, was a large framed poster of a young couple locked in a passionate kiss. At the bottom of the poster, a slogan written in large letters announced: "WE'LL PUT YOUR NAME ON EVERYONE'S LIPS." Underneath that, in tiny lettering, it said: "The best advertising is the advertising people talk about. Do something different and you stand out. Do something different with relevance and you're famous. Together we'll give London a KISS they'll never forget. BBDO."[659]

It was a very grand gesture for an advertising agency to make, but it certainly had the desired effect. We had never heard of BBDO until then, but now we were interested to find out exactly what the agency felt it could do for KISS FM. McNamee phoned BBDO and its new business director, Nick Thurlow, admitted that the 'creative mailer' delivered to us had taken ten hours to make. McNamee made an appointment to meet the agency and agreed that its staff should pitch for our launch advertising account. KISS FM would make a final decision about which agency to use in about three weeks' time. Before then, both BBDO and Saatchi & Saatchi had wanted to meet us in our office to get a better feel for KISS FM and to understand our hopes for the radio station's future.[660]

The next day, Friday, McNamee was once again embroiled in a meeting with the company's board of directors all morning. His absence left me, Greenwood, Laurence and Wesker on our own in the office. The issue of the employment contract, which I had still not signed and returned, rested heavily on my mind, so I started to talk to the others about my fears. They admitted that they too had misgivings about the whole direction in which KISS FM seemed to be heading. McNamee was acting very differently these days. He was no longer his normal, chatty self when he was in the office, and he refused to share any information with us about all the meetings he had been attending in recent weeks.

Before KISS FM had won the licence, the Blackstock Mews office had been a very enjoyable place to work. Everyone had shared their worries and problems and we had all, McNamee included, helped each other to overcome them. But McNamee already seemed to be growing apart from the rest of us and, now that he had taken delivery of a very expensive company car and had taken to wearing flashy suits, he seemed to be spending as much time out of the office as he could justify. None of us really knew any longer what was being planned in those boardroom meetings for KISS FM's future, and Heddi Greenwood was suffering the indignity of McNamee not having even offered her a contract with the station, despite her key role in winning it a licence.

There was one particular incident that seemed to have turned McNamee away from us more than any other. The previous week, he and his wife had attended a dinner party at the home of the station's new financial director, Martin Strivens, in Wandsworth, one of the more affluent parts of London. Also in attendance were the chairman of Centurion Press, Martin

Evans, and his wife; Tim Schoonmaker, from EMAP, and his wife; and new KISS FM chairman Keith McDowall and his wife. During the weeks preceding this occasion, McNamee had been full of himself, talking to us continuously in the office about the preparations for the dinner party, as if it were the first such event he had ever attended. However, if we were already bored by McNamee's chatter before the event, afterwards we became positively sick of his endless stories. Although McNamee was continuing to tell us almost nothing about the business aspects of KISS FM, he regaled us for days with details of the gossip that had been traded at the party, the dinner table games that the guests had played, the marvellous food they had eaten and the fun they had all had that evening.

The event seemed to have been a turning point in McNamee's redefinition of himself, his position in KISS FM, and how he related to the rest of us in the office. Until recently, we had all worked together as a team and McNamee had been 'one of the lads,' sharing our setbacks and our triumphs. Now, he seemed to be redefining his own position, so that he was no longer one of us, but instead considered himself to be a member of the company board, one of its shareholders, and a managing director who kept his staff in the dark and in their rightful place. It was no longer fun to work in the office when McNamee was around. He barked orders at us, complained constantly and kept himself to himself in a corner of the large room. It felt as if the desks that had originally been randomly situated in the centre of the huge office space had become more carefully located of late. McNamee now had his own little corner of the room where he would reflect, sulk or talk to people in lowered tones on the phone. Now, we too had our own designated spaces, away from McNamee, and we were expected to stay in them unless called for by him.

That morning, while McNamee was out, the four of us remaining in the office talked about this change in attitude we had all observed. We decided that we could not continue to work productively in such an increasingly hostile environment. We agreed that we should talk to McNamee as a group about our feelings. We decided that the best option was to nab him when he first came into the office in the morning, before he had the chance to go to any 'meetings.' It was now Friday. Laurence checked McNamee's diary and found that he was busy all day on Monday, interviewing for new staff. So we settled upon Tuesday. We would not warn McNamee in advance. We would just ask him in the morning if we could have a staff meeting, and then we could express our feelings to him directly. The office's newest recruit, Fran Andrews, could answer the phones while we were talking.

It was only two months since KISS FM had won the licence, but the radio station's previous existence already seemed like a world away. So much had changed since that fateful day in December 1989 when the Independent Broadcasting Authority had made its licence announcement. So much within the company seemed to be completely confused that none of us, with the possible exception of McNamee, knew exactly where we were heading. It was high time we talked about such things openly with McNamee. Surely that would help, would it not?

---

[652] letter from Grant Goddard to Martin Strivens, KISS FM, 22 Feb 1990.
[653] letter from Gordon McNamee, KISS FM to Grant Goddard, 19 Feb 1990.
[654] employment contract for Grant Goddard, KISS FM, 19 Feb 1990.
[655] ibid.

[656] ibid.
[657] ibid.
[658] letter from Gordon McNamee, KISS FM to Grant Goddard, 19 Feb 1990.
[659] Emily Bell, "Hungry Agencies Hit Fever Pitch", The Observer, 1 Apr 1990.
[660] ibid.

February 1990.

Gordon McNamee spent the whole of that Monday interviewing candidates for the newly created 'head of marketing' post within KISS FM. The other members of the interview panel, ensconced in the EMAP office in Farringdon, were Martin Strivens of Centurion Press, Tim Schoonmaker of EMAP, and me. I was uncertain as to precisely why I had been invited, when I had been excluded from a similar set of interviews three weeks earlier for the 'head of sales' post. Perhaps it was because my publicity and marketing ideas for KISS FM's licence application had worked successfully and, in the office, I was now drafting most of the station's press releases.

Each of the half dozen interviews lasted the better part of an hour, and the whole day was relieved only by a brief break for sandwiches at lunchtime. By the end, our heads were spinning with the pro's and con's of employing each of the interviewees, so the four of us convened to a pizza restaurant across the road to discuss our opinions. Initially, we all seemed to be in agreement that the sole female candidate had offered the most satisfactory response to our questions, she seemed to have the most relevant experience, and she displayed the kind of get-up-and-go attitude that KISS FM would need to achieve a successful launch. Unfortunately, despite agreeing with the rest of us about each of these assertions, McNamee seemed particularly reluctant to appoint this woman for reasons that he found difficult to articulate. Instead, his choice was one of the male candidates who, although satisfactory, had proved less impressive during the interview.

This was not the first time that McNamee had seemed uncomfortable about having powerful women in his employment. At the Blackstock Mews office, it was obvious that his relationship with Heddi Greenwood had broken down almost entirely, seemingly because she had more experience and expertise in office management, marketing and business than did he. Greenwood was certainly not a woman whom McNamee could trample upon, and he appeared to have difficulty dealing with her because his male charm, persuasion and sexist attitudes had absolutely no effect. I had observed that McNamee experienced similar difficulties dealing with Lyn Champion, KISS FM's head of talks designate, because she too refused to he bullied into submission or to blindly agree to his ideas and plans. McNamee liked Champion when she agreed with him, but he became exasperated when she disagreed. Rosee Laurence was the only woman in the office with whom McNamee seemed to get on well, simply because she seemed to do absolutely anything he asked of her, without complaint or opposition. Besides, McNamee and Laurence were close personal friends, which made the relationship in the office between them far more informal than McNamee's attitudes to Greenwood or Champion.

The woman we had interviewed for the head of marketing post appeared to know exactly what she was doing, and she displayed all the signs of being a thorough, professional worker who craved success. Although such attributes should have proven the perfect combination to win her the job, McNamee persisted in finding niggling little things about her that he disliked. It became obvious to the rest of us that she was not McNamee's favoured candidate and so, not wishing to prolong the day's deliberations any further, we eventually agreed to appoint McNamee's preferred male candidate. In the end, it was McNamee to whom the new person would be directly answerable. If McNamee felt that the female candidate was not someone with whom he could work satisfactorily, that was his prerogative. The decision was made. We finished our pizzas and headed home our separate ways.

The next morning, Tuesday, McNamee arrived at work to be met by the rest of us – Greenwood, Wesker, Laurence and me – asking if we could have a meeting together, there and then, to discuss how things were going with the radio station. Initially, McNamee seemed slightly shocked by the suggestion, but agreed that we could convene in the Free! office, sat around his glass-topped meeting table. As planned, new recruit Fran Andrews was left alone upstairs to answer the phones and to take messages whilst we were in deepest discussion.

The five of us assembled downstairs, with McNamee at the head of the table. The meeting started with a horribly stony silence as everyone looked at each other, expecting someone else to start discussion of the issues we wanted to raise. McNamee, meanwhile, simply looked perplexed. The obligation seemed to fall to me to get the meeting going, so I explained hesitantly that the four of us had decided we should meet together with McNamee to discuss the trepidation we shared about the way KISS FM had been going since the licence win in December. I explained that all of us had enjoyed working in the office until now, and that we had always put our utmost effort into tackling the work at hand with enthusiasm and diligence. The Blackstock Mews office had always been a great place to work, and all of us had contributed equally to the work required to win KISS FM a licence, often putting in horrendously long hours without complaint.

However, more recently, I suggested to McNamee, the feeling in the office had somehow changed. The strong sense of camaraderie was rapidly disappearing, and little was now left of the friendly give-and-take that we had taken for granted in the old days. All of us were being constantly bombarded with requests for information about KISS FM's plans, by the station's DJs, by staff like Lyn Champion who did not yet work full-time in the office, and by the companies we were dealing with on a day-to-day basis. How could we answer these questions when none of us were being informed of the board's plans for the station, what had been achieved to date, what remained to be done, what the time scale was, or what the hurdles were that still had to be overcome?

I continued to explain that, these days, McNamee spent more time out of the office than in it. I suggested that he was communicating with us far less than ever before. There was no explanation or feedback offered to us from all the meetings we knew he attended almost every day of the week. We were never briefed about the decisions of the company's board of directors, who now seemed to be running the station, what they expected of us, or what they thought the station was going to become when it was re-launched. With the exception of the celebration party held before Christmas, we never had opportunities to meet the directors because they never came to the Blackstock Mews office. We had been excluded from all the meetings that they and McNamee convened.

McNamee just sat there at the table, seemingly unmoved by my words. If he was feeling any emotion, he certainly did not show it. I continued to explain that he risked losing our enthusiasm and commitment to KISS FM because he was no longer sharing with us, as he had always done before, the trials and tribulations of getting the station re-established and back on-air. We could not work effectively for KISS FM if we were being totally cut off from his world. If he wanted to get the best out of us, then he needed to talk to us, communicate with us, and inform us what he had been doing when he spent the greater part of each day 'out.' I had almost run out of things to say, so I looked around the table at the others for help. Firstly Heddi Greenwood, and then Lindsay Wesker, took up the same theme. Greenwood was more forthright than me, telling McNamee bluntly that the radio station would not work properly if, at this early stage, we were already facing difficulties managing ourselves. Wesker was less bold, assuring McNamee that we were not criticising him, or his actions, but that we merely wanted to assist him more directly in making KISS FM a success.

But it was Rosee Laurence who, having kept quiet until now, suddenly burst into life and made the most vitriolic speech of all of us. Something inside Laurence snapped that morning and, as a result, her feelings and emotions gushed from her end of the table, past the rest of us sat on either side, and straight towards McNamee sat at the table's other end. She accused McNamee of having changed beyond all recognition during the last few weeks. She accused him of having changed his mode of dress, of having taken delivery of his ostentatious company car, of smoking cigars, and of generally acting as if he was someone completely different from the McNamee she had known for several years. She accused him of being secretive, of being rude to everyone, including herself, and of suddenly wanting to disregard his old friends, so that he could replace them with a new group of high-flying executives whose company he now seemed to crave, both in and out of work.

Laurence's words became increasingly emotional and she burst into tears as she sobbed across the table: "You've changed, Gordon. You're just not the same person any more that you used to be. You don't care about me and you don't care about us any more, Gordon. You seem to be embarrassed by who your friends were and you don't want us around you any more. You're not the Gordon we used to know. You've changed, Gordon. You've completely changed, and it's not a change for the good."

McNamee still sat unmoved at the end of the table. I recognised the same mood building in him that I had encountered the previous summer when I had told him of my decision to relinquish the editorship of Free! magazine to work on the second KISS FM licence application. Then, he had just stared at me blankly, making it difficult to tell whether it was anger, hatred or loathing that was building up inside him. Whatever it was, just like now, he did not let it out. He just sat there, betraying no emotion, as if he were simply a spectator of somebody else's life. Now, once Laurence's words had trailed away and she started to sob uncontrollably, I could see McNamee behaving in exactly the same way. I tried to bring the meeting back to some kind of order. I did not want it to turn into a slanging match between McNamee and Laurence, whose close personal relationship put their problem on a somewhat different plane than the grievances of Greenwood, Wesker and me.

I talked about how vital it was to ensure that proper communication existed within any organisation; how each worker had to know and understand what the others in the company were doing in order to function properly; how each of us could not afford to work only within our own area of responsibility and ignore everything else going on. These notions, I felt, applied as much to McNamee as to the rest of us, and all of us should take deliberate, purposeful steps to ensure that communication between us worked more productively. Otherwise, we would end up being totally unproductive and would fail to get KISS FM on-air within the agreed time scale. We needed to do something about these problems now, BEFORE it was too late, rather than wait until some unforeseen disaster occurred within the organisation. That was why we had asked for a meeting that day, whilst we believed that the situation was still salvageable.

Laurence was still sobbing into a tissue when McNamee finally stopped staring at us blankly and started to speak. He was surprisingly unemotional as he talked slowly and deliberately, though he made no attempt to directly address our criticisms. Instead, he suggested that these were difficult times for everyone involved in KISS FM, including himself, as we were all heading very quickly into unknown territory that none of us had experienced before. McNamee emphasised that he too was facing problems, that he had never managed a legal radio station before, that he had not had to cope with a board of directors before, and that he had never had shareholders with which to contend. He admitted that this was all a very new experience for him and asked that we understand that he too was under immense pressure, and that we should recognise that things might not always run smoothly. It was bound to be a difficult time for all of us, he said, but it would not always be like this.

McNamee said that he would look at ways to improve the means of communication within the company, but he made no promises to involve any of us more directly in his meetings or to inform us of their business or decisions. Laurence had almost stopped sobbing by now and was re-composing herself at the opposite end of the table to McNamee. The emotion had been diffused from the situation and our conversation around the table started to become more constructive. However, McNamee did not answer our main accusation that he was deliberately deserting us now that he had acquired a new set of colleagues. He offered no response to the accusation that he had changed in himself. Then, suddenly, after more than an hour's discussion, he effectively ended the meeting by announcing that he would appoint me as the channel of communication between himself and everyone else in the office. He explained that, because I was already working as his assistant in getting the station on the air, I would in future also be responsible for communicating all the news and developments about what was going in KISS FM to everyone else in the office.

The meeting ended abruptly, we went back to our desks upstairs, and McNamee promptly left the building. Laurence was still too upset to talk about the meeting properly, though the rest of us agreed that we had handled the meeting the best we could. McNamee had displayed little understanding of the true nature of our grievances. I felt that his sudden appointment of me to some new kind of internal communications role was merely McNamee desperately grasping at straws. In reality, I knew no more about what was going on within the company than the others in the office. There were only a handful of meetings, such as the interviews for the head of marketing post, to which I had been invited and, like the others, I too was being kept at arm's length from the shareholders and the board of directors. All McNamee had done that morning was transfer the burden of responsibility for action off of his shoulders and onto mine, without giving me the necessary information or access to meetings that I needed to carry out the role. I believed that this idea would be unworkable, and I anticipated that nothing at all would change.

McNamee had avoided answering our direct criticisms because he must have known that he was unable to rebuff the specific accusation that he had changed his own character. In fact, he now seemed largely unaffected by our opinions of him. It was good that we had called the meeting, but I was entirely sceptical that we would witness any change in his attitude towards us. My worst fear was that the current state of affairs was to become the way that KISS FM was going to be run. That would be a huge disappointment after so many years of toil and sweat during the station's pirate years, during which everyone involved had been fuelled by common hopes and dreams. Already, we were facing divisions amongst ourselves, and McNamee in particular seemed to have already written his own personal agenda for the future, one that no longer seemed to involve the rest of us in his plans.

By lunchtime, McNamee had sulked back into the office, still saying very little to us. It was not long before he and Laurence disappeared out of the office for the rest of the afternoon. It was obvious that McNamee felt his main priority now was to rekindle the close personal relationship he shared with his personal assistant, whilst the rest of us were a long way down his list of problems, if indeed we were there at all. The net outcome of the morning's meeting might be, in the long run, that Laurence would be able in some way to re-negotiate her position with McNamee, whilst the rest of us could go begging. Was the whole affair really to have been entirely in vain?

By five o'clock, McNamee and Laurence returned to the office, saying nothing, as we made preparations for Mentorn to start filming in the Free! office for the TV documentary it was making about KISS FM. Mentorn wanted to record a meeting at which the station's staff was planning its re-launch, so a 'committee meeting' was staged at Blackstock Mews, attended by McNamee, Schoonmaker, Strivens, McDowall, Laurence, Wesker and me. We had to pretend to discuss amongst ourselves a variety of topics that were pertinent to KISS FM's future, whilst the camera crew strolled around the table, filming us. I felt disgusted by the whole sad affair, particularly since Laurence, Wesker and I had sat around the very same table, only hours earlier, for our emotional meeting with McNamee.

Here we were, pretending for the cameras that the entire KISS FM staff was actively involved in planning the station's future when, only this morning, our main grievance with McNamee had been our deliberate exclusion from real meetings such as this. McNamee played up to the camera, discarding the sulky persona he had exhibited since our morning meeting, while the rest of us just sat there meekly, playing the parts that he and Mentorn had assigned to us. It was a farce of the grandest proportions, but we had all been told beforehand how important it was for Mentorn to capture some footage of the types of discussion and meeting that were supposed to be typical of the former pirate radio station's management style.

Following this faked meeting, Mentorn moved its film equipment to one of the large empty office units at the far end of Blackstock Mews, which McNamee had hired for the evening. A memo had been circulated to all the KISS FM DJs, asking them to attend a meeting that evening for which McNamee had explained: "Primarily the meeting is to allow Mentorn Films ([producers of] '01 For London') to film, with a view to making a three-minute trailer to present to Thames TV. Eventually, they plan to document the KISS FM story for a TV programme."[661]

Offered an unmissable opportunity to appear on television, almost all of the KISS FM DJs turned up for the meeting, despite there being very little news to tell them. McNamee gave a long, rambling speech, summarising the latest developments within the station for the aid of the cameras, more than the participants. It was followed by questions from the floor, though most of these proved unanswerable. No, premises had not yet been found. No, there was still no firm on-air date for re-launching the station. No, the programme schedule had not yet been decided. No, employment contracts were not yet ready to be issued to the DJs. No, the station had not decided who would be presenting its high-profile daytime shows. No, the station had not yet appointed an advertising agency. And no, there was no new station merchandise. Once the filming ended, a photographer took individual shots of the station's DJs and staff to use in future KISS FM publicity campaigns.

It ended an extremely crazy and emotionally charged day at the Blackstock Mews office. It seemed to me that the KISS FM bandwagon had already starting to develop a momentum all of its own. Despite any reservations that the rest of us working there might express, it was McNamee alone who knew the path down which the radio station was travelling now. And it was us, the office staff who had helped him win the licence in the first place, who now seemed like the last people on Earth to whom McNamee was going to disclose the details of his KISS FM master plan.

---

[661] memo from Gordon McNamee to "all KISS team", 15 Feb 1990.

February 1990.

Gordon McNamee may have seemed rather sulky in the Blackstock Mews office in the aftermath of the emotional staff meeting but, the following day, he made obvious attempts to be friendly towards his staff. Although he displayed a more positive attitude towards us than we had witnessed recently, nevertheless it became evident that the underlying attitude had not changed. He remained a very different Gordon McNamee to the one we had known only a few months earlier, and it began to look as if we would just have to live with his new persona.

That evening, the third programming meeting was convened in the office for a discussion between McNamee, Lyn Champion, Lindsay Wesker, Rosee Laurence and me of the detail of the station's programme schedule. After some debate, we agreed that, in addition to the broadcast of 'The Word' magazine show each evening at 7 pm, a further edition would be scheduled during weekday lunchtimes. We discussed the idea of broadcasting chart-based shows, where the DJ runs down a top ten list of records, and decided that each weekday evening at 7.30 pm, there would be a chart for a particular style of dance music, such as reggae, rap, house or soul. Additionally, each weekend, there would be an overall KISS FM chart that reflected retail sales of all dance music records in London during the previous seven days.

There was some disagreement about the exact time during the weekend that the main chart show should be broadcast. McNamee and Wesker were keen to schedule it at 7 pm on Sunday, when it would compete head-to-head with the two existing weekly chart shows broadcast across the whole country – the BBC chart on Radio One, and the Network Chart carried by commercial radio. I expressed the view that such a move was suicidal, since these two charts already captured most radio listening at that time. It would prove impossible for KISS FM to entice listeners away from two of the most popular radio programmes for music fans. I had examined the available radio audience data for London and had concluded that Saturday afternoon was the one time during the weekend when existing radio stations were failing to capture a sizeable audience. Why not schedule our chart show then, promote it heavily and hope to attract listeners who might not otherwise be bothered to listen to the radio at all at that time?

This argument over the best time during the weekend to schedule the chart show raged for a while, until we agreed to hold over the final decision to the next programming meeting. Other matters we discussed included the idea of producing a documentary each week. Lyn Champion and I explained to McNamee and Wesker how time consuming it could be to produce speech-based programming for radio, but neither of them had experience of such work. It proved extremely difficult to convince them that it could take ten or twenty times as long to produce a one-hour documentary as it would to make a one-hour music programme. Eventually, Lyn and I were forced to accept the scheduling of a documentary programme on Sunday night, another time in the week when radio listening was usually low.

McNamee and Wesker proposed several other ideas for programmes that they wanted to include in the schedule. Both of them suggested the production of a short, daily soap opera that would run and run, just like a television soap. They thought it would be easy to produce, with McNamee and Wesker playing the main characters, and supporting roles provided by other station staff. Fortunately, Champion and I were able, after much discussion, to convince them that radio drama was not only extremely time consuming to produce, but that it was far more difficult to do well than might be apparent to the average radio listener. We argued that the whole of KISS FM would be far too busy in its early days to make a commitment to drama in the programme schedule. Thankfully, the two budding thespians eventually agreed to hold over their idea until KISS FM had been firmly established on the airwaves.

The meeting continued to drag on late into the evening, with McNamee and Wesker coming up with increasingly elaborate and irrelevant ideas for crazy things that KISS FM could do on-air. Eventually, we closed the discussions and I went away pleased with the decisions that had been made, but frustrated by McNamee's lack of understanding as to how much work was involved in programming a seven-day, twenty-four hour radio station. In the pirate days of KISS FM, McNamee had simply told the DJs to turn up at the studio at a particular time, bring their own records and play whatever music they wanted. A proper commercial radio station could not be organised in such a haphazard way. The new KISS FM needed more management and more planning. McNamee had to understand that, if the station's audience failed to reach the promised target of one million, the entire company would be riding for a fall. Now that the scale of the station had been increased dramatically, the stakes were higher than ever. KISS FM needed to plan strategically to win.

The next afternoon, I met Lyn Champion, on my own, at the office to discuss the progress we were both making. Our experiences in the radio industry were complementary. Champion had only worked in the BBC, whilst I had only worked in commercial radio. The two of us had more radio experience than the others involved in KISS FM. We agreed that it was proving extremely difficult to make the others in our team, particularly McNamee and Wesker, understand how demanding it was to run a full-time radio station, because they had never worked in one. At times, it seemed like an uphill struggle just to deal with the station's internal wrangles, though both of us were fully committed to the idea that KISS FM, despite its inexperienced staff, could be made to work. It was an immense challenge, but a challenge that was definitely worth winning.

The other topic of conversation in the office that day was the start of test transmissions by the new incremental station for South London, Choice FM, in preparation for its launch at the end of March 1990. We tuned the radio expectantly to Choice and, much to our delight, we found that the station's music policy, as evidenced by the pre-recorded tapes of back-to-back music it was broadcasting, was going to be far more conservative than that of KISS FM. There were lots of Motown soul oldies from the 1960s, but very few records that were on the 'cutting edge' of current dance music trends in London. If its test transmissions were anything to go by, Choice FM sounded as if it was going to play very safe in its music policy and, as such, would prove no threat to KISS FM's more radical programming that would be aimed squarely at young Londoners.

The other new station launch that was of immense interest to KISS FM was that of Jazz FM, which started full programmes for the first time that Sunday. It was the first of the three, new London-wide music stations on the air, to be followed later by Melody Radio and KISS FM itself. Jazz FM had spent £1m on advertising to promote its arrival, including full-page announcements in several national newspapers, a decision that seemed rather grand given that the station was only audible in London. Because it was the first completely new London-wide station to be launched since 1973, Jazz FM attracted a huge amount of press coverage and became a big topic of conversation across the capital. Of particular interest to KISS FM was a public statement by the station's director, Ron Onions, which said that Jazz FM would play a high percentage of soul and blues music to broaden the station's appeal to non-jazz fans, particularly in its daytime output.[662]

However, Jazz FM's official launch on Sunday morning proved to be far from auspicious. A live interview in the initial programme with jazz veteran Ella Fitzgerald was a disaster, both technically and artistically. The DJs sounded completely unexcited by their station's birth, even on its very first day. And the station's music policy proved to be a constant jumble of different styles, veering from a pre-war blues record one minute, to a modern George Benson song the next, to some obscure 1960s jazz album track the next. Music Week magazine commented: "Jazz FM's programmes are disorientated, satisfying neither dedicated jazz fans nor general audiences."[663]

That afternoon, I called in at a KISS FM record fair that Lindsay Wesker had organised in North London. McNamee and I agreed that Jazz FM seemed to pose no threat whatsoever to KISS FM and, although there were a handful of soul records in the station's output, there was certainly not sufficient contemporary black music content to attract the loyal audience of young listeners which KISS FM hoped to achieve. Both of us heaved a huge sigh of relief. I celebrated by buying a second-hand copy of Linda Lewis' first album, 'Lark,' a record I had owned in the 1970s but had since lost. McNamee celebrated by buying several hundred pounds worth of old soul albums. Somebody joked to him that he must have just spent the whole of KISS FM's profits from its first year on-air, even before the station had launched. We all laughed. We all believed that KISS FM was bound to be successful and, as the business plan had forecast, would make a profit.

Unfortunately, the signs of profitability were slim from some of the other incremental stations that were already on-air. Sunset Radio, the black community station in Manchester that had been the first of the new stations to launch in October 1989, had made three staff redundant by January in an effort to cut costs. Its finance director, David Oakes, denied that the station was facing a major crisis. News had spread within the radio industry that the station founder, Mike Shaft, who had campaigned over many years for Manchester to be given its own black station, had just been sacked. Sunset issued a statement admitting that "Shaft ceased to be managing director with immediate effect" and the station's chairman, Peter Chui, added that "Sunset has had a number of early difficulties but these are behind us."[664]

Closer to home, North London black station WNK's head of programmes, Mark Damon, had left the station after only three months on-air. WNK managing director, Joe Douglas, temporarily took over responsibility for programming, before appointing former BBC Radio One DJ Dixie Peach to the post. These abrupt changes to key management positions did not bode well for the new stations. It looked as if their failure to achieve immediate success was leaving the founders vulnerable to replacement, and was making their businesses susceptible to takeover. KISS FM would be the last of the new incremental stations to arrive on-air, and it already seemed as if we had a lot to learn from the terrible experiences suffered by some of the earlier licensees.[665]

The start of the following week demonstrated how little things had improved in the disintegrating KISS FM office environment. Gordon McNamee spent the whole of Monday morning in a meeting elsewhere with the station's shareholders, but told us absolutely nothing about it when he returned to the office. We were obviously destined to remain in the dark as much as ever. On Tuesday, McNamee went out for lunch with the station's newly appointed head of sales. Afterwards, McNamee brought him back to Blackstock Mews and introduced him to everyone in the office for the first time. Thirty-two year old Gary Miele was a tall, overweight Canadian with a thick black moustache. He had emigrated to Britain in 1985 and had worked for the small Gloucester commercial radio station Severn Sound as sales director, before taking the same position at the larger Liverpool station, Radio City, in 1989.[666]

My first impression of Miele was that he was a typical salesman, with a loud voice and arrogant manner, who knew nothing about KISS FM, nothing about the dance music industry, and had never worked in London. However, McNamee seemed to have a particular liking for Miele and seemed proud to show him off to us in the office, as if he was just the sort of person the station needed. I was not so sure. The press advertisement for the job had specified that the applicant should fit in well with the rest of the KISS FM team, but Miele did not seem overly concerned about such matters and, even at that first meeting, he seemed to consider himself to be far more important than the rest of us in the office.

While McNamee was having lunch with KISS FM's latest recruit, I had had a meeting with a radio syndication company called Rock Over London at its office above the Globe Theatre in Shaftesbury Avenue. The managing director, Steven Saltzman, had told me on the phone that he had an interesting proposition to put to KISS FM. Now, I listened patiently while he described a plan he had hatched to link up several stations around the world that all shared the 'KISS' name. He suggested that these stations could swap programmes with each other and arrange visits to each other's cities. Once Saltzman had finished his pitch, I had to point out to him that the most important aspect of the London KISS station's ethos was its dance music policy, not its name. I was certainly interested in making links with other radio stations, particularly in America, who shared a similar music policy. However, I did not think that KISS FM's listeners would be interested in foreign stations that just happened to share the same name.

Afterwards, I reflected that Saltzman had proven to be another of the many people in the British radio industry who seemed to miss the whole point of KISS FM's impending arrival on London's airwaves. The station was important because it would be very different from all the pop music radio that the government had licensed until now, not because of its name. The most significant thing about KISS FM was that it would be a dance music radio station specifically aimed at young people. Why should London's KISS FM have anything in common with a station of the same name playing country music in America?

Later that week, McNamee brought KISS FM's other new recruit to the office to meet the staff. Twenty-nine year old Malcolm Cox, who was to be the station's head of marketing, seemed more likely to fit into the KISS FM team than Miele. Cox was quiet, thoughtful and had a considered manner that made him appear slightly vulnerable. He had an HND certificate in business studies and, since 1981, had worked in the marketing departments of Capital Radio, London Weekend Television, Tyne Tees Television and Anglia Television. Cox had always worked in London and already knew something about KISS FM's former pirate existence, even if he had not been a listener to the original station.[667]

Both Cox and Miele would start work in the Blackstock Mews office at the beginning of April. I drafted a four-page press release to announce their appointments, attached short biographies for each of them and included an updated list of the 'KISS FM Management Team.' The nine-person team now comprised: Keith McDowall as chairman, Gordon McNamee as managing director, Martin Strivens as financial director, Gary Miele as head of sales, Malcolm Cox as head of marketing, Grant Goddard as head of programmes, Lyn Champion as head of talks, Lindsay Wesker as head of music, and Rosee Laurence as "press & PR." The order in which these staff were listed had been specified by McNamee in order to demonstrate that the new recruits, Miele and Cox, were considered more senior than the rest of us in the office.

The details of Miele and Cox's remuneration were not made known to us, but McNamee intimated that substantial salaries and benefits had had to be offered to staff of their calibre to persuade them to join a new, untested venture such as KISS FM. The licence application had envisaged employing one sales & marketing director at a salary of £40,000 per annum. Now that this function had been split into two separate senior management posts, it was obvious that the budget for the re-launched station had required substantial amendment.

Some questions remained unanswered. Where was the extra money coming from to pay for these posts, seemingly at higher salaries than had been envisaged? I had been told that there had been no money to pay me at all during January, and now I was being paid only half my salary until the summer. So how come, within weeks, there was suddenly enough money to pay these two new staff their full generous salaries, and from the outset?

---

[662]"More Soul For Jazz FM", Broadcast, 16 Feb 1990.
[663]Bob Tyler, "Jazz FM Makes Its Debut After 10 Years' Work", Music Week, 17 Mar 1990.
[664]"Staff Axe", Broadcast, 9 Feb 1990.
"Staff Axed At Sunset", Radio & Music, 31 Jan 1990.
Edwin Riddell, "Shaft Leaves Manchester Incremental", Broadcast, 16 Mar 1990.
[665]"WNK Departure", Broadcast, 9 Mar 1990.
"Peach Picked", Broadcast, 16 Mar 1990.
[666][untitled], press release, KISS FM, 12 Mar 1990.
[667]ibid.

March 1990.

For each of the new incremental radio stations it was licensing, the Independent Broadcasting Authority [IBA] required a one-page document called the 'Promise of Performance' that specified precisely what sort of programmes the station was obliged to broadcast. This Promise of Performance was included in the licence contract agreed between the IBA and the radio station. The ethos of the incremental radio scheme was that each new station must widen the choice of radio programmes available to listeners within its geographical area. That is why every new station had to promise to broadcast programming that was markedly different from anything already offered by existing commercial stations in its vicinity.

During the initial period of the incremental radio scheme, the IBA had been relatively relaxed about the wording of the Promise of Performance. The regulator had seemed content to rely upon a station's good intentions rather than upon explicit wording to make it stick to a particular music format. For the first of the three new London-wide stations, Jazz FM, the IBA had agreed a Promise of Performance that included a remarkably generous definition of the station's jazz music format. The description of 'jazz' included "big band music, vocal and instrumental standards, Latin American music, traditional jazz, Afro-American music, urban contemporary dance, Afro-Caribbean music, soul, blues and bebop, ragtime, rhythm and blues, swing, reggae, gospel music, freeform jazz, future developments of these, and all other forms of music which can be said to have been influenced by jazz or to have been instrumental in its evolution."[668]

When the management team of Jazz FM had opened the letter from the IBA offering this wording, they must have jumped for joy. This definition of jazz somehow managed to include almost every style of popular music known to man. If its management had wished, Jazz FM could legitimately have played most of the pop songs from the current top forty singles chart. The station could have claimed, with some justification, that all these records had been influenced, somewhere along the line, by jazz music.

However, by the time the IBA came to license KISS FM, one of the last of its incremental radio stations, it had evidently learnt the lesson that its Promises of Performance needed to be drawn more tightly. Already, predictions had been published in the media trade press that KISS FM intended to compete head-on with London's pop music station, Capital Radio, rather than concentrate on soul and dance music. This obliged the IBA to be more careful with its wording. Paul Brown, the IBA head of programming, sent KISS FM a draft Promise of Performance that seemed particularly restrictive, allowing the station to play only a very small number of records each hour that were in that week's current top forty chart.

Gordon McNamee and I arranged to meet Brown on 13 March 1990 at the IBA office, where we outlined our objections to some of the wording in his draft Promise of Performance. I expressed the fear that, although I acknowledged that KISS FM should not play the same hit records as Capital Radio, I did not want KISS FM to be prevented from playing the large number of dance music records that dominated the current singles chart. It would be particularly bizarre if KISS FM were initially to offer heavy airplay to a new dance record that other stations, such as Capital, did not play but, once that record had become a big hit, KISS FM would be prevented from playing it because it had entered the chart.

Instead, I suggested that the issue of KISS FM's music policy should be approached from the opposite angle. Rather than prohibit the station from playing too many records from the hit chart, why not require KISS FM to play a certain amount of newly released records that were not in the chart? The station had always been committed to popularising new artists and new records. The inclusion of such a statement within KISS FM's Promise of Performance would merely make explicit the station's long-standing music policy. That way, KISS FM would be free to fill the rest of its output with chart records, but never to the extent that they dominated the whole station. During an hour of discussion, Paul Brown was sympathetic to my request and seemed to understand why I was desperate to find a form of wording that would prove less restrictive. By the time McNamee and I had left the meeting, we were pleased that Brown could see our point of view and hopeful that he would allow us the greater flexibility we believed was imperative to KISS FM's success.

At the end of the week, the revised document Brown sent to the Blackstock Mews office proved to be as good as I had hoped for. The new draft Promise of Performance defined KISS FM's dance music format as "soul, R&B, funk, house, garage, hip-hop, rap, urban contemporary dance, Afro-American, Latin, salsa, samba, fusion, future developments of all these and other forms of dance music which may be popular with a young audience from time to time, and including, to a lesser extent, reggae, ska, gospel, blues, soca, Afro-Caribbean and world music." At least fifty percent of the music played on KISS FM at peak times, defined as the hours between 6 am and 7 pm on weekdays, would have to be new material, defined as current releases not in the top forty chart. Up to forty percent of the remaining music at peak times could comprise records currently in the top forty.[669]

I was elated by this revised Promise of Performance because it freed my hand to programme the music on KISS FM pretty much as the station wanted, without the need to constantly refer back to the exact wording to ensure that I was not exceeding the IBA's limitations. A breach of a station's Promise of Performance could have resulted in the imposition of IBA sanctions that commenced with fines and, ultimately, could have led to the withdrawal of a station's licence. Brown had proven to be particularly adept at understanding my concerns about executing my programming responsibilities whilst, at the same time, allowing the IBA to impose a Promise of Performance that appeared to be tightly drawn. The successful conclusion of this part of the station's contract was a huge relief to me.

The evening after our meeting with Brown, McNamee and I went for a meal at a restaurant in Islington, accompanied by Rosee Laurence and the station's new head of marketing, Malcolm Cox. It was the first opportunity I had had to talk with Cox since his interview for the post two weeks earlier. For Laurence, it was the first occasion she had to talk to Cox (except for the brief visit he had made to the KISS FM Office). The evening proved very enjoyable, and it was on occasions like these that I felt privileged to be party to the creation of the new KISS FM. Cox was a new member of the team I would be working with quite closely, so McNamee was keen that I get to know him better. On the contrary, in McNamee's view, the station's directors and shareholders were off limits to me, and their regular meetings were outside the scope of the information that McNamee felt I needed to know. This remained the case, despite my new responsibility to inform the others in the office. In truth, I was still being kept just as much in the dark as they were.

The next morning at ten o'clock, the expanded KISS FM team, including new recruits Miele and Cox, met in Regent's Park at the office of BBDO, one of the two advertising agencies pitching for the station's launch account. For two hours, the BBDO creative staff suggested ideas that could be used to attract the public's attention to the station's launch, using advertisements on television, in the press, in cinemas and on billboards. Their work showed a clear understanding of KISS FM and the young audience it was hoping to attract. The poster designs included stark black and white photographs of couples kissing, dancers and surreal images. A rough version of a TV advertisement that they had created in only a few days conveyed lots of images of London and trendy young people that seemed to fit perfectly with KISS FM.

That afternoon, a similar presentation by the other agency pitching for the KISS FM account, Saatchi & Saatchi, could not have proved more different. Its designs consisted of bold slogans in a very large typeface, without any accompanying photographs or graphic images. The slogans tried to emphasise how different and how exciting KISS FM was, but this effect was achieved only by making comparisons between the newcomer and existing stations such as Capital Radio and Radio One. The slogans were quite damning of the competitors and succeeded perfectly in conveying the anti-establishment feel of KISS FM. They gave the assembled KISS FM team plenty of opportunities to break into a wry smile, but they communicated only the fact that KISS FM would be different from existing radio stations, without explaining how it would be different.

After the presentation, the KISS FM team met with a photographer whom McNamee had booked to take photos of Miele and Cox to accompany the press release announcing their appointments. The photos were taken in a back street just around the corner from the Saatchi & Saatchi headquarters, combining various members of the KISS FM management team standing against a blank brick wall of an office building. When the resulting prints were delivered to the office the next day, we realised how dreadful they looked but, because these were the only available photos of the new staff, we had to send them out anyway. Media Week used one of the photos, even though it made Miele and Cox look like East End criminals.[670]

Returning to the Blackstock Mews office, McNamee and I convened a quick meeting downstairs on our own to discuss the presentations of the two advertising agencies. I voiced the opinion that, although Saatchi & Saatchi's ideas fitted perfectly with the notion of 'Radical Radio,' they might make KISS FM seem as if it could do little more than knock the competition. Both Radio One and Capital Radio were established in the London marketplace over many, many years and had built loyal audiences. We would never be able to convince these stations' listeners to try KISS FM if we simply criticised their favourite station. I felt strongly that a knocking campaign was not appropriate when KISS FM had so much to offer that was genuinely positive. On the other hand, BBDO's campaign captured the mood of the station perfectly and emphasised the positive aspects of tuning to KISS FM. I recommended to McNamee that KISS FM go with BBDO, despite the fact that it was me who had originally suggested that Saatchi & Saatchi should pitch for our account. McNamee agreed with my sentiments and, later that day, the recommendation to contract BBDO was agreed by the rest of the board.

The next day, I met Capital Radio DJ Tim Westwood to discuss the possibility of him re-joining KISS FM as a daytime presenter. Although McNamee and I held differing opinions as to the suitability of DJs such as Graham Gold and Mark Webster for daytime shows on the station, we both agreed that Westwood was a very popular and very credible presenter for KISS FM to sign. He was easily the most knowledgeable and influential rap music DJ in London, and the switch he had made the previous year from pirate KISS FM to high-profile Capital Radio had increased both his reputation and his popularity amongst young dance music fans.

Westwood and I arranged to meet for lunch at Kettners restaurant in Soho, which he felt was sufficiently secluded that we would not bump into other people from the radio industry. Westwood was very scared that Capital Radio might find out he was talking to KISS FM. He had already seen how Capital had summarily sacked DJ Peter Young, who had been with the station for many years, as soon as they found out he was in discussions with Jazz FM about presenting a daytime show. I had met Westwood once before, when I interviewed him at Capital for a magazine article I was writing so, when we arrived at the restaurant, we each knew who we were expecting to meet. Sat in a quiet corner, eating our pizzas, I offered Westwood the same deal that McNamee and I had suggested to David Rodigan a few weeks earlier. We wanted Westwood to present a daytime show on weekdays that would play all styles of dance music, plus he would have one evening show a week devoted to the rap music in which he specialised.

Westwood was very keen to catch up with the latest news about KISS FM and so, without giving away too many secrets, I told him how busy we had become since winning the licence and how eager we were to find new premises and re-launch the station in August or September. Westwood and I talked a lot about the dire state of the mainstream radio industry in Britain, and I tried to persuade him how different KISS FM would be and how successful we anticipated it would be in attracting London's many disenfranchised young radio listeners. He asked me how McNamee was getting on these days and I told him that his former boss, from KISS FM's pirate days, was swiftly becoming the stereotype of a company man, wearing expensive suits, driving his expensive new company car, and smoking cigars. Westwood and I got on well, particularly as I was a big fan of his radio shows (I had anonymously been sending him examples of break-beat samples to use in his weekly on-air competitions). The two of us parted on good terms and agreed to meet again to discuss Westwood's possible defection to KISS FM in more detail.

Another matter requiring my attention was the growing realisation that it could still be a very long time before KISS FM had its own radio studios in which to train the DJs and let them rehearse their shows. KISS FM had won the licence the previous December, it was now mid-March and the station still seemed no closer to acquiring new premises. In the meantime, I would have to hire someone else's studio, so I phoned around several London radio facilities and decided to visit a new company called GDO in West London's Kensal Road. One of the partners in the business was Mark Oliver, whom I had worked with previously when he was the engineer at Radio Luxembourg's London studio, where I had produced music radio programmes for Japanese radio.

I explained my requirements for KISS FM to Oliver and he showed me around the two completed studios he had recently built. We agreed a discounted rate for which I promised to use his facilities for a minimum of one hundred hours between now and the station's launch. I also explained to him the importance of keeping KISS FM's bookings completely confidential. I would need to bring DJs such as Tim Westwood and David Rodigan here to rehearse programmes for KISS FM, even while they were still employed by Capital Radio. I could not risk rumours that might jeopardise their present positions or my negotiations with them. Oliver said he understood and so KISS FM, in the shape of me and several presenters, made GDO its regular studio home during the next few months.

The next day, Friday, Lindsay Wesker and I attended the annual UK Music Radio Conference, organised by the Radio Academy at the Barbican Arts Centre in East London. The conference itself was quite boring, but I came across several people whom I already knew in the record industry, including promotion man Scott Piering, for whom I had worked in 1987 at Rough Trade. He was very enthusiastic about KISS FM's prospects for success and promised to supply the station with copies of all dance records he was promoting. I also ran into Roger Lewis, who had recently been appointed Radio One's head of music and whom I had known since 1982 when he had presented an evening show on Northeast England commercial station Radio Tees. Lewis looked very different now than he did then. At Radio Tees, he had looked a bit of a hippy with long hair and a beard whereas, now, he was a young businessman with closely cropped hair and a smart suit. Lewis mentioned to me that he had a trainee producer working at Radio One, named George Ergatoudis, who he thought would fit in perfectly at KISS FM because of his passion for dance music. I told Lewis that I would bear the name in mind, but explained that the station's business plan unfortunately did not provide for the employment of music producers.

There was another full-day conference the following Tuesday, entitled 'UK Radio In The 90s,' held in the plush Selfridge Hotel. Although the event cost more than £100 per person, McNamee booked places for himself and me to attend, more because he felt it was important for KISS FM to have a presence at such industry events than for anything we might learn from it. The day provided little of interest except for the revelation by one of the IBA's radio officers that the Authority was not planning to license any further London-wide stations for at least four years. This ensured that KISS FM would have no new competitors on London's airwaves until at least 1994!

More interestingly, I had bought the latest issue of Record Mirror magazine on my way to the conference and, perusing it during a break in proceedings, I was surprised to read in its news columns that "London's KISS FM seems likely to be gaining the services of a certain superstar reggae DJ when it comes on-air in August." The inference would have been obvious to anyone working in the radio or music industries because David Rodigan was the best known reggae DJ in Britain and had won several awards for his shows. This revelation came only weeks after the same magazine had predicted that "Dave Pearce will be among the KISS FM presenters come August." The last thing that McNamee and I wanted to do was to precipitate the immediate dismissal of Rodigan or Pearce by their respective stations. We found a public phone in the hotel lobby and phoned Rodigan to explain that KISS FM had definitely not been responsible for the leak of this information, and that we hoped his position at Capital Radio would not be jeopardised by the rumour. McNamee phoned Rosee Laurence at the office and asked her to contact the article's author, James Hamilton, to explain to him the delicate position of these two DJs, and to request that he refrain from printing further gossip that could damage all parties involved.[671]

The last thing we wanted was for professional DJs such as Pierce, Rodigan and Westwood to fear that KISS FM was an amateur organisation that could not respect the need for total confidentiality in its negotiations to poach them from rival stations. KISS FM was still desperate to dispel the myth that it was merely a two-bit pirate radio station, which is why it needed to present a very professional image to the world. McNamee and I spent the rest of the day's conference worrying whether Rodigan would still trust us. We had already lost Peter Young to Jazz FM. To lose Rodigan as well would have dealt a huge blow to McNamee's plan to offer KISS FM's daytime programmes to established, well known radio presenters.

The question was: how was this secret information about KISS FM's plans being leaked to the press?

---

[668] "Jazz FM: Promise Of Performance", IBA, [undated].
[669] letter from Paul Brown, IBA to KISS FM, 16 Mar 1990.
[670] Richard Gold, "BBDO Steals KISS FM £1m Launch Account", Media Week, 23 Mar 1990.
[671] James Hamilton, "Beats & Pieces", Record Mirror, 3 & 23 Mar 1990.

March 1990.

Bad news about the incremental radio scheme continued to fill the media trade press. Sunset Radio in Manchester, the first of the new stations, continued to grab headlines, following the board's dismissal of its founder, Mike Shaft. Music Week reported ominously that Shaft's departure "raised a question mark over the financial viability of the UK's new breed of local black music stations." The magazine predicted that Sunset's music policy would be diluted by its new management "in order to attract mainstream advertisers." Shaft himself vowed: "It took me ten years to get the station on the air. I will get it back if it takes me another ten years."[672]

The remaining staff at Sunset lobbied Members of Parliament to stop their community station from being taken over by commercial radio interests, but it was too late. Terry Smith, managing director of the Liverpool commercial station, Radio City, was already acting as Sunset's spokesman to the press, and he was elevating his own position on the station's board of directors. Smith claimed that the board's decision to sack Shaft had been unanimous, and he said: "The station has potential but it is costing too much to run and is still losing substantial amounts of money."[673]

The following week, the situation at Sunset became even more confused when Shaft claimed to have been re-instated as managing director of the station. Then, it was reported that Terry Smith had resigned from the board at the company's first annual general meeting. The turmoil at the station received extensive coverage in the trade press and provoked much uncertainty in the radio industry about the viability of the incremental scheme and, in particular, of new black community and black music stations.[674]

The long established commercial radio companies suddenly appeared to want to play a more active role in the incremental scheme, now that all the licence winners had been announced and their launch plans were underway. Bristol commercial station GWR took a ten per cent stake in the city's new black community station, For The People, whose director Babs Williams explained: "Although we previously operated as a pirate station, we do not know all the ins and outs." Similarly, the Mid-Anglia Radio group took a shareholding in North London black community station WNK, whose managing director Joe Douglas explained: "They'll be a guiding light for us." Both WNK and For The People had desperately needed more capital to launch their stations and the industry's big boys had been happy to help them out, at a price. Other new stations were encountering similar problems. Isle of Wight Radio, due to launch in April, admitted that its launch costs were now expected to be double the £240,000 amount that had originally been budgeted. In London, after only three weeks on-air, Jazz FM had revamped its daytime programme schedule "in an effort to broaden its appeal."[675]

The music trade magazine, For The Record, reported (rather prophetically): "The long awaited expansion [of radio stations] may however have arrived at the wrong time. By the end of the year, London will have thirteen commercial radio stations. All will be looking for new advertising business from a currently depressed retail climate. The present advertising spend on London radio is about £36m. Trying to prise this away from the established Capital and LBC will be a difficult task … Under this climate, Jazz FM, and later KISS and Melody Radio, will need to survive until the economy lifts. It will be a sad and bleak couple of years for the new stations that will be over-burdened with high administration costs and royalties ... Just when specialist music radio has come into fruition, audience numbers rather than music policy will be the key to survival ... For the new music stations, how much watering down of the music will there be before the numbers go up? For the time being at least, accountants will be programming these radio stations."[676]

The signs began to look rather ominous for KISS FM, with so many new radio stations already faltering at such an early stage in their lives. At the same time, the expectation was being stirred by the media that KISS FM would somehow slay Capital Radio in London and steal most of its audience. Media Week suggested that "KISS FM would seem to pose the least threat to [LBC's FM/AM stations] Crown and Talkback, and the most to Capital." The Evening Standard asserted that "KISS FM will provide the first real competition for Capital Radio." Marketing Week reported that KISS FM would "attack the audiences of Capital FM and Radio One," an assertion fuelled by an unfortunate quote from KISS FM's new head of sales Gary Miele that "we are going to have some fun with Capital." Pat Falconer, managing director of sales house IRS, was similarly aggressive about his recent win of the KISS FM contract: "This gives us the opportunity to bring in all those advertisers who've been waiting to drop Capital for ages. They will be queuing to come in with us in the next month." Falconer added that KISS FM "should be the market leader in London."[677]

In their efforts to whip up a good story, the media was creating a phoney head-to-head war between KISS FM and Capital Radio, aided and abetted by the bluster of eager salesmen such as Miele and Falconer. If any of these journalists had ever heard KISS FM in its pirate days, they would have realised that its programmes were so different from those of Capital Radio that KISS FM could never attempt to compete with a pop music radio station. For all its popularity amongst young people and its significant showing in the top forty singles chart, dance music remained a minority interest, a fact that KISS FM had always understood. There was no way that the ex-pirate station could ever hope to attract as many listeners in London as a competitor with a pop music format.

This bizarre notion that KISS FM was suddenly about to metamorphose into a pop music station began to trouble many loyal KISS FM DJs. At the previous month's DJ meeting staged for the TV film crew, many presenters had expressed concerns that KISS FM sounded as if it was about to become a very different station from its pirate incarnation. Since that meeting, several DJs had expressed their view privately to me that they had noticed McNamee adopting a quite different persona. They felt that his performance in front of the cameras at the meeting had been just that – a performance – and that his expensive suits and cigars signalled a changed man. Most galling to them was McNamee's brand new Mercedes company car which he had parked at the end of the Mews, right outside the office where the meeting had been staged, for everyone to see. What these DJs wanted to know was: how come they were being paid nothing at all until KISS FM re-launched, and then they would receive only £50 for each show they presented? Why, at the same time, did McNamee already seem to be earning a small fortune, even before KISS FM was back on the air?

McNamee became increasingly defensive about his expensive Mercedes car, justifying it as an asset of the company, rather than a personal perk. He argued that it was important for the managing director of a new London radio station to inspire confidence in the business people whom he met and the companies with whom he was dealing. However, the murmurs and whispers amongst the DJs continued, until the dissatisfaction with McNamee's apparent new found wealth burst into the open. Time Out magazine published an item in its gossip column that said: "Heard the rumour about KISS FM supremo Gordon Mac who had his car clamped outside Friday's Upfront club and promptly (well, two weeks later actually, but you've got to spin a yarn) went out and bought a Mercedes Benz! Well, it's true! 'Vorsprung durch Technik,' as they say at KISS-ion Control in Finsbury Park."[678]

Despite the jokey nature of the story, McNamee erupted in a fury that Time Out, a magazine that had until now always been so positive in its coverage of KISS FM, should print such gossip. The fact that the essence of the story was true did not seem to bother him. McNamee demanded that Rosee Laurence must phone Time Out and complain in the strongest terms about the item, pointing out that the Mercedes was a company car, not his own, and that it was part of his remuneration package from the new KISS FM company which was funded by the station's shareholders. Laurence obeyed her boss' orders, as she always did, but it was obvious to everyone else in the office that McNamee was losing his sense of perspective over such things. Until now, he had always relied upon the press to support KISS FM because, firstly as a pirate station and then as a licence applicant, it had always been portrayed as the underdog, battling valiantly against the established radio order. Now that it seemed as if McNamee was desperately trying to elevate himself to the status of some kind of media mogul, he hated any criticisms those same journalists might make of his new persona.

The rumblings about McNamee's extravagance, at the expense of the rest of the KISS FM staff, continued within the ranks of the station's DJs, although McNamee managed to stifle any further outbursts in print. He was pre-occupied with finalising the details of the exact FM frequency the station would occupy when it came back on the air. The Department of Trade & Industry had made available two FM frequencies – 100.0 and 104.9 – to the Independent Broadcasting Authority [IBA] for the new London stations, KISS FM and Melody Radio. McNamee wanted KISS FM to be allocated the 100 channel because it was a nice round number which would prove invaluable in the station's marketing campaign. All the other London stations had fractional frequencies – Capital was on 95.8, GLR on 94.9, LBC on 97.3, and Jazz FM on 102.2 – which would make KISS FM the only FM station with a simple, whole number.

McNamee lobbied the officers at the IBA to offer KISS FM the 100 FM frequency. They eventually agreed, although they stressed that the assignment could not be officially announced to the public for several months. However, it was the IBA itself that accidentally broke the news of KISS FM's channel when it updated its annual Pocket Guide which listed all the existing and planned stations it had licensed. There, in print for everyone to see, the booklet showed that KISS FM was scheduled to transmit on 100 FM from the IBA facility in Croydon, South London. Now that the frequency had been made public, it was decided that the station would, in future, be named 'KISS 100 FM' in its publicity material, although it would still refer to itself as 'KISS FM' on-air.[679]

I was busy sorting out the jingles for the new station. As a pirate, KISS FM had used several identification jingles 'borrowed' from stations in America and France that were named KISS FM, in addition to some custom-made recordings by the Coldcut production team who were DJs on the station. I was very keen to give KISS FM a unique and identifiable sound, without using a set of jingles similar to those syrupy, cloying packages used by just about every other commercial radio station in the country. I contacted every jingle production company I knew of in Britain, as well as several in America, to solicit examples of their work, though nothing they sent me seemed to capture the contemporary, dance music sound that I felt would prove an ideal accompaniment to KISS FM's music programmes. The jingles needed to flow effortlessly in and out of the records being played, and they must not jar the listener with a clash of sounds.

I also obtained copies of other new stations' jingle packages to see if they had managed to create something different from the usual fare. To my disappointment, I found nothing that impressed me in their work. Although the Manchester black music station, Sunset Radio, had employed singer Lisa Stansfield to sing several of their jingles, the overall result was far too soft and lightweight for a station as radical as KISS FM. In London, both Choice FM and WNK had bought jingle packages that could be heard on almost any type of radio station and which gave no hint or indication that these stations played black music.

I decided that, if no one could supply the jingles that I required, then we at KISS FM would just have to make them ourselves. I contacted the Coldcut team – Jonathan More and Matt Black – to ask if they would be interested in producing KISS FM's jingle package. Although they were immensely busy, following their recent chart successes with Lisa Stansfield, Yazz and in their own name, they agreed to squeeze the project into their work schedule before KISS FM launched in the autumn. I visited Livingston Studios, just a few hundred yards behind WNK's studio in Wood Green, to discuss the idea with them further. Livingston was where they recorded most of their songs and also where they had built their own workshop, a tiny room brimming over with electronic gadgetry and obscure, old soul records which they loved to sample in their productions.

Coldcut played me a few of the ideas they had been working on for KISS FM jingles, but my immediate reaction to their initial efforts was that they were far too lengthy. I explained that a jingle should be between only one and five seconds long because, if it were longer, it would not bear repeated plays on a radio station. Until now, the only jingles that Coldcut had produced were the efforts (voiced by Yazz) that KISS FM had used in its pirate days. I shared with Coldcut the lessons I had learnt from my earlier experiences. When I had worked at Metro Radio ten years ago, my boss, Malcolm Herdman, had spent six months producing a new jingle package for the station that was performed and sung by a local group named Lindisfarne. After spending a lot of money and studio time on the project, the station had to scrap the resulting jingles because they were too long and unsuitable for playing regularly between records. Lindisfarne had written mini-songs of nearly a minute in length, rather than jingles that lasted a few seconds.

I explained to Coldcut that, although each jingle needed to be no more than a few seconds long, it nevertheless should have a definite introduction, a definite ending and something easily identifiable in the middle. Coldcut should treat the production of a jingle as the world's shortest pop song, and fill it with a single 'hook' that listeners would quickly warm to and recognise, even after only a few plays. We all agreed that making successful jingles was a tall order, but that the finished results would make KISS FM sound very different from any other radio station in Britain. If Coldcut's work proved successful on KISS FM, they might in future be able to convince other stations to let them produce a jingle package that suited their particular needs. Coldcut agreed to do the work and charge KISS FM only the cost of the studio time. I agreed to help them co-produce the jingles as much as I was able, and so I went home after the meeting and scribbled several pages of detailed instructions as to how to produce particular types of jingle for the different needs of the station.

Later that week, I attended a meeting of a more formal nature with Brian West, director of the Association of Independent Radio Contractors [AIRC], the trade organisation for the commercial radio industry. The AIRC had always been a wicked bogey man in the eyes of pirate stations, because it had exerted pressure on the government for so many years to act against illegal radio broadcasters. It seemed ironic that ex-pirate station KISS FM should now be enquiring about becoming a member of the AIRC, something that would have been unthinkable only a year earlier. Accompanied by McNamee and Strivens, I visited West at his office in Westbourne Grove and bombarded him with a list of questions I had prepared about the cost of membership and the benefits, if KISS FM were to join. West was very patient with us and explained in detail how the AIRC worked. After the meeting, McNamee and Strivens agreed with me that membership of AIRC was necessary, if only because it allowed KISS FM to participate in the radio industry's quarterly 'JICRAR' audience research. If KISS FM could not publish JICRAR-approved figures about the size of its listenership, the station would find it very difficult to sell advertising airtime. On that score alone, AIRC membership was worthwhile.

I wrote to West the next day (in McNamee's name), requesting membership of the AIRC, and West responded that "your trio gave me the most comprehensive 'interview' of any of our recent joiners." The fee to join AIRC was £1,500 and, additionally, members contributed £1,000 for every £300,000 of advertising revenue they earned. KISS FM's estimated first year revenues were £2.5m, which would have resulted in a further payment to AIRC of around £8,000 at the end of the first twelve months.[680]

The next weekend saw the launch of Choice FM, the South London station whose management had made scathing comments about KISS FM's licence win at the beginning of the year. There was very little evidence of a promotional campaign to announce the arrival of the new station, except in the specialist black press. There appeared to be a dichotomy between the IBA's licensing of Choice as a community radio station for South London and the station's determination to be a direct competitor to KISS FM. Choice FM's launch brochure explained the station's aims as: "Our main target audience is the sixteen to thirty-five age group ... The music programming will cover the whole spectrum of black music, though there will be a strong emphasis on dance music, which is currently the most powerful force in the music industry." This wording was almost identical to the stated objectives of KISS FM, which the IBA had licensed as a specialist music station. Where was the community programming that Choice was meant to be broadcasting?[681]

When Choice FM launched on the morning of 31 March 1990, it was obvious that, despite its public statements, the station was adopting a far softer music policy than that of KISS FM. Choice played very little music that was on the cutting edge of current dance music trends. In the station's first programme, the second record played was an old Marvin Gaye song. This was followed by an embarrassing series of interviews with the station's DJs, offering each an opportunity to publicise their career to date, as if this should be of interest to listeners. Choice FM sounded desperate to prove that it knew what it was doing, probably because it had won its licence against stiff competition from several popular South London pirate stations. Its own management team had very little radio experience and no history in pirate radio.[682]

All of KISS FM's potential competitors were now on the air – WNK in North London, Choice FM in South London, and Jazz FM across the whole city. None of them had delivered anything particularly revolutionary in their programming. Despite Jazz FM's recent revamp, its music policy was still rather chaotic. Both WNK and Choice FM had suffered from a lack of launch promotion, so that few Londoners even knew of their existence, let alone their programmes. As a result, the future for KISS FM's launch in the autumn still looked particularly bright.

---

[672]"Sunset Shake-Up Casts Shadow Over Black Music Stations", Music Week, 24 Mar 1990.
[673]"Sunset Staff Lobby MPs In Radio Protection Bid", Marketing Week, 23 Mar 1990.
"Angry Sunset Staff To Lobby Labour Broadcasting Man", Campaign, 20 Mar 1990.
Sean King, "Shaft Steps Up Sacking Battle", Broadcast, 23 Mar 1990.
[674]"Shaft Returns As Sunset MD", Media Week, 23 Mar 1990.
"Shaft Back At Sunset", Broadcast, 23 Mar 1990.
[675]William Arnold, "Profits Of Boom", Media Week, 23 Mar 1990.
"Jazz FM In Programme Shake-Up", Broadcast, 30 Mar 1990.
[676]Chris North, "Commercial Catastrophe?", For The Record, Apr 1990.
[677]Liz Roberts, "Lessons From London", Media Week, 23 Mar 1990.
Sarah Griffin, "London's Advertisers Get A Radio Double", Evening Standard, 23 Mar 1990.
"KISS FM Blows Own Trumpet", Marketing, 22 Mar 1990.
"IRS Plans To Kiss Capital Goodbye", Radio & Music, 28 Mar 1990.
[678]"KISS And Tell", Time Out, 28 Mar 1990.
[679]"IBA Pocket Guide", IBA, 1990.
[680]letter from Gordon McNamee, KISS FM to Brian West, AIRC, 30 Mar 1990.
letter from Brian West, AIRC to Gordon McNamee, KISS FM, 2 Apr 1990.
[681]"Choice FM's Audience", Choice FM launch brochure, 1990.
[682]author's recording, 31 Mar 1990.

April 1990.

The beginning of April 1990 saw some major changes in the KISS FM office at Blackstock Mews. A few more battered, second-hand desks were acquired, apparently from the office of Gordon McNamee's father, and some additional phone extensions were wired into the network. To make better use of the huge floor space, the desks of existing office staff were re-positioned around the edges of the room, rather than being randomly scattered in the middle as they had been until now. The newly delivered desks were set up in the previously unused space in front of the large double doors that opened onto the Mews. New recruits Gary Miele and Malcolm Cox were sat there, the first new additions since Fran Andrews had joined six weeks earlier.

After a rather rocky start, Andrews was starting to get to grips with her job. She had never worked in an office before and, initially, had no idea how to answer the phone, take messages or transfer calls. At first, when she answered the phone, she was so embarrassed that she either cracked up into giggles or there was complete silence. She was too scared to ask callers their names, and too disorganised to take messages if the required person was not in the office. Fortunately, after much coaching from Rosee Laurence, Andrews started to understand better her duties. The first few weeks of her tenure had been disastrous because she must have lost or aborted more phone calls than she managed to connect to the right person.

Miele and Cox could not have been more different to Andrews, since they had both worked in regimented office environments. Blackstock Mews still retained a very laid back feel because, most days, McNamee brought his dog Aster to work, the stereo system was cranked up loudly, and friends and acquaintances of the station called in continuously for a chat and a cup of tea. Miele and Cox were what the rest of us in the office referred to as 'suits,' because they wore suits to work at all times, while the rest of us, except for the newly regimented McNamee, continued to dress casually. McNamee had copies of the office keys cut for Miele and Cox, and additionally for me after my having worked several months at Blackstock Mews.

Miele and Cox's contracts offered each a company car up to the value of £15,000. Miele chose a BMW, while Cox selected a red Mazda, both of which were delivered in time for their first week of work. Miele and Cox were used to relying on secretarial assistance, rather than typing their own correspondence as the rest of us had to do, so McNamee employed a new secretary. Debbi McNally, who had previously worked at a radio saleshouse, IRS, was recruited as administrative assistant to both the newly created sales and marketing departments. Where there had been four of us working in the first floor space at the beginning of the year, there were now eight employees. The office suddenly seemed crowded.

Confirming our earliest suspicions, Miele did not seem to fit in well with the KISS FM ethos. He was loud, he was gruff, he barked orders at the new secretary, and he seemed to treat everyone in the station, other than McNamee (who had appointed him), with contempt. During the first few weeks of the expanded KISS FM team, it became obvious that things were no longer quite as they should be. KISS FM DJ Paul Anderson was still using the office as his 'home,' although he was out during most daytimes and working in clubs at night. He complained to McNamee that, on several occasions, he had returned late at night to find Gary Miele fast asleep on his sofa bed. McNamee was forced to make it clear to Miele that Blackstock Mews was only his workplace and that he could not sleep there. However, Anderson continued to complain that he was still finding Miele fast asleep in the office at night.

McNamee had similar cause to complain about Miele's behaviour. On the shelf unit behind his desk, McNamee kept an opened bottle of brandy, from which he poured himself an occasional glass when there was an occasion to celebrate in the office. One morning, McNamee arrived at work to find that the bottle had been mysteriously emptied. No one else in the office was particularly interested in alcohol, so McNamee took up the matter with Miele, who admitted he had finished off the bottle one night and offered to replace it.

Until now, the atmosphere within the office had always been one of complete trust in each other's integrity, despite any differences we might have had in recent weeks with McNamee's new persona. Each night, I habitually cleared all the papers from my desk into its drawers, but only so that I would not find them dusted with Anderson's and his associates' recreational remains the next morning. Now, for the first time, when I took my papers out in the morning, I started to find they had been disturbed overnight and put back in the wrong places. On one occasion, some papers about my plans for the station mysteriously disappeared and I could not understand where they had gone, having searched everywhere without result. Then, the next day, these papers suddenly re-appeared in one of my desk drawers.

A similar mystery was posed by the office fax machine. After every few dozen faxes had been received or sent, the machine automatically printed a summary of the numbers that had been called and the number of pages that had been sent. These diagnostics were usually discarded in the nearest waste paper bin but, one afternoon, I happened to notice that there were a series of very long numbers on the print-out I was about to throw away. Closer examination showed that some very long faxes had been sent from the KISS FM office late at night to numbers in North America. Since none of our work in the office usually involved American contacts, I drew McNamee's attention to this anomaly. He raised the matter with Miele because he was Canadian. Later, McNamee told me that Miele had admitted to sending the faxes, but had explained that they had been related to his work responsibilities.

On several occasions, McNamee was quizzed by me and the others in the office about Miele's behaviour, but his responses were that KISS FM needed an aggressive salesman, that Miele knew more than any of us about radio advertising and that, even if Miele had some character deficiencies, they were part and parcel of a salesman's life. Nevertheless, McNamee took delivery of a very secure, lockable filing cabinet, the first piece of brand new furniture ever seen in the office. For the first time, McNamee made sure he cleared all the papers from his desk every night into the cabinet, for which only he and Rosee Laurence had keys. The cabinet even remained locked during office hours. When I asked McNamee why such high security had become necessary, he admitted that KISS FM was no longer in a position where it could trust all of its staff. From then on, I always took home with me my most important papers about the station's plans. Whatever he was up to, my feeling was that Miele could not to be trusted.

The arrival of the new staff also heralded a much needed system for improving communication between everybody involved in the station. From the first week of April onwards, the station held a 'Monday morning meeting' at 9 am, attended by McNamee, Laurence, financial director Martin Strivens, Miele, Cox and me. The meetings were initially called 'head of department meetings' but this title failed to explain the presence of McNamee's personal assistant. Initially, I took the minutes of these meetings and typed them up afterwards, but it proved difficult to both write and be involved in discussions, so Laurence assumed the role of secretary to the meetings.

At each meeting, there was a regular, fixed agenda. We would look through the minutes of the previous meeting and ensure that they were correct, that each person had accomplished the things they had promised to do, and we would then update the others on the outcomes. Next, in turn, each person would detail what they had achieved during the previous seven days and how far their plans were progressing towards the station's launch. Then, the rest of the meeting would be spent considering specific issues about station policy in which we all needed to be involved to make a decision. During the first few weeks, these meetings lasted an hour or two. As the station's plans became more complex, the meetings lasted the entire morning and sometimes late into the afternoon, broken only by a short break to eat sandwiches purchased from a café down the road.

Soon after their appointments, Miele and Cox held a series of meetings with Martin Strivens to determine what resources they needed and how their departments were to be structured. Savings would have to be made to finance the appointment of Cox, because a separate head of marketing post had not existed in the station's original business plan. One media magazine passed comment on KISS FM's "unusual step of appointing separate heads of sales and marketing." Now, Miele and Cox were proposing their own ideas as to their staffing requirements.[683]

I was concerned that Malcolm Cox was going to be responsible not only for all the promotional aspects of the station's launch, but also for off-air activities such as the sale of KISS FM merchandise and the organisation of the station's popular club nights and concert events. Not only did this seem to be a lot of work, but Cox had no prior experience of club promotions. Although the station was still off-air, KISS FM's weekly club nights were still earning thousands of pounds in cash that Laurence counted and banked every Monday morning.

I had several private conversations with Heddi Greenwood who, although still working full-time in the office, had been offered no position, other than as a freelance DJ, in McNamee's plan for the re-launch of KISS FM. Greenwood was keen to be involved in the marketing of the station and, although McNamee had thwarted her proposal to attend a marketing course, I asked if she would consider working in Cox's department. I thought she could take responsibility for the station's music-orientated activities, of which Cox had little knowledge or experience. Greenwood agreed that such a job would be better than no job at all within the station, so I lobbied McNamee. Although he still seemed somewhat disinterested in his business partner, McNamee eventually came around to the idea that Greenwood could sustain KISS FM's highly profitable club activities. As a result, Greenwood became the first member of Cox's marketing department and, from now on, could start discussing with him directly, rather than with me, her ideas for the radio station.

At the same time, Cox was arguing to McNamee and Strivens that he needed an experienced sponsorship manager who could devote their time to exploiting the potential links between KISS FM and outside companies to sponsor the station's programmes, club events and the launch ideas he was planning. Cox was also arguing for a full-time press officer to be appointed who could organise the station's ongoing relationships with the media. Until then, it had been envisaged that Rosee Laurence would combine the responsibilities of McNamee's personal assistant and station press officer. However, McNamee's new role as corporate man was demanding even more of Laurence's time. McNamee told Laurence to choose between either continuing as his assistant, or taking on the public relations role for Cox. Laurence chose to remain as McNamee's assistant, so Cox was given approval to employ a press officer. The marketing department was about to expand from one to four staff.

Meanwhile, Miele was arguing that the five salespersons included in the original budget were insufficient to launch a new radio station. He proposed a more hierarchical structure for the sales department, with two group heads each responsible for a team of three salespersons. This was a significant departure from the original plans. McNamee and Strivens bowed to Cox and Miele's experience in the media industry, which they lacked, accepting that the pair must know what they were doing, and so they acceded to these additional demands on the station's limited budget.

Strivens had no desire to make cuts to his finance department in the station, which would consist of five full-time staff, so he sought cutbacks in the one remaining department, which was programming. From his perspective as an accountant, both the sales and marketing departments generated revenues that were crucial to the station's survival, while his own department ensured that the finances of the station were maintained in an orderly fashion. Whereas, the programming department generated no revenue directly, employed the most people, cost the most of all the station's departments and probably seemed to be the least productive. Consequently, the programming department's budget would have to be pruned in order to divert funds into the newly enlarged sales and marketing departments.

McNamee was very particular about the items that could and could not be cut from the programming budget. He had promised the thirty-odd DJs who had been with the station, as a pirate, that they would all be employed by the new company. He had reiterated this promise at the most recent DJ meeting and had told them that they would be paid £50 for each two- or three-hour programme they presented. This was one area that McNamee was not prepared to have cut. He had also promised the three people who had worked on the pirate station's magazine show, The Word, that they would be employed by the newly legalised station. This too was a commitment upon which he was not prepared to renege. This left the options very limited for cutbacks to the programming budget.

I had already been offered a job as head of programming, Lindsay Wesker as head of music, and Lyn Champion as head of talks. The cuts would have to be found elsewhere. Over the following weeks, Champion and I entered a difficult period that required a large number of very long meetings with McNamee and/or Strivens in which we had to argue the case for the remaining posts within the programming department. These discussions became frustrating and exhausting because neither McNamee nor Strivens had any concept of the essential roles that production and administrative personnel played within a radio station.

Lyn Champion and I spent hour upon hour explaining the role of each person within our department, as well as outlining on paper their responsibilities and a list of tasks they would be expected to perform during a working day. Despite our best efforts, Strivens and McNamee still insisted that cuts had to be made. The one change to which I had no objection was a reduction in the number of daytime DJs from five to four, an issue I had already argued for in a programming meeting, though on programming rather than cost grounds. McNamee had been opposed to the idea then, but now he was very much in agreement because it saved £15,000 per annum. Further cuts remained on the agenda for debate.

It was Champion's budget for talk programmes that had to bear the brunt of the cutbacks, the prospect of which she was understandably outraged. She insisted that it would prove impossible for her to produce the volume of talks programming that had been promised in the licence application and to which KISS FM had always had a firm commitment. At first, Champion argued that it would prove impossible to produce any substantial content with a reduced level of staffing, an argument which infuriated McNamee. Then, Champion would agree to the cuts during one meeting, only to have changed her mind at the next, and would become difficult for McNamee to pacify.

Champion wrote long memos for both McNamee and me that ran to many pages, arguing that she was being asked to perform impossible tasks with fewer staff, and constantly referring back to the promises that the station had made in its licence application and in public statements. McNamee was unconcerned by such changes in station policy because he, more than anyone in the station, understood from his elevated vantage point that KISS FM would become a completely different radio station from anything that had happened during its pirate incarnation. He became outraged by Champion's attitude and was beginning to find her particularly difficult to deal with. On several occasions, McNamee asked me if I wanted him to sack Champion, which he said he was prepared to do. I rejected the offer because, although Champion might occasionally be difficult to work with, she was the only other full-time person in the programming department with previous experience in legal radio. I knew that I was going to need all the help I could get in order to launch the station's programming successfully. I could not do my job without someone like Champion to contribute significant experience in radio production.

It was never clear to me from McNamee's offer to sack Champion whether he was thinking of replacing her with someone else, or whether it was merely a way to save £22,500 per annum that could be re-allocated to the sales and marketing departments. Whatever he was thinking, I was shocked by the callous way in which he had so quickly suggested dropping Champion from the team. If he could consider such an action against Champion, whom he had known longer than me, then how precarious was everyone else's future within the radio station? I had already seen the way in which McNamee had omitted one of his original business partners, Heddi Greenwood, from the plans for KISS FM. Only my intervention had helped restore her to the team.

Once again, was McNamee demonstrating how difficult he found it to deal with women who were strong and assertive, as Champion and Greenwood both were? Or was it simply that McNamee dealt with anyone in this way who did not agree with absolutely everything he said? I was not sure and it left me feeling very uneasy.

[683] "KISS FM Blows Own Trumpet", Marketing, 22 Mar 1990.

April 1990.

Gary Miele, KISS FM's new head of sales, told the 'Monday morning meeting' that he needed a recording of what the new radio station would sound like to play to potential advertisers. He said it would be impossible to convince people to advertise on a radio station that did not yet exist, unless they were offered some idea of the audio environment in which their advertisement would appear. To solve this problem, McNamee and I listened to several cassette recordings from the pirate days of the station that he kept in the bottom drawer of his desk, but there was nothing suitable. We listened again to the cassette that had been mailed out nearly a year ago as part of the station's campaign to win a licence, but it only served to remind us how dreadful that recording had been.

To solve Miele's problem, I booked four hours of studio time at GDO Studios and McNamee selected about twenty records that he felt were typical of the music that KISS FM would be playing. These included old songs, new releases, soul, reggae, rap, and other styles that represented the breadth and variety of the music played on KISS FM. McNamee suggested that KISS FM DJ Paul Anderson could subtly blend excerpts of these records together into a two- or three-minute mix. Anderson was undeniably the most accomplished mixer on the station and his services were increasingly being employed by record companies that wanted their latest single releases tweaked.

Arriving by taxi at GDO, Anderson and I established ourselves in one of the studios and started to record the requested mix. Anderson had brought with him one of Coldcut's earliest recordings which had some useful spoken introductions, so we recorded those to start with. As we moved on to mixing the songs, Anderson admitted that he had not listened to them or planned what he was going to do. I was surprised because I had arranged the studio booking several days in advance and had asked him to prepare what he intended to do. Anderson looked at some of McNamee's records, said he was bored and then wandered out of the studio, explaining only that he had to go and visit a friend, but would be back shortly.

The studio engineer and I proceeded with the mix ourselves. I quickly scanned through each of McNamee's songs, searching for the most well known section of each. Then, I assembled them into an order that I thought might blend together well. Anderson had still not returned, so we started to edit them together ourselves. We finished the whole job to our satisfaction just inside the four-hour booking. Suddenly, Anderson re-appeared without explanation of where he had been or what he had been doing all that time. I hid my annoyance and took the finished recording back to the Blackstock Mews office. McNamee liked it, Miele liked it and everybody else seemed pleased with the work that they thought was Anderson's. In confidence, I explained to McNamee that Anderson had not produced the mix, but he did not seem concerned. Copies of the tape were duplicated on cassette for potential clients, who were told it was a special KISS FM mix by the station's top DJ, Paul 'Trouble' Anderson.

The next day, Miele gave me a lift to a significant meeting. Although he had only taken possession of his BMW company car a few days earlier, it already smelt like an ashtray and there were pieces of paper and rubbish scattered everywhere. Miele was playing a cassette of Canadian rock band Bachman-Turner Overdrive in the car's stereo system and I could not help but wonder whether he was even trying to understand anything about the black and dance music that KISS FM would be playing. During the journey, Miele asked me a lot of probing questions about McNamee, as if he believed I had inside information that might prove useful to him. I evaded his interrogation and vowed to myself that this was the last time I would accept a lift from Miele.

I travelled to the Holiday Inn on Edgware Road to meet the editor of Independent Radio News [IRN], John Perkins, in the lobby. Although the contract between KISS FM and its newly appointed saleshouse, Independent Radio Sales [IRS], had not yet been signed, it remained only a matter of agreeing the detail. Now seemed like a good opportunity to investigate the offer of the free customised news service from IRN that was being included in the deal. Perkins asked me how I envisaged the KISS FM news bulletins should sound. I explained that I was thinking of hourly two- or three-minute bulletins that focused on a number of short news stories, without flannel, without contributions from correspondents, and without the silly items that often seemed to characterise the final story in bulletins produced for other local commercial radio stations.

Perkins asked me if I wanted the news to be read over the top of background music throughout the bulletins. He asked if I wanted stories about the entertainment and music industries positioned first in the bulletins. He asked if I wanted stories of concern to young people or the black population to be prioritised. He asked if I wanted 'heavy' stories, such as political news and foreign affairs, omitted altogether. I was aghast. The ideas he was suggesting sounded more appropriate for a radio network aimed at children. KISS FM's audience was young people in their late teens and twenties, who were intelligent, interested in the world around them and, like me, probably read a newspaper every day. In common with other people in the British radio industry, Perkins had a notion of KISS FM that was far removed from its reality. I told him that, if anything, I wanted hourly news bulletins on KISS FM to sound more authoritative, more concise and less lightweight than those broadcast by most commercial radio stations. Young people were as serious about current affairs as anyone else.

Perkins listened to me carefully and seemed relieved that the content I was asking him to produce was not substantially different from the bulletins that IRN provided to other clients. The only aspect that I wanted to be markedly different was the use of younger voices who did not sound like graduates of the rigid BBC style of news reading. Additionally, I wanted the service to be called 'KISS FM news' and not to mention IRN. To the station's listeners, it should appear that KISS FM had its own news team, rather than buying in the content. I promised that I would discuss the finer points of the service with KISS FM's head of talks, Lyn Champion, before Perkins and I met again.

That afternoon, I returned to the Blackstock Mews office to meet once more with GLR DJ Dave Pearce and update him about the progress we were making with the station's launch. He was still very keen to join KISS FM because recent programme changes at GLR had further reduced his time on-air and had marginalised the dance music that he played. We discussed an appropriate date to make the announcement that he had joined KISS FM, and I explained that I would like him to record some fake KISS FM programmes at GDO Studios before I could make a final decision as to which daytime programme he would present.

Meanwhile, McNamee was looking around another set of potential premises for KISS FM in North London's Holloway Road. The station's chairman, Keith McDowall, had been driving across London from his home in Islington recently when he had noticed a newly renovated office building that was being offered for rent. On his return to Blackstock Mews, McNamee was full of enthusiasm for the building. Although it occupied five floors, it was relatively cheap and, importantly for McNamee, it included secure private car parking space at the rear. To the rest of us in the office, the building sounded far too large for our needs, considering that much smaller offices had already been rejected for being too large. McNamee insisted it felt like the right place to install KISS FM.

Although it now seemed certain that Dave Pearce would join KISS FM, particularly as his future at GLR was decidedly insecure, our negotiations were nowhere near as advanced with the two Capital Radio DJs, David Rodigan and Tim Westwood, whom McNamee wanted to employ. A secret meeting was organised with Rodigan at the Centurion Press office in George Street to discuss some sponsorship ideas he wanted to share. McNamee, Malcolm Cox and I met Rodigan there, aware that he was very worried about his present employer rumbling his plans. Luckily, since the time that the gossip item had appeared in Record Mirror, no further speculation had been published about Rodigan joining KISS FM. We discussed Rodigan's proposal to organise a Sunsplash reggae festival in London during the summer of 1991, similar to the annual event that took place in Jamaica. Being reggae fans, McNamee and I were both keen to see the station associated with a style of music that was neglected by most other media and which was played very little on the radio.

The Easter holidays came and went without any significant progress made to secure a new home for KISS FM. Back in January, the KISS FM board had insisted that new premises had to be finalised by Easter. Yet here we were, no further forward than then. KISS FM's new saleshouse, IRS, and its new advertising agency, BBDO, were both insisting that the station must fix its launch date, without which it would prove difficult for them to sell advertising on the station or to book space in other media to announce the station's arrival. The KISS FM board decided that 1 September would be the launch date, come hell or high water. I expressed my concern to McNamee that this date would be cutting it far too tight. I had already told him that I needed at least one month to train the DJs in how to use a radio studio. To launch at the beginning of September, test transmissions would have to start at the beginning of August, DJ training should start at the beginning of July, and the studios would take a month or more to build before then.

I was not present at board meetings and had no access to the directors, so I was unsure whether any of my recommendations and worries had been raised by McNamee before they had fixed the launch date. Decisions about the station's future were now being made by a small group of people who had no previous radio industry experience and who had almost no contact with the 'shop floor' of the business, except through McNamee. Suddenly, all of the station's staff had been committed to a 1 September launch date.

One morning, McNamee, Martin Strivens and I went to look at another two offices that estate agents had suggested might be suitable. Both were in North London, one just off the Euston Road near Capital Radio's headquarters. It was an old building that had previously been used as a photographic studio, but it seemed particularly unsuited to our needs. The remains of the photography business were still scattered all over the floor. Before leaving, I selected a beautiful colour photo of what looked like a church on a small Greek island, beside a perfectly translucent blue sea. I took the photo home and stuck it on my kitchen wall.

The other premises were even less suitable, so McNamee, Strivens and I spent lunchtime in a nearby pub, where I began to feel increasingly frustrated about McNamee's insistence that any building meet very particular criteria, especially the need for a secure car park. I broached the touchy subject of how seriously behind schedule we already were. If we really wanted KISS FM to launch on 1 September and not embarrass ourselves, as several other new stations had done, we had to move fast to give ourselves sufficient time to complete the training, the test transmissions, and the dozens of other smaller tasks that a station had to do. I was gloomy and I did not hide the fact from McNamee. I felt that his stubbornness was beginning to hold up the whole company.

It was nearly the end of April and I had still not signed or returned the contract of employment that McNamee had given me in February. That afternoon, back in the office, McNamee asked me to give him the contract. I asked if he had taken up the matter with the board that I had asked him to. I was still concerned that McNamee was my line manager, the arbiter of any grievance I might raise, and the final determinant of a dismissal notice. He told me that he had asked the board, and that they had wanted to keep the contract exactly the way it was. Their decision, he said, was final. If I did not sign and return my contract by the end of the month, not only would I not be paid, but it would be assumed that I no longer wanted the job with KISS FM. That was the way it was and the way it was going to stay, McNamee told me. I could take it or leave it.

I recalled how callous McNamee had been earlier in the month, when he had suggested that Lyn Champion could be dismissed. I remembered that he had intended to cut Heddi Greenwood out of KISS FM completely, until I had helped to rescue her position at the last moment. There were other people whom I knew had worked for KISS FM and had apparently played significant roles in the station's development, but whom were now rarely mentioned positively in the office – Tosca, Guy Wingate, Sandra Charlemagne, Helen Needham. Where were these people now? Had KISS FM dropped them? Had they left of their own accord? Or had they merely fallen from McNamee's favour?

From these few things that I knew, I felt that McNamee must not be bluffing about my contract. I still wanted to be part of KISS FM. I wanted to be the person who made KISS FM a success. More than anything, I knew I had the skills to achieve the station's target of one million listeners per week in its first year on-air. I did not want someone else to take my job in KISS FM and screw up that responsibility. This was the first, and possibly the only, opportunity for London to have a black music radio station. I had spent almost twenty years in anticipation of this moment.

So, on 20 April 1990, I signed the KISS FM contract, just as it was, without alteration, and returned it to McNamee. The deed was done. I would have to face the consequences, whatever they might be.

April & May 1990.

The continuing recession continued to cause financial problems for the commercial radio industry. Yorkshire Radio Network announced that its advertising revenues for the first quarter of 1990 were down seventeen per cent year-on-year, prompting a 55p fall in the public company's share price. In London, Crown Communications, owner of commercial talk station LBC, announced that it was making seventy staff redundant. At newly launched Jazz FM, managing director Peter Gelardi announced that he would leave as soon as a successor was found. The incremental radio stations that had only been on-air a few months seemed the most vulnerable. Broadcast magazine commented: "The new wave of smaller community-based stations may have increased interest in radio, but they have not made any significant inroads into their established competitors' advertising market."[684]

Several of the new stations were coming under fire for the lack of originality in the music they were broadcasting. Chris Cracknell, A&R director of reggae record company Greensleeves, said he was "disgusted, disillusioned and disappointed" that black music radio stations such as Choice FM in London and Sunset in Manchester were "playing housewives' soul to get the advertisers ... not what the local communities want to hear." Jazz FM continued to draw criticism from listeners who complained that it played too much easy listening and soul music, rather than bona fide jazz.[685]

The misfortunes of these radio stations were very worrying for KISS FM, but they also made me more determined to ensure that absolutely everything should be made perfect for the station's launch. Many of the DJs were becoming impatient to get the station back on the air. It was now sixteen months since they had presented their final shows on the pirate KISS FM. McNamee was too pre-occupied to call a further DJ meeting to keep them informed of new developments, so Rosee Laurence started a newsletter that was sent to all the DJs to keep them involved in the station. The first edition ran to four pages and informed them of the 1 September launch date. It also explained that the station's staff complement had grown. Laurence wrote: "You may or may not know but, in order to obtain a licence, a number of very valuable people were taken on board. Some of them may seem unconnected with 'the scene' but they were all very helpful in a variety of ways. The staff of Goodfoot Promotions could only do so much, it was necessary to bring in experts from other fields."[686]

The newsletter hinted at the station's increasingly desperate search for premises: "One way or another, even if we have to broadcast from a mobile unit, we will be on-air on September 1, 1990." McNamee had already asked me to investigate the possibility of hiring a mobile studio that the station might have to use for its launch, if suitable premises could not be readied in time. Although the idea sounded abhorrent, I duly tracked down a caravan unit equipped with a radio studio. I started negotiations as to how much it would cost for KISS FM to hire for several weeks or months.[687]

There were other tasks I was being given that I felt were distracting my attention from the priority of preparing the station for launch in September. McNamee had become particularly keen on the idea of KISS FM owning a mobile outside broadcast unit that could transmit programmes live to air from locations such as the Notting Hill Carnival and outdoor concerts. Head of marketing Malcolm Cox had convinced McNamee that this new project could be self-funded through sponsorship, so I was told to investigate the costs and draft a proposal to show to potential sponsors.

Suddenly, I was spending much of my working day meeting builders of caravan units, drawing up budget proposals, discussing artwork designs and working out timescales for construction. I spent a whole day visiting Southend's commercial station, Essex Radio, to look at its outside broadcast unit and take photos. I spent a weekend standing in a cold, wet field somewhere on the North Downs, looking at a similar caravan used by Guildford commercial station County Sound. I spent another weekend at a stately home in Newbury, photographing a tiny trailer used by Reading commercial station Radio 210. In the end, all this work was in vain because Cox could not secure a sponsor and McNamee's enthusiasm for the project quickly waned.

Another tangent that pre-occupied McNamee for a time was his opinion that the station needed a new logo for its re-launch. I felt that it would be stupid to suddenly ditch the current KISS FM logo that had been used since 1985. It would negate all the merchandising and publicity work that had made the station such an instantly recognisable brand in London. McNamee disagreed and told me to find the logos used by radio stations named KISS in other parts of the world. It took some time to locate the designs used in America, France and Ireland, which were passed to the station's graphic artist, Nick Crossland, to be re-designed with the '100' FM frequency. Eventually, McNamee dismissed Crossland's efforts and dropped the idea.

There was also a proposal by KISS FM's advertising agency, BBDO, to use the soul oldie 'Bus Stop' by The Fatback Band as the soundtrack to the station's television commercial. Everybody within KISS FM agreed that the song was typical of the funky, but popular, music for which the station had developed a reputation. The rights to the track were owned by the record company I had worked for until the previous year, so I was asked to organise the song's use. The record company suggested they would be interested in releasing a remixed version of the song, so I suggested they commission KISS FM DJ Paul Anderson, who I convinced them was in demand as a mix specialist. They agreed and paid for Anderson to spend a day in a studio working on the track. However, when he returned to the office and played us the results, everyone had to agree that they were awful. Anderson had somehow destroyed the essence of the song and created something different instead. The record company rejected his remix and I was left feeling embarrassed about the money they had wasted using Anderson on my recommendation. Instead, the record company commissioned another DJ (unconnected with KISS FM) to make a remix which was used when the song was reissued.

The inexorable increases in the budget for KISS FM were evident in a half-page recruitment advertisement that head of sales Gary Miele placed in Media Week magazine. Two newly created 'group head' positions were promised £35,000 each, while 'sales executives' would be paid £25,000. The licence application had budgeted for sales executives to cost £20,000, and there had been no group heads. The stylish advertisements asked in big letters "What would you be prepared to do for a KISS?" and were overprinted with a pair of red lips.[688]

In early May, further programme changes at GLR brought DJ Dave Pearce's five-year tenure at the station to an end. Like the DJs from KISS FM's pirate days, Pearce was now without radio exposure until the station launched in September. He was concentrating on his record label, Reachin' Records, which focused upon releasing British dance music artists. I arranged to meet Pearce at the office to discuss his employment contract with KISS FM. He was enthusiastic about every aspect, except for the £15,000 salary. I explained that I was constrained by the station's budgets, that all the daytime DJs would be paid the same amount, and that all the programming staff were being paid relatively low salaries. McNamee took Pearce out for dinner and must have promised him something in addition to the salary he was being offered, because he eventually agreed to take the job for £15,000.

Rosee Laurence had been busy for weeks, organising a surprise thirtieth birthday party for McNamee at Flynns nightclub in London's West End. She had printed and distributed specially printed invitation cards to everyone involved in KISS FM and to the media contacts the station had built up over five years. Laurence asked me if I would make a speech at the event, trumpeting McNamee's successes and congratulating him on behalf of everyone involved in the station. I was very reticent as I had always hated making public speeches. However, Laurence insisted that I should make the speech, though she agreed that I could share the task with KISS FM DJ Dean Savonne, who was one of McNamee's oldest friends.

On the evening of 10 May 1990, several hundred people gathered inside Flynns club to see McNamee arrive in the company of his parents, who had pretended they were taking him out for a meal to celebrate his birthday. As he was shepherded through the front door, the whole room burst into a chorus of 'Happy Birthday,' followed by tribute speeches from Savonne and me, along with a brief introduction by KISS FM financial director Martin Strivens. The whole event was rather flamboyant, worsened by McNamee's expression of blank surprise at the huge welcome he had been given. Mentorn Films was present with cameras and floodlights to commit the whole event to videotape for inclusion in the documentary about KISS FM. This made the evening much more of a media spectacle than a private birthday celebration.

That evening, and the next day in the office, it was obvious that McNamee was not at all pleased by Laurence's organisation of the surprise event. He showed no gratitude and acted as grumpily as he had ever done in our company. I had given him a pair of solid silver cufflinks as a birthday present, though he had hardly even thanked me for the most expensive gift I had ever bought for anyone. The only thing that seemed to concern him was Mentorn's filming of the event. His mood did not improve until he had persuaded the company to agree not to use any footage from that evening in its documentary. It appeared that, because McNamee had been unable to rehearse his performance for the surprise birthday party, he did not want to be seen on film as he really was – a moody, often grumpy, man who seemed to like to feel in control of people around him and who liked to appear sufficiently powerful to make them jump to his commands.

McNamee continued to fill most of his working days with meetings away from the Blackstock Mews office. There were more board meetings, more shareholder meetings, meetings with IRS to finalise the saleshouse contract, meetings with BBDO to finalise the launch marketing campaign, meetings with Gary Miele to interview candidates for the sales jobs, meetings with the company that KISS FM was sub-contracting for transmitter installation, and more. Although no one else working in the office had yet viewed the potential premises in

Holloway Road, McNamee seemed certain that this five-story building was the one that KISS FM would eventually occupy, though contracts had still to be finalised.

So certain was McNamee of securing these premises that he asked his father, who was apparently an interior designer, to come up with plans for the inside of the reception area of the new KISS FM building. The designs, of which McNamee was sufficiently proud to show everybody in the office, looked absolutely ghastly. The plans were pretentious, over-cluttered and many of the surfaces in the reception area seemed to be painted silver, like a cheap science fiction movie from the 1960s. The designs reeked of someone who had more money to spend than common sense. McNamee tried to persuade the KISS FM board to approve the idea. The immense cost of the work dissuaded them. It had been another of McNamee's pet projects designed to 'payback' those to whom he felt loyalty. Instead, the board opted for a design from another contractor that was more practical and frugal.

The first good news about the new incremental radio stations arrived in the form of Jazz FM's initial audience figures. The statistics showed that fourteen per cent of Londoners had listened to the station during its first six weeks on-air. Managing director Peter Gelardi commented: "We told the industry we'd get a thirteen per cent reach. At this stage, we would have been quite happy with ten per cent. As it is, we recorded fourteen – that makes us the third biggest station in London." The newspaper headlines were upbeat: 'Jazz FM Strikes A Major Chord,' 'An Upbeat Jazz FM Defies Recession' and 'Jazz Station Tunes In To Early Success.' However, the station's research had not been conducted to radio industry standards and so was not directly comparable to other stations' results. Confirmation of Jazz FM's success would have to wait until the next official JICRAR audience research was published in the autumn.[689]

The Jazz FM figures managed to instil a little confidence in an industry where, until now, the only news about incremental radio stations had concerned boardroom coups, sudden programme changes, internal conflict and outright failure. EMAP Radio, which already held a twenty per cent stake in KISS FM, announced that it was looking to invest in other new radio stations and wanted to be involved with rock music formats aimed at 25 to 44 year olds. EMAP invested £350,000 in a 29.9% stake in Stockport station KFM which, after only three months on-air, had run out of money. The station had generated only £60,000 of advertising revenue during that period, compared to the £150,000 required by its business plan. KFM had originally been a pirate station, but its founder and managing director for the launch, Charles Turner, had resigned after disagreements about where the blame lay for the station's failure.[690]

Already, at two incremental stations, Sunset and KFM, the founders turned managing directors had been kicked out (although at Sunset, Mike Shaft had been temporarily reinstated). One station had been a successful pirate, while the other had campaigned during many years for a licence. These were scary developments to observe, only months prior to the launch of KISS FM.

One evening in the office, after work, when McNamee seemed to be in a quite receptive mood, I talked to him about the problems that had arisen elsewhere from stations' transformations from pirate to legal broadcaster. I asked whether these recent events at Sunset and KFM had made him wary of the KISS FM shareholders and the possible axe they might wield over his own head in future.

McNamee told me that he was presently embroiled in negotiations with a remuneration sub-committee that the KISS FM board had convened in order to finalise his employment contract. He admitted that the discussions had dragged on for many weeks and had taken up a lot of his time. Letters and draft contracts were being sent back and forth, he said, and a lot of the work was being done by his solicitor. McNamee reassured me that he had every intention of securing his own future within the station. He would only agree to a contract that enabled him to retain the post of managing director of KISS FM for several years to come. Yes, he admitted, he had observed the pitfalls that Mike Shaft at Sunset and Charles Turner at KFM had encountered, and there was no way that he would allow himself to fall into a similar trap. KISS FM was his station, he emphasised. If the shareholders did not keep him as managing director, they could not have KISS FM either. But, he admitted, the details of his personal contract had still not been settled, although he was hoping for a sensible conclusion as early as possible, so that he could get on with the rest of his responsibilities.

I left the office that night hoping that McNamee would manage to maintain his position within KISS FM. I knew that KISS FM could succeed with its present team of staff, but expected that it would fail if it fell into the hands of a large company such as Capital Radio. Whilst I hoped that McNamee could hang on to his job, it was frustrating that the rest of the KISS FM application team seemed to have been hired on a 'take it or leave it' basis without any of the guarantees that he was seeking for himself.

---

[684] Peter Goodwin, "Can UK Radio Ride The Recession?", Broadcast, 27 Apr 1990.
"Jazz FM Chief To Step Down", Broadcast, 27 Apr 1990.
[685] Stu Lambert, "'Get Real' – Reggae Label Boss Berates Stations' Policy", Music Week, 28 Apr 1990.
[686] "Newsletter", KISS FM, 25 Apr 1990.
[687] ibid.
[688] KISS FM recruitment advertisement, Media Week, 27 Apr & 4 May 1990.
[689] Susannah Richmond, "Jazz Gets 14% Reach", Campaign, 27 Apr 1990.
Sean King, "Jazz FM Strikes A Major Chord", Broadcast, 4 May 1990.
Susannah Richmond, "An Upbeat Jazz FM Defies Recession", Campaign, 4 May 1990.
Steve Clarke, "Jazz Station Tunes In To Early Success", Sunday Times, 13 May 1990.
[690] "EMAP Planning New Moves Into Local Radio Market", Media Week, 18 May 1990.
Sean King, "KFM Suffers Ad Revenue Crisis", Broadcast, 25 May 1990.
Sean King, "EMAP And Signal Bid To Rescue KFM", Broadcast, 1 Jun 1990.
"EMAP Share In KFM", UK Press Gazette, 28 May 1990.
"KFM Confirms Cash Boost", Media Week, 1 Jun 1990.

May 1990.

Following Rosee Laurence's decision to remain as McNamee's personal assistant and to relinquish her press and publicity responsibilities within the station, McNamee amended her job title to 'general manager.' This change was baffling because Laurence's role did not expand and she continued to show no inclination towards managing anything more than the affairs of her boss. The rest of us in the office presumed it must have been some kind of reward for her personal loyalty to McNamee, despite the changes he was evidently going through, or it might have provided a reason for him to argue to the board that her salary should be increased from the £16,000 earmarked in the business plan.

Now, head of marketing Malcolm Cox had to advertise for "a public relations person to look after KISS FM's media image." The office was inundated with job applications as the result of a recruitment advertisement published in The Guardian newspaper which was headed, in large letters, "Wanted – someone for a KISS." A whole day was set aside for interviewing the shortlist of candidates, each of whom was asked to write a brief strategy whilst they awaited their appointment with Cox and McNamee. The decision was eventually made to appoint Anita Mackie, who was working for Lynne Franks' PR company.[691]

In addition to employing a full-time press officer, KISS FM chairman Keith McDowall insisted that the station must use the services of a well known public relations firm, at least for the duration of its launch in September. Several companies were approached to take on the work and, after another day of interviews, it was decided to hire Rogers & Cowan. This was the company that had worked on the launch of Jazz FM and had secured it an enormous amount of press coverage.

It was now little more than three months until KISS FM was to re-launch and I too needed to recruit new staff for the programming department. The following week, another advertisement was published in The Guardian under the headline "What would you be prepared to do for a KISS?" For the station's talks department, I required producers, researchers and freelance reporters "to produce a daily 30-minute specialist programme about dance music, style and culture." Again, the office was inundated with job applications and enquiries which kept Lyn Champion and me busy, reading all the letters and listening to examples of previous work that candidates had submitted on cassettes.[692]

By the end of May 1990, KISS FM had signed its contract with Independent Radio Sales [IRS], the station's advertising saleshouse. The entire full-time KISS FM team trooped down to the company's new headquarters in Hammersmith one evening after work to attend a special presentation. The staff showed us a series of slides and gave us a commentary about what they believed KISS FM could offer potential advertisers. Unfortunately, it was evident that, although they had tried very hard, they had not understood how different KISS FM was going to sound compared to Capital Radio and Radio One. The IRS presentation had failed to communicate the uniqueness of KISS FM as a specialist music radio station for young Londoners.

After the late May Bank Holiday, Rosee Laurence compiled and mailed out a second KISS FM newsletter to update the station's DJs about recent progress. The letter explained that a lease for the building in Holloway Road had still not been signed, although the DJs were assured that "if not, we will still be coming on-air September 1, but from an outside broadcast unit."[693]

I was becoming increasingly concerned that the finalisation of premises was so late that I would not be able to offer the presenters a full month to learn how to use professional radio equipment. Many of the KISS FM DJs were expressing similar concerns to me, and several suggested they could enrol for DJ training courses offered by commercial companies in London. The newsletter explained: "Grant will be organising 'practice sessions' for everyone in our studios (once they are completed!) at the beginning of August … Throughout August, presenters will book our two self-operated studios for their own use to practice, and they will be expected to come in all hours of the day and night (literally!) … There are 'DJ training courses' offered commercially by other companies in London, but they largely train people to sound like BBC or Capital [Radio] presenters in studios that will not necessarily be similar to ours. Such training is not particularly relevant to KISS and will not compensate for hard graft in our very own studios nearer the time."[694]

Two internal tussles were still ongoing, one between Gordon McNamee and Martin Strivens, the other between Lyn Champion and me, both about the precise cuts to be made to the programming department budget. The newsletter hinted that cuts to the radio station's original programme plans were in the air: "There are currently some changes taking place within the 'Word' department. This doesn't affect the station's commitment to the speech output, which remains solid, but, during the first few months, we'll be producing interviews and information etc. in a different form."[695]

The newsletter also publicised, for the first time, six statements about the radio station that I had written and which Malcolm Cox had agreed to use in the marketing of the station. To me, they summarised the positive aspects of how different KISS FM was going to be. The newsletter explained that they were now part of what Cox referred to as KISS FM's 'brand positioning.' The statements were:

- KISS FM is London's all-music station
- KISS FM plays tomorrow's hits today
- KISS FM reflects the sound of the street
- KISS FM sounds exciting and different
- KISS FM is the city's dance music authority
- KISS FM has presenters who know their music.[696]

While these statements were going to be used in the station's off-air publicity, I had written another set of slogans that were to be used in jingles and read out by DJs within the station's programmes. Twenty-four of these were published in the newsletter, including some that dated back to the station's pirate days:

- KISS FM – Dead On Your Dial
- Your Radical Radio – KISS FM
- Check Us Out – On KISS FM

and new ones such as:

- London's Music Leader – KISS FM
- The Sound Of Young London – KISS FM

- London's Music Authority – KISS FM.[697]

The newsletter also carried word of a huge, public launch event that KISS FM was planning. This had already proven to be one of the biggest headaches for us to organise. The initial idea had been to stage a concert of soul and dance music at London's Royal Albert Hall, similar to the previous year's Disco Mix Club Awards held at the same venue. Then, the location was switched to Docklands in London's East End, and then to a greyhound racing stadium in South London. The newsletter explained the latest plans: "We're looking at having a launch event to coincide with the station coming on-air. This will probably take place on Sunday September 9 at Highbury Fields. It will be a free, open-air event for 20,000 people, and we are looking to put on a spectacular line-up of US and UK live acts and PAs with, of course, you [the KISS FM DJs] supplying the music."[698]

On the front of the newsletter was printed a huge KISS FM logo, almost identical to the one used in pirate days, but with '100 FM' substituted for '94 FM.' The newsletter explained: "You will see a copy of the official KISS 100 FM logo. This is about to be trademarked so I hope you like it!" To the DJs, it must have looked as though little had changed, but this 'new' logo had been the outcome of a fierce internal battle within the station. Although McNamee had rejected the new designs suggested recently by KISS FM designer Nick Crossland, he remained unconvinced that the station logo should stay exactly the same as it always had been.

Whilst creating the station's launch advertising campaign, BBDO had suggested to McNamee that the logo design should be changed. Within the proofs of the press advertising that the creative team had shown us at regular review meetings, a new logo had been included as part of their overall marketing package for the station. I was as impressed as the rest of the KISS FM team had been with the high quality and suitability of BBDO's work, but I repeatedly had to raise the issue that their designs had included a new logo that was not the station's own. McNamee became irritated by my ongoing objections to BBDO about this particular point, but I persisted. He and the rest of the KISS FM team had spent five years raising the profile of that logo in London. I still felt that it would be suicidal to ditch it now.

During one meeting with BBDO, I raised my usual objection to the new logo and McNamee told me bluntly that, since the previous meeting, he had agreed with the agency to adopt its new design. I was amazed but I waited until later to argue the point with him. Could he not understand that any advertising agency would love to be able to say that it had designed a successful client's logo? Did he not realise that the creative department at BBDO would like to feel that it had control over all of our station's publicity material, including its logo? Why was he prepared so easily to throw away five years' hard work building up the brand name 'KISS FM' and such a well know logo in London, just because BBDO was advising him to?

McNamee listened but refused to change his mind. I set about lobbying others in the station to try and make McNamee see how ridiculous it was to change the station's logo. It was one of the few remaining links that the public could make between KISS FM's former pirate existence and its new status as a legal radio station. Why was McNamee so determined to pretend that the illegal history of the station had never existed? Other members of the original KISS FM team continued to chivvy McNamee to change his mind, though it was me who bore the brunt of his stubbornness. Now, whenever I raised the matter, he huffed and he puffed and told me how boring I had become.

However, I believed that the logo was a crucial part of the station's marketing plans and I continued to press my case at all the relevant meetings going on within the company. In the end, McNamee said that, although the station would not revert back to the original logo design, he would let me talk to BBDO about making amendments to its new one. This was done more to placate me than through any change of heart on his part, but I was pleased to have secured a concession on this issue. I took up his offer and, during the course of several bizarre meetings at BBDO that I had to arrange myself, the agency's creative department agreed to 'amend' its logo through a series of minute changes until it closely resembled the original pirate design. BBDO fought to the bitter end to use a new typeface for '100 FM,' but I insisted it should remain the same. The only noticeable change was the re-design of the red lips within the logo to make them look less like a tulip lying on its side.

BBDO probably billed KISS FM for 'redesigning' the logo through many different draft versions with which I was not satisfied. The agency's frustration at not being able to use its own logo became evident in the proofs of the poster designs and press advertising that we were asked to approve. The 'old' KISS FM logo had been positioned at the very bottom of the text and was now so small that it was hardly visible. In the magazine advertisements, BBDO now wanted the logo to be no more than a few millimetres high. When McNamee and I suggested that it was too small, its size was increased, but only marginally. Even in the finished posters that appeared in print, the logo was much smaller than in any previous KISS FM publicity. For the most recent KISS FM newsletter sent to DJs, Rosee Laurence had ensured that the logo covered the whole front page.[699]

Also included in the newsletter was the proposed floor plan of the radio studios, as they would be built within the Holloway Road premises if and when the lease on the building was agreed. After many days of discussions with the station's engineering sub-contractors, and several visits to a studio construction company called KFA based in Wood Green, it was agreed that KISS FM would have two identical on-air studios from which DJs would present live programmes. There was a separate production studio that would be used to pre-record interviews, jingles, documentaries and promotional trailers. On the same floor, there was also a tiny transfer booth where tapes could be copied from one format to another, and the station's record library.

Recently, McNamee had taken me to view the Holloway Road premises for the first time. It looked perfect for the station's needs, even though builders had not yet completed their work on the interior. Holloway Road was an extremely busy major road running northwards from the centre of London. Although the vicinity was quite a rundown area, a lot of nearby properties were also being renovated into office blocks. Our building was light and airy, with plenty of windows. A short flight of steps led up to the entrance of the building, which opened into a large reception area, the left side of which was to be partitioned as the office for Free! magazine. The basement floor was to be occupied by the sales and marketing departments, the first floor was to be the studio complex, the second floor was for the programming department, and the top floor was for McNamee and the finance department.

McNamee was working with a firm of architects to determine the detail of where the partitioning was to be erected, where the power points were to be installed, the telephone sockets and the like. He showed me the plans for each office floor which he had designed without consultation with the relevant departmental heads. The basement was intended to be entirely open plan, though Gary Miele and Malcolm Cox subsequently insisted that they occupy partitioned offices to allow them to have private conversations with staff. The top floor was McNamee's pride and joy, where he had designed an enormous boardroom to be filled with a massive boardroom table that took up most of the floor. The remaining floor area was allocated to private offices for himself and Rosee Laurence, with an interconnecting door, a large office for Martin Strivens, and an open plan area for the rest of the finance team.

It was the programming department floor plan about which I was most concerned. McNamee had created a floor filled with lots of tiny offices for each of the programming staff. I had to explain to him that such a plan was unworkable. Having never worked in a radio station, McNamee had failed to grasp that people worked in teams in the production and presentation of programmes, not in little offices on their own. Rather than lots of individual offices, it would be more productive to build several large open plan areas designated to specific areas of the station's output. I took a copy of the floor plan home and completely redesigned it. A long time ago, I had worked in an architect's office and I had learnt how to design efficient office space. I replaced the little offices with one large room for music production staff, one room for talks production staff, one listening room for people to listen to records, and separate offices only for me, and for the head of talks and the talks producers. I presented this revised arrangement to McNamee and overcame his initial resistance by insisting that this configuration was used in most radio stations.

The same week that Rosee Laurence had sent out the second newsletter, the first KISS FM advertising rate card arrived from the printers, designed by advertising agency BBDO to convince potential advertisers to spend money with the new station. It looked fantastic and was easily the most expensive item of KISS FM promotional material produced to date. Printed on thick glossy card, the rate card opened out into a three-page A4-size folder, with 'KISS 100 FM' printed in eight-inch high letters on one side, while the other comprised a montage of dozens of small black and white photographs of young people kissing each other. The caption underneath asked 'What do one million young Londoners do every day?' This referred to the station's promise to attract at least one million listeners a week during its first year on-air.

Advertisers were guaranteed a core audience of young Londoners aged between 15 and 34. A single 30-second advertisement would cost £150 between 6 am and midday, £75 between midday and 6 pm, or £25 between midnight and 6 am. The differences between these rates were based upon the patterns of listening to pop music commercial radio stations, whose audiences declined steadily from breakfast time onwards, making the cost of advertising cheaper later in the day. This system was adopted by the KISS FM board, despite the fact that I had predicted in an earlier programming meeting that the station's audience in the evening would probably be the same size, or perhaps greater, than during the day. A radio station with a specialist music format had not existed in London until now, so both the board and the saleshouse must have felt there was no reason that the KISS FM audience would be different than that of any other station.

Press announcements followed about several new appointments to the KISS FM team. Two group heads had been recruited to the sales department – John Devine from Capital Radio and Gary Smith from LBC. In the marketing department, a new sponsorship manager, Gordon Drummond, was recruited from Jazz FM. In the programming department, I wrote a press release to announce that Dave Pearce was to become a KISS FM daytime DJ. Interviewed in one magazine, Pearce explained that morale at his former station, GLR, was low. He said that the station's manager, Matthew Bannister, and programme organiser, Trevor Dann, had wanted him "to change the music to hit a much wider spectrum of young people and to include people like Jason Donovan, Bros and Kylie Minogue which I've got no real interest in, and I don't believe that's what the programme was supposed to be about. So, over a period of months, we started to disagree on the music policy of the show."[700]

Commenting on his new job, Pearce said: "KISS FM is a station I've been wanting to work for, as an idea of a radio station, since I started DJ-ing. It's a realisation of a dream of seven years and, for many music fans, the felling is the same. I've never understood why there's so little black music and dance music on the radio, on legal stations, and now, congratulations to the Independent Broadcasting Authority that they saw the light at last. It's very exciting."[701]

---

[691] advertisement, KISS FM, The Guardian, 14 May 1990.
[692] advertisement, KISS FM, The Guardian, 21, 26 & 28 May 1990.
[693] "Newsletter no. 2", KISS FM, 1 Jun 1990.
[694] ibid.
[695] ibid.
[696] ibid.
[697] ibid.
[698] ibid.
[699] ibid.
[700] Sarah Davis, "Pearce Kisses GLR Goodbye", Music Week, 2 Jun 1990.
[701] ibid.

June 1990.

It was only three months away from the scheduled re-launch of KISS FM, even though the lease on the Holloway Road premises had still not been signed. It was only two months until test transmissions were due to start and the intensive training of the DJs had to begin, yet the work to start building the studios could not start until the lease was signed. I was becoming very worried because there were only so many things I could achieve without having studios in which to work. It looked as if KISS FM might be broadcasting from a caravan at the rear of the building for several weeks, using the private car park which McNamee had desired so much.

The economic recession continued to have a negative impact on the viability of the commercial radio industry. Crown Communications, owner of London station LBC, reported profits of £2.95m for the previous six months, down 22 per cent year-on-year. The Yorkshire Radio Network reported profits down from £619,000 to £410,000. Invicta Radio reported that profits had fallen from £420,000 to £116,000. London station Jazz FM announced that its American shareholder, Westinghouse, was injecting a further £1m to clear some of the debt that had accumulated during its first three months of broadcasting.[702]

There were further management rifts at some of the new incremental stations. John McDowell, chief executive of Belfast Community Radio, quit the station less than three months after its launch, following revelations that its launch capital of £250,000 had already been used and that the business was now overdrawn. A month earlier, the station's programme controller, Mike Gaston, had been dismissed following "irreconcilable differences" with McDowell. An industrial tribunal awarded Gaston £22,000 compensation for his dismissal. At KFM in Stockport, the station recently acquired by EMAP Radio, programme controller Steve Toon quit after the new owners suggested the station should broaden its musical output by playing mainstream records "such as Abba." Toon commented: "The new KFM will attempt to take on the Manchester station Key 103. This was not the point of KFM or incremental radio."[703]

There was still public concern about the surfeit of soul, blues and easy listening music that was being broadcast by London's Jazz FM. Laurie Staff of London record shop Honest Jon's commented: "At least fifty per cent of the programming should be jazz, and I don't think it is at the moment, although it is getting better." Alan Sage of Mi-Price Records said: "Before the station came on the air, everyone was full of optimism, but the reality is that they are satisfied in getting the audience they want to, but it has very little to do with jazz." At times, it seemed as if the entire incremental radio scheme was about to self-destruct, with so much negative news reported about the new stations. The task remained to make KISS FM an exceptional success.[704]

Even if disunity or disagreement existed within the station's management team, it was vital that KISS FM presented a unified front to the rest of the world and, in particular, to the press that was so interested in the rags-to-riches story of the radio station. From the time when KISS FM had won its licence the previous December, I had emphasised to everyone in the office how important it was for the media to be given a consistent story about the station's plans. For this reason, McNamee had continued to act as the KISS FM spokesman, even though his 'quotes' or 'statements' were usually written by me or Rosee Laurence. The earlier faux pas committed by Lindsay Wesker, in conversation with Broadcast magazine about Dave Cash's role in the first licence application, was still on my mind. The station could not afford another PR error like that.

The recent recruitment of new staff had made the task of controlling the station's publicity much harder. Rumours suddenly started coming back to the office from outsiders that DJs such as David Rodigan and Tim Westwood were to have daytime shows on the station. McNamee took to task the new staff for the serious damage such leaks could cause, and he traced the source to the station's head of sales, Gary Miele. Problems had already been caused by Miele's insistence in stating publicly that KISS FM was going to take on the might of Capital Radio, so McNamee disciplined him and banned him from talking to the press. This was the first occasion we knew of that someone working for KISS FM had deliberately, rather than accidentally, divulged the station's plans in a way that could have seriously damaged Rodigan's and Westwood's relationships with their current employer, Capital Radio.

On McNamee's instruction, KISS FM head of marketing, Malcolm Cox, issued a two-page memo to everybody involved in KISS FM, which emphasised that "only nominated spokespeople have direct contact with the press" in order "to ensure that KISS FM speaks with one voice." The "KISS FM spokespeople" were listed as: "Gordon McNamee, Rosee Laurence, Grant Goddard and Malcolm Cox." The recent newsletter distributed by Laurence to the station's DJs had similarly emphasised that "KISS FM representatives should not be seen to be contradicting each other."[705]

At the same time, Gary Miele was also proving to be a more direct source of frustration to me. Both he and Malcolm Cox had taken delivery of their £15,000 company cars as soon as they had started work, but I was still awaiting my £10,000 car. Financial director Martin Strivens had asked me to select a car and inform him to arrange its purchase. I had only ever owned one car – a second-hand Datsun Cherry that I had bought in 1977 and run into the ground until it had to be scrapped in 1985. I knew very little about cars and had to buy a car magazine to understand which models were within my price range. I asked Strivens if I could save the station money by buying a second-hand car, but he insisted that it had to be brand new.

One day, walking from my home to the railway station, I noticed a car parked in my road that looked quite suitable. It was a hatchback that would enable me to transport a large amount of radio and recording equipment in the back, should the need arise. I noted down its name, Toyota Corolla, and found that it cost just over £10,000. I asked Strivens if this price was acceptable, but he insisted that it could not be a penny over the specified amount. Over several days, I phoned most of the Toyota dealers in Southeast England, asking if they could sell me the car for under £10,000. I had no luck, but Miele insisted that he could arrange 'a good deal' for me with the garage in Cheltenham where he had purchased his BMW company car. Every week, I would enquire to Miele about the progress with my car and, every week, he would assure me that it would be only a matter of days before it was delivered. In the meantime, I continued to use public transport at my own expense to travel around London for the many appointments I was keeping.

One of these appointments was a second meeting with John Perkins of Independent Radio News [IRN] to finalise details of the KISS FM news service. Perkins showed me a spare studio in his new building in Hammersmith that could be used to present the KISS FM news bulletin which would be sent down a British Telecom landline to the station's studios in Holloway Road. We agreed that IRN would employ two newsreaders, working on a shift system, who would read live news bulletins each hour throughout weekday daytimes and during weekend mornings. IRN would pay the newsreaders' salaries and the cost of the landline as part of the package agreed between KISS FM and its saleshouse, Independent Radio Sales. Listeners would assume that the news bulletins were being broadcast from KISS FM's own studios, and the station would promote the newsreaders as part of its presentation team. All that remained was for IRN to recruit the two staff, train them and start rehearsing bulletins ready for the 1 September launch. I wanted two young and enthusiastic voices with London accents who did not sound like 'professional' newsreaders but fitted in well with the station's DJs. Perkins promised he would start the recruitment process.

In its ongoing battle against a competing radio news service offered by Independent Television News [ITN], IRN had signed contracts with six of the new incremental stations, compared to ITN's seven. IRN was particularly keen to attract London stations because, in the capital, ITN had already snatched Jazz FM, Sunrise Radio, WNK and Choice FM. IRN's John Perkins told Broadcast magazine: "KISS and Melody are the key ones we wanted. They're going to be the two biggest incrementals in the current phase – much bigger than Jazz FM."[706]

KISS FM head of talks, Lyn Champion, was very insistent that IRN should use young newsreaders and she was keen for them to employ staff without the usual radio newsroom experience. John Perkins had given me a cassette tape of some newsreaders he suggested KISS FM could use, but Champion and I rejected them all as too old-sounding, too formal and not vibrant enough to fit in with KISS FM's music programming.

Champion was still only working part-time at KISS FM, whilst finalising her departure from the Pressure music video company in which she had been involved. One day, after Champion had left the KISS FM office, Rosee Laurence whispered conspiratorially to me: "You know, Lyn looks different and I think she might be pregnant." It was true that Champion's wafer thin body was looking slightly heaver than usual, but I had never entertained the idea that it might have been caused by pregnancy. However, the next time she visited the office, Champion told me privately that she was indeed pregnant and that the baby would be due sometime before the end of the year.

When McNamee learnt of Champion's pregnancy, once again he asked me if he should sack Champion and employ someone else to do her job. Once again, I argued that she was the only other management person who had production experience in legal radio. I needed her to be part of the programming department team. I would discuss with Champion the ways in which we could accommodate her pregnancy and the maternity leave she would have to take. McNamee was not happy. He seemed to take it almost as a personal insult that Champion was due to have a baby coincidental with the launch of his radio station. He seemed to believe that, just by being pregnant, Champion would be unable to do her job properly. What kind of personal commitment did he expect his staff to make to KISS FM, particularly when he seemed to treat them as if they could be so easily disposed of or replaced?

I had several long talks with Champion and explained that I would be happy to make any arrangements necessary to keep her as part of the KISS FM team and to keep her in her post as head of talks. She was not yet sure of the baby's due date, since she said the pregnancy had been an accident. We agreed that she would need at least two months of maternity leave and that KISS FM should employ a replacement temporarily during her absence. McNamee and Strivens were still demanding cutbacks to the programming department budget, so Champion and I created an arrangement that would cost the company no more than if Champion had not become pregnant.

Champion agreed that her maternity leave of two months from mid-October would have to be unpaid, and that her temporary replacement would be paid a slightly lower salary whilst she was away. The savings made would be put towards employing the replacement for an overlap period before Champion left, so that person could learn the ropes. Once Champion had returned, another overlap period would ensure that she was fully briefed on what had happened in her absence. The proposal was put to McNamee and Strivens who, after some persuasion, accepted the idea because it did not require additional funds. The deal was agreed and all that remained was for me to learn more precisely when Champion's baby was due, so that her leave could be scheduled far enough in advance.

Although new premises for KISS FM had still not been agreed, I had to forge ahead to recruit the remaining programming department staff that were required. A further job advertisement was published in The Guardian under the same headline: "What would you be prepared to do for a KISS?" This time, I was seeking an administrator to support the whole department, a record librarian and programme assistants to work on the station's music output. Once again, the office was deluged with hundreds of applications and enquiries from all over the UK and abroad. The public interest in KISS FM was proving to be phenomenal, and the enthusiasm of the people who wanted to work for the station was incredible.[707]

I had to keep Tim Westwood and David Rodigan updated on our progress and persuade them that their futures lay with KISS FM, rather than with Capital Radio. I met Westwood at Kettners restaurant again one Monday night, as it had been three months since our last meeting. I updated him on our likely premises and gave him some indication of how the station was going to sound. I asked him to come with me to GDO Studios to record a sample programme to see what he sounded like on daytime radio. Westwood had only presented specialist rap shows on Capital Radio. Now, I needed to hear how he could cope with the regular features of daytime shows such as weather and travel reports, what's on information and station promotions. After our meal, Westwood gave me a ride home in his customised Jeep, which had a huge loudspeaker propped up on the rear seat that was so powerful it vibrated your bodily organs. As we hurtled down the outside lane of the A40 out of London, Westwood cranked up his tape of the debut Ice Cube album, 'AmeriKKKa's Most Wanted.' We had to shout to each other over the din. Westwood seemed genuinely enthused about KISS FM. I was looking forward to working with him.

One of the documents that KISS FM still lacked was an employment contract to offer its presenters. Martin Strivens and Gordon McNamee were under the impression that the station's full-time DJs could be offered the same dreadful contracts that I and the other office staff had been given. I had to explain that it was particularly important to specify in a presenter's contract precisely what they could and could not do on-air. Strivens, McNamee and KISS FM's solicitor (which was Centurion Press' solicitor) had no understanding of these issues, so I was asked to draft a contract that would be suitable for the station's presenters.

The weather in London had turned hot for a brief summer, so I spent the next three weekends sat on the grass in my local park, surrounded by a pile of legal papers I carried there in a holdall. I had several radio station contracts from my previous employment in the industry, and I had acquired several contracts from friends who had been employed in radio. Taking a paragraph from here and a paragraph from there, I drafted a contract that ran to around a dozen pages when typed. It might have looked lengthy, but at least I had ensured that the contract considered all eventualities. It was particularly important not to allow KISS FM DJs to over-expose their own music recordings, as many of them were also producers or artists, or to over-publicise their own club events, so these issues had to be considered in the contract.

Strivens gave my draft document to the company's solicitor, who simply added numbers against the paragraphs and shuffled their order. My work probably saved the station several thousand pounds in legal fees, though I seemed to receive no gratitude from Strivens or McNamee. It was typical of my involvement in the station that many such tasks fell outside my responsibility as head of programming. In many matters, I was the only member of the KISS FM senior team with relevant experience in radio management. I felt that, if I did not offer my expertise, the task at hand might be executed poorly and, inevitably, I would end up picking up the pieces afterwards.

In the end, I felt that it was better for me to offer my services in areas where I had expertise, such as employment contracts and the design of office accommodation. The outcome was that my role had already developed into more of a general manager, in addition to my creative responsibilities as head of programming and my technical responsibilities. McNamee liked to deal with what he saw as the big issues involved in getting the radio station on-air: liaison with the board, the shareholders, the estate agents, the architects, the building contractors. This meant that organisation of the radio aspects of the company were left almost entirely to me.

My biggest challenge was that there were not enough hours in the day to accomplish everything I needed to within the required timescale. I was already working all week and every weekend. I desperately wanted KISS FM to succeed, so I just got on with the necessary work. I had to keep believing that, if the station's re-launch proved successful, I must earn some sort of reward for my endeavours. That was the one thing I wanted and hoped for.

---

[702] Sean King, "Crown And YRN Profits Hit By Advertising Slump", Broadcast, 15 Jun 1990.
"Invicta Slumps", Broadcast, 22 Jun 1990.
Sean King, "US Shareholder To Raise Jazz FM Stake", Broadcast, 22 Jun 1990.
[703] "McDowell Quits Job At Cash-Strapped BCR", Broadcast, 22 Jun 1990.
Bob Tyler, "KFM Management Fired Over 'Play Abba' Furore", Music Week, 16 Jun 1990.
[704] Nick Robinson, "Jazz FM Starts To Tickle The Tills", Music Week, 23 Jun 1990.
[705] memo from Malcolm Cox, KISS FM to all staff, 7 Jun 1990.
"Newsletter no. 2", KISS FM, 1 Jun 1990.
[706] Cameron Balbirnie, "IRN Plans Second Service", Broadcast, 8 Jun 1990.
[707] KISS FM advertisement, The Guardian, 2 Jun 1990.

June 1990.

Gordon McNamee had not convened a meeting of the KISS FM DJs since the one four months earlier that had been staged for the benefit of the documentary film crew. He seemed to be too busy attending endless meetings with many other parties to be bothered with another DJ meeting. In the meantime, I had been interviewing each DJ to discuss what they wanted to do in their shows once the station re-launched, while Rosee Laurence's newsletter had tried to keep them updated about developments within the station.

KISS FM's public relations company, Rogers & Cowan, asked to use some of the station's DJs as part of its publicity campaign. A select group of about ten DJs, hand picked by McNamee as the most likely to approve the station's marketing direction, were invited to an evening meeting. The event, held in the office of the station's advertising agency, BBDO, was the first opportunity for the DJs to see the creative work that would be part of the launch campaign. McNamee chose the venue over the KISS FM office to try and create an air of slight intimidation. The last thing he wanted was for these spokesmen (there were no females) for KISS FM not to support the station's new style of advertising.

The staff from BBDO and Rogers & Cowan explained their plans for the launch that would use TV, cinema and press advertising to bring the station to the public's attention. As McNamee had hoped, most of the DJs went along with the argument that, although some of the publicity might not seem appropriate to the 'old' KISS FM, it was important now to persuade Londoners to tune in and give the station a try. The threat that McNamee articulated was that if, as a team, we did not try our hardest to attract an audience, we might miss our target of one million listeners per week, the station would fail and then we would all be out of a job. This tactic worked well, except with the more opinionated DJs, such as Norman Jay, who objected in the meeting to some of the ways that KISS FM was being described and to the image of the station that was being presented to the public. McNamee endured these criticisms and politely ignored them. In the end, he told the DJs, what we had just seen was the plan of action decided by the station's board. This was exactly what was going to happen. It had already been decided. The station had no choice now.

In recent months, McNamee seemed to have increasingly enjoyed moving in the worlds of advertising and public relations. The staff at BBDO and Rogers & Cowan treated him with a lot of respect, as managing director of a large radio station. He loved their work, they loved treating him like a valued client, and the shareholders were picking up the bill for this mutual admiration. McNamee was having meetings at BBDO at least once a week. There was nothing more he liked to do than to park his Mercedes immediately outside BBDO in a 'no parking' zone, glide into a meeting in a beautifully air-conditioned room, eat the exquisite food that was always laid on for clients, and wait to be called, should the company's receptionist spy a traffic warden walking along the street, handing out parking tickets. This was McNamee's world now. The likes of Norman Jay who, until very recently, had commanded more money and more respect than McNamee in the music industry, were already being left behind. McNamee was streaking ahead of the rest of the KISS FM team and occupying a new position in a whole new world.

Besides, McNamee already had plenty of other projects up his sleeve with which he was keeping busy. Many of them had nothing to do with ensuring that the radio station arrived on-air on time, but they propelled him along with the notion that he must be some kind of media magnate and that KISS FM must already be so successful that he could start diversifying his interests. McNamee met Steve Ripley at CBS Records to discuss a possible compilation album branded with the KISS FM name. He met EMAP Metro, the magazine publishing division of EMAP, to discuss the possibility of a KISS FM magazine. He met David Trott, of the advertising agency Gold Greenless Trott, to discuss KISS FM's possible involvement in the 'Cancel The Third World Debt Campaign.' He met a television production company, Channel X, to discuss the possibility of a regular KISS FM dance music TV show. And he met clothes designer Paul Smith to discuss the possibility of a limited edition KISS FM shirt that he wanted made. These days, McNamee hardly wore anything that was not designed by Paul Smith whereas, a year earlier, he was usually dressed in a baggy jumper and jeans. Smith showed his appreciation by offering McNamee a discount on future purchases.

I had more mundane problems with which I was struggling. KISS FM head of marketing Malcolm Cox had renewed his interest in securing sponsorship for an outside broadcast vehicle, and he was now suggesting a less grand vehicle than his earlier plan. I was asked to draw up a budget for a converted self-drive van, rather than the earlier plan for a caravan unit that would have had to be towed. This task required phone calls to van suppliers, new estimates for equipment costs and more plans to be sketched of what such a vehicle might look like, demonstrating the opportunities it would offer to a sponsor. Once again, eventually Cox found no company that would commit itself to sponsorship before KISS FM arrived on-air, and so these endeavours came to nothing.

Now that the lease for the Holloway Road premises was almost finalised, KISS FM's engineering contractor, Phoenix Communications, had started to determine its staffing needs for the station. It was agreed that two studio engineers would be employed by Phoenix to work solely at KISS FM on a shift system. Phoenix arranged the recruitment and invited me to attend interviews of three suitable candidates. In turn, I invited Lyn Champion to join us because the engineers would be working extensively on the station's speech output. Of the three candidates, one was entirely unsuitable, one had more experience with transmitters than studio work, and another had experience of engineering speech, but not music, programmes. Neither Champion nor I were entirely happy with Phoenix's shortlist, but the company insisted that these were the only three people it had found with relevant experience who would work at the budgeted pay rate.

Champion felt particularly uneasy about having to rely upon contracted staff that, she felt, did not come up to the standard she expected. I had to remind her that she was no longer working in the BBC, and that the contracting arrangement upon which McNamee had insisted was tying our hands. The two engineers would not be KISS FM employees, although they would be under our day-to-day supervision because, ultimately, they reported to Phoenix Communications. I was not convinced that this contracting out arrangement was by any means the best way to organise the radio station, but I had no choice in the matter, particularly as the entire engineering department included in the original business plan had been abolished. We decided, with much reluctance, to accept Phoenix's proposal to employ the best two of the three candidates we had interviewed.

That evening, after these interviews, news arrived at the Blackstock Mews office that the lease had just been signed for 80 Holloway Road. At last, our new home was official! The 8,100 square foot premises were taken on a 25-year lease at an annual rent of £140,000. There was a collective sigh of relief because work could now start on building the station's studios. It was now 15 June 1990. The station was due to start test transmissions on 1 August, less than seven weeks away. The board's original plan had been to finalise the premises by Easter. We were now two months behind schedule. Undoubtedly, it was going to be a very tight squeeze for us to be fully prepared for the launch.[708]

Ever since KISS FM had won its licence, applications had been pouring into the office from DJs wanting jobs. At first, I had stored them in a drawer of my desk. Then, it became two drawers. Soon, I had to transfer them to a large cardboard box. As the station's imminent launch garnered more and more coverage in the press, applications flooded in at an unprecedented rate. Although McNamee had fixed ideas about the presentation team he wanted for the station, I felt a duty to at least listen to the cassettes that these hopefuls had submitted to the station. I set aside an entire day and evening to spend at home, reading several hundred application letters and listening to a similar number of demonstration cassette tapes. Sadly, the majority of them were awful, leaving only a handful worthy of consideration. I put these to one side, hoping there might be a use for them in future. Most applications had been sent by pop music DJs who had no understanding that KISS FM would only be playing black music. As one magazine reported: "KISS have had demo tapes from aspiring presenters from as far away as Radio Gloucester. 'I don't think some of them realised what we are about,' confided my informant. 'They used things like Shakin' Stevens.'"[709]

More urgently, I still had to recruit the remaining DJs that McNamee wanted to poach from other stations. Now that Dave Pearce's appointment had been announced, he was already acting as an excellent spokesperson for KISS FM. He told one magazine that he would be presenting a daily show, "but the time of it is not yet decided. The programme controller will decide after he has heard all the presenters doing dry runs. Then he will fit it in to the best suitable time slot." And Pearce told one newspaper: "What's interesting, from my point of view, is that all the [KISS FM] managers have come up through the same music. It's important, if you're playing a Public Enemy record, that your boss understands why."[710]

I had already taken Pearce to GDO Studios to make a recording of the afternoon drive show for which I was considering him. Now I needed to try out that same programme with Tim Westwood. I met Westwood again for an evening meal at Kettners restaurant and explained to him the detail of the show I wanted him to record at GDO, what the format of the programme would be, and how I wanted it to sound. We arranged a recording date in two weeks' time.

By now, the other DJ from Capital Radio that KISS FM wanted, David Rodigan, had agreed to join the station and I had hand delivered a copy of the employment contract to his agent's office in Swiss Cottage one evening. All that remained now was to agree upon a salary. One lunchtime, McNamee and I met Rodigan at the office of Centurion Press, in order to maintain confidentiality. We were offering a £15,000 salary to each daytime DJ, plus £50 per week for a specialist show. Rodigan explained patiently that the £17,500 we were suggesting was far below what he was earning at Capital Radio and that he would not be able to support his family on those earnings. He was very open about his pay at Capital and explained that, however much he supported the idea of KISS FM, he could not afford to leave Capital for a lower paid job. To my surprise, McNamee agreed to raise Rodigan's salary to £23,000. It was clear that McNamee felt Rodigan was an essential part of his masterplan for KISS FM. All three of us left the meeting satisfied.

I was, however, concerned on two counts. Where was the extra money going to come from to pay for Rodigan's salary, which was now substantially more than the figure in the budget? Secondly, I was worried about the consequences of employing several, supposedly equal, daytime DJs on vastly different salaries. Dave Pearce had already expressed his concern about being paid only £15,000. If Tim Westwood was going to join KISS FM as well, how much would he want? The disparities between different presenters' salaries seemed like a ticking time bomb that might not be important right now, but which could explode at some moment in the future.

The radio show that Dave Pearce had recorded at GDO Studios, as well as serving as a good demonstration tape for my purposes, was also used for some market research I was conducting before the station's launch. McNamee scoffed at the importance of research, but I had insisted that a certain amount be carried out amongst KISS FM's potential audience, prior to the station's launch, to help me determine the finer points of how the station should sound. Fortunately, KISS FM's new head of marketing, Malcolm Cox, was also convinced of the value of market research and agreed to designate some of his departmental budget for this purpose. The station's advertising agency, BBDO, suggested we use a company called Sirius Research which it had successfully contracted for the launch of other consumer products. After meeting the company's staff, I was convinced they could be of more use to me than one of the specialist radio industry research companies. My experience of the latter was that you might pay them merely to produce the answers that they thought you wanted to see, confirming both your suspicions and their affability. This was not what I needed.

I provided Sirius with a comprehensive briefing document about the issues I wished to uncover. For example, were young people already aware of KISS FM, what did they expect to hear on the station, and who were their favourite DJs? Over several meetings, I briefed Sirius about the important decisions I needed to make about how the station would sound when it re-launched. Sirius set up a number of field research groups in different parts of London, where they randomly recruited a group of young people of different ages and varying musical interests. Some of these participants were interviewed in groups, while others were interviewed individually. All of them listened to excerpts of the Dave Pearce programme and were encouraged to pass comment on his style of DJ-ing and the music he played.

On the evening of 21 June, a KISS FM contingent, that included Gordon McNamee, Rosee Laurence, Malcolm Cox, Lyn Champion and me, travelled in a convoy of cars to Hemel Hempstead in Hertfordshire. Sirius had organised one of its research sessions in specially converted premises that enabled us to privately view and hear the group's comments relayed by video from an adjacent room. For me, the evening proved very instructional because the comments about KISS FM were lively and opinionated. For McNamee, the evening seemed to be an opportunity to gorge the mountains of sandwiches and snacks that had been provided for us while we watched and listened to the discussion.

The group of young men had strong opinions about the Dave Pearce tape. Howard said he "did not like it at all" because he "did not like the music." Michael thought it was "good in places" but that "it went on and on and on." Jim said he "did not like the tape" because "it wasn't a particularly good station to listen to." Andy said it was "alright" but "it did not grab my attention at all." Dave thought it sounded "like something you would hear in Top Man shop while you buy your clothes." Martin thought it was "airhead music – brainless disco doodles – wish wash." Alistair said it was "alright" but sounded like "a watered down version of Capital Radio" and that he "would have changed channels." Other comments included: "it was pretty bland" and "sack the DJ – he's got too many words in his mouth, trying to spit them out before the next record." Another said: "the style of the DJ-ing was exactly the same as has been going on for years and years. There's nothing new about the DJ at all. He could have come from anywhere."[711]

KISS FM's mission statement was read to the group. This declared that the station was "a new, exciting radio station for young Londoners, playing the best dance music around in a new style that reflects the sound of the street." One of the group responded: "whoever wrote that – it's very naff, it's crap." Another suggested: "they should find out why they were successful in the first place, as a pirate station, and retain all the good qualities that they had, which were spontaneity, vitality and the fact that they really did care about the music." One person commented: "if it was so popular as a pirate station, why don't they just keep the same format – that seems to be the sensible thing to do." Another added: "they could be the LEGAL pirate station and they wouldn't have to worry about being chucked off the air, but they'd still have that pull that other major stations don't. They wouldn't be competing against Capital [Radio] and all that."[712]

One participant summarised the station's dilemma astutely: "What would probably make it more attractive would be if it were still a pirate, because there's probably an image connected to listening to a pirate station. As soon as KISS FM becomes legal, then probably, in its own way, although it's still trying to be exciting, it is then mainstream ... and it has to conform."[713]

After the meeting, McNamee was very dismissive of the two-hour discussion we had just witnessed. He expressed his view forcefully that the evening had been a waste of time because the young men who had participated were obviously not typical KISS FM listeners. He seemed almost personally insulted by some of the negative comments that had been made about the station and about Dave Pearce's programme. I felt that, increasingly these days, McNamee was surrounded almost entirely by people from KISS FM's saleshouse, its advertising agency, its PR company, its board and its shareholders, all of whom supported the notion that KISS FM was going to be a fantastically successful business enterprise (for them). McNamee was no longer used to hearing dissent voiced about his radio station, since he had so little contact with the general public these days. The voices heard that night – those of real people – came as a bit of a shock to McNamee, so he wanted to dismiss their opinions as irrelevant.

I understood that KISS FM could not possibly achieve its target of one million listeners if it only attracted an audience that was already convinced of the station's worth. To succeed, KISS FM would have to persuade, cajole and interest people in its programming. It would have to persuade them that it was more worthwhile to listen to than its competitors. To only win over the hardcore dance music fanatics would spell the failure of the new KISS FM, since they alone probably did not number one million people. While McNamee wanted to reject the opinions of those people who were not already confirmed fans, I knew that our hardest task ahead was to bring these people around to our point of view by any means possible.

On the other hand, McNamee seemed increasingly to be coming around to the viewpoint that KISS FM could be a direct competitor to pop music stations such as Radio One or Capital Radio. Although these two viewpoints were inconsistent – that KISS FM would appeal only to the converted, but that it would compete directly with pop stations – McNamee and other members of the station's board had become increasingly open about their desire for KISS FM to 'take on' competing pop music radio stations in London.

In an article for the EMAP in-house newspaper, KISS FM director Tim Schoonmaker wrote that the station's "prize is reaching the region's 15 to 34 year olds, a radio market which has remained the exclusive preserve of Capital Radio for nearly twenty years." This perception that KISS FM would become a mainstream radio station was also shared by at least one of its competitors. Joe Douglas, managing director of the North London black community station WNK, responded in the press to a question about the threat of KISS FM's launch: "KISS won't worry me. They'll go for a mainstream audience ... like Capital [Radio]."[714]

The agenda for the re-launch of KISS FM seemed to be shifting from the creation of a successful dance music radio station towards the creation of a money-making machine that would smash Capital Radio's stranglehold over commercial radio listening in London. It seemed as if McNamee was becoming caught up in the 'corporatisation' of KISS FM and was beginning to forget why the pirate station had proved so successful in the first place. Some of the opinions voiced by participants in the focus group had been too close to the truth.

McNamee did not want to listen to people who believed that KISS FM would sell out, who thought that KISS FM should stick more closely to its pirate radio roots or that, if it tried to imitate existing commercial stations, KISS FM would prove a disaster with listeners. Many of those around McNamee were telling him that KISS FM could take on Capital Radio and win. He seemed to have had it with pirate radio. He felt that he had hit the big time now, and he was thoroughly enjoying the ride. How dare the public tell him what to do! What did they know about radio?

---

[708] "A KISS For Islington", Estates Gazette, 30 Jun 1990.
[709] Sarah Kilby, "Radio Daze", Midweek, 12 Jun 1990.
[710] Bob Tyler, "Airwaves", Jocks, Jul 1990.
Simon Hills, "7 Days", Sunday Telegraph, Jul 1990 [exact date unknown].
[711] Sirius Research recording, 21 Jun 1990.
[712] ibid.
[713] ibid.
[714] Tim Schoonmaker, "On The Air!", EMAP, Jul 1990.
Ian Nicolson, "Beat Dis!", Radio & Music, 20 Jun 1990.

June & July 1990.

My world was becoming more and more dominated by paperwork relating to KISS FM's impending launch. Piles of papers were all over my desk, some needing reading, some needing replies, and others were internal documents about one issue or another that had yet to be determined. I had asked the station's advertising agency, BBDO, to lend me copies of any research they had in their library concerning the youth market. The result was another pile of documents, more than a foot high, that addressed every aspect imaginable of young people's tastes and interests. I was determined to understand as much as I could about KISS FM's target audience before the station's launch. I took these reports home and spent the next few weekends sitting outdoors in the brief British summer, consuming them avidly to learn what I should include in KISS FM's programmes to attract young people's attentions.

Additionally, I still had hundreds of job applications to sort through for the remaining vacancies in the programming department, though there was never enough time during my day in the office to study them carefully. Inevitably, I had to take these papers home as well. My evenings became filled with scanning hundreds of CVs, listening to cassette tapes of applicants' radio work, and writing notes about each person's suitability for posts in the station. I still had no administrative help, so all the replies, correspondence and filing had to be organised by me in what little spare time remained.

Now that KISS FM had announced that DJ Dave Pearce would be presenting a daytime show, and now that the defection of David Rodigan from Capital Radio was only waiting for him to return the contract, it was time to determine the remainder of the daytime programme line-up. Although negotiations with Tim Westwood about his move from Capital to KISS FM were still in their early stages, I knew that internal candidates would still be needed to fill one or more remaining slots. I called a meeting of those KISS FM DJs who had expressed an interest to me in becoming a full-time daytime DJ, rather than presenting one show per week on a freelance basis. Amongst them were Graham Gold and Tony Monson, to whom I knew Gordon McNamee had already made promises of specific daytime shows. However, I needed to treat everyone fairly, because the rest of the DJs had no knowledge of Gold and Monson's privileged positions.

The meeting was held on a Monday evening at BBDO's office and included around ten DJs. I explained to them that KISS FM was to have five weekday daytime shows, and that Dave Pearce was the only person to have signed a contract to host one of them. I also explained that the daytime shows, unlike the specialist shows, would have to be heavily formatted to ensure that KISS FM maintained a consistent sound. These shows would not be an opportunity for individual DJs to give exposure to their favourite records of the moment. The objective was to communicate a KISS FM 'feel' to the audience, not the personal tastes of each DJ, which would be the province of evening and weekend specialist music shows. I announced that each daytime hour would comprise around twelve records, ten of which would be selected from KISS FM playlists of current hits and oldies. A daytime DJ would be able to choose the remaining two records per hour, though these would still have to fit within the overall sound of the station and could not be anything too off-the-wall or inappropriate for daytime radio.

My announcement was greeted with uproar from the assembled DJs. Ever since KISS FM had announced its intention to apply for a licence, McNamee and Lindsay Wesker had stated that the station's daytime programmes would comprise fifty per cent of records selected from the playlist, with the remaining fifty per cent chosen by the DJ. These pronouncements had been made time and time again at DJ meetings, in KISS FM's newsletters and in interviews in the press. Now, I was telling them that this was not to be the case. Surely, they asked, if the DJs did not choose their own records, KISS FM would end up sounding no different than Radio One or Capital Radio?

I answered by explaining that it was the particular records that were included in a playlist that made the difference. KISS FM would certainly not be including pop records on its playlist, though it would need to include hit dance music tracks that listeners would hear throughout the day in every show. This could only be achieved by organising a playlist. There was simply no room in daytime radio to allow every DJ to satisfy their own indulgences. Each daytime DJ would HAVE TO play the records on the KISS FM playlist and endorse them on-air, whether they personally felt a particular record was excellent or terrible. Daytime radio was not the place to air DJs' personal prejudices about particular records or musical styles. Every daytime programme would have to be representative of the broad range of dance music tastes, including soul, reggae, rap, house, garage, etc.

The DJs at the meeting were obviously unhappy about this new revelation concerning the station's daytime music policy. I expressed sympathy with their feeling that they had repeatedly been promised one thing, and now were being told it would be something quite different. However, this was not my fault. Statements had been made in the past by McNamee and Wesker, without them having had experience of how commercial radio operated to attract listeners and revenues. If I were a DJ, I would love to be able to play my own favourite records every day of the week, but that was not how a radio station could become successful during weekday daytimes. KISS FM, like other stations, needed to attract listeners who would stay tuned during several shows throughout each day. That could only be achieved by providing the audience with a consistent daytime sound.

Despite the evident concerns over this issue, I went on to explain that I would be inviting each of the DJs present to record a fake KISS FM daytime show at GDO Studios to hear what they might sound like. Before each booking, I would brief each presenter about the format and give them the records they would play. They would be instructed at what time to play advertisements, when to read out travel and weather information, what competitions to use in their show, and the other elements that go to make up a regular daytime show. I would let them have several hours on their own to practice before the recording, as I realised that several of those around the table had never used a professional radio studio, having only worked in pirate radio. Then, I would listen to the results before McNamee and I decided who was best equipped for a daytime programme, and which time most suited each presenter. Not everyone at the meeting would win, but this seemed like the fairest way to assess each person's talent.

The meeting ended at ten o'clock with the DJs still not pleased about my apparent desire to take away their creative input from the daytime programming. I was repentant, but unrepentant. I knew that it would be me, as the only person on the KISS FM launch team with previous commercial radio experience, who was going to be held responsible for the station's success or failure with listeners. I could not afford to leave an element as important as the station's daytime programmes to chance. Those shows would be the 'shop window' of the station and would inevitably be judged far more harshly than the more specialist evening and weekend shows. My experience at Metro Radio, a decade earlier, had demonstrated that a carefully implemented playlist system made all the difference between a successful radio station and an unsuccessful one.

The next day, Tuesday 26 June 1990, was spent interviewing candidates for three researcher posts to work on the station's speech output. The shortlist included the three people – Lisa I'Anson, Tony Farsides and Eko Eshun – who had worked on the station's speech programmes in its pirate days, and whom McNamee had made clear he felt to be the most appropriate applicants for the jobs. I had insisted that the posts must be advertised and recruited in a competitive manner, which was why head of talks Lyn Champion and I spent a whole day interviewing candidates. By the end, it was obvious that several of the external applicants had extensive and relevant experience. I'Anson, Farsides and Eshun had no radio experience before working for KISS FM, where they had used domestic cassette machines to produce their programmes. Like the DJs, none of them had worked in a professional radio studio. I felt that Champion and I should objectively choose the best candidates for these jobs because we were being required by the board to attract one million listeners per week. Champion was more reticent and seemed acutely aware of McNamee's intention to fill the posts with people to whom he had already made promises. It had been an exhausting day, so we agreed to postpone the decision to a later date.

On Wednesday evening, McNamee held a meeting of the station's entire staff at the future KISS FM premises in Holloway Road. Building work had not yet been completed, so that each floor of the place seemed incredibly cavernous and bare. McNamee explained to the large group where each of the offices would be built and who would occupy each floor. This was the first opportunity for the DJs to see the premises. There was no doubt that they were suitably impressed by the sheer scale of the building. The evening had the desired effect of leaving the whole KISS FM team enthused and inspired. After what had seemed like months and months of anticipation, the station at last had a new home, much grander than anything of which we had dreamed. McNamee announced that the 80 Holloway Road office would be named 'KISS House,' a name that I had invented in jest in the office as a reference to the station's creeping 'corporatisation.' McNamee had quickly adopted it, without a hint of the irony I had intended.

The following day, McNamee left for a week's holiday abroad, accompanied by his wife. I used the rest of the week to finalise the details with Independent Radio News of the customised news service it would provide, and to brief the station's aspiring daytime DJs as to what they should do for their audition shows. Also, I was busy writing, producing and collating several hundred copies of a KISS FM information pack that I wanted to take to the annual Radio Festival event, to be held in Glasgow the following week. McNamee had approved the funds for Lyn Champion and me to attend as ambassadors of KISS FM. With the station launching in only two months time, everyone seemed to want to know more about what it would sound like and what it would be doing. The Radio Festival provided an ideal opportunity to raise KISS FM's profile within the radio industry and to generate some publicity for the station's innovative programming.

The Radio Festival started on Monday night, but I already had meetings scheduled in London across the whole day, so McNamee agreed that KISS FM would pay for Champion and me to fly to Glasgow from London's Heathrow Airport on Monday night. Stupidly, I had crammed all the information packs into one very large cardboard box that was almost too heavy to move. At the end of the day, Champion and I caught a taxi to Finsbury Park Underground station, and then negotiated our way across London, with me dragging both a suitcase and the huge box, up and down escalators and onto tube trains. By now, Champion was obviously pregnant and there was no way that she could help. The plane had only a handful of people aboard, which made the journey very enjoyable, and more so as it was the first occasion I had caught an internal UK flight. No passports or customs checks to worry about! When we arrived at the Hospitality Inn in Glasgow, there were no standard rooms available, so Champion and I had to take two luxury rooms with huge beds and bathrooms that were big enough to house an entire family.

The next morning, I got up early and dragged the overweight box from the hotel and along the streets to the Festival venue. In preparation for the opening of the event, Champion and I stood outside the entrance door and handed each of the 350 delegates a copy of the information pack. There was no doubt that, over the next two days, the Festival was buzzing with people who were keen to find out more about KISS FM. All the preparation work had been worthwhile and I felt that I had achieved the aim of putting the station firmly on the map in the minds of the rest of the radio industry. Between conference sessions, I was approached by a journalist working on the weekly BBC Radio Four show about radio, The Radio Programme, to explain more about KISS FM's programming. I willingly obliged.

Champion and I returned to London the following evening on a flight that, once again, carried only a handful of people. An important football match was taking place that night, so the captain gave regular updates of the score over the aircraft's public address system. I talked to Champion further about the appointment of the three researchers in her talks department. I told her that, whoever she decided to appoint to the jobs, I would support her decision, even in the face of opposition from McNamee. She still seemed undecided as to whether to appoint the three pirate radio staff for whom McNamee had been rooting, or whether to appoint the three best people for the job.

The next morning, I met McNamee (who had just returned from his holiday) at the Blackstock Mews office to discuss this problem. He was adamant that he had promised the three, ex-pirate radio staff full-time jobs within the station. I explained to him that the task I faced – to attract one million listeners to KISS FM within the first year – was difficult enough as it was, without being forced to employ inexperienced staff in some of the key jobs. KISS FM was already committed to employing a DJ team, almost none of whom had ever seen the inside of a professional radio studio. The station could not afford to handicap itself further by wilfully taking on people who might not be up to the tasks at hand. The meeting ended cordially, but without agreement. McNamee said he would talk to Champion on his own, which I felt might mean he would try bullying her into submission. I told him, as I had already told Champion, that I felt she needed the best people for the job. We left it at that.

The next job appointment I needed to make was the station's record librarian, who would be supervised by KISS FM's head of music, Lindsay Wesker. Since taking over the editorship of Free! magazine from me the previous year, Wesker had had little involvement in the re-launch of KISS FM. He seemed almost obsessed with the monthly magazine, spending many late nights in the ground floor office writing articles and reviewing records. Since Wesker had no prior commercial radio experience to contribute, I had not been particularly worried by his absence. However, the person appointed as record librarian would report to Wesker, which is why it was vital for him to be involved in their selection. I loaned Wesker a large folder of all the applications I had received for this job and I asked his opinion of which might be the most suitable to interview.

The next day, Wesker returned the folder to me, having marked the handful of candidates he felt were most suitable. I looked through his selection and was puzzled by his choices. I asked him why he had chosen those particular applicants, none of whom had previous library experience. He explained that there were two qualities he had been looking for – the candidates had to demonstrate knowledge of dance music, and they had to be female. At first, I thought he was joking, but I quickly discovered that he was not. Wesker explained to me his theory that a record librarian had to be a woman, and stated that he was not interested in working with someone who was not a proven expert in dance music. I was shocked that Wesker could be so irrational in choosing a suitable person for the job. His method of appointing staff was proving to be as bizarre as that of McNamee.

I patiently explained to Wesker that his own post, as KISS FM's head of music, was to be the station's expert in dance music. We were now looking to appoint a librarian who would complement his skills. Did Wesker know anything about organising a record library? No. Had he ever worked in, or visited, a radio station record library? No, he had not. So, what we needed was someone who could apply their librarian skills to KISS FM. Yes, it was important that we appoint someone who had sympathy with dance music. However, if we were to select a dance music expert, all he or she might want to do was to listen to records or discuss music all day. KISS FM needed someone who was efficient, organised, and had proven librarian skills.

Wesker bowed to my arguments in the end. I searched the application forms and selected a shortlist of seven candidates, none of whom had been on Wesker's shortlist, and the majority of whom turned out to be male. Wesker and I spent an entire day interviewing these people and, in the end, decided to appoint a young man, Alexander Donelly, who had previously worked in the database section of the MCPS rights organisation. I was pleased to have found someone I believed would do the job well, but chastened by Wesker's preferred system for making the appointment. If he could be so obtuse in choosing the one person who would be working in his department, what would he be like dealing with other tasks within his KISS FM responsibilities?

That Sunday, BBC Radio Four had broadcast a special edition of the Radio Programme that focused entirely on The Radio Festival in Glasgow. The show's presenter, Laurie Taylor, reported: "Looking around, there seemed to be slightly less animation among the delegates this year than last year. Perhaps it was because there aren't quite so many new radio stations on offer this year. The only sign of pizzazz or showmanship that I've seen so far comes from KISS FM, the new London black/dance music station which is coming on-air in September. They've been busy handing out brochures of the new station, featuring pictures of the pirate DJs who are going to find themselves now legitimately re-employed, and boasting about their completely new, young sound."[715]

Taylor went on to interview Simon Bates, a DJ on BBC Radio One, and asked him if he thought KISS FM was going to make a large impact on London's radio listeners. Bates replied: "KISS FM will be swings and roundabouts. It will go for success and then, when it doesn't get it, it will panic, go into retrenchment, then come back again with a slightly different format. It will be one of those oscillating stations that you have so often in Australia and Canada and in America. I wish them luck. I think their success is a lot more questionable than they imagine it is. It sounds brusque and sounds dismissive, and I don't mean it to be, [but] I think it will be popular with Time Out [magazine]. I suspect that the listeners will be hard coming."[716]

Then, the programme cut to my response to a question I had answered about whether KISS FM would be a failure in London and would be sacking staff after its first six months on-air. I replied: "If you look at the pop charts these days, you'll see that the type of music we're playing – dance music – currently constitutes about half of the top seventy-five [singles]. Dance music generally is a very popular music form amongst young people, and that's why we firmly believe that our specific music format will succeed in London." I was asked about the use of the station's former pirate status in the publicity I had been distributing at the Festival, to which I replied: "KISS FM, as a pirate station, was very successful. It was very much the support and audience we had from being unlicensed that enabled us to campaign and then succeed in getting the licence that we've got now. An Evening Standard readers' poll in 1988 voted us second most popular radio station in London. So, there is no way in which we want to try and deflect from the history of the station as it was. That's a very, very important part of what KISS FM will be when it comes back on in September."[717]

This was the only part of the half-hour programme that mentioned KISS FM. I felt particularly pleased that Laurie Taylor had highlighted my work handing out brochures for the station. I had wanted to create a positive impression in advance of KISS FM's launch and it felt as if this objective had definitely been achieved.

The next day, in the KISS FM office, I was very surprised to find that Gordon McNamee was not at all pleased with my contribution to the Radio Four programme. He felt that I should not have emphasised KISS FM's pirate history so much, and that I should have responded more directly to Bates' criticism. I explained that I had not heard Bates' opinions until the programme was broadcast. Although the programme running order had been edited so that I followed Bates' words, I had been interviewed on my own at the Festival and had not even seen Bates at the event. McNamee did not seem convinced.

Later that day, I was even more surprised to receive a phone call at the office from Keith McDowall, the KISS FM chairman. McDowall had never had regular contact with me, so I was astonished to learn that he too was calling to complain about my contribution to the Radio Four programme. He too expressed unhappiness about my replies to Simon Bates' criticisms of KISS FM. I explained once again that I had not been party to Bates' comments when I was interviewed. With his extensive experience in public relations, surely McDowall must realise that radio and television programme producers piece together different interviews to fit their purposes. In Glasgow, I had been asked specific questions, to which I gave specific answers. Whatever BBC Radio did with the results was out of my hands. McDowall still seemed very unhappy about the whole business.

I was shocked by this incident. Working entirely on my own initiative, I had organised a KISS FM presence at the Radio Festival and had succeeded in blitzing the event with the station's publicity. For this achievement, not only had I received no thanks but, instead, I was being criticised for something that a BBC Radio One DJ had said about a future competitor. I could only presume that McNamee must have been jealous of the fact that I had been KISS FM's spokesman in Glasgow, whilst he had been abroad on holiday.

I was even more appalled that McNamee should have arranged for McDowall to barrack me. Since the station had won its licence the previous December, McNamee had kept me (and the rest of the office staff) as far away as possible from KISS FM board members. For the first time, I had an inkling that this incident might be something that McNamee was using to tarnish my name at board level. The phone call from McDowall had been my first contact with the chairman for months. Why had he been so exercised about such a minor incident in which, I still felt, I had done nothing wrong whatsoever?

I knew that, in future, I would have to be very careful about my visible role in re-launching KISS FM. McNamee wanted to be seen publicly as the person responsible for the station's programming. He would be quite happy for the rest of the world not even to be aware of my existence. Although this situation was entirely unfair, if it avoided further conflict with McNamee and the board, I felt I had little choice but to bow to his inflated ego.

All I could hold on to was the knowledge that, if KISS FM's programming proved successful with listeners, I had been largely responsible for creating that success. Regardless of whether McNamee would let me speak to the media, I was determined to press on with making the station's launch, in less than two months' time, a huge success. McNamee was becoming more and more distant. If this is what was occupying his days, I would leave him to it. I knew that I had far more pressing matters to resolve.

---

[715] The Radio Programme, BBC Radio Four, 8 Jul 1990.
[716] ibid.
[717] ibid.

July 1990.

At seven o'clock in the morning on Monday 9 July 1990, Melody Radio launched in London with the words: "Good morning. This is James Hanson introducing you to London's first easy listening music station on behalf of the owners, the shareholders of Hanson plc and the staff of Melody Radio. We will be bringing you the best of melody, twenty-four hours a day, seven days a week." Melody had been awarded its FM licence by the Independent Broadcasting Authority [IBA] at the same time as KISS FM, the previous December. That now left KISS FM as the one remaining incremental radio station to launch on-air in the capital.[718]

Much to KISS FM's distress, horror stories continued to arrive from new stations that had launched recently in other parts of the country. At Belfast Community Radio, it was now being reported that managing director John McDowell had resigned after the station's board had passed a vote of no confidence in him for his handling of the dismissal of programme controller Mike Gaston. The station's commercial manager, George Lamour, resigned three weeks later. Bradford City Radio had attracted only £15,000 of advertising revenues in its first six months on-air and was effectively taken over by the London Asian station, Sunrise Radio. Bristol black community station For The People had used up its £210,000 launch fund, after only three months on-air, and was now appealing to its investors for a further £250,000 to see it through the next six months.[719]

At KFM in Stockport, new co-owners EMAP Radio and Signal Radio announced plans to "change the station's original programming policy," a move that drew much criticism from the radio trade press. At Manchester station Sunset Radio, managing director Mike Shaft finally decided to throw in the towel and resign, but not without criticising the IBA for its regulation of the new incremental stations. He said: "If you are going to have specifically targeted stations, why let them do other things? There is no control from the IBA."[720]

Meanwhile, KISS FM's public relations company, Rogers & Cowan, countered the launch of Melody Radio with a press release the same day, entitled 'It Started With A KISS.' Five pages of gushing prose credited Gordon McNamee alone with having founded the station, having won its licence application and having launched Free! magazine. An explanation of the station's ownership structure noted that forty per cent of the company's shares were "split between the management team, with a number as yet unsold." This was a reference to the tranche of shares that had been promised to staff involved in the licence application, but which had never been issued to me. Nobody from the original radio station team, other than McNamee, warranted a mention in the press release. Increasingly, the public accounts of KISS FM's seemingly benevolent ownership structure held less and less truth.[721]

Further fictions emerged in the press when KISS FM head of music Lindsay Wesker discussed the station's music policy with a journalist from the weekly trade magazine, Music Week. The resulting article noted that "Programme Controller Grant Goddard has planned KISS's daytime programming around two three-minute blocks of advertising per hour, allowing half-hour sweeps of records or mixes to be played between quarter-past and quarter-to the hour." This was completely untrue. Wesker had spoken to the press without any prior discussion with me. According to the internal memo issued some months earlier, Wesker was not even a designated spokesperson for the station.[722]

In fact, my plans for the daytime output involved four commercial breaks each hour, allowing DJs to play three records in a row at most, but not the half-hour sweeps to which the article referred. Another aspect of the article that horrified me was Wesker's assertion that "guest artists" from the music industry would be invited to join a panel of people who would meet each week to select the station's playlist. The Music Week article was even headlined 'Artists To Take A Hand In KISS FM's No-Hype Playlist.' The notion was clearly preposterous and must have made KISS FM a laughing stock within the radio industry. The most important tool over which a radio station has control is its music playlist, whose every record determines the station's sound. Why would a station ever turn that power over to a complete outsider?[723]

I decided that it was time to have a talk with Wesker about the methods used to determine the station's music playlist. I showed him the 'clocks' I had carefully drawn up for every hour of each daytime show. The clock told the DJ which record to play at a particular time, when to broadcast the advertisements, when to read the travel news, and the like. There were three categories of record on the KISS FM playlist: new releases that KISS FM predicted would be hits, records that were already hits, and current dance records that were not hits but sounded good on the radio. The list of records on these three playlists would be re-assessed each week.

Wesker discussed his idea of a playlist panel with me. I explained why the idea of inviting 'guest artists' to participate was a complete no-no. Instead, Wesker said he wanted to call a meeting each week of representative people from within the station, who would listen carefully to every new dance record released that week and decide which were the most appropriate for the KISS FM playlist. I told him that the idea sounded fine in principle, but would never work in practice. I had seen the notion of a 'playlist committee' disintegrate at other stations where I had worked. At Newcastle's Metro Radio, we had pretended to record companies that playlist decisions were made by a committee. However, none of the DJs had shown much interest in the process, so it had been left to me to make all the decisions, and then to seek approval each week from my boss.

Wesker argued that KISS FM DJs were different, that they were passionate about music, and that they would relish the prospect of helping to choose the station's playlist each week. I responded that, however interested DJs might be initially, they would quickly have better things to do. Anyway, the playlist was not intended to be the sum product of a few individuals' favourite records. The playlist was a tool of the radio station that had to be used very carefully to make KISS FM's daytime output sound appropriate and appealing to its audience. This was Wesker's main responsibility. He could not devolve the decision to others within the station. He argued forcibly that I was wrong, that a weekly playlist panel would work for KISS FM, and that he intended to chair the meeting each week. I told him that I would not be at all surprised if such an arrangement collapsed after only a few weeks on-air. I had seen such idealism before and I knew that it would not work.

I sensed that Wesker's inexperience in commercial radio might prove a costly barrier to making the station successful. Wesker would have to grasp the concept that the playlist was his responsibility to objectively update each week. It was not a list of records that he or anyone else within the station might want to hear on the radio themselves. It needed to be full of records that KISS FM listeners wanted to hear on the radio, regardless of whether Wesker liked those records or not. KISS FM's future success depended not upon preaching to people, but upon determining what THEY wanted to hear and satisfying that need, however uneducated or philistine their tastes might appear to some.

This issue raised its head again the very next day when KISS FM DJ Tony Monson asked me if he could come to the office for an early morning meeting. He told me that he had been thinking about the recent briefing I had given to potential daytime DJs, and he had decided to drop out of the competition. He explained that he had always played exactly the records he wanted to in his shows for both pirate and legal radio stations. He said that he could not face the prospect of having to play records, day after day, that were dictated to him by a station playlist. I sympathised with his viewpoint, but explained again that the use of playlists during daytime shows was the only way I could ensure that KISS FM's output remained consistent for its audience. I asked that, if he was so certain he did not want to host a daily show, would he consider presenting the weekend breakfast shows, where I could guarantee him a free hand. Obviously, this would only be a part-time job, compared to the full-time post of a daytime DJ, but it was the most prestigious and important time slot outside of the weekday schedule. He accepted the offer and I respected him enormously for the difficult decision he had made.

Monson had been promised a daytime show by McNamee long ago, so his withdrawal greatly impacted the proposed KISS FM programme schedule. For the five daytime shows, I now had: Graham Gold, who had been promised the breakfast show by McNamee; Dave Pearce, whose appointment had already been announced; David Rodigan, who was about to sign his contract and leave Capital Radio; and Tim Westwood, with whom I was still in negotiation to leave Capital Radio. This left only one empty space for an internal candidate. Undoubtedly, the loyal KISS FM DJs would not be pleased to discover that only one of their number would be promoted to a daytime full-time job, but this outcome had been McNamee's doing. If Monson had not dropped out, the situation would have been impossible. Sadly, Monson was one of very few people in the original KISS FM DJ team with legitimate radio experience, and he was widely recognised as a very able radio DJ. I was both disappointed to lose Monson and, at the same time, relieved that there was now one space during daytime for an internal candidate.

That evening, I met Tim Westwood once again at Kettners restaurant to brief him about the details of the fake KISS FM drivetime show we were going to produce at GDO Studios the following afternoon. Capital Radio would have sacked Westwood immediately if they knew he was contemplating leaving the station, so I had to book him into GDO under a pseudonym and emphasise to the staff there that no-one was to breathe a word about his presence. The three-hour recording session went well and, by the end of it, I was convinced that Westwood would make an ideal drivetime DJ for KISS FM's weekday programme schedule.

I had arrived at the GDO Studios after having spent the whole day ensconced in advertising agency BBDO's office, attending a de-briefing session about the results of the audience research that I had commissioned from Sirius Research. I was very satisfied with the work they had done and I endorsed almost all of their recommendations. Many echoed the opinions voiced by respondents in the focus group session that had been organised in Hemel Hempstead the previous month.

The main recommendations of Sirius Research were:

- "KISS FM need to focus on retaining the best of their old identity, rather than emulating Capital Radio. People wanted KISS to be a 'legalised pirate' – young, brave, real, sexy, stimulating.
- KISS FM DJs need to be individuals in their own right, as well as distinctive in style from Capital/Radio One DJs. Maybe there should be a KISS FM style of presentation.
- KISS FM need to sound distinctive. The music should span the whole range of dance music and be identifiable as KISS FM.
- To avoid disappointment/rejection, KISS should flag the fact that weekends/evenings is [sic] the same format as before [when a pirate], but that daytime is different.
- The daytime positioning needs to be more single-minded and punchy.
- There is a need for broadest appeal at breakfast time but, throughout the day, KISS can afford to become more radical. Daytime programming should not be homogenous throughout the day. Opportunity for variety.
- In IMAGE terms, KISS should strive to retain the rebelliousness/excitement of their pirate roots."[724]

The barrier I faced in implementing these recommendations were the forces within the embryonic radio station that did not want KISS FM to sound radical and different. Instead, they wanted it to become a competitor to Capital Radio by playing as much pop music as possible in as similar a style to legitimate radio as possible. McNamee endured the research de-briefing session, but still demonstrated little faith in the value of the work or the accuracy of its findings. Because he showed such little interest in taking these recommendations to heart, it was left to me to try and implement them as far as I could within the station's programming.

McNamee was pre-occupied with another swingeing round of budget cuts that he and financial director Martin Strivens were imposing upon the programming and engineering departments of the station. The expansion of the sales and marketing departments, following the appointments of Gary Miele and Malcolm Cox respectively, was necessitating further cutbacks elsewhere, as I had anticipated. The station's technical needs had to reduced, with McNamee and Strivens insisting that the studio mixing desks be downgraded from MBI to Soundcraft, the cheapest brand available. In the studios, the CD players with professional specifications had to be downgraded to domestic machines of the kind that could be bought in a hi-fi shop.

In other changes, McNamee insisted upon cuts to the budget for building the studios within the Holloway Road premises and suggested removing the external windows. I resisted this change as strongly as possible. I had spent many hours working in radio station studios and, without any means of visual contact with the outside world, it can feel like working in a badly lit prison cell if there is no source of natural light. Eventually, I managed to gain a concession on this issue. The windows would be retained but were to be reduced in size. On the other points, the cuts were made despite my opinion that they were a false economy because buying cheaper equipment meant that it was more likely to go wrong and need repairs.

McNamee also insisted upon cuts in the staffing of the programming department. In Lyn Champion's talks section, the £20,000 budget for freelance reporters was to be axed, and three producer posts costing £15,000 each were to be removed. Champion's entire talks section would now consist of only herself and three researcher/reporters. Elsewhere in the programming department, McNamee insisted that the music royalties administrator, at £11,500, would have to go. Champion and I were both furious about these latest cutbacks, particularly at such a late stage in the station's launch plans. Was it coincidence that the only three remaining posts in the talks section would neatly fit the three people from KISS FM's pirate days to whom McNamee had already promised jobs?

Champion and I had a succession of very fraught meetings with McNamee to try and make him understand that a new radio station could not produce good speech programming out of thin air. On the one hand, he and other board members were espousing the idea that KISS FM would give Capital Radio a run for its money. On the other hand, he was substantially reducing the available staff to produce the programmes. The only concession we wrung from McNamee was that two of the producer posts, instead of being axed completely, would be reconsidered once the station was on-air. Following these cuts, Champion and I told McNamee that the daily magazine show, 'The Word,' would have to be reduced from twice a day to once a day, broadcast at seven o'clock in the evening, and its length would have to be reduced from half an hour to fifteen minutes. McNamee resisted these changes until Champion made it plain that she was on the verge of quitting KISS FM if he continued to ignore her recommendations. The outcome was that the budget cuts were implemented and the station's commitment to speech programming was reduced substantially.

I had already arranged for the five short-listed candidates for the producer posts to be interviewed the next day, so Champion and I went ahead with the process and had to hide our embarrassment at telling the candidates that these appointments had now had to be postponed until the station was on-air. The interviews proved to be particularly frustrating because three candidates were very strong. They were George Ergatoudis, who BBC Radio One's head of music, Roger Lewis, had recommended to me earlier in the year; Richard Hopkins, who was working at the North London black community station WNK; and Lorna Clarke, who had worked for BBC Radio London. KISS FM desperately needed experienced radio people such as these to be involved in its launch because Champion and I were still the only full-time staff in the programming department with professional radio experience. It would have been so useful for the station to hire these three skilled candidates, but McNamee was adamant that these cuts had to be made.

After several weeks of indecision, I needed Champion to make a firm choice about the successful candidates for the three researcher posts. In the end, she bowed to pressure and decided to select the three staff from KISS FM's pirate days to whom McNamee had promised the jobs. One of the three, Eko Eshun, subsequently contacted Champion to tell her he was no longer interested in the post because he felt that the £10,000 salary was insufficient. As a result, Champion's team ended up comprising Lisa I'Anson and Tony Farsides from KISS FM's pirate days, along with Sonia Fraser, who had worked with Dave Pearce at BBC Radio London. Fraser had far more radio experience than the other two, and I wondered if

Champion might eventually regret having given in to McNamee. To celebrate the new appointments and to get to know each other, Champion and I invited the three new staff for lunch at the Italian restaurant just around the corner from the Blackstock Mews office.

The following week, I had the task of interviewing candidates for the five programme assistant posts, three of whom would work on the station's daytime programmes and the remainder on the evening and weekend output. The job advertisement placed in The Guardian had produced more applicants for these posts than all the other vacancies added together, maybe because these positions were a good entry point to the radio industry as they required only minimal experience. I had whittled down the applications from many hundred to around a dozen people I thought were worth interviewing. Many applicants had written bizarre letters to try and attract my attention. One woman wrote that she would do literally anything to work for KISS FM and, as if to emphasise her promise, had surrounded her message with impressions of her lipstick-covered lips. Another woman wrote her letter in the form of a spiral that, like a record, worked its way from the outside edge towards the middle of the page. Although ingenious, such attempts to attract my attention did not compensate for an application that was straightforward and easy to read.

I interviewed the short-listed candidates over two days during some of the hottest summer weather. The Blackstock Mews office had become very overcrowded and noisy, following head of sales Gary Miele's appointment of two group heads and several sales staff, whom he was busy training. Gordon Drummond had started work as the station's sponsorship manager in the marketing department, and Lyn Champion and her talks team were planning their programmes. There was no space left in the office to use for interviews, so I had to set up two chairs facing each other outside in the Mews. I proceeded to interview candidates while cars and pedestrians passed by, probably wondering what on earth I was doing. In one sense, it was a relevant, gruelling test for the applicants because I knew that they would need to be able to cope with working inside a very busy, open plan radio station office that could be noisy and distracting.

Sitting in the sunshine over two days proved enjoyable for me, although some of the interviewees seemed rather flummoxed by the unorthodox interview environment. While several of the candidates seemed eminently suitable for the programme assistant posts, there was one young woman who arrived wearing the shortest skirt and a most plunging neckline, who excitedly told me she wanted the job because she was dying to meet lots of stars in the pop music industry. Needless to say, she was not one of the people I thought would be good for the job.

The deadline for KISS FM's re-launch was a little over a month away now. It started to seem as if the plans that had been in preparation for more than a year were coming to fruition. With so many new people being recruited, KISS FM finally seemed on its way to becoming a fully fledged radio station, rather than just a crazy idea that we had talked about in the office for so many months. Nowadays, time was running away with us and it always seemed as if there were far too many different things to accomplish. It was hard to believe: KISS FM's re-launch as a legal radio station was only weeks away.

---

[718] author's recording, 9 Jul 1990.

[719] Julian Clover, "McDowell Walks Plank After BCR Mutiny", Radio & Music, 20 Jun 1990.
"BCR Chief Quits", Broadcast, 6 Jul 1990.
"Lit And Sunrise To The Rescue At Struggling BCR", Radio & Music, 6 Jun 1990.
Sean King, "Storm Clouds Gathering Over Bristol's Ex-Pirate", Broadcast, 27 Jul 1990.
[720] "New KFM Team Promises Major Policy Changes", Radio & Music, 20 Jun 1990.
Stu Lambert, "Fear Is In The Air", Music Week, 21 Jul 1990.
"Shaft Outburst At IBA", Broadcast, 13 Jul 1990.
[721] "It Started With A KISS", Rogers & Cowan/KISS FM press release, 9 Jul 1990.
[722] Bob Tyler, "Artists To Take A Hand In KISS FM's No-Hype Playlist", Music Week, 7 Jul 1990.
[723] ibid.
[724] "Understanding Radio Listening In Relation To KISS FM – Debrief Notes", Sirius Research, Jul 1990.

July 1990.

Lyn Champion was still far from happy about the extent of the most recent cuts that had been imposed upon her talks department. She wrote long memos to Gordon McNamee and to me, outlining how difficult it would be for KISS FM to fulfil the promises that had been made in its licence application about the extent of speech programming included in the station's output. I met privately with Champion at the Blackstock Mews office on a Saturday morning to try and calm the situation. I did not tell her how close McNamee had been to sacking her on several occasions for no good reason. If she persisted with her complaints, I was worried that McNamee might simply override any concerns I expressed and decide to abolish her and her department altogether.

I had to explain to Champion that what had been written in the licence application would not be legally binding. If McNamee or the board decided to do things differently, it was entirely their prerogative. However much we might dislike it, we had no power of redress, and neither did the Independent Broadcasting Authority. I did not like, any more than she did, the way that the sales and marketing departments had been expanded exponentially since the original business plan, whilst the programming and engineering departments had borne huge cutbacks. There was little we could do. Both of us had to work through McNamee, who was denying us any contact with the board of directors. Our line manager was McNamee and we had to carry out his orders. For both Champion and me, it was a very different set of circumstances than the period before KISS FM had won the licence, when decisions were reached by consensus in the office. We both had to recognise that McNamee's character had changed almost beyond recognition since then. He was a very different man now, and KISS FM was a very different organisation now than it was then. I hoped I had convinced Champion of the worth of trying to keep her job.

I ordered a taxi to take me to McNamee's new home in South London, into which he had moved during the previous few weeks. He had been incredibly secretive about the move and had refused to tell anyone in the office where he lived now or his new home telephone number. Only his personal assistant, Rosee Laurence, knew that information and she was telling no one. McNamee hinted darkly that there were certain people who would like nothing better than to know where he lived, though he would not elaborate. For some time afterwards, McNamee continued to suggest to the outside world that he still lived at his former East London address – 155 Ernest Richard Tower, Colchester Road, Walthamstow, London E17. (KISS FM Radio Limited's mandatory Annual Return to Companies House, dated as late as 21 August 1991, still insisted that McNamee lived in Walthamstow, although he had moved more than a year earlier. In the subsequent Annual Return, undated but received by Companies House on 17 February 1992, McNamee was initially still listed as resident at the Walthamstow address, although someone had subsequently corrected this record by hand.)[725]

I had had to phone McNamee from my home to ask for his address, despite the fact that he had invited me there, and he made he swear that I would pass this information on to absolutely no one. I was astounded by the extent of the man's increasing secrecy. In its pirate days, KISS FM's on-air phone number for advertising enquiries had been McNamee's home telephone in Walthamstow. Now, even the people with whom he worked most closely were not allowed to know where he lived.

In recent weeks, Rosee Laurence had organised a KISS FM account with a local minicab company, so that everyone working for the station now had to order taxis through this system. Unfortunately, Laurence's chosen company proved far from reliable. The minicab driver I was given that Saturday had no understanding of where I wanted to go, so I had to map read for him from a London 'A-Z' book. When we eventually reached the one-way traffic system in Camberwell, the taxi ran out of petrol. Without attempting to try and move the car out of the way of busy Saturday traffic, the driver told me to stay where I was, then leapt out of the car and ran down the road in search of a petrol station. I exited the taxi and stood helplessly on the pavement, rueing the fact that I had still not taken delivery of my promised company car. I had informed the station's financial director, Martin Strivens, that the cheapest deal on the Toyota I wanted was only slightly over the £10,000 limit I had been given. I had given him the details of a South London car showroom where I had arranged a substantial discount, and I had asked him to proceed with the purchase the car. However, he seemed to be stalling and could still offer me no date by which he might have sorted out the arrangements.

The taxi driver eventually returned, poured in some petrol and I arrived, somewhat belatedly, at McNamee's address – 17 St Aidan's Road, Dulwich, London SE22. The Edwardian terraced house, which McNamee said he had just bought from his step-father, was in a very desirable area of South London. On the outside, the house looked as ordinary as any other in the street. However, on the inside, McNamee had decorated the place as a shrine to his own ego. In the hallway and the living room, photos of McNamee had been blown up to mammoth size and stared down at you from their imposing black frames on the walls. Where the pictures were not of McNamee, they were huge blown-up versions of KISS FM's poster campaign for the station's September launch. McNamee gleefully gave me a guided tour of his home and I found every room to be expensively and lavishly decorated with every modern convenience. The whole house reeked of opulence and was filled with the decadence of someone who probably had more money than taste, and whose new found wealth was being spent on acquiring anything and everything he thought he might not actually need, but nevertheless ought to have.[726]

The ostentatiousness of McNamee's home shocked me and brought home to me how much profit he must have siphoned out of KISS FM and its related businesses during the previous five years. Whilst the story given to the press had always been that the pirate version of KISS FM had never made any money for its participants, the truth must have been somewhat different. It was barely seven months since KISS FM had won its legal licence. Surely, McNamee could not have earned these riches in that short space of time, even before the station was re-launched? Or had McNamee already received a gigantic bonus payment from the company's shareholders for winning the licence on the second attempt? These were affairs about which McNamee never talked, particularly to those of us who worked in his office.

I knew that McNamee's motive for wanting to hold this meeting at his house was to intimidate me into accepting his decisions without challenge concerning the precise details of the KISS FM programme schedule. Here, on home turf, he was the boss and I was a mere visitor. We moved into the dining room, so dominated by an absolutely huge dining table that there was barely room to squeeze around the edges to sit down. McNamee regaled me with stories of the time he had invited the KISS FM board of directors for dinner and he told me what fun the group had had, talking, drinking and dining together. The effect was to make it clear that I was only here on sufferance. McNamee wanted me to know that I was definitely no longer a member of his select group of business acquaintances. The days had long gone when he and I might pop round to the local Italian restaurant for a meal together. He moved in different circles now. Neither I, nor any of his other former colleagues from the station's pirate days, moved in his newly refined circle.

Firstly, we discussed the progress we had made with the recruitment of new DJs. McNamee told me that he had finalised negotiations on his own with Robbie Vincent, a former BBC Radio One soul DJ and now host of a daily phone-in show on London's talk station, LBC. McNamee wanted Vincent to present a weekly soul music show on KISS FM and he had offered Vincent more than the £50 per show promised to other DJs in order to secure his services. An announcement about Vincent's new weekly show would be made to the press the following week. The week after that, KISS FM would announce David Rodigan's defection from Capital Radio. If the timing worked out well, Tim Westwood's move to KISS FM would be trumpeted the week after that. McNamee and I had met Westwood at the West London office of his solicitor, music industry specialist John Kennedy, three days earlier to discuss the details of the contract I had prepared. Their objections seemed confined to a few minor clauses that I was happy to amend.

The next task that McNamee and I tackled was the detail of the station's evening and weekend programme schedule. I had prepared a large sheet of paper on which I had mapped out all the programme times across a whole week of broadcasting. I had also made several dozen little cards, each of which bore the name of one KISS FM DJ. The task at hand was to match up the programme times with the most appropriate DJ. Initially, McNamee insisted that the weekend programmes should stay exactly as they had been in the station's pirate days, eighteen months earlier. I managed to convince him that there were several new programmes that had to be accommodated, which necessitated some changes. McNamee accepted this argument, but then insisted that his own weekly show should be Saturday morning between 11 am and 1 pm, and that he must be followed by Norman Jay, who must be followed by Paul Anderson. There may have been no logic behind his argument, but he insisted bluntly that these shows were sacrosanct and could not be moved.

I managed to bring more sense to the remaining parts of the schedule. Monday night was to showcase reggae with David Rodigan and house with Judge Jules; Tuesday night – hip hop with Max LX & Dave DJ, followed by techno with Colin Faver; Wednesday night – house with Steve Jackson and R&B with Jay Strongman, Thursday – soul with Bobbi & Steve and Jay Strongman; and Friday night – Jazzie B and Coldcut, the best known DJs on the station who were having commercial success with records in the pop music charts.

At weekends, I finally managed to convince McNamee not to schedule KISS FM's weekly dance music chart at the same time as Capital Radio's and BBC Radio One's charts on Sunday afternoon but, instead, during Saturday afternoon. There was to be a two-hour Saturday night 'KISS FM Master Mix' where a DJ would blend together records, uninterrupted by announcements or advertisements. Each week, the show would highlight a different DJ. On

Sunday evening, there was room for a one- or two-hour 'Sunday Night Special,' a weekly documentary for which Lyn Champion's talks department would be responsible. This would enable us to include longer interviews and features in the schedule.

There were a handful of late night and early morning slots that remained unfilled. Instead of simply offering one of the thirty-odd KISS FM DJs a chance to present two, rather than one, shows a week, McNamee insisted that additional staff must be recruited for these slots. He was acutely aware that Heddi Greenwood was the only female DJ on the KISS FM staff, and he wanted to improve the situation by appointing at least one other woman. I played McNamee a tape of Angie Dee, one of the few good unsolicited demonstration tapes I had received from a female DJ. Dee had worked on the former soul pirate TKO and for the London community station, Radio Thamesmead. McNamee agreed to hire her but insisted she take an early morning slot. Additionally, McNamee had other people in mind. He wanted to recruit Clive Richardson who, a year and a half earlier, had written to McNamee, asking to be involved in the KISS FM licence application. McNamee also wanted Dennis O'Brien, who had presented shows on KISS FM in its early pirate days, but had left before the 1988 shutdown. Although it seemed folly to add more people to what was already the largest DJ complement of any legal British radio station, McNamee made it clear that these were people he had to recruit. I had to yield.

It took the rest of the day to agree these matters with McNamee, so that it was evening by the time I ordered a taxi to take me twenty miles to the other side of London where I lived. Yet again, my driver (though different from the morning's) did not know his way around London and I had to navigate the entire route home. McNamee and I had agreed to meet again the following Sunday to discuss and finalise the weekday daytime schedule. I anticipated that this discussion would be even tougher, because of the offers that McNamee had already made to several DJs to present certain shows when the station re-launched.

The next week proved to be extremely busy. I had to phone each DJ and inform them of the time of their evening and weekend shows in the new schedule. Some were very pleased, while others were angry at not being offered the slot they thought they deserved. I took delivery of Coldcut's finished version of the new KISS FM jingle package, which turned out far better than I could ever have expected. Recorded on several tapes were hundreds of variations of different themes and slogans for the station. An entire day had to be spent at home, selecting which jingles were the most appropriate to use for the station's launch. A further afternoon was spent at GDO Studios, transferring this selection to a Digital Audio Tape, which was then couriered to a CD factory in Wales to be pressed onto a limited edition compact disc for use in the station's studios.

One morning, Lyn Champion and I met a television researcher, Richard Godfrey, for breakfast at a patisserie in Old Compton Street. He was working on a new music show for Channel Four television to be called 'The Word.' This had been the name of KISS FM's magazine show since the station's pirate days. We discussed various ways in which the two parties might collaborate, though none of these came to anything in the end. The overriding feeling on our part was that the TV production company had stolen its programme name from KISS FM without so much as a request or an apology. KISS FM had never registered 'The Word' as a trademark, so there was nothing we could do about it. The most unfortunate aspect was that the TV show was due to launch before KISS FM, which might lead new listeners to imagine that we had stolen the name from them, rather than the other way around.

Rosee Laurence circulated her third occasional KISS FM newsletter to the staff and promised that, in future, it would be published weekly. Its main news was that KISS FM had finally been granted a licence to stage its open air launch concert at Highbury Fields on 9 September. The newsletter also confirmed that an official launch party for all the station's staff and guests would be held on the first day of broadcasting, 1 September. And the move to the Holloway Road premises was scheduled to take place during the first weekend in August.[727]

The arrangements for the new office were causing me increasing concern. It was now only five weeks until the station's launch, though the radio studios were still nowhere near completion. McNamee had insisted upon handling the contracts for the studio construction company, so I had to harangue him to get the contractors moving faster on the few occasions he was in the Blackstock Mews office. Test transmissions were due to start next week, which would prove impossible without the use of a studio. I still needed at least a month to train all the DJs in studio practice. How could I accomplish that when the equipment had not yet been installed? McNamee promised me that he was doing his utmost to cajole the contractors. I still felt that he had little understanding of how impossible it would prove to launch the station properly without sufficient time for preparation.

There were other areas of the new building about which I was not happy. KISS FM financial director Martin Strivens insisted that the whole building must be wired with a computer network and VDU terminals on the staff's desks. The idea sounded very progressive, but the reality was less impressive. During the course of several long meetings with Strivens and a computer consultant, it became apparent that only four terminals were going to be installed in the programming department, despite it having more than sixty staff. Whereas, Strivens' own floor was to have six terminals for use by six staff. Because neither Strivens nor the computer company had any experience in radio, I had to explain in detail why more computer resources would have to be allocated to the programming department. Eventually, it was agreed that the number of terminals would be increased from four to eight. However, Strivens refused to provide me or Lyn Champion with a terminal. His belief was that managers had no need for computers, despite the fact that neither Champion nor I had secretarial help on which to call. In the end, Strivens bought Champion and me a number of second-hand IBM golfball electric typewriters on which to type our scripts and memos. Although the company was spending a huge sum on a computer network, it apparently could not afford to give its own managers access to the technology! Champion and I were flabbergasted.

Another issue of concern to me about the new building's infrastructure was telephones. Strivens insisted that the whole programming department must share a handful of phone extensions. I had to insist forcibly that phones were the lifeblood of a radio station's production teams. He eventually agreed to install a phone extension for each person's desk. Similarly, I had to insist that the company purchase answering machines on the desks of daytime presenters and programme assistants, who were likely to be spending a lot of time in the studios but still needed a system to retrieve messages. With no secretary in the department, there was no one specifically assigned to take messages. I wanted to avoid the chaos that would inevitably ensue if all the phones rang endlessly without reply in the offices.

I also needed a computer programme to manage the database of the station's record library. There were several such systems on the market that could be bought relatively inexpensively. However, Strivens insisted that KISS FM's computer requirements must all be handled by the one company, so I was prevented from ordering the off-the-shelf system I required. Instead, Strivens told me to brief KISS FM's computer contractor, which would then write the required programme from scratch. To me, this seemed like the least efficient way to achieve the end result. Strivens' inexperience in radio led him to imagine that any computer company would be able to accomplish such a task, rather than choosing to purchase existing software.

Strivens' learning curve could have been faster if, when I told him that I needed an item for the radio station, he simply believed me. Instead, he seemed to begrudge spending money on even the most basic supplies of a radio station. Each request for the purchase of items, almost all of which had already been included in the station budget, was accompanied by an interrogation session, during which I had to argue that the station could not launch without it. In these matters, McNamee provided no support, because he too had no knowledge of the way that commercial radio stations were organised.

We were already running so far behind schedule, though the station's board was determined not to postpone the launch date under any circumstances. This constant battle for essential resources wasted far too much time and involved far too many meetings. I felt that there were a thousand and one more essential things I needed to be doing, rather than spending what had turned out to be an entire working day arguing about the number of telephones needed in an office. KISS FM was starting to drown under the weight of its own self-imposed bureaucracy, even before it had arrived on-air. Was this really the way the former pirate radio station was going to be run?

---

[725] KISS FM Radio Limited, Companies House no. 02378790.
[726] Judi Bevan, "Treasures Of The Pirate", Evening Standard, 7 Jul 1993.
[727] "Newsletter no. 3", KISS FM, 24 Jul 1990.

July & August 1990.

It was five o'clock on a Wednesday morning. I was standing on the deserted street corner outside my flat, waiting for KISS FM DJ Graham Gold to arrive in his car, from his home in Watford, to offer me a lift to GDO Studios. He and Mark Webster, who had arranged to meet us there, were about to record a dummy breakfast show together between six and nine o'clock. I wanted the show to incorporate the reality of having to get up that early in the morning. If we were going to record a breakfast show, it should to be done at that time.

McNamee remained convinced that Gold and Webster were the ideal pairing for the re-launched KISS FM, although I had strong reservations that the GDO recording session only served to confirm. Gold was a very competent, very professional radio DJ but, on-air, he sounded very similar to dozens of other local radio presenters up and down the country. There was nothing unique about his style that would mark him out, particularly in the competitive London market, as someone who was worth making an effort to listen to every day. On the other hand, Webster had a wicked sense of humour and an exceptional intelligence that made him worth listening to. The problem was that Gold and Webster together just did not work well. They were just too dissimilar to each other.

A few days later, I ordered a taxi on the KISS FM account to pick me up from home at five o'clock in the morning to travel once again to GDO Studios to try another combination of breakfast presenters. This time, Webster was paired with Dave Pearce, a blend that seemed more compatible because Pearce had a stronger character and shared Webster's sly sense of humour. I thought that this combination would prove far more productive and could bring something special to the most important show in KISS FM's schedule. Pearce, however, complained that he had never got up that early in the morning in his life. He told me that I was crazy to even consider him as a breakfast show presenter because he did not feel he functioned properly at that hour.

That same week, I tried out several of the internal KISS FM candidates for daytime shows at GDO Studios. Trevor 'Madhatter' Nelson's show was particularly impressive and he demonstrated an incredibly natural rapport with his audience, without sounding at all like a typical commercial radio DJ. His audition proved particularly memorable for the fact that he brought a new record – 'Groove Is In The Heart' by Dee-lite – to the studio which we both agreed was the best soul record to be released for a long time. Another internal candidate, Steve Jackson, proved to be incredibly creative in the studio, but lacked the professionalism and polish to be put immediately on daytime radio. With more practice, I considered Jackson to be a future candidate for a daytime slot on KISS FM.

That Sunday, I took a taxi once again the twenty miles from my flat to McNamee's home in Dulwich. After a very amenable Sunday lunch cooked by McNamee's wife, Kim, we set about the business of deciding the station's daytime DJ line-up. I had made cassette copies of the shows I had recorded at GDO Studios that week for McNamee to listen to and consider. We had already agreed that there would be five daytime shows, rather than the six in the original plan. Dave Pearce, David Rodigan, Graham Gold and Tim Westwood already occupied four of those slots, and McNamee was quick to agree that Trevor Nelson was the most suitable internal candidate for the fifth show. McNamee and Nelson had been long-time friends and McNamee had already selected Nelson to be the director who would represent the other DJ shareholders at board level.

I was determined to make McNamee understand how strongly I believed that Graham Gold was not the most suitable DJ for KISS FM to schedule in the station's most important daytime programme. All the market research had shown us that young radio listeners in London wanted KISS FM to be different from existing radio stations. To achieve that objective, it needed to employ daytime DJs who did not sound as if they aspired to jobs on BBC Radio One or Capital Radio. Gold sounded too ordinary to entrust with the breakfast show. McNamee hated research and had often said that he did not consider the work I had commissioned from Sirius Research to be worthwhile. He solemnly rejected any attempt to persuade him that Graham Gold and Mark Webster were not ideally suited to the breakfast show. Besides, he would say, these are jobs I have already promised them. What your job is now, he said, pointing at me, is to make them a winning combination. I persisted that I could not create a successful and popular breakfast show out of presenters who I did not feel were suitable for the job. But McNamee refused to accept any notion that Dave Pearce was a more appropriate choice for the breakfast slot. I was saddled with his stubbornness.

At the other end of the daytime schedule, I did manage to convince McNamee that Tim Westwood was the most suitable DJ for the drivetime show. Westwood was already very popular amongst young people who listened in to his hip hop shows on Capital Radio. I wanted to build up that audience by attracting kids to tune in to KISS FM after school each weekday. If they tuned to KISS FM to listen to Westwood, they might stay listening the rest of the evening. McNamee agreed although, because negotiations with Westwood had still not been concluded, we could not publicly release his name.

That left three other daytime slots to fill on KISS FM. I suggested to McNamee that, if he was not going to let Dave Pearce present the breakfast show, he should at least give him the next show during the morning period. I recommended that Pierce was followed by David Rodigan at lunchtimes, and by Trevor Nelson in the afternoon. Eventually, McNamee agreed to this line-up.

During the hour-long taxi journey home that evening, I could not help but consider the extent to which McNamee's judgement in these critical commercial issues was being clouded by promises he had made to people before KISS FM had won its licence. I had advised him, categorically, that Gold and Webster would not prove successful on the breakfast show. Why was he so determined to ignore that advice? Why was he prepared to risk the economic viability of the entire radio station by damaging what should potentially be its most lucrative show in terms of advertising revenues? McNamee's decisions were frustrating me more and more. My role was going to be reduced to one of damage limitation, rather than effective programme management. The journey gave me time to mull over these issues, though I knew that there were too many urgent things I had to do to get the radio station on-air by 1 September to worry too much about McNamee's psyche.

The next day, another new recruit started work at the KISS FM office in Blackstock Mews. Philippa Unwin, with whom I had worked at community station Radio Thamesmead four years earlier, was recruited to be the programming department administrator, handling all the office routines that the radio station needed. Having handled all this paperwork myself until now, it was an immense relief to be able to share the burden with someone else at last. With the recruitment of Unwin, two new receptionists selected by McNamee for the new premises, and a full complement of sales staff, the overcrowded Blackstock Mews office had become almost unrecognisable from the expansive, airy place it had been at the beginning of the year. Everyone was agreed on one thing – the sooner we could move to the new building, the better for all of us.

That Monday, I met David Rodigan once again at the Centurion Press office in the West End to discuss the details of how he should inform his current employer, Capital Radio, of his decision to join KISS FM. As agreed, Rodigan subsequently made an appointment with Capital's programme director, Richard Park, on Wednesday 1 August. Rodigan told Park that he wished to give the required one month's notice of his decision to leave the station. Park thanked him and told him to pack his belongings and leave the station there and then. Understandably, Rodigan was particularly upset that he had not been allowed to present a farewell reggae show on Capital Radio after eleven years at the station. Without explanation, Capital simply wiped his show from its programme schedule.

The media trade press lapped up the story of Rodigan's departure from London's most successful radio station. 'Capital Loss,' said Broadcast. 'Top Reggae DJ Quits Capital For KISS FM,' said Music Week. It commented that, "in luring the DJ from its closest rival, Capital, KISS has scored its most prestigious presenter appointment to date." Capital's Richard Park told Music Week he was sorry to lose Rodigan, but that "the station's commitment to reggae is undiminished." However, Capital Radio did not appoint another reggae presenter and it quietly abandoned the weekly reggae show that had been present in its schedule since Tommy Vance's trail-blazing 'TV On Reggae' in 1975. Music Week's article was unintentionally ironic because it was accompanied by a photo of Tim Westwood, whose hip hop show Capital Radio had extended to fill the gap vacated by Rodigan. Little did the magazine know that Westwood was KISS FM's next intended defector.[728]

In addition to Westwood, there were still a few more staff appointments to be made. The deal with Independent Radio News [IRN] to provide KISS FM with a customised service of news bulletins had proven very slow to implement. IRN had still had not identified two newsreaders that Lyn Champion and I considered to have suitable voices for a radio station aimed at young people. In desperation, IRN agreed to pay for a job vacancy advertisement in The Guardian newspaper that asked for a "KISS FM Newsreader/Writer" with "a fresh, young, lively style." There was only a month until the station's launch and this important part of KISS FM's on-air sound had yet to be finalised.[729]

The rest of the work week was consumed with the packing of everyone's office belongings and paperwork into large cardboard boxes, to be ready for the move to Holloway Road over the weekend. Rosee Laurence had issued everybody with a one-page memo that contained detailed instructions of what we should do. The empty crates were delivered to Blackstock Mews on Wednesday and had to be packed by Friday, ready for collection on Saturday morning. All KISS staff were expected to spend Saturday and Sunday (unpaid) unpacking their possessions in the new office for "work as normal" on the Monday. Laurence's memo ended poignantly: "Bye Bye Blackstock Road (tear, tear, tear)."[730]

I spent the whole of Friday interviewing eight short-listed candidates for the music royalties administrator post in the programming department. Financial director Martin

Strivens had wanted to axe this post. It had taken me several weeks of argument to persuade him that, because the company was not implementing a computer system to handle the task of royalty accounting, it was essential to employ someone specifically to handle this painstaking task. KISS FM would be required to pay substantial sums of money to the two main royalty collection agencies, the Performing Right Society and Phonographic Performance Limited, both of which required a regular, detailed analysis of every piece of music that the radio station had played.

It was a particularly sad moment when I left the Blackstock Mews office late on Friday night for the very last time. Since January 1989, I had spent most of my waking hours in this office, working long days, late into the night, and most weekends. It was here that all of KISS FM's plans to win the coveted radio licence had been hatched. It was here that Gordon McNamee, Rosee Laurence, Lindsay Wesker, Heddi Greenwood and I had shared the most emotional moments in our recent lives – planning the first licence application, losing to Jazz FM, campaigning for further licences, winning the argument, planning the second licence application, the ecstasy of winning, and the sheer hard work of getting the station on the air. Never again would the five of us be so closely entangled in each other's lives, sharing all the ups and downs as a team of close friends.

An era in our lives was ending with the move to the new office block in Holloway Road. KISS FM was no longer the funky little outfit hidden away behind the bleak streets of Finsbury Park. KISS FM was no longer a people-orientated group of friends who shared the same dreams and loved the same music. The new KISS FM was a hard-nosed business venture. The new KISS FM was a corporate entity, rather than a collection of like-minded misfits. KISS FM was no longer fun and laughter. It was now pure cut-and-thrust. McNamee had blazed the trail with his sudden metamorphosis from streetwise friend of music to corporate friend of the nouveau riche. The rest of us were being asked to follow in his wake ... or be damned. Now, more than ever, if we did not agree wholeheartedly with McNamee's way of doing things, he seemed to consider us his enemy.

That evening, before making my way home, I paid a private visit to KISS FM's new home which, from tomorrow morning, I knew would be buzzing with activity. But for now, it was still dark and empty. There was something foreboding about making the move from two open-plan offices linked by a rickety wooden staircase to a brand new concrete and glass building on five floors linked by a lift. As I wandered alone around the cavernous spaces of 80 Holloway Road, I realised that, from Monday, I would no longer be able to simply shout across the room to McNamee, Laurence, Wesker or Greenwood. We would all be occupying different offices on different floors from now on. Gone was the camaraderie that had once made KISS FM such a productive, invigorating place to work. No longer would we be sharing the same experiences in our working lives at the radio station.

I was sad. Sad for the good times that the five of us had shared together in our intimate surroundings. And sad for my realisation that things at KISS FM would never be like that ever again. But I was also afraid of the future. Afraid that things would never again be so brotherly and sisterly within KISS FM. Afraid that we were all changing in our different ways. Frictions had already emerged between us that none of us would have predicted, even a few months ago. The move to Holloway Road would mark the pinnacle of the station's successful campaign to be a legitimate radio station in London. But I knew that it also marked the start of a completely new era in the station's history. For all of us, I wondered what fortunes that future would hold.

And then I caught the train home – tired, exhausted from interviewing people all day, and slightly apprehensive about the future. KISS FM's future. Our future – McNamee, Laurence, Wesker, Greenwood ... and me.

---

[728] Sarah Davis, "Top Reggae DJ Quits Capital For KISS FM", 18 Aug 1990.
"Capital Loss", Broadcast, 10 Aug 1990.
Grant Goddard, "Sold!", City Limits, 11 May 1989.
[729] "KISS FM Newsreader/Writer", recruitment advert, The Guardian, 30 Jul 1990.
[730] Rosee Laurence, "Shedule [sic] For Move To KISS House", KISS FM memo, 30 Jul 1990.

August 1990.

More bad news arrived about the increasingly perilous economic state of the British commercial radio industry. The latest figures showed that six local commercial stations had suffered slumps of more than twenty per cent in their revenues from national advertisers between October 1989 and March 1990, including Plymouth Sound whose revenues had declined by forty-nine per cent. The GWR Radio group announced that its half-year pre-tax profits to July 1990 had fallen by forty-three per cent year-on-year to £454,407. At London talk radio station LBC, staff voted for industrial action over the management's move to axe twenty-three jobs and its refusal to negotiate increased pay rates.[731]

News about the new incremental radio stations continued to cast a shadow over their viability. At the troubled Belfast Community Radio, executive chairman John Simpson resigned. At the new London multi-ethnic station, Spectrum Radio, sales manager Dick Seabright resigned only five weeks after the station's launch. To cut costs, Spectrum had dismissed five newsroom staff and a senior presenter. At Bristol station For The People, executive chairwoman Babs Williams declared that, if a £250,000 rescue package was not secured by mid-August, the station would be in "desperation." At London's Melody Radio, its former music consultant, Andy Park, admitted that the station "was a difficult birth" and complained of "constant interference" from its owner, Lord Hanson: "It was bad enough trying to do two jobs at once – then Hanson would phone or fax in and you would have to turn your attention to a third."[732]

At the new KISS FM premises in Holloway Road, there were inevitable teething problems. The phone system did not work properly for the first few days. The computer system did not work for the first few weeks. The lift refused to move between floors for the first few months. Construction of the radio studios had still not been completed, despite there being only three weeks until the station's launch. The contractors had barely started to install the huge air conditioning system that the soundproofed studios required. There remained several areas of the new building that were still unfinished, despite the staff having moved in over the weekend.

In the basement, there were ominous signs of a rift between the station's sales and marketing departments that shared the floor. Over the weekend, head of sales Gary Miele had come to work and moved dozens of shoulder-height filing cabinets so that they stretched in two back-to-back lines the whole length of the floor, dividing it into two very unequal parts. Naturally, the larger part was to be occupied by Miele's sales staff, whilst the smaller part, barely a fifth of the floor space, was intended for the marketing staff. Head of marketing Malcolm Cox was furious at Miele's cavalier attitude but, despite his complaints to Miele and McNamee, nothing was done to rectify this situation. Only a handful of the filing cabinets were ever used by Miele's staff, though they served their purpose by demarcating the limits of his fiefdom.

These filing cabinets were part of a large delivery of second-hand furniture that Martin Strivens had purchased for the new building. The cabinets must have come from a local authority 'rates' department, because several of them were still filled with files labelled with individual addresses and containing correspondence related to the recently dismantled system of local household taxation. Many of the filing cabinets had drawers that were impossible to pull out due to their old age or lack of maintenance, and none of the cabinets came with keys, making them all but useless for storing confidential documents.

The other part of Strivens' furniture delivery was a large number of very battered second-hand office desks of varying shapes, sizes and ages. The only staff to have been granted the luxury of new office equipment were the heads of each department and those that worked on the top floor of the building, where Strivens and McNamee resided. The programming department floor was filled with the old furniture from the Blackstock Mews office, including the desks we had painted black the previous summer, plus a huge quantity of filing cabinets without keys. I had to complain to Strivens that the department needed secure lockable cupboards to store valuable tapes, records and portable recording equipment. All these items had been included in the budgets I had drawn up with him, but they had not been purchased.

I also had to complain to Strivens and McNamee about the work of the contractors who had assembled the partitions in the programming department. They had ignored the plans and seemed to have used their own judgement over the size of rooms and the materials they used. My office had ended up being much bigger than was planned, while Lyn Champion's adjoining office was too small and had no windows (a visiting fire officer said that Champion's office was illegal because it had no outlook onto the rest of the floor). The producers' office had only one door, instead of the two that were on the plan, so that it lacked any flow of fresh air as it had no external window. The corridor on the floor had ended up twice as wide as it should have been, so that you could have driven a car down it. This made the office shared by the presenters and programme assistants too small – nine people were being asked to work in a room no larger than an average kitchen. Conversely, the partitioning had been wrongly erected so that the office for the three talks researchers was large enough to hold an intimate party.

Despite my complaints and the obvious errors the contractors had made, Strivens and McNamee refused to recall the contractors to rectify their mistakes. I could not understand their reticence, since they were condemning many of the programming staff to work in unnecessarily overcrowded conditions, simply because of errors in construction. The shoddiness with which the whole building had been finished was further confirmed when a heating system engineer insisted that, in my office, he needed to move three filing cabinets away from the wall so that he could test the heating system. He sounded confused when he told me that the radiator was not there, even though it existed on the floor plan of the building. The contractors had omitted to install heating in my office! Again, Strivens and McNamee refused to recall the contractor to rectify the mistake.

The austerity and overcrowding of the programming department on the second floor contrasted sharply with the opulence and spaciousness on the top floor of the building. Although the two levels occupied roughly the same floor space, the programming floor serviced more than sixty staff, whilst the top floor housed only eight people. All the furniture on the top floor was brand new, the staff benefited from a kitchenette with a fridge and a microwave oven, and McNamee's corner office housed a huge colour television set, a private fridge inside one of his office cupboards, and a bar. All the windows and clear plastic partitioning on the upstairs floor were fitted with expensive black, floor-to-ceiling venetian blinds, while the other floors had neither blinds nor curtains, not even across the external windows that looked out onto the busy Holloway Road.

During that first week in the new premises, two delivery men arrived unannounced in my office. They brought several heavy cardboard boxes from downstairs and started to empty the contents onto my office floor. I asked them what they were doing, and they replied that they had instructions from Martin Strivens to deliver and construct one table and chairs unit in the office of each head of department at the station. The table was low and circular in heavy, black wood and was accompanied by several matching heavy black chairs. I phoned Strivens to explain that I did not particularly want such a table in my office because it would not leave enough room to hold a meeting with several staff at once. Strivens was outraged. How could I not want such an expensive table that he had ordered specially for each of the station's heads of departments? He informed me that, because it had already been delivered, I would have to have it in my office. As a compromise, I suggested that it would be better to install the table in the small meetings room on the programming floor, where weekly playlist meetings were to be held.

The next thing I knew was when the workmen stopped assembling the expensive table and started to put all the pieces back into their cardboard boxes. I asked what they were doing and they told me that they had new instructions to take the table away. I phoned Strivens again to ask why they were not assembling the table in the meetings room. He told me bluntly that the table had been specifically designated for my office and, since I did not want it, he had arranged for it to be returned to the manufacturers, saving the station several hundred pounds. I asked him why the table could not be installed in the meetings room. He responded that it was a wholly inappropriate table for such a room. So neither I, nor the meetings room, benefited from this expensive table. Despite the refund, the department never received the more essential lockable filing cabinets and storage units that could have easily been purchased using the money that had been saved.

This incident, though minor, typified the attitude with which both Strivens and McNamee seemed to treat the rest of the staff in the building. Even by the end of that first week, it became obvious that the top floor worked to one set of rules, whilst expecting the rest of us to live by another set of rules. We were required to be excessively frugal, totally undemanding and to put up with under-resourced offices and inferior equipment. Even in that first week, I had to listen to and placate a torrent of complaints from my departmental staff about the lack of this or the need for that, almost all of which were met with firm 'no's or vague promises and platitudes when I presented my case to Strivens and McNamee. The money that I had already agreed with them would be part of my department's first-year budget was being denied to me, without any explanation as to why.

Though the radio station might be going through turmoil on the inside, to the world on the outside, the impending launch of KISS FM was starting to gather a lot of attention in the press. Even the local newspaper, The Islington Chronicle, reported KISS FM's move to Holloway Road and noted that one local resident, in adjacent Horsell Road, believed that the station would create "a lot of noise and commotion, with many people going in and out late at night." Councillor Paul Convery told a meeting of the Islington Council development control committee that "residents are worried that this place will be a noisy, good time place."

However, a report from the council's planning department suggested "there will be little noise generated" because "an elimination of background noise is required for broadcasting purposes." Planning officer Keith Sheffield admitted: "I have visited another 24-hour radio station and it was like a morgue, even during the day." The committee granted KISS FM the required planning permission, even though it would have been too late by then to stop the station moving in.[733]

Fashion Weekly reported that KISS FM was producing a special commemorative T-shirt for the station's launch, designed by Paul Smith. Gordon McNamee confessed that he was "a great fan of Paul's clothes." Smith returned the compliment: "I am proud to have been associated with KISS 100 FM and wish them every success for the future."[734]

On a less parochial level, The Guardian's media supplement ran a front-page feature to trumpet the imminent arrival of KISS FM, using a huge photo of six of the station's DJs (including a rare appearance by Heddi Greenwood) stood in front of the huge double doors at the former Blackstock Mews office. McNamee told the newspaper that the station would be unbiased in choosing the particular records it played: "Listeners aren't silly. In the pirate days, we flatly refused to do any payola or anything like that. By doing that, it earned us more credibility. Our whole credibility and name lives and dies by what we play in our music."[735]

Media Week magazine reported that KISS FM's launch would be "backed by a £1m advertising campaign, through BBDO, using cinema, television, outdoor and print." Marketing Week magazine carried the headline 'KISS FM Pulls In £1m Sponsorship' and reported that three major sponsors – LA Gear, NME and Purdey – had boosted the station's sponsorship revenues by this amount, even prior to launch. Both figures should have been taken with a pinch of salt, though they gave the desired impression to the advertising industry that KISS FM presented an opportunity it would be wise not to miss.[736]

McNamee's attempts to cultivate a new, more sophisticated image were evidenced in his contribution of an editorial column to Campaign magazine which argued the value of radio advertising. McNamee wrote: "Advertising creatives look forward to making ads specifically for the style press and soon they will get excited about creating different treatments for radio" and: "Previously a station's remit has been geographically driven or simply catering for the lowest common denominator." These were not the sort of phrases likely to be heard in conversation with McNamee. In the blitz of publicity leading up to the station's re-launch, McNamee was continuing to create a public relations image of himself that was further and further removed from reality.[737]

Talking to Time Out magazine, McNamee expressed no self-doubt about KISS FM's ability to attract the one million listeners it was promising its advertisers: "If we can't get a million listeners out of thirteen million in London, when Capital's got five-and-a-half million ... And we don't need five-and-a-half million people listening to our station to make it a sound investment for our investors." Time Out noted that, during the interview with McNamee, "he tips back his chair and spreads his palms as magisterially as a man can who has two-foot dreadlocks and excitement leaping in his eye."[738]

Interviewed in Radio & Music magazine, McNamee admitted that "launching a radio station is always one of the most difficult things going, and it's not a good time to start with the present economic situation." Quizzed as to why KISS FM had seemingly reversed its music policy since he told the magazine, seven months earlier, that it would stop playing records as soon as they entered the Top Fifty singles chart, McNamee replied: "Yes, that was crap, that. But we got a lot of publicity on it." Radio & Music asked Capital Radio DJ Tony Blackburn his opinions about KISS FM's launch, and he said: "I'm pleased KISS FM is coming on air. I think it's good for radio, but it isn't guaranteed to get an audience. It's not enough to play the right music any more – it has to be presented well."[739]

A rare criticism of KISS FM was published in the gay and lesbian newspaper Pink Pages, criticising the station's launch publicity campaign for including thirty-five photos of heterosexual couples kissing, but no lesbians or gay men. An unnamed KISS FM spokesperson explained to the paper: "It's a commercial concern. It's nothing more than a business. We were trying to create an attractive proposition." Pink Paper commented: "The gay market is, as usual, very good as a sounding board for record companies and radio stations to try out new material but, as soon as riches beckon, it's no longer 'attractive.'"[740]

To my surprise, just prior to the station's launch, extensive profiles of KISS FM head of talks Lyn Champion appeared in both The Guardian newspaper and Broadcast magazine. Both correctly credited Champion with helping to write the station's winning licence application and detailed her previous experience working for BBC Radio. My surprise was that neither KISS FM's recently appointed publicity officer, Anita Mackie, nor the station's PR company, Rogers & Cowan, had managed to arrange similar profiles for me, as the person within the company responsible for the station's programmes and overall sound. During the busy pre-launch period, I was only called upon to give two short interviews – one which I was approached to do directly by a journalist colleague who worked for Broadcast magazine, and the other which McNamee asked me to do for Radio & Music magazine after head of music Lindsay Wesker unexpectedly became unavailable. Once again, I suspected that McNamee wanted to hog the limelight by acting as if it was he who was solely responsible for the station's programmes, though he acknowledged that Wesker controlled the station's music policy. My name had been almost completely drowned out by the pair's self-promotion efforts.[741]

---

[731]"Southern Revenue Slumps", Broadcast, 3 Aug 1990.
"GWR 'Will Recover' From Profits Drop", Radio & Music, 1 Aug 1990.
"Staff To Hold Strike Ballot At Crown", Radio & Music, 29 Aug 1990.
[732]"BCR Reshuffle As Chairman Resigns", Radio & Music, 29 Aug 1990.
"Seabright Quits Spectrum", Radio & Music, 29 Aug 1990.
"Bristol Station Seeks Investor", Broadcast, 3 Aug 1990.
Bob Tyler, "Melody Launch Problems Put Down To Record Companies", Music Week, 18 Aug 1990.
[733]"Residents Fear 'Noisy' KISS", Islington Chronicle & North London Advertiser, 1 Aug 1990.
"Radio Station Passes Noise Test", Islington Gazette & Stoke Newington Observer, 2 Aug 1990.
[734]"Paying Lip Service", Fashion Weekly, 9 Aug 1990.
"A Paul Smith KISS For KISS 100 FM", Rogers & Cowan/KISS FM press release, 26 Jul 1990.
[735]Edwin Riddell, "Old Pirate Ready To Return To The Waves", The Guardian, 6 Aug 1990.
[736]"£1m Campaign Will Back KISS FM Launch", Media Week, 3 Aug 1990.
Sarah McDonald, "KISS FM Pulls In £1m Sponsorship", Marketing Week, 10 Aug 1990.
[737]Gordon Mac, "Head To Head", Campaign, 17 Aug 1990.
[738]Nick Coleman, "KISS Of Life", Time Out, 29 Aug 1990.
[739]Brian Tottle, "KISS And Tell", Radio & Music, 29 Aug 1990.
[740]Hercules, "Sharp Words", Pink Paper, 18 Aug 1990.
[741]"Champion Of The Airwaves", The Guardian, 30 Aug 1990.
"Profile - Lyn Champion", Broadcast, 17 Aug 1990.
Sean King, "Can Capital Be Caught By KISS FM?", Broadcast, 17 Aug 1990.
Brian Tottle, op cit.

August 1990.

It was less then three weeks until the station's launch on 1 September 1990 and there were still several major tasks to complete. KISS FM's test transmissions should have started two weeks earlier, but were delayed due to problems that the engineers of the Independent Broadcasting Authority [IBA] had encountered while installing the station's transmitter facility in Croydon. The IBA told us that test transmissions were unlikely to commence until a week before the station's launch.[742]

Even if the transmission facilities had been ready, the contractors had only just completed one of the three KISS FM studios. I had always emphasised to Gordon McNamee that I would need at least one month's use of all three studios to train KISS FM's large complement of presenters, few of whom had ever seen a professional radio studio, let alone knew how to use it. It had become obvious that, with the delays, I alone would not have time to organise the necessary training. I managed to convince McNamee that, unless I could call upon outside help, the station's launch could prove disastrous. He agreed to let me hire two radio professionals – Daniel Nathan and Eugene Perera – whom I knew would be capable of the task. At short notice, they proceeded to work all hours of the day and night, training the DJs, whilst the contractors continued to finish building the studios around them.

Another pressing task was the conclusion of negotiations with Tim Westwood over his KISS FM DJ contract. KISS FM's Free! magazine wanted to publish a special issue, timed to coincide with the station's launch, that would include the complete programme schedule. The station's PR company, Rogers & Cowan, was also desperate to release the full details of KISS FM's programme line-up. As a result, I was forced to leave a gap in the published schedule where Westwood's daily shows were to be broadcast. The words 'to be confirmed' looked particularly untidy on the station's first programme schedule, though I had no choice. Until Westwood's defection from Capital Radio was definite, I could not even allude to his involvement in the station.

McNamee and I had a further meeting with Westwood at the office of his solicitor, John Kennedy, on 14 August. This time, Westwood was accompanied by his manager, Phil Ward-Large, the former programme controller of Radio Luxembourg. After going through the specific points in the contract that Westwood had queried, Kennedy astutely concluded that Westwood's main concern about joining KISS FM seemed to be creative, rather than contractual. Westwood had always been offered an entirely free hand to choose the records for his specialist hip hop shows on Capital Radio. Presenting a daytime show on KISS FM would require Westwood to sacrifice a large amount of creative control to the playlist system, which accounted for ten out of the twelve records played each hour. Kennedy suggested that this was an issue in which he could be of little assistance. It was something that Westwood needed to discuss in more detail with me, until he could be assured that the mandatory playlist would not detract from his credibility as a hip hop DJ, which he had spent years cultivating.

The meeting concluded quickly and I assured Westwood that we would talk in more detail about his concerns. During the next two weeks, I spent a lot of time, in the office and at home, on the phone to Westwood, explaining in detail what he was expected to do on his show, how the playlist was going to be selected each week, and what I was trying to achieve with the station's daytime sound. I worked my way down the current Top 75 singles chart and indicated to him the records that I anticipated he would have to play as part of the playlist. I also emphasised to him that he still had a separate specialist music show, at a prime time each weekend, where he had a completely free hand to chose whatever he wanted to play. However, it was some of the dance records in the chart that Westwood felt would most damage his credibility if he had to play them on the radio regularly. Around half of the current chart was composed of dance-orientated records and Westwood seemed happy to play crossover hits such as 'U Can't Touch This' by MC Hammer and 'Rockin' Over The Beat' by Technotronic. But the one record he could not see himself playing was 'Where Are You Baby?' by Betty Boo.

To Westwood, Betty Boo's recent records were not the sort of tracks that KISS FM should be playing, despite the fact that Boo had been a member of one of the earliest British female hip hop groups, the She Rockers. Westwood asked if he could be given the right, in his contract, not to have to play such records in his daytime show if he objected to them that strongly. I expressed sympathy with him but had to explain that, if I let him exercise creative control over some elements of his daytime programme, I would have to offer the other daytime DJs the same prerogative. The playlist system would break down completely if each DJ felt he did not have to play particular records that he did not like. I was sorry to seem so inflexible, particularly as I understood his desire to maintain his street-wise image as a hip hop DJ, but there were certain concessions I simply could not grant him, and this was one of them. Relations between the two of us remained cordial (I even lent Westwood a book on hip hop that he had not seen) and I felt that Westwood would eventually succumb to the spirit of KISS FM and re-join the station in the end.

To the outside world, and to everyone in the station except for McNamee and me, the delicate negotiations with Westwood were completely unknown. Rosee Laurence's latest internal newsletter made no reference to the gaping hole in the newly published KISS FM programme schedule but, instead, dwelt on other burning issues. Addressing the continuing major problems with the new computer system, Laurence assured staff that "a call-out engineer is being arranged, so don't despair." No company had yet been contracted to clean the offices or to dispose of its rubbish, so Laurence requested that "everybody take care of their own rubbish etc. at the moment." On the issue of the single studio that had been completed, the newsletter assured staff that "Martin and Lawrence [of engineering contractor Phoenix Communications] are working flat out to finish the other two, which should be ready soon-ish."[743]

At Independent Radio News [IRN], two newsreaders were finally appointed to read the KISS FM bulletins each hour. Although Lyn Champion and I had some reservations about the new recruits – Suzi Pote and Paul Munn – it was too late in the day to place another job advertisement. The two started to prepare and read hourly bulletins from IRN's headquarters in Hammersmith, which were sent down a British Telecom landline to the KISS FM studios in order for presenters to practice integrating them into their programmes.[744]

Now that we were close to the launch date, KISS FM's head of music, Lindsay Wesker, stopped working full-time as editor of Free! magazine and started to tackle his responsibilities within the station. A new editorial team was appointed to run the magazine, although Wesker still contributed articles to the next few issues. Wesker's workspace was the station's record library on the same floor of the building as the studios, and his first task was to put the records into some sort of order. Wesker had never seen a radio station record library, so I had to explain to him how it should work, how he should consider security to be of the utmost importance, how he should carefully note every record loaned to a member of staff, and never let anyone rifle through the racks and take records out of their own accord.

All the major record companies had been sending the station their new releases for several months, and many had contributed as much of their back catalogue as they could manage, so the library was already quite large. Robbie Vincent had sold his considerable record collection to the station, 4,000 albums and 2,000 singles which formed the bulk of the initial stock, in a deal that McNamee had negotiated. The press was told that Vincent had donated these items.[745]

I explained to Wesker the details of the playlist system that I had devised for the station. There were three playlists of current records. An A-list for new releases that were destined to be big hits, a B-list for new releases that were not going to be hits but sounded good on the radio, and a C-list for records that were already hits. It was the simplest system I could create for operation and maintenance by a head of music with no previous experience in these matters. Wesker's job was to add and subtract records to and from each list week-by-week, according to how many good new records were released. I had also designed a rotation pattern for every hour of each daytime programme, which would instruct the DJ which playlist record to play at a particular time. KISS FM, unlike most stations of comparable size, had no computer software for its playlist system. Everything would have to be done manually. Wesker said he understood and would get on with drawing up the station's first playlist.

Wesker and I also had to get on with the task of recording the test transmission tapes that KISS FM would broadcast prior to its first live programmes on 1 September. Wesker chose eight hours of music, mixing new releases with some old favourites and then visited a local video shop to buy a blank four-hour VHS videotape. In addition to the music, the IBA insisted that certain scripted announcements had to be broadcast at regular intervals during the test period. For this purpose, stations commonly used an authoritative man with a rich, BBC-style voice in a style that was a throwback to the earliest days of radio. Even the recently launched South London station, Choice FM, had used such a voice, despite targeting the black community.

I felt that KISS FM needed to project a more youthful and less establishment sound in its first transmissions. Listeners would judge the station by what they heard when they tuned in for the first time. I wanted to make them feel that this was a new radio station that reflected their own personalities. Instead of using a plummy, BBC-type voice, I decided that a selection of young, female voices would be far more appropriate. It was late in the evening at the Holloway Road office, but there was still a group of people working in one of the downstairs offices, collating a huge mail-out to be sent to the people on the list that KISS FM had established in its pirate days. I went and asked the women who were there – head of talks Lyn Champion, DJ Heddi Greenwood, and office staff Fran Andrews and Debbi McNally – to come to the studio and record the scripted announcements. They obliged and, although Andrews and McNally were nervous because they had never been on the radio before, I felt that their voices captured the spirit of KISS FM much more than would a professional DJ.

After Wesker had returned from the shop with the VHS videotape, the two of us set up camp in the one operational studio and recorded an eight-hour block of continuous music, interrupted only by the pre-recorded announcements and a few KISS FM Jingles. The entire eight-hour session had to be completed in one sitting without errors. It was an exhilarating feeling for me to be sat at the mixing desk, pressing the appropriate buttons and knowing that what I was recording would be the public's first experience of the re-launched KISS FM. During those eight hours, which stretched far into the night, Wesker and I had a great time together, singing along to the records, dancing around the studio, ordering pizza deliveries to sustain us, and turning up the studio monitors as loud as we dared. Suddenly, all the hard work, frustration and setbacks of the last few months all seemed worthwhile. Right there in the studio, we were creating the future sound of KISS FM, exactly as we wanted it to be. This was OUR radio station and we felt that nobody could take that away from us.

Once we had finished the recording, we were both elated but exhausted. It was almost sunrise, so I ordered a taxi to take me home. KISS FM had switched its account to a different cab company, but the drivers' abilities seemed no better than the previous contractor. My driver that morning, who had assured me he knew the way to Harrow, somehow ended up on a deserted industrial estate in Colindale, miles away from the route he should have taken. I had been too tired to keep a check on where he had been driving. Then, he suddenly stopped the car, jumped out and started walking away, leaving me on my own. I got out and ran after him, asking him what he was doing. He said he was going to look for somebody to tell him how he could get from Colindale to my home. I asked why he could not use the A-Z map of London in his car and he replied that he could not read maps. There was no one around for him to ask at that early hour in the morning, so I told him that I could read maps and ended up guiding him. Once I reached home, after a journey that was three times longer than normal, I was so pleased to arrive that I did not even argue with the driver when he insisted on charging me the full amount for the miles he had clocked up.

After I had snatched a few hours sleep, I took public transport to Holloway Road and marched into the office of financial director Martin Strivens. I wanted to know when I was going to take delivery of my company car, and I wanted to know now. McNamee had had his car seven months, the head of sales and head of marketing had had theirs three months, Strivens had had his company car since I don't know when, and still I had nothing. Since the move to Holloway Road, every single day I had worked past midnight, long after everyone else had left the building. Every night, I was spending £25 on a taxi to get me home. My contract had promised a company car from 1 June. I had already given Strivens details of the car I wanted, the garage it could be bought from, and the discounted price I had negotiated. I could no longer suffer incompetent taxi drivers who wasted hours of my time meandering around the backstreets of North London. I wanted my car. And I wanted it now!

Strivens promised he would deal with the matter as quickly as possible, though I still needed to remind him several more times before it was resolved. Eventually, a few days before the station launched, my company car was delivered – a red Toyota, registration H81 XYF. It only remained for the car insurance policy to be arranged. Strivens asked if there were other people I wished to add to the policy so that they could drive the car. I suggested two KISS FM staff whom I knew could drive and whom it would be useful to be able to rely upon, should I be busy but need something picked up by car. Strivens looked aghast. He said he was

375

thinking more along the lines of a wife, a girlfriend, a son or daughter whom I might want to add. I explained that I would much prefer to add another KISS FM worker, and he looked at me as if I was mad to even consider letting anyone in the radio station drive my company car. I was confused. Was working for KISS FM and having a company car supposed to be about nothing more than receiving a subsidised perk?

For me, there were still not enough hours in the day. I held long meetings to brief the daytime presenters more precisely as to how their programmes should sound. I had meetings with the new programming department staff to explain everything about the station and their jobs. I still had the weekly Monday morning meetings with McNamee and the other heads of department, each of which was now lasting almost the whole day. I had meetings with the DJ team, one for full-timers and another for part-timers, to drive home to them the findings of the Sirius Research study I had commissioned. They must understand that KISS FM needed to be different from existing radio stations and they should not try to emulate or imitate them. Additionally, there still seemed to be a thousand and one minor problems that had to be solved before 1 September.

At last, the IBA finished installing the new KISS FM transmitter, enabling test transmissions to start on 21 August, three weeks later than planned. McNamee called a staff meeting that evening for all the full-time staff, but not for the thirty-odd freelance DJs, cramming us all into the boardroom to wish us luck with the station's launch. As soon as the test transmissions started, the phones started to ring with listeners calling to congratulate us on our arrival at long last. As part of my station plans, I had organised a specific phone number that was mentioned in the test transmissions, to which I had attached an answering machine. That night, before making my way home after midnight, I listened to the first few messages that had been left by listeners.

The building was empty now apart from the engineers downstairs, hurriedly trying to complete the studio installation. There was nobody left in the programming department except for me, crouched on the floor, bending my ear over the answering machine on the floor (there was still a lack of office furniture). Out of the speaker came the voices of people phoning in from all over Southeast England, and those voices were tinged with excitement and emotion about the long promised KISS FM. Those voices, which quickly filled an entire cassette tape on the first day of test broadcasting alone, made me feel extremely proud to have played my part in creating a black music radio station for London, almost out of thin air. It was late, I was alone in the office, and I started to cry with emotion. The long and arduous struggle to win KISS FM a licence had finally proven worthwhile when a listener, any listener, had responded that first night by phoning in to say 'thank you.'

If the test transmissions were causing such a positive response from Londoners, how would they react when the proper programmes started in ten days time?

---

[742] Sarah Davis, "Engineers Delay KISS FM Test Transmissions", Music Week, 25 Aug 1990.
[743] "Newsletter no. 5", KISS FM, 13 Aug 1990.
[744] "IRN Starts Work On KISS News", Journalist's Week, 17 Aug 1990.
[745] "Robbie Vincent", Radio & Music, 1 Aug 1990.

August 1990.

It was one week before the station's launch when I received a phone call from an officer at the Independent Broadcasting Authority [IBA], asking politely why he had yet to receive an outline of KISS FM's programme plans. This was a document that all new radio stations were required to submit before coming on-air. I admitted to him that, in the frenetic rush to get everything ready for 1 September, I had forgotten about this formality. I promised to submit the necessary paperwork as soon as possible.

The next two nights were spent, without sleep, scribbling pages and pages of explanations as to how KISS FM was to be programmed and why these decisions had been made. It was the first opportunity I had been given to encapsulate, on paper, all the policies and principles that I had spent the last few hectic months trying to turn into reality. The result was a detailed manifesto of what KISS FM planned to do when it arrived on-air, and how these plans would attract the one million listeners that KISS FM had promised its advertisers. I knew that the document would remain confidential, so I offered the regulator as much information as I could muster to explain why everything broadcast on KISS FM would sound the way it did.

Once this document had been typed, a courier was dispatched to deliver it to the IBA. I was delighted and gratified when word came back quickly from the IBA officer that not only had KISS FM's programme plans been approved without reservation, but also that my document was considered a 'model answer' that would be used as an example to other new stations of how best to present their case. It was not often that I had been offered such generous praise for my work. I was particularly pleased to have entered KISS FM's launch period on such a positive footing with the IBA.

I had just reached the end of a very tiring, totally exhausting week. Two nights had been spent working on the IBA document, and a further night I had been working out a complicated shift pattern system for the programme assistants that were allocated to evening and weekend duties. Now, it was late on Friday night and I was ready to drive home in my new company car and collapse into bed. Although tomorrow was Saturday, I still needed to work all day, but at least I would not have to be back for nine o'clock in the morning. I looked out of the window of my new second floor office and noticed that Gordon McNamee's car was still in the car park, although I had not seen him around the building. It was unusual for him still to be at work this late. I had never seen him leave after midnight.

The lift in the building was still not working, so I walked up the flight of stairs to the top floor. It was completely dark and it seemed as if no lights had been left switched on. Then, pushing open the double fire doors, I noticed a dim light in McNamee's office. The floor was very spooky with all the main lights turned off, but I walked over and knocked on McNamee's door. There was a pause before he answered and shouted for me to enter. I opened the door and found him sat behind his desk, leaning back in his expensive padded executive chair, seemingly doing nothing at all. There was no music on his stereo system, his widescreen television was not on, and there were no papers on the desk in front of him. I sat on the hard chair on the opposite side of his desk and tried to engage him in small talk. I told him I had just finished work for the night and was about to go home. I told him that I was exhausted, but determined to organise a great launch for the station the following weekend.

He had not said anything of substance until now, but he suddenly raised his eyes from the desk that separated us, leaned forward in his chair and said to me: "I know what you're doing, don't think I don't realise." I was taken aback. What was he talking about? He continued: "I know you're going to ruin this station. You are going to destroy KISS FM." I was shocked. I asked him what on earth he meant. He replied: "I know what you're up to. You and Malcolm [Cox, head of marketing], you've been planning this together. It's going to fail. And it's going to be all YOUR fault." I could not believe my ears. What on earth was he going on about? McNamee continued: "You and Malcolm, your plans to make this a station for young people will destroy what KISS FM is about. It will fail ... and it will be all YOUR fault."

I found it very hard to believe the scene that was unfolding in front of my tired eyes. It was very late on Friday night. I desperately needed some sleep. I had only come upstairs to say goodbye to McNamee out of courtesy. It had been one of the few occasions that he was still in the building when I was ready to leave. I had come up to his office for a quick, friendly goodbye. Had he ever sought me out in the building to say goodbye before he departed, usually several hours before I did? I was working as hard as I possibly could. Yet now, he was accusing me of trying to destroy the station? I was outraged.

I kept calm and, despite his ridiculous accusations, I told him that the decision to target young people as KISS FM's audience had not been mine at all. Neither did I believe the decision had been Malcolm Cox's. I was simply carrying out the tasks I had been told to do. It was certainly not me who had decided the station would succeed by being a young people's station. That decision to determine KISS FM's target audience had been made by those who were running the company. But McNamee was having none of it. He continued to snarl at me: "You're going to ruin it. It will be a failure and it will fail because it is not what KISS FM is about. KISS FM was a soul station, and now you and Malcolm are trying to turn it into something else, something that you wanted it to be. And it will all be YOUR fault."

I could not take any more of these preposterous accusations and lies. I knew that McNamee had changed a lot over the last few months, but I had not realised that he might be on the verge of paranoia. I told him: "Why do you think I have spent every waking hour for the last few months building this radio station piece by piece with my own hands? Do you really think I would work harder than I have ever done in my life just to see this station fail? Do you really think I've done all I could do to make things happen for KISS FM over the last two years, just to destroy KISS FM? I don't need to stand here and take this sort of shit!"

I got up from the chair, charged out of McNamee's office, slammed his office door and walked back down the stairs to gather together my things. I was stunned. I was absolutely stunned. I just could not believe the conversation I had just endured. And my immediate reaction was to say 'fuck you!' and never to come back. After all the lies McNamee had spun me in the past, all the promises he had broken, all the rewards he had refused me, all the thanks he had never given me, and all the recognition for my achievements he had denied me. I got in my car and drove home, numbed by the whole encounter. What the hell was I doing, working my arse off for someone who not only did not seem to respect me, but who somehow believed that I was out to destroy his radio station? I arrived home and went straight to bed.

Unlike recent nights, I could not even face the prospect of shuffling any more bloody KISS FM paperwork before I went to sleep. This was crazy.

The next day, I was just as angry at McNamee's outburst and expected he might phone me to explain why he had felt so bitter and aggrieved. He needed to offer me some kind of apology for his outrageous behaviour. But the phone did not ring. It was Saturday, so I did some shopping in the supermarket and then drove to Holloway Road to get on with the work at hand. However much I had felt like quitting the previous night, I knew now that I could not do it. Too many people had worked too hard for me to abandon this radio station right now. I had dozens of people working for me in the programming department. I would be letting them down to walk out the door. Anyway, I was not a quitter by nature. When I decided to do something, I would see it through to the bitter end. But I did expect McNamee to apologise for the ridiculous things he had said to me. However, I did not hear from him on Saturday, I did not hear from him on Sunday, and I did not hear from him on the Bank Holiday Monday. On Tuesday, when I entered the KISS FM boardroom for the weekly nine o'clock meeting of heads of department, McNamee acted as if nothing had ever passed between us.

The rest of the week was bedevilled by problems that left me little time to think any more about what had happened on Friday night. Tim Westwood phoned McNamee to say that, after lengthy consideration, he had decided not to defect to KISS FM and, instead, had just renewed his contract with Capital Radio. McNamee was absolutely furious and he raged for the rest of the day to anyone in the building who was within earshot. He shouted and screamed that Westwood had only used KISS FM as a means to improve his contract at Capital, and that Capital must be ecstatic to know that it had destroyed our plans for the KISS FM daytime programme schedule. McNamee shouted that he would never ever let Westwood even consider working for KISS FM in the future. And he vowed, rather ominously, to destroy Westwood's career as much as he could in the future.

I knew from my own dealings with McNamee, and from conversations I had had with others who had crossed his path, that these outbursts occurred after he felt he had been wronged by someone. You were either someone that McNamee liked, or you were someone that he hated. There seemed to be very little space in between for tolerance or understanding. But even I had never seen McNamee articulate so openly, in front of station staff, how much he hated someone as he did on that day. For my part, I viewed Westwood's decision more with sadness than anger. I had been looking forward to working with him and I believed that he would have been a real asset to the station. My biggest problem now was what to do with the gap that Westwood had just created in the KISS FM weekday programme schedule.

Once he had cooled down somewhat, I asked McNamee what he wanted to do. However much it might ruin the programme schedule that the station had already published, I was in favour of shuffling around the programmes. The drivetime show that Westwood would have presented was vitally important to attract young listeners, and I felt it should be filled by Dave Pearce, who would have to switch from his planned morning slot. David Rodigan could stay where he was on the lunchtime show. I suggested switching Trevor Nelson from afternoons to mornings. That still left a hole to fill in the afternoon, between the end of Rodigan's show and the start of Pearce's drivetime slot.

McNamee suggested that we should fill the gap with a daily mix show of records played back-to-back, without announcements or a DJ, broken only by advertisements. He felt that this had been successful on American stations and would work in London as well. I told him that I was not so sure, because the market research had shown that Londoners liked DJs who kept them company during the day. Mix shows would be fine during evenings and weekends, but I was not sure that audience tastes were mature enough yet to inflict a daytime mix show upon listeners. Besides, the engineers had still not installed the equipment in any of the studios that was necessary to produce a mix show. Although KISS FM's publicity had heralded the promise that back-to-back mixes would be a regular feature of its programmes, the facilities were not ready yet.

Instead, I suggested that another of the KISS FM DJs I had tried out at GDO Studios could be recruited to fill the afternoon show. Steve Jackson had demonstrated that he had the right talent to be a daytime DJ, although I had considered him as a 'reserve' until now, because his technical skills still required a considerable amount of practice. McNamee said he was not so sure that Jackson was ready for a daytime show. He still felt that the mix show was a better idea. Even though the necessary equipment had not yet been installed, he suggested that KISS FM could hire time in an outside recording studio in the interim to produce daily mix shows. I had to explain that I was still much too busy to organise the production elsewhere of a show every day. It was too much work to do at the same time as launch a brand new radio station.

Eventually, McNamee told me frankly that, if I really wanted to hire Jackson, the decision was to be on my own head. If the idea failed, it would be my fault because it did not have his endorsement. I realised there and then what a terrible manager McNamee was turning into. If I had introduced a daily mix show and it failed, which I felt sure it would, it would have been my fault. If I introduced Steve Jackson and he failed, it would have been my fault. On the other hand, I also felt certain that, if I introduced Jackson and it worked well, McNamee would probably claim it had been his idea all along. This was not management by any standard. However, I decided I had to take on the challenge. I knew that Jackson MIGHT work, but I knew that daily mixes certainly would not. I could only do what I thought was right, under the circumstances. So I phoned Jackson and told him that, in addition to his weekly show of house music, he now had a daily show on KISS FM every afternoon. Jackson was over the moon.

I sat in my office and reflected on the fact that Tim Westwood seemed not to have joined KISS FM in the end, partly because he was so principled about the music he played in his programmes. I had to admire someone who could stick so closely to his ideals, refusing a prime daytime slot on what might become one of the most popular radio stations in the country, simply because he did not like the prospect of having to play a record by Betty Boo. As McNamee had indicated, there was also the possibility that Westwood had played off KISS FM against Capital Radio to renegotiate his current contract. However, there was no doubt that I had never had such lengthy discussions before with anyone other than Westwood over the artistic merits of a Betty Boo record. I suddenly recalled that the latest issue of Smash Hits magazine had a full-colour poster of Boo as its centrespread. I carefully eased the pages out of the staples and stuck the poster on my office wall. It would serve as a reminder to me that, if it were not for Betty Boo, I might have had Tim Westwood on KISS FM's daytime DJ team. How crazy it was when the seemingly small things in life were the very ones that become the greatest obstacles to your plans.

The other problem I was faced with was Lyn Champion's tardiness in transforming the KISS FM daily magazine show 'The Word' from a good idea on paper into a real programme on the radio. I had offered Champion as much studio time as she needed at GDO Studios over the previous few months, but she and the three researchers had still not managed to produce a pilot programme until now, for reasons that were unclear. Given the same amount of time, and having had to work almost entirely on my own, I had piloted all the daytime shows at GDO and had set up the necessary equipment and systems for a 24-hour, seven-day programme schedule. How was it that Champion still seemed so unprepared for a daily programme that lasted fifteen minutes?

After much discussion with Champion, I went to consult with an angry McNamee and, once again, resisted his suggestion to fire her. In the end, we agreed that, during the station's first weeks on-air, the speech programme would be broadcast three, instead of five, times a week on Monday, Wednesday and Friday. Champion was rightly arguing that the engineers had still not finished building the radio studios, though I too had been forced to work around these problems and find alternate solutions. Champion also argued that two of the three researchers were still not capable of recording or producing good interviews for radio. With this argument, I had less sympathy. It was Champion who had buckled under pressure from McNamee to appoint them, even when there were more experienced candidates on the shortlist. Now it was her task to achieve what she needed from them.

There was another area of unease that had been niggling me about Champion's work. During the drafting of KISS FM's licence application the previous year, and during the planning of the budgets and policy for the station since that January, Champion had proven to be extremely articulate and forthright in her discussions and on paper. At times, McNamee and I had felt that we were drowning under the weight of the memos, policy documents and counter-arguments that Champion invariably produced at every twist and turn along the way. But somehow, despite her certainty in planning her ideas on paper, Champion seemed to have more difficulty translating them into action. She was now charged with leading a team of three researchers, only one of whom had professional radio experience. Champion would need a particularly 'hands-on' approach, to use McNamee's favourite phrase. It was not enough now to expect the others to do all the work. It seemed sometimes that Champion might be reluctant to leave the confines of her office to put the effort into doing radio production herself.

My concerns about Champion were exacerbated by the arrangements made to cover for her maternity leave. I had agreed that Champion would take maternity leave from 13 October, six weeks after the station's launch. To cover her absence, Champion and I had agreed to offer a temporary contract to Lorna Clarke, one of the candidates whom we had interviewed earlier for the postponed producer posts. There would need to be an overlap period before Champion left, so that Clarke could learn the basics of the job. I agreed with Champion that this overlap should be two weeks. However, I discovered later that Clarke had been told to start work on 17 September, which would have given the pair a full month together. How this mistake had been made I never understood but, as Clarke had already been offered this start date in writing, I felt obliged not to change it.

The matter became even more confused when, before the station's launch, Champion pleaded with me to allow Clarke to start work two weeks earlier. In this case,

Clarke's temporary contract would have commenced precisely at the station's launch. I explained to Champion that my budget did not allow for these extra staffing costs. Clarke was already starting considerably earlier than intended and I could not justify more than one month's overlap period. Next, Champion went to McNamee and pleaded her case for employing Clarke earlier, but he too turned her down. In the end, Champion must have persuaded Clarke to start work at KISS FM two weeks earlier, but without pay. I only learnt of this arrangement when I expressed surprise to see Clarke in the building much earlier than I had anticipated, and she told me that Champion had specifically asked her to come in earlier than had been planned.

    I was becoming worried by Champion's behaviour in recent weeks. I could not understand why her previously confident attitude seemed to have given way to slowness in executing the tasks at hand. Now was the time for urgent action. We were all under such immense pressure to succeed and we were so close to the launch of KISS FM.

August & September 1990.

The final few days before KISS FM's official launch were a blur of frenetic activity and outright panic. It was only at this late date that construction of the three studios was completed by the contractors. Now, at last, they were ready for the engineers from the Independent Broadcasting Authority [IBA] to test and inspect. Much to my relief, their report required only a few minor alterations to the air conditioning system, after which the IBA issued KISS FM with a certificate of technical competence. I affixed it to my office wall, alongside the poster of Betty Boo.

With only days to go, I held two long, evening meetings with all the part-time DJs to explain what they could and could not do legally on-air. As former pirate DJs, they were unfamiliar with the conventions of libel, slander and other legal niceties which legitimate radio DJs have to learn. It was important for me to emphasise how essential it was for KISS FM to protect itself against prosecution or rebuke by the commercial radio regulator, the IBA. I went through their employment contracts, page by page, explaining what the jargon meant and what implications the clauses had for their radio shows. Also, I had to stress the importance of playing the right advertisements at the right time. This was a contractual requirement that had been relatively relaxed on pirate stations.

The night before the station's launch, I was still busy putting the finishing touches to the inside of the studio until the early hours of the morning. Although two on-air studios had been built, there was only time to bring one of them up to scratch with all the accessories required for live broadcasts. With only hours to go, the engineers and I were frantically drilling holes in the studio walls to hang the storage racks for audio cartridges used to play advertisements, as well as wiring up the studio lights on the ceiling. I handwrote several large posters in thick felt pen to remind the presenters of the station's address, its phone number for requests, and what to say about the station's launch. Then, I had to spend several hours making labels with a Dymo and sticking them onto each piece of equipment in the studio for the presenters to know precisely which button performed which task. Finally, when everything was ready, I drove home and collapsed into bed.

The next morning, Saturday 1 September 1990, was the biggest day of our lives. Some weeks earlier, Gordon McNamee had hung a handwritten sign on his office wall that read "X DAYS TO GO" with the number being changed daily. That number was now down to zero and the sign had finally become redundant. The day had arrived at last, whether we were ready for it or not. McNamee and I met at the station in the morning and locked ourselves away inside the production studio. McNamee wanted to perform a countdown to the station's launch at midday but, in order to ensure that it went perfectly smoothly, he wanted to pre-record it. I set the timer on my digital wristwatch to five minutes and recorded McNamee's voice, counting down at one minute intervals from five minutes to one minute, and then counting down the seconds during the final minute until the alarm sounded. It took two attempts to get it right.

After that, we moved to the main on-air studio, taking the tape of the countdown with us. We had decided not to allow anyone other than essential station personnel into the studio for the launch. It was not a big enough room to comfortably accommodate more than a few people, and the presence of journalists would only have made us even more nervous. McNamee had arranged for Mentorn Films, which was making the television documentary about the station, to erect a tripod camera in the corner of the studio to record the whole event. A video link had also been booked to relay the picture live to a large screen in Dingwalls nightclub, where the official KISS FM launch party was being held that day.

With all the tension that surrounded that historic day, we quickly forgot that we were being watched by a video camera from the corner of the room. I spooled McNamee's countdown recording onto a tape machine and started it at precisely five minutes to midday. McNamee's countdown was now automatically being superimposed over the music from the test transmission VHS cassette that had been playing continuously for the last ten days. Over the beats of the Kid Frost hip hop track 'La Raza,' McNamee's voice coolly counted down the minutes. At the one minute point, McNamee counted "59, 58, 57, 56...." and I slowly faded out the music to increase the suspense of the moment. Accompanied by the pre-recorded sound of my digital watch alarm, McNamee said the magic words "twelve o'clock."[746]

I turned up the microphone in the studio for McNamee to make KISS FM's live opening speech: "This is Gordon Mac. There are no words to express the way I feel at this moment. So, with your permission, I'd just like to get something out of my system. Altogether – we're on air – hooray!" Everyone in the studio joined in a loud cheer, before McNamee continued: "Welcome, London. Do you realise it's taken us fifty-nine months, four hundred and sixty-five thousand, seven hundred and twenty working hours, plus three and a half million pounds, as well as all of your support over the last five years, to reach this moment? As from today, London and everywhere around the M25, within and without, will have their own twenty-four hour dance music radio station. I'm talking to you from our new studios in KISS House, which is completely different from the dodgy old studios we used to have in the past [laughter in the studio]. The odds were against us. None of the establishment fancied our chances but, with the force of public opinion and our determination, the authorities had to sit up and listen and take notice. Today, I'm being helped by Rufaro Hove, the winner of the Evening Standard KISS 100 FM competition. Refaro was chosen from thousands of people who entered and she will press the button for the first record. But before that, the first jingle."[747]

McNamee pushed the cartridge button to play a lo-fi jingle from KISS FM's pirate days. The sound of a telephone answering machine tone was followed by McNamee's personal assistant, Rosee Laurence, saying: "It's me again. I forgot to say – hooray, we're on. Bye bye." The jingle ended with the sound of a phone being put down.[748]

McNamee continued: "There we go, Rufaro, now you can press the first one. Go!" The first record played on the new KISS FM was the reggae song 'Pirates' Anthem' by Home T, Cocoa Tea & Shabba Ranks. The song was a tribute to London's pirate radio stations. The rallying call of the chorus was:[749]

Them a call us pirates
Them a call us illegal broadcasters
Just because we play what the people want
DTI tries [to] stop us, but they can't[750]

One of the song's verses narrated the story of pirate radio in the UK:
Down in England we've got lots of radio stations

Playing the peoples' music night and day
Reggae, calypso, hip hop or disco
The latest sound today is what we play........
They're passing laws. They're planning legislation
Trying their best to keep the music down
DTI, why don't you leave us alone?
We only play the music others want[751]

These lyrics were the perfect choice for the station's first record. KISS FM's pirate history may have been behind it now, but the station had proven that pirate broadcasting had been necessary to open up the British airwaves to new musical sounds and fresh ideas for the 1990s. 'Pirates' Anthem' was followed by the personal choice of the Evening Standard competition winner, 'Facts Of Life' by Danny Madden. In the studio, the atmosphere was electric. It was difficult to believe that the few of us crowded into that little room were making broadcasting history. This was the creation of the dream that some of us thought we might never witness – a legal black music radio station in London, at last. It was difficult to believe we were really on the air.[752]

Next, McNamee thanked "all the original disc jockeys, all the backers, all the new staff and last, but not by any means least, all of the listeners that have supported us over the five years." He introduced the record that he had adopted as KISS FM's theme tune – 'Our Day Will Come' by Fontella Bass. The station's first advertisement followed, booked by the Rhythm King record label to publicise its latest releases. Soon, McNamee's stint as the station's first DJ came to an end and his place was taken by Norman Jay, whose croaky voice betrayed the emotion of the day.[753]

Jay told listeners over his instrumental 'Windy City' theme tune: "After nearly two very long years, all the good times, all the bad times we shared on radio ... Thanks to all of you. Without your help, this day could not have been possible. On a cold and wet October day in 1985, KISS FM was born. Gordon Mac, George Power and a long time friend of mine, Tosca, got together to put together a station which meant so much to so many. And thanks to those guys, Norman Jay is now on-air."[754]

Once Jay was on the air, McNamee said farewell to the rest of us in the studio and left to attend the station's official launch party at Dingwalls. We stayed in the studio, still thrilled to be part of the celebration of that historic moment and enjoying the music that Jay played. Throughout the rest of the weekend, each KISS FM DJ presented their first show on the newly legal station. Many of them reminisced about the pirate days of KISS FM and played music from that era, when they had last graced the airwaves of London. To the majority of the station's audience, who might never have heard of KISS FM until now, the weekend's broadcasts must have sounded rather indulgent. Far from most of the records played that weekend reflecting the cutting edge of new dance music that the new KISS FM had promised, the songs mostly reeked of nostalgia and the station's former glory days as a pirate station. This brief moment of indulgence was a healing process that was necessary for the station's staff.

I remained in the studio the rest of the day, helping the DJs to grapple with the unfamiliar equipment and showing them the new systems with which they had to contend. Despite the intensive training they had been given in the last ten days, it had been twenty months since any of them had spoken a word on the radio, let alone presented a professional show. Nearly all the DJs looked incredibly nervous, and several seemed gripped with terror at the prospect of having to present a show from a fully equipped radio studio for the first time in their lives. I stayed there until the early hours of Sunday morning, with only an occasional break for a takeaway pizza.

Everybody involved in KISS FM, apart from the small group of us left in the studio – the DJ on the air, me, Lyn Champion and programme assistants Colin Faver and Hannah Brack – were at Dingwalls, enjoying the party celebrations. It felt strange, during the station's first day on-air, that the rest of the huge KISS FM building was entirely empty. In the evening, the only lights visible from outside were in the tiny studio on the first floor. By two o'clock in the morning, I was absolutely exhausted. It had been an incredibly exciting day and everything had run much more smoothly than I had expected. I drove home, having left Champion and Brack to 'babysit' the studio overnight to ensure that the rest of the presenters could cope with the equipment.

When I returned to the station on Sunday, everything still seemed to be going well. The one thing that surprised me was the absence of Gordon McNamee. After his opening announcement in the studio the previous day, he had returned to present his own two-hour show on Sunday and then had left straight away. I was surprised because I had expected McNamee to be present most of the weekend to experience the birth of the radio station. During the run-up to KISS FM's re-launch, McNamee had had little involvement in the day-to-day preparations of the programmes and studios. This was expected because he had effectively passed to me the responsibility of launching the station on-air. However, I had thought he would have wanted to be around more of the time now, if only to offer encouragement and support to the nervous team of DJs. In fact, McNamee was nowhere to be seen.

I had one occasion to contact McNamee on his mobile phone during that first weekend, to explain that there was a minor problem with the British Telecom line that supplied news bulletins to the studio. When he answered his phone, it sounded as if he was in the middle of a busy shopping centre. I asked if he was able to talk, or should I call him back later? He answered that it was fine to talk and that he was in a very expensive restaurant in Knightsbridge, having a meal with his wife. I soon learnt that this incident would become typical of McNamee's much vaunted 'hands on' management technique now that KISS FM was on-air. McNamee seemed happy to swan around London and enjoy himself, whilst his employees were left to do the work on his behalf.

For me, the successful launch of the radio station had proven in itself to be a great achievement. However, at the same time, it had left me absolutely no room to draw breath or to recover from the tribulations of the previous months. We had just given birth to a brand new seven-day, 24-hour radio station, whose live programmes would now be broadcast without cease. It was as if I had turned on a fast flowing tap that would prove impossible to turn off. That tap would be flowing from now until ... until forever ... and my job was to make sure that the water that came out was always the right colour, the right consistency and flowed for every second into exactly the required places. The task was incredibly daunting, if I ever stopped to think about it too much.

I quickly learnt that, in the same way that McNamee had passed to me the responsibility for so much of KISS FM's plans prior to its launch, I was now expected to be in charge of much more than the station's programming. McNamee's job may have been entitled managing director, and his personal assistant may have been promoted to general manager, but, in practice, many problems seemed to fall to me! I quickly understood that, although McNamee had given me a mobile phone to keep in touch with the radio station, wherever I was, it quickly became a millstone in my back pocket.

When a foreign journalist turned up at KISS House in the early hours of the morning, who was it that the security guard on duty that night contacted? Me. When a DJ working on an overnight programme was not sure which advertisement to play in a commercial break, who did he contact? Me. When some fans of the station turned up at KISS House late one night, insisting they had come to pick up tickets for a competition they had won, who was called to sort out the problem? Me. If a security guard on duty at night was unsure as to whether he was allowed to let a DJ into one of the studios, rather than tell the DJ to sort out the problem during office hours, he rang me. Aware that I was required to maintain twenty-four hour contact with the station, everyone knew that I was available, at any time of the day or night. Other staff in the station might turn off their mobile phones at night, but there was one person who could be guaranteed to always answer a phone call.

As a result, the first few weeks that the station was on-air became one long blur of requests, demands and urgent problems in my mind, all of which needed to be solved within an impossible time frame. It felt as if I had gone straight from the frying pan and into the fire. If I had been able to enjoy even one private moment to draw breath and reflect on what had already happened, I might have realised that the achievement of getting an ex-pirate radio station, staffed almost entirely by enthusiastic amateurs, on the air on time was an incredible challenge to have overcome. However, when there is no time to reflect, you simply carry on facing up to the next challenge.

Much to my disappointment, I received very few words of personal encouragement from McNamee after the station had launched. His top floor office seemed to be overflowing with congratulatory bottles of champagne, greeting cards and telegrams from well-wishers. Very few of these gifts or messages were ever communicated to me or the other staff working long hours in the programming department. The most recognition I received for achieving a successful station launch came from McNamee's assistant, Rosee Laurence, who regularly expressed admiration that I could cope with so many simultaneously pressing demands, prioritise them, keep them all in mind and try to solve them successfully.

There was only one occasion during that first week on-air that the pressure and the exhaustion proved too much for me. I had worked too many hours and had had too little sleep when, one morning, my head began to ache as if a bomb was exploding inside. I took some aspirins but still needed to escape from the manic activity of the programming department. I went upstairs to the quiet solitude of the top floor executive suite and laid flat on my back on the floor of the empty office adjoining that of Rosee Laurence. With a newspaper placed over my face to blot out the sunlight, I must have looked ridiculous. It was the first and only time that the whole business of launching a radio station seemed to have become too much for my brain to process.

The one thing with which I tried to console myself was the thought that, at some point in the future – even though it might still be several months away yet – I would be able to reclaim part of my life for myself. Leisure time and a social life had not existed for me for many months. Surely, one day, things must quieten down at KISS FM sufficiently for me to regain some time outside of this building in Holloway Road. On that morning, laid flat out on Laurence's office floor, I was very much looking forward to the day.

---

[746] author's recording, 1 Sep 1990.
[747] ibid.
[748] ibid.
[749] ibid.
[750] 'Pirates Anthem' Words and Music by Calvin Scott and Michael Bennett and Rexton Gordon and Winston Tucker and Stephen Bishop © 1990 Reproduced by permission of Dub Plate Music Publishers Limited, Kingston, Jamaica
[751] 'Pirates Anthem' Words and Music by Calvin Scott and Michael Bennett and Rexton Gordon and Winston Tucker and Stephen Bishop © 1990 Reproduced by permission of Dub Plate Music Publishers Limited, Kingston, Jamaica
[752] "Switch In Time", Evening Standard, 4 Sep 1990.
[753] author's recording, 1 Sep 1990.
[754] ibid.

September 1990.

During September 1990, London was splattered with reams of publicity about KISS FM's launch. The paid-for advertising seemed to stare out from every glossy magazine and from poster sites right across the city, communicating the launch slogan: 'KISS 100 FM – the station on everyone's lips.' Every morning, driving into work, I chuckled to myself when I passed a huge billboard site, next to the Archway bridge in North London, which proclaimed KISS FM's arrival. There were advertisements on television, in cinemas and in newspapers, all of which grabbed people's attention in exactly the right way and reflected the youthful spirit of the radio station.

Andrew Niccol, creative director of KISS FM's advertising agency, BBDO, explained: "The kind of advertising we did … has never been done before. It's taking advertising to the consumers, rather than just sitting back and expecting them to see it. It's important the advertising doesn't alienate listeners who tuned in to KISS as a pirate station." One of the BBDO creative team, Walter Campbell, concurred: "We needed a campaign that would get new listeners to tune to 100 FM. Once they're there, KISS will do the rest. But we also wanted to assure the old crowd that KISS hasn't sold out just because it's gone legal."[755]

The contract between BBDO and KISS FM was novel for the inclusion of a 'payment by results' clause. The success of the agency's advertising campaign was to be measured through three marketing metrics: volume, awareness build and movements in "key image dimension." KISS FM's head of marketing, Malcolm Cox, explained: "The aim of the advertising is to get people to try KISS once, to draw them in, and once there, it is up to us to keep them. BBDO will be measured against our aim to get one million ten to thirty-four year olds to try the station in its first year, and we'll reward the agency for achieving more than one million."[756]

While the paid-for advertising was proving to be incredibly effective, the work of KISS FM's PR agency, Rowers & Cowan, was just as productive. Almost every publication devoted many inches of column space to announcing the launch of KISS FM and many heralded it as one of the media events of the year in London. Journalists swallowed whole the rags-to-riches story of KISS FM, without needing the detail of the station's press releases. Gordon McNamee's photo appeared all over the media, accompanied by witty sound bytes that only served to emphasise how brilliantly he dealt with the hordes of enquiring journalists. One magazine commented: "Mac's virtue is that he is a nice guy, with his feet on the ground." The Independent newspaper commented that, if KISS FM achieved its target of one million listeners, "Mac could be swapping the Mercedes for something even more befitting a hip young media mogul."[757]

KISS FM's head of music, Lindsay Wesker, was wheeled out to assure journalists of how credible the station would remain: "There was a certain underground apprehension on the part of a few people that we couldn't be legal and credible, that we couldn't be a corporation, have control and be groovy at the same time. But how can we fail? The music's going to be incredible! … Even up until a month ago, [BBC Radio One DJ] Simon Bates was declaring that KISS won't work. We'll have a crisis of confidence after a few months, he says, and end up going mainstream. I find that unbelievable: we've got a licence, we're up and running, and the public can't wait!"[758]

Whilst the music magazines and style-orientated publications lapped up the idea of ex-pirate station KISS FM's legal re-launch, there were other areas of the press that expressed their doubts about the station. The Financial Times commented that "frankly, if you have reached your thirties, KISS is not meant for you" and went on to prove its point by referring to the "wrap" music that the station played. The Sunday Telegraph's radio critic, Gillian Reynolds, said: "To look at the [PR] campaign on behalf of KISS FM, you'd think there had never been a radio station before it. On the other hand, to listen to KISS FM is, for anyone over twenty, to suddenly understand apartheid by age." MidWeek magazine noted: "KISS will have a problem convincing listeners, especially the hard core fans who have supported them for the twenty-one months they've been off the air, that the new KISS is just as credible as the old one ... KISS now has to prove whether radical radio and the profit motive can co-exist in the same radio station." However, the article concluded that "with someone like Mac at the helm, maybe it's possible."[759]

Vox magazine commented that "the youth of the greater London area will have already decided if the new, legit KISS FM is crass or crucial." The article noted: "Even before the [launch] celebrations had ended, some uncomfortable rumours were flying around. Rumours of 'mainstream' daytime soul shows with middle-of-the-road playlists being MC'ed by ex-Capital [Radio] presenters. And all this was surely designed to appease middle-aged investors and advertisers – all despite the fact that hard dance tracks were now regularly hitting the charts."[760]

Vox asked Chris Cracknell, managing director of reggae record label Greensleeves, for his comments on the 'new' KISS FM: "What the kids want to hear, and what I want to hear, are the original KISS [disc] jockeys who won the station its popularity and licence in the first place. I'm sure you can get adverts for hardcore dance shows, but the advertising men are too lazy. Instead, they say 'We've got loads of ads for fitted kitchens and jacuzzis, so your daytimes have to be more mainstream.' I know it's going to be difficult for KISS to fight that sort of business pressure ... If KISS is bland, it won't satisfy anyone at all, really."[761]

The Independent newspaper commented: "Some purists remembering the old KISS might be disappointed with its new wider appeal." It described the recruitment of 'outsider' DJs to present some of the KISS FM daytime shows as "a somewhat unimaginative move" and noted that "most incongruously of all, Graham Gold has been brought in to do the breakfast show."[762]

The recruitment of new names was also the main bone of contention of a two-page feature in Soul Underground magazine on the launch of KISS FM. The article complained that "several commercial radio DJs from stations such as GLR and Capital [Radio] are sitting in the hot seats during peak daytime broadcasting hours, while original DJs have been allocated night-time slots, mainly between 10 pm and 12 pm." It went on to reveal that "one presenter, who has been with the station for a long time, was expecting to present a breakfast show, until discovering at the eleventh hour that the slot had been assigned to a DJ previously unconnected with KISS." Another of the station's DJs was reported to be "slightly miffed that, now a budget is in place for DJs, the fee for a two-hour show after 7 pm is only £50."[763]

Soul Underground quoted one unnamed KISS FM DJ who said: "There's a lot of unhappiness among KISS DJs at the moment. We used to be one big happy family, but that has changed. Beforehand, we were all responsible for the format of KISS, but now shareholders such as EMAP and Virgin have a say in the running of programmes ... KISS is supposed to be the 'sound of young London' but, while DJs such as Robbie Vincent and Tony Monson are highly respected on their own scene, they don't necessarily represent young Londoners. The whole thing is a farce. KISS is supposed to play multi-cultural music, but it's being managed by white, middle-aged businessmen."[764]

An unnamed record company executive told the magazine that KISS FM had taken on corporate values and was distancing itself from its previous pirate radio audience: "Instead, the station is veering dangerously towards Capital [Radio] listeners. I know they have to make their money, but did they really have to drag in Graham Gold and Dave Pearce? [KISS FM head of music] Lindsay Wesker says their style of broadcasting is what the listeners want but, from where I stand, they're attracting the wrong following ... You go into the [KISS FM] offices now and they're full of men in business suits with calculators. If they continue in this way, they're going to find themselves rivalling Capital sooner or later."[765]

The Soul Underground article concluded with a quote from another unnamed KISS FM DJ: "I don't know of one original KISS DJ whose morale isn't pretty low right now. I have been at KISS long enough to expect a good slot, but didn't get it. I could have applied for a job on another station, but I didn't because I was holding out for KISS. We all were. There is simply no communication and there doesn't need to be. The KISS big boys know that, for as long as KISS is the only dance music station on-air, it'll do well. They'll be in for a shock when, in two years' time, another dance station comes along and stays a dance station. Believe me – it will happen. I strongly recommend that Gordon Mac holds a big meeting for all DJs before it's too late."[766]

By now, rumblings of discontent amongst the original KISS FM DJs had been breaking out periodically over several months. However, the Soul Underground article was the first public manifestation of a growing feeling of unease felt by many of the DJs. There was no doubt that things had changed considerably since the station's pirate days. More than anything else, it seemed to be McNamee who had changed his attitudes towards his DJs. In the days when KISS FM was still at Blackstock Mews, McNamee had remained accessible to anybody who cared to drop in to the office or call him. DJs would regularly arrive and regale the office staff with news of their adventures. Nothing was thought to be more normal than for everyone to crowd around the office stereo system to listen intently to a new record that someone had brought to the office.

Things were very different now. If it was proving difficult even for me to pin down McNamee during office hours, it must have been ten times as difficult for the part-time DJs to have a casual chat with their ultimate boss. These days, if you did not have something of worth in business terms to discuss with McNamee, it might seem that you had nothing to discuss with him at all. The bad feeling amongst the DJs had started as early as January 1990, when McNamee had taken delivery of his Mercedes company car. The discontent had reached its peak just before KISS FM moved to Holloway Road, when DJs had learnt that three 'outsiders' were to be given daytime shows. McNamee was well aware of the DJs' increasing suspicions about his decisions and motives.

The day of the DJ meeting before the station had launched, McNamee had confessed to me that he expected a rough ride from many of those present. Fortunately, however much the DJs liked to grumble amongst themselves and to me, they were still wary of being outspoken directly to McNamee. That meeting had passed off with little bad feeling being aired. Since then, McNamee had handed me the responsibility for day-to-day relationships with his long-time associates. Despite still presenting a weekly show on the station, McNamee no longer bothered to turn up to his own radio station's DJ meetings. Such things seemed beneath him now. Maybe he had more enjoyable things to occupy his time. As a result, the close relationships he had established during the pirate years with most of the DJs who had supported him and his pirate station were now starting to disintegrate. Now, rather than tackle the DJs' concerns head on, McNamee chose to ignore them.

Bathed in the glow of the voluminous media attention he had captured during KISS FM's launch, McNamee now seemed supremely confident that he could do anything that he wanted. The press would always believe him, whatever he said. The Evening Standard's monthly colour magazine included a regular feature on prominent people and their cars. It reported: "Most company directors have a radio in their company car. Gordon 'Mac' McNamee, managing director of the new dance music station KISS FM has two. When he acquired his 1971 Mercedes 280SE ('the last of the hand-built Mercs'), the car radio only received long and medium wave. But, obviously, KISS FM is an FM station, so Mac had another Blaupunkt fitted. The car is a two-door coupé with electric windows and a sun roof – 'it's lovely because when the windows are open, it's like having a convertible' – which was his choice, though not his perfect choice, which would have been a silver Mercedes Gullwing."[767]

This article, and an accompanying photo of McNamee sat inside the 1971 Mercedes, would have been unremarkable except for the fact that McNamee did not own the car that was featured, let alone drive it around London. Everyone at the radio station knew that he drove a brand new Mercedes company car, in which he had been photographed for an article in the Sunday Correspondent newspaper four months earlier. I happened to notice the Evening Standard article and asked McNamee how it had got its facts so wrong. He shrugged his shoulders and said that, to him, it seemed to make a better story.[768]

I was beginning to learn how lightly McNamee could treat the truth, and that this was by no means a recent phenomenon in KISS FM. One of McNamee's staff from the pirate days, Guy Wingate, wrote an article about the station's history in MixMag magazine to coincide with the re-launch. Wingate admitted: "The history of KISS is well documented, though the truth was often much distorted. Much of the time, this was due to the station's original management team having to pervert the stories to keep the government authorities off their backs … In many of the articles written in the press over the last few years, there has always been pointed (and instructed) mention of the fact that KISS was very heavily raided by the Radio Investigation Service of the Department of Trade & Industry. Yet, despite all their press releases, KISS sometimes went through weeks where the transmitter wasn't taken … As for the studios reportedly changing location after every weekend broadcast, the logistics of this were impossible … KISS the pirate has been glamourised into KISS the legend."[769]

Not only were critics of KISS FM emerging anonymously from within the station and in the press, but also from the established radio industry. The most vociferous of these was Capital Radio DJ Tony Blackburn. He had been a very successful breakfast show DJ in the 1960s and 70s, whose career had started in offshore pirate radio, and he had always demonstrated a love of soul music. Nowadays, he had been relegated to lower profile programmes on Capital's oldies station. Following the launch of KISS FM in London, it would have been disingenuous of Capital Radio to say anything critical about a former pirate station that had threatened publicly to steal its audience. Instead, it seemed that Blackburn had been pushed into the spotlight to tell the world that, as a professional DJ of several decades' standing, and as a recognised soul music man, he thought that KISS FM was a disaster. Only days after the station's launch, Blackburn appeared on the national television station, Channel 4, during primetime to explain that he considered London's KISS FM to be a terrible radio station.

The same views were aired in an opinion piece that Blackburn contributed to Jocks magazine: "KISS FM didn't so much open up on September 1st, it staggered onto the air with all the professionalism of a British Rail station announcement, infact [sic] I think some of the station announcers have better voices than a lot of the KISS FM DJs. For a whole weekend, we were subjected to humourless, badly spoken amateurs thanking the management and telling us all that they were now legal, something we'd all worked out for ourselves. At least every half hour, I was told how much the DJ loved me and that everything was 'crucial.' At one stage on the first day, I heard a DJ actually play a record for 'everyone who knows me' and then invited listeners to send in 'fax messages on a fax 'cause our phones ain't workin'.'"[770]

Blackburn continued in this vein for a further three paragraphs before concluding: "On radio, a good voice is important and the ability to use it properly, a lot of the DJs on KISS talk on a monotone, all sound the same and are not a bit entertaining. These people might be very good in clubs but make the station sound so bad I would go as far as to say it is not professionally acceptable. Naturally these remarks don't apply to the professionals they have on the station such as Robbie Vincent, David Rodigan and a few others."[771]

At the same time, a profile of Blackburn appeared in the Sunday Telegraph, in which he said: "When you listen to those new stations like KISS FM, it shows up how good these old guys are." The interviewer noted, with understatement, that Blackburn "has a bit of a bee in his bonnet about KISS FM."[772]

Five years earlier, it had been reported that Tony Blackburn and fellow DJ Tony Prince were considering a licence application for a soul radio station in London. Nothing had happened. In recent months, Prince had been invited to join the KISS FM board as a non-executive director. Some of Blackburn's fellow DJs at Capital Radio – Peter Young, David Rodigan and Tim Westwood – had been asked to join KISS FM. Even Blackburn's former colleague at BBC Radio London, Robbie Vincent, had joined KISS FM to present a weekend show. However, Blackburn seemed aggrieved that he had never received a call from KISS FM to ask him to be part of the venture.[773]

At the next Monday morning meeting of heads of department, McNamee insisted upon playing Blackburn's television commentary from videotape in its entirety. He seemed to take Blackburn's criticisms very personally and asked me what was to be done. I expressed the opinion that the commentary, and Blackburn's similar press articles, had been cleverly staged by Capital Radio, but gave KISS FM nothing to worry about. After Blackburn had left BBC Radio One in the 1980s, he had criticised the station in the harshest tones. Then, after he had left BBC Radio London, he had criticised that station too. Blackburn was highly self-opinionated and conveniently seemed happy to damn any station that was not his current employer.

I suggested that, if Blackburn's main criticism of KISS FM was that it sounded very different from Capital Radio, then it should be taken as a compliment. The market research had shown conclusively that, if KISS FM had launched sounding the same as every other music radio station, it would fail. It was our station's very differences from the others that would make us successful. In fact, Blackburn's stance in criticising KISS FM should only demonstrate to us that he had no idea what young people wanted from a radio station. His criticisms might even encourage more young people to listen to KISS FM than if he had said that he loved the station.

McNamee seemed unconvinced by my arguments. He was wounded by Blackburn's comments and suddenly seemed filled with self-doubt about the station's 'different' sound. I was reminded of the accusations he had lobbed in my direction late that night before the station's launch – that it was I who would be personally responsible for the station's failure. Now, at this management meeting, I was feeling that McNamee was too eager to blame me for Blackburn's criticisms. Neither did I feel I was receiving support from the other heads of department present.

I could not understand what was going on inside this man's head. Had McNamee lost the courage of his convictions about the radio station he had founded? Rather than be a strong leader who demonstrated commitment to his loyal staff, McNamee already seemed to be floundering, only days after the station had launched. Through Tony Blackburn's criticisms, Capital Radio had scored a direct hit on the managing director of its first competitor in the London commercial radio market. It seemed to be left to me now to hold the ship steady and to demonstrate that KISS FM would only succeed if it refused to follow Tony Blackburn's 'advice.'

---

[755] "BBDO Takes Aggressive Line On KISS FM's Autumn Launch", Campaign, 30 Mar 1990.
Jane Alexander, "Making Noise With Silence", Evening Standard, 24 Aug 1990.
[756] Louise Atkinson, "BBDO Offers 'Payment By Results' On All New Pitches", Media Week, 27 Apr 1990.
[757] Chris North, "Sealed With A KISS", For The Record, September 1990.
Martin Wroe, "No Longer An Illicit KISS", The Independent, 30 Aug 1990.
[758] Andrew Smith, "KISS FM", Melody Maker, 1 Sep 1990.
[759] "Sound Profit In Hip Hop", Financial Times, 29 Aug 1990.
Gillian Reynolds, "Radio's Fairy Godmother To The Rescue", 7 Days magazine, Sunday Telegraph, 23 Sep 1990.
David Davies, "Lip Service", MidWeek, 4 Sep 1990.
[760] Phil Strongman, "KISS FM: No Sell Out?", Vox, October 1990.
[761] ibid.
[762] James Style, "Kissing In Public", The Independent, 31 Aug 1990.
[763] Lisa Brinkworth, "Sealed With A KISS", Soul Underground, Sep 1990.
[764] ibid.
[765] ibid.
[766] ibid.
[767] [untitled], Evening Standard magazine, Sep 1990.
[768] Cynthia Rose, "Pirate Enterprise", Sunday Correspondent, 29 Apr 1990.
[769] Guy Wingate, "Lip Service", MixMag, October 1990.
[770] Tony Blackburn, "Airwaves: Tony Blackburn Comment", Jocks, Oct 1990.
[771] ibid.
[772] Martyn Harris, "The Soul Survivor Of DJ-Speak", Sunday Telegraph, 23 Sep 1990.
[773] The Mouth, "Street Noise", Blues & Soul, 3 Sep 1985.

September 1990.

Eight days after KISS FM's arrival on the airwaves, the station staged a huge public launch party in the form of a daytime open-air concert on Highbury Fields, only a few hundred metres away from the Holloway Road office. Although publicity for this event had initially been very slow, by the beginning of the month the event had gathered a momentum that seemed impossible to stop. Naturally, the station had promoted the concert extensively on-air during its first week, and new acts were being added to the all-star line-up on a daily basis.

Driving into work that Sunday morning, my journey came to a standstill a mile from the office. Cars had already been parked along the roads leading to the event, and the pavements were jammed with people walking to the event. It took me an hour to travel the final mile to the radio station, a distance that usually only took a matter of minutes, even in the weekday rush hour. Suddenly, it was brought home to me very clearly how enormous KISS FM's listenership must be after only a week. At the radio station, everybody was excited because we could look out of the office window at the back of the building and see, literally, thousands of people teeming into Highbury Fields. These were our listeners! For the last week, we had been broadcasting into the ether above London, never knowing whether more than a few hundred people were listening to us. But here was the proof. If any one event made the entire KISS FM staff believe that the station was already a success, it was the sight of all those people who had decided to spend a sunny September day with us ... just because we had invited them.

Although most of the day's activities were taking place at Highbury Fields, the KISS FM building was also very busy. The entire floor used by the programming department had been turned into a changing room for the artists to use. This proved very convenient for us to grab interviews with each of them before they went on-stage. Sufficient material was gathered during that one day to make dozens of editions of 'The Word' programme over the following few weeks. I went downstairs to the production studio and found a very fraught Lyn Champion, head of talks, in animated conversation on the phone. She put the phone down and told me that Gordon McNamee had been calling her, demanding that she put on-air a live link from the Highbury Fields stage. I was surprised. During all the preparations, McNamee had not mentioned to me anything about a live link-up.

Investigating further, I found that McNamee had unilaterally arranged for the station's engineering contractor to set up a microwave radio link from the event stage to the studio, without informing us. Champion was very concerned that the quality of the audio received from the stage was so awful that it did not bear transmission on the radio. I listened too and indeed, it sounded like someone playing a stereo system very loudly in a bathroom. The quality was appalling and would sound exactly that way coming out of listeners' radios. I felt that it would do neither the station, nor the artists who happened to be performing at the time, any service to broadcast such poor quality sound. Besides, I was not sure that KISS FM had even sought permission from any of the artists to relay their live performances to the whole of London.

I contacted McNamee on his mobile phone at the event and told him that, after listening to the microwave link, I agreed with Champion that the sound quality was too poor to put on-air. McNamee exploded with anger and called me every swear word under the sun. However, I refused to lose my temper and told him that, from where I was standing in the studio, the quality would sound dreadful for the stations' listeners, a fact that he would not be able to appreciate himself, being at the event. Everybody in the studio had agreed upon this – Champion, me and the DJ on-air at the time. It would be crazy to put something on-air that sounded so bad. McNamee raged at me some more and then the phone line went dead.

I imagined that McNamee might turn up at the studio and put the live link on-air himself, but maybe he was too busy enjoying the privileges of the VIP Enclosure he had organised backstage at Highbury Fields. I never saw McNamee visit the station studios that day, but I realised that I would bear the brunt of his bitterness at some point in the future, so I would not have escaped unscathed.

More importantly than putting the event on-air, by mid-afternoon the police and transport authorities were asking the station to broadcast appeals asking people not to try and travel to the event because the area could not cope with more visitors. I happily obliged. These announcements only served to reinforce in the minds of our listeners the power that the station was able to wield after only one week on-air.

At the very end of the day, when the crowds had finally dispersed happy and fulfilled, I cleared up the debris that the artists had left in their 'dressing room' and drove a mile or so down the road to the after-event party that had been organised. There were bouncers on the door of the venue, to whom I identified myself as a KISS FM staff member and showed my ID card. They made me wait ... and wait ... and wait. Then, one of them came back and told me that I was not on their list of approved guests. I told them that I must be. I worked for KISS FM and this was the radio station's party. They insisted that I was not one of the invited guests of whom they had been made aware. I realised that there was little point in getting angry with two very large bouncers that KISS FM had contracted for the event. The only person I knew that would be inside the event with a mobile phone was McNamee. This was not a good time to ask him a favour. Instead, I drove home frustrated and angry at my exclusion.

If the acres of press coverage that KISS FM had attracted a week earlier for its launch were not enough, the Highbury Fields event resulted in more positive attention for the radio station. The day was expected to attract 30,000 people, though the police estimated that 100,000 people were present. Even by six o'clock in the evening, newcomers were still arriving at the rate of five hundred per minute. The final line-up included appearances by stars such as LL Cool J and Toni Tony Tone who flew in from America, Aswad, Caron Wheeler, Maxi Priest, Sybil, The Pasadenas and Beats International.[774]

Blues & Soul magazine referred to the "enormous audience" that turned up, and commented that it was "the sort of event which would never happen in New York." Unfortunately, local residents in the area seemed less pleased about the 100,000 people who had disturbed their weekend. The Islington Gazette asked: "What about the consideration of all the people who live within a mile's radius of the Fields, whose quiet Sunday was affected as Highbury became like Wembley on Cup Final day? Even their local tube station had to be closed twice because of overcrowding. And should Islington poll tax payers be expected to pick up the tabs for clearing up the mess? Islington Council handed over the Fields free of charge to

KISS FM – then had to pay rubbish collectors to clear up the sea of litter and cans, when they could have been employed clearing up our filthy streets. All KISS FM had to pay was the standard £165 licence fee to stage the event."[775]

KISS FM chairman Keith McDowall replied that "the number attending surprised everybody, including the council and the police. And yet the crowd was very well behaved, there were few incidents and the police have congratulated us on the good behaviour ... But, just for once, couldn't we look on the bright side and see that some young Londoners of all ethnic backgrounds worked hard, achieved a local success, provided some employment and economic activity, and actually gave 100,000 well-behaved people a bit of fun."[776]

Buoyed by the success of the launch party in the park, McNamee was very keen to organise more live events for the radio station. Leisurewear company LA Gear had sponsored the concert, encouraging McNamee to believe that further revenues could be earned from similar tie-ins. After only five days on-air, a live broadcast was organised from the HMV record shop in London's Oxford Street during KISS FM's lunchtime show. During the following months, there were many more outside broadcasts from jeans shops, record shops, nightclubs and concert venues, each of which produced valuable revenue.

For the programming department, these sponsored outside broadcasts brought with them immense logistical problems, which the organisation could barely cope with so soon after the station's birth. McNamee and the head of sales, Gary Miele, charged sponsors several thousand pounds for each live broadcast, justified by their argument that the station had many extra costs to cover, including the hiring of engineers, production staff and overtime payments for the DJs involved. However, almost all of that revenue went straight to the station's bottom line. The truth was that the only additional cost was the lease of a British Telecom landline for a few hours to send the signal from the location back to the studio. As soon as a sale was made, McNamee and Miele dumped the organisation of the whole event in my lap, without any budget to achieve it. This meant me having to beg the necessary staff, including the DJ, to work extra hours for no pay. Worse, it detracted everyone involved from the most important task of ensuring that the radio station's programmes sounded good during those important first few weeks on-air.

The situation was exacerbated by the fact that the station had no in-house engineering department. By default, I became responsible for the technical, as well as the production, elements of each of these outside broadcasts. McNamee seemed to have no idea how much effort it required to ensure that a one- or two-hour sponsored event would run smoothly. As a result, the first few weeks of KISS FM were littered with such affairs, each making a profit of several thousand pounds but, at the same time, taking the station's programming team almost to breaking point from the amount of extra work generated. When I raised this issue, McNamee told me that the station needed any revenue it could find and that, if it meant extra work for everyone, so be it. I tried to explain to McNamee that, if KISS FM's programmes sounded sloppy, the station would not succeed in attracting the one million listeners it had promised. The outside broadcasts continued to pile up regardless.

KISS FM's lack of an in-house engineering department quickly proved to be unworkable. McNamee's insistence on contracting this work to his former pirate radio friends, Phoenix Communications, was a disaster. Phoenix never moved into the office allocated to it in the KISS FM building. Now that the equipment had been installed in the KISS FM studios,

Phoenix seemed to be very busy selling its services to other radio stations in the UK and abroad. During those first few months, many problems arose with the studio equipment but, when I needed Phoenix to attend and assist, it proved notoriously hard to pin down. Often, its office in the Midlands would be unattended, its answering machine tape would be full and its fax machine would have run out of paper. As a last resort, I had to contact a local engineer in London for help with emergencies, and he would then invoice Phoenix for his services.

Some elements of the radio studios were still incomplete. KISS FM's launch publicity had announced that back-to-back music mixes would be an important part of its output. However, the mixing equipment that Phoenix had installed still did not work. To work around this problem, I had to ask DJ Richie Rich to bring all his own equipment from home, which I then wired up to a tape recorder and edited the results as we went along. The resulting two-hour mix was recorded and produced by me, late one night in the station's production studio. It was brilliant fun, knowing that together we were producing the very first 'KISS FM Master Mix,' but it would have been made a lot easier if the correct studio equipment could have been used.

Worryingly, there were several occasions when KISS FM went off the air completely due to a fault with the digital section of the British Telecom landline that connected the Holloway Road studios to the transmitter in South London. If the station had employed a chief engineer, as planned, these problems could have been solved quickly. Instead, I found myself trying to deal with highly technical matters about which my understanding was quite limited. One morning, as I drove to work, the station went completely off the air – first, one channel of the stereo signal, and then the other. I stopped the car and phoned the station to find out what had happened, only to learn that a British Telecom engineer had visited the building, without an appointment. He had pulled out the plugs in the main connection box, without even realising that he had taken KISS FM off-air. I spoke to the engineer and demanded to know exactly what he thought he was doing, but he remained completely nonchalant about the fact that he had destroyed any audience the KISS FM breakfast show might have had that day.

One problem that quickly became apparent was that one of the two on-site technical staff that Phoenix had employed to work at KISS FM was not up to the job. With regret, I had to ask Phoenix to replace this person with someone who could cope more skilfully with the equipment and the production work that we needed. I pressed McNamee to acknowledge that the contracting out arrangement was not working, and that it should be replaced by an in-house engineering department, as used by every other London-wide station. He and Martin Strivens eventually responded by commissioning a report from the London-based engineer who Phoenix regularly sub-contracted, to outline how the station's technical needs might be organised. After the barest amount of research, the report's main recommendation was that KISS FM should hire the engineer himself as a consultant.

Neither McNamee not Strivens had consulted me beforehand about the commissioning of the report or its aims. I had to reject its main recommendations as totally unworkable. KISS FM needed its own engineering department and there was no way to avoid that issue. I could not endure the struggle any longer of having to be responsible for all the station's technical aspects whilst Phoenix Communications, which had been contracted by McNamee to do the job, was rarely seen. Strivens countered that there was no budget available to change the arrangement, and McNamee explained that he had personally promised Phoenix the contract. The matter remained unresolved.

Another technical aspect of the station that was not functioning properly was the computer network linked to terminals on every floor. The whole system crashed almost daily and there had been no computer training organised for the staff. When I requested training for the programming department staff, Strivens told me that this could not be undertaken during office hours, so would have to be organised at weekends. I explained that, because most of my staff worked on shift systems and were already labouring much longer hours than they were supposed to, I could not expect them to attend a weekend training session without extra pay. Strivens was unmoved – it was either weekends or nothing. So it remained 'nothing,' and the staff remained untrained in how to use the expensive technology.

However, several of the programming department staff tried to master the computer system themselves by playing around with different commands and written instructions. They soon found that one advantage of a network was the ability to look into everybody else's computer files in every other department. The computer company had apparently installed no security barriers. It was not long before those programming staff who had terminals on their desks were telling me the intricate details of other people's employment contracts, including their salaries, and asking if I was aware of several pieces of highly confidential correspondence written by McNamee's personal assistant, Rosee Laurence. I made McNamee and Strivens aware of the potential breaches of confidentiality caused by the unsecured network. However, the computer company failed to fix the problem. Soon, several members of my staff were more aware than I was of indiscretions that were taking place within the company.

Similarly, the computer company failed to deliver the database system for the record library which I had requested in the summer to be ready for the station's launch. As an interim measure, head of music Lindsay Wesker and the new record librarian had organised all the records on the shelves into alphabetical order. The computer contractor's failure to supply the programme meant that no data about the station's stock of records could yet be entered into the computer system. Once again, I asked Strivens if I could buy one of the many off-the-shelf library systems that were available. Again, he insisted that there was no additional budget available outside of the one computer company he had contracted to do all the station's work.

It seemed to be the same story so much of the time, now that KISS FM was on-air. When staff problems, bad workmanship or malpractice were identified within the station, neither McNamee nor Strivens seemed willing to take the necessary action to solve them appropriately. Whilst the creative shop floor of KISS FM was buzzing with activity, the top management of the radio station seemed unable to respond to even the simplest demands. My staff was starting to ask me regularly – what the hell is going on here?

---

[774]"The Revellers Welcome KISS", South London Press, 14 Sep 1990.
[775]The Mouth, "Street Noise", Blues & Soul, no. 570, [exact date unknown].
"Never Say 'Never Again'?", Islington Gazette & Stoke Newington Observer, 20 Sep 1990.
[776]Keith McDowall, "Let's Look On The Bright Side", Letters, Islington Chronicle, 29 Sep 1990.

September & October 1990.

By the end of KISS FM's first week of broadcasting, it was evident that the programming department was woefully under-resourced. The severe budget cuts that had been implemented since the station had won its licence were now inhibiting the ability of its inexperienced staff to sustain a 24-hour music radio station. Out of the complement of fifty-seven people employed in the programming department, only three had previous experience of commercial radio (David Rodigan, Tony Monson and Robbie Vincent), whilst a further three had BBC radio experience (Lyn Champion, Sonia Fraser and Dave Pearce). The remainder had experience that had been limited to pirate or community radio operations. Many of them had never been involved in any radio station other than KISS FM.

Amongst the DJs I had assigned to present overnight shows were some whom I felt had the least potential. Very quickly, some of them were found to need the most assistance. At night, the building was empty except for the security guard on duty and the DJ on-air. During the first week of programmes, many of the overnight DJs found it hard to cope with the unfamiliar studio equipment on their own. They pleaded with me, and with Gordon McNamee, to provide them with a programme assistant who could help them produce their programmes and prevent the mistakes that I had heard in their first shows. Amazingly, McNamee agreed to fund a further programme assistant to be paid £10,000 per annum. I immediately interviewed a possible candidate, Alan Russell, who had worked with Dave Pearce at GLR, appointed him, and he started work at KISS FM two days later on the overnight shift.

During those first few weeks, it started to become clear why head of talks Lyn Champion had been so insistent on wanting her maternity leave replacement, Lorna Clarke, to work at KISS FM from its first day on-air. It appeared that Clarke was doing most, if not all, of the hands-on production of 'The Word' programme, whilst Champion mostly stayed in her office and instructed Clarke and the three researchers as to what to do. Champion's office had been wrongly built without windows by the contractors, so it was impossible to see what she was doing with her time. However, I rarely found her getting her hands dirty in the studios downstairs.

I was still up to my ears in work. However much I wanted to transfer my radio skills to the fifty-seven people I was managing, the process was inevitably slow and, at times, proved quite frustrating. I had asked each specialist music presenter to produce a 'trail,' which was a very short, pre-recorded tape to advertise their programme on-air during the rest of the output. I thought that they had understood my instructions, and several DJs presented me with tapes into which they had undoubtedly put hours of painstaking studio work. However, many of their efforts were more than a minute in length, when I required something that was either fifteen or thirty seconds, and some DJs had forgotten to mention either the day or the time of their own programme. It made me realise that it was going to take time for many of them to improve their radio skills.

I arranged a meeting with Champion, Clarke and the department administrator, Philippa Unwin, to try and re-distribute some of my workload. Although I did not say it explicitly, I felt that Champion could be doing more to help me with the organisation of the department, particularly as she possessed the prior experience in radio that so many of the other staff lacked. I drew up a list of the priority tasks I needed to solve urgently and asked Champion to take responsibility for some of these areas. She agreed and I heaved a sigh of relief that she would provide me with the practical assistance that I so needed.

However, a few days later, I was surprised to find that Champion's offer of 'assistance' to me seemed to have been interpreted as a call to write another huge memo, rather than practical action. In it, she set out what she felt should be my work priorities, and she detailed those areas in which she thought I was failing my duties. Paperwork seemed to be the main way in which Champion could function. Perhaps she considered herself an ideas person, and maybe 'management' was about telling others what to do, rather than doing it herself. I started to feel sad and extremely disappointed with Champion's contributions, now that the station had launched. She had proven to be an excellent work colleague throughout KISS FM's licence application, and during the planning of the radio station. But now, when I desperately needed practical help from a radio professional, she wrote me memos. Worse, she copied them all to McNamee, which annoyed him (and me) immensely. These latest memos from Champion only offered McNamee a stick to help beat me with.

The inexperience of the KISS FM staff continued to consume a lot of my time and energy. Steve Jackson, to whom I had offered a daytime show only days before the station's launch, was extremely nervous in the studio and tended to panic when any little thing went wrong. For his first few days on-air, I had to stand at the back of the studio, reassuring him and instructing him as to what he should do next. Eventually, I shared these duties with others in the department. We quickly established a rota to 'babysit' Steve Jackson until such time as he felt confident enough to present the two-hour daily show on his own. However chaotic his programme might have seemed to those of us working with him, it quickly became obvious that my decision to hire him had been the right one. The audience reaction to Jackson's programmes, in phone calls and letters, was extremely positive, even during those first few weeks.

Another production chore that took up a considerable amount of my time was the KISS FM chart show presented by Graham Gold on Saturday afternoons. Only days before the station's launch, I had concluded four months of negotiations for the company Chart Information Network to supply KISS FM with a weekly chart based on sales of dance records across the previous seven days. The problem I faced was that nobody else in the station had produced a chart music show. The chart arrived at KISS FM by fax on Friday afternoon, which meant I had to prepare the records every Friday night and then come to work on Saturday to supervise the show as it was broadcast live.

After several weeks of following this routine, I asked Lindsay Wesker if he might like to learn how to produce the chart programme. Perhaps I could alternate the task with him week by week. He agreed and came to the studio one Saturday to watch me produce the show. Because the last record played in the show would be that week's number one, you had to work from the end of the programme backwards, timing each record and making sure there was room to fit in all the necessary records. I explained to Wesker that the appropriate records to play were those that either had risen in the chart that week or had stayed in the same position, but not those that had fallen.

Wesker looked at that particular week's chart and told me that I should play this record and that record. I explained that the ones he was choosing were not the records showing increased sales. He replied that the ones he had selected were definitely the best records, regardless of their movement in the chart. I reminded him that the whole idea of a chart show was to provide the listener with an objective opportunity to hear the records that the public was buying. Wesker told me, in no uncertain terms, that if he were producing the show, he wanted to play the records he considered to be the best. "What is the point of playing bad records?" he asked me. I explained that, were he to listen to every other chart show on radio, he would find that their criteria for playing a record were exactly the same as mine. This was not my idea. This was the system for producing a definitive, objective chart show. Wesker was not satisfied with my answers and walked out of the studio.

Another of Wesker's convictions was that a weekly playlist meeting, that he wanted to chair, would be the perfect way to select the station's playlist. However much I tried to convince him that there was more to selecting the records for a playlist than a show of hands, he was adamant that it should be the task of a carefully selected sample of KISS FM DJs whom he would invite to a meeting every Thursday afternoon. I attended the first of these meetings and it quickly degenerated into nothing more than a shouting match between people who were passionate about their particular musical interests, but intolerant of others. At that first KISS FM playlist meeting, I had to expel DJ Steve Jackson from the room because his only contribution was to complain about any record we tried to listen to that did not fit his definition of 'house music.'

After the initial few weeks of playlist meetings that started early, finished late and were filled with arguments, rather than rational discussion, Wesker abandoned the idea altogether and replaced it with one that seemed just as nonsensical. Each week, he filled several sides of paper with the titles of every new record that he knew to be released that week, and then circulated the list to staff in the building, asking people to put their initials by their favourite records. It was not only the DJs whose opinions were solicited, but everybody from secretarial staff to sales people, many of whom must have known little about the records listed. Each Thursday, Wesker could be seen stalking around the building with his clipboard, soliciting people's views. The one person he never consulted about the station's music playlist was me.

Initially, I felt that it was best to let Wesker consider his prime responsibility to be the production of the KISS FM playlist. However, after only a few weeks on-air, I sensed that his policies towards the station's music were changing. Throughout the station's planning period, Wesker had always said that KISS FM's music policy would not be dictated by the record companies. If a record was good, it would be played on the station, even if it was not yet released in the UK. The overwhelming majority of dance music still originated from America. KISS FM's policy would be to play the best music it unearthed, even if that music was not commercially available to record buyers in Britain. Before the station's launch, Wesker had even told the press that he would not welcome visits to the station by promotional representatives of the record labels, whose role was to persuade radio stations to play particular new releases. Radio & Music magazine had noted that "KISS doesn't allow pluggers into the station." Wesker was adamant that KISS FM's music policy would not be at the mercy of the record industry.[777]

During the first few weeks, Wesker carried out that policy to the letter, choosing records for their intrinsic worth. Then, after a month on-air, Music Week published a front-page story headlined "North-South Divide Knocks Dance Sales." It argued that sales of dance music records were not reaching their full potential: "The problem is most keenly felt in London's specialist dance shops, particularly since incremental dance radio station KISS FM came on-air with its promise to be the first with new tracks. London retailers say they are turning away customers who want to buy singles they have heard on the radio or in clubs three or four weeks before release."[778]

A more detailed story inside the magazine complained: "KISS 100 FM has made an immediate impact on London's record stores but, thanks to the station's playlisting policy, they are being besieged by listeners clamouring for records that are either not due out commercially for weeks (in particular the Ten City newie, which was being played off tape), or old and out of stock. This is frustrating for the independent dance music dealers, who are having a tough enough time as it is at the moment. There are still far too many dance records coming out for any dealer to stock them all in depth, but a fashionable 'buzz' can still grow rapidly around certain records and then fade almost as fast, the novelty of new records being what keeps dance music buyers (who are spoilt for choice) coming back for more – and the danger is that KISS 100 FM's listeners will have lost interest by the time that the records being plugged way in advance are finally out."[779]

The Following month, Billboard magazine in America picked up the same story: "While British labels and artists continue to enjoy the widespread public interest generated by the recently introduced KISS 100 FM dance music outlet, independent dealers are singing a different tune. It seems they are having difficulties filling requests for singles heard on the station. One of the playlist policies at KISS 100 FM is advance airplay of upcoming releases, and occasional rotation for out-of-print singles. For instance, the station played the new Ten City single 'Whatever Makes You Happy' off a cassette two weeks before it was shipped commercially. 'There is a definite danger that [KISS 100 FM] listeners will have lost interest [in the single] by the time we stock it,' says one UK dealer."[780]

KISS FM's response to these criticisms should have been to shrug its shoulders and reply "tough." KISS FM was not in business to help either record companies or record shops sell records precisely when or how they wanted to. KISS FM was an entertainment business in its own right and had to determine its music policy without reference to external commercial forces. The proportion of listeners to KISS FM who visited record shops to buy records they had heard on the station must have been tiny. Anyway, the overlap between radio listeners and record buyers was very small, so the overlap between KISS FM's listeners and the handful of record shops in London that specialised in dance music must have been even smaller. Music Week's criticisms were those of the determinedly self-interested music industry and should have been ignored.

Instead, it appeared that Wesker took these criticisms to heart and, almost overnight, instigated a complete about turn in KISS FM's music policy. Suddenly, he would only add an imported record to the station's playlist after verifying with the British subsidiary or licensee when it was to be released in the UK. Although KISS FM's music policy had been promoted as breaking new records that were ignored by other radio stations, soon Wesker was holding back records from airplay that he had possessed for months. On several occasions, I asked him why a particular dance music hit in America was not yet on the station's playlist, and he replied that the British record company had postponed the single's release in Britain by a further few weeks. He argued that he did not want to play the record 'too early.'

Wesker now seemed to see his role within the radio station as helping record companies to maximise their sales of dance music records, rather than choosing records that would entertain KISS FM's audience. Wesker seemed to be trying his utmost to remain in favour with the record companies, who supplied their releases free of charge to the station. By remaining on the best of terms with the record companies, he could request and receive just about any record release he requested. Wesker was like a kid let loose in a sweet shop on his own. Suddenly, he appeared to be doing all he could to please the record companies. Their representatives started to make regular visits to the station, and Wesker was regularly out of the office at lunchtimes, enjoying expense account dinners with record company executives. The determined independence in music policy that the pirate KISS FM had worn so proudly on its sleeve was now in danger of being replaced by corporate back-scratching between two highly interdependent parts of the incestuous music industry.

In one of its earliest manifestos, when it was a pirate radio station, KISS FM had declared: "We are a taste-making station. Our playlist is built up from PRE-RELEASE RECORDS ... We spot 'hits' before anyone else, which is one of the reasons why our audience follows and trusts us." Only months before its re-launch, McNamee had promised: "Our playlist is mainly for new music that is from new albums, unreleased or pre-released tracks, or maybe even a demo tape that's been sent in by some obscure band that we think is extremely good." Wesker had promised: "The most happening records will be on that playlist, and that's it. And it will be the first playlist in history to feature imports. This is the beginning of a black music industry."[781]

Between then and now, what had happened? Had KISS FM sold its soul? Had Wesker, whose determination to build an independent playlist had always been so strong, started to lose the plot?

---

[777] Ian Nicolson, "Are We Being Served?", Radio & Music, 7 Nov 1990.
[778] "North-South Divide Knocks Dance Sales", Music Week, 6 Oct 1990.
[779] James Hamilton, "James Hamilton Column", Music Week, 2 Oct 1990.
[780] Larry Flick, "Dance Trax", Billboard, 3 Nov 1990.
[781] "A Bid To Be Legal", KISS FM manifesto, [undated].
Paul Easton, "UK Now Moving To Urban/Dance Beat", Billboard, 2 Jun 1990.
Debbie Kirby, "KISS FM Goes Legal", Echoes, 6 Jan 1990.

October 1990.

The harsh criticisms that Tony Blackburn had made on television of KISS FM's DJs, immediately after the station's launch, were soon followed by similar opinions in the press. Record Mirror commented: "KISS 100 FM sounds best when, with the honourable exception of a few such obviously experienced radio presenters as Dave Pearce, David Rodigan and Graham Gold, most of its other DJs shut up and let the music do the talking. Their enthusiasm for and knowledge of the music cannot of course be faulted, but enthusiastic amateurs are still to be found on the many remaining pirates, to whom kids will tune if that's what they want while, unfortunately, the big budget advertisers the station needs in order to pay the bills now that it's legal are not particularly interested in that young demographic and could well be frightened off completely by an overly amateurish approach, regardless of the size of the audience ..."[782]

Record Mirror subsequently published several readers' letters that agreed with this viewpoint. One correspondent wrote: "Imagine my dismay after tuning in and listening to what can only be described as a bunch of complete and utter amateurs attempting to be broadcasters." Another said: "The presentation on KISS 100 FM is absolutely diabolical. The presenters act as though they are still a pirate station ... This isn't radio presentation. It's shabby. Send the jocks to radio presenting school or seek out better ones."[783]

BBC Radio One DJ Mark Goodier told Record Mirror: "I admire their loyalty to the DJs they had when they were a pirate station but I think, in a major market like London, if they want to convince the public that it's good music they're playing and that they know what they're doing, they need DJs who can string words together a bit better – they need good BROADCASTERS. I think they're going to have to sharpen up a bit if they're going to maintain their success, and that's not a bad thing because, if you're playing good music, it'll sound that much better. I don't think that KISS FM should still sound like a pirate station."[784]

Another BBC Radio One DJ, Andy Kershaw, filmed a ten-minute commentary that was broadcast by Channel 4 television and criticised KISS FM with as much vitriol as had Tony Blackburn. This programme was produced by Mentorn Films, the company that had made the documentary about KISS FM's launch which was to be broadcast by the same television channel the following day. Kershaw said: "I'm sure the KISS FM guys are dynamite in the clubs, but they are not used to communicating. Put them on the radio and, understandably, they shout as though they are addressing a crowd. They are neither exciting, nor authoritative. They are, by and large, incompetent, lacking in humanity and have nothing to say. I have listened fairly solidly since last Saturday, and I have not heard one DJ say anything interesting all week ... Unless the audience expectations are as minimal as the abilities of the presenters, I wouldn't be too optimistic about [KISS FM's] future."[785]

Already, I was becoming used to hearing highly critical opinions expressed publicly about KISS FM. The station was being targeted by the DJs of radio stations competing with KISS FM, and by people who were themselves probably outside of the youth audience the station was seeking to attract. For me, the fact that long established radio stations were bothering to criticise KISS FM on national television must have meant that our new, little

London radio station was worrying them considerably. They had not made similar comments when Jazz FM or Melody Radio had launched. I felt that this validated what we were doing. However, these issues would not go away and, if anything, they had started to become more significant within the station.

At the beginning of October, Gordon McNamee showed me a two-page letter that KISS FM non-executive director Tony Prince had written to him, criticising the station's unprofessionalism and expressing doubts about the daytime music policy. I met with McNamee and head of marketing Malcolm Cox and, together, we drafted a detailed response for McNamee to send back to Prince. It explained that KISS FM sounded this way not because we were sloppy or unprofessional, but because all the pre-launch market research that the station had commissioned demonstrated that this was the style of broadcasting that would prove popular with young people. KISS FM's potential audience had stated categorically that they would not tune to a new radio station that sounded like a pale imitation of BBC Radio One or Capital Radio.

Having received McNamee's reply, Prince still expressed reservations about the station's direction, so I was asked to meet him in the boardroom to discuss the matter. This was a rare occasion for me to chat with one of the station's directors. Prince's main criticism was that there were insufficient features in KISS FM's daytime programmes, something that, he believed, made successful radio. Why, he asked me, were there not more competitions in the morning show aimed at housewives? Could not the station introduce recipes or features that would specifically attract housewives to listen? I explained to Prince that the notion that housewives constituted the majority of radio's daytime audience was a myth. I had painstakingly analysed the radio industry audience data to determine KISS FM's likely audience during the day, and it was certainly not housewives. The commercial radio industry had propagated the myth of the 'housewife' listener since its inception in 1973. I was programming KISS FM to appeal to the agreed target audience of fifteen to thirty-four year olds. I did not believe that they wanted silly competitions or recipes. Prince listened to me, but still seemed unconvinced.[786]

I knew that the only incontrovertible proof of the appropriateness of KISS FM's current programming policy would be statistics that showed the station was attracting a significant audience. Fortunately, only a few days later, the station received the results of a market research survey that its advertising agency, BBDO, had commissioned. It showed that the station had just over 750,000 listeners between 19 and 25 September. These numbers were a solid indication that KISS FM was already on target to achieve the one million listeners it had promised advertisers by the following September. The figures also showed that 96% of listeners were within the ten to thirty-four year old demographic that the station was targeting. McNamee called a meeting in the boardroom to inform the staff of this good news, and the station issued a press release the same day. More than anything, this press release helped calm the internal rumblings from Tony Prince.[787]

Whilst I was pleased with the 750,000 figure, I knew that the only data that mattered were the official JICRAR radio industry numbers that would not be published until January 1991. Neither did I want the programming staff to think that the battle for listeners had already been won and that they could work less hard from now on. I circulated a note to all fifty-seven personnel in my department: "Many thanks for all the hard work you've put in to help achieve these impressive results. We all need to keep it up so that we reach our ultimate goal of getting one million listeners tuned in ... In the meantime, it's worth remembering that that our first full-scale audience research is underway. JICRAR started last month and continues into December. Thousands of people all over London are filling in diaries right now every day with what they listen to on the radio hour by hour ... So, we've come a long way in the first month. Let's carry on in the knowledge that we're on the right course and can turn KISS into the most successful new radio station ever heard in London."[788]

In order to discover, in more detail, what the audience perceived as KISS FM's strengths and weaknesses, I commissioned a further survey from Sirius Research, the company that had provided such useful insights prior to the station's launch. From a series of group interviews with people who either liked or disliked the station, Sirius concluded that "KISS has succeeded in establishing a strong, distinct image," but suggested some areas where improvement was required. The breakfast show, for example, "currently fails to appeal to anyone much" so that "KISS is in a no-lose situation" and should aim for "a different character" of programme. Also, listeners had "currently very little knowledge of who presenters are" and "even more limited knowledge of scheduling – who is on when."[789]

The potential problems with the station's breakfast show had been evident even before the launch. Once again, I suggested to McNamee that Graham Gold and Mark Webster were not the most appropriate duo to be given responsibility for the most important show on the radio station. McNamee would have none of it and told me to spend more time improving the show. Sensing my exasperation, he even gave head of music Lindsay Wesker special responsibility for the programme. Having no professional radio experience, there was little Wesker could do to help. When Gold was sick for a few days, Wesker seized the opportunity to replace him as the breakfast DJ. It made no difference. Eventually, McNamee ordered a meeting with Gold, Webster and me in the boardroom and told us all to pull up our socks, or else. His threat was irrelevant. Graham Gold did not make a good KISS FM breakfast show DJ and there was nothing any of us could do about that. McNamee steadfastly refused to admit that his choice of Gold had been wrong.

As for the other issue raised by Sirius, I too had become concerned about the lack of promotion the KISS FM DJs had enjoyed since the station's launch. The newly appointed PR person, Anita Mackie, seemed happy producing reams of press releases for the station about new station sponsorship deals that had been signed, and new advertisers that had booked airtime. She did not seem particularly interested in alerting the press to the activities of the station's huge roster of DJs or to the programmes the station was broadcasting. Suddenly, it seemed as if all the excellent public relations work that Rosee Laurence had achieved at Blackstock Mews was being squandered. Laurence had been superb at keeping in regular contact with journalists working for all the music and style magazines, and the rest of us in the office had been roped into helping her with huge press release mail-outs every few weeks.

Now that the re-launch of KISS FM was over, publicity for the station had ebbed to a level that seemed lower than it had been during the station's pirate days. I talked about this deficiency to McNamee, but he did not seem overly concerned. To tackle the problem, I instituted a weekly newsletter from the programming department that was mailed to relevant music and what's on magazines, informing them of programmes and KISS FM activities in which their readers might be interested. I also mailed them the weekly KISS FM chart and playlist, which several publications started to print. Nevertheless, it seemed a shame that the station was no longer extending the close relationships with the many journalists who had supported it in its pirate days.

Another area of concern to me were the news bulletins supplied to KISS FM by Independent Radio News. A host of technical problems had dogged the news reports at first but, additionally, there had been editorial problems. During its first month on-air, KISS FM had co-promoted a reggae concert by Shabba Ranks at the Brixton Academy venue. Unfortunately, there was a shooting at the event and one member of the public had been injured. It was bad enough that KISS FM's name had been attached to such an unfortunate event, but the station's own news reports had mistakenly informed listeners that the injured person had died. I had not been particularly pleased with IRN's performance, so there followed a series of meetings with the two newsreaders to ensure that they understood why KISS FM required accurate, informative news bulletins, rather than inaccurate tabloid sensationalism.

KISS FM's head of talks, Lyn Champion, had been instrumental in helping me plan the news service and other important elements of the station's programming. When she took maternity leave in mid-October, I was very sad to see her go, after having worked closely together for the last year and a half. Champion's temporary replacement, Lorna Clarke, had already proven to be very impressive, right from the station's launch. Now, she provided me with much more assistance in sharing the workload than Champion had done. Clarke and I got on well and tackled the frustrations of working in a radio station where the top management often seemed to know nothing about how a radio station should be run.

McNamee appeared to have remarkably few practical responsibilities to execute within the station, so he seemed to enjoy calling and attending internal meetings on any topic that he wanted to discuss. Often these meetings would ramble on for hours, stretching right through lunchtime (when McNamee would order Rosee Laurence to bring him his required food) and often flowing straight into the next meeting, attended by almost the same combination of staff in the same boardroom. McNamee or Laurence would ring me most days and ask me to insert a series of 'important' new meetings in my diary on whatever topic McNamee felt should occupy his time that day. From my perspective, I had a large and extremely busy department to manage. It became a source of frustration that I had to spend so much of my working day away from my department, sat in the boardroom upstairs, participating in directionless discussions about relatively minor issues.

These endless meetings also proved frustrating for the staff in the programming department who sometimes had to form a queue outside my office door, when I was there, to ask advice on some aspect of radio in which they were not yet sufficiently experienced. Often, I only appeared in my office at the very end of the working day, having been in a constant round of meetings in the upstairs boardroom since having arrived early in the morning. On more than one occasion, someone in the department would greet me and ask if I had enjoyed my day off, assuming I had been away from the building the whole of the previous day. On such days, once I was free to tackle the mound of papers and messages left on my desk, I knew I would not be leaving the station until well after midnight.

I recognised that this situation was not sustainable for any period of time. I was at risk of burning myself out. I had not had one day off work since the previous Christmas. I had never anticipated that so much of my time would be occupied with internal meetings. I raised the problem with McNamee and explained that not only was I working fifteen-hour days and all weekends, but also I was being contacted night and day on my mobile phone to deal with the station's programming and engineering problems. I no longer could even make time to visit the supermarket to buy food, let alone do mundane chores such as housework and washing my clothes at the launderette. McNamee suggested that I employ a housekeeper, as he had already done. I thought he was being flippant, but then he said: "The problem we both have is that we're earning so much money, we don't have enough time to spend it in."

I assured McNamee that this was certainly not my problem. Rather, I had too much work to do and I felt that KISS FM should help me resolve the matter. I proposed that two additional staff should be employed in the programming department – one producer to take responsibility for the daytime shows, and another to be in charge of evening and weekend programmes. These two sets of shows were very different – the former were focused upon the music playlist, whilst the latter were specialist programmes, each of which showcased a particular music genre. McNamee agreed to discuss the matter with the financial director, Martin Strivens. Much to my surprise, my proposal was quickly agreed. The caveat was that these two posts would effectively replace the two producer posts in the talks department that had been frozen before the station's launch. I readily accepted this condition because I felt that the station's immediate needs were greater than those of the talks department. I wrote a job description and advertised the two new posts.

The decision to employ producers to work on the station's music programmes was a delicate one. McNamee had always voiced his dislike of producers, believing that it was producers who dictated the content of the shows on stations such as BBC Radio One and Capital Radio, rather than their presenters. McNamee empathised with radio presenters and had always promised: "On KISS, it's the DJs who'll pick the records, not the producers." In several interviews, he had said that KISS FM would never employ producers because the station's DJs had been "picked for their knowledge of music." However, McNamee now seemed convinced by my argument that the station might disintegrate if I did not enrol some experienced staff to assist me in programme production.[790]

One person who did not welcome the prospect of programme producers at KISS FM was Lindsay Wesker, who told me categorically that he was against the idea when I explained my plans. Wesker disliked the idea of producers telling DJs what to do. In one press interview, he had promised that "there will be no producers hovering in the background" at KISS FM. However much I tried, Wesker remained unconvinced that enrolling two producers would improve the station's programmes and, most importantly, relieve some of the burden on me of the station's production work.[791]

It was paradoxical that Wesker himself was a major reason for my need to recruit outside help. He did not see his role, as head of music, as assisting me in the production of radio programmes. He wanted to listen to records, talk to record companies and determine the playlist. That was it. I had asked him to monitor closely the ways in which presenters were selecting records to play in their shows, because I felt that some of them might be cheating the system in some way. However, Wesker seemed to have no interest in ensuring that his playlist was being implemented properly. Once he had chosen the records and typed up the week's playlist, that was it. As a result, production chores which, in a typical radio station, would be performed by the head of music, were being left to me.

Wesker clearly resented the idea that producers were going to be employed to meddle, as he saw it, in the production of the DJs' shows. On this issue, he made his dissatisfaction perfectly clear to anyone in the office who cared to listen to him complain and argue. Consequently, my proposal to recruit producers to ensure KISS FM's success, which had been uncharacteristically approved by McNamee in record time, only served to sow more seeds of discontent in one of McNamee's fiercest allies.

---

[782] James Hamilton, "Beats And Pieces", Record Mirror, 8 Sep 1990.
[783] Tom Dunman & Tee Dee, "KISS Off", Letters, Record Mirror, 22 Sep 1990.
[784] Mark Goodier, "Goodier For The Roses", Record Mirror, Nov 1990 [exact date unknown].
[785] Andy Kershaw, "First Reaction", Channel 4, 7 Sep 1990.
"Radical Radio: The Story Of KISS FM", Channel 4, 8 Sep 1990.
[786] Patricia Tisdall, "Radio Appeal", The Times, 2 May 1973 had written:
"The mass audience for radio is predominantly female with around two-thirds of all women using it at some time on each day … These are some of the facts which have emerged from a recent survey commissioned by J Walter Thompson as part of its preparations for commercial radio, to begin broadcasting this autumn. Although male audiences were not included in the research …"
[787] "Published Audience Results", press release, KISS FM, [undated].
[788] Grant Goddard, memo to Programming staff, KISS FM, 5 Oct 1990
[789] "Reactions To KISS FM: Debrief Notes", Sirius Research, Nov 1990.
[790] Phil Cheeseman, "Sweet FM", Record Mirror, 28 Aug 1990.
Steve Clarke, "The KISS Of Life As Radio Station Reopens", Evening Standard, 27 Dec 1989.
Jack Barron, "The Embrace Is On", NME, 1 Sep 1990.
"Sealed With A KISS!", Blues & Soul, 16 Jan 1990.
Matthew Gwyther, "Dance Music Master", GQ, May 1990.
[791] Debbie Kirby, "KISS FM Goes Legal", Echoes, 6 Jan 1990.

November 1990.

The Monday morning meetings that had commenced when KISS FM was based at Blackstock Mews continued now that the station was on-air. During the pre-launch period, those meetings had become very long, sometimes lasting five or six hours. I had presumed that they would return to a sensible length once the launch was over. I was wrong. The meetings still rumbled on interminably and, each week, removed most of an entire day from my diary.

Every Monday morning at nine o'clock, six people assembled around the huge boardroom table on the top floor – managing director Gordon McNamee, financial director Martin Strivens, head of sales Gary Miele, head of marketing Malcolm Cox, me as head of programming, and Rosee Laurence, McNamee's personal assistant. McNamee sat at one end of the table and Laurence sat at the other. Every week, the rest of us sat in exactly the same positions on either side of the table. McNamee chaired the meeting and worked his way around the table anti-clockwise, asking each of us in turn to explain what we had been doing the previous week.

Sat directly on McNamee's left, I was always the penultimate person to explain the issues, problems and policies I had been working on. By default, I was responsible for both the engineering and programming departments, which meant that there was always a lot to explain, discuss and debate. By the time it was my turn, McNamee had often become impatient to take the floor and would guillotine some of the points I tried to raise. McNamee might have been an inadequate chairman of these meetings, letting them meander and wander for hours, but he made up for it by being a brilliant raconteur. Once it was his turn, McNamee regaled us with stories of all the important people with whom he had lunched the previous week, all the evening social events he had attended, and all the people he had invited to his office. These events were not retold as statements of fact. Rather, they were incorporated into an act that included jokes, anecdotes and anything that McNamee considered was interesting and entertaining.

The rest of us had to sit there and endure this huge waste of our time, allowing McNamee to replay the highlights of his week. Sometimes, when there was very little of substance that McNamee could report, he resorted to passing comment on things the rest of us had already said. Often, anticipating that he would have little to offer during his turn, McNamee would punctuate my list of work activities by making comments such as "well, you have been finding lots of things to tell us about, Grant" or "are you sure you've finished, Grant, or am I getting in your way?" Following my very factual contributions, McNamee was in his element telling stories. This was the only part of the meeting in which he became animated.

Each Monday meeting, Laurence made copious notes of what had been said and decided. Afterwards, she typed them up and McNamee would edit them before they were circulated to the heads of department and, importantly, to each of the directors. Every week that the minutes were delivered to my desk, strangely my contribution to the meetings had been reduced to a small paragraph, whilst McNamee's had been enlarged and included items that he had not even raised during the meeting. Annoyingly, many of the accomplishments that I had related about the programming of the station ended up in McNamee's section of the minutes, as if he had originated them.

Apart from my recent boardroom discussion with Tony Prince, I had had no contact with the board of directors since the station had come on-air. I was becoming increasingly concerned that my work efforts were being marginalised in the directors' eyes. To them, from the minutes, it might appear that I was contributing little to the running of the station. I attempted to counter this impression by giving Rosee Laurence a handwritten list of the points I had raised in the meeting each week, as a reminder of what she should attribute to me in the minutes. It made no difference. Next, I typed a list of the tasks I had achieved each week and asked Laurence to attach my notes to the minutes. It made no difference. When the minutes arrived on my desk, there was no sign of my achievements or my list.

At the end of October, McNamee attended a four-day radio sales conference in Portugal, an event that provided him with many anecdotes and funny stories to tell the rest of us during the Monday morning meeting on 5 November. As a result, the meeting dragged on for three hours, at which point McNamee looked at his watch and suddenly drew it to a close. Then, he announced that he would meet Miele, Cox and me in the foyer in five minutes to go the Savoy Hotel for a luncheon organised by the Radio Academy. I walked downstairs to my office and found not only a pile of urgent messages on my desk, but also a queue of people waiting outside my office to see me. My time was tight and I still had an immense amount of work to do. I looked at my diary. That afternoon, McNamee had instructed me to attend a meeting with a potential sponsor in the boardroom. The next day, I had four meetings (three with sub-sections of my department) that would last from 9 am to 10 pm. The day after that, I was reviewing shows with each DJ throughout the entire day. On Thursday, I had seven consecutive meetings from 9.15 am to 9 pm.

I felt that that I would be unable to attend that day's luncheon without seriously neglecting my work responsibilities. If I had to put off several urgent matters until Friday, I could be subject to criticism for not performing my duties. I went down to the foyer to apologise to McNamee that I felt I was too busy that day to go with him to the Savoy for a social event. He reacted furiously and stomped out of the building with Miele and Cox. What could I do? I needed to get on with making decisions, dealing with the station staff, and getting things done. However, I realised that McNamee did not see things this way. I was not at all surprised to find that I did not see McNamee during the rest of that week.

Early on Thursday morning, Rosee Laurence arrived unannounced in my office, handed me a sealed envelope, and went out again without saying a word. I knew that something must be wrong because, these days, Laurence was rarely seen visiting the programming floor. When she had letters or memos to distribute, she would usually give them to someone else to deliver. With trepidation, I opened the envelope and found a two-page letter from McNamee typed on KISS FM stationery. This was definitely no ordinary memo. It was not yet nine o'clock and I had been the first person to arrive on my floor of the building. I sat in my chair, uninterrupted by the usual hustle and bustle. I could not believe what I was reading.

McNamee had written: "The lack of communication which exists between you and I, between you and the Heads of Department, and between you and your staff, has created uncertainty and mistrust of management and concern from members of Programming personnel. Your inability to communicate and delegate work is also hampering the ambitions of those who wish to further their careers at KISS FM. I know from personal experience that trying to speak to you is almost impossible. While I appreciate that you have a very busy schedule, that is true of all the Department Heads."[792]

I was astounded. How could he accuse me of a lack of communication when I always left my office door open, I encouraged everyone to come in and talk to me, I worked in the office longer hours than any other executive, and everybody had both my home and mobile telephone numbers? If there was one person who had become out of touch with his staff, then it was certainly not me. Furthermore, I was desperate to delegate some of my work, which is why I had recently proposed employing two producers.

I read on: "Your behaviour of Monday 5th is a typical example of your lack of respect to me as your Managing Director and to your colleagues, which I have felt for some time now. The way in which KISS FM has been set up, is that I run the company as Managing Director and in order to achieve this, I have a day-to-day relationship with every department head within the station. As your Managing Director, I require you to respect this."[793]

What I was reading in the letter seemed unbelievable. I could not fathom how McNamee might believe that the way to deal with my over-burdened schedule was to admonish me for not wanting to attend a social event, rather than attend to tasks within my department. Was I being told off for taking my work too seriously?

The letter continued: "On the subject of OB's [outside broadcasts] I hope to set the record straight. Most OB's that are commissioned will be sponsored. The cost of the OB is built into the sponsors [sic] payment. OB's naturally fall within the Programming Department's brief regardless of whether you feel it [sic] makes good programming or not. I accept that within the coming months we will receive proposals to do many OB's which are unsuitable for programming. However every OB that we take on must be looked upon as a challenge."[794]

McNamee was putting in writing what he had already made clear to me on several occasions. Outside broadcasts were sold by the station's sales staff, whether or not they made sense to broadcast on-air, and my job was to make them work, even if they were unworkable. McNamee knew full well that, although the sponsor was being charged for the additional costs the station incurred to stage the outside broadcast, in reality none of that payment ever reached my budget. I was having to ask my already overworked staff to commit an increasing number of late nights and weekends without any extra payments. Their goodwill was being exhausted at an ever increasing rate.

McNamee's letter concluded: "Take this letter as an official warning which I shall keep on file. I suggest you arrange a time to talk to me about the points I have raised above when you have had time to think about what I have said. I should just like to add that of all the departments within the company, my largest interest lies with the Programming Department. I have spent years building a rapport with the DJs and my staff and continue to think of this as being a very important role within my job. It grieves me to think that you have undone some of the work and enthusiasm which went into making the DJs at one with the station and that you are unable to share the experiences of being Head of Programming with me, be they good or bad. Yours sincerely, Gordon McNamee, Managing Director."[795]

This final paragraph really upset me. McNamee and I both knew that there had been a whispering campaign amongst the DJs since the beginning of the year, expressing concerns about the direction the station was heading. It was McNamee who was the target of the DJs' suspicions and fears. The DJs had seen McNamee's character change since KISS FM had won the licence, just as I had. The relationship that was changing was the one between the original KISS FM DJs and McNamee, of whom they saw very little these days. If McNamee felt that I was not spending as much time with each DJ as he would like, that was because I had forty-four DJs to manage. This was a direct result of McNamee's insistence not only that the entire pirate radio team was employed, but also that new recruits were added.

I was dumbfounded because the very criticisms that McNamee was laying at my door in his letter were the very criticisms that I had heard staff in my department whisper about McNamee. How was it that he could blame me for his own deficiencies? Why had he not raised these matters with me before now? Why did it have to be in a formal disciplinary letter? Should not an employee in a company be given the benefit of a verbal warning, before being issued with a two-page written warning like this? It was only nine weeks since I had launched KISS FM successfully on-air without a hitch. The first audience figures had shown that I was well on the way to achieving the target of one million listeners that I had been set. I was working for the station's success harder than I had ever worked for anything in my life. What more did McNamee want?

I sat in my chair, still alone in the department, re-reading the letter over and over again. It seemed plainly obvious what McNamee wanted. He wanted my head. I had served my purpose now. McNamee was ready to dispose of me. I was not needed any more. I had helped win the station its licence. I had launched the station on time, against all the odds. Now it looked as if I was going to achieve my audience target. There was nothing left that McNamee needed me to do. My time was up. He had used me up. Now I was on my way out the door.

McNamee had already cheated me several times. He had promised me a reward if my co-ordination of the second KISS FM application had won the licence, but I had received nothing. He had promised to pay me a wage from 1 January, but I had received nothing. He had promised me the unallocated shares in the company for my efforts, but I had received nothing. And he had offered me to purchase shares in the company, but I had received nothing. Whilst the newly recruited heads of department – Gary Miele and Malcolm Cox – had been offered executive contracts with excellent perks, I had been given a standard contract of employment that was identical to that of the receptionist working in the foyer. I had clung on to my job in the face of this provocation, but McNamee's letter was the hardest blow. Did he expect me to give up and quit now, just to suit him?

If that was what McNamee wanted, I was determined not to give him the pleasure. As I sat there, alone in my office, I realised that the rest of that day was filled with meetings, tomorrow was filled with work, and the next day was filled with meetings. I had managed to get this far making KISS FM a success, and I was sure as hell not going to let McNamee force me out before I fulfilled my plan to attract one million listeners per week to the station. Why quit now, just when KISS FM was on its way up? I had never been a quitter. McNamee would have to find more reasons than those in his letter to force me out. I folded the letter back into its envelope, hid it at the bottom of my briefcase, and tried to forget about it during the rest of the busy day ahead of me.

It was only at the very end of that Thursday, when the programming administrator Philippa Unwin and I were the only people left in the office, that McNamee's letter came back into my mind. Unwin said something quite casually to me about how difficult the day had been, and how there must come a time when running a radio station becomes a little easier. Her words touched me unexpectedly and, without thinking, I responded: "It doesn't really matter anyway, because I'll be out of here by Christmas." She was shocked and asked me what I meant. Reluctantly, I explained that I thought that myself, and probably several other staff, would be forced out of KISS FM by Christmas. She said that she did not believe me and asked me to expand upon my theory. But I could not. I could not tell her about the letter I had received that morning. I could only tell her that I knew my time was almost up.

When I reached home that night, I did not look at McNamee's letter again. I had read it and I knew its real meaning. McNamee's message to me was "Go! I don't need you any more!"

I sat on my bed – one of the few pieces of furniture remaining in my cold, empty flat – and I cried.

---

[792] letter from Gordon McNamee to Grant Goddard, 8 Nov 1990.
[793] ibid.
[794] ibid.
[795] ibid.

November 1990.

Whilst it appeared that the programmes on KISS FM were proving successful in attracting radio listeners, there were other areas of the station's activities that appeared to be having less success. The financial director, Martin Strivens, managed only four staff within his department, but seemed to be experiencing problems. In the post of secretary, three different women had been employed during the first few months, one of whom only lasted a week. One of Strivens' accounts assistants had to be hurriedly dismissed after several months, once it was discovered that she had embezzled substantial sums from the company. And Strivens' accounts manager was mugged and robbed of several hundred pounds in cash, walking from the office in Holloway Road to the bank one Monday morning.

From the time that KISS FM had won its licence nearly a year earlier, I had lost count of how many meetings I had attended with Strivens to discuss departmental budgets. Both before and after the station had been launched, the budgets had been constantly revised, almost always downwards. Although I had provided Strivens with masses of detailed information about the anticipated costs of running the radio station, the one document I had never received in return was a straightforward itemised list of my department's annual budget for its various activities. Strivens was regularly telling me I could not have money for 'this,' or I would have to cut out 'that,' but how much these amendments left me to spend remained a complete mystery.

Furthermore, when I asked for an up-to-date budget, Strivens told me that it could not be produced until he had finalised the 'allocated overheads.' These were the overall costs of running the building – the rent, heating, lighting, phone charges, etc. – that he wanted to split between the different departments within the building and include within their budgets. I was puzzled by this strategy on two counts. Firstly, I had seen such systems operate in large companies where there were autonomous subsidiaries based in different buildings, but the principle seemed inappropriate for a company as small as KISS FM. Secondly, there was little point in allocating these overheads to individual departmental budgets because each head of department had little or no control over whether this money was spent or not. How could any one head of department save money on the rent for the building or on the water rates?

When I asked Strivens how the allocations were to be decided, he explained that different criteria would be used for each budgeted item. For example, the rental costs were allocated according to the floor area of each department – my department had the most space, so I would pay the most. The phone charges would be allocated according to the number of phone extensions in each department – my department had the most phones, so I would pay the most. The costs of the computer system (which still barely worked) would be allocated according to the number of terminals installed in each department – my department had the most, so I would pay the most. The costs of the payroll system would be allocated according to the number of staff in each department – my department had fifty-eight staff, whereas most of the others had less than ten. And so on.

This system seemed crazy for a brand new company that needed to implement some kind of central control over costs, rather than devolving those overheads to each departmental head. I could foresee what might happen. Strivens would be able to blame me for overspending my budget, because I had spent too much on rent, heating, lighting and phones – items over which I had no control. Rather than Strivens himself taking responsibility for the company's general overheads, he was creating a financial system in which the blame for overspending could be shifted elsewhere within the company. As a result, Strivens was spending much of his time dividing the cost of these items into theoretical portions.

Eventually, at the end of October 1990, I received the first budget print-out for the current financial year. By then, I was hardly surprised to find that the programming department had been charged £42,058 per annum for rent, £18,472 for phones, £14,950 for security and £16,214 for depreciation of equipment. Furthermore, I was required to contribute £10,415 legal and professional fees, £6,726 audit and accountancy fees, £5,034 for insurance, £9,694 for the interest payments on hire purchase deals, £9,505 bank charges and interest, and £24,949 for repayment of the company's loan stock.[796]

In addition to these allocated costs were the real costs of running the programming department – £524,915 for wages, £13,200 for records and jingles (mainly comprising McNamee's purchase of Robbie Vincent's record collection) and the running costs of my company car. The programming department's total budgeted costs for the first year came to £729,844. However, I was still puzzled as to how some of the figures had been calculated. I wrote a memo to Strivens, asking for clarification of the bare totals on the print-out: "Please can you supply an itemised budget that details for example, the projected cost of individual staff, and which also states assumptions that have been made ... Without this information, I am not in a position to be able to say whether the figures within the print-out are relevant and appropriate."[797]

With McNamee already on the warpath to eject me from the company, I realised that I had to be more careful than ever to cover my back. If Strivens or the board should later accuse me of overspending, I needed to be able to demonstrate, in writing, that I had done everything within my power to ensure that the budgets were realistic and that I had tried to keep within them. My memo to Strivens elicited no response. Within a matter of days, my request was out-of-date because Strivens had once again amended the budgets downwards, though he did not circulate a new print-out to help me understand the consequences of his latest actions.

On a practical level, it was still proving almost impossible to prise even small amounts of money out of the company coffers. Before the station's launch, I had ordered several small cheques from Strivens so that I could subscribe to music magazines for the department to use in its research. By November, several of these cheques had still not arrived. Furthermore, the two trainers I had enrolled to assist the DJs prior to the launch were complaining to me that they had still not been paid. I had finally taken delivery of a stereo system for my office, but there was still no office furniture on which to install it. Eventually, I was forced to pay for many things out of my own pocket and then try and reclaim them as 'expenses,' which Rosee Laurence paid out weekly in cash. I spent £200 at the MFI furniture warehouse in Wembley on much needed office furniture, and I spent £114 on subscriptions to publications. It seemed a crazy way to run a business, but I found it was the quickest practical solution to gain access to the budget I was meant to have.

The next accounts information I received from Strivens was a forty-two page computer print-out that summarised the amounts I had apparently spent from my budget during October. However, the figures were aggregated totals that did not itemise individual payments or explain who had authorised or received each amount. I had to write another memo to Strivens: "Further to my memo of 26 October, I would still like to have a breakdown of how the figures in the original budget were arrived at. Because the figures include so many staff costs and running expenses, it is important to know the assumptions behind them, in order to determine if they are workable. I have asked Adam [Lewis, accounts manager] on every occasion for such a breakdown and, whilst I realise how busy you both are, I can't be expected to meet budget projections that I don't understand." I received no response.[798]

If these problems hinted that the station's expenditure might appear to be somewhat out of control, then the figures for KISS FM's revenues seemed even murkier. The licence application had anticipated that the station would earn £2.5m from advertising in its first year on-air, but it was proving difficult to believe that these expectations would be met. During the station's first few weeks on-air in September, there had been many advertisers that had tested a few short advertising campaigns. However, the novelty of KISS FM seemed to have worn off quite quickly. Now that the station's arrival was no longer plastered over billboards and written about in the press, the volume of advertising spots had dropped markedly. Even a casual listener to the station would have noticed that whole hours passed without a single paid-for advertisement.[799]

KISS FM's head of sales, Gary Miele, seemed to have little or no understanding of the station's youth audience, and he never seemed the slightest bit interested in the dance music culture from which the business had emerged. Neither did he recruit one person to his sales team who had had any direct involvement in the dance music industry. As a result, most of the potential local advertisers who were approached to spend money on KISS FM were the same mainstream companies that any radio station or newspaper might approach. KISS FM even ended up with a short campaign for the exclusive, high class London department store, Harrods, whose advertisements comprised a posh-voiced man saying what a wonderful place it was to shop. When I first heard this advertisement, played in the middle of a hardcore hip hop show, I thought it had been a fake spot inserted by the DJ. I was shocked to find that it was a real advertisement, booked into entirely the wrong show on a wholly unsuitable radio station.

At every Monday morning meeting, Miele would say what wonderful advertising contracts he was just about to sign. He would try to convince everyone around the table that he was well on the way to achieving the station's revenue targets. However, it seemed that the good news was always just around the corner, if we were to believe Miele, whilst very little of it seemed to have materialised to date. In the end, Miele resorted to selling advertising space on KISS FM for whatever money he could get. He cared not who the advertiser was, or whether they would benefit from using the station. He would take whatever money they offered him and, literally, threw their advertisement onto the station.

A thirty-second spot booked for broadcast on KISS FM between six o'clock in the evening and midnight should have sold for £25, according to the official ratecard, but it was known that many of these spots were going for as little as £10. Most of these remarkably cheap advertisements were booked by organisers of raves (one-off music events where DJs played techno and house music). Once Miele had sold an advertisement and had extracted his commission, he considered that to be the end of his responsibilities. Often, the recording of the advertisement for a rave would arrive at the station on an audiocassette, often recorded on a home stereo system with the rave promoter (or more frequently, his girlfriend) listing all the DJs who were appearing, over the top of a record being played too loudly in the background. Frequently, what was being said proved unintelligible. Often, the advert would turn out to be a minute long, rather than the thirty seconds that Miele had sold.

When advertisements arrived at the radio station, neither Miele nor anyone in the sales department listened to them. The recording was sent upstairs to one of the technical assistants to be transferred to an audio cartridge, which was then placed in the studio. The station's traffic manager typed out a list of the new advertisements, with details of when they should be played, to be placed in the studio. The first time that anyone, other than the technical assistant, heard each advert was when it appeared on-air, often unintelligible, occasionally completely the wrong advert, and usually nothing close to the duration that the DJ had been told on the label.

These mistakes with advertisements were a common occurrence that infuriated me and the DJs. They made KISS FM sound more amateurish than a pirate station. They made the DJ sound incompetent, particularly if the thirty-second advert he had played to lead up to the news at four o'clock turned out to be a minute long. I complained to Miele that he needed to vet each advert before it went to air, but he did nothing. I raised the matter at a Monday morning meeting, but he did nothing. I told McNamee that the system needed to be changed, but he did nothing. I told Strivens something needed to be done, but he did nothing. I continued to raise the matter at every Monday morning meeting, but still nobody did anything about it. I was astonished.

Advertisements were going straight onto the airwaves without any clearance procedure. They might be libellous, defamatory, illegal, abusive or inciting racial hatred. Nobody was bothering to check them at all. It was only when I heard a particularly bad advert, or when a DJ complained to me, that an error would be identified and, by then, it was too late. I explained to McNamee that it was common practice in every radio station for somebody with a degree of authority to listen to each advertisement before it was broadcast. In KISS FM, the only person who heard each advertisement was a technical assistant employed by Phoenix Communications, who had no knowledge or ability to judge editorial matters. I felt that someone in Miele's department, or the traffic manager, should be given responsibility for approving each advertisement.

McNamee was unmoved and responded that every advertisement made the station some money and that, whatever its quality might be, it was contributing to the station's revenue which paid my wages. I recalled the warning letter that McNamee had sent me, and the part that had told me I was responsible for organising outside broadcasts "regardless of whether you feel it makes good programming or not." McNamee seemed not to care any more about what was broadcast on KISS FM, as long as it made the station money. It seemed crazy to me that he had spent several years building up the brand name of KISS FM as a pirate radio station with integrity, good taste and a degree of quality control unheard on other unlicensed stations. Yet now, he seemed willing to throw all that hard work away by allowing anything onto the station that generated money. Outside broadcasts, sponsorships and advertisements all made money. Whoever they were booked by and whatever the quality of the end product, it seemed to be alright with McNamee.[800]

There was one advertising campaign booked on KISS FM by a men's magazine that included a series of distasteful and derogatory remarks about women. When staff in the programming department heard the advertisement on-air, they complained to me that it was sexist and not something they felt KISS FM should be broadcasting. As requested, I took the matter up with McNamee, but he rejected the staff's complaints. Next, several staff wrote a joint letter to McNamee, complaining that they felt the campaign was totally inappropriate for the station and insulted women. McNamee replied curtly that anybody who paid money to advertise on the station could say exactly what they liked within their advertisement, and neither he nor his staff should say anything against the advertisement, however sexist it might appear to them.

The personnel in the programming department were understandably upset by McNamee's response. It seemed that McNamee had adopted the philosophy that it was money alone that would make the station successful and, it followed, would make him successful too. He no longer seemed to give a damn about the radio product, just the money he could squeeze out of it for himself and the shareholders.

This philosophy was very evident in one of McNamee's weekly Saturday morning shows on KISS FM. A live advertisement to be broadcast from a jeans shop had been scheduled within the programme. McNamee insisted on mentioning this event frequently from the beginning of his show. His sales patter ran directly counter to one of the regulations of the Independent Broadcasting Authority [IBA] which insisted that a clear distinction must be maintained on-air between advertising and editorial content. McNamee completely blurred that line between his radio show and the paid-for advertisement. As a result, the IBA made a formal complaint to KISS FM that it had breached radio regulations. McNamee was forced to make a written and on-air apology to the IBA about the behaviour of one of the radio station's longest serving DJs – himself. Significantly, it was the first complaint that KISS FM station had received about its programmes from the IBA, and the only complaint while I was in charge of the station's programming.

---

[796] "Budgeted Profit & Loss Account: Detail For The Year Ended 30th September 1991", KISS FM, [undated].
[797] "90/91 Budgets", memo from Grant Goddard to Martin Strivens, 26 Oct 1990.
[798] [untitled], memo from Grant Goddard to Martin Strivens, 6 Dec 1990.
[799] "IBA Incremental ILR Contract Application Form", KISS FM, Nov 1989.
[800] letter from Gordon McNamee to Grant Goddard, 8 Nov 1990.

November & December 1990.

While the view of KISS FM from the inside might have started to look precarious, outside in the world, news that the station had attracted three quarters of a million listeners was viewed as an indication of how successful the ex-pirate had become. Broadcast magazine commented that "KISS FM leads the incremental [radio] challenge." Music Week wrote an article headlined "Sales Reflect KISS FM's Success." Announcing EMAP's interim financial results, its chief executive, Robin Miller, mentioned "the highly successful launch of London's newest radio station KISS 100 FM" in which EMAP was reported to hold a twenty-nine per cent stake. Debbie Garvey, account director at KISS FM's advertising agency, BBDO, told Music & Media magazine: "We're pleased with the figures." One investment magazine described KISS FM as "Capital [Radio]'s biggest potential rival."[801]

None of these public plaudits for the station's programming seemed to improve my standing with the station's managing director, Gordon McNamee. I asked him, as he had told me to in his warning letter, to suggest an appropriate time to discuss with him its contents. He responded that we could talk about it further while we both attended a four-day conference for UK commercial radio programme controllers, to be held in Spain during mid-November. Initially, McNamee had offered me a lift from KISS FM to the airport but, in the end, he took the day off work. I still had a morning filled with meetings, before I rushed off at lunchtime to catch the flight. On the plane to Gibraltar, and then on the bus from Gibraltar across the Spanish border to the hotel, McNamee said very little to me. I felt like a child whose parents refused to talk to him because he had done something naughty.

At the conference, McNamee threw himself into the social activities, whilst I studiously attended all the presentation sessions and remained sober. Over breakfast one morning, one of the delegates told me that he had accompanied McNamee and Richard Park, programme director of London's Capital Radio, into town the previous night and had participated in the merriment until he felt that it had started to become excessive, at which point he had bowed out and returned to the hotel. The delegate alleged that he had left McNamee and Park when they visited a whore house and started imbibing narcotic substances. Although I could not confirm the veracity of this account, I was not surprised by the story. McNamee knew how to have a good time. Other delegates had already told me of his antics in a jacuzzi at the hotel.

Apart from the occasional appearance at a few conference sessions, including one at which he was booked to make a speech, I did not see McNamee during the event. He returned to London on a different flight than me and did not contact me before he left. It seemed that McNamee had become uninterested in talking to me. In his mind, he had probably already ejected me from the company. I felt that it was only a matter of time before he turned that idea into reality. He seemed to have nothing to discuss with me about the warning letter he had sent. It was merely a prop which he could use to justify my eventual execution. I returned to London completely fed up with McNamee's attitude. Despite my success launching KISS FM, I was being excommunicated.

On his return to London, McNamee became immersed in a new project that he must have been negotiating for some time. He finalised a deal with the Trocadero shopping centre in London's West End that required KISS FM to rent two retail units there. In one, a fully equipped radio studio was built which McNamee promised would be used to create a new radio service for broadcast via loudspeakers in the shopping centre. In the second unit, KISS FM would establish a retail outlet from which to sell its merchandise. This deal was finalised between McNamee and the Trocadero while Malcolm Cox, the station's head of marketing, was away on a two-week holiday. After Cox returned, McNamee announced that he had irrevocably signed the deal and that Cox had to implement it. Cox was furious, since KISS FM had been on-air barely three months. Already, McNamee wanted to expand into a new venture that was not directly related to the KISS FM radio licence.

A new radio studio was quickly built at the Trocadero, and McNamee appointed KISS FM DJ Tee Harris to run the operation. Without informing me, McNamee and Cox removed a lot of records from the record library to use at the new station, as well as dozens of cartridges, jingles, tapes and other materials from the programming department. Then, Harris tried to recruit other KISS FM DJs to assist him in presenting programmes on the new station, which was broadcasting daily from 10 am to 8 pm. Many of the DJs were not interested because Harris could not pay for their time, and the audience in the shopping centre was likely to be minimal. Next, Harris started asking the KISS FM office staff if they were interested in taking on some DJ work. Many of the administrative and production staff were keen to be on the radio themselves and jumped at the opportunity, even without pay.

The situation with this second KISS FM radio station quickly got out of hand. Some of my staff started to ask if they could change their shifts, swap days with other staff, or take time off in lieu so that they could go to the Trocadero and present programmes. Not only was the project draining much needed physical resources from the programming department, but also it was starting to encroach upon personnel I needed to devote their working hours to running the real KISS FM.

Once again, the press applauded KISS FM's success. MixMag magazine announced: "Just three months after KISS 100 FM started broadcasting, Gordon Mac and his entrepreneurial team are at it again. Not satisfied with 800,000 listeners already, the radical radio is out to take over London's West End by launching its second radio station at the Trocadero Centre in Piccadilly Circus." However, within weeks, Tee Harris was having immense difficulty persuading enough people to work at the Trocadero to keep the second station on-air. Additionally, the retail shop that was meant to generate profits for KISS FM from the sale of branded clothing proved to be a disaster. Two staff had been recruited to run the shop, but the turnover was so dismal that this was quickly reduced to one.[802]

Only a few weeks after its launch, the Trocadero studio and shop were quietly closed, much to everyone's relief. Malcolm Cox had never wanted the project in the first place, whilst I was concerned about the drain on the programming department's resources. Only McNamee mourned the project's passing. The whole episode had been slightly surreal. It almost seemed as if McNamee had yearned to create a new radio station that he could call his own, a station where he could do what he liked without the meddling of others. The closure of the Trocadero radio station ended that particular dream.

I was relieved to see the back of the project, as I still had other problems to deal with. More and more staff within the radio station were complaining to me about the playlist that head of music Lindsay Wesker was updating each week. Several of them felt that the selection of new records that Wesker was choosing was becoming more and more esoteric, and further away from what the general public was buying. I checked Wesker's recent playlists and discovered, to my horror, that he seemed to have virtually abandoned the principles of the three separate lists that I had asked him to implement. Instead, he seemed to be choosing the records that he liked the most and ignoring those he disliked. Wesker had recently told Radio & Music magazine: "Sure, some of our [playlist] tracks are turn-offs to a pop audience ... At least now there's a station in London that provides me with no turn-offs at all."[803]

It appeared that Wesker could not separate his job function of choosing the most appropriate records for the playlist from his own personal taste in music. As a result, there were several dance music records near the top of the singles sales chart that KISS FM had not played at all during its daytime shows. The station had been busy marketing itself as the 'music leader' in dance music, yet there were immensely popular dance records that a radio listener would have had to tune to BBC Radio One or Capital Radio to hear. The drift in music policy was my fault. Since the September launch, I had been too busy with other matters to keep an eye on Wesker and his weekly playlist. It appeared that, during that period, he had been executing his weekly task with less and less objectivity.

I explained the problem to Wesker, but he refused to change his ways and include in the playlist the records that were popular. In the end, I had to tell him that I was left with no alternative but to produce the playlist myself each week from now on. Before the station's launch, I had set up the system and instructed him how to run it, but he was now ignoring my directions. Wesker was absolutely livid. He saw the playlist as his territory, to do with what he liked. How dare I intrude on his work! Anyway, he asked, what did I know about music? I explained patiently to Wesker that he had never seen a radio playlist system until I had shown him how it worked. I had started my career in commercial radio more than ten years earlier, compiling the playlist for a radio station that had more listeners than KISS FM. Wesker was still very unhappy.

I explained to McNamee the problem with the playlist. He ordered Wesker to a meeting in the boardroom and, in front of me, told Wesker that I knew what I was doing and that I was his line manager. It was tough if Wesker did not like it. After that intervention, I had to produce the playlist on my own, adding several records that, until now, had never been played on daytime KISS FM. Vanilla Ice's 'Ice Ice Baby' was number one in both that week's singles chart and dance chart, but had never been included on Wesker's playlists. I also added 'Sucker DJ' by Dimples D, 'Mary Had A Little Lamb' by Snap and 'Are You Dreaming?' by Twenty 4 Seven. For a soul music fan like me, these were not records I would have purchased for personal listening, but there was no doubt that the public loved them. Besides, these particular tracks were being played only occasionally on daytime KISS FM, alongside a much greater number of more 'credible' songs. I was determined not to make the station sound elitist in its choice of music.

However, the issue did not end there. One after another, several daytime presenters came to me and complained about the changes I was making to the playlist, almost as if they had been told what to say. Fortunately, once I had explained that my only motivation was to reflect public tastes, they were happy to comply with the new playlist. There were occasional attempts to boycott certain records, but their resistance quickly evaporated.

I realised that this episode had ruffled Wesker's feathers immeasurably. I also knew that the playlist was too vital to the station's success to let it become a personal indulgence of any one member of staff. Wesker was already furious about the imminent appointment of two producers, so the decision to relieve him of his power over the playlist merely exacerbated the situation. He failed to understand that the producers had become necessary partly because of his disinterest in helping me to produce the station's output. As a result, I had neglected to pay sufficient attention to his work on the playlist in recent weeks.

The job advertisements for the two producer posts produced a flood of applicants. McNamee and I interviewed a clutch of candidates over several days and then shared our opinions. McNamee was keen to appoint one particular applicant, a good looking woman, so I had to point out that she had very little radio production experience and might prove to be of little practical assistance to me. I eventually persuaded McNamee to appoint the two most qualified candidates – George Ergatoudis whom Radio One's Roger Lewis had recommended to me many months earlier, and Richard Hopkins who had been interviewed by Lyn Champion and me previously for the postponed talks producer posts. McNamee agreed to pay each producer £16,500 per annum and they would start work in January.

After the failure of the second radio station at the Trocadero, McNamee busied himself with the organisation of a staff party to celebrate KISS FM's one hundredth day on-air. On the evening of Sunday 9 December 1990, the station's entire staff, accompanied by members of the board and several journalists, filled The Underworld club in Camden, a venue that was only a few yards away from KISS FM's first office in Greenland Street. The event was an updated version of the annual KISS FM awards ceremony that had started in the station's pirate days. McNamee thoroughly enjoyed taking the role of circus ringmaster for the night and, just like the Oscars event, he announced the short-listed candidates for what seemed like a never ending succession of prizes.

Some of the awards were serious in nature – David Rodigan won 'Best Daytime Show,' Tee Harris won 'Best Specialist Show,' and Paul Anderson won the prize for 'Best Mixer.' There were also many joke awards with which McNamee could thoroughly enjoy embarrassing his staff – Sonia Fraser won the 'Biggest Flirt Award,' and Malcolm Cox won KISS FM's 'Worst Dancer Award.' During several hours of ceremonies, McNamee ensured that just about everybody at the station was either nominated or won an award. After a stage show in which three members of the programming department dressed up to present a skit on stage of a soul song by The Supremes, the guests were left to mingle, accompanied by music selected by former LWR DJ Elayne who had been hired for the night.

It was an enjoyable evening and a good way for everybody to relax after three months of hard work. Once the awards section of the evening was over, several of the staff from my department came up to me, one by one, to express surprise that I had not been mentioned at all in McNamee's ceremony or been nominated for any prize. One concerned member of my team expressed outright indignation that I had not even been thanked for my contribution to the station's successful launch. "Have you not worked harder than anybody to make this whole thing work?" she asked.

I shrugged off these comments as if I was not bothered about my complete omission from the night's events. But I too could not have helped but notice that McNamee had left me out. I was not at all surprised. McNamee usually made no bones about snubbing in public those former colleagues who had fallen from his favour. That night, everybody celebrated the fact that KISS FM had already won 750,000 listeners. McNamee seemed to be celebrating the fact that he did not need my services anymore.

---

[801] Ed Shelton, "More Gloom For GLR", Broadcast, 9 Nov 1990.
Sarah Davis, "Sales Reflect KISS FM's Success", Music Week, 17 Nov 1990.
"EMAP Confident Despite Standstill In First Half", The Scotsman, 20 Nov 1990.
"Awareness Of New London Stations Increases", Music & Media, 24 Nov 1990.
"Capital Radio", Investors Chronicle, 7 Dec 1990.
[802] "KISS FM Opens Second Station!", MixMag Update, 13 Dec 1990.
[803] Ian Nicolson, "The Hitlist", Radio & Music, 21 Nov 1990.

December 1990 & January 1991.

KISS FM's first legal Christmas on-air was only a few weeks away and, despite McNamee's increasing ambivalence towards me, I was pleased to see that some of the problems that had dogged the station since its launch were finally being resolved. Suddenly, McNamee and Strivens admitted that the arrangement with Phoenix Communications for KISS FM's engineering needs had been a failure and they agreed to terminate the contract. Instead, the station would appoint a head of engineering and one technical operator. The outsourcing arrangement had proven disastrous, despite McNamee's initial insistence that the plan would work well.

This decision made a big difference to me because it relieved me of the unacknowledged burden I had been bearing until then for the station's entire technical operation. Phoenix seemed to have been paid by KISS FM to do very little, whilst I was paid nothing extra for doing their work. The move to appoint two engineering staff, along with the recent approval of two producers to start work in January, was a great relief to me. Until now, it felt as if I had being doing the workload of around half a dozen people. Four extra pairs of hands would make a huge difference.

The other good news was that head of talks Lyn Champion had given birth to her baby without incident and, within a couple of weeks, she had proudly brought her first offspring to the station to show her off to the staff. Although Champion was not yet due to resume full-time work at KISS FM, she made it clear to me that she intended to start calling in more often to pick up the threads of activities that had been happening in her absence.

Shortly after Champion's initial re-appearance, McNamee called me to his office and told me that I had a difficult decision to make. He told me that KISS FM could not afford to employ both Champion and her temporary replacement, Lorna Clarke. I would have to choose between one or the other. The original idea was that Clarke would be appointed to a producer post once Champion returned to work. McNamee explained that this was no longer an option. The two producer posts in the talks department, the appointment of which had been frozen in the summer, had since been abolished. I had to make a choice. Who did I want to stay and who did I want to go?

I was appalled. It was a terrible decision to have to make. Champion had been a pillar of strength during the licence application process and had supported me in the difficult task of shaping KISS FM's future. However, since the station's launch, Champion had appeared not to be such a productive hands-on manager. McNamee had even dared to allege to me, without any grounding in fact, that Champion had become pregnant to avoid being under pressure on-site during the station's first few months. On the other hand, Clarke had proven to be an excellent work colleague over the last three months. The pressures on KISS FM to succeed were still immense, and I had to have someone working alongside me who I believed could help achieve the goal of attracting one million listeners by the end of the first year.

With a great amount of regret, I told McNamee that I believed Clarke would be more essential to the success of the station, now that it was on-air, than Champion. McNamee agreed. Finally, he seemed pleased that I would sanction his frequent suggestions to kick

Champion out of the company. I had been defending Champion against McNamee's exit plans for the last year. Now, it seemed that McNamee had got his own way at last. He phoned Champion and broke the bad news. Then he circulated a brief memo to everyone in the building, explaining that Champion would not be returning to the station. He called Clarke into his office and offered to make her a full-time member of staff. Without any prior consultation with me, McNamee offered her a new post of senior producer he had created at a salary of £15,000, considerably less than Champion's £22,500. In the end, the whole affair had been just another money-saving exercise.

The mood in the programming department became horribly gloomy upon the news of Champion's departure. She had been universally liked and she was recognised as one of the founders of the newly legalised KISS FM who had helped transform it from a pirate radio to a commercial station. Everyone loathed the way in which her dismissal had been handled. She had been given maternity leave and only then, once the baby had been born, was she told that there was no longer a job for her. It was a very underhand way of getting rid of one of the company's senior members of staff, and everybody knew it. Champion phoned me at home that evening and asked me what the hell was going on at KISS FM. She was understandably very angry. I felt that there was nothing I could say by way of explanation. I knew only too well how precarious my own job had become at the radio station, but it would achieve nothing to share my concerns with Champion. If Champion was now suddenly out of KISS FM, I knew that I was only hanging on by the barest thread.

I never spoke to Champion again. She arranged for someone in the programming department to gather up her personal possessions from the office, which Clarke now occupied, and take them to her house. Much to my surprise, nothing about Champion's sudden departure appeared in the press, despite the high profile she had achieved prior to the station's launch. It was only several months later, when I queried a sum of several thousand pounds that had been deducted without warning from my budget, I was told that McNamee had made a financial settlement with Champion. She had been paid her full salary for the duration of her maternity leave, although McNamee had never mentioned this fact to me.

Eight days before Christmas, McNamee invited the whole station to a staff party at the Brasserie Julius in Islington. The evening should have been an enjoyable event, if I had not been instructed to sit at a table with McNamee, financial director Martin Strivens and their wives. I should have felt amongst friends, sitting with the station's senior management, but it seemed that McNamee could barely conceal his disdain for me these days. I would much rather have been sharing a table with the staff in my department. Instead, I was forced to share stiff conversations with two work colleagues who treated me as if I was the enemy these days.

McNamee continued to exercise his authority over my working hours. Every day, he would tell me of urgently convened meetings which he insisted I must attend, many of which turned out to be things to fill his day, and which took me away from running the station's operations. It was not unusual for McNamee to ask his personal assistant, Rosee Laurence, to phone me at home before eight o'clock in the morning and tell me that I had to squeeze in at least one more important meeting that same day. One morning, whilst driving to work, Laurence phoned to say that McNamee was insisting I attend a newly created nine o'clock meeting. I explained that my entire day was already clogged up with meetings, some of which I could not postpone. Laurence reiterated that McNamee had insisted that I must attend and that I would have to deal with my other commitments as best I could. I was so furious that I gritted my teeth and promptly broke off one complete front tooth. After a series of hastily arranged visits to a dentist, the incident cost me £340 to fix.

Despite McNamee's lack of goodwill towards me, I felt eternally grateful towards the staff in my department who had persevered under sometimes atrocious working conditions to help make KISS FM's launch so successful. I thanked them personally by spending £100 on chocolate eggs and using an evening at home to gift wrap one for each member of staff in paper covered with red lips, similar to the KISS FM logo. It was a small token of my respect for them and the commitment they had demonstrated.

The survey period for KISS FM's first official JICRAR radio audience survey had started in October and finished in December, after which I could breathe a huge sigh of relief. I had insisted that none of the programming staff could take holidays during this important period. Now, all of them were keen to take days off, particularly over the Christmas holiday period. From the time that KISS FM had moved to Holloway Road, financial director Martin Strivens had insisted that I complete a staff register every day. It listed everyone in my department and noted who was present at work and who was absent due to holiday or sickness. Initially, the form only offered days between Monday and Friday because Strivens had failed to consider that programming staff worked during weekends. He rectified this, but still failed to understand that the shift system meant that not everyone who worked full-time was in the building during five days per week. For some staff, I had had to create complex shift patterns to ensure they had a sensible amount of time away from work, whilst ensuring that the station's programming requirements were being met.

Now, I anticipated that the huge amount of paperwork that Strivens had required from me would come into its own. I would be able to determine exactly how much holiday was due to each of the nineteen full-time staff in the department, all of whom were clamouring for time off. However, it was not to be. Strivens explained to me that, because so many secretaries had come and gone in his department, he had transferred responsibility for this documentation to Rosee Laurence, McNamee's personal assistant. Laurence told me that she had not had time to do anything with the staff register and pointed to a huge pile of paper, comprising four months of returns from each department that had not yet been processed.

I was in disbelief that, despite the insistence upon detailed attendance records, no one on the top floor had been executing the most basic personnel functions. I promptly visited a local stationery shop and purchased several large wall planners. I realised that, during the Christmas break and while the rest of the building was relatively quiet, I would need to spend a few days compiling a personnel chart for everyone in my department. After all, I had drawn up the presenter contracts, I had negotiated and haggled over the clauses within them, I had interviewed staff and I had trained them. If no one else in the building was performing basic personnel functions, I might as well complete the circle and work out the staff's holiday entitlements myself. The wall planners would go on the office partition behind my desk.

However, if I had anticipated that the Christmas period at the radio station would be quiet, I was proven wrong. Upon McNamee and Lindsay Wesker's insistence, a revised programme schedule was drawn up for the holiday period that scheduled two presenters for each show, instead of the customary one. This gave the evening and weekend DJs an opportunity to be heard during weekday daytime broadcasts. I was told that this arrangement had been a tradition during KISS FM's pirate days which it was important to continue. The practical problem was that Christmas was the busiest and most lucrative time for DJs who earned their living from club work. As a result, given a choice of earning several hundred pounds from a few hours work in a busy club, or earning £50 for presenting an extra show on KISS FM, many DJs chose the former.

Despite issuing every DJ with a detailed schedule of specific programmes that they were assigned to present, many failed to turn up at the allotted times, without warning or apology. As a result, the whole Christmas programme schedule sounded like a shambles on-air, with the DJs having little idea if or who would be on next. Since KISS FM had been re-launched, some DJs had only just managed to get to grips with turning up for their shows on time each week. This sudden variation proved too complex for many of them to understand. I had to learn this valuable lesson during many hours spent on the phone trying to organise replacement DJs over Christmas at short (and sometimes no) notice. In future, I vowed to keep it simple and not to try and stretch DJs' abilities too far too quickly, as McNamee and Wesker had demanded.

Another change during Christmas was the need to give the station's six programme assistants a break from their shifts on public holidays. I suggested that the rest of us in the programming department should offer to replace them on those days, so a rota was passed around the office for people to volunteer their services. When the sheet of paper arrived on my desk, I realised that I had been the last person to be asked. There were only two spaces left for me – the overnight shift between Christmas Eve and Christmas Day, and the overnight shift between New Year's Eve and New Year's Day.

In the end, both nights turned out to be very memorable occasions and a lot of fun. During Dave Pearce's New Year's Eve show, we let off dozens of streamers in the studio, took hundreds of phone calls from well-wishers, and enjoyed ourselves thoroughly. One listener phoned from Canada to tell us that he was listening to KISS FM on his local cable television system. At first, we thought this was a hoax but Martin Charman (chief engineer of Jazz FM and a long time friend of Pearce), who was a guest in the studio, explained that somebody at a satellite switching station had probably relayed KISS FM across the Atlantic as a New Year's joke.

One programme broadcast between Christmas and the New Year that had been heavily trailed on-air was an overnight reggae music special that promised records exclusively from Jamaica's legendary Studio One studio. As with so many other programmes, when the time came, the presenter did not arrive at the studio. That night, I was staying at my mother's house in Surrey when a phone call woke me up to tell me that no one had arrived to present the reggae special and that there were no appropriate records at the station. I soon discovered that all the station's reggae presenters were working in clubs that night. I had to quickly get dressed and drive twenty miles to my flat to pick up some reggae records from my collection, before driving to the radio studio. I arrived within an hour of the phone call and, unrehearsed, presented my first show on the radio station. KISS FM DJ David Rodigan later told me that, coming home from a club booking in the early hours of the morning, he had had the shock of his life to hear his boss' voice coming out of the car radio.

Another incident at the station over Christmas was less entertaining. There had been an excellent reaction to several of the KISS FM Mastermix shows that had been broadcast since September, so I felt that the holiday period was a good time to repeat the most requested mixes. However, one day, I was called urgently to the station and found the security guard alleging that one of the station's DJs, Paul Anderson, had arrived unexpectedly and had threatened him to open with his master key the room in which the station's master tapes were stored. Then, Anderson was alleged to have stormed into the studio, shouted abuse at the DJ on-air at the time, and demanded that the programme assistant on duty must open the locked tape cupboard. When I went to the cupboard, I found that all the tapes of Anderson's mixes had gone. Apparently, he had been angry that KISS FM was about to repeat one of his mixes.

I was horrified by the incident, particularly as the staff involved had been so upset by Anderson's behaviour. I knew how volatile Anderson could be. He had stormed into my office on several occasions and sworn at me because I was not prepared to give in to his demand for a second weekly show on the station. I was not intimidated by this sort of behaviour, but it was quite another thing for him to forcibly steal KISS FM property. Since September, he had produced several KISS FM Mastermixes and had been paid for them. They were not his property to repossess, and certainly not in this manner. I told McNamee about the incident and suggested that disciplinary action was appropriate. McNamee reluctantly agreed but did not seem overly concerned.

I wrote a formal letter to Anderson, demanding he make an apology to the staff he had allegedly threatened and insisting that the tapes he had stolen be returned at once. Anderson did not reply. When I took up the matter again with McNamee, requesting his permission to take disciplinary action against Anderson, McNamee backed down and said I should not pursue the matter further. He offered no reason for this decision, though I knew it left me in an impotent position in my department. On the one hand, the staff who had been affected by Anderson understandably wanted to know that something had been done about it. On the other hand, Anderson must have realised that he could get away with behaviour that would not be tolerated in most organisations. I was left in the middle, unable to deal properly with either party and without an adequate explanation as to why no sanctions had been taken.

The incident only served to increase the suspicion with which many of the staff viewed the senior management of the station. It might appear to them that Lyn Champion had been sacked for becoming pregnant, whilst Paul Anderson had not even been warned about his behaviour. One of the KISS FM DJs, who had been with the station since its pirate days, explained to me privately that McNamee and Anderson's relationship went back a long way and that McNamee would do nothing to cross Anderson's path. My confidant alleged that Anderson knew considerable dirt that could be dished about McNamee's past, facts which McNamee wanted kept secret at all costs. Additionally, Anderson was supposedly a good friend of McNamee's wife, and McNamee certainly did not want her to know why he was spending so much time in the company of his personal assistant, Rosee Laurence. The DJ also alleged that Anderson was receiving other perks from McNamee, including a salary for DJ-ing at KISS FM club nights (whilst other DJs were paid a fee per night), and that KISS FM was paying the rent on Anderson's home, the station's former office in Blackstock Mews. I could not substantiate any of these allegations.

However, it was evident that a 'special relationship' existed between McNamee and Anderson which seemed to allow Anderson to do almost whatever he wanted within KISS FM. McNamee's style of management bore no relation to how able or successful a member of his staff might be at their job. In McNamee's world, it was more a case of who had the knowledge to ransom whom. Those who knew dark secrets were those whom McNamee favoured. Those who had no dirt on McNamee seemed to have no power.

January 1991.

The re-launch of KISS FM in September 1990 figured favourably in many magazines' round-ups of the year. In his list of the five best events of 1990, City Limits music critic Rick Glanvill included "KISS FM goes legit." The Listener magazine remembered 1990 as the year when "ex-pirates like KISS FM finally went legit." The Face described 1990 as the year London "listened to a legal KISS." Record Mirror's readers' poll listed "KISS FM legalised" in its top ten events of the year, and KISS FM was voted the fifth best radio show. Readers of Melody Maker voted KISS FM their tenth favourite radio show. Unsurprisingly, the station's competitors were not so congratulatory. BBC Radio One DJ Mark Goodier described KISS FM's launch as the "non-event of 1990" and commented: "What could be great is still run-of-the-mill."[804]

While the media and the public applauded the success of KISS FM, the radio industry was still speculating about the dismal performances of most of the other new incremental radio stations. An extraordinary general meeting was called at Manchester's Sunset Radio to discuss "alleged financial difficulties." Birmingham station Buzz FM was effectively taken over by established commercial radio group Radio Clyde after running out of money. Scottish community station CentreSound was taken over by Radio Forth, whose marketing manager Brian Hawkins described the station as "the result of a romantic notion that well meaning volunteers can compete with the commercial sector." Jazz FM managing director John Bradford was forced to deny press reports that his London station had suffered "a considerable shortfall in current earnings."[805]

North London black community station WNK was thought likely to fall under the full control of the Midlands Radio Group, which had already acquired twenty per cent of its voting shares. London's multi-ethnic station Spectrum Radio was said to be organising a refinancing package. Bristol black music station For The People was re-launched as Galaxy Radio by new owners Chiltern Radio, and the ex-pirate's founders, Babs Williams and Clem McClarty, had left the station. Galaxy promised that "music from chart-topping artists such as Lisa Stansfield, MC Hammer and George Michael will feature regularly in programmes."[806]

Observing these problems, Music Week commented: "The incremental stations are in danger of failing in their first purpose, to represent the music and the voice of their community, and KISS comes as a surprise, paradoxically because it has retained its baseball cap atmosphere ... There's been a constant drizzle of disappointment elsewhere: [South London black community station] Choice [FM] seems intent on showing how jolly nice and ordinary the black people of Brixton can be, rather than pumping out seismic reggae. And other incremental stations, a majority of those on-air, have gone soft or had to sell some of their independence to mainstream radio ... At worst, future innovators in radio will find their opportunities restricted because the current situation has put off investors and regulators. The music industry badly needs KISS to succeed to give radio people faith in a bold future."[807]

The acid test of KISS FM's success would be its first JICRAR radio audience survey, which would hopefully demonstrate its ability to go against the grain of all the other failing new radio stations. The JICRAR results arrived at KISS FM at four o'clock in the afternoon on 18 January, sealed in a brown envelope. Gordon McNamee, Gary Miele, Malcolm Cox and I gathered in the boardroom to witness the opening of the envelope. Miele was chain smoking, Cox was nervous with excitement, whilst I nonchalantly ate my sandwiches, having been too busy until then to take a lunch break. McNamee opened the envelope but, not understanding statistics, had to ask Cox to interpret the information inside. We all knew that the future of KISS FM depended upon whether we had achieved anywhere near the figure of one million listeners that had been promised to advertisers by September 1991.

Cox announced to us that KISS FM had attracted 1,078,000 listeners per week over the age of five years. We had managed to beat our first-year goal after only four months on-air. We were jubilant at the fantastic news. After reading so much bad news about the other incremental radio stations, it seemed amazing that we had succeeded where so many other hopefuls had failed. KISS FM had obviously got it right, when just about everybody else must have got it wrong. It was an amazing feeling to know that all the theories, knowledge and experience that I had poured into the radio station, along with all the hours of hard work, had been worth it at last. My ideas had worked. KISS FM was a winner![808]

McNamee quickly called a meeting in the boardroom with each department to break the good news. At the gathering of the programming staff, he handed everyone a glass of champagne and congratulated us heartily on our hard work and the success we had reaped. Afterwards, many of my staff came up to me and congratulated me personally on my success. However, several of them asked me why McNamee had not made any mention of me in his glowing tribute to the department's work. They viewed me as the architect of the new, legalised KISS FM's programming. I could say nothing. McNamee seemed to resent my success and, even in front of my own staff, was not afraid to make his contempt obvious.

A two-page press release was hastily drawn up to announce the station's success attracting one million listeners. I wrote out a suitable quote for attribution to me, but was not surprised to find it omitted from the final document. Instead, there were quotes from McNamee and head of marketing Malcolm Cox. Neither I, nor the station's successful programming, were mentioned anywhere within the press release. There was only a banal statement that KISS FM "joins radio's millionaire's club, six months ahead of schedule, with a weekly audience of 1,078,000 listeners." This inaccurate reference to "six months" was reprinted in the press.[809]

I still imagined that I might receive some sort of formal letter of congratulation for my success from either McNamee or the board of directors. I was being far too hopeful. I received nothing at all, not even a congratulatory card from the station's management. McNamee's office soon became filled with bottles of wine and champagne sent by well-wishers, as news of KISS FM's success quickly travelled across London. I received nothing except the respect of the huge team of people I had nurtured in my department. It was only their commitment and determination to learn how to make successful radio that had kept me going in the face of hostility from other quarters. I had no intention to desert the fifty-seven staff I had built into such a fantastic team.

Although I was extremely pleased to have achieved the audience target, paradoxically I knew that it made me more vulnerable to being expelled from the station. Whether the figures had been good or bad, I was in a no-win situation. If the figures had been bad, McNamee would have blamed me for the station's poor performance and sacked me. If the figures were good, McNamee would know for certain that he no longer needed my services.

He could take the credit for the station's success, bathe in the glory of adulation for his skilful capabilities in radio programming, and then quietly dispose of me out of the back door. I had been McNamee's fall guy, ready to take the knocks, whichever way the station went. McNamee did not need me around any more. I was only getting in his way.

The day after the audience results arrived, I took a plane to the annual MIDEM Radio Conference in the south of France. Whilst I spent the daytimes attending the sessions and debates on radio, my evenings and nights were passed in the hotel room, equipped with a pad of graph paper, a ruler, a calculator and some coloured felt pens. The pressing task for me was to carefully analyse this first set of KISS FM audience data to determine exactly who was listening to the station and when. I needed to know which aspects of the station's programming were proving successful, and which were disastrous. The key to the station's future success would depend upon offering the audience more of what they liked and less of what they hated. My job was to work out what those things were.

Just as I had predicted before the station's launch, KISS FM's audience was unlike that of most pop music stations, which attracted their biggest audience at breakfast time, but whose listenership diminished through the rest of the day. KISS FM had a slight audience peak in the morning but, during the rest of the day, the numbers remained pretty constant, before there was a huge surge in listeners to the specialist evening programmes. KISS FM's listenership only started to fall dramatically after 11.30 at night, a time when most pop music stations hardly had any listeners at all. There were other interesting phenomena: more than one third of all fifteen to nineteen year olds in London were listening to KISS FM; the proportion of housewives listening to daytime shows fell as low as 9% (as I had tried to convince KISS FM director Tony Prince); and the evening magazine show 'The Word' was proving very popular.

One of the station's programmes that proved most disastrous with listeners was Gordon McNamee's Saturday morning show. McNamee started at eleven o'clock, inheriting 76,000 listeners from the preceding breakfast show but, by the end of the show at one o'clock, KISS FM's audience had fallen to 26,000. Even less popular were the Saturday shows by McNamee's most favoured DJs which followed him – the audience for Norman Jay and Paul Anderson fell as low as 14,000. In determining the re-launched station's new programme schedule, these three slots had been the ones that McNamee had insisted must remain where they had been in KISS FM's pirate days.

Whilst in Cannes, I discovered a wealth of detail amongst the audience data which told me that changes would be necessary to parts of the programme schedule. However, I knew that the most important change, the replacement of Graham Gold and Mark Webster as breakfast show hosts, remained an issue that McNamee refused to countenance. This was the one change that could have improved the whole weekday listening pattern, but McNamee refused to budge. He had no interest in statistics and was inclined not to believe them. For me, it was unimportant whether McNamee believed the validity of the figures or not. These statistics were made available to the entire radio and advertising industries, which would enable them to see that KISS FM had an evident problem with its breakfast show. It was important for the station's much needed revenues to be seen to be doing something about that problem.

On my return to London, I was surprised to find that there had been little press coverage of KISS FM's success in achieving its audience target. The few publications that ran stories did not mention the station's successful programming. The Daily Mail story was headlined 'Sealed With A KISS' and only quoted Malcolm Cox saying: "Our popularity has taken us by surprise. Now we aim to consolidate." McNamee was away on a two-week holiday in Jamaica with his wife, having pre-arranged to leave the day after the JICRAR results arrived, possibly in anticipation that they would be bad. On his return, McNamee told me that I must attend part of the next meeting of the company's board. He said only that there were matters the directors wished to discuss with me. I did not know quite what to expect, not having been invited to attend any of their previous monthly meetings.[810]

The afternoon of the board meeting, word came down from the boardroom upstairs that my presence was required. I had still not been briefed by McNamee what any of this was about, so I joined the meeting with some trepidation. I was asked what audience figures I expected KISS FM to achieve from the next JICRAR survey that commenced in April. I explained that I did not think there was sufficient information yet to determine what the next set of figures would be. The audience of one million had been achieved immediately following KISS FM's launch, when awareness of the radio station had been very high as a result of the marketing campaign. My job was to try and keep all those people listening, but only time would tell us the size of the station's 'core' audience. Lots of people would have tuned in to KISS FM during those early months out of curiosity and, as yet, I had no information to know how many of them had gone back to listening to their favourite station.

The board members persisted in asking me to give them a precise figure that I expected KISS FM to achieve in the next JICRAR survey. I explained that it was impossible to extrapolate the future trend from one solitary set of statistics. Once KISS FM had a second set of figures, then it would be possible to estimate how quickly or slowly the audience might grow in the future. This was impossible as of yet. KISS FM had been on the air barely five months. Never in the history of radio had so many new stations launched in London during such a short period of time. The London radio market was in a state of turmoil that had not been experienced previously. It would take some time before listening patterns settled down to give us a realistic view of the impact that the newcomers, including KISS FM, were having on established stations.

I suggested that the board only had to consider the recent experiences of another new London station, Jazz FM, to see how wrong it was to predict audience numbers in a station's early days. Only weeks after its launch, Jazz FM had released the results of a privately commissioned survey which showed that it had achieved a substantial share of radio listening in London. However, the official JICRAR figures that just been released showed Jazz FM's audience to be lower than that of both KISS FM and the other new London-wide station, Melody Radio. The headline in Media Week, announcing the survey results, had been 'Jazz FM Suffers Body Blow As JICRAR Shows 5% Reach.' Its story said: "The latest JICRAR figures showed disastrous results for the first London-wide incremental station, Jazz FM. The data ... showed Jazz FM with a reach of just five per cent."[811]

I knew that this bad news would cripple Jazz FM's future ability to sell advertising. Everybody loves a radio station that is on the rise, but no one wants to know it on the way down. Jazz FM had tried to impress the radio advertising industry too quickly that it was a runaway success. Already, it had fallen flat on its face. For the first few months, everybody had been talking about what a great success Jazz FM was, but now everybody was damning it as an outright failure. I did not want the same thing to happen to KISS FM. I urged caution before the station could set itself future targets for its audience. The original aim had been to attract one million listeners by the end of the first year of operation. That remained the aim, since there was no guarantee whatsoever that the station's audience would not decline between now and the next survey. I urged the board to wait until the next survey was published in July to plot the next goal. Only then could we get a better long-term view of the realistic growth path.

I was politely ushered out of the board meeting and it resumed its discussions without me. The whole experience was disorientating because no explanation had been offered to me of what they had been discussing or what decisions they were trying to make. I had been wheeled in and wheeled out without any information to place the board's questions into context. Furthermore, they had barely acknowledged the fact that I had already achieved the first year target within only a few months. There seemed to be no gratitude.

That was why, later that day, something happened which particularly surprised and delighted me. After the conclusion of the board meeting, two directors – KISS FM DJ Trevor Nelson and footballer John Fashanu – sought me out and thanked me personally for my work on the successful programming that had attracted one million listeners to KISS FM. This was the first time that anyone at board level had offered appreciation for my work. It was very gratefully received.

---

[804] Rick Glanvill, "Boxing Days", City Limits, 20 Dec 1990.
Anne Karpf, "Waves Goodbye", The Listener, 20 Dec 1990.
Mark Goodier, [untitled], NME, 22 Dec 1990.
"1990 Was The Year We....", The Face, Jan 1991.
"The Record Mirror Readers' Poll", Record Mirror, 5 Jan 1991.
"Best Radio Show", Melody Maker, 5 Jan 1991.
[805] "Briefs" & "Clyde Takes Buzz Stake", Radio & Music, 24 Oct 1990.
"Forth Takes Over At CentreSound", Radio & Music, 10 Oct 1990.
"'No Shortfall At Jazz' – Bradford", Radio & Music, 12 Sep 1990.
[806] "Midlands May Buy WNK", Radio & Music, 7 Nov 1990.
"Spectrum Talking", Broadcast, 11 Jan 1991.
Michael Kavanagh, "Galaxy To Redirect FTP", Broadcast, 18 Jan 1991.
[807] Stu Lambert, "Giving Radio The Kiss Of Life", Music Week, 22 Sep 1990.
[808] JICRAR, Q4 1990.
[809] "KISS 100 FM: One Million Listeners", press release, KISS FM, 21 Jan 1991.
[810] "Sealed With A KISS", Daily Mail, 22 Jan 1991.
[811] Richard Gold, "Jazz FM Suffers Body Blow As JICRAR Shows 5% Reach", Media Week, 25 Jan 1991.

February 1991.

I continued to work as hard as ever to improve KISS FM's programmes. I knew it was essential to the station's continued success for the results of the next JICRAR audience survey to be higher than the one million that had already been achieved. As of yet, I had no idea how much higher KISS FM could go. However, I knew that there would have to be some increase if I was to stand a chance of hanging onto my job in the face of McNamee's attrition.

One evening after work, I held a seminar for the staff in the programming department in order to explain the adjustments to the output that I was trying to achieve. This was part of my ongoing mission to educate everyone who worked for me in the techniques of radio management. I had to make them understand why certain things needed to be done in certain ways in order to achieve the necessary results. We met together in the upstairs boardroom, with me pointing to my flip chart and scribbling in felt pen when, suddenly, the lights went out. Looking out the windows from the top floor, we could see that the whole of Holloway Road had been blacked out by a power cut. Straight away, I knew that there was no way to keep the station on the air. In the initial KISS FM budget, there had been provisions for back-up electrical generators, but these had been one of the first items to be cut after winning the licence.

I carried on with my seminar, using torchlight, hoping that the power cut would last no more than a few minutes. After an hour had passed and the meeting had finished, I phoned London Electricity Board to ask when power might be restored. They told me that they had no idea and, what is more, they did not care that I was phoning from a radio station that they had taken off the air. I was told I would just have to wait, like everyone else. After a break of several hours, the power returned, although it resumed in fits and starts that confused the electronic equipment in the radio studio for a while. Eventually, the DJ was able to resume his programme. The incident demonstrated how vulnerable KISS FM was, as a result of having done away with back-up systems that had been considered too costly. That evening's power cut would become a portent of imminent events at KISS FM.

Gordon McNamee suddenly announced that the station would no longer publish Free! magazine after the January 1991 issue. I was proud to have created the idea for the magazine a year and a half earlier. Although I was no longer associated with its editorial team, I was sad to see Free! close just as KISS FM was proving to be a success with listeners. McNamee explained that the magazine was no longer earning sufficient revenues from advertising to cover its printing costs. However, there were rumours of other reasons for the closure. It was alleged that two KISS FM directors wanted to close Free! because it clashed with their publishing interests. Tony Prince owned the monthly MixMag magazine which had recently switched from subscription-only to retail sales. Free! would be a direct competitor. It was also alleged that KISS FM shareholder EMAP planned to launch its own monthly dance music magazine. Free! would be a direct competitor. Fortunately, Free! found an alternative financial backer and was reborn as 'Touch' magazine, which published similar editorial content.[812]

Once Free! had moved out, the large downstairs room on the ground floor of the Holloway Road building suddenly looked very empty. I spent an evening picking through the debris left in the office of the magazine that had started life as '94' in July 1988, and which had been such an important part of the pirate station's campaign to win a licence. Free!'s sudden closure was a bad omen. Staff in the building started whispering about further cuts that might be made to save the company money. These rumours were reinforced by news that Jazz FM had just axed four staff, reducing its workforce to forty. Negotiations had taken place with the remaining personnel for them to work longer hours rather than take pay cuts. Then came news that Jazz FM had axed a further sixteen jobs. Its director of programmes, Ron Onions, and marketing director, Mike Bernard, were amongst the one-third of the workforce that had lost their jobs.[813]

Within days, McNamee ordered me into his office and told me he had some bad news to share. There were going to have to be cutbacks at the station, and the programme department was going to have to accept the lion's share. McNamee insisted that one member of the talks department had to be made redundant, record librarian Alexander Donnelly would lose his job, one programme assistant would have to go, and several DJs. McNamee had already decided that part-time DJs would have to be paid £25, rather than £50, for each show they presented. He gave me the total amount by which I had to cut the wages bill in the department and he told me to go away and work out the specific details. I was asked to come back later that week with my recommendations.

For the next few days, I grappled privately with a further substantial revision to the budget for the programme department, behind the (unusually) closed door of my office and during evenings at home. I decided that, in order to maintain KISS FM's audience at the current one million per week level, I would have to preserve the present amount of resources allocated to daytime and evening programmes. That would require KISS FM to cut the overnight broadcasts that attracted very few listeners. Instead of live programmes, the station would have to broadcast pre-recorded tapes on weekdays between one o'clock and six o'clock in the morning. This was the only way to concentrate the station's resources on improving the daytime shows, which were by far the most important for listeners and advertisers.

I recommended to McNamee that seven part-time DJs would have to lose their weekly shows, all of which had been broadcast late at night or early in the morning. I also recommended Lisa I'Anson to be the researcher in the talks department to go because, although she presented 'The Word,' she brought fewer skills to the show than the other team members. McNamee rejected this suggestion and, instead, insisted that Tony Farsides must be made redundant, despite him having been one of the three people McNamee had demanded that Lyn Champion employ. I disagreed because Farsides was the only member of the team with detailed knowledge of dance music. As a music station, KISS FM needed that expertise. Although I'Anson was an excellent front person for the show, she could more easily be replaced. Eventually, after several days of discussion on this point, McNamee relented and decided that neither I'Anson nor Farsides would lose their jobs.

McNamee then distributed memos to all personnel, calling them to two meetings, one for full-time staff and the other for part-time staff. The note emphasised: "ATTENDANCE IS COMPULSORY ... All other appointments are to be cancelled until after mid-day. All visitors will be refused entry to the building during the meeting. The switchboards will close down for the duration of the meeting ... This may be short notice but it is a very important meeting ... ATTENDANCE IS COMPULSORY."[814]

On 18 February, the usual Monday morning meeting was cancelled. Instead, McNamee arranged a succession of short meetings in his office to fire those people who were to help the station save money. Record librarian Alexander Donnelly was told to leave work that day. After his meeting with McNamee, I spoke to him alone in the boardroom to explain that I had been given no choice about his dismissal. I assured him that it was not because he had not performed well in his job. He had been an excellent worker and I hoped that, if the station's finances improved, I might be able to re-employ him in the future. He cried before he left, and he made me cry too. He politely wished everyone in the department a final farewell. It made everybody incredibly sad to see such a valuable team member go.

McNamee met seven part-time DJs to inform them that they had lost their shows. Two of them – Heddi Greenwood and Tony Farsides – still had full-time jobs with the station that were unaffected by the cutbacks. The remainder – Peter Davis, Haitch, Nick Power, DJ André and Clive Richardson – were told to collect their possessions from their lockers on the programming floor. Then, they were escorted out of the building by one of the station's security guards. It was another dismal day in the department because everybody had seen people who had been loyal to KISS FM since its pirate days suddenly being ejected. It was only two months since the news of Lyn Champion's sacking had depressed the whole mood of the department. Now, another purge of McNamee's team was underway.

That evening, the remainder of the DJ team drifted into the building for the important meeting to be held in the recently vacated Free! office. The air was thick with anticipation because news of their sacked colleagues had already circulated during the day. McNamee and financial director Martin Strivens eventually addressed the gathering from one end of the cavernous room that had been a busy office until Free!'s recent closure. McNamee explained that everybody in the station was being forced to contribute to the station's financial cutbacks. There would be no pay rise for any staff during 1991, the company's directors had agreed to take no payment for attending future board meetings, and Strivens and he were taking pay cuts. The cutbacks meant that some DJs who had been with the station a long time had to lose their jobs, whilst the remainder had to take a pay cut from £50 to £25 per programme.

There was uproar amongst the DJs. Here was McNamee, dressed in his customary expensive suit, with his brand new Mercedes company car parked in the private car park behind the building, telling DJs who were earning only £50 per week from their work for KISS FM that it was they who would have to take a pay cut! This meeting was taking place in a brand new building that seemed to have all the modern conveniences of a successful business and which was filled with dozens of full-time staff who had only joined the station a few months ago, yet it was the DJs who had been involved with KISS FM for the longest time who were being asked to suffer the greatest blow! Was not this whole cost cutting exercise upside down? Was it not the KISS FM DJs who had made the radio station successful in the first place? Yet, now, these same DJs were being treated as if they were the least important asset of the station?

McNamee replied uncharacteristically cautiously to a barrage of criticism. He explained that most of the DJs present earned their living not from their one show a week on

KISS FM, but from the club work they did. KISS FM's full-time staff had no other source of income and most were already low paid. McNamee told the DJs that it would prove impossible to cut the salaries of the full-time staff because they would leave the company and then the radio station would fail. However much he disliked having to do it, he had to make cutbacks and it was the DJs who would have to take a pay cut. McNamee argued that the original payment of £50 per show had been generous by most radio stations' standards anyway, but it had proven impossible to sustain. He blamed the economy, he blamed the recession, he blamed reluctant advertisers, and he blamed the government. But the meeting did not hear him blame the station's sales department, or Strivens' budgets or the station's accounting practices, and he certainly did not blame himself for having failed to manage the station appropriately.

There was much dissent in the room about the seven DJs who had been sacked. McNamee was asked why it had to be those particular seven, why they had been ejected from the station completely rather than just temporarily 'rested,' and why no promise had been made to re-employ them when the station's financial situation improved. McNamee skirted around these questions, partly blaming the DJs themselves for not having produced shows of sufficient quality while, on the other hand, half-promising to take them back once there was enough money to produce live programmes overnight. However, I knew from the way the DJs had been escorted out of the building that McNamee had no intention of bringing them back.

There were questions about the other cuts that McNamee said he was making. The DJs wanted to know who else was going. McNamee told them that one of the receptionists had been made redundant, the record librarian, one programming assistant and a member of the finance department (in fact, the financial post was already vacant and was not going to be advertised because there was not enough work to warrant it). The DJs also wanted to know about the cuts that were taking place at board level. Why, they wanted to know, had board members been paid until now just for turning up to monthly meetings? Was that not a waste of money anyway? And how much of a pay cut were McNamee and Strivens actually taking? McNamee explained, with much embarrassment, that he and Strivens were effectively taking a pay cut because they had both been due to receive pay increases in April 1991 and, now, neither was going to take them. The DJs responded to this explanation with bitter comments. So, in fact, McNamee and Strivens were not taking pay cuts at all. They were simply not extending their already privileged existences.

The questioners persisted. Why did McNamee have to have such an expensive company car? He explained that it was owned by the company and was part of his employment contract. He said that some workers had wanted to be paid a lot of cash but he, instead, had opted for much of his remuneration to be taken in the form of a company car. Anyway, he added, pointing to Strivens standing alongside him, this man had actually taken a cut in pay to join KISS FM. When he had worked at Centurion Press, Strivens had had a Porsche whereas, now, at KISS FM he only drove a Jeep. It was a stock line in McNamee's repertoire that I had heard him say dozens of times before when he had wanted to impress people to imagine that Strivens had made sacrifices to work for KISS FM. However, to the assembled DJs, this explanation smacked of condescension. McNamee's ill-judged comments only served to further fuel their fury.

They wanted to know how McNamee could justify telling them only now that their pay was to be cut by half, starting less than two weeks hence. In an attempt to offer some kind of compromise to the meeting, McNamee agreed to delay the implementation of the pay cut by a further month. Those DJs who presented shows in duos wanted to know how they would be affected. For Coldcut and Bobbi & Steve, did this mean that, in future, each DJ would be paid only £12.50 per show? Again, McNamee relented and promised to maintain their fees at £25 per person per show. Sitting in the audience, I was unsettled that McNamee was rashly making such promises. I had been forced to lose good staff in order to save the amounts he had demanded from me, and now McNamee was handing out concessions that screwed up my budgets. Who was going to pay for these spontaneous decisions?

By the end of the meeting, it was clear to everyone that the KISS FM of pirate radio days had been well and truly laid to rest with these announcements. Not so long ago, McNamee had promised all the DJs that they would share in the radio station's success, that the business ran along the lines of a family, and that everybody had an important part to play. Now, by the end of that meeting, it was clear that KISS FM was a completely different operation these days. McNamee appeared to be giving up nothing of his new-found wealth. Instead, when cuts had to be made, he was inflicting them upon people who had worked for him for several years and who had always been promised some sort of reward. Suddenly, the DJs had seen through McNamee's external facade of bonhomie and camaraderie. He seemed to have moved beyond their reach now and seemed determined to stay there. The greater the distance he could build between him and them, the more secure he must feel. Never again would there be a meeting in which McNamee was treated as one of the boys.

In stark contrast, the similar meeting held the following morning for the station's full-time staff passed almost without incident. With the exception of a small number of us, most of those present had been recruited after KISS FM's licence had been won. These people knew little of the station's history, which is why the sacking of a few late-night DJs meant very little to them. What they did know was that, when a company hits hard times, people have to go. What they could not see was that McNamee was rooting out former colleagues, replacing them with more pliant, less principled workers who viewed KISS FM as a job, rather than a calling. A means to pay their bills, rather than the culmination of a twenty-year effort to get a soul radio station licensed in London.

McNamee unveiled the new programme schedule and explained that pre-recorded tapes would be broadcast overnight on weekdays, whilst evening shows would be extended in length from two to three hours, now ending at 1 am. The reaction from those present was quite muted, although the sales department was critical of the idea to play tapes overnight as it could no longer sell advertising spots during those hours. The truth was that there were several hours during the station's daytime output that were almost bereft of paid advertisements, so the loss of night-time opportunities was hardly an issue.

Much to McNamee's personal amusement during the meeting, a completely different argument broke out when DJ David Rodigan started to criticise my policy preventing daytime DJs from playing oldies that dated from earlier than 1980. There followed an uninformed debate amongst staff who had nothing to do with the station's programming that this policy was a silly idea. This distraction suited McNamee perfectly since it removed the heat from him and Strivens, standing vulnerably at the front of the gathering. For his part, Strivens waffled about the poor state of the economy, the difficulty all radio stations were encountering with advertising sales, and the need for everyone to tighten their belts. The meeting ended quickly and everyone went back to their desks to gossip in private about the implications of the cutbacks.

Afterwards, McNamee asked me to talk to Colin Faver and explain to him why he was losing his full-time programme assistant post, though he would still be paid for his weekly show on the station. I felt that McNamee wanted me to take the blame for Faver's dismissal because he was a shareholder in the station who might create problems for McNamee at board level. McNamee needed Faver on his side, so it was me who was forced to explain why I had chosen him to go, rather than any of the other programme assistants. (Several months later, I discovered in the accounts that Faver was still being paid £50 per show while every other DJ had been cut to £25. Asked about this anomaly, McNamee admitted he had made a special deal with Faver to continue paying him at the old rate, though I would never have known if I had not discovered the inconsistency.)

The previous week, when I had discussed with McNamee the details of which part-time DJs would be made redundant, I had proposed one name that McNamee had responded was definitely not for inclusion on the list. This DJ was also a KISS FM shareholder, although McNamee justified his exclusion by arguing that he did not wish to make three people redundant who all worked in the same record shop, Music Power Records, which had been KISS FM's mailing address in its pirate days.

One person within the company who remained unhappy about this wave of job losses was Lindsay Wesker. He seemed to blame me directly for the loss of his one member of staff, the record librarian. Again, I sensed that McNamee might have laid the blame at my doorstep, even though it was he who had insisted that this particular post disappear. Wesker ranted and raged at me for some time, asking how I could justify the recent employment of two new producers in the department, whilst at the same time losing a record librarian. Wesker predicted that the organisation of the music library would completely disintegrate now because he would have no time to undertake those duties. He suggested that I ask the producers to assist him with library duties, a proposal I rejected. Wesker continued to argue that the two new producers were a waste of money and something that KISS FM could do without, while the librarian was vital to the smooth running of the station.

Once news of the job cuts reached the outside world, the press were on the phone to me at work and at home, begging for information. Despite my misgivings over McNamee's actions, I was not going to jeopardise my own fragile position within the station. I said nothing, but others must have spoken, because the media were soon running stories about the cutbacks. Echoes music paper ran a story, headlined 'KISS Before Crying,' that reported: "Last Monday morning at 10.30 am, KISS MD Gordon McNamee sacked seven DJs, a receptionist, the record librarian and programme assistant Colin Faver. Several of them were apparently escorted from the building by security staff."[815]

Broadcast magazine reported that McNamee "blamed the advertising recession" and he was quoted saying: "This is fine-tuning ... We aimed to give everyone a chance when we went from being a pirate to being legit[imate]. Some people made it, some didn't." The article commented: "The station's presentational style, aimed at preserving a pirate's raw edge, has been criticised by some within the radio industry for often lacking polish, consistency and professionalism." Campaign magazine quoted an unnamed KISS FM spokesman saying that the sacked DJs "are a victim of a schedule change which will come into effect from 17 March. The new schedule is being kept under wraps but sources say it will incorporate a bid to make KISS sound more professional." I was baffled. The new schedule had nothing to do with making KISS FM sound different. The station had already achieved its target of one million listeners per week, regardless of critics' accusations of its unprofessional sound.[816]

UK Press Gazette reported that KISS FM had "adjusted its budgets downwards four times since its launch in September" and quoted financial director Martin Strivens saying that "firm budgetary controls were essential." Strivens asserted that the station's first year was still on target for advertising revenues of £2.5m: "We were quite close to budget in our first quarter. The second quarter is bound to be impacted by the recession however." McNamee promised that "despite the adjustment of business forecasts, KISS is cushioned against severe reorganisation by its audience and advertising base." These public pronouncements hardly squared with the information the staff had been given, particularly as there had been no promise that further redundancies might not prove necessary. The most unexpected revelation reported alongside the redundancies was that "the station is thought to be hiring new staff, including a sponsorship manager." Despite nothing having been said at the two staff meetings, head of marketing Malcolm Cox confirmed the following week that two new posts were being created in sponsorship and promotions. How could this be true if the station had needed to make such severe cutbacks?[817]

There was one published comment about the messy business of job losses at KISS FM that should not have been made to a journalist, but which was closer to the truth than McNamee or Strivens had admitted. Asked about the response to KISS FM from advertisers, Lindsay Wesker responded: "Well, the major problem has been the recession. There hasn't been a lot of money about – November, December, January were really, really grim, and we had redundancies in February, which was very sad for us. Up 'til then, it had been nothing but growth."[818]

The 'growth' evident in September and October 1990 had been the result of the station's high profile launch marketing campaign. After that, even though I had delivered the promised volume of listeners, KISS FM had seemed completely unable to convert its substantial audience into revenues. The question everyone within the station was asking privately was: maybe this was just the beginning of a complete restructuring of KISS FM?

---

[812]"Touch Is Free", press release, Freud Communications, 8 Feb 1991.
Joseph Gallivan, "They're Going To 'Touch' You For A Pound", The Independent, 19 May 1993.
[813]"Jazz Joins Avalanche Of Radio Job Cuts", Broadcast, 25 Jan 1991.
Alice Rawsthorn, "Jazz FM Cuts One In Three Jobs", Financial Times, 12 Feb 1991.
Michael Kavanagh, "Hard Times Hit Staff At Jazz FM", Broadcast, 15 Feb 1991.
[814]"Staff Meeting 19.2.91", memo from Gordon McNamee to full-time staff, KISS FM, 13 Feb 1991.
[815]"KISS Before Crying", Echoes, 2 Mar 1991.
[816]Michael Kavanagh, "Pirates Walk Plank As KISS 'Fine Tunes'", Broadcast, 1 Mar 1991.
"Staff Cuts Bite Hard At KISS and Parent Crown", Campaign, 1 Mar 1991.
[817]Terence Kelly, "Thornton Out In Latest Round Of Redundancies", UK Press Gazette, 4 Mar 1991.
"Airborne Warning", UK Press Gazette, 4 Mar 1991.
Caroline Marshall, "Print And Radio Sealed With A KISS", Litho Week, 20 Mar 1991.
"Staff Cuts Bite Hard At KISS and Parent Crown", op cit.
"Authority Invites Radio Applications", Marketing Week, 8 Mar 1991.

[818] Andy Smith, "Dancing Feats", For The Record, May 1991.

February 1991.

Early one morning, I was sat at my desk when one of the programme staff entered the office and whispered to me in a conspiratorial tone: "You know that Heddi has gone?" I was confused. "Gone where?" I asked. I assumed that Heddi Greenwood must either have gone on vacation or have moved office within the building. I was wrong. I was told that she had gone for good. She had left KISS FM and was not coming back.

I sat at my desk in total shock. Greenwood had been with KISS FM before my involvement in the station. She was as much a part of the KISS FM fabric as the rest of us who had worked in the Blackstock Mews office. How could she have gone? I was informed that she had been told to go. I was too shocked and too frightened to ask for the gory details. Knowing the full story would only have made me more angry and upset. Besides, there was absolutely nothing I could have done about the situation. I was powerless against the tide of dismissals that was sweeping through the organisation.

From my perspective, it was the news of Greenwood's departure that made it feel as if a purge was taking place within KISS FM. First it had been Lyn Champion. Then, it had been some of the DJs who had been loyal to the radio station for years. Now it was Heddi Greenwood. I felt wounded. I had lost count of how many occasions I had sought to dissuade Gordon McNamee from sacking Lyn Champion since KISS FM had won its licence. But I had lost that argument in the end. Similarly, I had fought to persuade McNamee to offer Greenwood a full-time job in the legalised KISS FM. Until that day, I thought I had won the argument. Now I had lost it too.

I felt far too affected to contact Greenwood to find out what had happened. What could I say to her? There was no hope I could offer her. I never learnt the detailed circumstances of Greenwood's departure from the radio station that she had helped create. I only knew that, without Greenwood's dedication and hard work, KISS FM would never have won its licence. During that critical period after the station had lost its first licence bid, when McNamee had drifted into a haze of inaction, it was Greenwood who had maintained the pirate station's campaigning strategy. It was Greenwood who had successfully mobilised London's dance music community to write their names on petitions that had helped persuade the government to relent and offer further FM radio licences in the capital.

Greenwood's sudden and unexpected departure from KISS FM had a horribly demoralising impact on me. My own experiences since the station had launched had made me anticipate that I would have been out of my job by Christmas. To my surprise, I had managed to last as long as February. Greenwood's exit made me think that I probably had only days or weeks left at KISS FM. I remained at the radio station more by luck than judgement. Soon, I knew that my luck would run out.

It became hard to motivate myself when, all around me, the people I had worked with were being expelled for all the wrong reasons. Greenwood's departure left only a handful of the original KISS FM office staff at the station: Gordon McNamee, Rosee Laurence, Lindsay Wesker … and me. The bond between the first three was long and strong. I was a relative newcomer compared to them. Laurence and Wesker had long demonstrated that they were much more prepared to do McNamee's bidding than ever I had been, or Lyn Champion or Heddi Greenwood. That had made the three of us less essential to McNamee and, ultimately, more expendable.

Heddi Greenwood's departure from KISS FM was one of my darkest days working at the radio station. In recent months, I had seen little of her. I worked on the second floor, while she worked in the basement. She and I rarely attended the same internal meetings. We had not talked privately for a long time. I had been too busy, desperately trying to make KISS FM a success. I had been pre-occupied with my own fragile position within the business. I sorely missed the times when we had worked in the same office at Blackstock Mews. Greenwood's talents had been wasted in the new KISS FM set-up. She should have been made a manager, she should have shared in the success, and she should have been rewarded.

Instead, it had ended horribly like this. No explanation was offered to staff about Greenwood's departure. She was there one day, but had gone the next. I knew that, whatever I did or said in the coming weeks, I must be next for the chop. The only thing I did not know was 'when' or 'how.'

The experience of working at KISS FM had somehow been transformed, within a matter of months, from a fantastic opportunity into a terrible nightmare. After Heddi Greenwood's sudden exit, KISS FM was never the same again for me.

March 1991.

KISS FM was not the only new radio station shedding staff. Jazz FM DJ Gilles Peterson was sacked for making on-air comments about the war in the Arabian Gulf that followed Iraq's invasion of Kuwait. Peterson allegedly made anti-war comments during one of his popular weekend shows and then played ninety minutes of records on the theme of peace, including Bobby McFerrin's 'Peace' and the Mighty Ryeders' 'Let There Be Peace.' He commented to the press: "It was a spontaneous and honest response to the impending threat of war and was not in any way a question of taking sides." However, Jazz FM managing director John Bradford responded: "No broadcasting organisation can express political opinions. That is the law."[819]

The following week, Jazz FM founder David Lee was ousted from the station. Former BBC producer Malcolm Laycock took over the post of programme controller and commented: "David is a jazz man, not a radio man. He has no experience in radio and, to be honest, he was floundering a little." Meanwhile, at Birmingham station Buzz FM, the black music format for which it had been licensed by the Independent Broadcasting Authority was rescinded by new owners in favour of a more pop music orientated sound. Newly appointed marketing director Peter Salt explained: "The music has been pretty obscure and has not been appealing to a broad enough audience. We will be playing chart music that fits into our format of 'Rhythm of the City' and golden oldies that people remember."[820]

In London, on local station RTM's first anniversary, fourteen staff were made redundant in an attempt to stem accumulated losses of £500,000. However, those personnel refused to complete their contractual commitments with the station, taking it off the air for most of the day. In the end, newly appointed station manager Rodney Collins offered to re-employ ten of the fourteen staff in order to settle the dispute.[821]

The track record of the new incremental radio stations had been quite appalling. Already, it was clear that the government could easily consider the entire incremental radio experiment to be something of a failure. The new stations were intended to increase the programme choices available to radio listeners in their areas, but many of them were already imitating the pop music formats of their competitors. To avoid public embarrassment, the authorities had allowed established commercial radio groups to acquire the new stations and merge them into their existing operations. More than ever, KISS FM seemed to be the exception to the rule, which is why the station continued to receive praise for having stuck to its original intentions.

Sponsorship manager Gordon Drummond secured a deal for David Rodigan's weekly reggae chart show to be sponsored by the health drink Supermalt. Drummond had promised the sponsor that the show would also be broadcast each week on Birmingham's Buzz FM and Manchester's Sunset Radio. He told the press: "It's rare for a station to approach other stations with programming direct[ly] like this, but this proves we can do it." What Drummond did not seem to have realised was that I would have to produce a completely different version of Rodigan's show for these two stations. During his programme for KISS FM, Rodigan played the station's jingles, advertisements, gave time checks, ran competitions and talked about other KISS FM shows. His show would have to be completely re-recorded for Buzz FM and

Sunset Radio. The press release included no mention of my role in the first syndication of a KISS FM show although, bizarrely, it did include a quote from Sunset Radio's programme controller. Sadly, the notion of a syndicated show was premature and the two stations quickly stopped broadcasting Rodigan's reggae chart once they had adopted more mainstream formats. The deal became another example of KISS FM's rush for revenues getting in the way of resolving the necessary details of a project.[822]

More successful was an exclusive prison interview that the station secured with legendary soul singer James Brown, who was expected to be released within a few months. The two-hour documentary made by Lorna Clarke attracted a lot of attention and returned KISS FM to the pages of the consumer press for the programmes it was broadcasting. Many magazines reprinted excerpts from the interview, mentioning the fact that it could he heard in full on KISS FM. A further boost to morale at the station came from Echoes music paper's annual readers' poll, in which KISS FM DJ Steve Jackson was voted 'Most Promising Newcomer' in the DJ category. I was particularly pleased that my decision to offer Jackson a daytime show, in the face of opposition from McNamee, had paid off.[823]

The imminent war in the Gulf had repercussions for KISS FM because I too needed to ensure that the DJs made no partisan statements on-air. I knew that radio was the medium that people turned to for immediate news during disasters or wars, so it was important for KISS FM not to lose its audience to more news-orientated stations when important developments occurred in the Gulf. Whilst tensions had been mounting over a period of weeks since January, I had been busy setting up new procedures to deal with the eventuality that a war might break out that involved British troops. KISS FM had no newsroom of its own, so responsibility for the station's editorial coverage rested with me.

The deal that had been struck with Independent Radio News [IRN] a year earlier to provide KISS FM with a customised news bulletin service had included several other facilities that had failed to materialise. IRN had promised to install a teleprinter at KISS FM, to be linked to its own service of hard-copy news and information. I chased this up and the printer was soon installed outside the main studios, churning out reams and reams of paper every day. When IRN had important news, KISS FM would be warned by teleprinter message that an unscheduled news bulletin was imminent. From now on, the programme assistants were charged with monitoring the printer's output during the day and evening, whilst I arrived early each morning to read the print-outs that had accumulated overnight.

I issued a five-page memo to all programming staff and DJs, to try and make them understand how important it was for the station to cover the impending war accurately and concisely. At the same time, I had to stress that no one should make personal comments on the situation within their programmes. Many of the staff thought I was being over-enthusiastic about the whole affair. However, I knew that, during the Falklands War in 1982, radio listening had increased dramatically at the height of the conflict. I could not afford for KISS FM to miss out on an increase in radio listening that might occur this time around.

After several weeks of mounting tension, it started to look as if British troops were going to be drawn into the war. Several evenings, I stayed even later than usual at the office, monitoring the news services, because I knew it was likely that the first air strikes would be made at night. One evening, by eleven o'clock, I had decided that war was probably not going to start that day. I drove home with the car radio tuned to London talk station LBC. I had reached within a few miles of my flat when the presenter, Robbie Vincent, suddenly announced that he was receiving unconfirmed reports of war having broken out in Baghdad. I pulled the car over and parked in Pilgrims Way, Wembley, sitting alone in the dark on a deserted street, listening to the radio intensely. A few minutes later, Vincent confirmed that Baghdad was being bombed and his station started to relay live commentary from CNN reporters in the city.

I phoned the DJ on-air at KISS FM, explained the situation and told him I would be there shortly. I turned the car around and headed back to the station at breakneck speed. When I arrived, a teleprinter message was waiting for me that announced: "ATTENTION NETWORK. WAR HAS BEGUN. WE WILL BE RUNNING TWO MINUTE BULLETINS ON THE HALF-HOUR. WE ARE EXPECTING TO EXTEND THE ON-HOUR BULLETINS … THAT WILL DEPEND ON THE MATERIAL WE HAVE. YOU WILL BE TOLD BY QUARTER TO EVERY HOUR. ANN BUSBY, IRN."[824]

I set up a war operations room in the KISS FM production studio, using two portable radios and two portable televisions to monitor developments. The teleprinter informed me of the bulletins that IRN was preparing, how long they would last, and when they were scheduled, so that I could decide swiftly which ones should be broadcast on KISS FM. I had to explain to the DJ the way they should introduce the bulletins and what should be said to keep listeners tuned to KISS FM, rather than them switching to competing stations.

I worked through the night until dawn and then right through the following day. I eventually drove home at the end of that afternoon, having to wind down my car window to keep myself awake. During the following weeks of outright war, Lorna Clarke and I shared the responsibility of making editorial decisions about the station's coverage, splitting each day into shifts. It proved to be exhausting for both of us and disrupted our other responsibilities immeasurably. I even failed to enter any of the station's programmes into that year's Sony Radio Awards because I was too busy with the war coverage. Although neither Gordon McNamee nor the other managers seemed to understand or appreciate the work Clarke and I were doing, the feedback from listeners and from news organisations, including IRN, was incredibly positive. I only hoped that our hard work had earned us listeners at a critical time in the station's history.

Once the war had ended, I put the finishing touches to the station's revised programme schedule which was to be introduced in mid-March. This timeline gave everybody two weeks to adjust to the changes before the station's second JICRAR audience research survey started at the beginning of April. From the statistics published in the previous survey, I had created dozens of graphs to add to the first few I had drawn whilst in Cannes in January. Having examined the data in minute detail for months, I had determined the good and bad points of the station's output, and calculated where exactly I felt KISS FM could attract more listeners. Some of this work I attempted to explain to McNamee, but he remained dismissive of statistics and accused me of taking them far too seriously. Many meetings to decide the changes had been held within the programme department, mostly between me, Lorna Clarke and the two producers. Initially, I had tried to involve Lindsay Wesker as well, but he had told the newly appointed producers during one such meeting that he thought they had no role within KISS FM and that the station would be better off without them. After that outburst, it proved difficult to get Wesker and the two newcomers to work together at all.

I presented the proposed programme changes to McNamee for his approval. In his eyes, the breakfast show remained sacrosanct, so there was no possibility of removing Graham Gold and Mark Webster from that timeslot, regardless of the fact that many within the station agreed that their show was still not working after seven months on-air. To try and alleviate the damage caused to the daytime audience, I recommended moving Steve Jackson from afternoons to the morning slot immediately after the breakfast show. The weekday evenings had already proved successful, so there were few changes necessary there, except to move some shows to compensate for the seven DJs that had lost their jobs.

In the weekend programme schedule, Saturday morning had proved the most disastrous with audiences. However, McNamee refused to move his show elsewhere, despite the adverse effect it was having on the station's figures. He told me that, only if his figures were still poor in the next audience survey, would he consider a different timeslot. The other poorly performing shows on Saturday were presented by Paul Anderson and Norman Jay. McNamee agreed to move Anderson to a more appropriate evening slot, though he was reluctant to move Norman Jay to Sunday. Jay had followed McNamee on-air during KISS FM's pirate days, as well as on the first day of the station's re-launch.

When I informed the DJs of their new programme times, most were happy with the changes, but Jay refused point blank to present his show on Sunday. He gave me an ultimatum – either to keep his show exactly where it was on Saturday, or he would leave the station. I did not feel intimidated by this tactic and told McNamee about the impasse. After much thought, McNamee told me that I could sack Jay if I wanted to, but that I should be prepared for the consequences. It still seemed as if McNamee was setting traps for me, hoping I would be snared by one eventually. I opted for self-preservation and acquiesced to McNamee's wish. Jay was another of the seven DJ shareholders whom McNamee needed onside at board level. Nevertheless, I shared with McNamee my concern that Jay consistently talked over all the records he played in his show. McNamee agreed that I should send him a polite letter, asking him to play more interrupted music ... or else. However, even after the new schedule had been implemented, in which Jay retained the same slot, he continued to talk too much. Predictably, McNamee insisted I should take no further action.

The knock-on effects of McNamee's decision to keep Norman Jay's show on Saturday were considerable. I had already told the DJs about their new timeslots, so now I had to revise several of them because of McNamee's reluctance to act in the best interest of the station's audience figures. The DJs I had to speak to for a second time were understandably annoyed, particularly when they realised they were being usurped to make way for the intransigence of Norman Jay. Once again, McNamee had seemed to find it easy to put his own interests above those of the company. The flaws in these judgements were beginning to become more evident to the staff within KISS FM.

A press release was drawn up to announce the revised programme schedule. The first draft contained only a quote from the station's head of marketing, Malcolm Cox. I raised my objection to always being excluded from the station's publicity materials and insisted that, since this entire press statement concerned programming, surely it was more appropriate for a quote from me to be included. The station's press officer, Anita Mackie, relented and, as a result and for the first time, I was given a little credit for the station's successful programme policy in a KISS FM press release. It would soon prove to be a pyrrhic victory.[825]

Within the radio station, I felt that it was important for everybody to understand why certain changes to the programming were being made. Using graphs and tables hand drawn on transparencies and displayed on an overhead projector, I made a presentation to the heads of department at one Monday morning meeting to explain my programming strategy. Then, a separate presentation was made to the staff in the sales and marketing departments, followed by a more detailed presentation to staff in the programming department. I had to emphasise how important it was that everybody must do their utmost to continue to expand the listenership of the station. At all costs, KISS FM had to avoid the 'Jazz FM' effect, whereby that station's audience figures had shown an initial interest to have quickly waned. These mistakes had already proven disastrous for Jazz FM. If the same thing happened at KISS FM, it could destroy the station. If the next set of audience figures did not demonstrate an improvement in listening, we could all lose our jobs.

The final presentation I wanted to make was to the KISS FM board of directors, in order to improve their understanding of the station's programming philosophy. I asked McNamee if I could use around thirty minutes of the board's March meeting for this purpose, but he said the agenda was already full with urgent business. I asked if I could make the presentation to the next board meeting in April, which he agreed. Although the programme changes would have been on-air for more than a month by then, I still felt it was important to explain to the board the driving principles within my department. Because many on the board had little experience of the radio business, I saw my role as to help them understand the intricacies of the industry and to explain why I was doing things in a particular way, just as I had done with all the departments in the company.

I was optimistic that I could win new listeners to the station with the changes to programmes I was making. I had to maintain the belief that, as long as I could demonstrate I was increasing the station's audience, McNamee might find it difficult to engineer my expulsion from the company. It had been four months since he had sent me the written warning. Despite KISS FM's successful launch, it still felt as if I was dangling over a cliff by my fingernails. I might lose my grip at any time.

---

[819] "Peace DJ Says Sacking Was Unjust", Music Week, 16 Feb 1991.
[820] "Lee Remains To Start Jazz Label", Music Week, 2 Mar 1991.
"Buzz Goes Mainstream", Broadcast, 1 Mar 1991.
[821] "Funds Slashed At RTM Radio", Broadcast, 22 Mar 1991.
"RTM Staff Switch Off", Broadcast, 28 Mar 1991.
[822] "Supermalt Joins Forces With KISS 100 FM In Programme Syndication", KISS FM press release, Jan 1991.
[823] "Readers' Poll", Echoes, 16 Mar 1991.
[824] IRN teleprinter message no. IRN0116, 00:13, 17 Jan 1991.
[825] "KISS 100 FM Announce New Programme Schedule", KISS FM press release, Mar 1991.

March 1991.

Since having met at the previous year's radio conference in Spain, KISS FM managing director Gordon McNamee and Capital Radio programme director Richard Park had seemed to have become good friends. Increasingly, McNamee would drop Park's name into informal conversations, telling me that he had learnt such-and-such from Park, or that Park had related to him a funny story about a particular radio station. I felt uneasy that the two of them should be on such good terms, considering that Capital Radio was KISS FM's closest rival in the London radio market. I was sure that Park had more to gain from the relationship than would McNamee, since he was a radio professional of considerable experience who would find it particularly useful to know what a rival station was doing. Already, Capital Radio had tried to launch a dance-orientated club night in London in direct competition with KISS FM's club events.

Another friendship that McNamee had forged in Spain was with the principals of Unique Broadcasting, a radio syndication and sponsorship broker established in 1989. Unique was the dominant company in the market for ready-made sponsored programmes for broadcast on local commercial radio stations. However, some in the industry disliked Unique for its allegedly strong-arm sales tactics and its alleged ability to cream off a significant proportion of sponsors' revenues for itself. Capital Radio owned a twenty-four per cent stake in Unique, which made some people wary because Capital already dominated the commercial radio industry, and Unique was quickly dominating a related sector.[826]

Advertising bookings at KISS FM continued to be poor, despite the station having already exceeded its first-year target of attracting one million listeners. By now, head of sales Gary Miele was resorting to bigger and bigger distortions of the truth at each successive Monday morning meeting, telling us that huge advertising campaigns were going to be booked on the station ... next week ... next month ... next quarter, but never right now. KISS FM sounded remarkably empty of advertisements throughout the day, and particularly during the flagship breakfast show. Advertisers had quickly realised that the low cost and high audiences available during weekday evenings represented a bargain, whilst the more expensive daytime shows delivered a smaller listenership at a higher price. At one of McNamee's interminable internal meetings, head of marketing Malcolm Cox and I tried to convince Miele that the advertising rates should be priced identically for day and evening in order to attract more advertisers. Miele refused, citing objections from KISS FM's saleshouse, Independent Radio Sales, while McNamee dithered, seeming unable to appreciate the importance of the argument raging around him.

McNamee had often described his entrepreneurial style as 'ducking and diving,' seemingly an apt description for the way he flitted from one project to another. He would quickly become bored or disenchanted with the success rate of the last one, but suddenly would be enthusiastic about the potential profit of the next. Sponsored outside broadcasts which, until recently, had been sold to any customer that wanted them, no longer seemed to be the flavour of the month. McNamee had moved up the scale to whole sponsored programmes and Unique Broadcasting, he believed, was going to help earn lots of income for the station. My problem was that all Unique's pre-produced programmes were geared towards the pop music stations that comprised almost the entire UK commercial radio industry. Specialist music stations, such as KISS FM, were a very new concept for which Unique's programmes did not cater.

These considerations no longer seemed to bother McNamee, as long as money was changing hands. He told me frankly that he would put anything on the air on KISS FM if the station earned some money from it. Any idea of maintaining standards or preserving the quality of the product had been flung aside in the pursuit of income. Initially, McNamee suggested to me that KISS FM could broadcast some of Unique's pop music programming. I objected so categorically that he relented, but he ordered me to find ways to accommodate Unique's ideas within the station's output.

The result was that, every week, Unique sent a list of ideas for potential sponsored programmes to McNamee and, every week, McNamee phoned Unique and told them they were great ideas (because they involved some payment) and passed them on to me. My job was to try and turn each idea into something that might fit within KISS FM's programming. I had to write a full proposal for each, detailing a format for a show that would please the sponsor, and explain how KISS FM could execute it. McNamee would then fax each of my proposals to Unique, which would present my ideas to the sponsor, alongside their own. More often than not, we would hear nothing further. Week after week, my days became filled with this time-wasting distraction, having to turn around the thinnest of ideas from Unique into programmes that might work. A day of activities in a sports centre? A programme of film reviews? A European show about fashion? A programme about a breakfast cereal? Lots of half-baked ideas landed on my desk and had to be transformed magically into something vaguely realistic.

None of these proposals came to anything until McNamee finally hit paydirt with a deal that involved Unique, drinks manufacturer Pepsi, and another sponsorship company called Broadcast Innovations. For several weeks, McNamee had become increasingly excited about this potential deal. Now, a meeting was held to explain the details. KISS FM would broadcast a weekly show sponsored by Pepsi, which Unique would then syndicate to other commercial radio stations. KISS FM would promote UK concert tours by Pepsi-sponsored artists, including Gloria Estefan and MC Hammer. KISS FM would participate in a Pepsi roadshow that would visit schools to explain how a radio station worked. And KISS FM would run a competition to send listeners to the United States, from where some of the station's DJs would broadcast live shows.[827]

A meeting was organised in the boardroom to consummate the deal, attended by senior KISS FM management and representatives of Unique, Pepsi and Broadcast Innovations, at which glasses of champagne were distributed to everyone present. McNamee was enjoying the glory of having forged the deal himself. He seemed proud that he had achieved what he called the biggest deal in the station's history. After everyone had gone, he pulled me aside and told me sternly: "I don't give a damn what you think about this deal. This is the most important deal that this station has pulled off so far. And YOU are going to make sure it works out on-air exactly as the sponsors want it to. And, if that means Pepsi being mentioned one hundred times a day, then that is what you have to do." The importance of the deal was underlined by Malcolm Cox, who said that the promotion was worth "several hundred thousands of pounds" to KISS FM.[828]

McNamee gave me the three-page letter that set out the entire agreement between Unique and KISS FM for the project that would run from then until September 1991. It detailed exactly what the station was expected to do every week, how many times Pepsi must be mentioned, and how many commitments KISS FM had to execute week by week. However, the agreement omitted to mention who was going to pay for all the extra work involved. In his haste to sign the deal, McNamee had failed to agree how the costs would be underwritten. In the end, the buck stopped, once again, on my desk. Neither KISS FM's sponsorship nor marketing department wanted anything to do with the Pepsi deal. McNamee had negotiated it on his own and, because he alone was claiming the glory, it would not help either department meet their revenue targets for the year. I was left to execute the deal which, I estimated, could occupy about two-thirds of my workload between now and September.

The whole deal was hampered by the fact that the original sponsorship contract for all these activities had been agreed between Pepsi and Capital Radio. Pepsi had taken the deal away from Capital midway, allegedly because it was not pleased that the station was promoting its rival, Coke, as the main sponsor of Capital's summer concert series. KISS FM was merely a convenient patsy in this disagreement, a radio station that Pepsi could use whilst renegotiating better terms with Capital Radio for a new contract to start in September. This situation was further confused by the role of Unique, which had long worked in tandem with its shareholder, Capital Radio. Unique was now being forced to work with Capital's rival, KISS FM. Unique would hardly want to help KISS FM win more listeners, and neither would it be enthusiastic to pass revenue from Pepsi's sponsorship to the station.

These conflicts of interest meant that my dealings with Unique quickly became quite tiresome. It was agreed that a new weekly, Pepsi-sponsored Saturday show on KISS FM would be presented by Dave Pearce. However, Unique's programme director, Tim Blackmore, insisted that the show must be produced by one of his staff. I was totally opposed to this idea because I had no intention of turning over any part of the station's output to an outsider who might not share my goal of increasing KISS FM's audience. Blackmore insisted that KISS FM would not be able to produce a good enough show on its own. He suggested that his colleague, Aidan Day, could produce the programme. Both Day and Blackmore had formerly held positions as head of programmes and head of music at Capital Radio. Neither of them knew the dance music scene in which KISS FM specialised and which, more importantly, the programme was intended to showcase. I continued to object until Blackmore eventually agreed to allow me to hire a freelance producer of my choice to produce the show. Subsequently, Unique failed to provide any assistance with the show, including a set of Pepsi jingles it had promised. Neither did it succeed in syndicating the programme to any other radio station. I was not surprised. Why would a friend of Capital Radio want to help market KISS FM's programmes?

As for the Pepsi-sponsored artists who were touring Britain, I managed to reduce KISS FM's contractual commitment to Gloria Estefan, who did not fit the station's music policy, to the giveaway of a few tickets and CDs in listener competitions. This concession was only agreed with Unique on the understanding that the station would support the visit by MC Hammer in a very big way. I understood completely that Hammer was not a credible dance music artist, as did the station's staff and, probably, most of its listeners. Until then, KISS FM had not played Hammer's records, even when his singles 'Have You Seen Her' and 'Pray' had reached the Top Ten during the previous six months. However, McNamee's instructions to me about the execution of his deal could not have been clearer. I called a meeting of the entire programming staff and explained to them frankly that, despite their and my reservations about the credibility of MC Hammer, we needed to hype the man's UK tour as if there was no tomorrow. All I could promise them was that, if this deal proved successful, in future, we might be able to promote an artist who better fitted the station.

To their immeasurable credit, the whole programming staff and the daytime DJs, who often had very strong opinions about music, went along with my plea and endorsed MC Hammer as if he was the biggest superstar we had ever seen. For the next month, the station went 'Hammer mad' and, amongst ourselves, the department re-christened the station 'Pepsi FM' because of the regularity with which the DJs were required to mention the drink. I even had to assign staff within the department to work full-time on different components of the Pepsi deal. The objective was to turn the promotion into exciting and appealing radio, even though I knew that Hammer was not a particularly appealing or appropriate artist for the station.

The Pepsi/Unique contract insisted that KISS FM had to broadcast a documentary about MC Hammer, for which Unique supplied us with what they promised was an exclusive pre-recorded interview. Listening to the tape, it became evident that this 'interview' was nothing more than a quick conversation with Hammer in the back of a car between engagements. Worse, it had been recorded many months previously and had already been broadcast in the UK. Lorna Clarke performed miracles with the interview and turned it into a two-hour documentary that included a lot of Hammer's music.

To generate listener interest in Hammer's forthcoming London concerts, I assigned talks researcher Sonia Fraser to follow him around the rest of his UK concert tour and provide daily reports on what he was doing. When I asked Unique for money to cover these costs, it was refused, so I had to fund Fraser's travels out of the programming budget. I also sent Fraser to cover an MC Hammer concert in Paris, prior to his arrival in England. Again, Unique would not pay her travel costs and neither would it provide a ticket for the Paris event. I had to pay for Fraser's £50 return flight with my personal credit card and she was forced to buy a concert ticket from a tout outside the venue.

When MC Hammer arrived in London, I was provided with an agreed number of concert tickets to give away to listeners in competitions. To my horror, these tickets had been printed with the Capital Radio logo on them. Although KISS FM was promoting itself on-air as 'the official MC Hammer station,' I had to send tickets to listeners inscribed with the name of a rival radio station. Worse, when I asked for tickets so that the staff that had worked on the Hammer campaign could attend his concert, the request was refused. This rebuttal so outraged everybody in my department that I had to ask McNamee to talk to Unique, or I would have had a mutiny on my hands. At the last minute, late on Friday afternoon, McNamee told me I could have tickets for the staff, but only if I gave away a further several dozen concert tickets on-air over the weekend. I was disgusted by this response because I had already carried out the Pepsi/Unique deal to the letter. It required me and another member of staff to stay at work very late that Friday night, arranging further competitions to be held on-air throughout the weekend.

When the MC Hammer concerts took place at London's Wembley Stadium, I was surprised to find not only that there was no KISS FM branding anywhere within the venue, but also that there was a massive Capital Radio banner inside the main hall. I later learnt that KISS FM had not been allowed even to promote itself inside the venue. A plan for some casual staff to be hired by head of marketing Malcolm Cox to distribute KISS FM car stickers in the venue's outdoor car park also failed to materialise. I went to one of the concerts and was frustrated to find no indication that KISS FM had had anything to do with the event.

Despite these setbacks, I still needed the DJs to enthuse about MC Hammer within their shows. The last few concert tickets that remained from the weekend promotion were given away in a stunt I had suggested. It was announced on-air one lunchtime that several KISS FM staff were in London's Piccadilly Circus to give away tickets. Despite having hired several security staff to marshal the stunt, things got out of hand and a mob fought for the tickets, knocking down Lorna Clarke in the process. The whole debacle was carried live on-air, with Sonia Fraser describing the scene using my mobile phone. I had made a bad decision and had to apologise profusely to Clarke. However, it had demonstrated the popularity of the radio station in London.

Without a budget to execute anything more technically professional, my mobile phone proved very useful to offer listeners a sense of immediacy. Fraser was excellent at reporting live events. This strategy was employed when MC Hammer made a surprise visit to a local school. Fraser's commentary via my mobile phone provided listeners with an eye-witness account of the children's delight when Hammer appeared at their school and talked with them about the importance of education and his career in music.

By the time Hammer had finished his UK tour, I was pleased with the success the station had brought to these events. We had produced exciting radio and generated an immense amount of interest in an artist who was of little interest to the staff within the station. It was a huge relief once the promotion of MC Hammer was over. There were other Pepsi commitments to execute through until September, but none as taxing as the last few months.

I asked for a meeting with McNamee and Martin Strivens, both of whom had negotiated the Pepsi/Unique deal, in order to 'post mortem' the MC Hammer part of the deal. I hoped that, in future, this would help us avoid some of the pitfalls that had resulted from a lack of co-operation from Unique. I suggested that head of marketing Malcolm Cox and PR person Anita Mackie should attend because it would help immensely if they were more involved in the execution of the Pepsi commitments. McNamee seemed unwillingly to hold such a meeting but I insisted and, after being abruptly postponed once, it was rescheduled. Only McNamee and Strivens attended, accompanied by myself and another person from the programming team. I carefully detailed all the problems I had encountered in recent weeks – from the lack of moral and financial support from KISS FM's partners in the deal, to the embarrassment of KISS FM branding having been excluded from the Wembley Stadium events. There were two things I wanted to know – what were McNamee and Strivens going to do about the numerous ways that we had been let down in these matters and, secondly, how were we going to avoid them happening again? The promotions had generated twice the amount of work they should have done, seemingly because of a lack of goodwill from our partners.

McNamee and Strivens refused to accept any of the criticisms I levelled at the station's partners. What is more, they refused to follow up any of the matters I had raised about the behaviour of the other parties, and refused to accept that similar problems might arise in future. On the contrary, McNamee told me that I had gone overboard in executing the deal. He said that I had tried too hard to turn the station into a shop window for MC Hammer. "Nobody ever said we had to be the official MC Hammer station in London," he told me. If there was anyone at fault, he continued, it was me, for trying too hard and doing too much. For him, there was nothing further to discuss. McNamee called the meeting to a close. He and Strivens walked off, leaving me and my colleague alone in the boardroom.

I was bewildered by McNamee's comments. He was the man who, only weeks earlier, had warned me in the sternest tones that if I did not make a huge song and dance about the Pepsi deal on-air, I would be suspected of treason. Yet here he was, now, saying that I had tried too hard. During the last month, I had spent most of my time untangling the intricacies of the Pepsi/Unique deal. It was a contract which, in his haste to sign, McNamee had failed to agree sufficient detail with his partners. Once McNamee had announced the deal and claimed the glory, he had shown no interest in its execution, except to chide me in the early days for not mentioning Pepsi a sufficient number of times on-air. Now he was telling me that I had tried too hard!

It seemed that what McNamee really disliked was my ability to turn what could easily have been a complete pig's ear into an acclaimed success. Everybody in the station had told me how marvellous they considered the MC Hammer tour promotion, but McNamee had reached the stage where he was not willing to offer me even grudging approval. In his eyes, I had failed because I had succeeded. The more I succeeded in my work, the more he wanted to expel me. I left the boardroom that day, almost not believing the meeting I had just attended. How many more times would I almost bust a gut to make KISS FM successful, and how many more times would McNamee proceed to kick me in the teeth? McNamee seemed to hate my achievements and seemed to hate the fact that I knew the answers to difficult problems.

I recalled one occasion, in the days soon after KISS FM had moved to Holloway Road, when I had been sat in McNamee's office, discussing the finer points of the station's re-launch on 1 September. I had run down a long list of the things with which I was dealing, and had explained what stage each of them had reached. Suddenly, McNamee leaned over his huge desk, looked me in the eye, and said to me in a voice dripping with contempt: "Do you know what I hate about you, Grant? You've got the answers to every bloody question. And they are always bloody right." I had offered no response to McNamee then. What was I supposed to say? I was doing my job. And it was a job I could do, and that I wanted to do well.

Remembering that dialogue, I consoled myself that, despite McNamee's comments, MC Hammer's UK concert tour had been transformed into excellent radio promotions on KISS FM. The next morning, on my way to work, I stopped off at a flower shop on the Holloway Road and, from my pocket, bought a huge bunch of flowers which I arranged on Sonia Fraser's desk before she arrived for work. Then, I wrote a note to everybody in the programming department, thanking them for the huge effort they had put into the MC Hammer tour. They deserved all the thanks they could get. I was not going to allow McNamee's attitude to stop me.

---

[826] "Ex-PPM Chiefs Get Capital Backing For Sponsor Firm", Campaign, 13 Oct 1989.
[827] "Pepsi-Cola Chooses KISS 100 FM As Their Radio Partner In London For 1991 Programme And Promotional Activity", KISS FM press release, Mar 1991.
[828] "Cola Giants Tune In To Music Radio", Music Week, 13 Apr 1991.

April 1991.

By the time that Easter 1991 had arrived, I could feel the pressure of work easing slightly. The recruitment of two producers in January and the appointment of the station's own chief engineer, Andy Howard, in February were finally beginning to pay dividends. My faith in Lorna Clarke's ability to function not only as a replacement for Lyn Champion in the talks department, but also as an assistant to me, had been proven correct. By now, I had trained a lot of people in the department as much as I could about how a radio station worked and they were rewarding me with loyalty and productivity. I took a week off work to attend my brother's wedding in Canada, the first occasion that I had taken leave from the station since I started full-time work fifteen months earlier.

While I was away, I gave Clarke responsibility for managing the department, which she handled without problems. This decision intensely annoyed Lindsay Wesker, who viewed himself as next in line and felt he should have been asked, rather than Clarke. Wesker did not seem to understand that not only did he have no legitimate radio experience, but also he had failed to appropriately perform many of the tasks for which I had initially given him responsibility. He loved music and he loved listening to records and arguing about the merits of particular artists. However, running a radio station's programme output was a role that required specific management skills.

While I was away, Gordon McNamee took the opportunity to commandeer the programme schedule and introduced, without prior discussion, a late night phone-in programme. When I found out, I was amused more than annoyed. McNamee never mentioned anything about the programme to me. It felt as if he were a child who could not help but interfere with his parents' hi-fi system while they were out. The station's second JICRAR audience survey was now underway and I felt that the best thing I could do was to bring a sense of stability to the department after the sackings of Lyn Champion and Heddi Greenwood, and the batch of DJ redundancies.

For the first time for more than a year, I managed to set aside a few evenings for my own enjoyment. I started attending soul concerts once again and visited some reggae clubs. I went to the final night of Dingwalls nightclub in Camden, before the building was pulled down for redevelopment. I made a digital recording, using equipment borrowed from the station's studios, of the night's showdown between the Joey Jay and Jah Shaka sound systems. I attended a launch party for The Sindecut's first album and the first UK concert by American soul singer Teena Marie. One evening, I went to an outside broadcast that KISS FM was making from the Mirage nightclub in Windsor. Afterwards, I drove down the M4 motorway into London to attend a special reggae night that KISS FM's David Rodigan was presenting at the Podium club in South London. I recorded the whole of that event as well, for possible broadcast in a future Rodigan show. My next objective for KISS FM was to bring the intimate sound of small London club nights to the airwaves.

Whilst I felt that, at long last, my life was returning to some semblance of normality, it seemed that McNamee's involvement in KISS FM was becoming more and more distant. After Easter, he started to work a bare minimum of hours at the station. My office overlooked the private car park to the rear of the building so that, every morning, I would hear him arrive at precisely nine o'clock in the morning and then leave at precisely five o'clock in the afternoon. During the day, McNamee was no longer seen around the building. Apart from his presence at meetings, I rarely saw him to talk to any more. There was a lot of whispering around the building that things were going very badly for McNamee.

One Monday morning, just prior to the regular meeting of heads of department, McNamee had shown me a story in one of that Sunday's tabloid newspapers. It revealed the horrific details of a drug dealer's business practices. McNamee pointed to the man's picture and asked if I knew who this person was. I had never seen him before. McNamee told me that, until recently, he had been employed by KISS FM as a security man for its club nights. He told me that, if ever anyone discovered the association between this man and the radio station, we were all ruined. "I don't just mean me," he said, looking terrified. "Me, you and everybody else and the whole radio station. We have ALL had it if this gets out." I had no idea what he meant by this.

After Easter, whenever I had to visit the top floor to see McNamee in his office, he would usually be sat behind his desk, doing nothing in particular. Often he would be staring at the latest share prices on the Teletext pages of his huge colour television. He seemed obsessed with the notion that he was some kind of entrepreneurial whiz-kid. He even started comparing himself to Richard Branson, the boss of the Virgin empire, in conversations. Often, I would find him listening to old soul or jazz records in his office, rather than to KISS FM. It seemed as if he was barricading himself into his corner office on the top floor, trying to ignore the realities of the radio station that were going on around him. Occasionally, he might phone down to Lindsay Wesker in the record library to dictate a list of new records that he wanted Wesker to obtain for free from record companies. I had noticed that McNamee and Wesker were becoming much closer these days. Wesker was increasingly becoming the 'voice of KISS FM' in press interviews that McNamee would arrange to publicise the station's activities.

Plenty of rumours were flying around the station that McNamee might be on his way out of KISS FM. One rumour alleged that McNamee had been caught in flagrante delicto, backstage at one of the station's club nights, with a young girl who was neither his wife nor his personal assistant, Rosee Laurence. Another rumour alleged that McNamee and Laurence had fallen out and that Laurence was about to spill the beans about their personal relationship. There were plenty of rumours that the station was running out of money and was about to be acquired by another company. Speculation was fuelled by the fact that, one month, the entire staff's salaries had been paid into their bank accounts later than the due date, causing inconvenience for many people who had regular standing orders or direct debits.

The air of increasing unease within the station was made worse by the evident problems in the sales department, including an alleged affair that had recently broken up acrimoniously between two staff. At a birthday celebration for one KISS FM salesman, held during lunchtime in a nearby public house in Holloway Road, another salesman had turned up who had just been fired. The two ended up in a brawl outside on the street. I happened to be in the station's reception area when one of the protagonists entered the building with blood pouring from his mouth, requesting medical assistance.

The sales department's apparent ineffectiveness in generating revenues was not helped by prolonged periods of absence from the building of the head of sales, Gary Miele. He would regularly inform the department secretary that he was away at this appointment or that appointment or some meeting, until it was discovered that many of these meetings did not exist. Instead, Miele had often been found holed up in some public bar.

The issue of Miele's absence from the radio station became so great that, one morning, McNamee suddenly appeared on the programming floor and wandered around the offices, shouting: "Gary Miele has not been sacked. Despite the rumours I am hearing, Gary is still employed by KISS FM. He has had to go away on urgent personal business, but he is still working for us. Ignore anybody who tells you otherwise." After McNamee had left the floor to broadcast this message to the rest of the building, we looked at each other amazed at what we had just witnessed. It was rare enough to see McNamee in person these days, let alone to see him going around the entire building in this manner. These events only fuelled internal speculation that something must be going seriously wrong within the station.

Because McNamee had become so inaccessible, a succession of staff would arrive in my office, close the door and ask if they could have a few private words with me. Many of them expressed concern about the radio station and felt that there were few signs of the business being managed properly any more. Many within KISS FM believed, mistakenly, that I still had some kind of direct private line to McNamee. The truth was that, like everybody else, I no longer had any personal dialogue with McNamee. There was nothing I could say to anybody in the building to relieve their anxieties. Little did they realise how precarious my own position within the company had become.

The station's sponsorship manager, Gordon Drummond, came to see me one day and moaned that he was nowhere near achieving the target that had been set for him for his first year. He told me that, if he did not reach this target, he would earn no commission, and he already felt that his salary was pitifully low. I sympathised, but there was nothing I could say to re-assure him. He did not even work in my department. Drummond also told me that he wanted a better company car, a complaint that found little sympathy with me. What was wrong with his current car? I asked. Drummond responded that, although it was a brand new car, it was unreliable and not sufficiently sporty. He wanted a car that was a bit different. "What? Like mine?" I asked him jokingly.

Although these internal doubts about the station's future troubled me, I knew there was nothing I could do except to make progress with the work at hand. I spent two days preparing a presentation of my programming policies for the board meeting on 24 April. By now, I had created more detailed explanations about the adjustments in programming policies I had implemented and the outcomes I thought that they would achieve. This would be the first opportunity I had ever been offered to address the company board in person with a prepared presentation. I knew how important it would be for me to demonstrate my knowledge of radio programming issues and to instil the board's confidence in my ability to build the station's future.

When word came down to my office from the top floor that my presence was required, I walked upstairs with trepidation and entered the boardroom, clutching my file of transparencies for the presentation. However, I was surprised to see that the overhead projector had not been set up. As had happened at the previous meeting I attended, no introduction or explanation was offered about what the board had been discussing. As soon as I sat down, questions were fired at me about very specific aspects of the revised programme schedule. I answered these as best I could and explained that I had a complete presentation with me that would greatly increase the board's understanding. One director told me that there was no time within the meeting for me to make a presentation and, before I knew what had happened, I was ushered out of the room.

It was evident that McNamee had not asked the board if they would view my presentation. It was also obvious from the questions I had been asked that someone had already sown seeds of doubt in their minds about elements of my revised programme schedule. I was outraged that McNamee could have been so underhand as to let me waste so much time preparing a thirty-minute presentation that he had no intention of letting me make. I also felt that, although he had agreed every minute detail of the new schedule with me, he might be working to discredit my efforts at board level. I could only dread to think what he might have told the board about my work and my role within the station, whilst he may have been attempting to steal the glory and credit for the one area of the radio station that had proven successful – its programming.

My worst fears were confirmed the next day when McNamee unexpectedly asked me if I would like to join him at a concert that evening by soul singer Alexander O'Neal at the Royal Albert Hall. McNamee and Lindsay Wesker regularly received free tickets from record companies and promoters to all the major soul and dance music events in London. Wesker's day-to day contact with the record industry ensured that the pair could take advantage of the 'perks' they felt they deserved, even though it was now my responsibility to update the station's music playlist each week. When the station had launched the previous September, Wesker had circulated a long list of KISS FM personnel to record companies, but the list had omitted my name, so I received no correspondence or invitations from the music industry. Blues & Soul magazine's gossip column had even commented: "KISS FM have arrived in no uncertain way at all the jigs going, and if I see Trevor [Nelson], Lindsay [Wesker], Gordon Mac and Steve Jackson propping up one more bar, I shall demand an immediate refund on my free ticket …"[829]

McNamee's invitation to join him at the concert was the first occasion in our two-year relationship that he had shared with me any of the perks that came with his job. For that reason alone, I would have been suspicious. The fact that the offer had been made one day after the board meeting had made it even more ominous. I agreed to join McNamee in the private box he had been given at the event, anticipating that he might have something private that he wanted to share with me. However, there was almost no conversation between us that evening. Leaving the venue alone afterwards, it felt as if I had just attended some kind of Last Supper. There was definitely a sense of occasion in me having been invited to spend time alone with McNamee outside of work, something he had never offered me since KISS FM had won the licence. Exactly what the occasion was I had no idea.

---

[829]The Mouth, "Street Noise", Blues & Soul, 6 Nov 1990.

May 1991.

In his speech to the University of Manchester Broadcasting Symposium, James Gordon, managing director of Radio Clyde, reiterated his scepticism that the new incremental radio stations were a viable commercial proposition. Referring to the speech he had made the previous year at the Radio Festival, Gordon said: "I caused offence by suggesting that twenty-five per cent of incrementals would go out of business within two years. That now seems a gross underestimate."[830]

In a sudden effort to put KISS FM back in the public eye, Gordon McNamee commissioned a new advertising campaign, the first since the station's launch eight months earlier. A series of posters, designed once again by BBDO, were displayed on London's underground trains. However, their content could not have been more different from the stylish, positive messages that had proven so successful the previous September. This new campaign was almost identical to the treatments that had been suggested by Saatchi & Saatchi in its earlier, unsuccessful pitch for the KISS FM account. Instead of emphasising the unique aspects of the radio station, the posters used knocking copy that asked in a huge font size: "Want to know what you'll be hearing on Capital in a couple of weeks? Tune to 100 FM" and "Find out how exciting KISS 100 FM is. Tune in to Capital first."[831]

KISS FM head of marketing Malcolm Cox argued that the campaign targeted young listeners to Capital Radio and was designed to differentiate the two stations. I could still see no value to KISS FM in merely knocking the competition. Capital Radio had been an institution in London since 1973. Even people who did not listen to the station were aware of its existence and probably respected its significance as the capital's first commercial music radio station. KISS FM was a new station that still needed to convince people of its own merit and it would seem to gain nothing from slandering its rival. Despite my reservations, the campaign went ahead during a four-week period and inevitably attracted headlines in the trade press such as 'KISS FM Poster Ads Hit Out At Capital.'[832]

The week these advertisements appeared, it was announced that EMAP, a major shareholder in KISS FM, had acquired Liverpool commercial station Radio City for £10.7m. The station's managing director, Terry Smith, welcomed the deal and promised that "Radio City will be the cornerstone of EMAP's overall radio strategy." Smith said he would join the board of the newly created 'EMAP Radio' company to work on the group's expansion plans. Tim Schoonmaker, now elevated to the post of managing director of EMAP Radio, promised that Smith would not be pushed out of Radio City, the station he had founded: "Terry's running the station. Part of the reason we were interested in the deal is because he is one of a handful of people who founded commercial radio in this country." Schoonmaker denied that Radio City was the first of several stations that EMAP intended to buy outright: "There's no shopping list. It's not tied to any other deals. It stands on its own. We'll look at each opportunity as it arises."[833]

At KISS FM, it was difficult to know how this deal might affect the station's future. EMAP already owned twenty-eight per cent of KISS FM, twenty per cent of the East Anglia Radio group, and sixteen per cent of Trans World Communications. Would Schoonmaker try and buy out the remainder of these partly-owned operations, or was he more interested in completely new acquisitions? McNamee was the only person in the building who seemed to have any contact with Schoonmaker these days, and he was saying absolutely nothing about what he knew of EMAP's game plan. The rest of us had to live with a horrible air of uncertainty over the future of KISS FM, and no idea whether our jobs would be safe.

That week, at the Monday morning meeting, McNamee issued each head of department with a photocopied page that was headed 'A Presentation Of Reassurance To KISS FM's Backers.' He explained that a board meeting and the company's annual general meeting were both scheduled to take place in the boardroom on the same day in three weeks' time. Each head of department would be required to make a presentation to the board meeting, explaining their targets for the next financial year which started in September 1991. On the sheet was typed the question "What are we aiming to achieve by end of Year 2?" Underneath were listed eight more specific questions, four of which McNamee told me that he and I would have to address together. These were:

- "How many listeners?
- How many hours (Ave)?
- What have we done or are going to do to improve listening hours and more listeners?
- How are we going to increase our listeners, i.e.: more 15-24 or 24-35, and if more 24-35 how are we going to achieve this?"[834]

To answer these questions, I went away and, once again, looked through all the statistics I had analysed about KISS FM's performance in its first JICRAR audience survey. I drew scattergrams and graphs, made extrapolations and examined in minute detail every section of the station's audience. A week later, McNamee called me into his office to discuss the progress I was making. Like everyone else in the building, I had seen little of him during the previous seven days. I was shocked to see how tired and haggard he looked, slumped in his expensive managing director's chair. He sounded exhausted when he spoke and told me, in an uncharacteristic drawl, that never in his life had be been under such pressure at work. He told me he had massive problems that he needed to solve, and that he needed to solve them very quickly. He did not elaborate further on what was troubling him, but it was evidently taking its toll on his health.

We talked about the progress I had made with answering the questions for the presentation to the board. McNamee told me that he considered I would need to achieve a one hundred per cent increase in the number of hours listened to KISS FM by the end of the second year. He told me that, in order to increase the station's revenue by fifty per cent, he understood that the hours listened would have to be increased by one hundred per cent. I was aghast. I explained that I thought a one hundred per cent increase was far too steep to accomplish within such a short space of time. The London radio market had become more intensely competitive than ever, due to the influx of new stations that had launched during the last two years. Doubling the number of hours listened, in my opinion, was unrealistic for any London radio station within the space of one year.[835]

McNamee told me that the target of one hundred per cent more listening was what I needed to achieve. He made it clear that I could consider absolutely any change in

programming policy to achieve that goal. He told me that there were only three limiting factors I needed to consider:
- the station's output still had to remain within the terms of the Promise of Performance that had been agreed with the regulatory authority
- there would be no increase in the programme budget for the foreseeable future
- there might have to be further redundancies to reduce the station's overheads.

I asked McNamee if he was saying that absolutely nothing within the programme schedule was sacrosanct in order to increase the station's audience. He agreed that, right then, increasing KISS FM's revenues was the only thing in which he was interested. I should recommend whatever strategy I thought appropriate to achieve this objective. I scribbled on my notepad: "100% hrs increase. How?"[836]

I went away and looked again at the current KISS FM programme schedule. The weakest part of it was still the weekday breakfast show. However, McNamee was still insisting that this could not be changed and, without an increased budget, there would be insufficient funds anyway to poach a successful, well known DJ from a rival station. I looked at the Promise of Performance and analysed the volume of specialist music programming it required KISS FM to broadcast. There was no denying that Saturday and Sunday had produced the station's weakest performances, largely because of McNamee's insistence upon modelling parts of the weekend schedule too closely on KISS FM's pirate days. The only way to encourage more listening at these times would be to make the shows less esoteric in their musical content and more similar in sound to the playlist format that operated during weekdays. It was very sad to have to make such fundamental changes but, if McNamee wanted a substantial increase in listeners, this is what we needed to do.

Friday night, similarly, should have been a stronghold for KISS FM, but it had fallen short of its potential. It might help to produce shows then that were more mainstream and, whilst not using the playlist, at least make them compete more effectively with dance music shows broadcast at that time by BBC Radio One and Capital Radio. Other, less significant changes could also be introduced to the existing daytime programmes which could make them more appealing to listeners, although creatively they would frustrate the DJs by removing much of their personal influence on the music content. And the pre-recorded tapes currently running overnight could be replaced by a CD jukebox formatted to provide a tighter station sound.

I typed these recommendations for programme policy changes onto a single sheet of paper to discuss with McNamee in more detail. It stated:
"DAYTIME
- extend definition of 'dance'
- reduce playlist size
- focus more on chart records
- rotate chart hits quicker (up to Promise of Performance limit – 40% max Top 40)
- eradicate free choice
- centralise oldies/recurrent choices
- reduce talk/features
- more back-to-back records

NIGHT-TIME
- CD jukebox/automated

SAT/SUN
- playlist/format all Sat 6am-11pm and Sun 6am-9pm
- either weekday copycat or alternative 'hits' format:
    - hits of 70s, 80s, 90s
    - soul weekend

[no Promise of Performance commitment to 'new' material evening/weekend]

FRIDAY NIGHT
- format heavily

SPECIALIST SHOWS
- Mon-Thu 7.15pm-1am
- Sat 11pm-6am
- Sun 9pm-6am."[837]

On 21 May, I met McNamee in his office to discuss my proposals. Initially, he was hesitant to agree to the changes because he realised, as did I, that they represented a fundamental change to the ethos behind the whole radio station. However, as he had instructed me, revenues had become the utmost priority, so I explained how each of these changes would attract more listening to the station. Eventually, he agreed to all the recommendations, except for the proposal to remove the two 'free choice' records per hour that daytime DJs enjoyed. This was a relatively minor change, so I was not bothered. During the conversation, I absent-mindedly scribbled "Gordon" in blue biro above the left-hand margin of my list and proceeded to tick off each policy recommendation that McNamee approved, with the exception of the one he rejected, against which I put a cross.[838]

Next, McNamee explained that the other departments within the station – sales, marketing and finance – had already completed their projections for the next financial year and, as a result, it remained the case that I needed to double the number of hours listened to the station by the end of the period. I told McNamee once again that I believed such a target would be impossible to achieve. A considerably lower growth rate would prove to be more realistic. KISS FM had only just achieved its first year target of attracting one million listeners per week. It would be crazy to set another target that was so much higher than the first. McNamee disagreed and insisted that the growth rate had to be one hundred per cent. I made it plain that I did not agree. Suddenly, he decided to call a meeting the following day for the heads of department to discuss the matter fully. I agreed and went away to examine once again my figures to make sure that I was not being unreasonable. I still concluded that aiming to double the amount of time listeners spent with KISS FM within the next year was unrealistic.

The following morning, at quarter to twelve, I attended the meeting in the boardroom about the proposals. There were only four of us in the huge room – McNamee, as usual, at the head of the table; on his right, financial director Martin Strivens and head of marketing Malcolm Cox; and, on his left, me. There was no sign of the station's head of sales, Gary Miele, though his absence from the building had become a way of life by now. The faces around the table looked grave. I sensed that this meeting was going to be very difficult.

McNamee and Strivens started by explaining the financial difficulties that KISS FM was suffering. They said that the consequences for the company would be dire if the situation was not improved. The company was now projected to lose £750,000 in the current financial year (1990/91), compared to the licence application's forecast of a £474,000 profit. The application had predicted that the station's advertising revenues in its first year would be £2.7m, but this had fallen short by at least £1m.[839]

If the station's costs were maintained at exactly the same levels during the station's next financial year (1991/92), and if the audience remained static, the company would lose a further £750,000. Such a situation was not sustainable, which is why the budgets were being adjusted to ensure that the company would break even next year (1991/92) and would generate a profit the following year (1992/93). There might have to be more redundancies to keep costs down. To achieve break even next year, advertising revenues would have to be increased by fifty per cent. McNamee and Strivens had consulted KISS FM's national advertising saleshouse, Independent Radio Sales [IRS], to determine what increase in listening would be necessary to produce fifty per cent more revenues. IRS had told them that the number of hours listened to KISS FM would need to double, which was the new target I needed to attain a year from now. It would be no good for KISS FM to achieve this target at the end of the second year, since that would prove too late to impact revenues. I had to achieve the target a year from now, roughly halfway through the next financial year.[840]

McNamee explained that every other department's plans for next year had already been prepared on the assumption of achieving this one hundred per cent increase in listening. Gary Miele had prepared revised advertising revenue projections, Martin Strivens had drawn up new budgets, and Malcolm Cox had created marketing plans for the second year. I was the only one left who needed to agree to the new strategy. Cox anticipated that the doubling of listening to KISS FM could be achieved by increasing two usage figures simultaneously: the number of listeners to KISS FM each week would have to rise from 1m to 1.3m, while the amount of time they listened would have to increase from 6.6 to 8.0 hours per week. Cox explained that the second year's marketing activity would focus on a small poster campaign around the theme that 'KISS FM changes your life' and a lot of on-air competitions. There was no money to mount a marketing campaign approaching the size of the launch publicity, but Cox anticipated using a lot of free, on-air promotion.[841]

McNamee asked me to expand upon the policy recommendations I had discussed with him the day before. I handed out copies of my proposals and explained the positive impact that each change would have on the station's audience. Strivens and Cox accepted all the recommendations without hesitation. McNamee asked me to expand upon my plans in writing, since they would need to be included in the presentation about the company's strategy that was to be made to the board the following week. I was instructed to write the expanded document that evening and give it to Cox the next day. Strivens explained that my presence at the board presentation was absolutely imperative. He said that I was the lynchpin of the revised budgets and that I had to convince the board that a one hundred per cent increase in listening to KISS FM was perfectly possible. Without my presence, the plan would not succeed.

I reiterated what I had said to McNamee the previous day. In my opinion, the one hundred per cent increase was unattainable. I could not endorse a strategy for the company's future that I knew was badly flawed. Strivens asked me what I thought was a more realistic target for the increase in listening.

"Fifteen per cent," I told him. "Given the intense competitiveness of the London radio market, I think fifteen per cent is a realistic growth rate for a year from now."

Strivens looked appalled. "Fifty per cent, but that's not enough. We need double that increase."

I realised there had been a misunderstanding. "Not fifty per cent," I told Strivens, "but fifteen per cent."

Strivens looked even more appalled. "But that's an impossibly low figure. The budgets simply will not work out if that is all we think we are going to grow the listening."

I asked the others around the table if they could suggest one example of a radio station in a competitive metropolitan market having doubled its listening within a twelve-month period. I had started analysing radio audience data in 1980 and I knew of no such example. There was silence. Of the three people I was facing, two had not previously worked in the commercial broadcasting industry and the other, Cox, had no experience in radio. However, the lack of a precedent did not deter McNamee and Strivens from insisting that my next target had to be a one hundred per cent growth rate.

McNamee asked: "Well, Grant, when we started up, you didn't seriously believe we were going to reach the one million target we had promised, did you? But we reached that, didn't we?"

I could not believe what I was hearing. McNamee seemed to have forgotten that it was I who had calculated very carefully in September 1989 that KISS FM could attract one million listeners.[842]

"Of course I believed it," I told him. "Do you think I would have worked this hard for this long, if I did not believe I could achieve the target? Of course I believed we could reach one million. Otherwise I would not have agreed to it in the first place."

With all the loathing he reserved for statistics, McNamee continued to insist: "Well, why don't you just accept this new target and see if you can reach it? How do you know that one hundred per cent is so impossible?"

"Because," I told him, "I've been working with radio audience figures for more than ten years now, and I know that this kind of increase is simply impossible when you're telling me that there's to be no big publicity campaign, no increased budgets, and there will probably be more redundancies from my department. Where exactly do you expect all the extra listeners to come from?"

There was no response. Instead, Strivens insisted once again that one hundred per cent was the target figure, whether I liked it or not, and that I was ordered to attend the presentation to the board next week, where I had to endorse the whole plan as fulsomely and enthusiastically as possible.

I told Strivens that I felt I could not lie to the other board members that this target for growth was in any way realistic. I knew that the target was unattainable and I was not prepared to lie about the company's future prospects to its board. Strivens looked me directly in the eye, as if I was his teenage son who understood nothing about his adult world.

"This isn't about lying," Strivens shouted at me. "It's about business. And, in business, this is simply what you have to do."

I recoiled in horror, not from Strivens' immediate remarks, but from my sudden realisation that, during all the craziness of the last two years, Strivens must have considered that lying was just part of what you had to do at work. I considered how many times Strivens had needed my input because he did not have the faintest idea how a radio station worked. And then I recalled how little help or information he had ever given back to me. Christ! I did not even know what my own departmental budget looked like anymore because Strivens had not answered my memos requesting this information.

I reminded myself of Strivens' lack of understanding about radio and tried to reason with him. I explained that the whole question of the revised budgets had been approached from the wrong end. The level of listening you anticipated that your radio station would achieve was meant to be the first element to be fitted into your business plan, and then you had to cut the cloth of your company accordingly. How many people listened to KISS FM, and for how long they listened, were figures that you could not manipulate, however hard you tried. Those figures were determined almost entirely by the marketplace. Everything else within KISS FM we had some kind of control over, but the level of listening we had no control over. For the advertising, we could set the rates high or low to either increase or decrease our revenues. For staff levels, we could sack people to cut costs. For overheads, we could move to a cheaper building. But for the volume of listening, we could do nothing other than make our programming as interesting and appealing as possible.

I offered Strivens an analogy with a newspaper, because he had worked in publishing. If, instead of having launched KISS FM, we had started a daily newspaper, what would happen to the business plan if we ignored until the very end the crucial statistic of many copies we could sell? We would work out what our costs were, how much advertising revenues we wanted to earn and then, finally, we would work out, as a result of our previous calculations, how many copies we needed to sell. Creating the business plan this way around, we might find that we needed to sell more copies of our newspaper than there were people in Britain, or we might find that we needed to publish the newspaper eight days a week. KISS FM's business plan was being approached this way and it seemed to make no sense to start the calculations from the wrong end.

Strivens rejected my analogy and said that he could see no similarity between a newspaper and a radio station.

McNamee chipped in: "So what are you saying we should do? Go to the board and tell them we can't run the radio station because we cannot get enough listeners? What are we meant to say? That we just give up because we can't work out the figures properly?"

I explained to McNamee that this was not at all what I was suggesting. "What we should be doing," I told him, "is working out realistic targets that we can genuinely achieve, and then seeing how much money that leaves us to operate the radio station. If that means more cuts, it means more cuts. But, doing it your way means the whole thing will come crashing down upon us in a few months' time. I won't be able to reach the audience targets, so the advertising revenues will then be too low, so the costs will be too high and we will lose even more money. Is that the right way to go about it?"

McNamee looked at me with a ruthless stare that communicated eye-to-eye exactly how much he must have hated me now. "Don't you think that we would all benefit from earning our nice little salaries for six months more? Why throw in the towel now, if we can all benefit from another six months' work here, rather than admitting defeat now?"

I was shocked by this confirmation that McNamee seemed to view KISS FM as little more than a way to finance his lifestyle. Here he was, admitting to me across this boardroom table, that he did not seem to give a damn about the radio station any more, other than what he could screw out of the business for himself. I told McNamee that my own motivation for saying these things was for the sake of the company, not for the health of my bank balance. If we wanted the company to survive, we had to come up with a realistic budget for the second year that included realistic targets. I wanted KISS FM to survive and I wanted it to grow, but we all needed to be realistic about its future.

McNamee sneered at me. "Are you telling me, Grant," he asked, "that you don't want your job any more? Because, if that's what you're saying, it can be easily arranged."

I ignored this threat. I had seen McNamee bully people many times previously. Because he was less articulate in situations that required rational argument, McNamee resorted quickly to the threat of brute force when words failed him. He was all smarm and bullshit when he wanted you to like him but, if you dared to disagree with him, he could be vicious and rude like a playground bully used to getting his own way. I ignored McNamee.

Instead, I repeated to Strivens my promise that I would happily attend the presentation to the board, but that I could not be ordered to lie about what I and the radio station could achieve.

Strivens looked at me patronisingly. "You know," he said, "perhaps we could send you on one of these acting courses you see advertised in the papers. You know – 'Learn Acting In Three Days' they promise. That sounds like the sort of thing you could do with. I'm sure KISS FM could pay for something like that."

My opinion of Strivens was diminishing exponentially with every minute I spent in his presence. Here was I, being deadly serious about putting the company's future first, while all he could do was think up ways to be rude and sarcastic about my integrity. I told Strivens that I cared nothing for acting. If I went to the board meeting, I was going to tell them the truth.

The argument went around and around in this manner for several more hours, without resolve. Everyone in the room had agreed wholeheartedly with my programme strategy for the station's future, but McNamee and Strivens refused to believe me as to the impact of those changes. They wanted one hundred per cent, and I was only offering them fifteen. Cox remained silent through most of the vicious argument that raged across the table between the three of us. If Cox agreed with me, he certainly was not going to jeopardise his relationship with the others by saying so. If he really agreed with McNamee and Strivens, then he certainly did not argue as dogmatically about it as they did. Cox was sitting on the fence. This was not his war and he did not seem to want to get involved.

When the meeting ended, Strivens once again asked me to write a more detailed document about my proposals, ready to give to Cox the next day. It was Wednesday, so he suggested that we all reconvene at nine o'clock on Tuesday morning (Monday was a Bank Holiday) to finalise the details of the presentation to the board. The matter would have to be resolved then, as the board was meeting the following day. We left the boardroom without any words of reconciliation between us.

I knew that I had raised McNamee's heckles to an extent that I had not seen since the occasion, two years earlier, when I had told him I would resign from Free! magazine. Then, he had not spoken to me for several days, despite the fact that my decision to pursue the second KISS FM licence application, which we had subsequently won, had put him where he was today. I was prepared for a similarly cold shoulder.

That evening, I went home and scribbled several pages of detail around the programming proposals I was recommending to the board. We might not yet agree on their impact but, at least, there was no disagreement amongst the station's management about KISS FM's future programming policies. I could only hope that McNamee and Strivens would realise that I was arguing in the best interests of the company, not from personal self-interest. Surely that was how it should be?

---

[830] Michael Kavanagh, "Gordon Attacks Authority", Broadcast, 19 Apr 1991.
[831] "KISS FM Poster Ads Hit Out At Capital", Media Week, 24 May 1991.
[832] ibid.
[833] Neil Hodgson, "Radio City In £10.7m Takeover", Liverpool Echo, 9 May 1991.
William Arnold, "EMAP Plans Radio Empire As Radio City Accepts Bid", Media Week, 17 May 1991.
Michael Kavanagh, "Radio City Takeover Lifts EMAP", Broadcast, 17 May 1991.
"EMAP Mood Bullish After Take-Over", Music Week, 25 May 1991.
[834] Gordon McNamee, "A Presentation Of Reassurance To KISS FM's Backers", KISS FM memo no. MAC/0010, undated [issued 7 May 1991].
[835] Grant Goddard, handwritten notes of meeting with Gordon McNamee, [undated].
[836] ibid.
[837] Grant Goddard, [untitled], [undated].
[838] ibid.
[839] Grant Goddard, "Board Presentation", handwritten notes, 22 May 1991.
[the projected Year One revenues in the application form were £2.5m from advertising and sponsorship, plus £0.4m from clubs and merchandising, totalling £2.9m]
[840] ibid.
[841] ibid.
[842] Grant Goddard, "Where Does KISS FM's Audience Come From?", 13 Sep 1989.

May 1991.

The next morning, Thursday 23 May 1991, I had to ask the programming department administrator, Philippa Unwin, to type my proposals for presentation to the board. The recommendations, which I had fleshed out in greater detail, filled three A4 pages. I introduced the document with a statement that summarised McNamee's instructions to me: "The aim of these changes is to increase the homogeneity of KISS' output, to reduce the variation between different shows and different timebands in the output, and to make KISS more of an 'on tap' service. Listeners should be able to tune in to 100 FM and hear a station that fulfils their expectations at all major times."[843]

The rest of that day I spent in the boardroom, chairing a meeting that had been arranged many weeks earlier by the station's press officer, Anita Mackie. In March, Record Mirror magazine had launched a competition in conjunction with KISS FM, the outcome of which was that three readers would "win the chance to be a DJ for a day." The first prize was a day at KISS FM and a ten-minute slot on-air. Two runners-up had been offered the chance to broadcast "in the heart of central London at KISS' latest station at the bustling Trocadero Centre in Piccadilly Circus." Contestants were required to send a cassette tape to the magazine, showcasing their DJ skills. The judges, which included me, would pick the winners.[844]

However, since the competition had launched, Record Mirror magazine and KISS FM's radio studio at the Trocadero had both closed. As a result, the station had been inundated with phone calls from competition entrants who wanted to know what was going to happen to their tapes. Anita Mackie had decided that KISS FM would continue to run the competition on its own. She had given me a cardboard box filled with hundreds of cassette tapes received by Record Mirror. I had spent a day and an evening at home, ploughing through the tapes and separating them into those that were good, bad and completely hopeless. Mackie had arranged a meeting in the boardroom for former Record Mirror deputy editor Tim Jeffery, KISS FM breakfast DJ Mark Webster, her and me to listen to the short-listed tapes and to declare the winners. The meeting dragged on for hours, during which Mackie thoughtfully provided us with sandwiches for lunch.

To my surprise, McNamee sat in on the whole meeting, despite not having been invited. It seemed an odd way for him to pass his time, given that the critical board meeting and company annual general meeting were in three working days' time. Did he not have more important things to do at this important juncture in the station's future? Only days earlier, McNamee had told me that he had never been under so much pressure in his job. I knew for certain that my desk downstairs must be piling high with things to do while I was sat in this meeting. However, McNamee was becoming more and more like a figurehead at the radio station, without a real job to do. His presence at the meeting disquieted me, but I could not be sure whether that was his deliberate objective, or whether he really just had nothing better to do.

McNamee said nothing further to me about our disagreement the previous day over the board presentation, so I presumed the issue was still to be discussed at the next meeting scheduled for Tuesday morning. After the judging had finished, I stayed at the station late into the evening, catching up on work. Then I went to the Astoria venue in Charing Cross Road, from which another sponsored event was being broadcast that night. Fortunately, Lorna Clarke had agreed to produce the show at the radio station, which gave me a rare opportunity to see how these events were organised on the ground. The broadcast finished at one o'clock in the morning and I returned home, tired but excited by the huge number of young people that had turned up for the event.

The next day was the Friday before a Bank Holiday weekend. On my desk, I found a package from Anita Mackie, thanking me for my work on the competition. Her letter said: "Having listened to eighteen tapes yesterday, I have realised just how many hours it must have taken you to plough through the entries. Please find enclosed a KISS T-shirt for your efforts!" I phoned to thank her for the gesture. It felt good to be appreciated, even though her gift of a promotional T-shirt seemed rather strange, given that I worked for the radio station.[845]

The rest of the day unfolded very slowly. Apart from drawing up the week's music playlist, a chore I was still doing instead of Wesker, there seemed to be very few tasks requiring my immediate attention. Normally, my phone would be buzzing with calls from McNamee or Strivens, asking me to attend this meeting or that committee, always at short notice and always because it was so very urgent. But that day, there was nothing. Nobody from the top floor was even seen in the rest of the building. I became suspicious because, suddenly, the demands on my time that McNamee usually made were no longer there. I called in the administrator, Philippa Unwin, and told her: "I just don't understand what's happening today. There doesn't seem to be anything to do." She could not explain it either. My department was functioning as normal, but the rest of the building had suddenly become ex communicado with this floor. It was almost as if everyone had already left for the holiday weekend although, as I could see from my office window, McNamee's and the others' cars were still parked at the back of the building.

I spent some time looking through recent press coverage that the station had received. I noticed three things that made me feel even more uneasy. In Music Week magazine, there was a profile of the station that listed its 'key staff' as "managing director Gordon McNamee [and] head of music Lindsay Wesker." There was no mention of me, despite the article's focus on KISS FM's programmes. In another profile of the station for the music industry trade magazine For The Record, Lindsay Wesker had been described as KISS FM's head of programming. Finally, in the newly published Radio Authority handbook, which listed key personnel of all UK commercial radio stations, I was omitted from the KISS FM entry. Every other radio station had listed its head of programming, but KISS FM had only listed its chairman, managing director and head of sales. It was difficult for me not to feel that I was being squeezed out of my job.[846]

I had understood from what had been said at the meeting two days earlier with McNamee and Strivens that their private plan seemed to be to set me up as the 'fall guy' who could help them save their own skins. They needed to persuade me to promise to the board that I could achieve an impossible target so that, in six months' or a year's time, when the target was not attained, they could pin the blame on me. I would be the one to lose my job, as they could explain away the fact that the rest of the station's budgets had failed by pointing the finger at my failure to achieve the promised audience growth. This must be why Strivens had been so insistent that I would be the "lynchpin" in the management presentation to the board, not because I was needed for what I had to contribute, but because I was needed to get the other senior managers off the hook.

That Friday seemed like the longest day of my working life at the station. It was the one day I did not feel totally at the beck and call of McNamee (except for the times he went away on vacation). There had not been a single phone call for me from the top floor all day, so I knew something was definitely wrong.

I gave a lift home that evening to Debbi McNally, who worked in the station's sales department and lived only a few miles up the road from me. The previous year, when she had driven her own car to work and I was using public transport, McNally had regularly given me lifts home. Now that I had a company car, I often returned the favour. (McNamee disapproved of my friendship with McNally and, in an attempt to convince himself that the two of us must be having a sexual relationship, he had once asked Rosee Laurence to contact each of us on our home phones one workday morning at half past seven with a fictitious message for the other person. Laurence had found each of us at our own homes, much to McNamee's likely disappointment.)

During the drive home, McNally suddenly said to me: "You don't get paid enough for the work you do, you know."

There was still no security system on the station's computer network and I knew that McNally was clever enough to locate the computer files of anyone in the building, if she had wanted to.

"You think I don't get paid enough," I told her. "You know, by next week, I probably won't have a job at the station, let alone get paid enough."

McNally said she could not believe I would be fired. I told her that I was even considering going to my office over the weekend to clear out all my personal possessions. There was something in the air at KISS FM that just did not feel right, and I anticipated that I would be bearing the brunt of it.

In the end, I decided not to take my things from the office that weekend. However, like every other weekend during the past nine months, I was to be found in my office, catching up with paperwork I never seemed to find time to do during the week. I started to think that I risked becoming paranoid if, at the hint of an internal conflict, I was to imagine that McNamee would throw me out without warning.

After finishing work on Saturday evening, I visited a friend who lived in Hornsey, quite near to the KISS FM office. We sat around talking and listening to old reggae records until the early hours of the morning. I had not realised how late it was until I left and got in my car to drive home. It was now the middle of the night and the residential roads in the area were completely deserted. I drove along a narrow road that linked to the main route north, carefully negotiating the gap between two solid lines of cars parked outside their owners' houses on either side. To my surprise, a car suddenly turned into the road and started heading towards me. The road was far too narrow to accommodate two cars comfortably, so both of us came to a halt, facing each other, as we evaluated our situation.

It was only then that I recognised the car facing me. It looked remarkably like the old Triumph Herald that Lyn Champion used to drive when she had worked at KISS FM. I looked more carefully at the driver and could make out, between the glare of the car's headlights, that it was being driven by a woman who had long kinked hair, just like Champion's. After some time sat facing each other, the other car slowly tried to squeeze past me. I pulled as close as I could to the cars parked on my left hand side and, as the Triumph Herald passed within inches of me, its driver raised a newspaper that she held against the window to shield her face from my gaze. It was definitely Lyn Champion. This was the first occasion I had had contact with her since she had phoned me five months earlier to ask why she had been sacked.

I drove home, startled by my experience, thinking what an incredible coincidence it was to have come face-to-face with Champion at that hour of the night, on that quiet back road, and during that weekend when I was having so many doubts about my own future with KISS FM. Had I been superstitious, I might have viewed it as some kind of omen. However, I knew that Champion used to live in Ferme Park Road in Hornsey, so it should not have been such a surprise to find her in her old stomping ground. Nevertheless, it was the timing of our chance meeting that shocked me and, like a ghost from the past, made me consider my vulnerability in the radio station that we had both worked so hard to create.

After the Bank Holiday weekend, I arrived at work on Tuesday morning and went straight to the boardroom for the nine o'clock meeting that had been arranged to finalise the board presentation. To my surprise, the boardroom was still locked, but I caught McNamee walking out of his office. I asked him what was happening with the meeting.

"It's cancelled," he told me. "We're too busy with other things."

He walked away from me without further explanation. It made no sense that a meeting that was so critical to the board presentation had been cancelled. Why had no one phoned to tell me? McNamee was always asking his personal assistant to call me at all hours of the day and night about some important meeting he had called, re-arranged or postponed. None of this made any sense.

McNamee seemed to have no interest in talking to me further, so I entered Martin Strivens' office and found him sat behind his desk, poring over pages of figures that I assumed were part of the board presentation. I asked him if the meeting scheduled to take place that morning was going to be re-scheduled later in the day. He told me that it was not. I asked him what was going to happen about my unwillingness to endorse the one hundred per cent growth figure he had required of me. He told me that the presentation to the board was going ahead exactly as planned, including the one hundred per cent growth target.

"Tomorrow afternoon," Strivens told me, "you'll be called in to the board meeting and you'll be explaining how you will achieve the hundred per cent growth rate. So be on standby, waiting to be called."

I told him, once more, that I did not agree with the one hundred per cent figure, but he waved me out of his office, insisting that he had important work to be getting on with.

It was just after nine o'clock when I walked downstairs to my office and sat at my desk, contemplating what I should do. The rest of the programming department was still deserted, which gave me an opportunity to think quietly about my best course of action. It seemed that McNamee and Strivens were determined to force through at board level a commitment to a one hundred per cent growth rate, despite my objections to the target I was being set. I had always been denied access to board members, so it would be possible for the two of them to say absolutely anything they wanted to the rest of the board about my supposed endorsement of the figures. I would be railroaded into certain failure, unable to achieve the one hundred per cent target demanded of me, but effectively gagged from telling the board that I had never agreed to the target in the first place. I considered that I could not let McNamee and Strivens brush me aside in this way, or set me up to fail, particularly when I felt that I was acting in the best interests of the radio station.

I decided to write a formal letter to McNamee and to copy it to the company chairman, Keith McDowall. I would point out my considered objections to the target of one hundred per cent and explain why I had felt it necessary to raise the matter in this way. McDowall was McNamee's ultimate boss. If I could not persuade McNamee to take account of my concerns, I had no option but to approach the next person up in the company's management hierarchy. I scribbled out the letter by hand on a notepad, being particularly careful to ensure that the wording did not make me appear negative about KISS FM's situation. After an hour or so working on the letter, I showed it in confidence to Lorna Clarke. I needed a second opinion on what I was doing, and I valued her judgement tremendously. She suggested some changes to the final paragraph, which I made, before heaving onto my desk the IBM golfball typewriter that I had to use to type my work, as a result of Strivens having denied me a computer terminal.

The letter was addressed to McNamee and started: "Following our discussions over the last week, I feel I must confirm in writing my unease with the presentation that it being prepared for tomorrow's board meeting. I am aware of the board's need for full confidence in the station's management team, and I also understand the need for a business plan that demonstrates the company's ability to produce a profit for its investors. On both these points, I have worked constructively and will continue to undertake such tasks as are required to make KISS a success.

"However, the plan being put to the board contains specific targets for KISS listenership in 1991/2 that are entirely unrealistic and, I believe, will fail to be achieved. I have expressed this opinion to you over the last week in explicit terms and at length, despite which you are determined to proceed using these targets. As you are aware, I do not disagree that there is great potential for the station's audience to grow. However, the target of a one hundred per cent increase in total hours listened (over the 1990 JICRAR Wave IV figure for 15+) is not merely ambitious, but is unattainable, given no intended accompanying investment in programming resources."[847]

I then proceeded to detail the discussions and meetings on this issue that had taken place during the previous week. I noted that "if the station's financial success depended so heavily on fixing a projected figure for 'total hours listened,' it was wrong to set a figure so unrealistically high." The memo concluded: "I feel I cannot give my assurance to the board that the audience target is attainable, and I feel it is far too important an issue to gloss over or ignore. I am more than willing to be involved in any further re-evaluation of KISS' potential audience, or in any re-assessment of the resources necessary to run the station profitably. However, I do not wish to be party to an unrealistic business plan that overestimates the station's potential for growth, and fails to build properly on the success that has already been achieved."[848]

Once I had typed the memo, I showed the finished version to Lorna Clarke.

"You don't think it's a bit heavy, do you?" I asked her. She read it once again.

"No," she replied, "it's definitely not a letter of resignation, if that's what you mean."

I made some photocopies of the memo, carefully signed and sealed two copies in envelopes, one of which I delivered to McNamee's office upstairs. At lunchtime, I drove to the chairman's house in nearby Islington and hand-delivered his letter. On my return to the office, I expected to at least receive a phone call from McNamee or the chairman in response to my letter. Instead, there was silence. Neither McNamee nor Strivens came down from their top floor offices to see me, not even to berate me. The silence was deafening.

That evening, KISS FM was co-promoting a music concert at the Town & Country Club venue in Kentish Town. I had stayed late at work to catch up with a tidal wave of paperwork, but stopped off at the concert on my way home. I walked inside the main hall just as the headline act was performing its last song. I had not realised that it was already so late in the evening. Otherwise, I might not have bothered attending. Although I knew it was the final song, I thought I might as well stay until the bitter end now that I was there. Standing at the very back of the hall, I suddenly saw the crowd in front of me part to allow someone to make their way to the exit at the back. It was only then that I recognised that the crowd was parting for Gordon McNamee. I offered him a reflexive smile of recognition, but he scowled at me as he brushed straight past on his way out. Behind him trailed his personal assistant, Rosee Laurence, and the station's head of music, Lindsay Wesker. None of the three said a word to me as they left.

I knew then that, as far as McNamee was concerned, I no longer had a part to play in his radio station. In his mind, I had already been banished. With him at that concert had been the last remains of his trusty crew, Laurence and Wesker. Already, during the last six months, Lyn Champion and Heddi Greenwood had been expelled. I knew that I must be next on McNamee's list for the chop, something he had been itching to do since the previous year. For McNamee, it was a case of out of sight, out of mind. He had demonstrated that philosophy to me that night.

The next day at work passed far too quietly for me. Despite Strivens' insistence that I must attend the board meeting when called for, no word arrived from upstairs. I sat in my office all day, wearing my best suit and tie, but nothing happened. Throughout the whole day, I never saw any of the senior management team.

In the evening, I chaired the monthly meeting in the boardroom of the station's DJs. Neither McNamee nor Trevor Nelson, who had both attended the board meeting, came to the DJ meeting. I sat in the boardroom, wondering what might have happened in that same room, earlier in the day, when the presentations on the station's future had been made. Why had neither McNamee nor McDowall responded in any way to my memo? What audience targets had the board agreed for the station's programming in my absence?

The DJ meeting dragged on interminably. I did not leave the radio station until eleven o'clock. It was typical of my work schedule at KISS FM. I was often one of the first to arrive at work, and almost always the last to leave the building each day. Sometimes the workload got me down and tired me out, but I loved the radio station and I was immensely proud of having made it a success with listeners in such a short space of time. I could not imagine ever wanting any other job.

[843] Grant Goddard, "Programming Changes", 23 May 1991.
[844] "Hey DJ!", Record Mirror, 9 Mar 1991.
[845] letter from Anita Mackie to Grant Goddard, 24 May 1991.
[846] "Focus: KISS FM", Music Week, 11 May 1991.
Andy Smith, "Dancing Feats", For The Record, May 1991.
"The Radio Authority Pocket Book", The Radio Authority, Jun 1991.
[847] "Presentation To Board", memo from Grant Goddard to Gordon McNamee, 28 May 1991.
[848] ibid.

30 May 1991.

It was a little after seven o'clock in the morning when the phone rang. Normally, I would already have been out of bed by that hour on a weekday. However, the previous night's DJ meeting had tired me out. I was awake, but I was still trying to urge my body to get out of bed. The mobile phone stationed beside my bed rang noisily and forced my brain into action far faster than it wanted.

It was Rosee Laurence on the line, asking if I could schedule a meeting that morning with Gordon McNamee. I scrambled out of bed to retrieve my diary from the battered WH Smith black plastic briefcase I always took to work. Requests for meetings at such short notice were common although, during the last few days, McNamee had had no contact with me. Laurence suggested ten o'clock. I explained that I already had an editorial meeting scheduled for half past ten, but I could fit it in as long as the meeting was not going to last too long. She assured me that it would not. I scribbled "10am – Gordon" in my diary, replaced the mobile phone in its charger and got on with the business of waking up properly.

My diary told me that I had two further meetings that afternoon – a weekly sponsorship get-together at one o'clock with Martin Strivens and the sponsorship manager, Gordon Drummond, followed by a debriefing session in the boardroom at three o'clock with KISS FM's partners in the Pepsi promotion. During the drive from my flat to the office, I reflected on the possible reason for the early morning phone call. Was McNamee going to tell me what had happened at the previous day's board meeting? Was he going to pretend that nothing untoward had happened and that the board had approved all his targets for Year Two?

I was already running late when I became caught up in the worst of the rush-hour traffic along Holloway Road. Although my work day officially started at half past nine, I liked to arrive at work earlier so that I could snatch a little time to myself before the inevitable mayhem started in the department. However, that day, there was only time to down a quick cup of tea before walking up to the top floor in time for my ten o'clock appointment. Gordon McNamee was sat in his corner office when Laurence ushered me in. After exchanging morning greetings, I sat facing McNamee across his huge wooden desk. He shuffled from side to side in his chair a few times, avoiding looking directly into my eyes, and he sighed unusually heavily. Several times, he looked up at me as if he was going to say something, but then stopped short.

I stared at him blankly, not knowing what to expect. Eventually, he started mumbling something apologetically, but still he was making little sense. I knew then that McNamee had bad news to break to me. He had always been excellent at whipping his team into a frenzy of enthusiasm when something good was happening, but he was almost incapable of breaking negative news to anyone. He started speaking slowly and managed to explain that he had been "extremely vexed" by the memo I had delivered to him two days earlier. 'Vexed' was one of McNamee's favourite words to use in situations when somebody had done something that displeased him. Anyone else might have been angry, but McNamee was always 'vexed.'

As he reflected upon the contents of my memo and how 'vexed' it had made him, McNamee seemed better able to talk to me directly and to break the bad news. He explained that the board had met the previous afternoon and had decided that the company no longer needed my services. He muttered something about this being the hardest thing he had ever had to do and how he regretted the decision, but I was barely listening to his words. Instead, I was thinking how cowardly was this man sitting in front of me. I was thinking that, even now, he had no intention of telling me the truth of what had taken place at the board meeting, or how he had probably acted to save his own skin. What I wanted to know was what he had told the board about my dissent and what he had told the board of my contributions to the station's success.

But there seemed little point in saying anything at all to the cowering figure sat in front of me, with whom I had worked so closely for more than two years. I got up to leave the room. McNamee had failed to deliver my promised rewards on so many occasions that I did not need to hear another fabricated story about why I was not getting things to which I felt I was entitled. As I left his office, McNamee said that it would be necessary for me to leave the building immediately, and he thrust some documents into my hand. I walked straight out of his office, shocked that, even at this stage in our relationship, McNamee was still incapable of telling me truthfully why I had to go.

Before I could reach the staircase to return to my office, McNamee had caught up with me and was asking me to stop. For a second, I felt as if I should ignore him totally and just carry on walking, but I turned towards him at the very top of the building's stairwell.

"We could say that you had resigned, to make it easier for you, if you wanted," McNamee suggested to me.

I stared at him coldly with a combination of anger and hatred that I could feel welling up inside me.

"Gordon, that's a fucking insult," I spat at him. Then I turned and walked down the staircase leading to my office on the next floor.

I was incensed. After all the sweat, blood and toil I had poured into this company. After all the personal sacrifices I had made to ensure that KISS FM succeeded. After my hard work had produced the required results more quickly than had ever been anticipated. Now, I was being asked to resign from a job in which I had achieved nothing but success. McNamee's cheek to even suggest such a thing had made me really angry. I was in a rage as I stormed into my office. The programming floor was starting to fill up, as staff trickled into work. My first thought was the speed with which McNamee had insisted I must leave the station. Rather than suffer the indignity of being forcibly removed from the building by the station's security guard, I started to pack up my possessions.

Lindsay Wesker caught my attention as he walked onto the floor from the staircase. He was one of my senior team members, so I felt I should break the bad news to him personally. The only private place I could think of to talk was the men's toilet in the stairwell of the floor, so we crowded into the tiny cubicle.

"I've just been sacked," I said to Wesker, "and I've been told to leave the building immediately."

Wesker looked thoughtful, but did not seem particularly shocked. I suddenly understood that Wesker must have been the only member of my team to know what was going to happen to me, before I did.

"Just as you've said before," said Wesker calmly, "it's always the programming department that gets the chop."

These were the very words I had shared with Wesker more than a year earlier, during the first programme planning meeting I had convened at Blackstock Mews. Wesker had mulled over my words carefully then and, now, I realised why he had found those words so interesting. In Wesker's eyes, he had got rid of me at last. I exited the men's toilet without saying another word.

Having received no sympathy from Wesker for my predicament, I walked back to my office and continued assembling my personal effects. I had spent far more of my waking hours in that building during the last year than I had at home, so many of my own possessions were intermingled with that of the company. There was the portable television I had brought to the office when the Gulf War had started, there was a portable cassette player I used, the records I had used to make station jingles, and unread magazines that were cluttering the floor. These were all mine. I started gathering them together into a manageable pile to take away with me. Other staff on the floor noticed me through the clear plastic partition of my office and started to wonder what was going on.

I told Philippa Unwin, who had worked with me closely as the department administrator since the Blackstock Mews days, what had just happened to me. She became visibly upset. As I told other members of my team, they stood around the floor in disbelief and shock.

Lorna Clarke said to me: "They can't sack you just like that. You're the only one who knows how this whole station works."

I felt pressured by the urgency to get out quickly, so I started carrying boxes of my things down three flights of stairs to put in my company car parked at the back of the building. I suddenly realised that my hasty and unexpected departure from KISS FM could be explained away to the staff on any pretext, unless I could make some kind of statement myself. The memo that had 'vexed' Gordon so much had recorded all the significant events of the previous week, as well as having stated my unambiguous position on wanting KISS FM to adopt a realistic strategy for its future.

After less than a year on-air, one of the staff's major criticisms was the lack of information about company decisions that trickled down to them from the senior management. Only those staff working most closely with me in the programming department understood that I was just as ill-informed about what was going on at board level as everybody else was in the building. Using a Pritstick from the top drawer of my desk, I glued a copy of my memo to Gordon McNamee onto the clear plastic partition of my office. My room opened onto the floor's entrance lobby and the partition could be seen by everyone passing through the department. Alongside the memo, I glued the document detailing the programming policy changes I had been ordered by McNamee to devise.

While I continued to gather together my possessions, staff in the department started to read my two memos, all the while expressing outrage that my dismissal could be so abrupt. Then, Wesker burst into my office and handed me a sheet of ledger paper.

"Rosee [Laurence] upstairs says these things are KISS property which you have to give back before you go," said Lindsay sheepishly.

Inscribed in red ink was a list:

"1) security tag 13-92 + ID pass.
2) office & studio keys.
3) car keys."[849]

It was evident that Wesker had been anticipating my dismissal and was acting as messenger boy for the management staff on the top floor who were too cowardly to talk to me directly. I snatched the piece of paper from him, but ignored it. I asked him, rhetorically, how I was expected to take home all my personal possessions without being able to use the company car?

Before leaving the station for the last time, I walked around the programming department and said my hurried goodbyes to the few staff who were already at their desks. Because the majority of my team worked shifts, there were only a few people there. In the DJs' office, David Rodigan was sat at his desk, facing the front windows that looked out over Holloway Road. His back was towards the office door, so I had to interrupt his preparations for that day's lunchtime show to bid him farewell. He expressed outrage at my sacking and seemed bewildered by the speed with which I was being forced to leave.

There was nothing left to do except thank everyone who was in the department for the good times we had spent together and to give many of them one last hug. Some of the staff were crying, others were visibly angry, and some did not seem to believe the events that were unfolding right in front of their eyes. Wesker was the only person who seemed unmoved by the whole scene. He was busy protesting that I had not left the company's property that he had been given responsibility to collect. I could not have cared less.

I got into my company car, half expecting someone to rush out and stop me driving it away. But they did not, and I drove away from the station's car park for the very last time. I had arrived at work barely two hours ago. Now, I was already on my way home again. It felt as if some ghastly mistake had happened, some chance mishap over which I had been able to exert no control. I could not believe that this would really be the very last day I ever worked at KISS FM. The traffic was much lighter on the roads, now that the rush hour was over, so I reached home within half an hour. By then, I was feeling neither upset nor angry about my dismissal. More, I was stunned that the end could have come so abruptly, and without McNamee having offered any gratitude for my significant contributions to KISS FM's success.

Once back home, I looked at the documents that McNamee had handed to me in his office. There was a P45 form for Inland Revenue, a £10,000 cheque in settlement of outstanding wages, and a yellow post-it note on which Martin Strivens had scribbled calculations about the money due to me. His notes included an assertion of the amount of holiday pay I was owed, although his figure was far too low, given that I had only taken one week's vacation during the seventeen months I had worked full-time at the station since it had won its licence. There was no letter of dismissal, nor any reason given for my sacking. Only these few bare documents.

I phoned my family and my close friends to break the bad news. Then I phoned Bob Tyler, a journalist who was now working for the trade magazine Now Radio. The previous weekend, we had traded radio industry gossip on the phone and, before ringing off, Tyler had warned me to watch out at work and be careful that nothing dreadful happened. I had maintained my usual diplomatic silence about the internal wrangles that had been happening within KISS FM. With hindsight, I now wondered if Tyler might have had inside knowledge of what McNamee had had planned for me. Ever since the 'Last Supper' music concert to which McNamee had unexpectedly invited me, I had sensed strange 'goings on' at the radio station to which I had definitely not been party.

It all began to feel quite bizarre, now that I was wandering around my flat, and I started to realise the full consequences of that morning's events. It felt particularly weird to suddenly have spare time on my hands, when my commitment to running the radio station had always left me so little private life. My flat was piled high with a hundred and one mundane household chores that I could never seem to get around to completing. So, having lost my job only hours beforehand, I decided that, rather than become upset, angry, or depressed, I would get on with the rest of my life. Out came the ironing board, on went the steam iron, and I set about ironing the dozen or so clean, but crumpled, shirts that had accumulated over the last couple of weeks.

That afternoon, my phone rang many times, with journalists wanting to know the story behind my sudden departure from KISS FM. It transpired that McNamee had met the station's press officer, Anita Mackie, at half past nine that morning and had instructed her to issue immediately a terse press statement stating that I had "relinquished" my post as head of programming. The reason why McNamee had wanted to meet me at ten o'clock was that Mackie did not start work until half past nine. I was incensed that such a blatant lie was being circulated to the press. It would be assumed that I had been asked to leave the station because I must have done something wrong. The reality was that I had not resigned. I had been fired. I had been offered no reason for my dismissal. I proceeded to put the record straight with the journalists who called me.

Whilst I was talking on the phone to the press, back at KISS FM, actions were being taken to tidy the loose ends surrounding my dismissal. Philippa Unwin phoned me and, in hushed tones, tipped me off that McNamee's personal assistant was arranging to send two security guards to my home address to repossess KISS FM property she said I still had. I was outraged. For the first time that day, I began to feel upset and a little frightened. Unwin's tip-off was confirmed only a few minutes later by a phone call from KISS FM financial director Martin Strivens. Without the slightest apology for the day's events, he told me that I still had KISS FM property – the company car, my office keys, ID tags and the bedside mobile phone charger – that had to be returned to the station immediately. Strivens confirmed that someone was already on their way to my home to collect these items. He acted as if this sort of thing was just part of a regular day's work.

Normally, I parked the company car in front of my block of flats, even though there was a garage to the rear of the property that was included in the lease. I rushed outside and quickly cleared enough space in the garage to park and hide the company car. Closing the garage door, I returned to the flat, double-locked the front door, drew the curtains and sat on the floor of the spare room, fearful of a heavy knock on the door from McNamee's security men. I recalled that, months earlier, McNamee had shown me the tabloid newspaper story which, he had admitted, somehow linked KISS FM with a violent criminal. It seemed crazy that, only a few hours ago, I had had an enjoyable job. Now, by that afternoon, it felt as if I were a fugitive on the run.

The phone continued to ring all afternoon with a mix of personal friends, work colleagues and journalists wanting to know what had happened, and expressing their sympathies. I did not dare go out again that day for fear of bumping into the heavies that had been sent to scare me. They arrived. They banged hard on my front door. I sat on the floor of the flat with the phone in my hand, ready to call the police if they started to break down the door. Eventually, they stopped and went away.

I could never have imagined that my involvement in KISS FM would have ended in such an abrupt way. This was the end of a relationship with Gordon McNamee in which, time after time, he had promised me rewards that he had never delivered. Never had he thanked me for my work at KISS FM, nor had he acclaimed the skills and expertise I brought to his company. Now he had finally kicked me out without apology.

---

[849] Rosee Laurence, [untitled], 30 May 1991.

PART THREE

Aftershocks: 1991

Journalist:

"What do you most hate about your job?"

Gordon McNamee, described as *"managing director (and head of programming and founder) at London dance radio station KISS 100 FM"*:

"Dismissing a member of staff, luckily a rare occurrence."

"And Finally…"
Broadcast
11 June 1993

"Tune in to Gordon Mac and 'lie like a guy!' Make Saturday mornings special by catching 'The Gordon Mac Show' and learn to 'lie like a guy!' … Talk your way out of a tricky situation by 'lying like a guy' and match your gab against Gordon's!!"

Programme Information
KISS FM
16 November 1992

May & June 1991.

Back at the KISS FM office in Holloway Road, Gordon McNamee followed through his plans for my dismissal, once I had left the building. He called into his office the three staff in my department with whom I had worked most closely – head of music Lindsay Wesker, senior producer Lorna Clarke, and programming administrator Philippa Unwin. He told them, in no uncertain terms, that if they had any misgivings about my sacking, they were welcome to leave KISS FM straight away. If they stayed, he would expect absolute loyalty from them and total respect for his authority within the company. He was offering them a choice but insisted they had to make up their minds there and then. All three declined McNamee's offer to resign.

McNamee explained that he would expect all three of them to share my former responsibilities in the department, and that he needed all three to work together with him in the best interests of the station's future. He dismissed them from his office and then called an immediate meeting of all the programming department staff in the boardroom in order to explain my sudden and unexpected departure. His assistant Rosee Laurence was reported to have cried during this meeting, not because of my absence, but because so many of my former staff refused to believe McNamee's assertion that my dismissal was in the best interests of the station. Laurence always demonstrated unswerving loyalty to McNamee, and she hated it when other staff did not agree wholeheartedly with his point of view.

After the staff meeting, McNamee phoned the station's former record librarian, Alexander Donnelly, whom he had insisted upon making redundant three months earlier, to ask him if he wanted to start work again at the station the next day. This was McNamee's pay-off to Lindsay Wesker. Perhaps McNamee had blamed me publicly for his own decision to force Donnelly's redundancy. McNamee knew that, more than anything else, Wesker believed he should have had my job as head of programming. In the early stages of the first KISS FM licence application in 1989, Wesker had provisionally been appointed the station's head of programming. It was only after I had joined the station that Wesker had been effectively demoted to the head of music post.[850]

Having accomplished all this dirty work by lunchtime, McNamee drove his Mercedes company car home and promptly flew away on vacation to his parent's villa in Spain for one week. He had taken similar evasive action the day after the station's first JICRAR audience ratings had arrived the previous December, having anticipated (wrongly) that they were going to demonstrate KISS FM's poor performance. When the going got tough, McNamee was often nowhere to be found. My dismissal was no exception. In McNamee's absence, Martin Strivens was left to tidy any loose ends surrounding my dismissal.

The next morning, Strivens phoned to tell me that he had cancelled the £10,000 cheque that McNamee had given me the previous day, because I had not yet returned the company car and other station property. I told him that I was about to take legal advice and that he would hear from me soon.

I also received a letter from McNamee, dated the previous day, which he must have signed before he left for Spain. In full, it said: "I regret to inform you that the board and I no longer have confidence in your ability to run the programming department. I am therefore forced to terminate your employment with the company with immediate effect. You have already received your P45 and final pay cheque." (The reference number on the letter was "MAC/0033," an indication of how few letters McNamee wrote.)[851]

That morning, I visited the local office of the Citizens' Advice Bureau, which gave me the names of several local solicitors who specialised in employment law. I made an appointment with one of them and took along all the documents that related to my dismissal. The solicitor read through my KISS FM contract of employment and told me it was the worst example of such a document she had seen in her entire career. She advised me that there was very little I could do. The contract gave me no right to keep the company car during the one-month notice period to which I was supposedly entitled. She told me that Strivens' action in cancelling the settlement cheque was completely illegal, but she recommended that I offer to trade the company car with KISS FM for an irreversible banker's draft for the same amount. She wrote a letter on my behalf to KISS FM, which pointed out that I had still not been given "proper reason for dismissal" and which lodged an appeal against my sacking.[852]

Although my letter was addressed to McNamee, the response had apparently been drafted by Martin Strivens (the letter's reference was "MRS/000223") but it was signed by McNamee, despite the fact that he was still in Spain. It said: "Contrary to your assertion, you are not entitled to appeal ... as you received payment in lieu of notice considerably in excess of your contractual entitlement. Nevertheless, I am prepared to address your appeal. I have re-examined the situation and discussed it with other members of the board. The decision and the reasons for it remain as stated in my letter dated 30th May 1991."[853]

It was evidently proving difficult for Strivens to offer a specific reason for my dismissal. While these letters went backwards and forwards between me and him, I continued to receive phone calls at home from staff within the programming department, asking what they should do about this problem, or what they needed to do to make such-and-such work properly. It was obvious that they were having as much difficulty as I was adjusting to the fact that I no longer worked for the station. I decided to write to all the full-time staff in my department in order to explain my sudden departure and to thank them for their contributions to KISS FM's success.

My letter said: "Because I was asked to leave the building immediately on Thursday morning, there was only time to have a very quick word with the few staff who were around then. So, I just want to say 'thank you' to you for all the work and effort you've put in to make KISS happen. I've enjoyed working with everybody in the department and I'm pleased the station has got such a good audience. I realise there is confusion about why I'm not there. I did not 'relinquish' my job. The fact is – I was sacked – without warning or proper reason. The closest to an explanation is the attached letter that I received by post from Gordon [McNamee] on Friday. Neither Gordon, nor any other member of the management, have attempted to tell me more.

"The aspect of all this that I find most personally hurtful is the complete lack of recognition or thanks for my work for KISS over the last two and a half years, and for the success that the whole department has achieved. I would not choose to leave the station in this way, with such haste or with any bitterness. KISS is too important in its own right for me not to want it to succeed. Despite all the crazy things that have happened over the past few days, I would still much rather be working at KISS than anywhere else. Maybe one day that will be possible. In the meantime, it's been good working with you and I hope our paths can cross again at some point. Good luck for the future and thanx [sic] for putting up with me."[854]

I photocopied the letter and mailed it individually to each member of the programming department at the station, with the exception of Lindsay Wesker. McNamee's response (or, maybe, Strivens' response in McNamee's name) was to issue a memo to all programming department staff which forbade them from having any contact with me, either within or outside the radio station. The memo threatened that if the station's management found anyone had made contact with me, they would be disciplined. It seemed that, if McNamee could not convince them that I had been some kind of traitor to KISS FM, then he had to threaten them, in much the same way as he had done to me during previous months.

Martin Strivens wrote me another letter, agreeing to my request to exchange the company car for a banker's draft, and suggesting that the swap should take place at Holloway Road on a Tuesday at noon. His letter concluded: "Gordon McNamee will be your point of contact." On the assigned day, I delivered the company car to the KISS FM office but, unsurprisingly, the receptionist told me that McNamee was not at work that day, despite having returned from his vacation. Instead, the exchange was made with Adam Lewis, the company's accounts manager. Whilst I was talking with Lewis in the reception area, one of my former staff came through the front door and, recognising me, came over for a brief chat. Later, I found out that someone had informed McNamee that the two of us had been in conversation and, as a result, my former colleague was disciplined for having made contact with me.[855]

During the period I had been locked in negotiations with KISS FM over the return of its company car and the replacement of my cancelled cheque, the trade press had gone to town over my dismissal. Music Week magazine was the first to publish the story on the Monday following the Thursday of my dismissal, under the headline 'KISS Fires Goddard.' The front page article noted my success in achieving the one million listener target, but explained that "McNamee will take over the role [of head of programming] he held in the station's pirate days."[856]

Three days later, Broadcast magazine headlined its front page lead story 'KISS Goes Mainstream.' The article focused upon the changes to the station's programming policy that had been approved by McNamee and the management team, which Broadcast said would "introduce more chart music to its schedules in a bid to challenge rival Capital Radio." The only comment from the station came in the article's last paragraph, which quoted an official statement that "Gordon McNamee, managing director, resumes the head of programmes position in addition to his other responsibilities."[857]

The same day, Campaign magazine reported my dismissal and included a quote from a KISS FM spokesman that "Goddard was told to quit because he remained unsupportive of company policies." Marketing magazine ran the story under the headline "KISS FM Row Sends Out Shockwaves" and commented that my dismissal "highlights the stresses and strains new commercial stations find themselves under." Now Radio magazine ran an article on its front page, under the headline 'Programme Head Axed,' which noted that "rumours of major programming changes are circulating around KISS House this week."[858]

While the trade press followed up the story, McNamee had been in Spain and was, therefore, conveniently unavailable for comment. KISS FM press officer Anita Mackie seemed to have had no previous experience of handling company dismissals. She had been given no information other than the one-sentence press statement McNamee had told her to issue before he left. Other staff in the building had been told not to talk about the matter, although one anonymous member of staff told Now Radio: "We can detect the hand of big business taking a grip. Most of us have suspected all along that Gordon Mac's idea of a legal dance station for London was hijacked by ambitious public companies who really wanted a chance to take on Capital [Radio], win some of its revenue and call themselves successful radio owners."[859]

Because KISS FM had issued a completely false statement that I had "relinquished" my job at the station, I felt that I had to explain to journalists that I had, in fact, been summarily dismissed without reason. I pointed out that the station's programming was one area in which KISS FM had achieved proven success. I explained that the policy recommendations I was asked to draft had been accepted by everyone involved in the station, and that there had been no disagreement over programming policy. The only area of dissent was the target figure for the station's audience in its second year, which I had pointed out was entirely unrealistic.

As a result of having presented the full facts to journalists who rang me for information, the resultant press coverage was fairly sympathetic to me, particularly as KISS FM was unable to offer a comment from McNamee or a reasonable explanation for my sudden departure. Journalists continued to phone the radio station wanting more detailed information, so the company chairman, Keith McDowall, was brought in to handle the matter in McNamee's absence. Having had no day-to-day involvement in the radio station, and having had no direct contact with me in over a year, McDowall resorted to inventing fantasies to explain my dismissal. Despite (or perhaps because of) his many years' experience in public relations, his strategy seemed to be to bully journalists into writing something that put over the opposite viewpoint, by phoning them persistently and writing long, angry letters.

McDowall responded to Broadcast magazine's front-page story about my dismissal by writing a remarkable letter to its editor: "Last week, I spent about twenty minutes putting the KISS FM point of view to your [reporter] Mr Michael Kavanagh about the departure of Grant Goddard. I repeated to him several times that we all regretted Goddard's departure but, for a number of reasons, the board had reluctantly concluded it either backed him or its management team. After about ten minutes, it became clear to me that your Mr Kavanagh's mind was closed to my board's point of view and was only interested in peddling that of Goddard's – that, like a radio transmitter, he was locked on 'transmit' and was incapable of receiving.

"As a lifelong member of the National Union of Journalists, which I joined in 1946, I suggested to him that his role was not one of protagonist or counsel for the prosecution, but that he should listen to both points of view and then try to reflect them in the space available. Today, in Broadcast, I find exactly what I expected – the knocking copy provided by a young man burning with indignation, and the deliberate leaking of our commercial decisions – but no attempt to provide the alternative arguments. Indeed, you do not even go through the motions of putting my case. Perhaps that is why I had to telephone Broadcast, rather than have you seek me out, and why Mr Kavanagh was so clearly not over-interested in what I was telling him.

"Therefore, I have no option but to ask you for a similar space to put the KISS FM point of view, or to tell you that we are so appalled at this partisan and destructive approach to this industry that we propose to pursue our case with the new Press Commission. This may not worry you overmuch, but it may indeed signpost the route for all the others who tell us that the treatment we have received from Broadcast is in fact par for the course."[860]

Aside from being a serious over-reaction to Broadcast's news story, McDowall's letter was ridiculous for his reference to me as a "young man," when I was older than KISS FM's managing director, and for my alleged leaking of "commercial decisions." All I had told the press were my own recommendations for programming policy changes which had already been approved by the management team. To their credit, Broadcast resisted McDowall's threats, although it did publish a short letter from McDowall, rebuffing the main points of its news story, three weeks after it had first appeared.[861]

Other publications proved not so determined to stick to their original story, in the face of such provocations. Music Week published both a letter from McDowall entitled 'KISS In The Pink' and an article, much larger than its original news story, headed 'KISS MD Slams Goddard Claims.' McDowall's letter asserted: "We received a recommendation for minor adjustments to programming from the management team which all participants – except Goddard – were prepared to support. We did not feel his support for them was one hundred per cent but, in fact, rather negative and we did not feel he was prepared to motivate his staff sufficiently. In those circumstances, we reluctantly concluded it was time to part company."[862]

In his desperate attempt to justify my dismissal, McDowall was moving further and further away from the facts. His letter represented a complete inversion of the truth, which was that the programme recommendations had been all my work, and that the rest of the team had approved them. This was confirmed by KISS FM head of marketing Malcolm Cox in his comment on my dismissal to Time Out magazine: "The irony is that the programming plans that [Goddard] set forward for this year and next are all going ahead."[863]

If McDowall's letter published in Music Week was inaccurate, then the news story that the magazine printed was a complete travesty of lies. Having by now returned from his vacation, McNamee told Music Week that my recommendations included the sacking of all of KISS FM's weekend DJs and the playing of more pop music to compete with Capital Radio. McNamee said that the station had not agreed to these proposals which were "a clear sign that Goddard was a face that didn't fit." Carried away in his own tissue of lies, McNamee continued: "I am really pissed off about this. Grant got together lots of ideas in a discussion document. Not all of them were put to the board and they were by no means accepted. The most damaging idea is the sacking of DJs. That has obviously worried a lot of our staff, but it's not an idea we are considering."[864]

Similarly, McNamee told Time Out magazine that my proposals were merely "a thinking document." McDowall complained that "this young man has decided, in his great protestations of loyalty and hurtness, to give away every commercial secret he can lay his hands on." In Now Radio magazine, McNamee claimed that I was sacked because I "did not fit in with the programme team," while McDowall claimed that I "was not prepared to work with the management team" and insisted that my policy proposals "were conceived by the whole management team."[865]

491

In Marketing magazine, McDowall claimed that I was sacked because of "personality problems." He told Music & Media magazine: "We have to reflect the fast-moving dance scene, and the depressed commercial scene means me have to cut our cloth accordingly. That means a team effort and everyone has to give a bit. Grant wasn't prepared to do that and, reluctantly, we've had to part company." McDowall explained that McNamee had pre-arranged a one-week holiday before taking on my role as programme controller. It was the first public admittance that my dismissal had been premeditated in order to make way for McNamee to usurp me.[866]

Finally, Television Today magazine reported that I had been dismissed "following personality clashes with other members of KISS' management team which came to a head at a meeting about 'minor adjustments to programming.'" Interviewed in the article, McNamee attacked me because I had been "stirring it up as much as possible" since I had left the station. He claimed that I was "not a team player," so it had been decided that I and the station should part company.[867]

By now, I had become far angrier about the lies that McNamee and McDowall had told the press than I had been about the dismissal itself. As the story had evolved, their fabrications had become more and more bizarre. It seemed that McNamee would stop at nothing to discredit me entirely for the last two and a half years that I had invested in KISS FM. I could just about accept the fact that I no longer had a job at the station that I had helped succeed, but I could not accept the fact that McNamee was so bitter in his determination to destroy my reputation and my character. After all, now that I was out of the radio station, McNamee had got what he wanted – my job and the success I had already brought to it. Was that not enough to satisfy him? Why did he feel he had to go to such extremes to try and destroy me?

I recalled the several occasions when I had been warned by different people to be careful about involving myself in KISS FM. In my determination to help create the UK's first licensed black music radio station, I had fallen into the traps that McNamee had set for me. It was too late now. My time was up.

---

[850] "The Team Behind KISS", KISS FM, [undated].
[851] letter from Gordon McNamee to Grant Goddard, 30 May 1991.
[852] letter from Grant Goddard to Gordon McNamee, 4 Jun 1991.
[853] letter from Gordon McNamee to Grant Goddard, 5 Jun 1991.
[854] memo from Grant Goddard to KISS FM full-time programming department staff, 2 Jun 1991.
[855] letter from Martin Strivens to Grant Goddard, 5 Jun 1991.
[856] "KISS Fires Goddard", Music Week, 8 Jun 1991.
[857] Michael Kavanagh, "KISS Goes Mainstream", Broadcast, 7 Jun 1991.
[858] "KISS Rebuffs Fired Director's Claims Of Financial Crisis", Campaign, 7 Jun 1991.
Valerie Latham, "KISS FM Row Sends Out Shockwaves", Marketing, 6 Jun 1991.
"Programme Head Axed", Now Radio, 6 Jun 1991.
[859] "Programme Head Axed", op cit.
[860] letter from Keith McDowall, KISS FM to The Editor, Broadcast, 6 Jun 1991.
[861] Keith McDowall, "'KISS Goes Mainstream'?", letters, Broadcast, 28 Jun 1991.
[862] Keith McDowall, "KISS In The Pink", Music Week, 15 Jun 1991.
[863] Sid Smith, "Mass Repeal", Time Out, 12 Jun 1991.
[864] "KISS MD Slams Goddard Claims", Music Week, 15 Jun 1991.
[865] Sid Smith, op cit.
"Mac Hits Back", Now Radio, 13 Jun 1991.

[866] Valerie Latham, op cit.
Hugh Fielder, "Goddard, KISS FM Split Over Programming Row", Music & Media, 15 Jun 1991.
[867] Angus Towler, "KISS And Tell Tales Denied", Television Today, 13 Jun 1991.

June to August 1991.

After a fortnight, the stream of vitriol against me in the press from KISS House started to subside. The magazines lost interest in the story and moved on to other tales of corporate horrors. My KISS FM company car, which had taken me so long to wheedle out of Martin Strivens, turned up parked outside the home of the station's sponsorship manager, Gordon Drummond, who lived less than a mile from me. Only days before my dismissal, Drummond had told me how much he had wanted a more sporty car. Now he had mine. I never heard anything further from Gordon McNamee or Strivens or the post-pirate team of 'suits' (including Drummond) whom they had recruited to work at the station.

However, I continued to receive sympathetic phone calls from the staff in my former department at the station. They were appalled at the treatment McNamee had meted out to me, but there was little they could do about the situation. I also received phone calls from other colleagues within the radio industry who told me that my experience was all too common within the scores of poorly managed commercial radio stations. One industry colleague kindly invited me out for lunch in London. John Catlett, who had managed the offshore pirate station Laser 558 in the 1980s, had recently been appointed general manager of the English service of Radio Luxembourg. I told him of my experiences with KISS FM. He suggested that I should write to those shareholders in the station who had other interests in radio. My letter would demonstrate that I had no negative sentiment about my dismissal from KISS FM and it might open up new employment opportunities for me.

I followed up Catlett's suggestion by writing to Virgin Broadcasting and to EMAP Radio, both of whom were shareholders in KISS FM, asking if they would consider me for any future radio projects in which they might be involved. Tim Schoonmaker of EMAP Radio phoned to say he would be happy to meet up, but that he was too busy at the moment. He promised to call me again later in the year. I received a written response from Charles Levison of Virgin Broadcasting who, like Schoonmaker, was a director of KISS FM: "I appreciate and respect the work which you did at KISS, but the interviews which you gave to the press when you left were most unhelpful and misleading. I hope you will understand that I would have considerable reservations, despite your abilities, in working with you on any radio projects at this time."[868]

I knew that, whatever story McNamee had told the press about the reasons for my dismissal, I could be sure that the reasons he must have offered to the company's board to ensure my sudden departure were probably much more lurid and fantastic. I dreaded to think what McNamee might have been saying, in confidence, to colleagues within the radio industry about what dreadful deeds I was supposed to have committed at KISS FM before he had found me out. Was there anything that McNamee would not do to try and destroy my reputation?

That question was answered three weeks after my dismissal. I received a phone call late one evening from Daniel Nathan, a colleague in radio whom I had employed at KISS FM temporarily to help train the DJs. The two of us regularly exchanged news about developments within the industry. At the end of the conversation, Nathan asked me how I had reacted to the newspaper report about my dismissal. "What report?" I asked him, knowing that the media trade magazines had already run out of steam with the story. He went away for a while and returned to the phone with the Independent On Sunday newspaper in which he had seen the article.

Under the headline 'KISS FM Keeps Status Quo,' the report said: "KISS FM, London's hippest radio station, has fought off an attempt to take it into the mainstream of pop music. But the former pirate has dismissed its head of programming after he suggested that 'the radical sound of young London,' as KISS calls itself, ditch the soul, Latin, house R&B, rare groove, salsa, blues, hip hop, reggae and bhangra music styles that made its name. Grant Goddard, head of programming at KISS, was sacked by the managing director, Gordon McNamee, after proposing to dismiss the weekend disc jockeys and play more commercial music to compete with Capital Radio."[869]

I could not believe the 'story' that Nathan was reading to me over the phone, but the article continued: "While a soured Mr Goddard fed the trade press stories of a crisis – 'Struggling KISS Goes Mainstream' declared the magazine Broadcast – Mr McNamee, or Gordon Mac as he is known, had gone to Spain for a rest. By the time he returned, the rumour was that Virgin, the principal shareholder, was selling out to the publishing company EMAP, who were to install a rock music supremo to win new listeners. 'That's all rubbish,' said Mac yesterday. 'We're not about to start playing pop music, although of course we are interested in taking listeners from other stations, including Capital.'"[870]

The article continued with a glowing biography of McNamee, trumpeting his abilities, accompanied by his photo. I could not believe what Nathan had just read to me down the phone line. This was the first national newspaper to pick up the story of my dismissal, but the newspaper had made no attempt to discover my side of the story. Furthermore, McNamee's lies had surely reached their zenith in this article. And the journalist had peppered the article with inaccuracies – Virgin was not the principal shareholder in KISS FM. EMAP, far from buying the radio station, already had a substantial stake in it. I was absolutely livid and was determined to do something about it.

Once I found the relevant issue of The Independent On Sunday in my local library the next day, I noticed that the article had been written by Martin Wroe. The name was familiar to me because Wroe had written regularly about KISS FM since January 1988, when a piece in The Independent, entitled 'Pirates Who Storm The Open Airwaves,' had been accompanied by a photo of McNamee standing in the pirate KISS FM studio. Wroe's first article had offered a glowing account of "Gordon Mac, the twenty-seven year old North London entrepreneur who controls KISS FM." In at least four further articles about the station, Wroe had described McNamee as "a hip young media mogul" and had referred to "the excellent audience figures of KISS FM." If I had wanted to choose someone to write a positive account of recent events at KISS FM, who better to ask than a journalist, on a national newspaper, who had never said a negative word about me?[871]

I was incensed that Wroe had made no attempt to contact me to discover my side of the story, despite the fact that the article had been published three weeks after my dismissal. Every other journalist who had written about my exit from KISS FM had at least spoken to me about the story, even if they had not believed my version of events. Wroe had written a straightforward character assassination piece, much as McNamee might have wanted. Just when I thought McNamee had finished sticking the knife into my back publicly, he had played his trump card.

I returned to the local Citizens' Advice Bureau and asked if they had information about solicitors who specialised in libel. The middle-aged woman I spoke to said that I was being ridiculous, since no ordinary person would ever consider taking out a libel action. "You're not a film star or a politician, are you," she chastised me, "so why do you think you want to get involved in a libel action?" Fortunately, the solicitor I had consulted about my employment contract proved more helpful and gave me the name of a central London firm that dealt with libel matters. I initiated an action for defamation against The Independent On Sunday which, after protracted correspondence, was settled out of court. However, it was not until three months after Wroe's article had been published that the newspaper printed a full retraction and apologised for Martin Wroe's wholesale inaccuracies.[872]

Whilst the legal wrangles had continued about Wroe's article, KISS FM's second set of JICRAR audience ratings were published, reflecting the station's listening during the three months from April 1991. There was a twenty-four per cent increase in the number of hours listened to the station, compared to the previous survey six months earlier. I was pleased to see it confirmed that the programming changes I had introduced in March had substantially boosted the station's audience. I also felt vindicated that the on-air enthusiasm I had generated around the Pepsi-sponsored MC Hammer tour had paid dividends, evidently managing to please not only the sponsors, but the KISS FM audience as well. Despite the programming team's understandable reservations about the credibility of Hammer, they had demonstrated their skills by turning the event into a huge success. I was satisfied in knowing that I had turned many other money-making promotions into creative, attractive radio.[873]

However, I was also very sad that I could not share in the success that I had created at KISS FM. For the last two and a half years, KISS FM had been my entire life. Never before had I worked so hard, and with such determination, to make something succeed, against such massive odds. It was seventeen years since I had listened to London's first soul music pirate station, Radio Invicta, and had dreamed that, one day, I would help to create Britain's first legal radio station devoted to black music. Since then, I had played my role and brought to fruition a dream that, for a long time, I almost lost hope could ever be transformed into reality.

If I had won that particular personal battle, then I had also lost a much more public war about my professional reputation. There was nothing in the public domain that verified the successes I had achieved at KISS FM, or my role in creating the legal version of the radio station. It seemed that history had repeated itself. In 1980, I had received no credit for my role in turning around Metro Radio's fortunes, and I had lost my job. Now, in 1991, I had received no credit for the successful launch of KISS FM in London, and I had lost my job.

One of my most important personal ambitions in life had been fulfilled, but I had almost nothing to show for it, apart from my own satisfaction and the knowledge of how I had achieved my goal.

In KISS FM, I had accomplished a dream that every soul music fan of every age should be proud of. I had successfully launched London's first black music radio station, and nobody could ever take that achievement away from me.

....

Several months later, I attended the annual Music Radio Conference in London, alongside executives from the British radio industry. I was chatting with journalist Bob Tyler, when he kindly introduced me to the programme controller of a metropolitan station in the north of England.

"I remember your name," the man said to me, "but I can't quite place you."

"KISS FM," I told him, "I used to be head of programming at KISS FM."

"Oh yes, I remember now," he said. "All those headlines in the papers. That sounded like a really nasty affair. ... But what are you doing now?"

"I'm looking for another job in radio at the moment," I told him.

"Yes, it must be difficult," he replied, "particularly when you've got morals."

I looked at him to determine whether he was trying to be witty, but he was deadly serious.

"You see," he said to me in a patronising tone, "you won't get a job in commercial radio if you've got morals. Commercial radio and morals just don't go together."

I thanked him for his advice and walked away.

By the end of the decade, he had been promoted to a very senior management position in one of the UK's largest commercial radio groups.

---

[868] phone call from Tim Schoonmaker, EMAP Radio to Grant Goddard, 8 Aug 1991.
letter from Charles Levison, Virgin Broadcasting to Grant Goddard, 8 Aug 1991.
[869] Martin Wroe, "KISS FM Keeps Its Status Quo", The Independent On Sunday, 16 Jun 1991.
[870] ibid.
[871] Martin Wroe, "Pirates Who Storm The Open Airwaves", The Independent, 13 Jan 1988.
Martin Wroe, "Making Radio Contact With 5m Listeners", The Independent, 12 Jul 1989.
Martin Wroe, "Cut The Chat; Play The Music", The Independent, 4 Jul 1990.
Martin Wroe, "No Longer An Illicit KISS", The Independent, 30 Aug 1990.
Martin Wroe, "Do I Hear A Bid For This Station? Well, Do I?", May 1991 [exact date unknown].
[872] "Mr Grant Goddard", The Independent On Sunday, 1 Sep 1991.
"Goddard Gets Retraction", Now Radio, 12 Sep 1991.
[873] JICRAR, Q2 1991.

EPILOGUE

"What would probably make KISS FM more attractive would be if it were still a pirate, because there's probably an image connected to listening to a pirate station. As soon as KISS FM becomes legal, then probably, in its own way, although it's still trying to be exciting, it is then mainstream ... and it has to conform."

member of public interviewed for KISS FM's pre-launch market research by Sirius Research
Hemel Hempstead
21 June 1990

"Fear not! Very little will change if KISS FM becomes legal."

KISS FM
'KISS FM Closes Down'
94 no. 3, December 1988

Gordon McNamee [before KISS FM's licence win]:

"We've grown up together as a family and we would like to think that a legal licence would consolidate our position without losing our underground family feel."

Dave Seaman
'The Story So Far'
MixMag
March 1988

Un-named KISS FM DJ:

"We used to be one big happy family, but that has changed."

Lisa Brinkworth
'Sealed With A KISS'
Soul Underground
September 1990

July 1991.

Broadcast magazine reported that KISS FM had contracted consultants to review the station's programmes, which were "to become more mainstream." However, for many months thereafter, the KISS FM programme schedule remained exactly as I had fixed it back in March 1991.[874]

On 10 July 1991, the Department of Trade & Industry struck off KISS FM managing director's Gordon McNamee's company 'Goodfoot Promotions Limited' and forcibly dissolved it, having received no details of the company's activities for more than two years. The only set of audited accounts ever filed for Goodfoot covered the period from the company's creation in September 1987 to the end of December 1988, when the pirate KISS FM had closed down. During that period, Goodfoot had made a loss of £4,989 on turnover of £18,419. It owed its creditors £6,743, including £4,310 to McNamee.[875]

The company's auditor, Barcant Beardon of Blackstock Mews, noted that "the company's system of control is dependent on the close involvement of the director [McNamee] who is the major shareholder. Where independent confirmation of the completeness of the accounting records was therefore not available, we have accepted assurances from the director that all the company's transactions have been properly reflected in the records."[876]

Although the audited accounts ended on 31 December 1988, Goodfoot might have appeared to have been busier than ever during 1989 and the first half of 1990, organising KISS FM club events whilst the radio station was still off the air. Every Monday morning, I had watched McNamee's personal assistant, Rosee Laurence, count out thousands of pounds in cash in the Blackstock Mews office, the proceeds of the weekend's club nights. Every Monday, Laurence had walked to the bank in Finsbury Park to pay in these proceeds.

In a survey of the performances of the new incremental radio stations, The Evening Standard noted that KISS FM "hopes to double its audience in the next year" but that the company "is said to require a new injection of finance." KISS FM's losses were reported to be £1.75m in the ten months since the station's launch.[877]

After months of speculation, KISS FM head of sales Gary Miele exited the station.[878]

August 1991.

Terence Smith was replaced as managing director of Radio City, the Liverpool station recently acquired by EMAP. Smith said he would be staying on with EMAP and would "be active in the development of EMAP's radio interests overall."[879]

September 1991.

After its first full year on-air, 'KISS FM Limited' reported losses of £728,000 on total revenues of £2,576,000. However, the start-up costs of the station had amounted to just over £1m, bringing the company's accumulated loss to £1,744,802. The company accounts revealed that, in February 1991, KISS FM's financial situation had required it to obtain an unsecured loan note for £352,000 and a mortgage debenture from its banker, NatWest Bank. Seven of KISS FM's non-executive directors had been paid up to £5,000 during the year, despite McNamee's assurance to the staff meeting in February 1991 (at which he had announced redundancies) that directors would make sacrifices by refusing payments for attending board meetings.[880]

Despite the company's losses, some executives had been paid handsomely. Managing director Gordon McNamee's salary was £66,160, greater than the £55,000 budgeted in the licence application. Financial director Martin Strivens earned nearly £50,000, compared to the £40,000 in the application.[881]

October 1991.

On 22 October 1991, the Department of Trade & Industry struck off and dissolved 'KISS Records Limited,' the record company that Gordon McNamee had created in partnership with Heddi Greenwood at the end of 1987. Only one set of accounts had been filed for KISS Records, for the year ending 31 March 1989, which recorded a loss of £10,533 on turnover of £61,371. At that time, the company's creditors included £2,000 in the form of a loan from Centurion Press, £8,584 owed to McNamee, £1,249 owed to Greenwood, and £3,942 owed to Customs & Excise. Like Goodfoot Promotions, it appeared from activity I had observed at the Blackstock Mews office that KISS Records Limited had continued to trade for at least a further year, though no further accounts had been filed.[882]

December 1991.

Although, at the time, no announcement was made to the radio station's staff, by May 1991, Virgin Broadcasting had purchased an additional £55,588 of shares in KISS FM Limited. For the first time, EMAP and Virgin had equal stakes of twenty-one per cent in the company. At the beginning of December 1991, a further 125,000 new shares were issued, of which 57,722 were acquired each by EMAP and Virgin Broadcasting. The remainder were purchased by other shareholders: David Evans (4,327), Martin Strivens (2,729) and Gordon McNamee (2,500). McNamee's control of the company was effectively reduced from twenty to nineteen per cent, whilst EMAP and Virgin had increased their command to twenty-three per cent each.[883]

In mid-December 1991, after several postponements, Tim Schoonmaker, KISS FM director and EMAP Radio managing director, agreed to meet with me. He asked me to go to

Hubbles winebar in London's Smithfield district one afternoon. When I arrived, I found Schoonmaker with a large crowd of EMAP staff who had just finished their company Christmas dinner at the venue. He invited me, rather bizarrely, to join in some of the party games he was playing with the staff at his table. He had nothing much to say to me about KISS FM and no explanation for my dismissal. I left wondering why he had bothered to invite me to such an inappropriate social gathering. The meeting had been a complete waste of my time.

Once I had returned home, I discovered that EMAP had just announced it had acquired Virgin Broadcasting's shareholding in KISS FM. This increased EMAP's stake to forty-six per cent, giving it near control over the company. Schoonmaker commented: "KISS is easily radio's most successful FM launch for some years. EMAP is looking forward to further success at KISS. We continue to support Gordon McNamee and his team." Virgin's Charles Levison resigned his seat on the company board. A KISS FM press release noted that the forthcoming audience figures "are expected to show a further significant improvement" in the station's listenership.[884]

January 1992.

Radio audience data for the final quarter of 1991 showed KISS FM having increased its hours listened by twenty-six per cent over the previous six months to 8,988,000 hours per week. This was the second successive increase since the station's launch and continued to reflect the appeal of the programme schedule I had introduced in March 1991.[885]

In an apparent effort to hinder EMAP taking complete control of KISS FM, Gordon McNamee and Martin Strivens sold some of their personal shareholdings in the company to their wives, thus increasing the number of shareholders entitled to attend the company's forthcoming Annual General Meeting.[886]

March 1992.

Asked about the success of the incremental radio station scheme, The Radio Authority's chief executive Peter Baldwin responded: "There were twenty-five licences [advertised], twenty-three of which came on-air. Two have failed and seven have experienced changes in ownership ... The incremental plan was an experiment. From our point of view, it has been a considerably successful experiment ... We are delighted with the success with audiences of stations like KISS....."[887]

Commenting on KISS FM's success, McNamee said: "If you plan something and say 'this is what we want to do, this is the audience we want to achieve' and you get it, the backers leave you alone because they know you know what you are doing. If it doesn't come, backers will want change. At this moment, and as far as I can see in the future, we are doing the first rather than the second. Tim Schoonmaker [of EMAP] is very pleased with the station.

But, if in years to come it lost audience, I'm sure he would come in and say it's time to move on."[888]

The following week, EMAP acquired further shareholdings in KISS FM that had been held by Centurion Press, Cradley Group Holdings, David Evans and Keith McDowall, increasing its stake even further. Resigning his seat on the company board, chairman McDowall commented: "We all worked together as a team to get the station off the ground and so, naturally, we wish the KISS venture well." EMAP Radio director Terence Smith was appointed to the KISS FM board. McNamee retained his shareholding in KISS and was appointed to the board of EMAP Radio. He said: "It has been an exciting first year and we're all sad to see our chairman and David Evans of Centurion go because they played important roles in our winning team. But EMAP has the resources and radio experience necessary to take the radio station to the next stage in its development, and that is very important."[889]

Evidence of McNamee's ego surfaced in the KISS FM press release to announce the deal, which claimed that "it was McNamee's ideas that led to the radical shake-up in commercial radio, giving London three new incremental stations." EMAP was reported to have invested a total of £4m in KISS FM to date.[890]

Accounts for the six months to the end of March 1992 showed that KISS FM had lost £319,000, although its revenues from advertising had increased to £1,666,000. The station's accumulated loss had increased to £2,063,802. The station's highest paid director (probably McNamee) had earned £99,621 IN SIX MONTHS.[891]

April 1992.

KISS FM announced a "new programme schedule" but, apart from changes to the times of some specialist shows, the daytime presenter line-up remained exactly the same as it had been a year earlier. "It's really a bit of streamlining," said Gordon McNamee. "We are very pleased with the way things are going, but we still have some way to push forward. The confidence that EMAP have in us is great."[892]

May 1992.

Commenting on EMAP's financial performance, The Sunday Times slammed the company's "ill-judged and expensive ventures in radio." City analyst Derek Terrington of Kleinwort Benson commented: "The doubts in the City are whether EMAP will produce a reasonable stream of earnings from its radio activities."[893]

June 1992.

EMAP admitted that the total profit returned from its £27m investment to date in commercial radio stations was just £100,000.[894]

July 1992.

Radio audience data for the second quarter of 1992 showed a fall in listening to KISS FM, down six per cent over the previous six months to 8,418,000 hours per week. The total growth in hours listened to the station since I had left had been eighteen per cent year-on-year. This outcome was slightly higher than the fifteen per cent growth figure I had predicted to the management team a year earlier, but nowhere near the one hundred per cent figure that Gordon McNamee had insisted would be possible. Finally, I had been vindicated for my stand on this issue.[895]

KISS FM non-executive director Tony Prince resigned his seat on the company board and joined rival London station Capital Radio to present a Sunday night show on its oldies AM service.[896]

KISS FM daytime DJ Steve Jackson was suspended for refusing to play the George Michael single 'Too Funky' during his shows. "He doesn't need our support," said Jackson.[897]

August 1992.

EMAP purchased half of Gordon McNamee's five per cent shareholding in KISS FM in a deal worth £149,000. The 'A' class shares had a face value of only £15,000, but gave EMAP much needed voting control over the company, increasing its holding of 'A' shares from 5.1 to 42.4 per cent, and of B shares to 99.7 per cent. McNamee was paid £26,358 cash and was offered 46,010 shares in EMAP. At the same time, EMAP acquired the 'A' class shares in KISS FM owned by Martin Strivens, along with the 'B' class shares that had earlier been transferred to Strivens' wife and to McNamee's wife. EMAP's Tim Schoonmaker described the move as a "tidying up operation." Trevor Nelson resigned his seat on the company's board.[898]

September 1992.

KISS FM DJs Tee Harris, Joey Jay, Norman Jay, Jonathon More, Trevor Nelson and Dean Savonne sold their shareholdings in the station to EMAP. It represented the death of a dream that had started in 1985 when McNamee had promised the DJs who worked for him that, at some point in the future, they would share in the success of KISS FM. Now, only McNamee had a remaining stake in the station. None of his former associates from the pirate radio KISS FM between 1985 and 1988 any longer held a seat on the company board, nor held any senior management positions in the business (except for Lindsay Wesker as head of music). The dream of the KISS FM 'family' had finally been destroyed.[899]

The presenter of KISS FM's evening magazine show, Lisa I'Anson, quit the station to join MTV Europe. KISS FM sacked rap presenter Richie Rich, who also switched to MTV to present a Saturday night soul show.[900]

October 1992.

After two years presenting the KISS FM breakfast show, Graham Gold and Mark Webster were finally dropped, a move I had begged McNamee to consider even before the station had launched. They were replaced by comedian Craig Charles "in order to target Capital [Radio]'s Chris Tarrant show," London's most popular radio breakfast programme. Pete Wardman was employed as producer and co-host of the show, moving from Southampton station Power FM. Despite being a minor celebrity, Charles' Liverpool accent and lack of radio experience did not seem to go down well with the London audience, and the station lost listeners. It was the first bold move that McNamee had made to change the station's daytime line-up, seventeen months after my departure, and it failed.[901]

In another change to the daytime schedule, McNamee dropped Trevor Nelson's afternoon show and expanded the remaining daytime slots. Nelson had been one of McNamee's inner circle of friends from the station's pirate days and had held the seat on the company board representing the other DJ shareholders until his resignation two months earlier. McNamee admitted that the changes to programmes had been caused by dissatisfaction with KISS FM's latest audience figures. Record Mirror magazine asked: "Is it a shake up or shake out at KISS FM?"[902]

At the same time, playlisting of current hits was extended to Saturday and Sunday shows between 6 am and 4 pm, one of the recommendations I had made to the board eighteen months earlier. Daytime weekend shows that had been presented by Tony Monson, Gilles Peterson (formerly of Jazz FM) and Norman Jay were moved to the evening, to make way for playlisted shows, including an additional show presented by Lindsay Wesker. McNamee insisted that KISS FM was not "selling out" and explained: "It is just five playlist records an hour. You wouldn't notice the difference."[903]

Colin Faver became the last DJ to sell his KISS FM shareholding to EMAP.[904]

November 1992.

Soul DJ Robbie Vincent joined London's Jazz FM, having quit his show on KISS FM.[905]

In his new Sunday night show on KISS FM, DJ Norman Jay reminisced about the radio station's pirate days and asked: "Whatever happened to KISS?"[906]

At the Dance Aid Trust fundraising dinner, KISS FM head of music Lindsay Wesker was the unanimous choice to be coated in green goo.[907]

December 1992.

KISS FM announced that EMAP director Martin Boase was joining the station's board as non-executive chairman. McNamee commented: "This is a great vote of confidence for KISS 100 FM. We are both honoured and proud to welcome Martin Boase as our chairman." Sixty-year old Boase, replacing former chairman Keith McDowall who had left in March, said that KISS FM had been anxious to hire someone "with an advertising and a general business background."[908]

January 1993.

Radio audience data for the final quarter of 1992 showed KISS FM had suffered a substantial decline in hours listened to 5,418,000 per week. During the previous six months, the station's listening had fallen by what one magazine referred to as "a massive thirty-six per cent." The audience for KISS FM was now lower than when the station had launched in 1990.[909]

February 1993.

As part of my efforts to secure another job in the radio broadcasting industry, I placed a full-page advertisement in Broadcast magazine. It displayed a graph of the audience for KISS FM, demonstrating that it had increased whilst I had been responsible for the station's programming, but had declined noticeably since I had left. Above the graph was the headline 'When it comes to successful radio programming, it's a station's audience who vote with their ears.' It was the first time that Broadcast had published a full-page 'situations wanted' advertisement. Amongst the replies I received was a letter from American radio consultant Robert Richer, congratulating me on "the great ad." A less welcome response was an agitated message left on my answering machine by Tim Schoonmaker, managing director of EMAP Radio, which said: "I saw your job ad. It's a real eye-catcher, that one. And I just wanted to say I've got somebody who wants to talk to you about a position. But I just have to get the STD [dialling] code for Antarctica. When I've got that, I'll call you back." The following week, EMAP acquired Broadcast magazine from International Thomson Publishing.[910]

KISS FM financial director Martin Strivens and head of sales John Reilly (who had replaced Gary Miele) announced they were leaving the station. Media Week commented: "Some observers see the moves as evidence of parent company EMAP's increasing involvement in the day-to-day running of the radio station." McNamee said of Strivens: "[He] is an old friend and we will all be very sad to see him go. However, new blood could be good for the station." Strivens also resigned his directorship of the station, and was subsequently appointed managing director of Centurion Press.[911]

March 1993.

Accounts for the year ended March 1993 showed KISS FM Limited had made a profit of £135,000, the first time the company had been in the black. Revenues from advertising had increased to £3,807,000 under EMAP's influence, and the number of full-time staff had been cut from eighty-three to sixty-seven. However, the accumulated deficit was still £1,929,000.[912]

KISS FM passed a special resolution to convert the company's former 'A' and 'B' shares into 'ordinary shares' that no longer offered preferential voting rights. McNamee's control over the company was instantly reduced to two per cent, with the remaining ninety-eight per cent held by EMAP.[913]

KISS FM appointed Fiona Driver from design company Fether Miles Group to replace Martin Strivens as financial director. Malcolm Cox was promoted to marketing director, while Gordon Drummond was promoted to sponsorship & national sales director. All three were appointed to the KISS FM board, the company's first non-shareholder executives to enjoy the privilege.[914]

April 1993.

Radio audience figures for the first quarter of 1993 showed that KISS FM's hours listened had fallen by a further sixteen per cent to 4,532,000 hours per week. The total hours listened to KISS FM now stood at half the level that had been achieved in 1991.[915]

KISS FM announced a new "one hundred per cent more music" programme schedule that introduced more substantial changes to the daytime line-up. Out went the unsuccessful Craig Charles from the breakfast show, to be replaced by Dave Pearce, who had hosted the KISS FM drivetime show since the station's launch. Record Mirror magazine reported that "KISS has given up its hunt for comic presenters to challenge Capital [Radio]'s far more successful Chris Tarrant breakfast show." Three years earlier, I had recommended to Gordon McNamee that Pearce should be offered the breakfast show for KISS FM's launch, a proposal he had rejected in favour of Graham Gold and Mark Webster.[916]

The Evening Standard profiled a newly recruited KISS FM DJ, Caesar The Bogeyman, who had been dismissed by his previous employer, Radio Invicta, allegedly for gross misconduct. Caesar had been charged with three counts of theft at Canterbury Magistrates Court under his real name, Chris Ryder. The article noted "the racism which you can almost guarantee to hear within a few moments of turning on" his new KISS FM late night show.[917]

June 1993.

KISS FM marketing director Malcolm Cox told Music Week: "We don't have a problem attracting advertisers. We could play artists like Ace Of Base and 2 Unlimited but, while that might attract new listeners, it would also turn off regular listeners."[918]

Commenting on EMAP's latest financial results, Media Week berated the company because "it does spend an increasing amount of money and time on forays into the low-yielding radio sector."[919]

July 1993.

Radio audience figures for the second quarter of 1993 showed KISS FM having increased its hours listened by fifty-four per cent to 6,979,000 hours per week since the previous quarter. Although this was the first increase in listening recorded for nearly two years, it still represented a seventeen per cent year-on-year decline.[920]

At the KISS FM Annual General Meeting, held at EMAP's headquarters in Peterborough, resolutions were passed that "the company shall not henceforth hold Annual General Meetings" and that "the company shall not lay accounts and reports before the company in general meetings." KISS FM had been totally subsumed into EMAP's media empire and had lost its independence.[921]

August 1993.

Lorna Clarke was promoted to the post of head of programming at KISS FM. Broadcast magazine reported that she "takes over responsibility for all the output from KISS FM managing director Gordon McNammee [sic]."[922]

Record Mirror magazine reported that "the number of pirate radio stations is on the increase again, particularly in the London area." The Department of Trade & Industry had raided twice as many pirate stations in 1992, compared to 1991. 536 raids had resulted in sixty-eight convictions, and three-fifths of all pirate stations were said to be broadcasting in London.[923]

September 1993.

DJ Norman Jay quit KISS FM after failing to agree a new time slot for his programme. He explained: "I could no longer be involved in a station I didn't believe in. I now feel sorry for the people left behind. The station has lost its credibility."[924]

Erskine Thompson, manager of artists such as Maxi Priest, Sly & Robbie and Loose Ends, told a music conference that KISS FM had "betrayed" the black music industry by opting to play rave music instead of R&B.[925]

October 1993.

Radio audience data for the third quarter of 1993 proved that the improvement demonstrated the previous quarter had been only a temporary blip in the station's continuing decline. The new figures showed that listening to KISS FM was down by fourteen per cent quarter-on-quarter to 5,983,000 hours per week.[926]

Four KISS FM DJs – Dean Savonne, DJ Tee, Jay Strongman and Jez Nelson – were axed.[927]

November 1993.

All the KISS FM weekday evening specialist music shows were cut in length from three hours to two hours.[928]

December 1993.

One of the most vociferous critics of KISS FM's increasingly weak programming was Touch magazine. This was the new name of the monthly dance music publication that I had created for KISS FM as 'Free!' in 1989. Touch chronicled the departure of more and more of KISS FM's original DJs and published this commentary:

"First, the issue of KISS FM's programming. The London dance station reorganised its weekday evening schedules once again in November, just two months after the last major revamp. No other radio station has undergone so much change this year, and it is surely a cause for concern. So what could be the reason for this? KISS FM has always been subjected to criticism for not playing more of the music that made them one of the finest pirates to ever come on-air ...

"However, this year has seen too many changes in KISS FM's programming. The departure of key DJs, and either the axing or curtailment of certain shows has all been too much. The direction of KISS is now to follow a more mainstream approach to their music policy, and it is now so apparent that their weekday daytime (revenue making) shows are basically duplicated at weekends, with the few remaining specialist shows programmed for late night/early morning. This is reminiscent of 1980s legal radio, who saw fit to schedule quality black music in the late night hours as a 'favour' because it was considered 'too specialist.' But KISS, as a black/dance station, have implemented exactly the same tactic as their legal predecessors like Radio London, Capital, etc. in their quest to satisfy their advertisers and financial shareholders.

"The autumn schedule changes came at a time when mid-year ratings showed an increase but, since then, the weekly London audience share has decreased (from 3.5% to 3.1%) for KISS, while commercial rival Capital has shown an increase. The loss of key shows has had a severe impact to the overall ratings as more of the original (pirate days) listeners now only tune in for one, or maybe two, specialist shows. KISS surely cannot expect their audience figures to remain consistent, especially if their daytime musical approach is now worse than ever … KISS have now introduced the playlist outside of its daytime scheduling, thus reinforcing its power. This tactical move must be seen as a measure to retrieve listeners lost over the years to Capital, Choice and the pirates. In fact, there is now less house, rap, reggae, jazz, soul – all the pure forms of popular music types on KISS FM, but more 'pop' dance, which illustrates their more bland direction."[929]

In the same article, Touch reported the resurgence of pirate radio in London: "Even the casual listener in London could not have failed to notice the rise of illicit stations this year. Despite the presence of the specialist legal stations, 1993 has seen the biggest influx of pirate stations in the capital than at any other stage in the history of illegal broadcasting, surpassing even the mid-1980s boom. Why is this? Is legal radio incapable of satisfying Londoners' needs in the rapidly progressing 1990s? Or is it that black music can only be properly represented by the rebel operators? …

"While the government are planning new frequencies to be made available from spring 1994, if none are allocated to specialist black music radio, the London pirate situation will become even more prevalent. The pirates will continue to dominate, with more stations establishing (reminiscent of ten years ago), and it seems ever more likely that a few 'big' soul/R&B/jazz stations will join the reggae/soul and house fraternity. 'What goes around comes around' and the second half of the 1990s will be a mirror image of post mid-1980s. The future of UK radio could and should be a first class service, but if government attitudes remain as in the past, without realising how important a medium radio is, then there will be no hope for the full potential of radio ever being reached in this country."[930]

January 1994.

Radio audience figures for the final quarter of 1993 showed that listening to KISS FM had fallen by six per cent since the previous quarter to 5,652,000 hours per week. The station's popularity was still below the level that had been achieved immediately after its launch, and the volume of listening to KISS FM was now about one third below the peak of the station's popularity, achieved two years earlier.[931]

April 1994.

Radio audience figures for the first quarter of 1994 showed that listening to KISS FM had fallen by a further fifteen per cent since the previous quarter to 4,794,000 hours per week. Each listener was spending an average 5.3 hours per week tuned to KISS FM, the lowest figure in the station's history.[932]

The same day that the audience figures were published, KISS FM DJ Tony Monson phoned me. It was the first time I had spoken to him since I had been sacked almost three years earlier. He called to let me know that he too had just been sacked without explanation from the station. Gordon McNamee had not bothered to speak to him but, instead, had arranged for Lorna Clarke to give him his redundancy papers and see him out the door. Monson told me that morale was very low at the station. He explained that several more of the station's launch staff (including Sonia Fraser) had recently been expelled. Monson said that he failed to understand what Gordon McNamee was doing with the radio station and expressed the opinion that he had been misled by McNamee from the very beginning about his promised role in the legal KISS FM. Monson told Music Week: "All I can say is that I am very gutted …"[933]

October 1994.

Although KISS FM had been licensed to broadcast a specialist music radio format, managing director Gordon McNamee and head of music Lindsay Wesker both seemed to enjoy presenting phone-in shows on the station. On 7 October 1994, Wesker was presenting his daily, early morning talk show when a woman called in and "gave a candid description of having sex with her dog," according to the regulator. She explained how she liked to cover her body with dog food and have her dog lick it off. This conversation took place in a section of his show that Wesker labelled 'Everything You Wanted To Know About Sex.'[934]

Three listener complaints to the regulator resulted in KISS FM being fined £10,000. The Radio Authority said that it "considered the [phone] call was disgusting and required the strongest signal that material of this kind must not be broadcast." A Radio Authority spokesperson commented: "Although it was KISS' first offence and the first time we've had to impose a fine against the station, the size of the fine reflects the seriousness with which the Authority viewed the topic. Bestiality is a totally prohibited subject under our regulations."[935]

Wesker resigned from KISS FM in December 1994. According to the Radio Authority, KISS FM "had taken disciplinary action." However, Gordon McNamee said: "[Wesker] didn't get sacked and I'm very sad to see him go." Record Mirror magazine noted that Wesker's resignation "will leave [Gordon] Mac as the only full-time KISS employee remaining from the original pirate team."[936]

December 1994.

Out of the blue, I received a handwritten letter from my former girlfriend with whom I had shared a flat in Harrow, until she had disappeared with much of our household contents in December 1989. The letter started:

"Dear Grant. I know that it has been a very long time – more than five years – since we last had any contact, but I am writing to you because, having recently been thinking over many aspects of my life, I came to the inescapeable [sic] conclusion that I owe you a long-overdue apology for the way I behaved during the break down of our relationship …"[937]

At least it was some kind of apology. From KISS FM, I had received no further communications since exiting the station. During the past three years, I had applied for every relevant job vacancy in the radio industry, but had been offered nothing. I had contacted every commercial radio station in the UK for work, but had been offered nothing. By 1994, I was working overseas in radio. I was in the process of relocating to another city, in another country, on another continent.

May 1998.

Pirate radio stations continued to flourish in London, just as they had in the 1980s. Ministry magazine commented: "They may not be household names like KISS or Radio One but, to an army of dedicated listeners, they mean more than the big-time legal stations could ever do. There are pirates covering most forms of music neglected by the mainstream, from soul and reggae to drum'n'bass."[938]

The Naturalist, a DJ on London pirate station Déjà Vu, said: "Stations like KISS can't be trusted to play [garage] music non-stop, like we do, and other stations don't play underground stuff at all. I can't even imagine London without pirates – they'd be nothing to listen to."[939]

Eastman, a DJ on pirate station Kool FM, added: "Jungle and drum'n'bass would never have come through like it did without the underground stations. KISS are always three years behind, and Radio One are five years behind."[940]

December 1998.

On the morning of 18 December 1998, after Steve Jackson had finished presenting the KISS FM breakfast show, he showed his studio guests to their cars. His return to the studio was blocked by a security guard who escorted him to the top floor boardroom, where he was dismissed. He was offered £10,000 in lieu of notice and an ex gratia payment of £10,000 if he agreed not to pursue the matter. Jackson rejected the offer. He said: "I was shocked by this. I was upset, very quiet and subdued. I was escorted out of the building by a security guard, watched by

KISS members of staff. I was not allowed back to get personal belongings. There was nothing in my behaviour that would have required me to be escorted."[941]

Three black or Asian presenters – Steve Jackson, David Morrissey and Janice V – were amongst twenty staff dismissed by the station's acting managing director, Dee Ford, on "organisational and economic grounds." A subsequent employment tribunal required KISS FM to face charges of race discrimination, unfair dismissal and breach of contract.[942]

Jackson told the tribunal: "I believe that the principle reason for my dismissal was my race. KISS has also changed its musical output from predominantly black dance music to predominantly white dance and pop music. I believe it has taken the view that only white presenters should be allowed to play white music in its peak-time spot."[943]

Morrissey told the tribunal: "Although I was told by Dee Ford that my dismissal was due to changes in management and strategy, I believe in retrospect that it was connected with my race … My impression from the radical changes to the presenters in the station was that KISS wanted to have male, white presenters."[944]

The tribunal upheld Jackson's claims for unfair dismissal and breach of contract, though it did not support the charge of race discrimination. When he left the tribunal, Jackson told a reporter: "The worst thing about it is that they have taken away the last dance music [radio] licence for black music in London."[945]

July 1999.

Back in 1991, KISS FM head of marketing Malcolm Cox had insisted that the station could achieve the required one hundred per cent growth in hours listened by increasing its weekly reach from 1.0 to 1.3 million adults, and its average hours per listener per week from 6.6 to 8.0, within the next twelve months.

However, by 1999, KISS FM's weekly reach was still only 1.1 million adults and its average hours listened had fallen to 5.6. Not only had the station failed ever to achieve the one hundred per cent increase in its hours listened, but its performance was below the level achieved during its first year on-air. KISS FM's share of radio listening in London was now 2.9 per cent, compared to the 3.4 per cent recorded in early 1991.[946]

In his new job as marketing director of EMAP Radio, Cox unveiled a £2m marketing campaign for KISS FM that used the slogan 'live sexy' and was intended to make it the number one station for fifteen to twenty-four year olds in London. "For years, we've had around a million listeners," said Cox. "It hasn't really gone up or down, and the audience has grown old with the station."[947]

In an article headlined 'A Kiss Goodbye To Radical Radio,' The Independent newspaper reported that KISS FM "wants to be like safe, old Capital Radio," having dropped ten DJs and many specialist music programmes. Rob Blake, a former KISS FM DJ, commented: "A year ago, they wouldn't play anything older than three years old and, if they heard tunes on other stations after they'd made them hits, they'd drop them. Now, they are playing the big classics of the last five years over and over again. Apart from a few late-night specialist slots, they are not interested in breaking new music any more."[948]

August 2008.

By 2008, I was back in London, working as a media analyst for a small, independent analyst company that specialised in the media and telecommunications industries. Part of my job was to sell consulting services to media owners, so I had arranged an appointment on 6 August to meet Dee Ford, the group managing director of Bauer Radio.

Ford had worked her way up EMAP Radio since joining the company in 1994, three years after I had exited KISS FM. In 2007, EMAP had sold its entire radio division to German publisher Heinrich Bauer. Bauer Radio was now the second largest commercial radio group in the UK.

I was sat in the reception area of Bauer Radio's corporate headquarters in Shaftesbury Avenue, awaiting my eleven o'clock appointment with Ford. I was dressed in the 'analyst' uniform mandated by my employer – a dark suit, white shirt, tie and black shoes.

Ford came out to greet me. She led me down a corridor and towards a conference room where we would talk.

"Someone mentioned that you had once worked for KISS FM," she said, as we walked.

What should I say? I wanted to tell Ford that Bauer Radio might never have existed if I had not met some EMAP executives in the HMV Megastore one evening in 1989 and talked to them about radio. I wanted to tell her that KISS FM might not exist now if I had not helped it win a radio licence and become EMAP's first significant radio investment. I wanted to tell Ford that her job, her radio empire and her company might never have happened if it were not for my efforts two decades earlier. But I knew that this was neither the time nor the place for such a conversation. My appointment that day had been arranged for me to market my employer's analyst services.

"Yes, I did," I replied to Ford. Even to my ears, these words sounded like a remarkably vague response.

Suddenly, Ford turned towards me and looked me up and down, seemingly puzzled.

"I can't imagine someone like you working at KISS FM," she said. "What exactly did you do there?"

---

[874] "Consortium To Bail Out Jazz FM", Broadcast, 5 Jul 1991.
[875] Goodfoot Promotions Limited, Companies House no. 02162147.
[876] ibid.
[877] Nicholas Hellen, "New-Wave Radio Stations Look To The Stars For Survival", Evening Standard, 15 Jul 1991.
[878] "KISS Man To Launch New Radio Station", Music Week, 20 Jul 1991.
[879] "Rival Boss To Radio City", Broadcast, 9 Aug 1991.
[880] KISS FM Radio Limited, Companies House no. 02378790.
[881] ibid.
[882] KISS Records Limited, Companies House no. 02213441.
[883] KISS FM Radio Limited, op cit.
[884] "KISS 100 FM Share Deal", KISS FM press release, Dec 1991.
[885] JICRAR, Q4 1991.
[886] KISS FM Radio Limited, op cit.
[887] Michael Kavanagh, "Turn On Tune In Drop Out", Broadcast, 27 Mar 1992.
[888] Michael Kavanagh, "KISS It Better", Broadcast, 27 Mar 1992.

[889] "EMAP Increases London-wide KISS FM Stake", KISS FM press release, 31 Mar 1992.
[890] ibid.
"EMAP Takes KISS In Shares Swoop", Music Week, 11 Apr 1992.
[891] KISS FM Radio Limited, op cit.
[892] "KISS 100 Announces New Programme Schedule", KISS FM press release, Apr 1992.
"KISS Streamlines", rpm, 25 Apr 1992.
[893] "Sharewatch – EMAP", The Sunday Times, 17 May 1992.
"City Concern Over EMAP", rpm, 23 May 1992.
[894] Jason Nissé, "EMAP In Cash Call As Results Beat Forecast", The Independent, 10 Jun 1992.
[895] JICRAR, Q2 1992.
[896] "Prince Of Capital", rpm, 1 Aug 1992.
[897] "Jackson Funks Off", Record Mirror, 18 Jul 1992.
[898] "EMAP Lifts Stake In KISS FM Radio", Financial Times, 18 Aug 1992.
"EMAP/KISS Stake", Media Week, 28 Aug 1992.
[untitled], Broadcast, 21 Aug 1992.
KISS FM Radio Limited, op cit.
[899] KISS FM Radio Limited, op cit.
[900] "Beats & Pieces", Record Mirror, 26 Sep & 17 Oct 1992.
[901] "KISS FM Revamps To Take On Tarrant", Media Week, 16 Oct 1992.
"KISS's Capital Breakfast", rpm, 3 Oct 1992.
[902] "All Change At KISS", Record Mirror, 3 Oct 1992.
"Beats & Pieces", Record Mirror, 10 Oct 1992.
[903] "Soul-ed Out", Record Mirror, 17 Oct 1992.
[904] KISS FM Radio Limited, op cit.
[905] "Revisionist Jazz", Broadcast, 6 Nov 1992.
[906] "Beats & Pieces", Record Mirror, 5 Dec 1992.
[907] "Dooley's Diary", Music Week, 21 Nov 1992.
[908] "KISS 100 FM Announce New Chairman For Board Of Directors", KISS FM press release, 9 Dec 1992.
Belinda Archer, "Elder Ad Statesman Boase Takes Senior Position For KISS FM", Campaign, 18 Dec 1992.
[909] RAJAR, Q4 1992.
"Commercial Radio In London Suffers Most In New Data", Campaign, 5 Feb 1993.
[910] Grant Goddard, advertisement, Broadcast, 5 Feb 1993.
letter from Robert Richer to Grant Goddard, 24 Feb 1993.
phone call from Tim Schoonmaker, EMAP Radio to Grant Goddard, Feb 1993 [exact date unknown].
[911] "Reilly Departs In KISS FM Restructure", Media Week, 12 Feb 1993.
"Strivens Quits KISS FM", Media Week, 8 Jan 1993.
[912] KISS FM Radio Limited, op cit.
[913] KISS FM Radio Limited, op cit.
[914] "Driver To Steer KISS", Media Week, 5 Mar 1993.
[915] RAJAR, Q1 1993.
[916] "KISS 100 FM Announce New Programme Schedule: 100% More Music", KISS FM press release, Apr 1993.
"Pearce Serves KISS Breakfast", Record Mirror, 17 Apr 1993.
[917] "Boogie In Court", Broadcast, 15 Nov 1991.
Jonathan Margolis, "Radio's Dawn Raider", Evening Standard, 7 Apr 1993.
[918] "Niche Work If You Can Get It", Music Week, 5 Jun 1993.
[919] [untitled], Media Week, 11 Jun 1993.
[920] RAJAR, Q2 1993.
[921] KISS FM Radio Limited, op cit.
[922] "Clarke In Charge At Kiss 100", Broadcast, 13 Aug 1993.
[923] "Newsfile" & "Pirates Slam Drug Slur", Record Mirror/Music Week, 28 Aug 1993.
"Pirates Again On The Increase", Broadcast, 20 Aug 1993.
[924] "Stormin' Norman Quits Kiss", Record Mirror/Music Week, 18 Sep 1993.
[925] "Radio Under Fire", Music Week, 25 Sep 1993.
[926] RAJAR, Q3 1993.
[927] "Kiss Axes Four DJs", Record Mirror/Music Week, 2 Oct 1993.
[928] "Kiss Cuts Back Its Specialist Shows", Record Mirror/Music Week, 20 Nov 1993.
[929] Stephen White, "Radio Waves", Touch, Dec 1993.
[930] ibid.
[931] RAJAR, Q4 1993.
[932] RAJAR, Q1 1994.
[933] "Kiss Eyes Specialist Spots", Music Week, 30 Apr 1994.

[934] "Complaints Bulletin – Q4 1994", unattributable guidance for journalists, The Radio Authority, 25 Jan 1995.
Torin Douglas, "Talking About A Revolution", Marketing Week, 3 Feb 1995.
"Kiss Blow As Wesker Quits", Record Mirror/Music Week, 7 Jan 1995.
[935] "Programming & Advertising Complaints: Quarterly Summary October-December 1994", The Radio Authority, Summary no.16, 25 Jan 1995, pp.9-10.
"Kiss Blow As Wesker Quits", op cit.
[936] ibid.
[937] letter from XXXXX XXXXXX to Grant Goddard, 2 Dec 1994.
[938] [uncredited], "It May Not Be Glamorous, But This Flat Is Home To One Of The Country's Biggest Pirate Radio Stations", Ministry, May 1998.
[939] ibid.
[940] ibid.
[941] Teri Judd, "Kiss FM Sacked Its Leading DJ 'Because He Was Black'", The Independent, 18 Aug 1999.
[942] ibid.
[943] Julia Hartley-Brewer, "Kiss DJ Sacked 'For Being Black'", The Guardian, 18 Aug 1999.
[944] Kim Sengupta, "Support For DJ Who Claimed Black Presenters Were Purged", The Independent, 19 Aug 1999.
[945] Katy Weitz, "DJ's Unfair Sacking Was Not Racism", The Independent, 13 Nov 1999.
Teri Judd, op cit.
[946] RAJAR, Q1 1999.
JICRAR, Q2 1991.
[947] Paul McCann, "A Kiss Goodbye To Radical Radio", The Independent, 13 Jul 1999.
[948] ibid.

EPITAPH

"Dear KISS FM,

First Norman Jay [exiting KISS FM], then Jay Strongman. Well, I am disgusted. I may live 400-odd miles away, but I was proud to have helped and supported (in my own way) the rise of Britain's first national black music-based station. The thrill of piracy and then the pride when you obtained your fiercely fought for legality ... 'Turn your radio to KISS and pull the knob off,' says your advertisement. How very apt.

Yours knobfully,
Pete Haigh,
Blackpool."

'Backchat'
Blues & Soul
23 November 1993

According to a newspaper profile, Gordon McNamee *"now shops almost exclusively at Paul Smith, Ralph Lauren and Cerruti"* and *"in the evenings, he can be found [dining] at Bibendum in Chelsea or the Pont de la Tour at Tower Bridge."*

Robert Ashton
'Root With A Suit'
Music Week
29 February 1992

Gordon McNamee told one journalist that he loved drinking port and smoking Monte Christo cigars, and he showed her his cuff links, saying: *"Aren't they wonderful? I bought these in Bergdorf Goodman, my favourite shop in New York."*

Judi Bevan
'Treasures Of The Pirate'
Evening Standard
7 July 1993

Asked to explain his success, Gordon McNamee said: *"People at KISS and I have worked bloody hard to get where we are ... it's one thing doing it all, but it's another thing to be allowed to keep it."*

Martin Hennessey
'KISS Unlocks A Treasure Chest For Pirate Mac'
The Mail On Sunday
20 June 1993

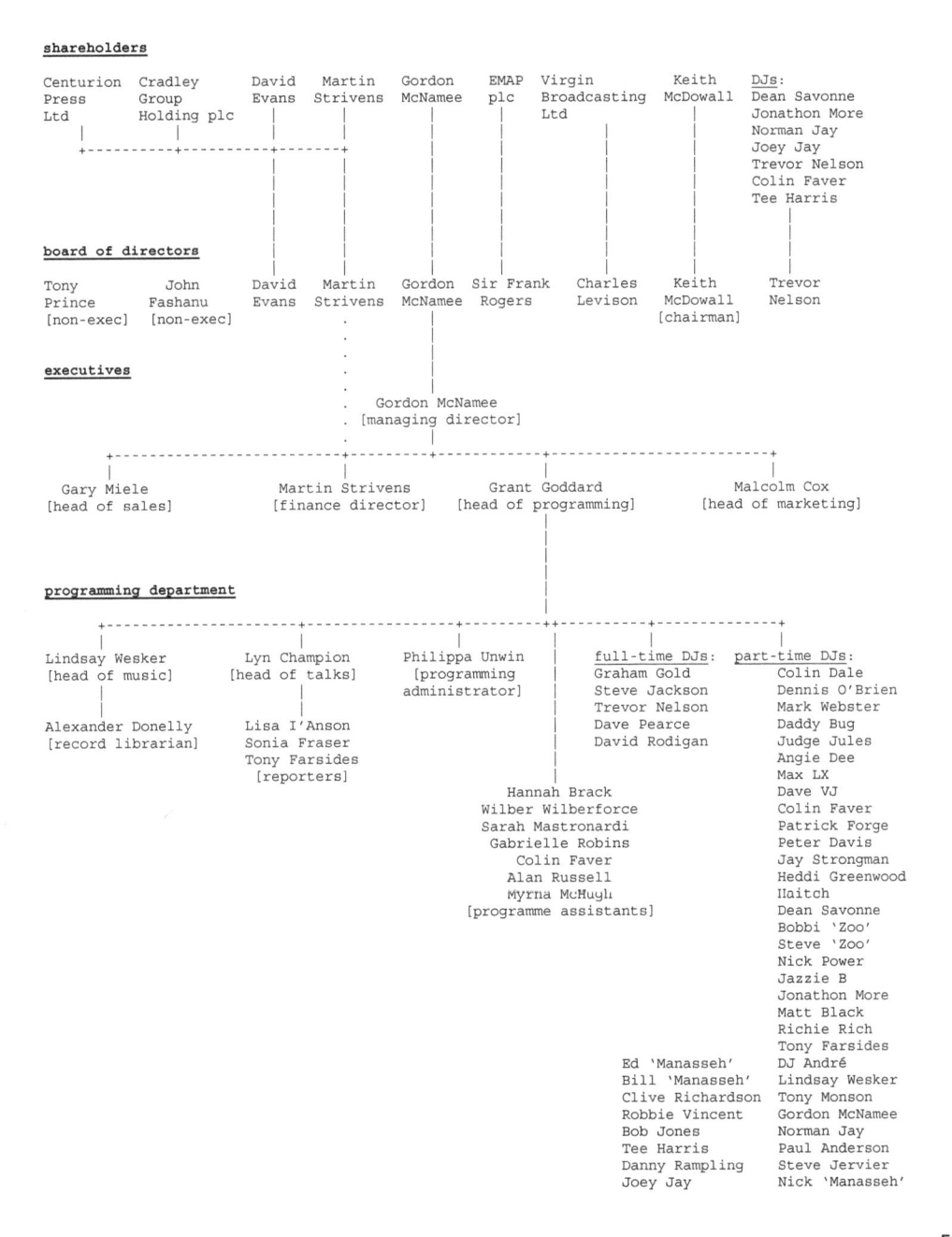

STRUCTURE OF KISS FM RADIO LIMITED: September 1990

shareholders

- Centurion Press Ltd
- Cradley Group Holding plc
- David Evans
- Martin Strivens
- Gordon McNamee
- EMAP plc
- Virgin Broadcasting Ltd
- Keith McDowall
- DJs: Dean Savonne, Jonathon More, Norman Jay, Joey Jay, Trevor Nelson, Colin Faver, Tee Harris

board of directors

- Tony Prince [non-exec]
- John Fashanu [non-exec]
- David Evans
- Martin Strivens
- Gordon McNamee
- Sir Frank Rogers
- Charles Levison
- Keith McDowall [chairman]
- Trevor Nelson

executives

Gordon McNamee [managing director]

- Gary Miele [head of sales]
- Martin Strivens [finance director]
- Grant Goddard [head of programming]
- Malcolm Cox [head of marketing]

programming department

- Lindsay Wesker [head of music]
  - Alexander Donelly [record librarian]
- Lyn Champion [head of talks]
  - Lisa I'Anson
  - Sonia Fraser
  - Tony Farsides [reporters]
- Philippa Unwin [programming administrator]
- full-time DJs: Graham Gold, Steve Jackson, Trevor Nelson, Dave Pearce, David Rodigan
- part-time DJs: Colin Dale, Dennis O'Brien, Mark Webster, Daddy Bug, Judge Jules, Angie Dee, Max LX, Dave VJ, Colin Faver, Patrick Forge, Peter Davis, Jay Strongman, Heddi Greenwood, Haitch, Dean Savonne, Bobbi 'Zoo', Steve 'Zoo', Nick Power, Jazzie B, Jonathon More, Matt Black, Richie Rich, Tony Farsides, DJ André, Lindsay Wesker, Tony Monson, Gordon McNamee, Norman Jay, Paul Anderson, Steve Jervier, Nick 'Manasseh'

Hannah Brack, Wilber Wilberforce, Sarah Mastronardi, Gabrielle Robins, Colin Faver, Alan Russell, Myrna McHugh [programme assistants]

Ed 'Manasseh', Bill 'Manasseh', Clive Richardson, Robbie Vincent, Bob Jones, Tee Harris, Danny Rampling, Joey Jay

KISS FM RADIO LIMITED: SHAREHOLDINGS

According to the Memorandum & Articles of Association of the company:
- each 'A' share entitles the holder to six votes
- each 'B' share entitles the holder to one vote.

11 OCTOBER 1990

SHAREHOLDER	A shares	B shares	£	votes	control
Gordon McNamee	60,000		30,000	360,000	21.7%
Centurion Press Ltd		360,000	180,000	360,000	21.7%
EMAP Investments Ltd		360,000	180,000	360,000	21.7%
Virgin Broadcasting Ltd		270,000	135,000	270,000	16.3%
Cradley Group Holdings plc		90,000	45,000	90,000	5.4%
Keith McDowall		45,000	22,250	45,000	2.7%
David Evans	4,500		2,250	27,000	1.6%
Martin Strivens	3,000		1,500	18,000	1.1%
Dean Savonne	3,000		1,500	18,000	1.1%
Jonathon More	3,000		1,500	18,000	1.1%
Norman Jay	3,000		1,500	18,000	1.1%
Joey Jay	3,000		1,500	18,000	1.1%
Trevor Nelson	3,000		1,500	18,000	1.1%
Colin Faver	3,000		1,500	18,000	1.1%
Tee Harris	3,000		1,500	18,000	1.1%
TOTAL	88,500	1,125,000	606,500	1,656,000	100.0%

3 MAY 1991

SHAREHOLDER	A shares	B shares	£	votes	control
EMAP Investments Ltd		381,176	190,588	381,176	21.2%
Virgin Broadcasting Ltd		381,176	190,588	381,176	21.2%
Gordon McNamee	60,000		30,000	360,000	20.0%
Centurion Press Ltd		360,000	180,000	360,000	20.0%
Cradley Group Holdings plc		90,000	45,000	90,000	5.0%
Keith McDowall		47,647	23,823	47,647	2.7%
David Evans	4,500	1,588	3,044	28,588	1.6%
Norman Jay	3,000	1,036	2,018	19,036	1.1%
Martin Strivens	3,000		1,500	18,000	1.0%
Dean Savonne	3,000		1,500	18,000	1.0%
Jonathon More	3,000		1,500	18,000	1.0%
Joey Jay	3,000		1,500	18,000	1.0%
Trevor Nelson	3,000		1,500	18,000	1.0%
Colin Faver	3,000		1,500	18,000	1.0%
Tee Harris	3,000		1,500	18,000	1.0%
Tony Prince		3,173	1,587	3,173	0.2%
TOTAL	88,500	1,265,796	677,148	1,796,796	100.0%

5 DECEMBER 1991

SHAREHOLDER	A shares	B shares	£	votes	control
EMAP Investments Ltd		438,898	219,449	438,898	22.9%
Virgin Broadcasting Lt		438,898	219,449	438,898	22.9%
Gordon McNamee	60,000	2,500	31,250	362,500	18.9%
Centurion Press Ltd		360,000	180,000	360,000	18.7%
Cradley Group Holdings plc		90,000	45,000	90,000	4.7%
Keith McDowall		47,647	23,823	47,647	2.5%
David Evans	4,500	5,915	5,207	32,915	1.7%
Martin Strivens	3,000	2,729	5,729	20,729	1.1%
Norman Jay	3,000	1,036	2,018	19,036	1.0%
Dean Savonne	3,000		1,500	18,000	0.9%
Jonathon More	3,000		1,500	18,000	0.9%
Joey Jay	3,000		1,500	18,000	0.9%
Trevor Nelson	3,000		1,500	18,000	0.9%
Colin Faver	3,000		1,500	18,000	0.9%
Tee Harris	3,000		1,500	18,000	0.9%
Tony Prince		3,173	1,587	3,173	0.2%
TOTAL	88,500	1,390,796	739,648	1,921,796	100.0%

3 MAY 1992

SHAREHOLDER	A shares	B shares	£	votes	control
EMAP Investments Ltd		877,796	438,898	877,796	45.7%
Gordon McNamee	60,000		30,000	360,000	18.7%
Centurion Press Ltd		360,000	180,000	360,000	18.7%
Cradley Group Holdings plc		90,000	45,000	90,000	4.7%
Keith McDowall		47,647	23,823	47,647	2.5%
David Evans	4,500	5,915	5,207	32,915	1.7%
Norman Jay	3,000	1,036	2,018	19,036	1.0%
Martin Strivens	3,000		1,500	18,000	0.9%
Dean Savonne	3,000		1,500	18,000	0.9%
Jonathon More	3,000		1,500	18,000	0.9%
Joey Jay	3,000		1,500	18,000	0.9%
Trevor Nelson	3,000		1,500	18,000	0.9%
Colin Faver	3,000		1,500	18,000	0.9%
Tee Harris	3,000		1,500	18,000	0.9%
Tony Prince		3,173	1,587	3,173	0.2%
C.L. Strivens		2,729	1,364	2,729	0.1%
Kim McNamee		2,500	1,250	2,500	0.1%
TOTAL	88,500	1,390,796	739,648	1,921,796	100.0%

On 8th March 1993, the company passed a special resolution that converted all the former 'A' and 'B' shares to ordinary shares with equal voting rights.

3 MAY 1993

SHAREHOLDER	ordinary shares	£	votes	control
EMAP Investments Ltd	1,449,296	724,648	1,449,296	98.0%
Gordon McNamee	30,000	15,000	30,000	2.0%
TOTAL	1,479,296	739,648	1,479,296	100.0%

BIBLIOGRAPHY

BOOKS

Stuart Henry & Mike Von Joel, **PIRATE RADIO: THEN AND NOW**, Blandford Press, Dorset, 1984.
John Hind & Stephen Mosco, **REBEL RADIO: THE FULL STORY OF BRITISH PIRATE RADIO**, Pluto Press, London, 1985.

PERIODICALS

TX, nos. 1-14 (October 1985 - April 1987), London.
RADIO TODAY [incorporating **TX**], nos. 15-18 (August 1987 - September 1988), London.
RADIO TODAY NEWSLETTER, no. 1 (4 January 1989), London.
AM/FM NEWSLETTER, nos. 1-3 (Spring 1990 - Summer 1993), London.

NOW RADIO, nos. 1-154 (May 1986 - November 1990), Kettering.
NOW RADIO, nos. 1-23 (May 1991 - October 1991), London & Petersfield.

94, nos. 1-3 (July 1988 - December 1988), London.
KISS FM'S WRITTEN WORD, nos. 4-6 (February 1989 - August 1989), London.
FREE!, nos. 1-15 (November 1989 - January 1991), London.

RADIO & MUSIC, nos. 0-38 (April 1989 - December 1990), London.

INSPIRATION

[uncredited], **RADIO IS MY BOMB: A DIY MANUAL FOR PIRATES**, Hooligan Press, London, 1987.
Louis Cantor, **WHEELIN' ON BEALE: HOW WDIA MEMPHIS BECAME THE NATION'S FIRST ALL-BLACK RADIO STATION**, Pharos, New York, 1992.
Sue Carpenter, **40 WATTS FROM NOWHERE: A JOURNEY INTO PIRATE RADIO**, Scribner, New York, 2004.
Frederic Dannen, **HIT MEN: POWER BROKERS AND FAST MONEY INSIDE THE MUSIC BUSINESS**, Vintage, London, 1991.
Charlie Gillett, **THE SOUND OF THE CITY**, Sphere, London, 1971.
Nigel Grant, **PIRATES OF THE AIRWAVES: THE STORY OF RADIO FREE LONDON**, ITMA, London, 1990.
Michael Haralambos, **SOUL MUSIC: THE BIRTH OF A SOUND IN AMERICA**, Da Capo, New York, 1974.

Local Radio Workshop, **CAPITAL: LOCAL RADIO & PRIVATE PROFIT**, Comedia, London, 1983.

Local Radio Workshop, **NOTHING LOCAL ABOUT IT: LONDON'S LOCAL RADIO**, Comedia, London, 1983.

Joseph Menn, **ALL THE RAVE: THE RISE AND FALL OF SHAWN FANNING'S NAPSTER**, Crown Business, New York, 2003.

Peter Mulryan, **RADIO RADIO: THE STORY OF INDEPENDENT, LOCAL, COMMUNITY & PIRATE RADIO IN IRELAND**, Borderline, Dublin, 1988.

Mark Newman, **ENTREPRENEURS OF PROFIT AND PRIDE: FROM BLACK-APPEAL TO RADIO SOUL**, Praeger, New York, 1988.

Robert Pruter, **CHICAGO SOUL**, University of Illinois Press, Chicago, 1991.

Thom Racina, **FM**, Harcourt Brace Jovanovich, New York, 1978.

Paul Alexander Rusling, **THE LID OFF LASER 558**, Pirate Publications, Herne Bay, 1984.

Ron Sakolsky & Stephen Dunifer [ed.], **SEIZING THE AIRWAVES: A FREE RADIO HANDBOOK**, AK Press, Edinburgh & San Francisco, 1998.

Andrew Yoder, **PIRATE RADIO STATIONS**, McGraw-Hill, New York, 2002.

George Zeller, **THE PIRATE RADIO DIRECTORY**, Tiare, Wisconsin, 1993 [updated annually].

ACKNOWLEDGEMENTS

This book would not exist without the immense generosity of my mother. Twenty years ago, when her accounts department in Woking closed and she was made redundant, she purchased one of the company's office computers and gave it to me. This entire book was written on that IBM XT, my first personal computer, in MultiMate.

Thank you to my wife and daughter for their unwavering encouragement and enthusiasm for my radio obsessions, and their unflinching loyalty to remain by my side through thick and thin. Without them, an old manuscript would never have been transformed into this book.

The story of pirate radio could not have been told so comprehensively without the resources of the library of the Independent Broadcasting Authority that had existed at 70 Brompton Road. Thank you to the then Librarian for his diligence in clipping and filing every news story about broadcasting from even the smallest local newspaper in those pre-internet days … and for letting me use the library photocopier for hours on end.

Thank you to the many thousands of musicians whose work has inspired me to do things in the radio and music industries. From the time in 1969 when I bought my first Stax single ('Time Is Tight' by Booker T & The MGs) and my first Laurel Aitken single ('Jesse James' on Nu Beat) from the record department in Harvey's of Guildford department store in Camberley, soul and reggae have been the soundtrack to my life.

Practical assistance was gratefully received from Charlotte Mortimer at Faber Music, Angus Fulton and Pete Beck at Warner Chappell Music, Leah Webb and Andre Carroll at EMI Music, Kathleen Luckey at the BFI National Archive and the staff of the Newspaper Library at Colindale. Special respect to Augustus 'Gussie' Clarke of the Anchor Group in Jamaica for his help.

A big thank you to Muema Lombe for his boundless enthusiasm for this project.

Lightning Source UK Ltd.
Milton Keynes UK
UKHW032137170822
407449UK00005B/603